C000084962

Six Years in Purgatory: The Story of Lincoln City in The Conference 2011-2017

Philip Priddle

DARK
RIVER

An imprint of Bennion Kearny

Published in 2017 by Dark River, an imprint of Bennion Kearny Limited.

Copyright © Dark River

ISBN: 978-1-911121-30-5

All Rights Reserved. No part of this publication may be reproduced, stored in a retrieval system, or transmitted in any form or by any means, electronic, mechanical, photocopying, recording or otherwise, without the prior permission of the publisher.

This book is sold subject to the condition that it shall not, by way of trade or otherwise, be lent, re-sold, hired out or otherwise circulated without the publisher's prior consent in any form of binding or cover other than that it which it is published and without a similar condition including this condition being imposed on the subsequent purchaser.

Dark River has endeavoured to provide trademark information about all the companies and products mentioned in this book by the appropriate use of capitals. However, Dark River cannot guarantee the accuracy of this information.

Published by Dark River, an imprint of Bennion Kearny Limited
6 Woodside
Churnet View Road
Oakamoor
ST10 3AE

This book is dedicated to Bob Dorrian,
without whom Lincoln City would not exist.

Main Sources Used

www.bbc.co.uk | www.lincolnshireecho.co.uk | www.redimps.co.uk | www.statto.com | www.scoresway.com
www.wikipedia.org | www.grimsbytelegtraph.co.uk | www.scunthorpetelegraph.co.uk
www.gainsboroughstandard.co.uk | www.bostonstandard.co.uk | www.thefa.com | www.thenationalleague.org.uk
www.footballdatabase.eu | www.soccerbase.com | www.fussball.wettpoint.com | www.flashscore.com
www.doingthe92.com | www.non-leagueclubdirectory.co.uk | www.aylesburyunitedfc.co.uk |

A large number of football club websites in the UK and Europe.
A large number of online national and local newspapers in the UK and Europe.
All statistics compiled by the author.

Acknowledgements

The author would like to thank Clive Nates and Bob Dorrian for their unstinting support during the creation of this book. Although the book does not always show Lincoln City in its best light, it would have been so much harder to complete without their commitment and honesty. Thanks also to Kevin Cooke for facilitating everything at Lincoln City; to Danny Cowley for kindly agreeing to write a foreword and extend his working day to 25 hours instead of the usual 24; to John Vickers at Lincoln City and to Mark Whiley of the Lincolnshire Echo for their assistance and enthusiasm; to Julian Burley at Vital Lincoln City for his permission to reproduce the original Danny Cowley article; to publisher James Lumsden-Cook for believing in such a ludicrous project and for translating everything into something presentable; and finally to a German Shepherd puppy called Cassie for allowing the author to type occasionally instead of playing catch.

Table of Contents

Preface   1
Foreword   3

Year 1: 2011-12   7
Year 2: 2012-13   25
Year 3: 2013-14   41
Year 4: 2014-15   57
Year 5: 2015-16   75
Year 6: 2016-17   93

Achievements: 2016-17   115
The Players   117
Trialists & Others   203
The Managers   209
Imperama   223
Bob Dorrian Review   237
Vital Lincoln City: Welcome Danny Cowley   245

Preface

In May 1987, Lincoln City became the first club to suffer automatic relegation from the Football League to what was then called the GM Vauxhall Conference. No one had any real idea what to do next. All player registrations reverted to the Football League, so theoretically City were left with no players whatsoever. Player-manager Peter Daniel had departed for Burnley, and the old wooden St Andrews Stand had been demolished in the safety-conscious aftermath of the appalling Valley Parade fire. Would City remain full-time? Would they even continue to exist? Because City were the first club to be relegated automatically, there was no established template to follow. They were to be the pioneers in the brave new world of the reconstructed football pyramid, and they had to do it with no manager, no players and no main stand. This was hardly the most auspicious of starts for a club about to enter the uncharted waters of non-league football.

At that point, a young City supporter living in Sheffield decided that 1987-88 would be a special season and began to collect newspaper cuttings, photographs and any other snippets of information about City's journey he could find. In these days of instant information, knowledge is very cheap and easy to come by, but 30 years ago it was a challenge to find anything relating to non-league football or to Lincoln City. That supporter had never felt the urge to collect these things before, and he has never done it since. Perhaps a guardian angel tapped him on the shoulder one day and told him that something special was about to happen. Despite the extremely unpromising beginnings, City stormed to the Conference championship under the mercurial Colin Murphy, and the young supporter in Sheffield was vindicated in keeping his scrap books. I still have them to this day, and I own a very special and personal record of a truly unique season.

When City returned to the Football League in 1988, they had escaped from the dank prison of non-league football at the first attempt, and they were never going back. Lessons had been learned, a solid platform had been established, and Lincoln City had been reborn. There were good times to be enjoyed, including a promotion in 1998 and five successive appearances in the League Two play-offs, achieved in the face of some very significant financial problems. The fact that all five shots at the play-off target were unsuccessful is, unfortunately, symptomatic of Lincoln City's history, as is the fact that their lack of success set a new Football League record which still stands. Worse was to follow. After a couple of seasons struggling to avoid the trapdoor at the foot of League Two, City finally fell through it in May 2011.

That is where the story told in this book begins, of course, but certainly not where it ends. There was to be no immediate return to the Football League this time around, and the next five seasons produced very little to be excited about. It presents a gruesome read at times, with five successive finishes in the bottom half reflecting the desperate state of a once-proud club. The financial challenges were sometimes so great that one has to wonder how the club still exists. It really should not. Optimism has not been on the menu at Sincil Bank in recent years, and for very good reason.

On 13 May 2016, Lincoln City confirmed the appointment of a PE teacher from Essex as their new manager. His brother was to be assistant manager, and he was a PE teacher too. They had made something of a name for themselves in non-league football over a protracted period, and they were taking their first steps into the dangerous world of the professional game. Although reaction from supporters was very positive, there was no reason to believe that something extraordinary was about to happen.

The following month, the young City supporter from Sheffield was on holiday in Somerset. He was no longer a young supporter by this stage, neither was he from Sheffield anymore. But that guardian angel was at it again, tapping him on the shoulder and whispering about an extraordinary season ahead. But how to mark it this time? A scrap book was inappropriate for a number of reasons, and perhaps a wider audience might be interested. As an established writer, a book on the subject seemed a viable option. However, it soon became clear that the 2016-17 season could not be considered in isolation of the previous five years. It was, without doubt, a product of those desperate seasons, and their very antithesis as it proved. A decision was made: the book would tell the story of Lincoln City in the Conference, but it would be published only once City were back in the Football League.

All that remained now - besides the small matter of last season's thirteenth-placed side having to win the National League - was to convince Lincoln City and a publisher to commit to a project that might never see the light of day. More in hope of gaining his support than expectation, I contacted Clive Nates and told him what I was doing. Far from calling in the men in white coats, Clive was immediately engaged and gave the project his enthusiastic backing. Bob Dorrian was more reticent to begin with for a variety of reasons, but soon proved eager to contribute. Publisher James Lumsden-Cook should have been a harder nut to crack, but he seems to love eccentric ideas. This was all too easy, and perhaps it was simply written in the stars. It was time to set to work.

It soon became apparent that the deluge of information pouring from six very complex years precluded any possibility of structuring the book in a regular prose format. Rather than omit much of that information to reduce the book to a manageable length, it was necessary to compile the main body of the book in note form. Anything of note that happened at Lincoln City in that time is listed day by day, defeat by defeat, crisis by crisis. It is all there, the all too infrequent smiles and the inevitable tears. As a natural consequence of that, it is a very factual book. I have tried to avoid offering any opinion, but there is no need to: the facts speak for themselves.

As we stand at the end of what has proved to be the most memorable season in the club's 133-year history, it is very easy to forget where the club has been, and very recently. To have won the National League championship, reached the semi-finals of the FA Trophy, and become the first non-league club in 103 years to reach the quarter-finals of the FA Cup against the backdrop of the previous five years is the stuff of fantasy. Written into a Hollywood movie, it may just be believable. Within the context of Lincoln City and its desperate struggle for survival, it is not. This book is a celebration of a quite astounding achievement, but should also serve as a frightening reminder of where this club has been. It must also stand as a warning never to go back there, because the contrasts within these pages are as stark as any story ever told within the history of football.

Philip Priddle, Ayrshire, May 2017

Foreword

I write this piece on the first night of my family holiday at the end of May. This is the first time I have been able to draw breath and reflect on the season just gone.

From the moment Nicky and I took the role we were taken aback by the sheer potential of this club. Whenever we take over at a new football club we spend the interim period learning about the DNA of the organisation and all of the little idiosyncrasies which make it unique. Quite quickly it became clear that Lincoln City's major strength was the people.

Part of the learning process involved watching the Aldershot Town game from the end of the 2010/11 season, the day the club got relegated from the Football League. The two things that stood out to me from that game were the fact that there were over 8,000 supporters crammed into Sincil Bank and the pain etched onto their faces at the final whistle. Both really resonated with Nicky and me, making us even more determined from the start to change the tears to smiles. It affected us so much that we decided to show the players the footage at our first meeting. We wanted to show the players the pain that the club had gone through and how much it meant to those people. In order to get to where we wanted to go, I felt it was necessary to show the group where it had been.

Having engaged the players, we wanted to engage the people, the supporters. We looked back at previous managers who had been successful at Lincoln City such as Graham Taylor, Colin Murphy and Keith Alexander. They all had one thing in common... they interacted with the local community, they went into the schools, the offices, the factories, they connected with the people. Instantly it become clear that if we could emulate this and bring the football to the people, then they could be the driving force behind the team.

From our very first interaction with the players they have been brilliant. We have increased their workload, the number of days they work, the duration of their day, the intensity that they work at, and not once have they complained. Our daily demands have been relentless. They have embraced the shift in culture and enjoyed working hard. They are an honest, hard working group and it has been one of my greatest privileges to work with them on a daily basis. We have learned and developed together, becoming stronger people and more unified as a consequence.

We had a really good start to the season which was both pleasing and surprising in equal measure. Nicky and I knew coming into August that we were a long way from implementing our method. We knew that this would take time, so we aimed to be competitive in the early period of the season while we were fine-tuning the important detail of our team strategy. So to be top of the league by the 10th of September wasn't in our script! The fact we then went on our worst run of the season was no surprise to us, and actually confirmed what we knew... we weren't quite right!

As a manager, you have a sixth sense: sometimes results can paper over it but in your heart of hearts you have a feeling when it is just not quite right. The art is to identify the issues and act quickly on them. Nicky has an unbelievable eye. The game happens in slow motion to him, and consequently he is able to dissect it and then influence it tactically.

We left the Dover away game at the end of September searching for some answers. Like always, we spent Sunday watching the game back and analysing the fine details. Nicky found the answer: a really small tweak, but a defining moment in our season. We switched Matt Rhead from our second striker to our first forward. This went against the textbook and probably made Rheady into the most unique number 10 in world football, but it worked because it suited our profile of players. All of a sudden we had pace beyond Rheady in central and wide areas. It allowed us to press more aggressively from the front which allowed our centre halves to play on the front foot. No longer were they worried about the space in behind because they had confidence in the ability of our front players to pressure the opposition into poor clearances.

This small tactical tweak made our players significantly better. Luke Waterfall and Sean Raggett's performances improved by the game. Our midfield players became second ball machines because they knew where the loose balls were going to land. Nathan Arnold and Theo Robinson excelled as the spearheads of our attack, and although we took goals away from Matt Rhead, his overall contribution to the team became even greater.

We went on a 17-game unbeaten run which coincided with us beating Forest Green Rovers and Tranmere Rovers as well as embarking on our FA Cup run. We had found winning football, a style that was the very best fit for our profile of players. The players took care of the rest; their relentless work ethic, determination and resilience allowed us to find the level of consistency needed to be successful.

The FA Cup run will live long in the memory of everybody who contributed to the journey. The Oldham game was the first of our giant killing acts, although we didn't really celebrate this victory because we were annoyed at the way we had lost our focus towards the end of the match. This was typical of our group... even when we were winning we always strived for more.

The Ipswich games were pivotal. The players were simply brilliant in the first game, but the supporters were even better! To take 5,000 supporters away from home, as a non-league team, will never be seen again in the history of the English game. The atmosphere that day will live with me forever.

The second game and Nathan Arnold's goal after brilliant work from Adam Marriott in the dying moments was special in itself. However, for me, more important than the goal and the victory was the change on the terraces from that night on. It felt like the supporters really started to believe in the team. Prior to this, it still felt like the supporters expected the team to let them down... probably when it mattered most. Maybe our supporters were still scarred by the past? After this game, a newfound trust had been built. A new, different Lincoln City had been born. This team knew how to win, they were determined and resilient, and were not going to let the supporters down. This trust gave the players real confidence which both enhanced and transcended their performances.

The second half performance against Brighton surprised me. I didn't think we could play that well. We didn't just win that game against the Championship leaders, we controlled it and in the second half dominated long periods of it.

At Burnley, we got the game plan right. We knew they wouldn't be used to being favourites. We let them have the ball, knowing that this would be different to what they were used to, week in week out, in the Premier League. It knocked them off their stride, and all of a sudden they were playing a different game to what they were used to. To score from a set piece and keep a clean sheet made the win even more special. The jubilation in the away end on both Sean Raggett's goal and the final whistle will stay with me forever. To beat a Premier League team on their own turf was what dreams are made of. To win and get into the last 8, the quarter-finals of the FA Cup, was too much... far too much for words. Again I have to credit the players. Not once did they get ahead of themselves, they just kept their heads down and continued to work hard, day in and day out.

Around 9,000 of you followed us to the Emirates. We didn't just take over Arsenal that day but the whole of London. The scenes in Covent Garden were unreal! You were Premier League that day and for 45 minutes the players matched your efforts. To this day, I lie awake wondering what would have happened if we had got in at half time all square. Unfortunately we didn't, and in the second half Arsenal found their confidence and subsequently their rhythm. Arsenal showed their class both on and off the field that day. The second half felt like the longest 45 minutes of my life. It was like watching your best mate get beaten up by 6 blokes while you are standing watching, holding the jackets!

The game prior to Arsenal, Braintree away, was one of our most professional performances of the season. To play with as much focus as we did that night, with the backdrop of Arsenal and the Emirates in the near distance, was testament to the players. As people you are defined by your actions. That performance against Braintree defined our players for me.

People would constantly ask me whether the cup run would be a distraction to our league form. We didn't see it like that, we genuinely felt that the cup run had given us confidence, created further connection with our supporters and provided us with the experience of playing and winning big games. We felt that would hold us in good stead for what was to come. However, we did anticipate a dip in form on the back of going out of the FA Cup.

The inevitable dip did arrive after the Arsenal game, but thankfully it was short-lived. Again, full credit to the players for their unwavering determination and grit to see us quickly through this period. They had to fight really hard after the disappointment of the loss in the FA Trophy semi-final and the Boreham Wood league game. Lesser teams with lesser characters would have gone under at this point. To beat Forest Green Rovers after these disappointments was just colossal. We won that game on sheer personality and will. It was an incredible win considering where we were as a team at that point. It was the beginning of another unbeaten run – this time 11 games – that would see us to the end of the season and rightfully crowned champions.

What happened to Lincoln City in the 2016/17 season was a football miracle. I am convinced of that. It will live with us all to the day we die and we will be forever proud of what we achieved. We beat a League One team, two Championship teams and a Premier League team away from home while reaching the quarter-finals of the FA Cup. However, that wasn't the real achievement. The real achievement was being able to maintain our consistency throughout a 46-game league campaign while enjoying this cup run. The gritty performances away from home at Solihull Moors and North Ferriby United on the back of our cup exploits made it possible.

To take 21 points out of the 21 competitive points available in April was a phenomenal return. When you consider that we played over 60 games in the season and 28 in just over 99 days, it makes it even more remarkable. The players' resilience and resolve was astonishing. We looked dead on our feet during the run in but as a group we refused to give up. We managed to stay in games when we didn't play well and fight right to the end. We never knew when we were beaten, and this was demonstrated in the number of games where we came from behind to win, and the fact that we scored a third of our goals in the last 15 minutes of matches. As a group, we just found a way.

People often ask me about my favourite moment of the season. For me, it is simple, the final whistle at the Macclesfield game; a realisation that we had got value for our hard work. From my point of view, to see everyone – players, staff, directors and supporters – get the success their hard work deserved was immensely rewarding. Whatever the future holds for Nicky and me, I am not sure we will ever feel better than we did on the final whistle against Macclesfield.

The celebrations that followed showed what a united football club this is. The open top bus parade around the city, and the awards evening, showed what it meant to the people. It is not the bricks and mortar that make a football club, it is the people. That means our football club has class and it has soul.

As a club we may have suffered six years in purgatory, but we have come out the other side bigger, stronger, and with a realisation of what this club can be. It may just be the making of this football club. Football in non-league is real, real football with real people. We must use our success this season as a springboard to push on, but we must never forget the lessons that non-league football has taught us. UTI!

Danny Cowley, Lincoln, May 2017

Year 1

2011-12

3 City announce they are to reduce admission prices for Saturday's decisive game against Aldershot Town.

6 City face their biggest game for many years against Aldershot on Saturday, needing a win to ensure Football League survival. They sit third from bottom of the table, 2 points ahead of Barnet; but with a vastly inferior goal difference to their old North London foe, a draw will not be enough should Barnet beat Port Vale at home.

7 **Lincoln 0 Aldershot Town 3**. Att: 7,932. Another desperately poor performance sees City relegated from the Football League. Barnet's 1-0 win over Port Vale sees them leapfrog City to safety. City's failure is dramatic, picking up just 2 points from a possible 33 in the closing weeks of the season; at the start of that run, they had been closer to the play-offs than relegation. Manager Steve Tilson's post-match reaction angers fans: 'I might come across as being OK but deep down this will hurt me.' Only deep down?

⇒ Chairman Bob Dorrian confesses it may take two or three years for City to regain their place in the Football League. His comments are met with criticism from fans, who believe they are defeatist.

9 Bob Dorrian confirms that ruthless cuts will have to be made following relegation, which is expected to cost the club £300,000 in solidarity payments from the Football League. He also states his belief that City were not helped by previous manager Chris Sutton's recruitment policy last summer, and that Steve Tilson is the right man to take Lincoln forward: 'As far as I am concerned, he can stay as long as he likes.'

⇒ Steve Tilson announces that he wants to stay at the club following relegation.

⇒ League Two side Oxford United are reported to be interested in City defender Paul Green.

10 Former City manager Chris Sutton insists he is not to blame for the club's relegation. Sutton resigned nine games into the season with City in 20th place in the table.

11 Steve Tilson announces his retained list. Just three players - Danny Hone, Luke Howell and Andrew Hutchinson - are offered new contracts, with every other player either released or made available for transfer as the Imps try to cut their cloth following relegation. Released are Delroy Facey, Joe Anderson, Drewe Broughton, Jamie Clapham, Paul Green, Cian Hughton, Patrick Kanyuka, Clark Keltie and Scott Spencer. Although still under contract for the 2011-12 season, Mustapha Carayol, Ali Fuseini and Gavin McCallum are all available for transfer, whereas Joe Anyon, Josh O'Keefe and Adam Watts have all been told they are free to leave the club.

13 In a letter published in the Lincolnshire Echo, former City chairman Rob Bradley blames 'years of fundamental mistakes' for City's relegation from the Football League. His concerns lie in the areas of player recruitment and failure to engage with the supporters in particular.

14 Director David Beck apologises to the fans for relegation and admits that mistakes were made which undermined the campaign. However, he lays the blame squarely at the door of the players.

⇒ Former City manager Peter Jackson injects a cold dose of realism by forecasting that City could take five or six years to return to the League.

16 CEO Steve Prescott announces that season ticket sales are holding up very well despite City's relegation from the Football League, with over 600 sold to date.

17 Defender Josh Gowling says he would not rule out a return to Lincoln City after being released by Gillingham. The centre half spent time on loan at Sincil Bank last season, but City's reduced budget makes a return unlikely.

18 Steve Tilson insists his reduced budget will hamper his chances of taking City back to the Football League this season. Tilson believes the budget is in the lower half of the Blue Square Bet Premier, and says the six transfer-listed players will be leaving because of budget constraints, not because they are not wanted. At the same time, he admits he had a problem with the attitude and mentality of some of his players but believes those problems arose before he came to the club.

19 City confirm that former player Chris Moyses has invested heavily in the club's Centre of Excellence to keep it going for the next year; City need to raise between £100,000 and £150,000 following the loss of central funding from the Football League. The deal includes an option for a further two years and a coaching role for Moyses. The former Lincoln Moorlands manager says it is 'a dream come true.'

⇒ Former captain Scott Kerr launches an attack on Steve Tilson's management of the club. The midfielder, who left the club for York City at the end of January, feels Tilson lost the dressing room very early in his tenure through poor man-management and trying to change too many things too quickly. Tilson disputes Kerr's version of events.

20 City defender Adam Watts says he is prepared to renegotiate his contract with City in order to stay at the club. He has one year left on his current deal but has been given a free transfer following relegation.

21 Defender Danny Hone admits he is considering his Lincoln City future very carefully, and that he is waiting to see whether his availability attracts interest from Football League clubs.

26 Chairman Bob Dorrian promises at a fans' forum that City will do everything in their power to return to the Football League as soon as possible; he explains his original comments as a heat of the moment reality check. He tempers the statement with the news that City are set to post a £400,000 loss for the current financial year with a projected loss of £80,000 for the season to come. He also confirms that Steve Tilson is looking to work with a squad of 18 professionals next season. In perhaps the most revealing statement of the evening, he labels the majority of last season's squad as 'absolutely gutless.' The training ground is to be mothballed to save money. Bob confirms that £120,000 was spent in paying off players last season and that failed centre forward Ben Hutchinson cost the club £1,000 per week. He also believes that the board did not watch the deals previous manager Chris Sutton was doing closely enough. Savings will be made this season by stopping appearance money, reducing accommodation costs for players and reducing relocation costs by 50%.

30 Steve Tilson admits he is not even close to making any summer signings. He blames the £80,000 cut in his playing budget for his inability to sign the players he wants, and the need to move out the six transfer-listed players first, as the six are taking up 30% of the playing budget.

31 City are linked with former Notts County defender Graeme Lee, whom Steve Tilson tried to sign in January. Lee is a free agent after being released and is believed to be very interested in a move to Lincoln.

June 2011

1 17-year-old youth team goalkeeper Nick Draper signs a one-year professional contract.

3 CEO Steve Prescott insists patience will pay dividends for City in the transfer market. Reacting to concerns from fans, Prescott believes being panicked into making signings would be a recipe for disaster and insists that City must ensure value for money.

7 City are linked with former Grimsby midfielder Mark Hudson, although the player confirms no contact has been received from Lincoln.

9 The coroner announces that former City midfielder Richard Butcher died of an undiagnosed heart abnormality. Butcher, who had moved on to Macclesfield Town, died on 10 January.

⇒ Former City striker Jamie Forrester says he is willing to come out of retirement to help Lincoln back to the League. The 36-year-old retired a year ago to concentrate on his business interests.

10 Steve Tilson confirms he is to hold talks with midfielder Luke Howell to try to persuade him to sign a new contract with City. Howell wishes to remain in the Football League.

13 Young striker Andrew Hutchinson signs a one-year deal and becomes the second player after Nick Draper to sign up for the new season.

⇒ City are set to reduce their £40,000 asking price on Mustapha Carayol as a League Two club closes in on his signature. Carayol has ruled out playing for City on reduced terms and wants to remain in the Football League.

15 Bob Dorrian promises that it is business as usual at Sincil Bank following the shock resignation of vice-chairman Chris Travers from the board.

17 Reserve goalkeeper/goalkeeping coach Paul Musselwhite leaves City to join Conference rivals York City. The 42-year-old had been offered a contract by City on the proviso that Joe Anyon left the club.

⇒ Mustapha Carayol joins Bristol Rovers for an undisclosed fee. Rovers have just been relegated to League Two.

18 It is revealed that former City associate director Michael Foley is to sue the club and chairman Bob Dorrian for slander and libel following comments made at the fans' forum last month. Foley tried unsuccessfully to join the board in March.

20 Steve Tilson confirms his interest in former Notts County defender Graeme Lee but fears his wage demands may be beyond City's budget. Tilson also rules out moves for Dover striker Adam Birchall and Morecambe midfielder Andrew Fleming.

⇒ A group of City shareholders dissatisfied at the club's poor performance on and off the field in recent years declares no confidence in Lincoln City's board of directors. The move calls for an Extraordinary General Meeting to take place.

21 City suffer a financial blow as new Nottingham Forest manager Steve McLaren cancels the pre-season friendly scheduled for 30 July. Forest confirm they have cancelled all pre-season friendlies for the time being.

⇒ The friendly against Nottingham Forest is confirmed as being back on after Forest confirm they have included the fixture within their revised pre-season schedule.

22 Chris Travers officially ceases to be a director of the club.

⇒ City are linked with former Forest Green Rovers midfielder Matt Somner.

23 Steve Tilson confirms he has tabled offers for a midfielder and a defender. He also dismisses speculation linking him with former Bolton Wanderers and Denmark striker Henrik Pedersen.

24 Steve Tilson confirms he is interested in former Oxford United right back Ben Purkiss but believes the player would like to stay in the Football League.

27 Steve Tilson confirms that young striker James Wilson has signed a one-year deal.

⇒ City confirm that season ticket sales have reached almost a thousand.

⇒ City announce admission prices for the coming season, with paying on the day costing up to £18 depending on the stand. The announcement is met with immediate criticism from fans who feel the pricing structure offers poor value for money. At £18, the matchday price is the most expensive in the Blue Square Bet Premier.

29 Steve Tilson announces he is close to signing an experienced non-league striker. Tilson also confirms he will be taking a look at a number of trialists over the next few weeks.

30 Danny Hone signs a new one-year deal.

⇒ Steve Tilson is set to make a bid for striker Sam Smith from crisis club Rushden & Diamonds.

1 Lincoln City Supporters' Society Ltd (The Trust) is appointed to the board of directors.

⇒ David Beck ceases to be a director of the club.

⇒ City sign 28-year-old striker Jamie Taylor from Eastbourne Borough on a two-year deal.

⇒ City are linked with Rushden & Diamonds midfielder Alan Power, former Southend United winger Francis Laurent and former Kettering midfielder Jon Challinor.

⇒ Bob Dorrian reveals that the uncertainty surrounding the club following the calling of an Extraordinary General Meeting is hampering negotiations to bring players into the club.

2 Steve Tilson reveals he is close to agreeing a deal with a big target man to play alongside new signing Jamie Taylor. Tilson confirms he has offers in for five players.

5 City sign 25-year-old French winger Francis Laurent from Northampton Town on a one-year deal.

⇒ It is revealed that the big target man City are pursuing is former Tamworth striker Kyle Perry. City face competition from Mansfield Town manager Paul Cox for the 6'4" striker.

⇒ Former Cambridge United striker Daryl Clare is on trial with the Imps.

⇒ The Extraordinary General Meeting called by a number of disgruntled supporters is set for 21 July. Among other demands, the group is calling for the dismissal of every current director and the appointment of former City director Chris Travers as the new chairman. It is revealed that former City director Keith Roe is one of the group.

6 City sign 23-year-old midfielder Alan Power from Rushden & Diamonds on a one-year deal. Power was voted Rushden's 'Player of the Season' for 2010-11.

⇒ City sign 21-year-old striker Sam Smith, also from Rushden & Diamonds, on a one-year deal.

⇒ The fixture list for the new season is published and sends City to meet Southport on the opening day. Southport enjoyed a reprieve from relegation at the end of last season when Rushden & Diamonds were expelled from the Blue Square Bet Premier for financial reasons.

8 City sign 29-year-old defender John Nutter from Gillingham on a two-year deal.

⇒ City also sign 25-year-old striker Kyle Perry from Tamworth on a two-year deal.

⇒ City also sign 26-year-old defender Tony Sinclair from Gillingham on a one-year deal. Sinclair states he will try to persuade his Gillingham colleague Josh Gowling to sign for City too. Gowling is currently on trial at Crewe Alexandra.

9 Bob Dorrian reveals he is to loan the club £100,000 from his own pocket to cover numerous expenses that would normally have been taken care of by the Football League solidarity payment. The new loan is in addition to £50,000 put in by Dorrian last month. Dorrian also confirms that the club has now made around £650,000-£700,000 in cuts as it prepares for life in non-league football.

11 The challenge to the board of Lincoln City by the group of disgruntled supporters descends into farce as it is revealed that Chris Travers has not been consulted regarding his part in their proposals. Travers confirms that he is not supportive of their action, calling their conduct 'discourteous' and 'unprofessional', and is to vote against every resolution. Keith Roe and Paul Wilson, two of the leading shareholders behind the action, admit they should have contacted Travers first.

12 City sign 27-year-old midfielder Nicky Nicolau from Boreham Wood on a one-year deal. Nicolau previously played under Steve Tilson for Southend United.

13 Premier Sports announces its schedule of matches for the opening months of the Conference Premier season. Three Lincoln City matches have been selected, meaning that they will move from their allotted Saturday afternoon kick-off times. The matches affected are Wrexham at home (now Friday 19 August), Braintree away (now Saturday 3 September at 7pm) and Fleetwood Town at home (now Friday 14 October).

14 City sign 27-year-old defender Josh Gowling from Gillingham on a two-year deal. Gowling is well-known to City fans, having impressed on loan in October and November 2010.

16 City open their pre-season with a 4-0 win at Northern Premier League Premier Division newcomers Ilkeston, the goals from Jamie Taylor, Gavin McCallum, Andy Hutchinson and Josh Gowling.

18 Manager Steve Tilson reveals that Bradley Barraclough has joined the club on trial after he sent Tilson a link to some YouTube highlights of him playing for Bellarmine University Knights in Kentucky, USA. Although Barraclough spent his formative years in Lincoln, he has been on a sports scholarship in America and has a degree in psychology.

19 City's pre-season continues with a 2-0 win at neighbouring Barton Town Old Boys, newly-promoted to the Northern Counties East League Premier Division, with Adam Watts and Sam Smith scoring. Full back Jason Beardsley - later to sign for the club on non-contract terms - plays as an unsuccessful trialist. Other trialists include midfielders Sam Clucas and Joe Fox, and strikers Aristote Guerin-Lokonga and Danny Kelly.

20 City sign 26-year-old midfielder/winger Simon Russell from Cambridge United on a one-year deal.

⇒ City pick up another pre-season win, this time at Brigg Town of the Northern Premier League Division One South by 4-1. City's scorers are Josh O'Keefe, Ali Fuseini, Jamie Taylor and Gavin McCallum. Stefan Cox from Tooting & Mitcham impresses as a trialist.

21 Bob Dorrian and the directors defeat a vote of no confidence in their leadership at the Extraordinary General Meeting, gaining 78.6% of the shareholder vote. Despite a substantial defeat, challenger Keith Roe still believes the board's position is 'untenable'.

22 David Parman is officially appointed to the board of directors.

23 City's home game against Stockport County scheduled for Saturday 27 August is brought forward to Friday 26 August on police advice.

24 Lincoln beat Scunthorpe United 4-3 on penalties in the semi-final of the Lincolnshire Cup at Sincil Bank after a 1-1 draw; Sam Smith scores City's goal. Steve Tilson announces he will play a youth team in the final, as he intends to take his first team squad away on a team building exercise.

26 City lose for the first time in pre-season, going down 2-1 at Gainsborough. Transfer-listed Gavin McCallum scores his third goal in four games, prompting manager Steve Tilson to predict that McCallum will 'rip up the Blue Square Premier' this season. City field a number of trialists in the game including Vincent Fernandes, former Grimsby defender Dallas Moore, right back Sam Eckhardt from Sheffield Wednesday, and goalkeeper Jamie Butler.

30 City lose by a single goal at home to Championship side Nottingham Forest in front of 2,863.

August 2011

1 City sign 22-year-old trialist Bradley Barraclough on a one-year contract with an option for a further year.

2 Steve Tilson signs trialists Stefan Cox, Doug Lindberg and Sam Eckhardt on short-term deals to enable them to play in tonight's Lincolnshire Cup Final. Only registered players may appear in the competition.

⇒ Grimsby Town score two goals in the final five minutes to beat City 4-3 in the final of the Lincolnshire Cup. Simon Russell, Bradley Barraclough and Kyle Perry score Lincoln's goals in front of 1,446 at Sincil Bank. Doug Lindberg, James Wilson and Sam Eckhardt make their first and only competitive appearances for the club as manager Tilson fields a very young side as he had indicated in the week.

4 City are to take a look at French midfielder Jean-Francois Christophe, who played under Tilson at Southend.

⇒ Steve Tilson says he would like to sign defender Sam Eckhardt if the budget allows.

6 City end their pre-season with a narrow 4-3 win at Boston United, the goals coming from John Nutter, Gavin McCallum, Alan Power and Bradley Barraclough in front of 982 at York Street.

9 Bob Dorrian believes City 'should be looking at the play-offs as a bare minimum' this season as they start their journey back to the Football League.

10 City sign Jean-Francois Christophe on a one-year deal, effective from 22 August. Christophe has been persuaded to sign by his friend Francis Laurent, a former team mate from French club FC Compiègne.

13 **Southport 2 Lincoln 2 (Smith, Perry).** Att: 1,687. City take the lead twice before drawing their first match in the Conference for 23 years, with Sam Smith and Kyle Perry scoring on their debuts. John Nutter, Alan Power, Jamie Taylor, Simon Russell and Bradley Barraclough also make their City debuts. Josh Gowling makes his second City debut. City sit 7th in the table after game one, 2 points behind early leaders Hayes & Yeading.

16 In an interesting sub-plot to tonight's game against Kidderminster, Kyle Perry reveals that Harriers' centre half Tom Marshall plays in the rock band 'Stubblemelt' with him.

⇒ **Lincoln 0 Kidderminster Harriers 1.** Att: 2,448. Tony Sinclair makes his City debut after recovering from pre-season injury, but a poor City performance extends the winless run at Sincil Bank to 5 matches. Only a fine performance from goalkeeper Joe Anyon keeps the score down. City slip to 17th in the table, 5 points behind leaders Gateshead.

18 Relations between the fans and the players deteriorate further as skipper Josh Gowling has exchanges with angry fans on Twitter.

19 **Lincoln 1 (Smith) Wrexham 2.** Att: 2,211. This game is played on a Friday evening for the benefit of the Premier Sports TV cameras but produces a painfully familiar outcome. The winless run is now 14 games. At least the television exposure brings in a welcome broadcast fee of £5,000.

20 No game this Saturday due to the Wrexham match being moved to last night. Once the Saturday round of matches is completed, City are down to 20th.

22 Businessman Michael Foley withdraws his legal action against the club after Bob Dorrian apologises for comments made during the fans' forum in May.

23 **AFC Telford United 1 Lincoln 2 (Perry 2).** Att: 2,323. The winless run stretching back five months is finally over, as two late Kyle Perry goals give City their first win back in the Conference. Nicky Nicolau makes his City debut as their league position improves to 14th, 6 points behind leaders Gateshead.

25 City defender Adam Watts is called up to the England C contingency squad for the game against India on 6 September.

26 **Lincoln 1 (Power) Stockport County 1.** Att: 2,152. Alan Power's early opener is cancelled out before half time, and City have to settle for a point after hitting the woodwork twice in the second half.

27 No Saturday game today due to the Stockport game being moved to last night on police advice. After the Saturday games are completed, City slip to 17th again, 8 points behind leaders Wrexham.

29 **Darlington 3 Lincoln 1 (Power).** Att: 2,252. A goal by Ryan Bowman after just 13 seconds sets City on their way to a disappointing day in the surreal atmosphere of the 25,000-seat Northern Echo Arena. Jean-François Christophe makes his debut as a 9th-minute substitute for Tony Sinclair, but City are well-beaten by Mark Cooper's side. Adam Watts misses the game after trapping a nerve in his back picking up his football boots. City drop a place to 18th, and are already 11 points behind leaders Wrexham.

30 The current injury crisis deepens as City are left with three fit defenders after the game at Darlington.

31 City sign 22-year-old defender Mitchell Nelson from Bournemouth on a one-month loan.

September 2011

2 City are investigating the possibility of receiving some money from the transfer of former striker Dany N'Guessan from Leicester to Millwall.

3 **Braintree Town 1 Lincoln 0**. Att: 1,182. City's first ever meeting with Braintree ends in defeat. Mitchell Nelson makes his City debut in a game that kicks off at 7pm for the benefit of the Premier Sports cameras. Jamie Taylor hits the woodwork but it is another poor performance from Tilson's misfiring team. Chairman Bob Dorrian is subjected to criticism from angry fans at the final whistle as City slip into the bottom 4, with just 5 points from 7 games.

6 Bob Dorrian says City were 'absolutely dreadful' in the first half against Braintree but gives his backing to Steve Tilson; he believes Tilson is too experienced not to salvage the current poor run of form.

7 City captain Josh Gowling also gives his support to manager Tilson, and blames the players for the current run.

9 Steve Tilson fails in a renewed bid to sign Oxford defender Ben Purkiss on loan; the player has opted to extend his loan deal at Darlington instead. Tilson believes that Darlington could offer to pay a larger percentage of the player's wages.

⇒ Goalkeeper Doug Lindberg joins Sleaford Town on loan.

10 **Lincoln 0 Kettering Town 2**. Att: 2,269. City go down to a dismal home defeat to bogey team Kettering, who had been in the bottom four prior to kick-off. Two second half goals give new manager Mark Stimson a win in his first game. A poor afternoon is compounded by a red card for Jean-François Christophe in injury time. City have still not won at home since March and have just 1 win in 19 games. They sit 22nd in the league, 2 points from safety.

12 Steve Tilson claims he is still the right man for the job and says he will never resign.

⇒ Captain Josh Gowling again issues a plea to the fans to be patient.

14 CEO Steve Prescott confirms that City have revised their projected attendance figures after gates fall below budget. The average of 2,270 is the lowest for 25 years.

15 Josh Gowling removes himself from Twitter after angry exchanges with fans online.

17 **Luton Town 1 Lincoln 0**. Att: 6,316. City suffer their fourth successive defeat as they go down to Gary Brabin's big-spending Luton side. They lose to an 85th-minute Stuart Fleetwood goal despite playing against 10 men for much of the game after the 23rd-minute dismissal of Luton defender Dean Beckwith. The result flatters the Imps after Fleetwood misses an astonishing 6 one-on-ones with keeper Joe Anyon. Mitchell Nelson is sent off for two bookable offences in the closing seconds. City stay 22nd, with just 5 points from their opening 9 games.

19 Pressure grows on manager Steve Tilson as Lincoln City Trust chairman Chris Ashton confirms the Trust has raised its own concerns with director David Beck. Defender Adam Watts admits he is too ashamed by Lincoln's poor form to leave his house, although Tilson confirms he has the full backing of the club.

20 **Lincoln 1 (Fuseini) Gateshead 0**. Att: 1,587. Ali Fuseini's header sees City beat the league leaders to win at Sincil Bank for the first time since 12 March. However, an inspired performance from goalkeeper Joe Anyon keeps City in the game in front of the lowest attendance at Sincil Bank for 10 years. City are up to 19th, out of the bottom 4 on goal difference.

24 **Lincoln 1 (Hone) Forest Green Rovers 1**. Att: 2,076. The first ever meeting between the two clubs sees the visitors take the lead after just 2 minutes. The goal angers City, as defender Tony Sinclair is off the pitch having been forced by the referee to remove a wristband. Danny Hone's 60th-minute equaliser means that Forest Green remain unbeaten away from home. City stay 19th, out of the bottom 4 on goal difference.

27 Steve Tilson bemoans the lack of overnight stays ahead of the 5-hour journey to Barrow. Budget constraints mean they can only afford one more this season. Tilson blames the fact that he has been unable to offload five of the six transfer-listed players on high wages.

⇒ City announce the signing of French defender Jean Arnaud, who has been on trial at Sincil Bank for the last three weeks. The 24-year-old has signed a short-term contract to the middle of January 2012.

⇒ **Barrow 1 Lincoln 0**. Att: 1,181. A first half penalty sees City go down to Barrow in their first meeting since 1972. Barrow striker Andy Cook is sent off late on but City produce yet another poor second half performance to slip back into the bottom 4, 2 points adrift of safety.

29 Skipper Josh Gowling assures City fans that there is no danger of relegation, and that he believes they have the players to make the play-offs.

1 **Lincoln 2 (Smith, McCallum) Bath City 0**. Att: 2,244. Relief abounds as City despatch bottom side Bath City with two goals in the first half-hour on a hot afternoon. Temperatures reach 28 degrees on Lincolnshire Day. City rise to 19th, 1 point above the drop zone.

3 Steve Tilson hopes that City's win over Bath is not a false dawn.

6 Former City manager Chris Sutton claims in his autobiography *Paradise and Beyond* that Lincoln are trying to sue him for breach of contract following his resignation last season.

8 **Tamworth 4 Lincoln 0**. Att: 1,232. In what proves to be Steve Tilson's last game as City manager, Tony Sinclair is sent off after 60 minutes for two bookable offences on a bad afternoon all round. Defender Jean Arnaud makes what turns out to be his only City appearance, as a 63rd-minute substitute for Nicky Nicolau. Steve Tilson lays the blame for the defeat on his players.

9 Doug Lindberg's loan at Sleaford Town is extended for a further month.

10 Manager Steve Tilson and assistant manager Paul Brush are sacked by Lincoln with the club languishing in 19th place in the table, one point above the relegation zone. Head of Youth Grant Brown is placed in caretaker charge of the club until a permanent replacement is found.

11 Former City players Mick Harford and Steve Thompson emerge as early favourites for the manager's job. The pair almost landed the job last year when it was given to Steve Tilson.

⇒ City re-sign defender Mitchell Nelson from Bournemouth on another month's loan.

⇒ **Alfreton Town 1 Lincoln 3 (Smith 2, McCallum)**. Att: 1,232. City coast to victory in Grant Brown's first game as caretaker manager, with all the scoring complete by the 24th-minute. Youth teamer Karl Cunningham makes his City debut in a game which bizarrely produces an identical attendance to the defeat at Tamworth on Saturday. City stay 19th but are now 3 points clear of the relegation zone.

13 Bob Dorrian says he regrets not sacking Steve Tilson following relegation and admits there was no bond between Tilson and the club. He claims it came as a relief to Tilson when he was finally dismissed. He also calls Tilson 'a catastrophe for Lincoln City', adding that his time in charge has cost the club £1m. The club is looking for a manager with experience in senior non-league football.

⇒ Ronnie Moore and Martin Foyle are the latest managers to be linked with the City job. The intention is to have the new man in place by the end of next week.

14 **Lincoln 1 (O'Keefe) Fleetwood Town 3**. Att: 2,332. This game is moved to Friday evening for the benefit of the Premier Sports TV cameras but results in a familiar outcome as City squander a half time lead. Danny Hone plays his final game for City.

15 A blank Saturday due to the match against Fleetwood being brought forward to last night. Saturday results see City slip back into the bottom 4 on goal difference.

17 City are drawn away to Conference rivals Alfreton Town in the fourth qualifying round of the FA Cup. City won 3-1 at Alfreton last Saturday and will be optimistic with the draw.

⇒ Former City striker Simon Yeo confirms that he has applied for the manager's job. City have received over 40 applications including Yeo's former City teammate Stuart Bimson.

18 **Lincoln 1 (McCallum) Mansfield Town 1**. Att: 2,944. An 86th-minute equaliser by Mansfield's Matt Green denies City a valuable win. Youth team striker Jordan Thomas becomes the youngest player ever to appear in a competitive match for Lincoln, at the age of 16 years, 71 days. Karl Cunningham makes his second and final first team appearance. Ali Fuseini also makes what proves to be his final appearance for the club. City stay in the bottom 4 on goal difference.

20 It emerges that Lincoln are to interview four candidates for the manager's job: Martin Foyle, David Holdsworth, former City manager Steve Thompson, and one unnamed candidate believed to be Grant Brown. Whoever gets the job will be rewarded by one of the lowest salaries in recent history, believed to be no more than £50,000 as City seek to reduce costs further.

21 City sign 18-year-old midfielder Curtis Thompson from Notts County on a one-month loan.

⇒ **Cambridge United 2 Lincoln 0**. Att: 2,875. A goal in each half from striker Ashley Carew sends the Imps to yet another defeat on a disappointing evening. Curtis Thompson makes his debut for City, appearing for the final 2 minutes as a substitute for Josh O'Keefe; he never appears again.

22 Interviews are held for manager's job throughout Saturday. Results elsewhere mean City stay 21st, in the bottom 4 on goal difference.

24 Former Watford, Sheffield United and Birmingham defender David Holdsworth is appointed manager until the end of the season.

26 Chairman Bob Dorrian says David Holdsworth was 'the stand-out candidate' and the most suitably qualified of those who applied for the manager's job.

27 In his first press conference, David Holdsworth confirms that his remit is to avoid relegation and is under no illusions about the size of that task. No money will be available for players unless substantial savings are made first. He is unsure about bringing in an assistant due to financial constraints and believes he may have to call in a few favours from friends.

29 FA Cup 4Q: Alfreton Town 1 Lincoln 1 (Smith). Att: 1,000. First-year professional goalkeeper Nick Draper makes his City debut as a substitute after Joe Anyon is sent off on half time; his first task is to pick Nathan Jarman's penalty out of the net. Francis Laurent, signed way back in July, makes his City debut at last.

30 City are drawn at home to League One Carlisle United in the first round of the FA Cup, if they can overcome Alfreton in Tuesday night's replay.

November 2011

1 FA Cup 4Q Replay: Lincoln 1 (Smith) Alfreton Town 2. Att: 1,728. City crash out of the FA Cup despite taking a first half lead. Nick Draper makes his second and final first team appearance despite being unwell. He has no choice but to play, as Joe Anyon is suspended after his sending-off in the original tie on Saturday. Draper is the only other goalkeeper on the club's books and FA rules state that a club cannot field a player who was not registered for the original tie. Football League leftovers Gavin McCallum and Adam Watts make what proves to be their final appearances for the club.

3 City sign 22-year-old goalkeeper Paul Farman on a two-month loan from Gateshead. He is new manager David Holdsworth's first signing.

⇒ 31-year-old former Sheffield Wednesday defender Richard Hinds starts a trial period at the club as manager Holdsworth promises 'radical changes'.

⇒ David Holdsworth bans players from using social media such as Twitter.

⇒ CEO Steve Prescott confirms that all 20 of the club's remaining full-time staff have been offered voluntary redundancy in order to reduce costs further. Prescott confirms that the club lost £680,000 from its budget in Football League, Premier League and television subsidies following relegation.

4 City quickly sign Richard Hinds on a short-term contract to the New Year.

⇒ City sign 25-year-old winger Conal Platt from Cambridge United on a two-month loan.

5 Lincoln 2 (Smith, Christophe) Barrow 1. Att: 2,090. A consolation goal in injury time from the visitors is not enough to overturn a two-goal half time lead. Paul Farman, Conal Platt and Richard Hinds make their City debuts as new manager Holdsworth picks up his first win at the third attempt. City are up to 18th, 2 points clear of the bottom 4.

8 Danny Hone joins Barrow on an emergency loan until 8 January.

9 Gavin McCallum is made available for immediate loan.

10 City extend Mitchell Nelson's loan for a further month.

⇒ New manager David Holdsworth confirms that on-loan midfielder Curtis Thompson has returned to Notts County before the scheduled end of his loan spell.

11 City make Ali Fuseini available for immediate loan.

12 City have no game due to being knocked out of the FA Cup at the 4th qualifying stage.

17 City sign 22-year-old striker Luke Medley on loan from Kidderminster Harriers until the New Year.

⇒ City also sign 25-year-old wide man Jake Sheridan on loan from Eastwood Town until the New Year.

⇒ City also sign 29-year-old midfielder Tyrone Thompson on a deal to 8 January. Thompson has been a free agent since leaving FC Halifax Town last month.

⇒ CEO Steve Prescott reveals that City have to halve their wage bill before the end of the season, and a period of consultation is under way. It is also revealed that the players are being asked to fund their pre-match meals from their own pockets.

18 David Featherstone is appointed to the board of directors.

19 Wrexham 2 Lincoln 0. Att: 3,424. A goal in each half sees City go down to their promotion-chasing hosts. Luke Medley makes his City debut as a substitute, whilst Mitchell Nelson and Josh O'Keefe play what turns out to be their final games for the club. Sam Smith breaks a bone in his foot and will be out for at least 6 weeks. City slip to 20th, 2 points clear of the relegation zone.

22 Gavin McCallum joins Barnet on loan until the New Year.

⇒ Goalkeeper Doug Lindberg leaves the club by mutual consent without making a competitive first team appearance.

25 City release Ali Fuseini by mutual consent after there are no offers for his transfer or loan.

26 Lincoln 3 (Platt, Russell, Nutter) Ebbsfleet United 0. Att: 2,111. A dominant performance from a new-look City side. Conal Platt, Simon Russell and John Nutter all score their first City goals, while Jake Sheridan and Tyrone Thompson make their City debuts. City are up to 18th, 5 points clear of the bottom 4.

28 City are drawn away to either Colwyn Bay or FC Halifax Town in the first round of the FA Trophy. The two Conference North sides drew 0-0 on Saturday in the third qualifying round and face a replay at the Shay.

29 York City 2 Lincoln 0. Att: 3,155. A goal after just 4 minutes sets City on their way to a disappointing defeat at play-off chasing York. City stay 18th, now 3 points clear of the drop zone.

⇒ City will travel to Colwyn Bay in the first round of the FA Trophy after the Welsh side wins 2-1 at FC Halifax tonight in their third qualifying round replay.

⇒ James Wilson joins Worksop Town on a one-month loan.

December 2011

1 It is revealed that the Lincolnshire Echo is paying for City's overnight stay prior to the game at Newport.

3 **Newport County 1 Lincoln 0**. Att: 1,270. City lose a very scrappy game to fellow strugglers Newport. City are 19th, 3 points clear of the relegation zone.

⇒ It emerges that on-loan defender Mitchell Nelson has been sent back to Bournemouth following a dressing room disagreement with manager David Holdsworth prior to the game at Newport. His loan period has been ended.

6 **Lincoln 1 (Hinds) Luton Town 1**. Att: 2,049. Richard Hinds scores his only City goal as promotion-chasers Luton end the game with 9 men. Former City defender Jamie Hand is one of those dismissed. City rise a place to 18th, still 3 points clear.

7 City release French defender Jean Arnaud after just two months of his contract, having clocked up just one substitute appearance in his time at Sincil Bank.

8 Former City midfielder Ali Fuseini, who left the club on 25 November, is jailed for 10 weeks for two counts of driving while disqualified; the original disqualification was given following a conviction for unauthorised taking of a motor vehicle shortly before he joined the Imps. His car is seized and crushed to prevent him driving again on release. It ends a poor 2011 for Fuseini, who had also been cleared of aiding and abetting an abduction and rape at Blackfriars Crown Court on 12 February.

⇒ Bob Dorrian assures fans that administration is not a possibility despite the severe financial limitations facing the club. At the Annual General Meeting he confirms a loss of £480,000 for the financial year ending 30 June 2011.

⇒ Michael Thompson, treasurer of the Lincoln City Supporters' Trust, is convicted of stealing £42,000 from a children's charity.

⇒ Manager David Holdsworth believes City can win the FA Trophy. City are at 25/1 with the bookmakers.

9 Striker Bradley Barraclough joins Buxton of the Northern Premier League Premier Division on loan until the end of the season.

⇒ 22-year-old defender Jason Beardsley signs for the club on non-contract terms. Beardsley had an unsuccessful trial at City during the summer, playing in the friendly win at Barton Town Old Boys.

10 **FA Trophy 1: Colwyn Bay 1 Lincoln 3 (Taylor 2, Platt)**. Att: 383. City coast to a comfortable win as Colwyn Bay play for the majority of the game with 10 men. Jamie Taylor scores his first goals for the club after an injury-hit start to his City career.

12 City are drawn at home to Carshalton Athletic in the second round of the FA Trophy. Carshalton play in the Ryman League Premier Division, two tiers below the Imps.

17 **Forest Green Rovers 0 Lincoln 2 (Power pen, Laurent)**. Att: 969. City continue their recent improvement with another comfortable win at Forest Green, who play for half the game with 10 men. The third game without defeat is the longest unbeaten run since February. City are up to 17th, 5 points clear of the bottom four.

20 Adam Watts and Josh O'Keefe are made available for loan.

21 Leicester City goalkeeper Adam Smith is on trial at Lincoln.

22 David Holdsworth reveals there is 'an army' of players wanting to join the Lincoln City cause but he doesn't want to change too much and risk derailing their form.

26 **Lincoln 1 (Platt) Grimsby Town 2**. Att: 5,506. Second half goals from future Imps Scott Garner and Liam Hearn give Grimsby the points after City lead at half time. Jason Beardsley makes his only appearance for City. Kyle Perry makes his final appearance, as does Paul Farman - although he will return. City remain 17th, 5 points clear of the danger zone.

⇒ Josh O'Keefe leaves the club by mutual consent.

⇒ Adam Watts leaves the club by mutual consent.

29 David Holdsworth is giving trials to Leeds United duo Sanchez Payne and Will Hatfield.

January 2012

1 City sign 24-year-old defender Robbie Williams from AFC Telford United on loan to the end of the season with a view to a permanent move.

⇒ **Grimsby Town 3 Lincoln 1 (Taylor)**. Att: 6,672. City are well-beaten by their neighbours in the second game of the festive double-header as future Imp Liam Hearn scores again. Richard Hinds and Luke Medley make their final appearances for City, while Robbie Williams makes his debut. City stay 17th, 4 points clear of the relegation zone.

4 Richard Hinds rejects a further contract and leaves the club. Manager David Holdsworth reveals that the club cannot afford his wage demands.

⇒ City sign 28-year-old striker Richard Pacquette from Maidenhead United until the end of the season.

⇒ City sign 19-year-old defender Karlton Watson from Nottingham Forest to the end of the season.

⇒ Striker Kyle Perry joins AFC Telford United on loan until the end of the season.

⇒ Danny Hone's loan at Barrow is extended until the end of the season.

5 Lincoln sign Leicester City goalkeeper Adam Smith on loan until the end of the season as cover for Joe Anyon. Smith has been training with the Imps for the last two weeks. Coincidentally, Manager Holdsworth is also chasing namesake and former Lincoln loanee Adam Smith of Mansfield as he seeks to overcome his shortage of fit strikers.

⇒ City sign 18-year-old defender Matty Pearson from Blackburn Rovers on a three-month loan.

⇒ Humberside police are investigating complaints from Lincoln fans after Grimsby striker Anthony Elding allegedly made a lewd gesture during the match on New Year's Day. The incident has also been reported to the FA.

⇒ Goalkeeper Joe Anyon reveals that things at the club had become 'really sloppy' under previous manager Steve Tilson.

6 City cancel the registration of defender Jason Beardsley after one appearance.

⇒ City sign on-loan winger Conal Platt from Cambridge on an eighteen-month deal.

⇒ City sign 20-year-old winger Danny Lloyd on a deal to the end of the season. Lloyd impressed playing against them for Colwyn Bay in the FA Trophy last month.

⇒ City sign on-loan winger Jake Sheridan from Eastwood Town on a permanent deal to the end of the season.

⇒ Tyrone Thompson extends his short-term deal to the end of the season.

⇒ In an interview with the Lincolnshire Echo, former City captain Scott Kerr reveals that he left Lincoln in January 2011 because he could not stand playing under Steve Tilson.

7 **Lincoln 0 York City 2**. Att: 3,048. Danny Lloyd, Karlton Watson and Richard Pacquette make their City debuts but are unable to prevent City going down to two second half goals. Tony Sinclair makes what proves to be his final City appearance. City slip to 18th, 4 points clear of the bottom four.

9 The former treasurer of the Lincoln City Supporters' Trust Michael Thompson is jailed for two years for stealing £42,000 from a children's charity.

10 City announce that prices will be reduced for Saturday's FA Trophy tie against Carshalton.

⇒ A City team containing reserves and trialists is beaten 2-0 by Gainsborough Trinity in a behind-closed-doors friendly. Trialists include Leeds United's Sanchez Payne and striker Jordan Burrow from Chesterfield.

⇒ City sign 18-year-old midfielder Tom Richardson from Sheffield FC on a deal to the end of the season.

12 Josh Gowling, Tony Sinclair and Gavin McCallum are spotted outside a Lincoln nightclub (*Home*) less than 48 hours before a game in breach of manager Holdsworth's strict code of conduct. None of the three appears in Saturday's FA Trophy tie against Carshalton, and McCallum and Sinclair never play for the club again.

⇒ David Holdsworth reveals he does not have a contract at the club.

13 City sign 28-year-old defender Paul Robson on non-contract terms. Robson has been a free agent since leaving Newport County in October.

⇒ New signing Tom Richardson joins Blyth Spartans on a one-month loan.

14 **FA Trophy 2: Lincoln 0 Carshalton Athletic 0**. Att: 1,743. Defenders Paul Robson and Matty Pearson make their debuts as City fail to beat opposition from the Ryman League Premier Division. Youth team player Jordan Thomas makes his second and final appearance for the first team.

⇒ Cambridge United's 4-1 FA Trophy win over AFC Telford means that their Conference Premier game against Lincoln, scheduled for 4 February, will need to be rearranged.

16 City agree to postpone tomorrow night's FA Trophy second round replay at Carshalton by 24 hours to allow the frozen pitch to thaw.

⇒ City are drawn away to either Worksop Town or Newport County in the third round of the FA Trophy, should they win Wednesday night's replay at Carshalton. Saturday's tie between Northern Premier League side Worksop and Conference Premier Newport was postponed.

18 **FA Trophy 2 Replay: Carshalton Athletic 3 Lincoln 1 (Sheridan)**. Att: 488. A hat-trick from Carshalton's Francis Vines ensures one of the worst results in City's history. Matty Pearson makes his second and final appearance for City. Reece Thompson makes his only appearance for the first team, as a late substitute.

21 **Gateshead 3 Lincoln 3 (Pacquette 2, Smith)**. Att: 870. City come back from 3-1 down with 8 minutes to play to snatch a draw with their promotion-chasing hosts. Alan Power is sent off with Gateshead's James Marwood in the second half. City are 18th, 5 points clear of the drop zone.

23 City announce the formation of a new 'holding company' designed to provide the club with a much-needed cash injection of £522,000 from a consortium including Bob Dorrian, Lincolnshire Co-operative and the Lindum Group. The money will go towards the running costs of the club and arises from problems caused by the club's relegation from the Football League. Dorrian states that the club would have run into serious financial problems in February and March had the move not taken place.

⇒ Alan Power receives a three-match ban for his red card at Gateshead.

24 **Lincoln 2 (Christophe, Pacquette) Southport 0**. Att: 1,615. Sam Smith breaks the same foot for the second time this season and will miss at least two months. City rise to 16th, still 5 points clear of the relegation zone despite their win.

25 City are linked with Grimsby striker Rob Duffy and winger Billy Gibson of Yeovil Town after Sam Smith is told he will not play again this season.

26 It is revealed that the Lincoln City Supporters' Trust forms part of the new holding company; as the largest shareholder, 1,000,000 Trust shares will be transferred to the new company under the agreement.

⇒ Bob Dorrian reveals that the club is to investigate building a new stadium, possibly in the Tritton Road area. With opportunities for growing commercial income limited at Sincil Bank, Dorrian believes a move is the best way to secure the long-term future of the club. With the cost of redeveloping the Echo (St Andrews) Stand believed to be £4.5m, the club believes it can build a replacement stadium for around £9m.

27 Karl Cunningham joins Worksop Town on a one-month loan.

⇒ James Wilson joins Holbeach United on a one-month loan.

28 **Kettering Town 1 Lincoln 0**. Att: 1,417. City lose for the second time this season to the team destined to finish bottom of the league. A first half penalty is enough to beat the Imps, who have just one fit striker available in Richard Pacquette. City stay 16th, 4 points clear of the relegation zone.

30 Striker Gavin McCallum leaves Lincoln by mutual consent. It is believed he was earning £1,300 per week.

31 City sign four players on transfer deadline day: 32-year-old much-travelled striker Jefferson Louis arrives from Brackley Town until the end of the season; 24-year-old utility player Peter Bore arrives from Harrogate Town until the end of the season; 20-year-old striker Nialle Rodney from Bradford City until the end of the season; and 20-year old striker Louis Almond joins on loan from Blackpool until the end of the season. Louis is the cousin of Richard Pacquette, who joined City earlier in the month.

⇒ Matty Pearson is recalled by Blackburn Rovers, as the young defender has played just twice.

February 2012

2 Manager David Holdsworth says he has signed Jefferson Louis, Peter Bore, Nialle Rodney and Louis Almond for less than half what they were paying Gavin McCallum. He explains that he is offering short-term deals to avoid having to pay players through the summer.

4 City's home game against Braintree Town is postponed due to a frozen pitch. The game had been rearranged for today to take the place of the postponed match against Cambridge United. The game is rearranged for Tuesday 14 February.

9 David Holdsworth reveals he has tried to sign defenders Guy Branston from Bradford City and Elian Parrino from Estudiantes, both without success. He will try to sign Parrino again in the summer if international clearance can be obtained for the former Sheffield United player.

10 City's game at Hayes & Yeading United tomorrow afternoon is postponed due to a frozen pitch at their temporary home, Woking's Kingfield Stadium. Temperatures nationally have fallen to -15 degrees.

11 No game today, with the visit to Hayes & Yeading being postponed.

14 **Lincoln 3 (Louis, Thompson, Almond) Braintree Town 3**. Att: 1,616. Jefferson Louis scores within a minute on his debut, but City need an equaliser 2 minutes into stoppage time from 67th-minute debut substitute Louis Almond to earn a point. Peter Bore and Nialle Rodney also make their debuts. City stay 16th, but the gap to the relegation zone is down to 3 points.

16 Grimsby striker Anthony Elding is charged with improper conduct by the FA following reports of a lewd gesture during the match at Blundell Park on 1 January.

18 **Kidderminster Harriers 1 Lincoln 1 (Louis)**. Att: 2,081. This time, it is Kidderminster snatching a point with a 92nd-minute equaliser. Jefferson Louis' first half goal is almost enough to beat their promotion-chasing hosts. City are 17th, 4 points clear of danger.

21 Winger Conal Platt suffers a bad leg break during a behind-closed-doors friendly at Doncaster Rovers. City suffer a morale-sapping 4-1 defeat.

23 Conal Platt is expected to miss four to six months after breaking his tibia on Tuesday.

24 City sign 33-year-old striker Mark McCammon on loan from Sheffield FC until the end of the season.

25 **Lincoln 1 (Blackburn own goal) AFC Telford United 1**. Att: 2,438. City's recent good run is extended to just 1 defeat in the last 6 games. However, they attract criticism from supporters after on-loan striker Kyle Perry scores for Telford. City are 17th, 5 points clear of the bottom four.

March 2012

3 **Mansfield Town 2 Lincoln 1 (McCammon)**. Att: 4,830. Mark McCammon scores on his City debut 4 minutes into stoppage time but is unable to prevent City slipping to defeat. Simon Russell makes his final appearance in a City shirt. City are 18th, 5 points clear of the bottom four.

⇒ Tom Richardson joins North Ferriby United on a one-month loan.

6 David Holdsworth admits he is still looking to add a couple of players to improve City's recent defensive record.

9 James Wilson joins Holbeach United for a second spell on loan.

10 **Lincoln 0 Alfreton Town 1**. Att: 2,253. Fears of a relegation battle deepen as City are beaten at home by fellow strugglers Alfreton. On-loan striker Louis Almond plays what turns out to be his final game for City despite having signed until the end of the season. City slip to 19th, 3 points clear of the drop zone.

13 City Under-18s are through to the Midland Youth Cup final after beating Port Vale 3-2 in the semi-final.

15 City confirm that David Holdsworth has funds available to prevent a further relegation. The manager is still trying to shore up his defence in particular.

17 **Bath City 2 Lincoln 1 (Lloyd).** Att: 760. City find themselves 2-down after 4 minutes against the bottom side. Danny Lloyd's first goal for the club is not enough to salvage a point as City's poor run against fellow-relegation candidates continues. City slip to 20th, and are only out of the bottom four on goal difference once more.

21 City sign 21-year-old defender Tom Miller from Newport County until the end of the season.

22 Joe Anyon once again acts as peacemaker between the club and its fans, who are becoming increasingly angry at the club's continued decline.

24 **Lincoln 2 (McCammon, Nutter) Newport County 0.** Att: 1,951. City pick up a vital win over relegation rivals Newport, their first win in 8 games. Tom Miller makes his City debut against his former club. A group of disgruntled supporters stages a demonstration against the club's hierarchy prior to the game. The club responds by calling the demonstration 'a disgrace'. City lift themselves above Newport into 19th, 2 points clear of Hayes & Yeading in 21st.

27 **Hayes & Yeading United 1 Lincoln 2 (Louis, Miller).** Att: 327. An improved performance gives Lincoln a vital win over relegation-bound Hayes. All three goals come within a six-minute spell midway through the second half, with Tom Miller's first goal for City proving to be the winner. City win two successive league matches for the first time this season. This is the game rearranged from 11 February, which was postponed due to a frozen pitch at Kingfield. City are up a place to 18th, 5 points above the drop zone.

30 Louis Almond is recalled from his loan by parent club Blackpool.

31 **Lincoln 4 (Bore, Power pen, Thomas 2 own goals) Tamworth 0.** Att: 2,213. City gain revenge for their 4-0 defeat at Tamworth in October, assisted by two own goals by Tamworth left-back Danny Thomas. The winning run is extended to three games. City are 17th, still 5 points clear of the relegation zone.

April 2012

3 **Lincoln 0 Cambridge United 1.** Att: 1,978. City's winning run comes to an end after three games despite a reasonably dominant performance. This game was rearranged from 4 February when Cambridge were involved in the FA Trophy third round. City stay 17th, 5 points clear with 5 games to play.

5 City look set to go into the next two crucial games with 9 players missing through injury.

7 **Stockport County 4 Lincoln 0.** Att: 3,975. Future Imp Danny Rowe scores twice as injury-hit City's relegation fears are increased by a rampant Stockport side. Mark McCammon makes the final appearance of his loan spell. Stockport lift themselves above the Imps, who slip to 19th, 4 points clear of Hayes & Yeading in 21st place.

9 **Lincoln 5 (Lloyd 2, Louis 2, Taylor) Darlington 0.** Att: 2,274. City lead 4-0 at half time against their relegation-bound visitors and go on to record their biggest win of the season. Francis Laurent makes his final appearance. City are up to 17th, now 7 points clear of the relegation zone with 3 games left.

11 City Under-18s win the Midland Youth Cup with a 3-0 win over Chesterfield at the B2net Stadium. The goals come from Jordan Thomas, Karl Cunningham and an own goal. Team: Draper, Leggett, Rawson, Cobb (Rice 77), Coupland, Green, Massen (Weaver 78), Cunningham, Thomas, Robinson, Taylor (Downey 73). Subs not used: Pannell, Green. Att: 575.

13 **Fleetwood Town 2 Lincoln 2 (Taylor, Louis).** Att: 4,511. Two goals in the first 20 minutes put City into a 2-0 lead against their promotion-seeking hosts in front of the Premier Sports TV cameras. Two goals by future England international Jamie Vardy earn a point for Fleetwood, but their promotion party is put on hold. Jean-François Christophe and Robbie Williams make their final appearances for the Imps. City are now 16th, 8 points clear with 3 games to play.

14 No game today due to the game against Fleetwood being moved to last night for television purposes.

⇒ Hayes & Yeading's 3-1 home defeat to Mansfield means City are safe from relegation.

18 David Holdsworth confirms that agreement in principle has been reached for him to continue as manager next season.

21 **Lincoln 0 Hayes & Yeading United 1.** Att: 2,585. City slip to a dismal defeat in their final home game of a terrible season. The win is not enough to keep Hayes in the Conference, as they are relegated following Newport's win over Alfreton. Former City defender Jamie Hand is sent off at Sincil Bank for the second time this season, having received his marching orders while playing for Luton in December. Youth team striker Conner Robinson makes his first team debut. Fellow-youth teamer Frazer Cobb makes his one and only Lincoln City appearance as a 62nd-minute substitute. Danny Lloyd, Sam Smith and Nialle Rodney make their final appearances. City are 19th, 5 points clear of relegated Hayes & Yeading.

⇒ Joe Anyon is voted *Player of the Season* by the fans, and also picks up the *Away Player of the Season* award.

26 David Holdsworth vows to put an end to player contracts that are disadvantageous to the club. He believes deals done by previous managers were too complex and rewarded failure.

28 **Ebbsfleet United 2 Lincoln 3 (Howe own goal, Bore, Taylor).** Att: 1,217. City end another very poor season with a win, only their fifth away from home. Joe Anyon, Jefferson Louis, Tyrone Thompson, Richard Pacquette, Karlton Watson and Josh Gowling make their final appearances for the club.

⇒ City end the worst season in their history in 17th place, 8 points clear of relegation.

May 2012

2 Alan Power signs a further one-year deal.

⇒ Sam Smith signs a further one-year deal.

⇒ City take up the option in Bradley Barraclough's contract and extend it for another year. He returns from his half-season loan at Buxton having scored 11 goals in 18 games, and is also the winner of their Player of the Season award.

⇒ Curtis Woodhouse, who has been working part-time as a coach with the Imps, is appointed manager of Northern Premier League Division One South side Sheffield FC.

5 The retained list is announced, dominated by the need to trade without the £225,000 solidarity payment from the Football League that the club enjoyed last season. Therefore the majority of players cannot be offered the terms they were on last season.

⇒ Nicky Nicolau and Jake Sheridan have already agreed deals, so they join Bradley Barraclough, Josh Gowling, John Nutter, Conal Platt, Alan Power, Sam Smith and Jamie Taylor under contract for 2012-13.

⇒ Talks are ongoing with Tom Miller, Danny Lloyd, Tyrone Thompson and Peter Bore.

⇒ Players who cannot be offered the same terms are Joe Anyon, Jean-Francois Christophe, Danny Hone, Andrew Hutchinson, Francis Laurent, Jefferson Louis, Richard Pacquette, Nialle Rodney, Simon Russell, Tony Sinclair, Karlton Watson and James Wilson.

11 Nicky Nicolau signs a one-year contract extension.

⇒ Jake Sheridan signs a new one-year deal.

17 David Holdsworth gives his backing to the *Name Our Stadium* campaign, which is to raffle the naming rights for Sincil Bank for the next 12 months in exchange for £50 per ticket. The campaign aims to raise over £50,000, which will go to Holdsworth's playing budget.

18 David Holdsworth signs a one-year contract as Lincoln City manager.

21 City sign 29-year-old striker Rob Duffy from Grimsby Town on a one-year deal.

⇒ City sign 31-year-old midfielder Gary Mills from Nuneaton Town on a one-year deal.

⇒ City sign 35-year-old defender Ashley Westwood from Kettering Town on a one-year deal.

⇒ Peter Bore signs a new one-year deal.

⇒ Paul Robson signs a new one-year deal.

22 City announce that Championship side Leicester City will visit Sincil Bank for a pre-season friendly on 4 August.

23 City sign goalkeeper Paul Farman from Gateshead on a one-year deal after a successful loan period last season.

25 City sign 22-year-old defender Andrew Boyce from Gainsborough Trinity on a one-year deal.

SEASON 2011-12

CONFERENCE PREMIER

No.	Date		Opposition	Res	Att	Scorers	Anyon, J	Watts, A	Hone, D	Gowling, J	Nutter, J	McCallum, G	Fuseini, A	Power, A	Russell, S	Perry, K	Smith, S	Barraclough, B	Taylor, J
1	AUG	13	Southport	2-2	1687	Smith, Perry	Y	Y	Y	Y	Y	Y#	Y	Y	Y	Y*	Y>	S#	S*
2		16	KIDDERMINSTER HARRIERS	0-1	2448		Y	Y		Y	Y	Y#	Y		Y	Y	Y	S*	S#
3		19	WREXHAM	1-2	2211	Smith	Y	Y		Y	Y	Y*	Y	Y	Y	S*	Y	S#	Y#
4		23	AFC Telford United	2-1	2323	Perry 2	Y	Y		Y	Y	Y>	Y	Y	Y	S*	Y*	S#	Y#
5		26	STOCKPORT COUNTY	1-1	2152	Power	Y	Y		Y	Y	Y	Y	Y	Y	S*	S*	Y#	S#
6		29	Darlington	1-3	2252	Power	Y		Y	Y	Y	Y	Y	Y	Y	Y>	Y*	S>	S*
7	SEP	3	Braintree Town	0-1	1182		Y			Y	Y	Y#	Y	Y	Y	Y*	S#		S*
8		10	KETTERING TOWN	0-2	2269		Y			Y	Y	S*	Y	Y	S#	Y#	Y		Y*
9		17	Luton Town	0-1	6316		Y	Y		Y	Y*	Y>	Y	Y	Y		S*	Y#	
10		20	GATESHEAD	1-0	1587	Fuseini	Y		Y	Y	Y	Y*	Y	Y	Y	Y#	S#	S*	
11		24	FOREST GREEN ROVERS	1-1	2076	Hone	Y		Y	Y	Y	Y	Y	Y	Y	Y#	S#		
12		27	Barrow	0-1	1181		Y		Y	Y	Y	Y	Y#	Y	Y		Y	S#	
13	OCT	1	BATH CITY	2-0	2244	Smith, McCallum	Y		Y	Y	Y	Y*	Y#	Y		S>	Y>	S*	
14		8	Tamworth	0-4	1232		Y	Y	Y		Y	Y*	Y*	Y		S*	Y		
15		11	Alfreton Town	3-1	1232	Smith 2, McCallum	Y	Y	Y		Y	Y*	S#	Y		S>	Y>		S*
16		14	FLEETWOOD TOWN	1-3	2332	O'Keefe	Y	Y	Y		Y	Y	S*	Y		S>	Y>		
17		18	MANSFIELD TOWN	1-1	2944	McCallum	Y	Y		Y	Y	Y#	Y		S*	Y*		
18		21	Cambridge United	0-2	2875		Y	Y		Y	Y	Y	Y		S#	Y#		
19	NOV	5	BARROW	2-1	2090	Smith, Christophe				S*	Y#					Y	Y	
20		19	Wrexham	0-2	3424						Y			Y	S>	Y	Y#	
21		26	EBBSFLEET UNITED	3-0	2111	Platt, Russell, Nutter				Y	Y			Y	Y*	Y		
22		29	York City	0-2	3155					Y	Y			Y	Y*	Y#		
23	DEC	3	Newport County	0-1	1270					Y	Y			Y*	S>	Y		
24		6	LUTON TOWN	1-1	2049	Hinds				Y	Y			Y	Y*	Y#		S*
25		17	Forest Green Rovers	2-0	969	Power (pen), Laurent				Y	Y			Y	S*			Y>
26		26	GRIMSBY TOWN	1-2	5506	Platt				Y#	Y			Y	S>	S*		
27	JAN	1	Grimsby Town	1-3	6672	Taylor	Y				Y			Y	S>		S*	Y
28		7	YORK CITY	0-2	3048		Y				Y			Y		Y>		S*
29		21	Gateshead	3-3	870	Pacquette 2, Smith	Y			Y	Y			Y			Y	
30		24	SOUTHPORT	2-0	1615	Christophe, Pacquette	Y			Y	Y			S*		Y#		
31		28	Kettering Town	0-1	1417		Y			Y	Y			S#				
32	FEB	14	BRAINTREE TOWN	3-3	1616	Louis, Thompson, Almond	Y			Y	Y			S>				
33		18	Kidderminster Harriers	1-1	2081	Louis	Y			Y	Y			Y	S*			
34		25	AFC TELFORD UNITED	1-1	2438	OG	Y			Y	Y			Y				S#
35	MAR	3	Mansfield Town	1-2	4830	McCammon	Y			Y	Y			Y	Y*			S#
36		10	ALFRETON TOWN	0-1	2253		Y			Y	Y			Y				S*
37		17	Bath City	1-2	760	Lloyd	Y			Y	Y			Y				Y>
38		24	NEWPORT COUNTY	2-0	1951	McCammon, Nutter	Y			Y	Y			Y				S*
39		27	Hayes & Yeading United	2-1	327	Louis, Miller	Y			Y	Y			Y				S*
40		31	TAMWORTH	4-0	2213	Bore, Power (pen), OG 2	Y			Y	Y			Y				S#
41	APR	3	CAMBRIDGE UNITED	0-1	1978		Y			Y	Y			Y				Y*
42		7	Stockport County	0-4	3975		Y			Y	Y			Y				S>
43		9	DARLINGTON	5-0	2274	Lloyd 2, Louis 2, Taylor	Y			Y	Y			Y				Y*
44		13	Fleetwood Town	2-2	4511	Taylor, Louis	Y			Y	Y			Y				Y#
45		21	HAYES & YEADING UNITED	0-1	2585		Y			Y	Y			Y			S>	
46		28	Ebbsfleet United	3-2	1217	Bore, Taylor, OG	Y			Y	Y			Y				Y
						Appearances	38	11	9	36	46	17	15	42	17	14	18	4	10
						Substitute appearances	0	0	0	1	0	1	2	0	9	10	6	8	14
						Goals	0	0	1	0	2	3	1	4	1	3	7	0	4

56 league goals

FA CUP

				Res	Att	Scorers													
4Q	OCT	29	Alfreton Town	1-1	1000	Smith	Y	Y				Y			Y	Y#	S*	Y*	
4Qr	NOV	1	ALFRETON TOWN	1-2	1728	Smith		Y				Y	Y		Y#		S*	Y	S>

FA TROPHY

				Res	Att	Scorers													
1	DEC	10	Colwyn Bay	3-1	383	Taylor 2, Platt	Y			Y	Y			Y#	S*				Y
2	JAN	14	CARSHALTON ATHLETIC	0-0	1743		Y				Y			S#	Y		Y		Y#
2R		18	Carshalton Athletic	1-3	488	Sheridan	Y			S>	Y			Y	Y#		Y		

LINCOLNSHIRE CUP

				Res	Att	Scorers													
SF	JUL	24	SCUNTHORPE UNITED	1-1*	1769	Smith	Y	Y	Y	Y	Y	Y*	Y	Y	Y#		Y		Y
F	AUG	2	GRIMSBY TOWN	3-4	1446	Russell, Barraclough, Perry		Y	Y			S*	Y#	S#	Y	Y	Y*	Y>	

* City won 4-3 on penalties

Key:
Y = full appearance
Y# = full appearance, first player substituted - by substitute S#
Y* = full appearance, second player substituted - by substitute S*
Y> = full appearance, third player substituted - by substitute S>

■ Red Card
▧ Yellow Card

Player substitution / appearance tracking grid.

	O'Keefe, J	Sinclair, T	Nicolau, N	Christophe, J-F	Nelson, M	Arnaud, J	Cunningham, K	Thomas, J	Thompson, C	Thompson, T	Farman, P	Hinds, R	Platt, C	Laurent, F	Medley, L	Sheridan, J	Beardsley, J	Williams, R	Lloyd, D	Pacquette, R	Watson, K	Robson, P	Bore, P	Louis, J	Almond, L	Rodney, N	McCammon, M	Miller, T	Cobb, F	Robinson, C	Draper, N	Pearson, M	Thompson, R	Lindberg, D	Wilson, J	Eckhardt, S
	S >																																			
	S >	Y																																		
		Y	S >																																	
		Y																																		
	Y #	Y		S #																																
				Y	Y																															
				Y	Y																															
	S >	Y		S #	Y																															
		Y			Y																															
	S *	Y		Y *																																
	S *	Y >		Y *	S >																															
	S #	Y																																		
	Y	Y	Y #	Y		S #																														
		Y	Y	Y	Y		Y #																													
	Y #	S #	Y	Y *	Y																															
		Y	Y	S #	Y		Y >	S >																												
	Y *	Y	Y	Y	Y				S *																											
	Y *	Y	Y	Y	Y					Y	Y	Y	S #																							
	Y >	Y	Y *		Y					Y	Y	Y	S #	S *																						
		Y							Y	Y	Y	Y	S *	S #	Y #																					
		Y	S >						Y	Y	Y	Y	S *	S #	Y >																					
		Y		Y					Y	Y	Y	Y #	Y >	S #	S *																					
		Y		Y >					Y	Y	Y	Y	S #		S >																					
		Y		Y					Y	Y	Y	Y #	Y >	S #	S >																					
		Y		Y					Y >	Y	Y	Y *			Y	S #																				
	Y		Y *						Y		Y	Y >	S #	Y #		Y																				
	Y	Y #	Y						Y		Y *				Y	S #	S >	Y																		
		Y *							Y		Y #			S *		Y	S #		Y																	
		Y >	Y						Y		Y *			S >		Y	S #	Y																		
		Y >	Y						Y		Y *			Y #		Y	S *	Y	S >	Y																
		Y #	Y						Y		Y *					Y >	Y		Y	Y	S #	S *														
		Y							Y							S #		Y	Y #	Y *	Y	Y #														
		S >							Y							Y #		Y	Y >	Y	Y *	S *														
		Y							Y							Y #		Y	Y >	Y	S *	S >														
		Y							Y					S #		Y		Y	Y #	Y	Y >	Y	S *	S >											
		Y #							Y				S >		Y		Y	S #	Y *	Y	S *														
		S >							Y				S #		Y		Y		Y	Y #	Y	Y *		Y #	Y										
		S #							Y				Y *		Y		Y		Y	Y >	Y	Y *	S *												
									Y				Y >				Y	S *	Y #	Y >	Y	Y *	Y	S >											
		Y #							Y						S *		Y >		S #	Y		Y	Y >	Y	S >	Y									
		Y #							Y >						Y *		Y		S #	Y		Y		S *	Y										
			S >						Y						S *		S #		Y	Y >	Y	Y #	Y >		Y										
									Y						S #	S *	Y >	S >	Y *	Y	Y	Y *	Y	Y	S #	S *									
		S *							Y						Y *				Y #	S >	Y >	Y	Y #		Y										

	4	23	14	22	9	0	2	0	0	26	8	9	14	5	0	12	0	10	3	9	3	16	11	14	3	2	2	8	0	0	0	0	0	0	0	0
	6	1	5	5	1	1	0	1	1	0	0	0	0	9	6	8	1	1	9	4	2	0	0	0	2	4	4	0	1	1	0	0	0	0	0	0
	1	0	0	2	0	0	0	0	0	0	1	0	1	2	1	0	0	0	0	3	3	0	0	2	6	1	0	2	1	0	0	0	0	0	0	0

Supplementary rows (lower block 1):

| | Y | Y | Y | Y > | Y | | | | | | | | | S > | | | | | | | | | | | | | | | S # | | | | | | | |
| | Y > | Y | Y * | Y | Y | | | | | | | | | S # | | | | | | | | | | | | | | | Y | | | | | | | |

Supplementary rows (lower block 2):

		Y	S >	Y							Y	Y		Y	Y >	Y *		S #															Y			
				Y *				S >	Y	Y				Y >			S *					Y	Y										Y			
				Y >					Y	Y				Y *			S #					Y	Y										Y	S *		

Supplementary rows (lower block 3):

| | S # | | S * | | | | | | | | | | | | | | | | | | | | | | | | | | | | | | | Y | S > | Y |
| | Y | | Y | | | | | | | | | | | | | | | | | | | | | | | | | | | | | | | | | |

Appearances & Goals 2011-12

	League Apps	League Subs	League Goals	FA Cup Apps	FA Cup Subs	FA Cup Goals	FA Trophy Apps	FA Trophy Subs	FA Trophy Goals	Totals Apps	Totals Subs	Totals Goals	Totals Apps	Totals Goals	Lincolnshire Cup Apps	Lincolnshire Cup Subs	Lincolnshire Cup Goals
John NUTTER	46	0	2	2	0	0	3	0	0	51	0	2	51	2	1	0	0
Alan POWER	42	0	4	2	0	0	2	1	0	46	1	4	47	4	1	1	0
Joe ANYON	38	0	0	1	0	0	3	0	0	42	0	0	42	0	1	0	0
Josh GOWLING	36	1	0	0	0	0	1	1	0	37	2	0	39	0	1	0	0
Jean-Francois CHRISTOPHE	22	5	2	2	0	0	3	0	0	27	5	2	32	2	0	0	0
Tyrone THOMPSON	26	1	1	0	0	0	3	0	0	29	1	1	30	1	0	0	0
Simon RUSSELL	17	9	1	1	1	0	2	1	0	20	10	1	30	1	2	0	1
Sam SMITH	18	6	7	2	0	2	2	0	0	22	6	9	28	9	2	0	1
Tony SINCLAIR	23	1	0	2	0	0	1	0	0	26	1	0	27	0	0	0	0
Jamie TAYLOR	10	14	4	0	1	0	2	0	2	12	15	6	27	6	1	0	0
Kyle PERRY	14	10	3	0	2	0	0	0	0	14	12	3	26	3	1	0	1
Jake SHERIDAN	12	8	2	0	0	0	0	3	1	12	11	1	23	1	0	0	0
Nicky NICOLAU	14	5	0	2	0	0	0	1	0	16	6	0	22	0	1	1	0
Gavin McCALLUM	17	1	3	1	0	0	0	0	0	18	1	3	19	3	1	1	0
Paul ROBSON	16	0	0	0	0	0	2	0	0	18	0	0	18	0	0	0	0
Ali FUSEINI	15	2	1	0	0	0	0	0	0	15	2	1	17	1	2	0	0
Conal PLATT	14	0	2	0	0	0	3	0	1	17	0	3	17	3	0	0	0
Francis LAURENT	5	9	1	0	2	0	1	0	0	6	11	1	17	1	0	0	0
Jefferson LOUIS	14	0	6	0	0	0	0	0	0	14	0	6	14	6	0	0	0
Richard PACQUETTE	9	4	3	0	0	0	0	0	0	9	4	3	13	3	0	0	0
Adam WATTS	11	0	0	2	0	0	0	0	0	13	0	0	13	0	2	0	0
Bradley BARRACLOUGH	4	8	0	0	0	0	0	0	0	4	8	0	12	0	1	0	1
Danny LLOYD	3	9	3	0	0	0	0	0	0	3	9	3	12	3	0	0	0
Mitchell NELSON (L)	9	1	0	2	0	0	0	0	0	11	1	0	12	0	0	0	0
Josh O'KEEFE	4	6	1	2	0	0	0	0	0	6	6	1	12	1	1	1	0
Peter BORE	11	0	2	0	0	0	0	0	0	11	0	2	11	2	0	0	0
Robbie WILLIAMS (L)	10	1	0	0	0	0	0	0	0	10	1	0	11	0	0	0	0
Richard HINDS	9	0	1	0	0	0	1	0	0	10	0	1	10	1	0	0	0
Danny HONE	9	0	1	0	0	0	0	0	0	9	0	1	9	1	2	0	0
Paul FARMAN	8	0	0	0	0	0	0	0	0	8	0	0	8	0	0	0	0
Tom MILLER	8	0	1	0	0	0	0	0	0	8	0	1	8	1	0	0	0
Karlton WATSON	3	2	0	0	0	0	2	0	0	5	2	0	7	0	0	0	0
Mark McCAMMOM	2	4	2	0	0	0	0	0	0	2	4	2	6	2	0	0	0
Nialle RODNEY	2	4	0	0	0	0	0	0	0	2	4	0	6	0	0	0	0
Luke MEDLEY (L)	0	6	0	0	0	0	0	0	0	0	6	0	6	0	0	0	0
Louis ALMOND (L)	3	2	1	0	0	0	0	0	0	3	2	1	5	1	0	0	0
Karl CUNNINGHAM	2	0	0	0	0	0	0	0	0	2	0	0	2	0	0	0	0
Jordan THOMAS	0	1	0	0	0	0	0	1	0	0	2	0	2	0	0	0	0
Nick DRAPER	0	0	0	1	1	0	0	0	0	1	1	0	2	0	0	0	0
Matty PEARSON (L)	0	0	0	0	0	0	2	0	0	2	0	0	2	0	0	0	0
Jean ARNAUD	0	1	0	0	0	0	0	0	0	0	1	0	1	0	0	0	0
Jason BEARDSLEY	0	1	0	0	0	0	0	0	0	0	1	0	1	0	0	0	0
Frazer COBB	0	1	0	0	0	0	0	0	0	0	1	0	1	0	0	0	0
Conner ROBINSON	0	1	0	0	0	0	0	0	0	0	1	0	1	0	0	0	0
Reece THOMPSON	0	0	0	0	0	0	0	1	0	0	1	0	1	0	0	0	0

| Own goals | 4 | | | 0 | | | 0 | | | 4 | | | 4 | | 0 | | |

Players Used	League goals	FA Cup goals	FA Trophy goals	Total goals
45	56	2	4	62

Plus appearances in Lincolnshire Cup: Doug Lindberg 1, Sam Eckhardt 1, James Wilson 1.

Squad Numbers 2011-12

1	Joe Anyon	19	Bradley Barraclough
2	Richard Hinds; Karlton Watson	20	Doug Lindberg; Frazer Cobb
3	John Nutter	21	Nick Draper
4	Adam Watts; Robbie Williams	22	
5	Josh Gowling	23	Josh O'Keefe
6	Danny Hone	24	James Wilson
7	Jamie Taylor	25	Karl Cunningham
8	Alan Power	26	Paul Robson; Curtis Thompson
9	Kyle Perry	27	Jean-François Christophe
10	Ali Fuseini; Jason Beardsley; Jefferson Louis	28	Paul Farman; Reece Thompson
11	Francis Laurent	29	Jordan Thomas
12	Conal Platt	30	Gavin McCallum; Louis Almond; Conner Robinson
13	Tony Sinclair	31	Adam Smith; Peter Bore
14	Sam Smith	32	Luke Medley; Matty Pearson; Nialle Rodney
15	Simon Russell	33	Mark McCammon
16	Mitchell Nelson; Richard Pacquette	34	Tyrone Thompson
17	Nicky Nicolau	35	Tom Miller
18	Jean Arnaud; Danny Lloyd	36	Jake Sheridan

Conference Premier Final League Table 2011-12

			Home					Away					Totals		
		P	W	D	L	F	A	W	D	L	F	A	F	A	Pts
1	Fleetwood Town	46	13	8	2	50	25	18	2	3	52	23	102	48	103
2	Wrexham	46	16	3	4	48	17	14	5	4	37	16	85	33	98
3	Mansfield Town	46	14	6	3	50	25	11	8	4	37	23	87	48	89
P	York City	46	11	6	6	43	24	12	8	3	38	21	81	45	83
5	Luton Town	46	15	4	4	48	15	7	11	5	30	27	78	42	81
6	Kidderminster Harriers	46	10	7	6	44	32	12	3	8	38	31	82	63	76
7	Southport	46	8	8	7	36	39	13	5	5	36	30	72	69	76
8	Gateshead	46	11	8	4	39	26	10	3	10	30	36	69	62	74
9	Cambridge United	46	11	6	6	31	16	8	8	7	26	25	57	41	71
10	Forest Green Rovers	46	11	5	7	37	25	8	8	7	29	20	66	45	70
11	Grimsby Town	46	12	4	7	51	28	7	9	7	28	32	79	60	70
12	Braintree Town	46	11	5	7	39	34	6	6	11	37	46	76	80	62
13	Barrow	46	12	6	5	39	25	5	3	15	23	51	62	76	60
14	Ebbsfleet United	46	7	6	10	34	39	7	6	10	35	45	69	84	54
15	Alfreton Town	46	8	6	9	39	48	7	3	13	23	38	62	86	54
16	Stockport County	46	8	7	8	35	28	4	8	11	23	46	58	74	51
17	**Lincoln City**	46	8	6	9	32	24	5	4	14	24	42	56	66	49
18	Tamworth	46	7	9	7	30	30	4	6	13	17	40	47	70	48
19	Newport County	46	8	6	9	22	22	3	8	12	31	43	53	65	47
20	AFC Telford United	46	9	6	8	24	26	1	10	12	21	39	45	65	46
21	Hayes & Yeading United	46	5	5	13	26	41	6	3	14	32	49	58	90	41
22	Darlington	46	8	7	8	24	24	3	6	14	23	49	47	73	36
23	Bath City	46	5	4	14	27	41	2	6	15	16	48	43	89	31
24	Kettering Town	46	5	5	13	25	47	3	4	16	15	53	40	100	30

Progress Chart 2011-12

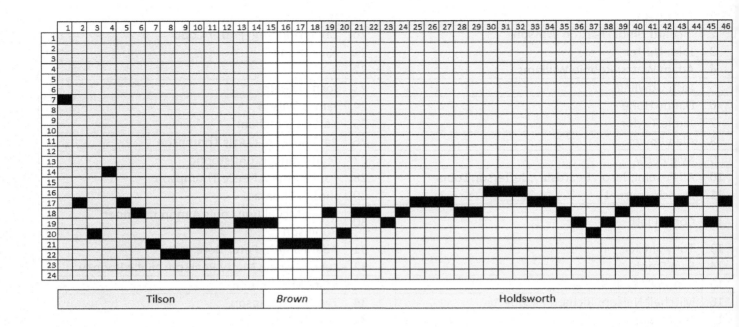

	Tilson	Brown	Holdsworth

Friendlies 2011-12

Jul	16	Ilkeston FC	4-0		Taylor, McCallum, Hutchinson, Gowling
	19	Barton Town Old Boys	2-0		Smith, Watts
	20	Brigg Town	4-1		O'Keefe, Fuseini, Taylor, McCallum
	26	Gainsborough Trinity	1-2		McCallum
	30	NOTTINGHAM FOREST	0-1	2863	
Aug	6	Boston United	4-3	982	Nutter, McCallum, Power, Barraclough

Does not include the behind closed doors friendlies against Gainsborough Trinity (10/1/2012) and Doncaster Rovers (21/2/2012)

Original Fixture List 2011-12

Aug	13	Southport		18	MANSFIELD TOWN		11	Hayes & Yeading Utd
	16	KIDDERMINSTER HARR		22	Cambridge United		14	BRAINTREE TOWN
	20	WREXHAM	Nov	5	BARROW		18	Kidderminster Harriers
	23	AFC Telford United		19	Wrexham		25	AFC TELFORD UNITED
	27	STOCKPORT COUNTY		26	EBBSFLEET UNITED	Mar	3	Mansfield Town
	29	Darlington		29	York City		10	ALFRETON TOWN
Sep	3	Braintree Town	Dec	3	Newport County		17	Bath City
	10	KETTERING TOWN		6	LUTON TOWN		24	NEWPORT COUNTY
	17	Luton Town		17	Forest Green Rovers		31	TAMWORTH
	20	GATESHEAD		26	GRIMSBY TOWN	Apr	7	Stockport County
	24	FOREST GREEN ROVERS	Jan	1	Grimsby Town		9	DARLINGTON
	27	Barrow		7	YORK CITY		14	Fleetwood Town
Oct	1	BATH CITY		21	Gateshead		21	HAYES & YEADING UTD
	8	Tamworth		24	SOUTHPORT		28	Ebbsfleet United
	11	Alfreton Town		28	Kettering Town			
	15	FLEETWOOD TOWN	Feb	4	CAMBRIDGE UNITED	May	12	FA Trophy Final

Year 2

2012-13

7 David Holdsworth announces that he has almost completed the rebuilding of his squad for next season.

14 City abandon attempts to re-sign winger Danny Lloyd for next season as contract talks stall over money.

21 City sign 27-year-old winger Adam Smith from Mansfield Town on a one-year deal. It is rumoured that Smith has signed for Lincoln despite having received offers from Football League clubs and has taken a substantial pay cut after leaving Mansfield. He made four previous appearances for Lincoln under Peter Jackson whilst on loan from Chesterfield in January 2008.

July 2012

1 Youth players Frazer Cobb and Karl Cunningham sign first-year professional contracts (one-year).

2 The fixture list is announced for the new season. It gives City a home game against Kidderminster Harriers on the opening day, with the double-header against Grimsby on Boxing Day (H) and New Year's Day (A).

3 The players return for pre-season training.

5 Ashley Westwood, who only signed on a one-year deal in May, asks Lincoln to cancel his contract so he can take up a coaching position at Portsmouth.

6 TV broadcaster Premier Sports announces that they are to show two Lincoln games in the first half of the season, necessitating a move from the scheduled Saturday afternoon to the previous Friday evening; the games are at Forest Green Rovers (now Friday 28 September) and at Southport (now Friday 30 November).

⇒ The transfer fee for Andrew Boyce will be decided by tribunal after City could not agree a figure with Gainsborough.

10 Former City kit man Matt Carmichael loses a claim for unfair dismissal. An employment tribunal accepts that the former City striker's redundancy in December 2011 was entirely due to the club's dire financial position.

12 David Holdsworth reveals that he has failed in a bid to sign two centre backs because of wage demands. The targets were Exodus Geohaghon, who has opted to join Kidderminster, and Crawley's John Dempster. City are short of defenders after Ashley Westwood unexpectedly left for Portsmouth.

⇒ City reveal that the *Name Our Stadium* campaign has raised just £15,000 with two weeks remaining. The total is £10,000 short of the budgeted figure of £25,000, and £35,000 short of the ideal.

18 City start their pre-season with a 2-1 win at Northern Premier League Premier Division side Worksop Town, the goals from Sam Smith and trialist Phil Bannister in front of 346 at Sandy Lane. Bannister is the second player to join City from the American university scene after Bradley Barraclough last year. Former Chesterfield defender Dan Gray and former City youngster Graham Hutchison also appear after joining the club on trial.

21 A paltry crowd of 199 sees City win 4-2 at struggling Northern Premier League Premier Division side Eastwood Town, just relegated from Conference North. Jake Sheridan scores twice against his former club, with Andrew Boyce and an Alan Power penalty rounding off a comfortable win. The friendly was agreed as part of the deal to sign Sheridan last season.

24 City's good pre-season continues with a 4-1 win at Newark Town of the Central Midlands League South Division. Goals from Graham Hutchison, Adam Smith, Rob Duffy and an own goal prove too good for their opponents in front of 302.

⇒ City sign 22-year-old midfielder Dan Gray on a one-year deal after the former Chesterfield man impressed in pre-season.

⇒ Lincoln sign 21-year-old American midfielder Geoffrey Gouveia on a one-year deal.

25 City re-sign 22-year-old defender Tom Miller on a one-year deal. Miller originally signed for City until the end of last season, but has chosen to return after evaluating options elsewhere.

26 City are set to receive a windfall of around £20,000 following the transfer of former goalkeeper Scott Loach from Watford to Ipswich. The amount is much less than expected as Loach moves for just £200,000.

27 Goalkeeper Nick Draper joins Sheffield FC on a season-long loan.

28 City's pre-season winning run comes to a halt as they are held 1-1 at Sincil Bank by Gainsborough Trinity. Rob Duffy bags his second goal in pre-season in front of 879 less than enthralled fans.

30 City sign 19-year-old defender Graham Hutchison on loan from Birmingham City following a successful trial period. The loan will run until the New Year. Hutchison has been here before - he started his youth career with Lincoln before being sold to Birmingham in April 2010.

⇒ City sign 19-year-old goalkeeper Jake Turner on a deal to the end of the season following a successful trial period.

⇒ City make Josh Gowling available for loan or permanent transfer with immediate effect.

31 Having received a bye straight through to the final, Lincoln lose to Grimsby Town in the final of the Lincolnshire Cup at Sincil Bank. Nicky Nicolau scores City's goal in a 1-1 draw, but Grimsby win 5-4 on penalties in front of 1,469. City field a very young side, with six players - Ryan Leggett, Will Rawdon, Frazer Cobb, Jake Turner, Karl Cunningham and the soon-to-depart Josh Gowling - making their only appearances of the season; it is also the last time any of the six appear in City's first team.

August 2012

1 First-year professionals Karl Cunningham and Dan Coupland join Goole on loan until 2 January.

⇒ City are set for another financial windfall after former striker Mustapha Carayol joins Middlesbrough from Bristol Rovers.

⇒ Last season's top scorer Sam Smith joins Cambridge United for an undisclosed fee, believed to be £25,000.

⇒ City announce that the ground will be known as the '12th Imp Sincil Bank Stadium' this season after the *Name Our Stadium* campaign raises £21,000 for the playing budget.

3 City sign 20-year-old former Sheffield Wednesday striker Vadaine Oliver on a one-year deal following an impressive performance in the Lincolnshire Cup Final against Grimsby.

⇒ City's scheduled friendly against Leicester City tomorrow is cancelled on police advice after they receive information that 'serious disorder' is planned for the match.

4 No game today due to the cancellation of the Leicester City friendly. The police still deploy 'a robust presence' in the city to deal with supporters arriving unaware of the cancellation. Despite this, several incidents are reported: two Leicester fans are arrested following an incident on Guildhall Street; another Leicester fan is arrested for being drunk and disorderly; and a female guard on the 18.34 train to Leicester is allegedly assaulted, causing the train to halt its journey.

6 The board of Lincoln City issues a statement explaining why the friendly match against Leicester was postponed, having received the information from Lincolnshire Police on Friday. They also state that the cancellation has cost them £30,000 in revenue and a further £30,000 from another high-profile friendly that they have been forced to decline.

8 Gary Mills is named team captain for the season, with John Nutter asked to be club captain.

⇒ Former City player Chris Moyses is to join the board as a full director.

10 City sign unattached 22-year-old defender Luke Daley on a non-contract basis.

11 **Lincoln 1 (Taylor) Kidderminster Harriers 0.** Att: 2,112. Seven players make their debuts (Andrew Boyce, Gary Mills, Dan Gray, Luke Daley, Adam Smith, Rob Duffy and Vadaine Oliver) as the Imps get off to a winning start in their opening game. Paul Farman makes his second debut, this time as a City player. City are in 6th place in the opening table of the season.

⇒ Youth team striker Conner Robinson signs his first professional contract (two years).

14 **Cambridge United 2 Lincoln 1 (Boyce).** Att: 2,546. Centre-back Andrew Boyce scores his first goal for the club, but City are beaten by an 80th-minute winner from Adriano Moke. City slip to 13th, 3 points behind leaders Newport.

17 A tribunal decides that City must pay Gainsborough Trinity an undisclosed five-figure sum (believed to be £12,500) plus a sell-on clause for Andrew Boyce. Chairman Bob Dorrian declares he is very happy with the arrangement.

⇒ Mark McCammon re-signs for City on a non-contract basis following a week training with the squad. The big striker played 6 games for the club on loan from Sheffield FC at the end of last season.

18 **Newport County 2 Lincoln 1 (Taylor).** Att: 3,024. Two goals from Aaron O'Connor send Newport back to the top of the Conference as the only side left with a 100% record. Striker Rob Duffy picks up a bad ankle ligament injury and never appears for the Imps again. City are down to 15th, 6 points behind Newport.

20 Striker Bradley Barraclough joins Gainsborough Trinity on loan until 2 January.

23 David Holdsworth is in a desperate search for bargain-basement players as 5 of his 18-man squad are out injured. He currently has Frenchman Mo Fofana and Kendal Town midfielder Ashley Dunn on trial.

24 City sign 30-year-old striker Colin Larkin from Hartlepool United until the end of the season.

⇒ Elliot Green joins Eastwood Town on a one-month loan.

25 **Lincoln 2 (Taylor, Boyce) Macclesfield Town 3.** Att: 2,009. Future Imp Waide Fairhurst opens the scoring as Macclesfield record their third straight win, while City go down to their third successive defeat. Tom Miller pulls up in the warm-up and is expected to be out for several weeks. Graham Hutchison and Colin Larkin make their City debuts as Mark McCammon makes his final appearance. City are 18th, just 1 point above the bottom four.

27 **Gateshead 1 Lincoln 1 (Robinson).** Att: 803. An 89th-minute equaliser by substitute Conner Robinson, his first for the club, earns City a point. Luke Daley plays his final game. City stay 18th, but are now level on points with the bottom four.

29 City sign unattached 24-year-old French midfielder Mamadou 'Mo' Fofana on a short-term deal until 2 January. Fofana has been on trial with the club since July.

⇒ Non-contract players Luke Daley and Mark McCammon leave Lincoln.

31 Josh Gowling leaves Lincoln by mutual consent with almost a year left on his contract and joins Kidderminster Harriers.

September 2012

1 **Lincoln 1 (Nicolau) Ebbsfleet United 1**. Att: 1,682. A goal in the third minute by Nicky Nicolau proves a false dawn as City misfire at home again. City are up a place to 17th, 1 point above the relegation zone.

4 **Lincoln 1 (Nicolau) Alfreton Town 2**. Att: 1,566. For the second match in a row, Nicky Nicolau's first half opener is all to no avail as Alfreton win at Sincil Bank for the third time in nine months. City have won just 1 of their opening 7 matches and have not won in 6; dissatisfaction grows among supporters as they slip to 20th, level on points with the bottom four.

6 It emerges that City are losing £10,000 per home match as attendances fail to reach the break-even figure. Fans' groups are to meet with the directors to raise their concerns.

7 Alan Power will miss the next three months with ruptured ankle ligaments suffered in the game against Alfreton.

8 **AFC Telford United 1 Lincoln 1 (Oliver)**. Att: 1,749. Vadaine Oliver scores his first goal for City in his first full start, but a late Telford equaliser means it is now 7 games without a win since the opening day. Mamadou Fofana makes his City debut. City slip to 22nd, 2 points from safety.

13 City sign 19-year-old midfielder David Morgan from Nottingham Forest on a one-month youth loan.

15 **Lincoln 3 (Larkin 2 pens, Oliver) Hyde 2**. Att: 1,745. Two penalties from Colin Larkin, his first goals for the club, and an 88th-minute winner by Vadaine Oliver give City their second win of the season. David Morgan makes his City debut against the side second from bottom. The win lifts City up to 18th, 1 point above the drop zone.

18 Fran Martin is appointed to the board of directors.

22 **Tamworth 1 Lincoln 0**. Att: 1,042. Normal service is resumed as City go down to a goal after 43 seconds. Gary Mills is sent off after 27 minutes against the club that sacked him in 2007. Graham Hutchison makes his final appearance as City slip to 21st and back into the relegation zone.

24 Gary Mills receives a three-match ban for his red card at Tamworth.

25 **Lincoln 2 (Nicolau, Miller) Nuneaton Town 1**. Att: 1,579. Two goals in the last 15 minutes give City their second successive home win. The victory over fellow-strugglers Nuneaton lifts City up to 15th, 2 points above the bottom four.

28 **Forest Green Rovers 3 Lincoln 0**. Att: 1,395. City suffer a convincing defeat to high-flying Forest Green, who have built a 27-man squad this season. Two goals from highly-rated Matt Taylor send his side to the top of the Conference table. This game is brought forward from Saturday for the benefit of the Premier Sports TV cameras. City are 19th, 1 point above the drop zone.

29 No game today due to the Forest Green game being shown on television last night.

October 2012

1 Goalkeeper Paul Farman is called up by England C for the match against Albania U21 in Durres on 16 October. He is the first City player ever to be called up at this level.

4 David Holdsworth claims City cannot afford proper medical care for the players. There is no money available for scans and assessments of injuries, causing the injury list and time for recovery to lengthen. City have their lowest playing budget for 40 years, believed to be around half of last season's.

⇒ City sign unattached 29-year-old defender Peter Gilbert on non-contract terms.

6 **Lincoln 1 (Taylor) Luton Town 2**. Att: 2,970. Paul Farman is credited with Luton's first goal as inconsistent City slip to another defeat. Peter Gilbert makes his City debut but cannot prevent his side dropping back into the bottom four (21st).

8 City are drawn at home to either Chester FC or FC Halifax Town in the fourth qualifying round of the FA Cup. Both clubs are in the top 5 in Conference North, and drew 1-1 at Chester on Saturday.

9 **Mansfield Town 0 Lincoln 0**. Att: 2,325. Jamie Taylor hits the woodwork but City stay fourth from bottom, 2 points behind safety at the foot of the Conference table.

⇒ City will play FC Halifax Town in the first round of the FA Cup after the Shaymen beat Chester 3-1 in tonight's replay.

⇒ City appoint directors David Parman and David Featherstone as co-Vice Chairmen.

12 Former City player Chris Moyses is formally appointed to the board of directors. Moyses is also helping manager David Holdsworth with training duties.

13 **Wrexham 2 Lincoln 4 (Nicolau, Taylor, Robinson, Larkin)**. Att: 3,809. Two late goals from promotion-chasing Wrexham spoil the scoreline a little as City record their first away win of the season. City climb to 20th, 1 point clear of the bottom four.

16 Paul Farman misses out on an England C cap when the game in Albania is called off shortly before kick-off due to flooding.

⇒ City win 1-0 at Sheffield FC in a hastily-arranged friendly. Designed to give players some much-needed game time, the winning goal is scored by Jake Sheridan in front of just 40 spectators on a bitterly cold night.

19 City extend David Morgan's loan until 1 January.

| 20 | **FA Cup 4Q: Lincoln 0 FC Halifax Town 0.** Att: 1,940. City fail to see off their opponents from Conference North and face an awkward replay. On-loan midfielder David Morgan is sent off in the closing stages.

⇒ 17-year-old youth team striker Jordan Thomas signs his first professional deal with the club (two years). Unfortunately, he is destined not to add to his two substitute appearances from last season.

| 21 | City are drawn at home to League One Walsall in the first round of the FA Cup, provided they can overcome FC Halifax in Tuesday night's replay.

| 22 | On-loan midfielder David Morgan receives a three-match ban for his red card against FC Halifax on Saturday.

| 23 | **FA Cup 4Q Replay: FC Halifax Town 0 Lincoln 2 (Sheridan, Taylor).** Att: 1,418. City turn in a much better performance in the replay and are through to meet Walsall at home in the first round. The win earns City a very welcome £12,500 in prize money.

| 25 | David Holdsworth hopes he will be allowed to use some of the FA Cup money to reinforce his squad.

| 27 | **Lincoln 3 (Taylor 2, Nutter) Stockport County 3.** Att: 1,873. A 90th-minute Jamie Taylor equaliser earns City a point to extend the unbeaten run to five games. Craig Hobson and Paul Turnbull, later to join the Imps on loan, score two of the Stockport goals. The draw lifts City to 19th, 1 point clear of the drop zone.

| 31 | Peter Gilbert signs a short-term deal until 2 January.

November 2012

| 1 | 30-year-old striker Adam Boyd is training with the Imps with a view to earning a contract. Boyd has joined on the recommendation of his former Hartlepool teammate Colin Larkin.

⇒ Jamie Taylor is named Blue Square Bet Premier Player of the Month for October for his 5 goals during the month.

| 3 | **FA Cup 1: Lincoln 1 (Taylor) Walsall 1.** Att: 2,032. City come close to a giant-killing against their opponents from League One, an 86th-minute equaliser preventing a famous win.

| 4 | City are drawn at home to either Conference rivals Mansfield Town or Slough Town of the Southern League Division One Central in the second round of the FA Cup, if they can win at Walsall in next week's replay. Mansfield and Slough fought out a 0-0 draw at Field Mill on Saturday.

| 5 | City sign 23-year-old defender Scott Garner from Cambridge United on a two-month loan.

| 6 | **Lincoln 3 (Sheridan, Boyce, Taylor) Braintree Town 0.** Att: 1,455. Jamie Taylor scores his 10th goal of the season as City extend their unbeaten run to 7 games in all competitions. The win lifts them to 15th, 3 points clear of Braintree who slip to fourth from bottom.

| 7 | City's opening goal at Braintree yesterday is officially awarded to Jake Sheridan after video footage shows that his shot was on target. Originally the goal had been given as an Alan Massey own goal after the Braintree defender deflected Sheridan's shot past his own keeper.

| 10 | **Barrow 1 Lincoln 2 (Power, Oliver).** Att: 987. Defender Scott Garner makes his debut after joining City on loan last week. City extend their unbeaten run to 8 games, 5 in the league, and are up to 13th in the table. They are 5 points clear of the bottom four, but still 9 points behind 5th-placed Dartford.

| 12 | City are drawn away to Conference Premier rivals Tamworth in the first round of the FA Trophy.

| 13 | **FA Cup 1 Replay: Walsall 2 Lincoln 3 (Oliver 2, Power).** Att: 1,762. Two goals in extra time by Vadaine Oliver earn City a famous victory and £18,000 in prize money. Peter Bore and John Nutter make their final appearances as City extend their unbeaten run to 9 games.

⇒ City will play Mansfield Town at home in the second round after the Stags beat Slough Town 4-1 on penalties in tonight's replay after the match finished 1-1 after extra time.

⇒ City's win at Walsall means that their Conference Premier game at Southport, scheduled for 1 December, will need to be rearranged.

⇒ Graham Hutchison returns to Birmingham City before the end of his loan, having picked up an injury. The loan was originally intended to run until 2 January.

| 15 | Chairman Bob Dorrian says he believes City are on the edge of a new era after five years of struggle.

| 16 | City sign 18-year-old winger Aristide Bassele on a youth loan from Bournemouth.

⇒ Striker Adam Boyd signs a short-term deal to 2 January after impressing on trial.

⇒ John Nutter joins Woking on a two-month loan. It is understood the defender wishes to be closer to his family in the south.

⇒ David Holdsworth insists City do not need to sell players after raising valuable funds through the FA Cup.

| 17 | **Lincoln 3 (Taylor, Larkin pen, Heath own goal) Hereford United 2.** Att: 2,233. An improved attendance sees City extend their unbeaten run to 10 games. Aristide Bassele makes his debut as City notch their fourth successive win. City are up to 9th, 6 points above the danger zone but now only 7 points behind the top five.

| 19 | City make Paul Robson available for immediate loan.

⇒ Dan Gray receives a one-match ban following his fifth yellow card of the season against Hereford.

| 23 | Elliot Green joins Sheffield FC on loan until the New Year.

⇒ Nick Draper is recalled from his loan at Sheffield FC

24 **FA Trophy 1: Tamworth 3 Lincoln 1 (Power).** Att: 726. The unbeaten run comes to a crashing halt as City exit the FA Trophy at the first time of asking. Marcus Kelly scores a second half hat-trick after City lead at half time. Adam Boyd makes his only appearance for City.

25 City legend Bert Linnecor dies at the age of 78. Linnecor scored 55 goals in 287 appearances for the Imps and is particularly remembered for his hat-trick at Anfield in April 1960.

27 City's game at Southport, originally scheduled for this Friday 30 November, is rearranged for Tuesday 8 January. The game is postponed due to Lincoln's involvement in the second round of the FA Cup.

28 Jordan Thomas joins Sheffield FC on loan until the New Year.

29 Manager David Holdsworth is named Blue Square Bet Manager of the Month for November.

December 2012

1 **FA Cup 2: Lincoln 3 Mansfield Town 3.** Att: 4,127. A 90th-minute equaliser by future City player Matt Rhead earns Mansfield a replay. It is the fifth successive Lincoln City FA Cup tie to go to a replay (Hereford United in the second round in 2010-11, Alfreton Town in 2011-12, and the three ties from this season).

2 Great excitement as the draw for the third round of the FA Cup gives Lincoln a home tie against Premier League Liverpool, if they can beat Mansfield in the replay next week. What a shame about that last-gasp Matt Rhead equaliser yesterday.

4 **Lincoln 0 Woking 2.** Att: 2,562. The unbeaten league run comes to an end after 6 games. City lose at home to a side beaten 7-0 at Hyde on Saturday. Aristide Bassele appears in his last game. The attendance is boosted through admission being slashed to just £5. City slip to 12th, still 7 points behind the top five, but only 4 points clear of the relegation zone despite the recent good run.

⇒ City sign 36-year-old goalkeeper David Preece from Barnsley on non-contract terms.

6 Jamie Taylor receives a one-match ban following his fifth yellow card of the season against Woking.

8 **Dartford 2 Lincoln 4 (Larkin 3, Gray).** Att: 1,466. A 22-minute hat-trick by Colin Larkin helps City to a 4-0 half time lead against fifth-placed Dartford. It is City's first hat-trick since relegation. Dan Gray scores his only goal for the Imps, while David Preece makes his debut in place of Paul Farman. City are up to 10th, 7 points behind the top five, and 6 points clear of the bottom four in a tightly-compacted league.

10 City confirm they have sold 1,300 of their 1,400 tickets for the cup replay at Mansfield tomorrow night.

11 **FA Cup 2 Replay: Mansfield Town 2 Lincoln 1 (Smith).** Att: 5,304. A 75th-minute winner by Louis Briscoe ends Lincoln's cup dream for another year, and the financial bonanza of that Liverpool tie goes to Conference rivals Mansfield.

13 City announce a loss of £230,053 for financial year ending 30 June 2012, which is less than half of the £484,752 lost the previous year. The trading loss is £134,000. The club is optimistic that its finances are back on a stable footing.

15 City have no game today, this being FA Trophy second round day.

21 Peter Gilbert signs a contract extension from 3 January 2013 to the end of the season.

⇒ Mamadou Fofana also signs a contract extension to the end of the season.

⇒ David Preece signs a contract to the end of the season; he will also assist with coaching.

⇒ Grimsby Town announce they have sold their allocation of 1,747 tickets for the game on Boxing Day.

22 City's scheduled game at Macclesfield Town is postponed due to a waterlogged pitch.

24 City's postponed game at Macclesfield, scheduled for last Saturday, is rearranged for Tuesday 5 March.

26 **Lincoln 1 (Power pen) Grimsby Town 4.** Att: 5,702. More Boxing Day misery for City at the hands of their neighbours for the second successive year. Joe Colbeck scores direct from a corner and Andrew Boyce scores an own goal in an error-strewn performance. Grimsby remain top of the league, while City slip to 13th, 9 points behind the top five, but only 4 points clear of the bottom four.

29 **Lincoln 1 (Robinson) Gateshead 1.** Att: 1,906. Gary Mills picks up an injury and never appears for City again. David Morgan makes his final appearance before returning to Nottingham Forest. City stay 13th, 8 points behind the play-offs but only 5 points clear of danger.

31 David Holdsworth confirms he is looking for a central midfielder when the transfer window opens.

January 2013

1 **Grimsby Town 1 Lincoln 1 (Power).** Att: 7,405. The Imps grab an unexpected point at Blundell Park, after the heavy defeat on Boxing Day. Both sides finish with 10 men, with 88th-minute substitute Adam Smith dismissed 3 minutes after coming on. Grimsby stay top, but City slip one place to 14th, 8 points behind the play-offs and 5 points clear of the relegation zone.

2 Aristide Bassele returns to Bournemouth at the end of his loan.

⇒ Adam Boyd leaves Lincoln at the end of his short-term deal after playing just 8 minutes for City.

⇒ City sign 23-year-old midfielder Jake Thomson from Newport County on a one-month loan. Thomson had been a City transfer target during the summer.

⇒ City decide to appeal against Adam Smith's red card at Grimsby.

3 City extend the loan of defender Scott Garner from Cambridge until the end of the season.

⇒ Bradley Barraclough returns from his loan at Gainsborough Trinity.

⇒ David Morgan returns to Nottingham Forest on completion of his loan period.

⇒ City's appeal against Adam Smith's red card at Grimsby is rejected. Smith receives a three-match ban.

⇒ David Holdsworth reveals he is trying to sign Notts County defender Hamza Bencherif on loan, with money the stumbling block. Bencherif made 13 appearances for the Imps on loan from Nottingham Forest in 2007-08.

4 City agree to cancel John Nutter's contract to enable him to join Woking on a permanent deal.

⇒ City announce that Lincoln City Ladies are to play their FA Women's Super League fixtures at Sincil Bank this coming season.

5 **Ebbsfleet United 1 Lincoln 1 (Robinson).** Att: 889. A 90th-minute equaliser by Conner Robinson snatches a point for City against their relegation-threatened opponents. Jake Thomson makes his City debut, while Bradley Barraclough makes his final appearance. City rise a place to 13th, 9 points behind the play-offs and 6 points clear of the bottom four.

7 City cancel the contract of utility man Peter Bore by mutual consent.

⇒ City sign 20-year-old Gateshead defender Chris Bush on a month's loan.

8 Goalkeeper Jake Turner joins Grantham Town on a one-month loan.

⇒ **Southport 4 Lincoln 2 (Taylor, Oliver).** Att: 815. City are 3-0 down after half an hour, with future Imp Karl Ledsham adding Southport's fourth late on. This game was rearranged from the original date of 1 December due to City's involvement in the second round of the FA Cup. Chris Bush makes his City debut as a substitute, having signed on loan this afternoon. Conal Platt makes his return after 11 months out with a broken leg as a second half substitute for Nicky Nicolau; unfortunately it proves to be his final game in City's colours. City slip back to 14th, 10 points behind the play-offs and only 5 points clear of the relegation zone.

12 **Lincoln 2 (Oliver, Bush) Newport County 4.** Att: 1,970. A late goal by on-loan Chris Bush on his first full start is to no avail as City are already 4-1 down at half time to their promotion-chasing visitors. City concede 4 goals for the third time in 6 games. Paul Robson makes his final appearance as City slip to 15th. The play-offs are over the horizon, with City only 5 points clear of the drop zone.

17 Bob Dorrian confirms that contract talks with manager David Holdsworth and the players are set to commence by the end of the month, with one-year deals being the maximum the club can afford. He also reveals the club is looking to build a 10,000-seat stadium on a 15-acre site within the city; the site will offer retail outlets to increase non-football revenue.

18 Tomorrow's home game against Wrexham is postponed due to a frozen pitch. Although under a covering of snow, the pitch is deemed unplayable.

19 No game today due to the postponement against Wrexham.

21 City manager David Holdsworth airs his concerns about Lincoln fans trying to make the journey to Luton tomorrow night in the current wintry conditions, which have left many roads treacherous. He calls for common sense to prevail.

⇒ City sign 19-year-old winger Jake Jones from Walsall on a one-month youth loan.

22 This evening's Conference Premier game away to Luton Town is postponed following a 10.30am pitch inspection. Despite having cleared the pitch of snow yesterday, it is still frozen in places. At the same time, City appeal to fans to assist with the removal of snow from the Sincil Bank pitch ahead of the scheduled game with Forest Green this coming Saturday.

23 City's postponed game against Wrexham, originally scheduled for last Saturday, is rearranged for Tuesday 12 March.

24 CEO Steve Prescott says City's attempts to bolster their squad are being hampered by the recent spate of postponed matches, which affects cash flow.

25 City sign 24-year-old midfielder Paul Turnbull from Northampton Town on loan until the end of the season. Turnbull scored against the Imps while on loan at Stockport in October.

26 **Lincoln 1 (Smith pen) Forest Green Rovers 2.** Att: 1,663. An own goal by Chris Bush in his final Lincoln appearance helps the visitors to a narrow win. Jake Jones and Paul Turnbull make their debuts, while Jake Thomson makes his final appearance. City have now gone 7 league games without a win, and the fans are becoming restless. The good form and promise of October and November seem a lifetime ago. They are now 17th, just 3 points above the bottom four.

29 Paul Robson, Jake Turner, Elliot Green and Dan Coupland all leave Lincoln in a cost-cutting exercise. Turner, Green and Coupland never made a first team appearance.

⇒ It looks unlikely that City can afford to extend the loans of Chris Bush and Jake Thomson.

⇒ Rumours suggest City have turned down an offer of £6,000 from Gainsborough Trinity for Bradley Barraclough.

February 2013

2 City's scheduled Conference Premier game at Braintree Town is postponed due to a waterlogged pitch at Cressing Road. It is the third game in two weeks to fall victim to the weather.

| 6 | City's postponed game at Braintree is rearranged for Tuesday 26 March.

| 8 | City sign 24-year-old midfielder Craig Hobson on loan from Stockport County until the end of the season. City fans have seen Hobson this season already - he scored one of Stockport's goals in the 3-3 draw at Sincil Bank in October.

| 9 | **Lincoln 2 (Oliver, Larkin pen) Dartford 1.** Att: 1,789. An 89th-minute penalty by Colin Larkin gives City their first win since they last beat Dartford in December, but unrest continues to grow. It proves to be Larkin's last goal in Lincoln's colours. Loanee Craig Hobson makes his City debut as Jake Sheridan is sent off in the first half. City lift themselves to 14th, and increase the gap to the bottom four to 6 points.

| 11 | City announce they are to appeal Jake Sheridan's red card against Dartford on Saturday.

| 12 | City's appeal against Jake Sheridan's red card against Dartford is unsuccessful; Sheridan receives a three-match ban.

⇒ **Stockport County 2 Lincoln 0.** Att: 2,769. Two goals midway through the second half send City crashing to defeat to relegation rivals Stockport, whose second goal is scored by future City defender Sean Newton. Colin Larkin misses a penalty as City slip to 18th, still 6 points above the relegation zone.

| 14 | Bradley Barraclough is released and signs for Gainsborough Trinity. City are criticised by fans, as they had allegedly turned down a £6,000 offer for the player on deadline day.

| 15 | Karl Cunningham joins Lincoln United for an initial one-month loan.

| 16 | **Hereford United 3 Lincoln 2 (Power pen, Musa own goal).** Att: 1,914. City blow a 2-1 half time lead, going down to two second half goals from future City loanee Chris Sharp. Peter Gilbert becomes the latest Lincoln player to be sent off. City have now taken just 6 points from the last 10 games.

| 17 | Manager David Holdsworth leaves the club by mutual consent after 16 months in the job. The change comes just four weeks after Bob Dorrian had spoken of a new contract for Holdsworth. He leaves City in 18th place, just 4 points above the relegation zone. City have not kept a clean sheet for 17 games.

| 18 | Peter Gilbert receives a three-match ban for his red card at Hereford.

⇒ City appoint Grant Brown caretaker manager for the second time since relegation.

⇒ Former City assistant manager Gary Simpson is believed to be a frontrunner for the manager's job. Former player and manager Steve Thompson, Premier League striker Dean Windass and former Conference Manager of the Year Dino Maamria are also linked with City.

| 19 | Former Luton Town assistant manager Kevin Watson has applied for the Lincoln job. Others believed to be interested include John Coleman, Marcus Law and Gary Brabin.

| 20 | City announce that Chris Moyses is to assist Grant Brown until a new manager is appointed.

| 21 | City legend Dick Neal dies at the age of 79. Neal made 169 appearances for the club in two spells between 1954 and 1964, scoring 17 goals. He is the only City player to be capped by the England U23 side, winning 3 caps during his first spell at the club.

| 23 | **Lincoln 0 Barrow 0.** Att: 1,830. Caretaker manager Brown gets off to a disappointing start with a draw against relegation rivals Barrow. City slip to 19th, now just 2 points above the bottom four.

| 25 | Former Hull and Bolton manager Phil Brown is believed to have applied for the City manager's job.

| 26 | **Lincoln 0 Mansfield Town 1.** Att: 2,734. City go down to a 90th-minute winner by Matt Green in Grant Brown's final game as caretaker manager. Dan Gray is sent off, as Colin Larkin makes his final appearance for the club. City stay 18th, still 2 points clear of the danger zone.

⇒ City extend the loan of winger Jake Jones to the end of the season.

| 27 | Lincoln appoint Gary Simpson as their new manager, initially until the end of the season. He will be supported by Grant Brown and Chris Moyses, who have been in charge since Holdsworth's dismissal.

| 28 | Dan Gray receives a three-match ban for his red card against Mansfield.

⇒ City's away game at Macclesfield Town, scheduled for next Tuesday 5 March, is put back by 24 hours to Wednesday 6 March to avoid Manchester United's Champions League tie against Real Madrid.

⇒ Gary Simpson sets his side a target of 12 points from their remaining 12 games to avoid relegation.

March 2013

| 1 | Gary Mills leaves Lincoln by mutual consent.

⇒ City sign defender Nat Brown on loan from Macclesfield Town until the end of the season. 31-year-old Brown originally spent three seasons at Sincil Bank between 2005 and 2008, and is new manager Gary Simpson's first signing.

| 2 | City sign 22-year-old French defender Tony Diagne on loan from Macclesfield Town until the end of the season. He played under Gary Simpson during his time as Macclesfield boss.

⇒ **Woking 1 Lincoln 1 (Oliver).** Att: 1,766. City fall behind in the 3rd minute at Kingfield but fight back to earn a point in Gary Simpson's first game in charge. Tony Diagne makes his debut, while Nat Brown makes his second debut for City. City remain 18th, still 2 points above the drop zone.

| 4 | Geoffrey Gouveia leaves Lincoln by mutual consent without making any first team appearances.

| 7 | Conal Platt leaves Lincoln by mutual consent. Platt broke his leg in a behind-closed-doors friendly with Doncaster Rovers on 21 February 2012 and has struggled to regain his first team place. He signs for Gainsborough Trinity.

⇒ **Macclesfield Town 2 Lincoln 1 (Power pen).** Att: 1,557. City lead at half time but a Scott Garner own goal helps Simpson's former club Macclesfield to a narrow win. Todd Jordan makes his debut, while Peter Gilbert makes his final appearance for the Imps. This is the game rearranged from 22 December. City slip to 19th, now just a single point above the bottom four.

8 Colin Larkin leaves Lincoln by mutual consent, the fourth player to leave this week.

⇒ Conner Robinson joins Worksop Town on a month's loan.

9 **Lincoln 1 (Power pen) Southport 0.** Att: 1,592. Another Alan Power penalty gives new manager Simpson his first win at the third attempt, whilst Paul Farman saves a Southport penalty to preserve the points for Lincoln. Power now has 10 for the season. Vadaine Oliver is sent off late in the game but City lift themselves to 18th, 4 points clear of danger.

11 Vadaine Oliver receives a three-match ban for his red card against Southport.

12 City sign 24-year-old French striker Gomez Dali from Droylsden on a non-contract basis.

⇒ The pitch passes an 11am inspection, and tonight's game against Wrexham goes ahead.

⇒ **Lincoln 1 (Westwood own goal) Wrexham 2.** Att: 1,379. City squander a half time lead against the league leaders. Gomez Dali makes his debut for City, while Scott Garner makes his final appearance. This game was rearranged from 19 January. City are 19th, 3 points above the relegation zone.

14 Gary Simpson emphasises the need for City to pick up a point per game from their remaining 9 fixtures.

16 **Nuneaton Town 1 Lincoln 0.** Att: 1,122. City go down to a 90th-minute goal by Wes York. They are now just one place above the relegation zone, with Nuneaton immediately behind them.

19 City drop into the bottom four as Nuneaton Town beat promotion-chasing Grimsby 1-0 to move above the Imps. City are now 2 points adrift with 8 games remaining. Gary Simpson issues a rallying cry for supporters to get behind the players for the run-in.

22 Karl Cunningham extends his loan at Lincoln United to the end of the season.

23 **Lincoln 3 (Taylor 2, Jordan) AFC Telford 2.** Att: 1,724. Two late goals by Jamie Taylor overturn a 2-1 deficit to give City a vital win over the league's bottom side. Todd Jordan scores his first goal for City. Before today's win, City had won just 2 league games in the last 17, both against Dartford. The defeat means that Telford set a new Conference record of 27 games without a win. City lift themselves back out of the bottom 4, and now sit 20th, level on points with Nuneaton.

26 City agree a three-year shirt sponsorship deal with Bishop Grosseteste University, effective from next season.

⇒ The pitch at Cressing Road, Braintree passes a 5.15pm inspection.

⇒ **Braintree Town 0 Lincoln 3 (Diagne 2, Boyce).** Att: 447. City coast to an easy victory despite having striker Gomez Dali sent off after 4 minutes on his only start for the club. All three goals come from defenders. It is the third game in a row City have scored 3 against Braintree. This game was rearranged from 2 February. City are up to 17th, 3 points clear of the drop zone.

27 City launch the *Future Imps Fund* initiative, designed to cover a £50,000 shortfall in funding following relegation two years ago. The Academy side of the club seeks to be self-funding, as the club itself can no longer afford to support it.

28 Peter Gilbert joins Dagenham & Redbridge on loan until the end of the season.

⇒ Gomez Dali receives a three-match ban for his red card at Braintree.

⇒ Gary Simpson is forced to revise his safety target from 12 points to 15 in light of several relegation rivals picking up unexpected points in recent weeks.

30 **Alfreton Town 0 Lincoln 2 (Hobson, Oliver).** Att: 1,189. Craig Hobson scores his only goal for the club as City ease to their third win in a week. Alfreton play for 85 minutes with 10 men as City lift themselves to 15th in the table. They have now taken 13 points from Gary Simpson's first month in charge, but are still only 3 points clear of fourth from bottom Stockport.

April 2013

1 **Lincoln 0 Cambridge United 0.** Att: 2,721. City slip a place to 16th but move 4 points clear of the relegation zone with a dour draw against Cambridge. It is City's third successive clean sheet and the fourth in 9 games since Gary Simpson was appointed. Tony Diagne makes the last appearance of his loan period.

4 Gary Simpson challenges his players to remain unbeaten to the end of the season.

6 **Kidderminster Harriers 3 Lincoln 0.** Att: 2,326. City go down to a heavy defeat to the league leaders. Rumours abound that Gary Simpson is saving the team for the final two games of the season, against easier opposition. Adam Smith makes his final appearance. City are back down to 19th, 2 points clear of the bottom four with three games to play.

9 **Luton Town 3 Lincoln 0.** Att: 5,393. A second successive 3-0 defeat leaves City in 20th place, just 1 point above the danger zone. Gomez Dali makes his final appearance for the Imps in an undistinguished spell. This game was rearranged from 19 January.

⇒ City release striker Rob Duffy, who has not appeared for the club since being injured in the third game of the season at Newport.

⇒ Cathedral Business Services extends its sponsorship of City's home and away shorts for a further three years.

10 Andrew Boyce receives a two-match ban for his tenth yellow card of the season at Luton. He will miss the final two games of the season.

11 Gary Simpson confirms that he protected certain players in the last two games because Tamworth and Hyde are more realistic targets for a win.

⇒ The board of directors issues a rallying call to supporters ahead of the Tamworth game on Saturday.

12 Gary Simpson also makes a personal appeal to the fans ahead of tomorrow's crunch game against fellow relegation strugglers Tamworth.

13 **Lincoln 2 (Taylor, Power pen) Tamworth 1.** Att: 3,174. An 83rd-minute penalty by Alan Power wins a nervy match as City overturn a half time deficit. Craig Hobson makes his final appearance. City lift themselves to 18th, 4 points clear of Stockport who have a game in hand.

⇒ Alan Power is voted *Player of the Season* by the fans, beating Jamie Taylor, Jake Sheridan and Tom Miller to the award. Tom Miller is voted *Away Player of the Season*, with Conner Robinson named *Young Player of the Season* by the management.

16 City's fight for survival goes to the final day as relegation-threatened Stockport postpone the drop by drawing with Gateshead this evening. Stockport are 3 points behind the Imps, meaning that City need a single point from Saturday's trip to Hyde to ensure survival. Stockport have a nightmare final day fixture - away to Kidderminster Harriers, who need a win to stand a chance of automatic promotion. Even if City lose, a five-goal swing is needed to relegate City. Barrow, Ebbsfleet and Telford are already relegated.

20 **Hyde 1 Lincoln 5 (Oliver 3, Power pen, Fofana).** Att: 1,390. A brilliant second half hat-trick from Vadaine Oliver ensures safety for the Imps in front of 850 travelling fans. They need not have worried - Stockport County are beaten 4-0 at Kidderminster and are relegated. It proves to be Oliver's final appearance. Jake Jones, Jamie Taylor, Nicky Nicolau and on-loan Paul Turnbull also play their final games.

⇒ City finish the season in 16th place, one place higher than last season, and 6 points clear of the drop zone. They have picked up 20 points from new manager Simpson's 13 games to secure Conference Premier status for next season.

⇒ Chairman Bob Dorrian pledges to increase the playing budget for next season in a bid to make the play-offs.

22 Gary Simpson agrees a three-year contract as Lincoln City manager.

⇒ City announce that the Stacey West Stand is to close for next season unless there is a large number of visiting fans expected. The move will produce significant cost savings.

25 Despite a pledge from the chairman to increase it, Gary Simpson's budget looks set to be the same as last season, at £400,000. Simpson has already opened negotiations with both existing squad members and potential new recruits.

⇒ Outgoing Gainsborough Trinity chairman Peter Swann continues to be linked with a place on Lincoln City's board.

29 Scunthorpe United announce that Peter Swann is to join their board of directors with a view to becoming chairman. The news comes as a blow to City, who believed Swann was coming to Lincoln on a similar deal.

May 2013

2 Gary Simpson reveals he is looking for players in their mid-20s with potential rather than seasoned professionals winding down their careers.

3 City confirm they are close to agreeing a deal with Jake Jones, who was released by Walsall this week.

6 Jake Jones confirms he has agreed a deal with City and calls his return to Sincil Bank 'a no-brainer'.

9 City announce the retained list for 2013-14 season. Just two players - youngsters Conner Robinson and Jordan Thomas - are under contract. Terms have already been agreed with Paul Farman, Dan Gray and Jake Sheridan. Deals have been offered to Andrew Boyce, Karl Cunningham, Tom Miller and Vadaine Oliver. The club is still in discussions with Mamadou Fofana, Todd Jordan, Alan Power, and David Preece.

Frazer Cobb, Gomez Dali, Nick Draper, Peter Gilbert, Nicky Nicolau and Adam Smith are all released. Also released is Jamie Taylor, who has elected to return to his native south-east for family reasons.

⇒ Jamie Taylor signs for Blue Square Bet South side Sutton United. He has taken a job as a painter and decorator to supplement his income. He reveals that his partner is expecting twins and they need the support of their families in the south-east.

10 Mamadou Fofana signs a new one-year deal.

⇒ Winger Jake Jones, who spent part of last season on loan from Walsall, misses a 5pm deadline to sign a permanent deal despite giving verbal assurances that he was keen to join.

13 City sign 24-year-old left-back Sean Newton from relegated Stockport County on a two-year deal. Newton scored against the Imps last season.

⇒ City also sign 24-year-old midfielder/striker Danny L Rowe from Fleetwood Town on a one-year deal.

14 Paul Farman signs his new two-year deal.

⇒ City discover that Jake Jones is set to sign for Tamworth.

15 Dan Gray signs a new one-year deal with the Imps.

⇒ City are believed to be interested in Bradford City defender Steve Williams and Elgin striker Craig Gunn.

16 Jake Sheridan signs a further one-year deal.

|17| City sign 24-year-old striker Waide Fairhurst from Macclesfield Town on a one-year deal.

|20| City announce that almost 700 season ticket holders have renewed at the special discount price.

⇒ City sign 21-year-old midfielder Jon Nolan from Stockport County on a one-year deal. Nolan is the second player to join from relegated Stockport after Sean Newton.

|22| Karl Cunningham signs a short-term deal to 31 December.

|23| Todd Jordan signs a permanent one-year deal after playing last season on non-contract terms.

⇒ City sign 21-year-old striker Adi Yussuf from Burton Albion on a one-year deal.

⇒ Tom Miller is believed to be attracting interest from Wycombe Wanderers, while Glasgow Rangers are monitoring Vadaine Oliver. The two players have yet to agree new contracts with City.

|24| Alan Power signs a new two-year contract.

SEASON 2012-13

CONFERENCE PREMIER

No.	Date		Opposition	Res	Att	Scorers	Farman, P	Nutter, J	Boyce, A	Miller, T	Mills, G	Power, A	Gray, D	Daley, L	Smith, A	Duffy, R	Taylor, J	Oliver, V	Sheridan, J
1	AUG	11	KIDDERMINSTER HARRIERS	1-0	2112	Taylor	Y	Y	Y	Y	Y	Y	Y	Y#	Y*	Y>	Y	S#	S*
2		14	Cambridge United	1-2	2546	Boyce	Y	Y>	Y	Y	Y	Y	Y	Y#	Y*	Y	Y	S#	S*
3		18	Newport County	1-2	3024	Taylor	Y	Y	Y	Y	Y	Y	Y	Y>	Y*	Y#	Y		S*
4		25	MACCLESFIELD TOWN	2-3	2009	Taylor, Boyce	Y	Y	Y		Y	Y	Y	Y#			Y	S*	Y>
5		27	Gateshead	1-1	803	Robinson	Y	Y			Y	Y	Y	S#			Y	S*	Y>
6	SEP	1	EBBSFLEET UNITED	1-1	1682	Nicolau	Y	Y	Y		Y#	Y	Y				Y	S>	Y
7		4	ALFRETON TOWN	1-2	1566	Nicolau	Y	Y	Y*		S#	Y#	Y				Y	S>	S*
8		8	AFC Telford United	1-1	1749	Oliver	Y	Y	Y		Y		Y				Y#	Y	Y*
9		15	HYDE	3-2	1745	Larkin 2 (2 pens), Oliver	Y	Y	Y		Y		Y				Y	Y	Y*
10		22	Tamworth	0-1	1042		Y	Y	Y		Y		Y		S*		S#	Y	Y*
11		25	NUNEATON TOWN	2-1	1579	Nicolau, Miller	Y	Y	Y	Y			Y		Y*		S#	Y	Y>
12		28	Forest Green Rovers	0-3	1395		Y		Y	Y			Y		Y*		S*	Y	S>
13	OCT	6	LUTON TOWN	1-2	2970	Taylor	Y		Y	Y>			Y		Y		Y		S>
14		9	Mansfield Town	0-0	2325		Y		Y	Y			Y		Y		Y		S#
15		13	Wrexham	4-2	3809	Nicolau, Taylor, Robinson, Larkin	Y		Y	Y	Y	S>	Y		Y#		Y*		S#
16		27	STOCKPORT COUNTY	3-3	1873	Taylor 2, Nutter	Y	Y	Y	Y		Y	Y		Y#		Y	S#	Y>
17	NOV	6	BRAINTREE TOWN	3-0	1455	Sheridan, Boyce, Taylor	Y		Y	Y	Y	Y#	Y		Y>		Y*	S#	Y
18		10	Barrow	2-1	987	Power, Oliver	Y		Y	Y	Y	Y>	Y		Y#		Y*	S#	Y
19		17	HEREFORD UNITED	3-2	2233	Taylor, Larkin (pen), OG	Y		Y	Y	Y	Y*	Y		Y>		Y#	S#	Y
20	DEC	4	WOKING	0-2	2526		Y		Y	Y	Y	Y	Y		S>		Y	S#	Y>
21		8	Dartford	4-2	1466	Larkin 3, Gray			Y	Y		Y	Y		Y#		Y		
22		26	GRIMSBY TOWN	1-4	5702	Power (pen)	Y		Y	Y	Y	Y	Y#		S*		Y	Y	Y>
23		29	GATESHEAD	1-1	1906	Robinson			Y	Y	Y	Y	Y				Y	Y	
24	JAN	1	Grimsby Town	1-1	7405	Power	S#		Y	Y		Y	Y		S>		Y	Y	Y>
25		5	Ebbsfleet United	1-1	889	Robinson	Y		Y	Y		Y	Y				Y		Y#
26		8	Southport	2-4	815	Taylor, Oliver	Y		Y	Y		Y	Y				Y#	Y	
27		12	NEWPORT COUNTY	2-4	1970	Oliver, Bush	Y		Y*	Y		Y	Y				Y	Y	
28		26	FOREST GREEN ROVERS	1-2	1663	Smith (pen)				Y			Y		S*		Y#	S#	Y*
29	FEB	9	DARTFORD	2-1	1789	Oliver, Larkin (pen)			Y	Y		Y	S#		Y>			Y*	Y
30		12	Stockport County	0-2	2769				Y	Y		Y	Y		Y*		S#	Y	
31		16	Hereford United	2-3	1914	Power (pen), OG			Y	Y		Y	Y		S*		Y#		
32		23	BARROW	0-0	1830		Y		Y	Y		Y			S*		Y#	S#	
33		26	MANSFIELD TOWN	0-1	2734		Y		Y	Y		Y	S#		S*		Y	Y	
34	MAR	2	Woking	1-1	1766	Oliver	Y		Y	Y		Y	Y		Y		Y	Y	Y#
35		6	Macclesfield Town	1-2	1557	Power (pen)	Y		Y	Y		Y			S#		Y	Y#	Y#
36		9	SOUTHPORT	1-0	1827	Power (pen)	Y		Y	Y		Y>			S*		Y#	Y	S#
37		12	WREXHAM	1-2	1379	OG	Y		Y	Y		Y	S>		S#		Y		
38		16	Nuneaton Town	0-1	1122		Y		Y	Y		Y			Y*		Y#		S#
39		23	AFC TELFORD UNITED	3-2	1724	Taylor 2, Jordan	Y		Y	Y		Y					Y		Y
40		26	Braintree Town	3-0	447	Diagne 2, Boyce	Y		Y	Y		S#	S*		S>		Y		Y>
41		30	Alfreton Town	2-0	1189	Hobson, Oliver	Y		Y	Y		Y	Y#		S#		Y>	S*	Y
42	APR	1	CAMBRIDGE UNITED	0-0	2721		Y		Y	Y		Y*					Y	Y	Y
43		6	Kidderminster Harriers	0-3	2326		Y		Y	Y		Y			Y#		Y	Y	Y
44		9	Luton Town	0-3	5393		Y		Y	Y		S#	Y		Y>		Y>	S*	Y
45		13	TAMWORTH	2-1	3174	Taylor, Power (pen)	Y			Y		Y	Y		Y		Y>	Y	Y
46		20	Hyde	5-1	1390	Oliver 3, Power (pen), Fofana	Y>		Y			Y	Y		S*		Y	Y	Y*
			Appearances				39	12	41	38	17	34	31	4	19	3	33	22	30
			Substitute appearances				1	0	0	0	1	3	4	1	11	0	7	15	10
			Goals				0	1	4	1	0	8	1	0	1	0	13	11	1

66 league goals

FA CUP

				Res	Att	Scorers	Farman, P	Nutter, J	Boyce, A	Miller, T	Mills, G	Power, A	Gray, D	Daley, L	Smith, A	Duffy, R	Taylor, J	Oliver, V	Sheridan, J
4Q	OCT	20	FC HALIFAX	0-0	1940		Y	S#	Y	Y	Y	Y		Y			Y	Y	
4QR		23	FC Halifax	2-0	1418	Sheridan, Taylor	Y	Y	Y	Y	Y	Y			Y*		Y>	S>	Y
1	NOV	3	WALSALL	1-1	2032	Taylor	Y		Y	Y	Y	Y#	Y		Y*		Y>	S>	Y
1R		13	Walsall	3-2	1762	Oliver 2, Power	Y	S>	Y	Y	Y	Y>	Y*		Y#		Y	S#	Y
2	DEC	1	MANSFIELD TOWN	3-3	4127	Power 2, Taylor	Y		Y	Y	Y	Y	Y		Y#		Y	S#	Y
2R		11	Mansfield Town	1-2	5304	Smith	Y		Y	Y	Y#	Y	Y		Y*		Y	S#	Y>

FA TROPHY

				Res	Att	Scorers	Farman, P	Nutter, J	Boyce, A	Miller, T	Mills, G	Power, A	Gray, D	Daley, L	Smith, A	Duffy, R	Taylor, J	Oliver, V	Sheridan, J
1	NOV	24	Tamworth	1-3	726	Power	Y			Y		Y					Y>		S*

LINCOLNSHIRE CUP

				Res	Att	Scorers	Farman, P	Nutter, J	Boyce, A	Miller, T	Mills, G	Power, A	Gray, D	Daley, L	Smith, A	Duffy, R	Taylor, J	Oliver, V	Sheridan, J
F	JUL	31	GRIMSBY TOWN	1-1*	1469	Nicolau				Y							Y	S*	Y

* Grimsby won 5-4 on penalties

Key:
Y = full appearance
Y# = full appearance, first player substituted - by substitute S#
Y* = full appearance, second player substituted - by substitute S*
Y> = full appearance, third player substituted - by substitute S>

■ Red Card
▨ Yellow Card

Main appearance grid:

Nicolau, N	McCammon, M	Hutchison, G	Larkin, C	Robson, P	Robinson, C	Bore, P	Fofana, M	Morgan, D	Gilbert, P	Garner, S	Bassele, A	Preece, D	Thomson, J	Barraclough, B	Bush, C	Platt, C	Turnbull, P	Jones, J	Hobson, C	Diagne, T	Brown, N	Jordan, T	Dali, G	Boyd, A	Rawdon, W	Leggett, R	Cobb, F	Cunningham, K	Turner, J	Gowling, J
S >																														
S >																														
S >		S #																												
S >	Y *	Y	S #																											
Y #		Y	Y	Y >		S >																								
Y *		Y	Y >	S #	S *																									
Y		Y	Y	Y >			Y																							
Y		Y	S #				S *	Y																						
Y >		Y	Y *			S *	S #	Y		S >																				
		Y >				S >	Y #	Y	Y																					
S >			S *			Y #		Y	Y																					
Y >			Y #	Y		S #		Y	Y																					
Y			S #			S *	Y *	Y #	Y	Y																				
Y			Y *			S *	Y #	Y		Y																				
Y			S *			Y >	Y			Y																				
S >			S *	Y *				Y																						
			S *					Y	S >	Y																				
			S *					Y	Y	Y		S >																		
			S *					Y	Y	Y			S >																	
			S *				Y *	Y	Y	Y	Y #																			
Y			Y		Y	S #		Y	Y			Y																		
Y *			S >						Y	S #																				
			Y			Y			Y	Y																				
			Y #						Y	Y							Y	S >	S *											
S >			Y #			S *			Y	Y		Y					Y	Y >												
			S >			Y *	Y		Y	Y		Y					Y	Y >	S #											
Y			Y >			S >	Y *			Y							Y	Y												
Y			S >				Y #			Y							Y >	Y *												
							Y										Y					Y	Y							
							Y		Y >	Y							Y *		S *			S >								
							Y			Y								Y *	S >	Y		Y								
							Y		Y >	Y								Y #	Y *	Y		Y		S *						
							Y *										S >	S *	Y #	Y	Y	Y								
							Y #										Y			Y *	Y	Y >		S #						
																	Y	S >	Y *			Y	Y							
			S *														Y #		S #	Y		Y	Y							
			Y																S #			Y	Y							
			Y														Y *					Y #	S >							
Y *			S >														Y	S #	S *			Y	Y #							
Y			Y									S >					Y	Y #				Y	S #							
18	**1**	**7**	**13**	**10**	**5**	**5**	**25**	**6**	**14**	**12**	**1**	**7**	**3**	**0**	**2**	**0**	**14**	**7**	**5**	**7**	**10**	**10**	**1**	**0**	**0**	**0**	**0**	**0**	**0**	**0**
8	*1*	*0*	*16*	*1*	*12*	*2*	*2*	*2*	*0*	*2*	*1*	*1*	*0*	*1*	*1*	*1*	*1*	*6*	*7*	*0*	*0*	*2*	*3*	*0*	*0*	*0*	*0*	*0*	*0*	*0*
4	0	0	8	0	4	0	1	0	0	0	0	0	0	0	1	0	0	0	1	2	0	1	0	0	0	0	0	0	0	0

Lower sub-grid:

Nicolau, N	McCammon, M	Hutchison, G	Larkin, C	Robson, P	Robinson, C	Bore, P	Fofana, M	Morgan, D	Gilbert, P	Garner, S	Bassele, A	Preece, D	Thomson, J	Barraclough, B	Bush, C	Platt, C	Turnbull, P	Jones, J	Hobson, C	Diagne, T	Brown, N	Jordan, T	Dali, G	Boyd, A	Rawdon, W	Leggett, R	Cobb, F	Cunningham, K	Turner, J	Gowling, J
Y >			S *			Y *	Y	S >	Y #																					
			S *	S #			Y #	Y																						
S #			S *				Y		Y																					
						S *	Y		Y																					
							Y		Y																					
			S *		S >		Y		Y																					

Single-row strip 1:

Nicolau, N	McCammon, M	Hutchison, G	Larkin, C	Robson, P	Robinson, C	Bore, P	Fofana, M	Morgan, D	Gilbert, P	Garner, S	Bassele, A	Preece, D	Thomson, J	Barraclough, B	Bush, C	Platt, C	Turnbull, P	Jones, J	Hobson, C	Diagne, T	Brown, N	Jordan, T	Dali, G	Boyd, A	Rawdon, W	Leggett, R	Cobb, F	Cunningham, K	Turner, J	Gowling, J
S #			Y *				Y	Y	Y	Y	Y #											S >								

Single-row strip 2:

Nicolau, N	McCammon, M	Hutchison, G	Larkin, C	Robson, P	Robinson, C	Bore, P	Fofana, M	Morgan, D	Gilbert, P	Garner, S	Bassele, A	Preece, D	Thomson, J	Barraclough, B	Bush, C	Platt, C	Turnbull, P	Jones, J	Hobson, C	Diagne, T	Brown, N	Jordan, T	Dali, G	Boyd, A	Rawdon, W	Leggett, R	Cobb, F	Cunningham, K	Turner, J	Gowling, J
Y						Y								Y *								Y	Y	Y #	S #	Y	Y			

Appearances & Goals 2012-13

	League			FA Cup			FA Trophy			Totals			Totals		Lincolnshire Cup		
	Apps	Subs	Goals	Apps	Subs	Goals	Apps	Subs	Goals	Apps	Subs	Goals	Apps	Goals	Apps	Subs	Goals
Andrew BOYCE	41	0	4	6	0	0	0	0	0	47	0	4	47	4	0	0	0
Paul FARMAN	39	1	0	6	0	0	1	0	0	46	1	0	47	0	0	0	0
Jamie TAYLOR	33	7	13	6	0	3	0	0	0	39	7	16	46	16	1	0	0
Jake SHERIDAN	30	10	1	5	0	1	0	0	0	35	10	2	45	2	1	0	0
Tom MILLER	38	0	1	6	0	0	1	0	0	45	0	1	45	1	1	0	0
Alan POWER	34	3	8	5	0	3	1	0	1	40	3	12	43	12	0	0	0
Vadaine OLIVER	22	15	11	0	5	2	0	1	0	22	21	13	43	13	0	1	0
Dan GRAY	31	4	1	5	0	0	0	0	0	36	4	1	40	1	0	0	0
Adam SMITH	19	11	1	6	0	1	1	0	0	26	11	2	37	2	0	0	0
Colin LARKIN	13	16	8	0	4	0	1	0	0	14	20	8	34	8	0	0	0
Mamadou FOFANA	25	2	1	5	0	0	1	0	0	31	2	1	33	1	0	0	0
Nicky NICOLAU	18	8	4	1	1	0	0	1	0	19	10	4	29	4	1	0	1
Gary MILLS	17	1	0	6	0	0	0	0	0	23	1	0	24	0	0	0	0
Peter GILBERT	14	0	0	5	0	0	1	0	0	20	0	0	20	0	0	0	0
Conner ROBINSON	5	12	4	1	1	0	0	0	0	6	13	4	19	4	1	0	0
Paul TURNBULL (L)	14	1	0	0	0	0	0	0	0	14	1	0	15	0	0	0	0
Scott GARNER (L)	12	2	0	0	0	0	1	0	0	13	2	0	15	0	0	0	0
John NUTTER	12	0	1	1	2	0	0	0	0	13	2	1	15	1	0	0	0
Jake JONES (L)	7	6	0	0	0	0	0	0	0	7	6	0	13	0	0	0	0
Todd JORDAN	10	2	1	0	0	0	0	0	0	10	2	1	12	1	0	0	0
Craig HOBSON (L)	5	7	1	0	0	0	0	0	0	5	7	1	12	1	0	0	0
Paul ROBSON	10	1	0	0	1	0	0	0	0	10	2	0	12	0	0	0	0
Peter BORE	5	2	0	2	1	0	1	0	0	8	3	0	11	0	0	0	0
Nat BROWN	10	0	0	0	0	0	0	0	0	10	0	0	10	0	0	0	0
David MORGAN (L)	6	2	0	0	1	0	1	0	0	7	3	0	10	0	0	0	0
David PREECE	7	1	0	0	0	0	0	0	0	7	1	0	8	0	0	0	0
Tony DIAGNE	7	0	2	0	0	0	0	0	0	7	0	2	7	2	0	0	0
Graham HUTCHISON (L)	7	0	0	0	0	0	0	0	0	7	0	0	7	0	0	0	0
Luke DALEY	4	1	0	0	0	0	0	0	0	4	1	0	5	0	0	0	0
Gomez DALI	1	3	0	0	0	0	0	0	0	1	3	0	4	0	0	0	0
Rob DUFFY	3	0	0	0	0	0	0	0	0	3	0	0	3	0	0	0	0
Jake THOMSON	3	0	0	0	0	0	0	0	0	3	0	0	3	0	0	0	0
Chris BUSH	2	1	1	0	0	0	0	0	0	2	1	1	3	1	0	0	0
Aristide BASSELE	1	1	0	0	0	0	1	0	0	2	1	0	3	0	0	0	0
Mark McCAMMON	1	1	0	0	0	0	0	0	0	1	1	0	2	0	0	0	0
Bradley BARRACLOUGH	0	1	0	0	0	0	0	0	0	0	1	0	1	0	1	0	0
Conal PLATT	0	1	0	0	0	0	0	0	0	0	1	0	1	0	0	0	0
Adam BOYD	0	0	0	0	0	0	0	1	0	0	1	0	1	0	0	0	0
Own goals			3			0			0			3		3			0

Players Used	League goals	FA Cup goals	FA Trophy goals	Total goals
38	66	10	1	77

Plus appearances in Lincolnshire Cup: Ryan Leggett 1, Will Rawdon 1, Frazer Cobb 1, Josh Gowling 1, Jake Turner 1, Karl Cunningham (1).

Squad Numbers 2012-13

No.	Player		No.	Player
1	Paul Farman		21	
2	Paul Robson		22	
3	John Nutter; Chris Bush; Tony Diagne		23	Craig Hobson
4	Gary Mills; Todd Jordan		24	
5	Andrew Boyce		25	Nat Brown
6	Scott Garner		26	
7	Adam Smith		27	
8	Alan Power		28	
9	Rob Duffy		29	
10	Jamie Taylor		30	Peter Gilbert
11	Conal Platt		31	David Preece
12	Jake Sheridan		32	
13			33	
14	Vadaine Oliver		34	Colin Larkin
15	Dan Gray		35	Luke Daley; David Morgan; Paul Turnbull
16	Nicky Nicolau		36	Gomez Dali
17	Bradley Barraclough		37	Mark McCammon; Mamadou Fofana
18	Peter Bore; Jake Jones		38	Adam Boyd
19	Graham Hutchison; Aristide Bassele; Jake Thomson		39	Conner Robinson
20	Tom Miller			

Conference Premier Final League Table 2012-13

				Home					Away					Totals		
		P	W	D	L	F	A	W	D	L	F	A	F	A	Pts
1	Mansfield Town	46	17	3	3	53	17	13	2	8	39	35	92	52	95
2	Kidderminster Harriers	46	15	4	4	49	22	13	5	5	33	18	82	40	93
P	Newport County	46	13	5	5	43	27	12	5	6	42	33	85	60	85
4	Grimsby Town	46	13	5	5	42	19	10	9	4	28	19	70	38	83
5	Wrexham	46	11	9	3	45	24	11	5	7	29	21	74	45	80
6	Hereford United	46	9	6	8	37	33	10	7	6	36	30	73	63	70
7	Luton Town	46	10	7	6	43	26	8	6	9	27	36	70	62	67
8	Dartford	46	12	4	7	41	26	7	5	11	26	37	67	63	66
9	Braintree Town	46	9	5	9	32	40	10	4	9	31	32	63	72	66
10	Forest Green Rovers	46	8	6	9	33	24	10	5	8	30	25	63	49	65
11	Macclesfield Town	46	10	6	7	29	28	7	6	10	36	42	65	70	63
12	Woking	46	13	3	7	47	34	5	5	13	26	47	73	81	62
13	Alfreton Town	46	9	5	9	41	39	7	7	9	28	35	69	74	60
14	Cambridge United	46	9	7	7	33	30	6	7	10	35	39	68	69	59
15	Nuneaton Town	46	8	9	6	29	25	6	6	11	26	38	55	63	57
16	**Lincoln City**	**46**	**9**	**5**	**9**	**34**	**36**	**6**	**6**	**11**	**32**	**37**	**66**	**73**	**56**
17	Gateshead	46	9	9	5	35	22	4	7	12	23	39	58	61	55
18	Hyde	46	9	5	9	35	31	7	2	14	28	44	63	75	55
19	Tamworth	46	9	4	10	25	27	6	6	11	30	42	55	69	55
20	Southport	46	7	4	12	32	44	7	8	8	40	42	72	86	54
21	Stockport County	46	8	2	13	34	39	5	9	9	23	37	57	76	50
22	Barrow	46	5	7	11	20	35	6	6	11	25	48	45	83	46
23	Ebbsfleet United	46	5	11	7	31	37	3	4	16	24	52	55	89	39
24	AFC Telford United	46	2	9	12	22	42	4	8	11	30	37	52	79	35

Progress Chart 2012-13

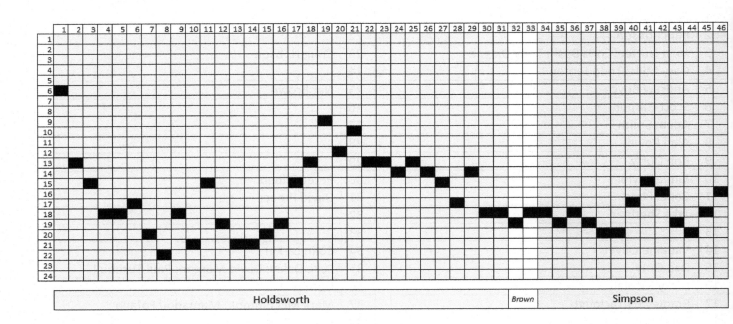

Holdsworth																	Brown		Simpson			

Friendlies 2012-13

Jul	18	Worksop Town	2-1	346	Smith, Bannister
	21	Eastwood Town	4-2	199	Sheridan 2, Boyce, Power (pen)
	24	Newark Town	4-1	302	Hutchison, Smith, Duffy, OG
	29	GAINSBOROUGH TRINITY	1-1	879	Duffy
Oct	16	Sheffield FC	1-0	40	Sheridan

Original Fixture List 2012-13

Aug	11	KIDDERMINSTER HARR
	14	Cambridge United
	18	Newport County
	25	MACCLESFIELD TOWN
	27	Gateshead
Sep	1	EBBSFLEET UNITED
	4	ALFRETON TOWN
	8	AFC Telford United
	15	HYDE
	22	Tamworth
	25	NUNEATON TOWN
	29	Forest Green Rovers
Oct	6	LUTON TOWN
	9	Mansfield Town
	13	Wrexham
	27	STOCKPORT COUNTY

Nov	6	BRAINTREE TOWN
	10	Barrow
	17	HEREFORD UNITED
Dec	1	Southport
	4	WOKING
	8	Dartford
	22	Macclesfield Town
	26	GRIMSBY TOWN
	29	GATESHEAD
Jan	1	Grimsby Town
	5	Ebbsfleet United
	12	NEWPORT COUNTY
	19	WREXHAM
	22	Luton Town
	26	FOREST GREEN ROVERS
Feb	2	Braintree Town

	9	DARTFORD
	12	Stockport County
	16	Hereford United
	23	BARROW
	26	MANSFIELD TOWN
Mar	2	Woking
	9	SOUTHPORT
	16	Nuneaton Town
	23	AFC TELFORD UNITED
	30	Alfreton Town
Apr	1	CAMBRIDGE UNITED
	6	Kidderminster Harriers
	13	TAMWORTH
	20	Hyde
Mar	24	FA Trophy Final

Year 3

2013-14

June 2013

3 City sign defender Nat Brown from Macclesfield Town on a one-year contract. Brown spent the last 2 months of last season on loan at Sincil Bank.

⇒ City reject an offer from Crewe Alexandra for Vadaine Oliver, believed to be £15,000.

4 Legendary City manager Graham Taylor gives his backing to the *Future Imps Fund*.

5 Tom Miller signs a new two-year contract to end speculation over a move to Wycombe Wanderers.

10 Vadaine Oliver officially rejects City's terms and signs for Crewe Alexandra. The deal is believed to be worth around £45,000 to City, with a £20,000 down-payment.

14 Andrew Boyce signs a new two-year contract.

17 Gary Simpson is believed to be tracking former Mansfield striker Nick Wright to replace the departed Vadaine Oliver and Jamie Taylor.

24 Gary Simpson confirms that Alan Power will continue as City captain next season. He is looking to sign four more players prior to the new season, but has ruled out a move for ex-Macclesfield striker John Rooney.

July 2013

1 City sign 25-year-old striker Nick Wright from Mansfield Town on a one-year deal.

⇒ City extend the deadline for discounted season tickets until 10 July. Sales are encouraging, with around 1,000 sold so far. The club is confident last season's total of 1,100 will be beaten.

⇒ The players return for pre-season training.

3 City will travel to Woking on the opening day of the season. They also retain the festive double-header against Grimsby.

⇒ New broadcaster BT Sport announces it will show 30 Conference Premier matches live per season including all 5 play-off matches. The deal is for the next two seasons.

9 City lose 3-1 at Chesterfield in a behind-closed-doors friendly, Adi Yussuf with the goal. The team is changed every 30 minutes, and includes 8 trialists.

11 City announce they are in a period of consultation with CEO Steve Prescott with regard to his position at the club.

⇒ City appoint the CEO of CARE International, Geoffrey Dennis, to the post of Non-Executive Director.

⇒ City are running an eye over several trialists including former Imp Luke Foster, defender Sean McCashin and winger Matt Rooney (both from Glenavon), and non-league striker Tom Williams.

13 City win 7-1 at Lincoln United in the first official pre-season friendly with trialist Bohan Dixon scoring two on his first start. City also take a look at two other trialists - former Imps Gary King and Luke Foster. New signing Danny Rowe hits a hat-trick, with Alan Power and Adi Yussuf rounding off the scoring on an easy night for the Imps at Ashby Avenue. It isn't all bad for United, though - they are delighted with the attendance of 721.

15 City sign trialist Bohan Dixon from Accrington Stanley on a one-year deal after his dominant performance at Lincoln United two nights ago.

16 City win 3-2 at Conference North side Harrogate Town, with new signing Nick Wright scoring a first half hat-trick in front of a sparse crowd of 256.

19 City announce that CEO Steve Prescott has been made redundant following a period of consultation. The post will no longer be used.

20 An Alan Power penalty is not enough to stop City slipping to a 2-1 defeat at Northern Premier League Premier Division neighbours Grantham Town in front of 236 at the South Kesteven Sports Stadium. Trialists Luke Foster and goalkeeper Matt Armstrong-Ford feature in the game.

23 City sign 23-year-old striker Ben Tomlinson from Alfreton Town on a two-year deal.

24 City go down 2-0 at home to Sunderland's U21 side in front of a disappointing crowd of 474 at Sincil Bank. Although a club from the Premier League, Sunderland U21s fail to draw the crowds. Future Imp Billy Knott features prominently in the game, creating the first half opener for his side.

26 E-commerce specialist Skrill becomes the new sponsor of the Football Conference.

27 Another U21 side from the north-east comes calling in the shape of Middlesbrough. Only 493 are there to see City win 2-1 with an 88th-minute Ben Tomlinson penalty and a third goal of the pre-season period for Adi Yussuf.

30 Lincoln beat Scunthorpe United 2-0 at Sincil Bank in the semi-final of the Lincolnshire Cup, both goals coming from Waide Fairhurst in front of 918.

August 2013

1 City sign 27-year-old defender Luke Foster on a one-year deal after a trial period. Former Imp Foster, who played for the club between 2005 and 2007, was latterly with Preston North End.

|2| Defender Tom Miller looks set to miss the start of the season with a persistent thigh injury.

|3| City's pre-season comes to a winning end as Sean Newton's piledriver three minutes from time is enough to see off Boston United in front of 1,008 at Sincil Bank.

|5| City confirm MANS Location Services as their new media sponsor for the season.

⇒ Damian Froggatt is appointed the new Head of Youth in succession to Grant Brown, who has been working with the first team.

⇒ It is revealed that Lincoln City Supporters' Trust chairman Steve O'Dare has resigned from the role and the board after he was challenged over his 'brusque style of leadership'. O'Dare succeeded Chris Ashton less than two months ago. Fellow directors Ty Corcoran and Dave Kirkbright are also rumoured to have resigned.

|6| City confirm 3e International as the new back of away shirt sponsor for the 2013-14 season.

|7| Lincoln City Supporters' Trust slips into further disarray as another board member resigns. Lee Thomas is also calling for an Extraordinary General Meeting after claiming no confidence in the remaining board.

⇒ Further problems arise in connection with the Trust after Lincoln City shareholder Michael Foley confirms he has issued legal proceedings against the club and the Trust over a variety of issues.

|8| David Preece signs a one-year deal as player/goalkeeping coach. He has been playing in Iceland for Keflavik during the summer to improve his fitness.

⇒ Director Roger Bates reveals that the club still needs £20,000 to keep the Academy going for this season.

|9| The Gelder Group secures naming rights to Sincil Bank as part of a sponsorship package for 2013-14.

|10| **Woking 0 Lincoln 0.** Att: 1,845. City get off to a reasonable start on the opening day. Sean Newton, Jon Nolan, Nick Wright, Ben Tomlinson and Bohan Dixon all make their City debuts, with Luke Foster making his second debut. City are 12th in the first league table of the season, 2 points behind early leaders Forest Green.

|13| **Lincoln 1 (Rowe) Macclesfield Town 0.** Att: 2,386. Danny Rowe's goal in the 27th-minute of his debut is enough to give City their first win of the season and their second clean sheet. City are up to 8th, 2 points behind new leaders Southport.

|15| Gary Simpson reveals he is still looking for a striker to take the place of the departed Vadaine Oliver.

|16| City designate Upper Block 7 of the Co-op Stand as the 'singing section' following incidents during the match against Macclesfield Town.

|17| **Lincoln 2 (Fairhurst 2) Forest Green Rovers 1.** Att: 2,290. Two goals from debutant Waide Fairhurst give City their second win in a week at Sincil Bank. They prove to be Fairhurst's only two goals for the club. City move up to 4th, level on points with new leaders Cambridge United.

|24| **Cambridge United 1 Lincoln 0.** Att: 3,022. City go down to their first defeat of the season, a goal just before half time proving enough for the league leaders. Alan Power is sent off in stoppage time. City slip to 10th, 3 points behind Cambridge.

|26| **Lincoln 2 (Tomlinson 2) Wrexham 0.** Att: 2,610. Ben Tomlinson's first two goals for City keep up the 100% home record against another of the title favourites. City are up to 5th after their best start to a season since 2006, 1 point behind new leaders Barnet.

|27| Alan Power receives a three-match ban following his red card at Cambridge on Saturday.

|30| Conner Robinson joins Gainsborough Trinity on a one-month loan.

|31| **Dartford 1 Lincoln 2 (Tomlinson, Boyce).** Att: 1,386. City end the month with four wins and a draw from their first six games; optimism abounds that a good season is on the cards at last. City are up a place to 4th, 1 point behind leaders Cambridge.

September 2013

|3| City field several first team players in a 4-2 friendly win at Sleaford Town to give them match time. The goals come from youth teamer Kieran Helsdown (2), Alex Simmons and Jordan Thomas in front of a token crowd.

|7| **Lincoln 0 Salisbury City 1.** Att: 2,646. City's 100% home record comes to a disappointing end as they are beaten by Conference newcomers Salisbury City in the first ever meeting between the two clubs. Adi Yussuf makes his City debut as the visitors keep 10 men behind the ball after taking a first half lead. City stay 4th, now 4 points behind leaders Cambridge.

|10| City play a behind closed doors friendly at Chesterfield to give some more game time to squad players and several returning from injury. They are beaten 4-0 on a wet and windy afternoon.

|13| City's game at home to Grimsby on Boxing Day is brought forward to 1pm on police advice.

|14| **Barnet 1 Lincoln 1 (Nolan).** Att: 1,913. A last-gasp equaliser from Jon Nolan, his first goal for the club, sparks scenes of wild celebration from City's traditionally large following at Barnet. It is City's first ever visit to Barnet's new ground, The Hive. City slip to 8th, 6 points behind leaders Cambridge, and 1 point behind fifth-placed Alfreton.

|17| **Lincoln 1 (Miller) Southport 0.** Att: 1,879. Tom Miller's first half header lifts City back up to 4th, 6 points behind new leaders Nuneaton Town.

|20| Gary Simpson insists his first target is to reach 50 points despite his side sitting in the play-off positions.

21 **Luton Town 3 Lincoln 2 (Power, Tomlinson).** Att: 6,203. City lead twice at Kenilworth Road before going down to two late Luton goals. City slip to 6th, 7 points behind leaders Cambridge, but level on points with fifth-placed Salisbury.

24 **Hereford United 1 Lincoln 0.** Att: 1,398. An 85th-minute winner from former/future Imps defender Chris Bush sends City to defeat against struggling Hereford. City are down to 10th, 10 points behind leaders Cambridge, and 2 points behind fifth-placed Luton.

27 Jordan Thomas joins Gainsborough Trinity on a one-month loan.

28 **Lincoln 3 (Dixon 2, Tomlinson) Hyde 0.** Att: 2,311. Two goals in the last 11 minutes by substitute Bohan Dixon - his first goals for the club - give Lincoln an unconvincing win over the league's bottom side. City rise to 7th, 8 points behind leaders Cambridge, and 1 point behind fifth-placed Braintree.

October 2013

2 Gary Simpson reveals he has spoken to Ben Tomlinson about talking back to referees and will fine him if he is booked for dissent.

5 **Nuneaton Town 2 Lincoln 2 (Miller, Nolan).** Att: 1,634. City pick up a useful point at second-placed Nuneaton. City are down to 9th, 10 points behind leaders Cambridge, and 2 points behind fifth-placed Luton.

7 Gainsborough Trinity are disqualified from the FA Cup due to an alleged registration error regarding loan player Jordan Thomas from Lincoln. The FA claims it never received the paperwork for his loan move before the deadline on 27 September, even though the Football Conference confirmed it did receive it, and Lincoln provided evidence to the FA that it had been submitted. Thomas played in the 2-0 win over Rushall Olympic in the second qualifying round on 28 September, believing that everything was in order.

8 **Lincoln 0 Tamworth 0.** Att: 2,603. City fail to break down their relegation-threatened visitors in a poor game. City stay 9th, 2 points behind fifth-placed Braintree. They are already out of touch with the leaders.

9 Ben Tomlinson receives a one-match ban following his fifth yellow card of the season against Tamworth.

10 Gainsborough Trinity lose their appeal against expulsion from this season's FA Cup.

11 Karl Cunningham rejoins Lincoln United on a one-month loan.

12 **Lincoln 0 Aldershot Town 1.** Att: 2,748. Ben Tomlinson's absence through suspension is felt as City fail to score for the second home match in a row. Adi Yussuf makes his second and final appearance as City lose at home to second from bottom Aldershot. City stay 9th, now 4 points behind the play-off zone.

13 Jean Foster ceases to be a director of the club.

14 City are drawn away to either Conference North side Worcester City or Southern League Division One Central side Rugby Town in the fourth qualifying round of the FA Cup. The two sides drew 1-1 at Worcester's temporary Aggborough home on Saturday in their third qualifying round tie.

15 City will be away to Worcester City in the fourth qualifying round of the FA Cup after Worcester won 2-0 at Rugby Town in tonight's third qualifying round replay.

19 **Kidderminster Harriers 4 Lincoln 1 (Wright).** Att: 2,103. City are well-beaten by second-placed Kidderminster. The only bright spot at Aggborough is Nick Wright's first goal for the Imps (albeit in his 11th appearance) against his former club. Ironically, Wright is to rejoin Harriers on loan later in the season. City have now won just 1 of their last 7 games and have slipped into the bottom half after a great start to the season. They are 13th, 5 points behind the play-offs.

22 City win the Lincolnshire Cup at the Northolme, beating Gainsborough Trinity 4-2 on penalties after a 0-0 draw, watched by 600. Youth teamsters Nick Green and Callum Ward make their first and last appearances for City's first team.

24 City recall Conner Robinson from his loan at Gainsborough Trinity.

⇒ Gary Simpson reveals he has failed in his attempts to sign a 6'3" striker this week. Simpson is keen to bring in a tall target man to replace Vadaine Oliver.

25 City sign 22-year-old winger Marlon Jackson from Bury on a two-month loan. Jackson had been a Gary Simpson target during the summer prior to joining Bury.

26 **FA Cup 4Q: Worcester City 1 Lincoln 1 (Boyce).** Att: 1,019. City make a quick return to Aggborough, temporary home of Conference North side Worcester. Marlon Jackson makes his debut, but City need a 77th-minute equaliser from defender Andrew Boyce to snatch a replay. It is the sixth successive Lincoln City FA Cup tie to go to a replay (Hereford United in the second round in 2010-11, Alfreton Town in 2011-12, FC Halifax, Walsall and Mansfield in 2012-13).

27 City are drawn at home to League Two side Plymouth Argyle in the first round of the FA Cup, provided they can overcome Worcester in Tuesday night's fourth qualifying round replay.

28 Jon Nolan receives a one-match ban following his fifth yellow card of the season at Worcester.

29 City's game at home to Gateshead, scheduled for Saturday 9 November, is rearranged for Tuesday 10 December due to Gateshead's involvement in the FA Cup first round on that date. City hope to join them in the First Round by beating Worcester in this evening's replay.

⇒ **FA Cup 4Q Replay: Lincoln 3 Worcester City 0.** Att: 1,344. City book an easy passage through to the FA Cup first round but lose Conner Robinson in the 3rd minute to a horror tackle by Worcester defender George Williams, who only receives a yellow card. Robinson will be out for at least 6 weeks with a broken leg. City bank a very useful £12,500 in prize money.

November 2013

2 **Welling United 1 Lincoln 0.** Att: 746. City have now gone 5 league games without a win. David Preece makes his final appearance as a player. City stay 13th, now 8 points behind the play-offs.

5 City's game at Alfreton Town, scheduled for Tuesday 19 November, is postponed due to two Alfreton players (future Imp Bradley Wood, and Dan Bradley) being called up for the England C match against the Czech Republic U21 side on the same night.

7 Striker Adi Yussuf joins Gainsborough Trinity on a one-month loan.

9 **FA Cup 1: Lincoln 0 Plymouth Argyle 0.** Att: 2,924. City are unable to find their way past a defensive performance by their League Two visitors. It is the seventh successive Lincoln City FA Cup tie to go to a replay (Hereford United in the second round in 2010-11, Alfreton Town in 2011-12, FC Halifax, Walsall and Mansfield in 2012-13, and Worcester this season).

10 City are drawn at home to Conference rivals Welling United in the second round of the FA Cup, if they can win at Plymouth in next week's first round replay. The Imps lost 1-0 to Welling a week ago.

11 City sign 27-year-old striker Chris Sharp from Hereford United on a one-month loan.

⇒ City's FA Cup replay at Plymouth is put back 24 hours from Tuesday 19 November to Wednesday 20 November.

⇒ Tom Miller receives a one-match ban following his fifth yellow card of the season against Plymouth.

12 **Southport 0 Lincoln 1 (Nolan).** Att: 818. Jon Nolan's 75th-minute winner gives City the points in their third away league match in succession. Chris Sharp makes his debut after joining on loan. City remain 13th, 5 points behind the play-off zone.

⇒ City's home match against Alfreton, scheduled for next Tuesday 19 November, is rearranged for Tuesday 7 January. City's FA Cup first round replay at Plymouth takes priority.

⇒ City's away game at Macclesfield Town, scheduled for Saturday 7 December, is rearranged for Tuesday 14 January. The postponement is due to Macclesfield's involvement in the second round of the FA Cup on that date (and hopefully Lincoln's if they can win at Plymouth next week).

14 Gary Simpson reveals that a Football League club has activated a release clause in Andrew Boyce's contract. City have rejected a request from that club to take Boyce on loan in the first instance, although the clause allows Boyce to leave in January.

15 Karl Cunningham and Jordan Thomas join Eastwood Town on a one-month loan.

⇒ Alex Simmons joins Lincoln United on work experience.

⇒ City reveal that Scunthorpe United is the club that has triggered the release clause for Andrew Boyce.

16 **Forest Green Rovers 4 Lincoln 1 (Sharp).** Att: 1,128. Chris Sharp's only league goal for Lincoln is not enough as City crash to defeat at Forest Green in their fourth successive away league game. Big-spending Forest Green win their second successive game under new manager Adrian Pennock. City slip to 15th, surprisingly only 6 points behind the play-offs.

18 City are drawn at home to Conference North side Stalybridge Celtic in the first round of the FA Trophy.

20 **FA Cup 1 Replay: Plymouth Argyle 5 Lincoln 0.** Att: 3,324. City are 2-down after 5 minutes, and 4-down after 35 minutes on a night to forget. The result is particularly surprising, as Plymouth had only scored 4 goals at home all season prior to the game. Andrew Boyce plays his final game for City amidst rumours that he is to join neighbours Scunthorpe United. His parting gift is an own goal in the second half.

22 Andrew Boyce joins Scunthorpe on loan until January, when the transfer will be made permanent.

23 **Lincoln 1 (Tomlinson) Hereford United 1.** Att: 1,874. Ben Tomlinson has a mixed day as he scores City's opener after 47 minutes but is then sent off in the 83rd minute. Frankie Artus equalises in the 89th minute to deny City 3 points. City slip a further place to 16th, 8 points behind the play-offs.

25 Ben Tomlinson receives a three-match ban for his red card against Hereford on Saturday.

28 Former City captain Delroy Facey is named as one of six people arrested on suspicion of match fixing.

⇒ Gary Simpson has failed in his attempts to sign two players ahead of today's loan deadline. The players are Fleetwood striker Jon Parkin and Southport midfielder Karl Ledsham.

30 **FA Trophy 1: Lincoln 5 (Power 3 - 1 pen, Jackson, Fofana) Stalybridge Celtic 1.** Att: 1,023. City coast into the second round with a comfortable victory over their Conference North opponents. Marlon Jackson scores his only goal for the Imps. Former Imp Conal Platt appears for the visitors.

December 2013

2 City are drawn away to Conference Premier rivals Braintree Town in the second round of the FA Trophy. The match will take the place of City's scheduled home game against Nuneaton Town, which is rearranged for Tuesday 4 February.

7 No game today, as City's scheduled game at Macclesfield Town is postponed due to Macclesfield's involvement in the second round of the FA Cup.

10 **Lincoln 0 Gateshead 1.** Att: 1,411. City's winless run at Sincil Bank is extended to 4 games as they fail to score for the tenth time this season. This game was rearranged from Saturday 9 November, when City and Gateshead were involved in the first round of the FA Cup. City stay 16th, 11 points behind the play-offs. Perhaps more worrying is the fact that they are now only 7 points clear of the relegation zone.

11 City extend striker Chris Sharp's loan from Hereford for a further month.

⇒ Alan Power receives a one-match ban after picking up his fifth yellow card of the season against Gateshead.

12 Gary Simpson is targeting three or four new signings when the transfer window opens in January in an attempt to reverse their current poor form. City have won just 1 of their last 9 league games.

14 **FA Trophy 2: Braintree Town 1 Lincoln 3 (Sharp, Foster, Hamann own goal).** Att: 410. City score three second half goals to overturn a half time deficit. Danny Rowe makes his first appearance since injuring an ankle at Luton in September. Marlon Jackson makes the final appearance of his loan before returning to Bury. Chris Sharp scores in his final appearance before returning to Hereford.

16 City are drawn at home to Conference North side North Ferriby United in the third round of the FA Trophy. Ferriby include former Imps Paul Robson and Danny Hone amongst their number.

17 The Lincoln City Supporters' Trust suffers a further blow as they fall victim to theft of unspecified amounts of money from their bank account. The police have been called in to investigate.

19 Chris Sharp is recalled by Hereford from his loan spell.

20 City announce that the match against Luton Town on 4 January will kick off at 1pm on police advice. The game is also all-ticket for away fans due to previous incidents in the city.

21 **Chester 3 Lincoln 3 (Dixon, Power pen, Robinson).** Att: 1,850. City grab a point after being 2 down after 10 minutes; Conner Robinson equalises in the 90th minute against 10 men. City have now won just 1 league game from the last 10, and slip two places to 18th, 7 points above the drop zone.

23 Sean Newton receives a one-match ban after picking up his fifth yellow card of the season at Chester.

26 **Lincoln 0 Grimsby 2.** Att: 5,421. City lose at home to Grimsby on Boxing Day for the third successive year in a game that kicks off at 1pm on police advice. Jake Sheridan is sent off as the poor league run extends to 1 win in 11 games. City stay 18th, 6 points clear of the relegation zone.

28 **FC Halifax Town 5 Lincoln 1 (Tomlinson).** Att: 1,979. Alan Power is sent off in the 12th minute for a two-footed tackle, and City crumble to another heavy away defeat. City manager Gary Simpson angers fans with some post-match defeatism: "We've got what we've got," is his response when asked about this latest defeat. They have just 1 win from their last 12 league games, and have not won in 6. City stay 18th, but the gap is down to 5 points above the bottom four.

30 Alan Power receives a four-match ban for his red card at Halifax; the longer ban is for Power's second straight red card of the season. Jake Sheridan receives a three-match ban after his red card against Grimsby.

31 Karl Cunningham is released by City by mutual consent. He signs for Gällivare FF in Sweden.

January 2014

1 **Grimsby Town 1 Lincoln 1 (Thomas own goal).** Att: 5,484. City snatch a point despite having Bohan Dixon sent off after just 23 minutes. Grimsby even up the numbers in the second half when former Imp Lennell John-Lewis receives two yellows. Kegan Everington makes his first-team debut while Waide Fairhurst plays his final game for City. The poor run continues, with 1 win in the last 13 league games. City stay 18th, 6 points above the relegation zone.

2 City sign 22-year-old winger Mitch Austin and 24-year-old striker Delano Sam-Yorke on loan from Cambridge. Austin joins for a month, with Sam-Yorke signing until 5 April.

⇒ Bohan Dixon receives a one-match ban for his red card at Grimsby on New Year's Day. Ben Tomlinson also receives a two-match ban for reaching 10 yellow cards for the season. City face a selection problem, with Jake Sheridan and Alan Power also currently serving suspensions.

3 Jordan Thomas joins Spalding United on a one-month loan.

⇒ City's home match against Welling United, scheduled for Saturday 11 January, is rearranged for Tuesday 11 March. The postponement is due to Lincoln's involvement in the third round of the FA Trophy on that date.

⇒ Gary Simpson assures supporters that there is no need to sell any of City's star players during the transfer window despite having already rejected one offer from a Football League club. He dismisses speculation that Jon Parkin is back on his radar on the basis that Parkin would take up half the wage bill.

4 **Lincoln 0 Luton Town 0.** Att: 2,928. Delano Sam-Yorke and Mitchell Austin make their City debuts in a match that kicks off at 1pm on police advice. City do well to hold the league leaders, but the poor run is now 1 win in 14 league games, and no win in 8. They stay 18th, 5 points clear of the bottom four.

6 Andrew Boyce signs a permanent contract with Scunthorpe United and officially leaves Lincoln City.

⇒ City's match at Macclesfield Town, scheduled for Saturday 14 January, is postponed due to the date being needed for Macclesfield's FA Cup third round replay against Sheffield Wednesday. The game will now take place on Tuesday 21 January.

| 7 | **Lincoln 4 (Wright, Nolan, Sam-Yorke, Kempson own goal) Alfreton Town 1.** Att: 1,877. Delano Sam-Yorke scores his first goal for City, while Nick Wright scores his second and final goal. This match was rearranged from its scheduled date of 19 November due to City's FA Cup first round replay at Plymouth. City's first league win in 9 games ironically comes against the team in third place in the table, and lifts the Imps to 16th, 8 points clear of the relegation zone.

| 11 | **FA Trophy 3: Lincoln 0 North Ferriby United 4.** Att: 2,037. City crash out of the competition at home to Conference North village team North Ferriby; some fans call it City's worst result ever and call for the head of manager Simpson. Nick Wright makes his final appearance for the club.

| 14 | City announce a trading loss of £102,000 for the financial year ending 30 June 2013, which is an improvement on the previous year's loss of £134,000. Chairman Bob Dorrian says the club is in a sound position financially despite the latest loss and states the club will remain full-time. Staff costs have reduced from £1,847,000 in 2011 to £937,000 in 2013. He also confirms that he put a further £20,000 into the club recently to pay wages following a string of postponements, taking his personal investment in the club to over £500,000.

⇒ No game today due to Macclesfield Town's involvement in their FA Cup third round replay against Sheffield Wednesday. They go down 4-1 at Hillsborough.

| 17 | Adi Yussuf joins Harrogate Town on a one-month loan.

⇒ Former City player Moses Swaibu is charged with conspiracy to defraud following ongoing investigations into match fixing.

| 18 | City's scheduled Conference Premier game at Braintree Town is postponed due to a waterlogged pitch; City's team coach has reached Newark when the news is received.

⇒ Manager Gary Simpson learns that his latest loan target - Luton Town's Shaun Whalley - has signed for AFC Telford United on loan instead.

⇒ City legend Andy Graver dies at the age of 86. Graver scored 150 goals for the club in 289 games in three separate spells and was voted in first place in the Lincoln City League Legends poll.

| 20 | Gary Simpson says he is not interested in signing Boston United striker Ricky Miller despite watching him hit a hat-trick against Solihull Moors on Saturday.

| 21 | **Macclesfield Town 3 Lincoln 1 (Tomlinson).** Att: 1,364. City are outclassed by Gary Simpson's former team and slip to defeat despite taking a half time lead against the run of play. Ben Tomlinson scores his 10th goal of the season. Pressure continues to grow on Simpson as City drop to 17th, just 5 points above the relegation zone.

| 23 | City are giving a trial to former Derby County and Luton Town midfielder Arnaud Mendy.

| 25 | **Lincoln 2 (Brown, Tomlinson) Woking 2.** Att: 2,017. Paul Farman saves a Giuseppe Sole penalty in the last minute to earn City a point. Mamadou Fofana makes what turns out to be his final appearance for City. The poor run extends to just 2 wins in 17 league games. City stay 17th, 6 points above the drop zone.

| 28 | City's postponed game at Braintree is rearranged for Tuesday 18 March, just three days after the scheduled home game.

⇒ Gary Simpson wants to keep on-loan striker Delano Sam-Yorke on a permanent basis and has made an offer to Cambridge for him.

| 29 | City draw 1-1 with Doncaster Rovers in a behind-closed-doors friendly, their goal from Mitch Austin. Arnaud Mendy appears as a trialist.

⇒ Striker Waide Fairhurst rejoins former club Macclesfield Town on a month's loan.

| 30 | Conner Robinson agrees a contract extension that takes him to summer 2016.

⇒ Cambridge United accept a bid from City for Delano Sam-Yorke. It is now up to City to agree terms with the player, although he is believed to want to keep his options open.

| 31 | Transfer deadline day. City sign 18-year-old Birmingham City midfielder Charlee Adams on a youth loan until the end of the season.

⇒ They also sign 27-year-old Crewe defender Thierry Audel on a one-month loan.

February 2014

| 1 | **Lincoln 3 (Tomlinson 3) FC Halifax Town 1.** Att: 2,077. Charlee Adams and Thierry Audel make their debuts after signing loan deals yesterday. City gain revenge on play-off chasing Halifax for the 5-1 defeat at the end of December. City are 17th, 9 points clear of the relegation zone.

| 3 | City extend the loan of Mitch Austin from Cambridge for a further month.

| 4 | **Lincoln 1 (Power) Nuneaton Town 2.** Att: 1,772. Another disappointing result as City are outplayed by play-off hopefuls Nuneaton. This game was rearranged from 14 December due to City's involvement in the second round of the FA Trophy. City are down a place to 18th, but still 9 points clear of danger.

| 7 | Jon Nolan signs a contract extension that takes him to the end of the 2014-15 season.

| 8 | **Hyde 3 Lincoln 4 (Sam-Yorke, Audel, Tomlinson, Miller).** Att: 646. Tom Miller's 90th-minute goal saves City from embarrassment against the league's bottom club, who have just one win all season. Paul Farman plays on with an injury until replaced in goal by Sean Newton after 75 minutes with City trailing 3-2. Unfortunately Farman is to miss the rest

of the season. This turns out to be Mitch Austin's final appearance in a City shirt as he is soon recalled by Cambridge. City are up to 16th, 11 points above the relegation zone but also 11 points behind the play-offs.

10 City sign unattached 24-year-old midfielder Arnaud Mendy on a short-term deal to the end of the season after a successful trial period. The Guinea-Bissau international was last with Luton Town, and played under Gary Simpson at Macclesfield.

11 City play a behind-closed-doors friendly against Notts County at Ashby Avenue.

13 City sign 19-year-old goalkeeper Nick Townsend from Birmingham City on a one-month youth loan as cover for the injured Paul Farman. Townsend has been training with City since Tuesday on the recommendation of his Birmingham City team mate Charlee Adams.

⇒ Gary Simpson reveals the club is no closer to persuading Delano Sam-Yorke to sign on a permanent basis.

14 Mitch Austin is recalled from his loan, as Cambridge have injury problems ahead of their FA Trophy semi-final first leg tie at home to Grimsby tomorrow. Austin is an unused substitute as Cambridge snatch a 2-1 lead.

⇒ Jordan Thomas extends his loan at Spalding United for a second month.

15 **Lincoln 2 (Tomlinson 2) Kidderminster Harriers 0.** Att: 2,012. Nick Townsend keeps a clean sheet on his debut as City win two successive league games for the first time since August. Their third win in four games lifts them to 14th, 12 points clear of relegation and only 8 points off the play-offs.

19 Tom Miller is placed on standby by England C for the match in Jordan on 4 March.

21 Youngsters Kegan Everington and Nick Green join Spalding United on loan.

⇒ Adi Yussuf joins Histon on a one-month loan.

22 **Lincoln 1 (Sam-Yorke) Chester 1.** Att: 2,354. Delano Sam-Yorke scores in what proves to be the final game of his loan spell from Cambridge. Alan Power's second half penalty miss prevents City winning three in a row for the first time since March last year. They are 15th in the table, 11 points above relegation but now 10 points behind a play-off place.

26 Delano Sam-Yorke is recalled by Cambridge after two months of his three-month loan.

March 2014

1 **Aldershot Town 2 Lincoln 3 (Miller, Audel, Tomlinson).** Att: 1,944. City lead three times before finally overcoming their relegation-threatened hosts. They are up to 14th, 13 points clear of relegation and 8 points behind the play-off spots.

3 Tom Miller receives a two-match ban following his 10th yellow card of the season against Aldershot.

4 Thierry Audel's loan from Crewe Alexandra is extended to the end of the season.

6 City cancel the contract of striker Waide Fairhurst by mutual consent.

7 Conner Robinson signs the contract extension that will take him to the end of the 2015-16 season.

8 **Alfreton Town 1 Lincoln 1 (Newton).** Att: 1,331. A fine performance from goalkeeper Nick Townsend earns City a point against promotion-chasing Alfreton. Sean Newton's 94th-minute equaliser is his first goal for the club in his 42nd game. Former Alfreton striker Ben Tomlinson is involved in verbal exchanges with his former supporters at the final whistle. City drop to 16th, 10 points behind the play-offs.

⇒ City sign globe-trotting striker Kris Bright on a deal until the end of the season. The 27-year-old New Zealand international has been playing in Finland and is seeking to establish himself in England.

10 Nick Wright joins Kidderminster Harriers on loan until the end of the season.

⇒ City fans are angered as Andrew Boyce joins promotion rivals Grimsby on loan from Scunthorpe.

11 **Lincoln 1 (Bright) Welling United 2.** Att: 1,623. City's unbeaten run comes to an end after 5 games. Kris Bright scores after 5 minutes of his debut, but City lose to Welling for the second time this season. This game is rearranged from its scheduled date of Saturday 11 January due to City's involvement in the third round of the FA Trophy. City slip a further place to 17th, still 10 points off the play-offs.

15 **Lincoln 2 (Miller, Audel) Braintree Town 0.** Att: 2,002. City beat Braintree for the second time this season and the fourth time in succession despite having striker Kris Bright sent off by referee Amy Fearn for an off the ball incident. They are back up to 14th, just 7 points behind the play-offs with 8 games to play.

17 City extend the loan of goalkeeper Nick Townsend to the end of the season.

⇒ Kris Bright receives a three-match ban for his red card against Braintree.

18 **Braintree Town 0 Lincoln 2 (Foster, Sheridan).** Att: 787. In a very quick turnaround, City play Braintree for the second time in four days, with an identical scoreline. Arnaud Mendy makes his City debut after signing last month. Youth team striker Alex Simmons makes his City debut as a late substitute. City have now beaten Braintree 5 times in a row. City are up to 12th, just 5 points off the play-offs; a play-off place looks unlikely, as City have played up to three games more than the teams above them.

20 Bob Dorrian reveals that the playing budget can only increase significantly if average attendances rise from the current 2,200 to around 2,900.

21 Ghanaian midfielder Koby Arthur becomes the third player from Birmingham City to join Lincoln on a youth loan this season. The 18-year-old signs until the end of the season.

22 **Gateshead 3 Lincoln 1 (Nolan).** Att: 804. City's outside chance of making the play-offs disappears on a disastrous afternoon at Gateshead. Koby Arthur makes his debut, but is substituted at half time with City already 2 goals down. Ben Tomlinson's 15th yellow card of the season and Thierry Audel's 90th-minute red card complete a bad afternoon for the Imps. City are 15th, 7 points behind the play-offs.

24 Ben Tomlinson receives a three-match ban after picking up his 15th yellow card of the season against Gateshead.

25 Thierry Audel receives a three-match ban for his red card at Gateshead.

⇒ Gary Simpson confirms he is not looking to make any more signings this season, preferring to wait for the close season. He admits that he does not know what his budget will be, but believes it will be unchanged.

29 **Tamworth 0 Lincoln 0.** Att: 979. City and Tamworth draw 0-0 for the second time this season. Another fine performance from on-loan goalkeeper Nick Townsend ensures a point against their relegation-threatened opponents. Bohan Dixon makes his final appearance. City are 15th, 9 points behind the play-offs.

⇒ City's U18 side wins the Midland Youth Cup with a 4-2 win over Shrewsbury Town at Greenhous Meadows. The goals are scored by Jenk Acar (2), Rob Smith and Mason Love. Team: Henry Smith, Marlon Grundy, Kieran Walker (Nick Green 58), Kegan Everington, Callum Ward, Jordon Cooke, Alex Simmons, Matthew Bowles, Mason Love (Jenk Acar 35), Matthew Cotton, Rob Smith (Josh Barr-Rostron 84). Unused subs: Andrew Wright, Richard Walton.

April 2014

2 City announce that the Lincoln Imp is to return as the official club logo and will appear on club documentation as well as team shirts from next season.

5 **Lincoln 0 Dartford 0.** Att: 1,947. City are held to a drab goalless draw by their relegation-threatened visitors in a game of few chances. They stay 15th but are now 12 points off the play-offs with 4 games to play. However, their poor goal difference means the play-off dream is all-but mathematically over.

12 **Salisbury City 1 Lincoln 2 (Newton, Rowe).** Att: 952. A superb 91st-minute winner by Danny Rowe gives City the points after they trail with 20 minutes to go against promotion-hopefuls Salisbury. Dan Gray makes his final appearance. City stay 15th, virtually equidistant between the play-offs and the relegation zone.

⇒ Gary Simpson reveals that he has been asked by the board not to discuss his budget.

15 Danny Rowe confirms that he wants to stay at Lincoln after suffering an injury-hit first season.

17 Bridge McFarland extend their sponsorship of the South Park Stand for a further three years.

⇒ Gary Simpson reveals he has already reached agreement with two strikers to join the Imps during the summer.

18 **Lincoln 1 (Tomlinson pen) Cambridge United 0.** Att: 2,535. A first half Ben Tomlinson penalty gives City a deserved win over second-placed Cambridge. Delano Sam-Yorke appears as a second half substitute for the visitors. This game has been brought forward 24 hours from its original Easter Saturday date. Charlee Adams plays the final game of his loan spell. City are up one place to 14th, 2 points behind what would be their first top-half finish since relegation.

⇒ Lincolnshire Co-op extend their stand sponsorship for a further two years.

21 **Wrexham 0 Lincoln 1 (Rowe).** Att: 2,714. A superb free-kick by Danny Rowe is enough to give City a third successive league win for the first time since March last year; it proves to be Rowe's third and final goal for City. They are up to 13th, 1 point behind a top-half finish with one game remaining.

24 Bob Dorrian says next season's budget is 'a moveable feast' as he tries to put the club on an even financial footing. Any increase in the budget that has been given to Gary Simpson will depend on season ticket sales over the summer and attendances early next season.

26 **Lincoln 3 (Brown, Bright, Tomlinson) Barnet 3.** Att: 2,812. City throw away a 3-1 lead in the second half of the game which kicks off at 5.30pm. An 88th-minute pitch invasion by a group of young City fans causes a delay; Barnet equalise in the stoppage time added at the end of the game. Ben Tomlinson becomes the first player in this Conference era to score 20 in a season (18 in the league). Kris Bright scores his second City goal in his final appearance. Luke Foster, Jake Sheridan and Danny Rowe make their final appearances for the club. Nick Townsend and Koby Arthur make their final appearances on loan from Birmingham. Thierry Audel plays his final game as his loan from Crewe comes to an end.

⇒ City end the season in 14th place, two places higher than last season, and 14 points clear of the danger zone. Had they beaten Barnet, they would have finished 11th.

⇒ Tom Miller is voted *Player of the Season* by the fans, with Sean Newton and Ben Tomlinson in second and third. Newton takes the *Away Player of the Season* award. Alex Simmons is named *Young Player of the Season* by the management team.

28 Joint vice chairman David Featherstone ceases to be a director of the club.

⇒ Lincolnshire Police confirm they are studying CCTV footage and numerous stills in order to identify the culprits responsible for the pitch invasion that marred the final home game of the season against Barnet.

⇒ The Football Association confirms that it is also investigating the pitch invasion against Barnet.

⇒ The club issues a formal statement condemning the pitch invasion and promises its full support to the authorities.

29 Gary Simpson reveals that he is to have one last meeting with Bob Dorrian before announcing the retained list next week.

| 30 | Birmingham City confirm that they have awarded one-year contract extensions to two of City's loan stars, Charlee Adams and Nick Townsend.

May 2014

| 1 | Bob Dorrian assures fans that any fine imposed by the FA following the Barnet pitch invasion will not affect the playing budget for next season. Dorrian also confirms that City have already been warned by the FA this season following four separate reports from referees regarding smoke bombs let off by their supporters.

| 4 | City receive a boost as Grimsby Town lose their play-off semi-final to Gateshead; the Lincolnshire derby will take place again next season after Grimsby lose the second leg 3-1 (4-2 on aggregate). Delano Sam-Yorke scores both goals against FC Halifax Town in the other semi-final second leg to take Cambridge to Wembley.

| 6 | City sign 26-year-old attacking midfielder Karl Ledsham from Southport on a one-year contract. He is City's first signing of the close season.

| 8 | The retained list is announced. Paul Farman, Tom Miller, Sean Newton, Jon Nolan, Alan Power, Conner Robinson and Ben Tomlinson are all contracted to the club for the 2014-15 season, as is new signing Karl Ledsham. Nat Brown and Todd Jordan have triggered appearance clauses in their one-year contracts and are automatically offered deals for next season. First-year professional contracts have been offered to youth players Kegan Everington, Alex Simmons and Callum Ward. However, manager Gary Simpson says he is not in a position to offer deals to any of the other out-of-contract players due to financial uncertainties. Included within this bracket are Jordan Thomas, Dan Gray, Bohan Dixon, Jake Sheridan, Danny Rowe, Mamadou Fofana, Kris Bright and Luke Foster, any of whom may be offered terms if the financial position improves. All are expected to leave the club accordingly.

| 12 | Defender Tom Miller is named on standby by England C for this month's internationals against Slovakia and Hungary.

| 13 | The FA is to take no further action against Lincoln following the pitch invasion at the Barnet match.

| 16 | Gary Simpson calls the FA's proposals to create a League Three featuring Premier League B teams 'a non-starter' and believes the idea will go no further.

| 21 | City sign 21-year-old striker Jordan Burrow from Stevenage on a 2-year deal.

⇒ Bob Dorrian says he would not dismiss the FA's plans for a new League Three if it meant Lincoln City regaining its League status.

| 22 | City appoint director Kevin Cooke as acting managing director.

| 24 | Bob Dorrian says he will only sell players if the offer is right for the club.

| 29 | Bob Dorrian calls for regionalisation of the Conference to reduce travel costs after Bristol Rovers, Torquay United, Eastleigh and Dover Athletic are set to join next season. He believes that merging League Two and the Conference under a regionalised structure will create significant savings. However, some number-crunching reveals that the savings would actually be minimal.

SEASON 2013-14

CONFERENCE PREMIER

No.	Date		Opposition	Res	Att	Scorers	Farman, P	Newton, S	Boyce, A	Brown, N	Foster, L	Fofana, M	Power, A	Gray, D	Nolan, J	Wright, N	Tomlinson, B	Dixon, B	Rowe, D
1	AUG	10	Woking	0-0	1845		Y	Y	Y	Y	Y	Y	Y		Y		Y# Y	S #	
2		13	MACCLESFIELD TOWN	1-0	2386	Rowe	Y	Y	Y	Y	Y	S *	Y	Y	Y		Y# Y	S #	Y *
3		17	FOREST GREEN ROVERS	2-1	2290	Fairhurst 2	Y	Y	Y	Y	S #	Y	Y	Y	Y		Y		Y
4		24	Cambridge United	0-1	3022		Y	Y	Y	Y	Y		Y		Y		Y	S #	S *
5		26	WREXHAM	2-0	2610	Tomlinson 2	Y	Y	Y	Y	S #	Y		Y	Y		Y	S *	Y *
6		31	Dartford	2-1	1386	Tomlinson, Boyce	Y	Y	Y	Y	Y	Y			Y		Y		Y
7	SEP	7	SALISBURY CITY	0-1	2646		Y	Y	Y	Y	Y #	Y			Y		Y	S *	Y *
8		14	Barnet	1-1	1913	Nolan	Y	Y	Y	Y		Y *	Y		Y	S #	Y >	S >	S *
9		17	SOUTHPORT	1-0	1879	Miller	Y	Y	Y	Y	S >	Y	Y >		Y	S #	Y #	S *	
10		21	Luton Town	2-3	6203	Power, Tomlinson	Y	Y	Y	Y	Y *	Y			Y	S *	Y		Y #
11		24	Hereford United	0-1	1398		Y	Y >	Y	Y		Y	Y		Y	S #	Y #	S >	
12		28	HYDE	3-0	2311	Dixon 2, Tomlinson	Y	Y	Y	Y	S *	Y *	Y		Y >		Y	S #	
13	OCT	5	Nuneaton Town	2-2	1634	Miller, Nolan	Y	Y	Y	Y	Y	S *	Y *		Y	Y #	Y	S #	
14		8	TAMWORTH	0-0	2603		Y	Y	Y	Y	Y		Y		Y	Y	Y #	S *	
15		12	ALDERSHOT TOWN	0-1	2748		Y	Y	Y	Y	Y		Y		Y	S *		S #	
16		19	Kidderminster Harriers	1-4	2103	Wright	Y	Y	Y	Y	Y >	S *	Y		Y *	S #	Y	S >	
17	NOV	2	Welling United	0-1	746			Y	Y	Y	Y #		Y			S *	Y	Y *	
18		12	Southport	1-0	818	Nolan	Y	Y	Y	Y	S >	Y	Y >	Y	Y	S *	Y	S #	
19		16	Forest Green Rovers	1-4	1128	Sharp	Y	Y	Y	Y		Y	Y	Y	Y	S #	Y	S *	
20		23	HEREFORD UNITED	1-1	1874	Tomlinson	Y	Y		Y	Y	Y	Y		Y #	Y *	Y	S *	
21	DEC	10	GATESHEAD	0-1	1411		Y	Y		Y	Y	Y *	Y			S #		S *	
22		21	Chester	3-3	1850	Dixon, Power (pen), Robinson	Y	Y		Y >	Y	Y #	Y			Y *	Y	Y	S *
23		26	GRIMSBY TOWN	0-2	5421		Y			Y	Y		Y	S #		Y		Y	Y
24		28	FC Halifax	1-5	1979	Tomlinson	Y	Y		Y	Y	Y *	Y		S #			Y	Y
25	JAN	1	Grimsby Town	1-1	5484	OG	Y	Y		Y	Y				Y		Y # Y		Y
26		4	LUTON TOWN	0-0	2928		Y	Y		Y	Y	Y			S *	Y *	S #		
27		7	ALFRETON TOWN	4-1	1877	Wright, Nolan, Sam-Yorke, OG	Y	Y #		Y		Y			S #	Y	Y	Y	S >
28		21	Macclesfield Town	1-3	1364	Tomlinson	Y	Y		Y	Y				S >	Y >	Y	Y #	S #
29		25	WOKING	2-2	2017	Brown, Tomlinson	Y	Y		Y	Y	Y #	Y		S #		Y		
30	FEB	1	FC HALIFAX	3-1	2077	Tomlinson 3	Y	Y		Y			Y				Y *		
31		4	NUNEATON TOWN	1-2	1772	Power	Y	Y			Y		Y				Y		
32		8	Hyde	4-3	646	Sam-Yorke, Audel, Tomlinson, Miller	Y *	Y		Y			Y	S *	S >		Y		
33		15	KIDDERMINSTER HARRIERS	2-0	2012	Tomlinson 2		Y		Y			Y				Y		
34		22	CHESTER	1-1	2354	Sam-Yorke		Y		Y			Y				Y		
35	MAR	1	Aldershot Town	3-2	1944	Miller, Audel, Tomlinson		Y		Y			Y				Y	S # Y	
36		8	Alfreton Town	1-1	1331	Newton		Y		Y			Y	Y	S >		Y	Y # Y *	
37		11	WELLING UNITED	1-2	1623	Bright		Y		Y			Y	Y	Y *		Y		
38		15	BRAINTREE TOWN	2-0	2002	Miller, Audel		Y		Y			Y				Y	S #	
39		18	Braintree Town	2-0	787	Foster, Sheridan		Y			Y			Y			Y #	S * Y	
40		22	Gateshead	1-3	804	Nolan		Y		Y					S #		Y		S *
41		29	Tamworth	0-0	979			Y *		Y	Y		S # S *	Y				S >	Y >
42	APR	5	DARTFORD	0-0	1947			Y		Y	Y		Y		Y #				
43		12	Salisbury City	2-1	952	Newton, Rowe		Y		Y	Y >		Y	S >					S *
44		18	CAMBRIDGE UNITED	1-0	2535	Tomlinson (pen)		Y		Y	Y		Y				Y		S *
45		21	Wrexham	1-0	2714	Rowe		Y		Y	Y		S #		Y		Y *		Y >
46		26	BARNET	3-3	2812	Brown, Bright, Tomlinson		Y		Y	Y		S #	Y		Y	Y *		Y

						Appearances	31	45	19	44	25	19	36	9	28	8	39	8	15
						Substitute appearances	0	0	0	0	6	3	2	8	4	11	0	21	8
						Goals	0	2	1	2	1	0	3	0	5	2	18	3	3

60 league goals

FA CUP

				Res	Att	Scorers	Farman	Newton	Boyce	Brown	Foster	Fofana	Power	Gray	Nolan	Wright	Tomlinson	Dixon	Rowe
4Q	OCT	26	Worcester City	1-1	1019	Boyce	Y	Y	Y	Y	Y *		Y		Y		Y # Y >	S #	
4QR		29	WORCESTER CITY	3-0	1344	Tomlinson 2, Dixon	Y	Y	Y	Y	Y * S *		Y				S # Y	Y	
1	NOV	9	PLYMOUTH ARGYLE	0-0	2924		Y	Y	Y	Y		S *	Y		Y *	Y >	Y	S >	
1R		20	Plymouth Argyle	0-5	3324		Y	Y	Y	Y	Y #	Y	Y		Y		S * Y *		

FA TROPHY

				Res	Att	Scorers	Farman	Newton	Boyce	Brown	Foster	Fofana	Power	Gray	Nolan	Wright	Tomlinson	Dixon	Rowe
1	NOV	30	STALYBRIDGE CELTIC	5-1	1023	Power 3 (1 pen), Jackson, Fofana	Y	Y		Y	Y >	Y	Y #	S >	Y		S *		
2	DEC	14	Braintree Town	3-1	410	Sharp, Foster, OG	Y	Y		Y	Y	Y					S #	Y	S *
3	JAN	11	NORTH FERRIBY UNITED	0-4	2037		Y	Y		Y	Y	S #			Y		Y * Y	Y #	S *

LINCOLNSHIRE CUP

				Res	Att	Scorers	Farman	Newton	Boyce	Brown	Foster	Fofana	Power	Gray	Nolan	Wright	Tomlinson	Dixon	Rowe
SF	JUL	30	SCUNTHORPE UNITED	2-0	918	Fairhurst 2	Y	Y	S #	Y	Y #	Y		Y >	Y	S *	Y	Y *	
F	OCT	22	Gainsborough Trinity	0-0*	600						Y	Y		Y		Y #	Y		

* City won 4-2 on penalties

Key:

Y = full appearance

Y# = full appearance, first player substituted - by substitute S#

Y* = full appearance, second player substituted - by substitute S*

Y> = full appearance, third player substituted - by substitute S>

 Red Card

Yellow Card

Fairhurst, W	Miller, T	Jordan, T	Sheridan, J	Yussuf, A	Preece, D	Jackson, M	Sharp, C	Robinson, C	Everington, K	Austin, M	Sam-Yorke, D	Audel, T	Adams, C	Townsend, N	Bright, K	Mendy, A	Simmons, A	Arthur, K	Ward, C	Green, N
Y #																				
	Y	Y #	Y *																	
Y #	S >		Y >																	
Y #	Y		S #																	
Y >	Y		S #	S >																
	Y	Y #	Y																	
	Y	Y	Y *																	
	Y	S #																		
S *	Y	Y	Y *																	
	Y	Y #	S >																	
	Y	Y																		
S #	Y	Y *																		
Y	Y	Y #			Y *															
	Y	Y #	Y																	
S #	Y	Y				Y	Y													
							Y #	Y *												
S >							Y	Y												
	Y	Y	S #																	
	Y	Y	Y			Y	Y #													
	Y	S >	Y																	
S *	Y #	Y	Y																	
S *	Y	Y																		
S #	Y	Y						Y *	S *											
	Y	Y						Y		Y #	Y									
	Y *	Y	S *							Y >	Y									
	Y							S *		Y *	Y									
	Y	Y						Y			Y									
	Y	Y	S *					Y #		S #	Y	Y	Y							
	Y	Y	S #					Y *		S *	Y	Y	Y #							
	Y	Y >	S #							Y #	Y	Y	Y							
	Y	Y									Y	Y	Y	Y						
	Y	Y	Y #					S #			Y	Y	Y	Y						
	Y	Y						Y #				Y	Y	Y						
	Y	Y >	S *					S #				Y	Y	Y						
	Y	S *	S #					Y #				Y	Y	Y	Y					
	Y	Y	Y #									Y	Y	Y	Y					
	Y	Y	Y *									Y	Y	Y			S #			
	Y	Y *	Y									Y	Y	Y		Y		Y #		
	Y	Y #	Y										Y	Y		Y				
	Y		Y *					S *				Y	Y	Y	Y			S #		
	Y		Y					S #					Y	Y	Y	Y *		Y #		
	Y		Y #							Y		Y *	Y	Y		Y		S #		
	Y		Y					S >				Y		Y	Y #	Y		S *		
	Y		Y									Y #		Y				S *		
5	**37**	**29**	**20**	**1**	**1**	**4**	**3**	**9**	**0**	**4**	**9**	**14**	**14**	**14**	**7**	**7**	**0**	**2**	**0**	**0**
7	*1*	*3*	*9*	*1*	*0*	*0*	*7*	*1*	*2*	*0*	*0*	*0*	*0*	*0*	*0*	*0*	*1*	*4*	*0*	*0*
2	*5*	*0*	*1*	*0*	*0*	*0*	*1*	*1*	*0*	*0*	*3*	*3*	*0*	*0*	*2*	*0*	*0*	*0*	*0*	*0*

Fairhurst, W	Miller, T	Jordan, T	Sheridan, J	Yussuf, A	Preece, D	Jackson, M	Sharp, C	Robinson, C	Everington, K	Austin, M	Sam-Yorke, D	Audel, T	Adams, C	Townsend, N	Bright, K	Mendy, A	Simmons, A	Arthur, K	Ward, C	Green, N
S >	Y					Y		S *												
	Y	Y	Y >			Y >		Y #												
	Y	Y	S #			Y #														
	Y		S #			Y														

Fairhurst, W	Miller, T	Jordan, T	Sheridan, J	Yussuf, A	Preece, D	Jackson, M	Sharp, C	Robinson, C	Everington, K	Austin, M	Sam-Yorke, D	Audel, T	Adams, C	Townsend, N	Bright, K	Mendy, A	Simmons, A	Arthur, K	Ward, C	Green, N
S #	Y		Y			Y	Y *													
	Y *	Y	Y			Y #	Y													
	Y	Y >	S >			Y														

Fairhurst, W	Miller, T	Jordan, T	Sheridan, J	Yussuf, A	Preece, D	Jackson, M	Sharp, C	Robinson, C	Everington, K	Austin, M	Sam-Yorke, D	Audel, T	Adams, C	Townsend, N	Bright, K	Mendy, A	Simmons, A	Arthur, K	Ward, C	Green, N
Y		S >	Y																	
Y		Y	Y	Y *	Y			S #								S *		Y >	S >	

Appearances & Goals 2013-14

	League			FA Cup			FA Trophy			Totals			Totals		Lincolnshire Cup		
	Apps	Subs	Goals	Apps	Subs	Goals	Apps	Subs	Goals	Apps	Subs	Goals	Apps	Goals	Apps	Subs	Goals
Sean NEWTON	45	0	2	4	0	0	3	0	0	52	0	2	52	2	1	0	0
Nat BROWN	44	0	2	4	0	0	3	0	0	51	0	2	51	2	1	0	0
Tom MILLER	37	1	5	4	0	0	3	0	0	44	1	5	45	5	0	0	0
Ben TOMLINSON	39	0	18	4	0	2	1	0	0	44	0	20	44	20	1	0	0
Alan POWER	36	2	3	4	0	0	1	0	3	41	2	6	43	6	0	0	0
Paul FARMAN	31	0	0	4	0	0	3	0	0	38	0	0	38	0	1	0	0
Jon NOLAN	28	4	5	3	0	0	2	0	0	33	4	5	37	5	1	0	0
Luke FOSTER	25	6	1	2	1	0	3	0	1	30	7	2	37	2	2	0	0
Todd JORDAN	29	3	0	2	0	0	2	0	0	33	3	0	36	0	1	1	0
Jake SHERIDAN	20	9	1	1	2	0	2	1	0	23	12	1	35	1	2	0	0
Bohan DIXON	8	21	3	1	2	1	2	0	0	11	23	4	34	4	2	0	0
Mamadou FOFANA	19	3	0	1	1	0	2	1	1	22	5	1	27	1	2	0	0
Nick WRIGHT	8	11	2	2	2	0	1	2	0	11	15	2	26	2	1	1	0
Danny ROWE	15	8	3	0	0	0	0	2	0	15	10	3	25	3	0	0	0
Andrew BOYCE	19	0	1	4	0	1	0	0	0	23	0	2	23	2	0	1	0
Conner ROBINSON	9	7	1	1	1	0	1	0	0	11	8	1	19	1	0	0	0
Dan GRAY	9	8	0	0	0	0	0	1	0	9	9	0	18	0	2	0	0
Thierry AUDEL (L)	14	0	3	0	0	0	0	0	0	14	0	3	14	3	0	0	0
Charlee ADAMS (L)	14	0	0	0	0	0	0	0	0	14	0	0	14	0	0	0	0
Nick TOWNSEND (L)	14	0	0	0	0	0	0	0	0	14	0	0	14	0	0	0	0
Waide FAIRHURST	5	7	2	0	1	0	0	1	0	5	9	2	14	2	2	0	2
Marlon JACKSON (L)	4	0	0	4	0	0	2	0	1	10	0	1	10	1	0	0	0
Delano SAM-YORKE (L)	9	0	3	0	0	0	0	0	0	9	0	3	9	3	0	0	0
Kris BRIGHT	7	0	2	0	0	0	0	0	0	7	0	2	7	2	0	0	0
Arnaud MENDY	7	0	0	0	0	0	0	0	0	7	0	0	7	0	0	0	0
Mitchell AUSTIN (L)	4	2	0	0	0	0	0	0	0	4	2	0	6	0	0	0	0
Koby ARTHUR (L)	2	4	0	0	0	0	0	0	0	2	4	0	6	0	0	0	0
Chris SHARP (L)	3	0	1	0	0	0	2	0	1	5	0	2	5	2	0	0	0
Adi YUSSUF	1	1	0	0	0	0	0	0	0	1	1	0	2	0	1	0	0
David PREECE	1	0	0	0	0	0	0	0	0	1	0	0	1	0	1	0	0
Kegan EVERINGTON	0	1	0	0	0	0	0	0	0	0	1	0	1	0	0	1	0
Alex SIMMONS	0	1	0	0	0	0	0	0	0	0	1	0	1	0	0	1	0

| Own goals | | | 2 | | | 0 | | | 1 | | | 3 | | 3 | | | 0 |

Players Used	League goals	FA Cup goals	FA Trophy goals	Total goals
32	60	4	8	72

Plus appearances in Lincolnshire Cup: Callum Ward 1, Nick Green (1).

Squad Numbers 2013-14

1	Paul Farman		17	Bohan Dixon
2	Tom Miller		18	Delano Sam-Yorke; Kris Bright
3	Sean Newton		19	Jon Nolan
4	Todd Jordan		20	
5	Andrew Boyce; Thierry Audel		21	
6	Mamadou Fofana		22	Kegan Everington; Marlon Jackson
7	Waide Fairhurst; Koby Arthur		23	Nat Brown
8	Alan Power		24	Karl Cunningham; Arnaud Mendy
9	Danny Rowe		25	Chris Sharp; Alex Simmons
10	Nick Wright		26	Charlee Adams
11	Ben Tomlinson		27	Luke Foster
12	Jake Sheridan		28	Mitch Austin
13			29	Jordan Thomas
14	Adi Yussuf		30	Nick Townsend
15	Dan Gray		31	David Preece
16	Conner Robinson			

Conference Premier Final League Table 2013-14

			Home					Away					Totals		
		P	W	D	L	F	A	W	D	L	F	A	F	A	Pts
1	Luton Town	46	18	3	2	64	16	12	8	3	38	19	102	35	101
P	Cambridge United	46	16	4	3	49	14	7	9	7	23	21	72	35	82
3	Gateshead	46	12	7	4	42	24	10	6	7	30	26	72	50	79
4	Grimsby Town	46	11	7	5	40	26	11	5	7	25	20	65	46	78
5	FC Halifax Town	46	16	6	1	55	19	6	5	12	30	39	85	58	77
6	Braintree Town	46	12	4	7	27	18	9	7	7	30	21	57	39	74
7	Kidderminster Harriers	46	15	4	4	45	22	5	8	10	21	37	66	59	72
8	Barnet	46	11	6	6	30	26	8	7	8	28	27	58	53	70
9	Woking	46	11	4	8	32	30	9	4	10	34	39	66	69	68
10	Forest Green Rovers	46	13	6	4	47	22	6	4	13	33	44	80	66	67
11	Alfreton Town	46	13	6	4	45	33	8	1	14	24	41	69	74	67
R	Salisbury City	46	13	6	4	34	21	6	4	13	24	42	58	63	67
13	Nuneaton Town	46	12	4	7	29	25	6	8	9	25	35	54	60	66
14	Lincoln City	46	10	7	6	30	19	7	7	9	30	40	60	59	65
15	Macclesfield Town	46	11	5	7	35	27	7	2	14	27	36	62	63	61
16	Welling United	46	10	5	8	31	24	6	7	10	28	37	59	61	60
17	Wrexham	46	11	5	7	31	21	5	6	12	30	40	61	61	59
18	Southport	46	13	5	5	33	23	1	6	16	20	48	53	71	53
19	Aldershot Town	46	11	6	6	48	32	5	7	11	21	30	69	62	51
R	Hereford United	46	9	6	8	24	24	4	6	13	20	39	44	63	51
21	Chester	46	5	12	6	26	30	7	3	13	23	40	49	70	51
22	Dartford	46	8	3	12	32	35	4	5	14	17	39	49	74	44
23	Tamworth	46	6	7	10	25	31	4	2	17	18	50	43	81	39
24	Hyde	46	0	3	20	18	57	1	4	18	20	62	38	119	10

Progress Chart 2013-14

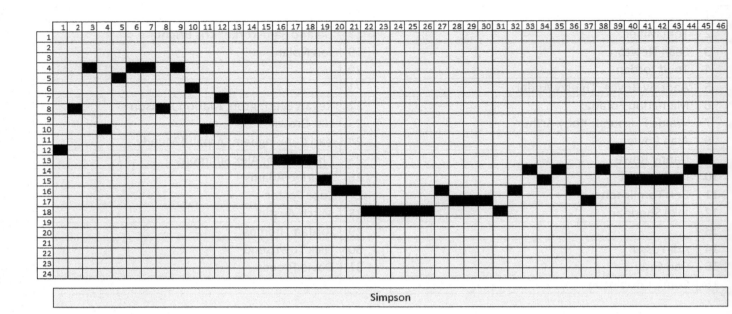

Simpson

Friendlies 2013-14

Jul	13	Lincoln United	7-1	721	Rowe 3, Dixon 2, Yussuf, Power
	16	Harrogate Town	3-2	256	Wright 3
	20	Grantham Town	1-2	236	Power (pen)
	24	SUNDERLAND U21	0-2	474	
	27	MIDDLESBROUGH U21	2-1	493	Yussuf, Tomlinson (pen)
Aug	3	BOSTON UNITED	1-0	1008	Newton
Sep	3	Sleaford Town	4-2	50	Helsdown 2, Simmons, Thomas

Does not include the behind closed doors friendlies against Chesterfield (9/7/2013), Chesterfield (10/9/2013), Doncaster Rovers (29/1/2014) and Notts County (11/2/2014).

Original Fixture List 2013-14

Aug	10	Woking	Nov	2	Welling United	Feb	1	FC HALIFAX TOWN
	13	MACCLESFIELD TOWN		9	GATESHEAD		8	Hyde
	17	FOREST GREEN ROVERS		12	Southport		15	KIDDERMINSTER HARR
	24	Cambridge United		16	Forest Green Rovers		22	CHESTER
	26	WREXHAM		19	ALFRETON TOWN	Mar	1	Aldershot Town
	31	Dartford		23	HEREFORD UNITED		8	Alfreton Town
Sep	7	SALISBURY CITY	Dec	7	Macclesfield Town		15	BRAINTREE TOWN
	14	Barnet		14	NUNEATON TOWN		22	Gateshead
	17	SOUTHPORT		21	Chester		29	Tamworth
	21	Luton Town		26	GRIMSBY TOWN	Apr	5	DARTFORD
	24	Hereford United		28	FC Halifax Town		12	Salisbury City
	28	HYDE	Jan	1	Grimsby Town		19	CAMBRIDGE UNITED
Oct	5	Nuneaton Town		4	LUTON TOWN		21	Wrexham
	8	TAMWORTH		11	WELLING UNITED		26	BARNET
	12	ALDERSHOT TOWN		18	Braintree Town			
	19	Kidderminster Harriers		25	WOKING	Mar	23	FA Trophy Final

Year 4

2014-15

5 City sign 25-year-old striker Sahr Kabba from Havant & Waterlooville on a one-year deal.

⇒ Gary Simpson expects to have a first team squad of 15 to 18 players this season due to budget constraints. He does not expect to make any more signings before the players return for pre-season training at the end of this month, although he has agreed deals with two unnamed players.

6 Seven directors of the Lincoln City Supporters' Trust resign their positions, citing 'negative campaigning' and 'intolerable pressure' as the reasons. The seven are Lesley Barker, Andrew Blow, Elaine Elvidge, Neil Ferguson, Helen Jacobs, Fran Martin and secretary Geoff Forbes. The resignations leave the Trust with just one director, Anthony Smith.

10 Hereford United are expelled from the Conference after failing to meet requirements laid down by the Board of the Football Conference. The decision means a reprieve for Chester, who filled the last relegation place.

12 An emergency working group is set up to help rescue the failing Lincoln City Supporters' Trust. The group consists of former Lincoln City club chairman Rob Bradley, Lincoln Sunday Football League secretary John Wilson, and the sole remaining Trust director Anthony Smith.

16 Salisbury City are demoted to Conference South after failing to provide financial guarantees to the Conference Board. The decision means a reprieve for Dartford, who finished in the third relegation place.

18 Former City player Moses Swaibu faces a retrial on match fixing allegations after the jury at Birmingham Crown Court fails to reach a verdict.

23 City confirm that they have received £8,000 from the new Premier League and FA Facilities Fund to enable them to buy a Charterhouse 1275 Overseeder for the Sincil Bank pitch.

27 Kegan Everington and Alex Simmons sign one-year contracts as first-year professionals; the contracts come into force on 1 July.

30 City agree terms with Morecambe's 23-year-old French defender Tony Diagne. Diagne previously made 7 appearances for the Imps on loan from Macclesfield Town in 2012-13, and has agreed a two-year deal.

⇒ City also agree terms with French-born midfielder Arnaud Mendy, who spent the second half of last season at Sincil Bank.

⇒ The players return for pre-season training. Kris Bright is the only player from last season's released list to attend, although Gary Simpson says it does not mean he will be offered a deal. Simpson made an open offer to all of those released to join pre-season training if they had not found clubs during the summer.

⇒ The emergency working group trying to salvage the Lincoln City Supporters' Trust holds an open meeting at Sincil Bank. More than 50 Trust members vote in favour of the working group, granting it a mandate to take the project forward. A Special General Meeting is to be held to elect a new board.

July 2014

1 Nat Brown signs a further one-year deal.

⇒ Todd Jordan also signs a further one-year deal.

4 The fixture list for the new season gives City a home game against Kidderminster Harriers on the opening day for the second time in three seasons. This year's festive double-header will be against Alfreton Town instead of traditional opponents Grimsby. City's general manager John Vickers confirms that City have requested Alfreton in a deliberate attempt to freshen up the fixture list.

⇒ City's pre-season campaign gets under way with a 3-1 win over Lincoln United. Goals from Alan Power, Jon Nolan and Tom Miller give City a comfortable run out in front of 650 at Ashby Avenue. City field a number of trialists including goalkeeper Luke Chambers, ex-Imp Hamza Bencherif, defender Michael Hollingsworth, and midfielders Harrison Biggins and Danny Meadows. Two unnamed trialists from Belgium also play part of the game in defence.

5 Gary Simpson believes trialist Hamza Bencherif is looking for a Football League club, and that money may also be a stumbling block to signing the experienced centre back.

8 Some poor defending sees City crash to an unexpected 4-3 defeat away to Basford United of the Midland League Premier Division, managed by former City striker Martin Carruthers. Jordan Burrow, Ben Tomlinson and Alex Simmons are on target for the Imps in front of 121 at Basford's Greenwich Avenue ground. City field 4 trialists - Michael Hollingsworth, Danny Meadows and the two unnamed Belgian defenders.

⇒ Tony Diagne signs after agreeing his deal last week.

⇒ Arnaud Mendy signs his one-year deal.

10 Gary Simpson allows all the trialists to leave Sincil Bank with the exception of goalkeeper Luke Chambers, who is to train with the Imps for the time being. Hamza Bencherif is training with Championship side Blackpool.

12 The defeat at Basford is forgotten as City ease past League One neighbours Doncaster Rovers, goals from Jordan Burrow and Alan Power giving them a 2-0 win in front of 1,144 at Sincil Bank. City field trialists Jake Caprice (defender), Hamza Bencherif and Luke Chambers as substitutes.

13 Gary Simpson refuses to confirm rumours that former Fleetwood striker Jon Parkin is to train with City.

15 Gary Simpson confirms that Jon Parkin is training with the Imps as he seeks a League club for the coming season. Defender Jake Caprice has also stayed on to train with the club, while Hamza Bencherif is now training with Cambridge United.

16 New signing Arnaud Mendy joins up with the Guinea-Bissau squad in preparation for their Africa Cup of Nations qualifiers against Botswana later this month.

19 City pull off another impressive pre-season win, this time over League Two champions Chesterfield. Goals from Jordan Burrow and Alan Power for the second match in a row give City a 2-1 win in front of 952 at Sincil Bank. French trialist Zak Belkouche makes a second half appearance, as do goalkeeper Luke Chambers and defender Jake Caprice.

⇒ Arnaud Mendy becomes the 11th player to win a full international cap whilst on City's books as he plays for Guinea-Bissau in an Africa Cup of Nations match against Botswana in Gaborone.

21 Striker Jon Parkin signs a one-year deal with big-spending Forest Green Rovers.

23 Lincoln win 1-0 at Scunthorpe United in the semi-final of the Lincolnshire Cup, the goal coming from Sean Newton in front of 729. Hamza Bencherif again appears for the Imps despite his attempts to find a Football League club.

24 Chairman Bob Dorrian says City must stay in the top 10 next season if the club is to remain financially stable. He reveals that the directors were forced to invest a further £150,000 in the club over the last seven months to shore up the club's finances.

26 City pick up their fourth win in a row with a 1-0 victory at Scarborough Athletic on a sweltering day in East Yorkshire. Tony Diagne scores with a header in front of 357 fans.

29 City's good pre-season run comes to an end at Sincil Bank as League Two Mansfield Town leave with a 3-1 win. Future Imp Liam Hearn scores twice for the visitors, with Hamza Bencherif replying in front of 924.

30 Van rental and sales specialist Vanarama are the new sponsors of the Conference.

August 2014

1 City sign 26-year-old defender Hamza Bencherif from Algerian club JS Kabylie on a one-year deal. Bencherif is no stranger to Sincil Bank, having spent part of the 2007-08 season on loan from Nottingham Forest and has been on trial on and off throughout pre-season.

⇒ City also sign 20-year-old defender Jake Caprice from Blackpool on a one-year deal. Caprice has been on trial at Sincil Bank for the last couple of weeks.

⇒ 24-year-old winger Marcus Marshall also signs for City, on a season-long loan from League Two side Morecambe.

2 City re-sign goalkeeper Nick Townsend from Birmingham City on a season-long youth loan. Gary Simpson immediately names Townsend as City's first choice keeper for the coming season, raising speculation over the future of Paul Farman.

⇒ City's pre-season campaign comes to an end with a disappointing 1-0 defeat at Conference North Stalybridge Celtic in front of 202 at Bower Fold.

7 City suffer a blow as defender Tom Miller is ruled out for six weeks after injuring a medial knee ligament in the Lincolnshire Cup tie against Scunthorpe.

⇒ Gold Members' Representative Fran Martin ceases to be a director of the club after resigning as a Trust director in the summer.

9 **Lincoln 0 Kidderminster Harriers 0.** Att: 2,598. For the third time in four seasons, City's first home game is against Kidderminster: one win, one draw and one defeat after today's drab encounter. Jake Caprice, Jordan Burrow and Marcus Marshall make their debuts, while Hamza Bencherif, Nick Townsend and Tony Diagne make their second debuts for the club. City are 12th in the first league table of the season, 2 points behind early leaders Barnet.

12 **Altrincham 1 Lincoln 2 (Burrow, Robinson).** Att: 996. A goal in stoppage time by the hosts cannot spoil a comfortable win for City. Jordan Burrow scores his first for the club, while Karl Ledsham makes his first appearance as a substitute after recovering from a hernia operation. City are up to 8th, 2 points behind leaders Barnet.

⇒ City announce that all youth team games will be played at Lincoln United's Ashby Avenue ground this season.

14 Alex Simmons joins Grantham Town on an initial one-month loan.

15 City's game at Braintree Town, scheduled for Saturday 4 April, is brought forward 24 hours to Good Friday by mutual agreement.

16 **Barnet 1 Lincoln 2 (Burrow, Bencherif).** Att: 1,529. City pull off a terrific win against a Barnet side which had scored seven goals in winning its opening two games. City are up to 6th, 2 points behind new leaders FC Halifax Town.

17 It emerges that the team bus did not turn up to take the team to Barnet yesterday, leaving the players and staff to make their own way in their cars. The team talk takes place using jelly babies instead of the usual tactics board.

22 Paul Farman vows to fight for his place despite being sidelined by loan signing Nick Townsend.

23 **Lincoln 3 (Newton, Bencherif, Tomlinson) Braintree Town 2.** Att: 2,231. City win their 6th successive game against Braintree despite having defender Tony Diagne sent off just after half time for denying an obvious goalscoring opportunity; City intend to appeal the decision. They are up to 3rd, 2 points behind leaders FC Halifax.

25 Tony Diagne's red card against Braintree is rescinded on appeal.

⇒ **FC Halifax Town 3 Lincoln 2 (Bencherif, Tomlinson pen).** Att: 2,369. City's 10-game unbeaten record (stretching back into last season) comes to an end against the league leaders, who maintain their 100% start to the season. Hamza Bencherif has an eventful afternoon, putting City ahead after 10 minutes and receiving a second yellow card in the 65th minute. Sahr Kabba makes his first appearance as a substitute. City slip to 5th, 5 points behind leaders FC Halifax.

26 | Hamza Bencherif receives a one-match ban for his red card at FC Halifax.

28 | Kegan Everington joins Lincoln United on a three-month loan.

29 | Delano Sam-Yorke rejoins City from Cambridge United on loan until 17 January.

30 | **Lincoln 1 (Tomlinson pen) Torquay United 3.** Att: 2,373. Everything goes wrong for City on a dire afternoon at Sincil Bank. Nat Brown is sent off after 8 minutes. Torquay enjoy 30 shots during a very comfortable win. City are down to 10th, 5 points behind new leaders Barnet.

September 2014

1 | Former City captain Delroy Facey is charged with conspiracy to commit bribery as part of the ongoing investigation into match fixing. Facey was originally arrested in November last year.

2 | City fail in their appeal to have Nat Brown's red card against Torquay rescinded. He receives a one-match ban.

⇒ It is confirmed that striker Conner Robinson broke his nose in two places against Torquay on Saturday.

6 | **Woking 3 Lincoln 1 (Burrow).** Att: 2,160. City slip to their third successive defeat, conceding three goals in each one. Delano Sam-Yorke begins his second loan spell against the club where he started his career, but City are well-beaten at Kingfield. They are down to 14th, 3 points behind the play-offs.

8 | Grimsby Town have sold their allocation of 1,750 tickets for tomorrow evening's game at Sincil Bank.

9 | **Lincoln 3 (Burrow, Newton pen, Bencherif) Grimsby Town 2.** Att: 5,209. An 87th-minute winner from Hamza Bencherif gives City their first win over Grimsby since relegation. Ben Tomlinson misses a first half penalty, and leaves Sean Newton to take one in the second half. City are back up to 9th, 2 points behind the play-offs.

11 | Sean Newton reveals that he has taken over penalty-taking duties from Ben Tomlinson after the striker missed in the first half against Grimsby.

12 | Paul Farman joins Boston United on a three-month loan deal.

13 | **Lincoln 2 (Newton pen, Burrow) Bristol Rovers 3.** Att: 2,933. City pull back from 2 down, only to lose to a 90th-minute winner. The defence is becoming a concern, having now conceded 16 goals in the last 6 games. Gary Simpson says he is to raid the loan market in a bid to improve things at the back. City slip back to 13th, 5 points below the play-offs.

15 | Striker Jordan Burrow and midfielder Jon Nolan are invited to attend an England C training camp at St George's Park on 21 and 22 September.

⇒ Alex Simmons extends his loan at Grantham Town by a further two months.

16 | **Welling United 2 Lincoln 0.** Att: 504. City slump to their fifth defeat in six league games, conceding two more goals in the process. They slip to 14th, 7 points behind the play-offs, but also now only 5 clear of the relegation zone.

18 | Gary Simpson confirms that he is looking for loan signings to shore up his leaky defence. He is close to sealing a deal for a Premier League centre half.

19 | City sign 21-year-old centre-half Tom Anderson from Premier League Burnley on a one-month loan.

⇒ Sahr Kabba joins Whitehawk on a six-week loan to build his match fitness.

⇒ Conner Robinson joins Boston United on a one-month loan.

20 | **Aldershot Town 1 Lincoln 0.** Att: 1,582. Tom Anderson's debut ends in a single goal defeat, City's sixth in seven games. Aldershot pick up their first win since August in a poor match. City slip two further places to 15th, 8 points behind the play-offs and 5 points above the danger zone.

23 | City lose 3-2 to Chesterfield in a behind-closed-doors friendly.

27 | **Lincoln 2 (Miller, Tomlinson) Macclesfield Town 0.** Att: 2,265. City hang on to a 2-goal lead despite having Jordan Burrow sent off after 38 minutes for a foul on Adriano Moke. City are 15th, 6 points below the play-offs.

29 | Jordan Burrow receives a three-match ban for his red card against Macclesfield on Saturday. Sean Newton also picks up an automatic one-match ban for his fifth yellow card of the season.

30 | **Lincoln 1 (Anderson) Gateshead 1.** Att: 2,394. Tom Anderson opens the scoring with his first goal in senior football and his only goal in City's colours. The point moves them up a place to 14th, 7 points behind the play-offs and just 6 points above the danger zone.

⇒ Jordan Burrow and Jon Nolan are named in the England C contingency squad for the upcoming game against Turkey B in Istanbul.

October 2014

2 | Gary Simpson is keen to retain Tom Anderson when his loan period ends on 18 October.

4 **Nuneaton Town 2 Lincoln 1 (Miller).** Att: 920. City go down to a disappointing defeat to the side sitting second from bottom of the Conference. Pressure builds on manager Gary Simpson, who says he cannot defend his team's poor performance. City drop a place to 15th, 6 points above the danger zone.

7 **Southport 3 Lincoln 3 (Sam-Yorke, Tomlinson, Brodie own goal).** Att: 746. City blow a 2-goal lead, with future City loanee John Marsden scoring an 86th-minute equaliser to give new Southport manager Gary Brabin his first point. Hamza Bencherif is red-carded after the final whistle for dissent. City now have just 2 wins from their last 11 games and have slipped to 16th, now just 4 points clear of the drop zone.

8 Hamza Bencherif receives a three-match ban for his red card at Southport last night. Gary Simpson will fine the defender heavily after his second red of the season.

10 Ben Tomlinson denies that Gary Simpson has lost the dressing room. Simpson says he is not worried about his future at the club and will continue his search for another defender.

11 **Lincoln 2 (Newton pen, Tomlinson) AFC Telford United 0.** Att: 2,529. City pick up a welcome win over the bottom side with two late goals, but the quality of the performance still leaves supporters dissatisfied. The league position improves to 13th, but still only 6 points clear of danger.

⇒ Striker Jordan Burrow receives a late call-up by England C for the International Challenge Trophy game against Turkey B in Istanbul on Tuesday. He has to drive back to Sincil Bank after the Telford game to collect his boots before linking up with the rest of the England squad.

13 City are drawn away to Conference rivals Alfreton Town in the fourth qualifying round of the FA Cup. It is the second time in three seasons that the two have been drawn together in the fourth qualifying round, with Alfreton winning a replay 2-1 at Sincil Bank in 2011.

⇒ Gary Simpson sets his side a target of 20 wins to make the play-offs.

14 Lincoln lose 2-1 at Grimsby Town in the final of the Lincolnshire Cup, Marcus Marshall scoring City's goal in front of 652 people.

⇒ Jordan Burrow makes his England C debut as a 64th-minute substitute for Louis Moult in their 2-0 defeat to Turkey B in Istanbul.

16 Bob Dorrian says the club is prepared to support Gary Simpson's search for a new defender despite having already exceeded the budget set pre-season.

17 City re-sign Crewe Alexandra defender Thierry Audel on a three-month loan. Audel made 14 appearances for the Imps on loan last season, scoring 3 goals.

⇒ Todd Jordan joins Stalybridge Celtic on a one-month loan.

18 **Lincoln 1 (Power) Wrexham 1.** Att: 2,360. Thierry Audel makes his second debut for City but is substituted after 56 minutes for Alan Power, who scores a late equaliser. Defender Tom Anderson makes his final appearance before he returns to Burnley. Nick Townsend makes what proves to be his final City appearance. City drop a place to 14th, 6 points clear of the relegation zone.

20 Defender Tom Anderson returns to Burnley after his loan period ends. Gary Simpson says a deal for Anderson to return has already been agreed.

22 City recall Paul Farman from his loan spell at Boston United after Birmingham refuse permission to play on-loan goalkeeper Nick Townsend in the FA Cup. Fortunately, City did not give Boston permission to play Farman in their own FA Cup qualifiers.

⇒ Forest Green Rovers confirm that their home game against Lincoln on 1 November will be the first all-Vegan football match in the world.

23 Bob Dorrian says that the FA Cup is the club's last chance to boost their playing budget this season. He confirms that falling gates mean the club is losing £3,000 per week.

25 **FA Cup 4Q: Alfreton Town 1 Lincoln 1 (Newton pen).** Att: 886. Despite earning a replay, City's players receive a negative reaction from fans at the final whistle. Gary Simpson angers fans further by saying he is fed up of hearing about the financial importance of the FA Cup to the club. It is the eighth successive Lincoln City FA Cup tie to go to a replay (Hereford United in 2010-11, Alfreton Town in 2011-12, FC Halifax, Walsall and Mansfield in 2012-13, Worcester and Plymouth in 2013-14).

27 City are drawn away to Conference rivals Eastleigh in the first round of the FA Cup, if they can win their replay against Alfreton at Sincil Bank tomorrow night.

28 Alfreton Town are to play an outfield player in goal in tonight's FA Cup replay. They do not have a fit goalkeeper after regular stopper James Severn ruptured a thigh muscle on Saturday, and are not permitted to sign a replacement under FA rules.

⇒ **FA Cup 4Q Replay: Lincoln 5 (Newton 3 - 1 pen, Sam-Yorke 2) Alfreton Town 1.** Att: 1,529. Left-back Sean Newton scores the first (and to date, only) hat-trick ever by a City defender. The unfortunate Alfreton goalkeeper was actually midfielder Anthony Howell, standing in for the injured James Severn.

30 Gary Simpson reveals he is set to make some surprising team selections as they embark on a run of long-distance away games.

1 **Forest Green Rovers 3 Lincoln 3 (Sam-Yorke, Ledsham, Burrow).** Att: 1,379. Karl Ledsham scores his first goal for the club, but City blow a 3-goal lead in the last 25 minutes. Gary Simpson accuses his players of poor game-management.

3 Manager Gary Simpson is placed on garden leave following a run of 2 wins in 10 games. Former City players Chris Moyses and Grant Brown are placed in charge until further notice. Simpson leaves City in 13th place, 8 points behind the play-off places and 7 points above the relegation zone.

Bob Dorrian reveals that the decision to replace Gary Simpson was taken prior to City's latest disappointment at Forest Green. He cites the lack of progress being made as the reason for Simpson's departure.

4 **Lincoln 1 (Robinson) Altrincham 2.** Att: 1,953. City's new management team of Moyses and Brown gets off to the worst possible start with a home defeat to lowly Altrincham. The performance leaves no doubt that there is a lot of work to be done if City are to salvage their season. Karl Ledsham makes his final appearance as they stay 13th, 7 points above the danger zone.

5 Chris Moyses reveals he has been given the next four games to convince the board to give him the manager's job on a permanent basis.

6 Bob Dorrian says the club is 'running on empty' and cannot afford to appoint a manager from outside the club. He also believes that Moyses and Brown are 'the logical next step', as they already know the players and have a good rapport with them.

7 Some City fans air their concern that the appointment of director Chris Moyses as team manager is a conflict of interest. Moyses responds by saying he will step down immediately if results do not improve.

8 **FA Cup 1: Eastleigh 2 Lincoln 1 (Sam-Yorke).** Att: 873. A 90th-minute goal by Eastleigh's Ben Strevens knocks the Imps out of the FA Cup and also ends City's record run of 8 successive FA Cup replays. Sahr Kabba makes his third and final appearance as a late substitute.

⇒ Chester's 2-1 win at Southend United in the FA Cup first round means that City's league game against Chester, scheduled for 6 December, will need to be rearranged.

10 Jordan Burrow keeps his place in the England C squad for the game against Estonia U23 at The Shay, Halifax on 18 November. Jon Nolan is included in the contingency squad.

11 **Gateshead 3 Lincoln 3 (Power 2 - 2 pens, Sam-Yorke).** Att: 1,211. City draw 3-3 for the third away league game in a row, but give third-placed Gateshead a good game. They stay 13th, 6 points clear of the relegation zone.

14 City re-sign Birmingham City midfielder Charlee Adams on a youth loan until 1 January.

⇒ Karl Ledsham joins AFC Telford United on a one-month loan to improve his match fitness.

15 City's Conference game at Eastleigh is postponed following a fire at the team hotel, the Hilton Southampton. The fire breaks out just after 11am, causing the evacuation of the building. The game is postponed when City are unable to re-enter the hotel to collect their belongings and specifically their boots in time for the match to go ahead. As City general manager John Vickers quips, "The players cannot be expected to play in flip-flops."

18 Jon Nolan starts for England C in their 4-2 win over Estonia U23 at Halifax. Jordan Burrow wins his second cap as a 67th-minute substitute for Grimsby's Omar Bogle.

⇒ City's game at Chester, scheduled for Saturday 6 December, is rearranged for Tuesday 20 January. The game has to be moved due to Chester's involvement in the second round of the FA Cup.

20 Todd Jordan's loan at Stalybridge is extended for a further two months.

⇒ Chris Moyses intends to train less on the artificial turf at Sincil Bank, as he feels the players are not used to playing on grass.

22 **Lincoln 1 (Miller) Dartford 0.** Att: 2,483. Tom Miller's first half goal gives new manager Moyses his first win despite having Delano Sam-Yorke sent off in the second half. Charlee Adams makes his second debut on loan. City are 15th, 7 points clear of the drop zone.

24 Delano Sam-Yorke receives a three-match ban for his red card against Dartford on Saturday.

⇒ Lincoln City Supporters' Trust suffers a further blow as Manchester County Court rules that candidates for election to the Trust board in 2013 had been wrongly disqualified from standing. The case, brought by former Lincoln City associate director Michael Foley, sought to prove that the Trust elections held in June 2012 and May 2013 were invalid. Rob Bradley, a member of the Trust working party, says he is unsure of the financial implications of the case. The Trust is also required to amend its rules accordingly.

25 The Football Association announces it is to investigate an unpleasant tweet about Grimsby by City midfielder Kegan Everington during transmission of the TV programme *Skint*.

26 Chris Moyses states the club will talk to Kegan Everington about his Grimsby tweet and will abide by whatever action is taken by the FA.

⇒ Rob Bradley hopes that an interim payment of around £12,000 incurred during the Michael Foley court action will be covered by insurance. The costs of the case were awarded to Mr Foley.

27 City sign 20-year-old striker Tyrell Waite from Notts County on a one-month loan. Waite has been training with the Imps for the last week with a view to earning a move to Sincil Bank.

29 **Lincoln 1 (Miller) Southport 0.** Att: 2,034. Tom Miller scores the only goal of the game for the second home match running to give City two successive league wins for the first time since August. City move up to 14th, but are now closer to the play-offs (9 points) than relegation (10 points).

December 2014

1 City are drawn at home to Conference Premier rivals Alfreton Town in the first round of the FA Trophy. The two sides also met in the fourth qualifying round of the FA Cup in October.

⇒ Chris Moyses reveals that City have turned down an offer from a fellow Conference club for striker Ben Tomlinson.

4 City announce that Gary Simpson has officially left the club after a severance agreement is reached between them.

⇒ Lincoln City Supporters' Trust releases a statement confirming that Rob Bradley has met with Michael Foley in France to discuss current differences and try to find a way forward. Mr Bradley admits that the Trust has been a disaster, and has been badly run. He also states that the Trust cannot move forward until the case has been fully resolved and all monies due are paid.

6 City have no game today, as scheduled Conference opponents Chester are involved in an FA Cup second round tie at Barnsley tomorrow.

8 Chris Moyses is appointed Lincoln's new manager on a 12-month rolling deal. As he is already a director at the club, he will not be paid for the role. Grant Brown will be assistant manager.

9 **Lincoln 3 (Burrow 2, Tomlinson) Nuneaton 1.** Att: 1,421. City make it three wins in a row for the first time since August. Tyrell Waite makes his debut against one of his former clubs, while Paul Farman makes his one hundredth appearance for the Imps. City are up to 13th, 8 points behind the play-offs.

12 Karl Ledsham's loan at AFC Telford United is extended for a second month.

13 **FA Trophy 1: Lincoln 0 Alfreton Town 2.** Att: 1,243. City's poor record in the FA Trophy continues with a disappointing defeat to a team they beat 5-1 in the FA Cup only 6 weeks ago. Thierry Audel makes his final appearance.

15 City release striker Sahr Kabba after six months on the books.

⇒ City's away game at Eastleigh, postponed from 15 November due to the hotel fire, is rearranged for Saturday 10 January, which is a blank day with both clubs being out of the FA Cup.

16 Lincoln beat neighbours Lincoln United 2-1 in a friendly at Ashby Avenue. Tony Diagne and Delano Sam-Yorke score the goals in a match arranged to give both clubs some valuable game time.

20 **Kidderminster Harriers 2 Lincoln 1 (Sam-Yorke).** Att: 1,784. City lose to a 93rd-minute winner after leading 1-0 at half time. Alan Power is controversially sent off in the 32nd minute with the score at 0-0. They stay 13th, 9 points behind the play-offs.

22 City extend Charlee Adams' youth loan until the end of February.

23 Alan Power's red card at Kidderminster is rescinded on appeal.

26 **Lincoln 3 (Bencherif, Tomlinson, Marshall) Alfreton Town 2.** Att: 2,685. Marcus Marshall scores his first goal as City notch their fourth home league win in a row. Despite the win, they slip a place to 14th on goal difference, 7 points behind the play-offs.

28 **Grimsby Town 1 Lincoln 3 (Adams, Power, Marshall).** Att: 7,136. City come back from a goal down to shock their high-flying hosts at Blundell Park. Charlee Adams scores with a spectacular long-range effort, while Marcus Marshall scores his second and last goal for the club, two days after he scored his first. City are into the top half (11th), just 4 points behind the play-offs.

29 City release Karl Ledsham from his contract; he is expected to sign for Conference North side Barrow.

30 Former City player and manager John Schofield returns to the club in a coaching capacity. He has been out of work since leaving Scunthorpe in October and approached Chris Moyses to offer his services.

⇒ City reach an agreement in principle for Delano Sam-Yorke to remain at the club for the rest of the season. The precise details of the deal are still to be confirmed.

31 Alex Simmons joins Boston United on loan to the end of the season.

January 2015

1 City's scheduled New Year's Day match at Alfreton is postponed following a 9am pitch inspection. A covering of snow has melted, causing it to be waterlogged.

2 Yesterday's postponed match at Alfreton is rearranged for Tuesday 3 February.

4 **Lincoln 4 (Tomlinson, Power, Nolan, Robinson) Barnet 1.** Att: 2,759. A thumping win over the league leaders gives City a third straight victory and their fifth straight home league win for the first time since relegation. The game is notable for a clash of shirts, as Barnet choose to play the game in purple and white stripes. City stay 11th, 4 points behind the play-offs.

⇒ Birmingham City recall goalkeeper Nick Townsend from his season loan, as he is not playing games. Townsend lost his place in the side in October when Birmingham refused City permission to play him in the FA Cup and has not appeared since.

6 Grant Brown believes that City's improvement in form is due in part to allowing the midfielders to go forward more than before.

8 City confirm that they have opened negotiations with several of the players due to be out of contract in the summer.

9 Chris Moyses confirms Grant Brown's statement when he says the shackles have been taken off the players, who are now allowed to play with more freedom. He also cites improvements in training and communication as factors in the overall upturn in form.

10 **Eastleigh 4 Lincoln 0.** Att: 1,492. City's recent good run comes to a crashing halt. Things go wrong from very early on as Jon Nolan is sent off after 18 minutes; Eastleigh also miss three penalties, two of them saved by Paul Farman. The game is rearranged due to both sides being out of the FA Trophy, which has its second round today. As this is the only league game of the day, City stay 11th, 5 points behind the play-offs.

12 City's match at Torquay United, scheduled for 24 January, will have to be rearranged following Torquay's 4-0 win over Bromley in the FA Trophy second round on Saturday.

⇒ Jon Nolan receives a three-match ban for his red card at Eastleigh on Saturday.

13 City's game at Macclesfield, originally scheduled for Saturday 21 February, is brought forward to Saturday 24 January to fill a blank date for both clubs due to FA Trophy postponements.

14 Chris Moyses promises that City will bounce back after the 4-0 hammering at Eastleigh and insists they are very capable of a play-off challenge.

15 Sean Newton reveals there has been interest in him from Football League clubs during the current transfer window. Newton has been offered a new contract by Lincoln but is keeping his options open.

⇒ Tom Miller also confirms similar interest from Football League clubs. However, he promises he will not leave during the transfer window and will stay at least until his contract expires in the summer.

16 City sign 19-year-old goalkeeper Aidan Grant on non-contract terms. The 6'6" stopper was recently on the books at Peterborough United and has been on trial at Sincil Bank this week.

⇒ City also sign on-loan striker Tyrell Waite on a permanent deal to the end of the season. Fans are surprised, as Waite has hardly featured for the first team.

⇒ City's postponed game at Torquay, scheduled for 24 January, is rearranged for Tuesday 24 February.

17 **Lincoln 3 (Adams, Tomlinson, Mendy) Aldershot Town 0.** Att: 3,022. City bounce back well after last week's defeat at Eastleigh to win their sixth successive home game in the league. Charlee Adams scores another spectacular goal, while Arnaud Mendy scores his only goal for the club. City are up to 10th, but now only 2 points behind the play-offs.

20 City's rearranged game at Chester is postponed due to a frozen pitch. The game is rescheduled for next Tuesday, 27 January.

⇒ City sign Delano Sam-Yorke from Cambridge on a permanent contract to the end of the season. It is the striker's 26th birthday.

21 City extend Charlee Adams' youth loan until the end of the season.

⇒ Alan Power agrees a new two-year contract, and calls on his out of contract team mates to do likewise.

22 City recall Todd Jordan from his loan period at Stalybridge Celtic.

24 **Macclesfield Town 3 Lincoln 0.** Att: 1,974. City's play-off ambitions take another knock as they are well-beaten by third-placed Macclesfield. This game was brought forward from the scheduled date of 21 February to fill a vacant date for both clubs. City are 11th, 4 points off the play-offs.

27 **Chester 4 Lincoln 0.** Att: 1,569. A night to forget, as City suffer their third heavy defeat away from home in a row. Todd Jordan is sent off after 15 minutes, by which time City are already 2 down. Chester add a third after 24 minutes before Alan Power is also sent off on 61 minutes. This is the rearranged game from last Tuesday, 20 January. This turns out to be Todd Jordan's final appearance for City, who have now had 10 players sent off this season. City stay 11th, 4 points behind the play-offs.

29 Chris Moyses reveals he is trying to bring in at least one new player ahead of Saturday's game against Dover to boost a squad depleted by injury and suspension.

30 City recall Alex Simmons from his loan spell at Boston United after a month; the loan was intended to run to the end of the season, but City have injury concerns ahead of tomorrow's game against Dover.

⇒ Todd Jordan receives a one-match ban for his red card at Chester on Tuesday; Alan Power will serve a three-match ban due to his challenge on Chester's Craig Mahon being viewed as dangerous.

31 **Lincoln 1 (Tomlinson) Dover Athletic 0.** Att: 2,509. Future Imp Sean Raggett hits the bar twice in the closing minutes, but Lincoln hang on for the win in the first ever meeting between the two clubs. It is City's seventh straight home win in the league in contrast to their recent form away from home. City climb to 9th, 2 points behind the play-offs.

[2] City sign 19-year-old midfielder Elliot Hodge on a deal to the end of the season after a successful trial. Hodge is the son of former England international Steve Hodge.

⇒ City sign 22-year-old defender Tom Davies on a month's loan from Fleetwood Town on transfer deadline day.

⇒ Chris Moyses fails in his attempt to sign former City defender Lee Beevers from Mansfield Town. He is to try to take the player on loan when the loan window opens next week.

[3] City's rearranged match at Alfreton Town is postponed at 6pm due to a frozen pitch despite the club being assured earlier in the day that the pitch was playable. Many fans feel a chance has been lost - City would have gone fifth with a win over a side in the bottom four.

⇒ Coach David Preece believes Jon Nolan has the ability to go as far as he wants to in the game.

[4] Jordan Burrow is called up for the England C friendly match against Cyprus U21 in Larnaca on 17 February.

⇒ City announce that they need to find £380,000 to repay outstanding debts to the Co-op Bank. The bank apparently told City to find alternative banking arrangements a year ago after changes to its business strategy, but the club has been unable to secure an alternative. The Co-op has now decided to call the debt in and is pressing for assets to be sold. Bob Dorrian appeals to supporters and investors to support the club by buying shares and three-year bonds.

[5] Lincoln supporters set up a fund-raising scheme using the Crowdfunder platform to raise money towards clearing the Co-op debt. The *Save The Imps* campaign aims to raise £350,000 by 5 March. Unfortunately this campaign is destined to be unsuccessful, with just £2,740 pledged.

[6] Aidan Grant signs a short-term deal until the end of the season.

⇒ City are to offer a *Name Your Price* ticket for the home match against Chester on 14 February. Supporters are invited to pay what they can afford, subject to a minimum of £1, in an attempt to attract new supporters to Sincil Bank.

[7] **Bristol Rovers 2 Lincoln 0.** Att: 6,528. City go down to their promotion-chasing hosts, with one of the goals scored by future loanee Nathan Blissett. Tom Davies makes his first and only appearance as a half time substitute for the injured Sean Newton. It turns out to be Newton's final appearance before his loan move to Notts County. City slip to 10th, 5 points behind the play-offs.

[9] City's visit to Alfreton Town, which has already been postponed twice, is rearranged for Tuesday 17 March.

⇒ Chris Moyses is set to use the loan market to revive his side's faltering play-off challenge.

[10] New signing Elliot Hodge and Alex Simmons join Spalding United on a month's loan.

[12] City sign 22-year-old striker John Marsden on loan from Southport until the end of the season. Marsden scored an 86th-minute equaliser against the Imps when the teams met in October.

[13] Defender Sean Newton joins Notts County on loan until the end of the season in exchange for a fee; the move is with a view to a permanent transfer when his contract expires in the summer. 21-year-old defender Jordan Cranston signs for City on loan until the end of the season as part of the deal.

[14] **Lincoln 0 Chester 1.** Att: 4,568. Another poor performance moves City further away from the play-off dream. The attendance is boosted by the *Name Your Price* offer, but City fail again. Jordan Cranston and John Marsden make their debuts while Tyrell Waite appears for the final time. City drop to 11th, 7 points behind the play-offs.

[16] City announce that pop group Madness are to play at Sincil Bank on 29 May as part of their Grandslam Madness Tour. It will be the first date of the tour, which will see the group play at different sporting venues throughout the UK. The gig will raise some much-needed revenue for the club.

⇒ City confirm that the *Name Your Price* initiative for Saturday's game against Chester was a success despite a number of supporters paying the £1 minimum.

[17] Jordan Burrow plays the whole game in England C's 2-1 defeat to Cyprus U21 in Larnaca, winning his third cap.

⇒ City play a behind closed doors friendly against Premier League Burnley to give the players game time. Tyrell Waite and John Marsden score City's goals in a 2-2 draw against a young Burnley side.

[21] City have no game today, as the scheduled visit to Macclesfield was brought forward to 24 January.

[24] City's rearranged game at Torquay is postponed just after lunchtime due to a waterlogged pitch. City are unhappy with the late decision, as they are just 90 miles from Torquay when they receive the news and have received constant assurances throughout the morning that there are no problems with the pitch. Manager Moyses brands the decision 'disgraceful'.

[26] Goalkeeper Paul Farman signs a two-year contract extension that takes him to the end of the 2016-17 season. The deal represents a rapid change of fortune for the keeper, who lost his place to Nick Townsend at the start of the season and was loaned to Boston United.

⇒ City announce a massive fundraising initiative designed to help pay off the club's £380,000 debts. The initiative, to be known as the *Dambusters* scheme, consists of installing new seats in the Co-op stand depicting an image of a Lancaster bomber flying over Lincoln Cathedral. The image has been created by renowned aviation artist Simon Atack, and has been inspired by Preston North End, who installed an image of Sir Tom Finney in a stand at Deepdale. Supporters are invited to sponsor individual seats ranging from £40 to £250. The target has been set at £150,000, with the cost of the work estimated at £100,000 of that; it will be the biggest scheme of its type ever if it is successful.

⇒ At the club's Annual General Meeting, Bob Dorrian reveals that the club was advertised for sale anonymously in two national newspapers three months ago. There were no serious responses. He also confirms that the club is in discussions with a potential investor. The operating loss for the financial year ending 30 June 2014 was £195,362.

28 **Lincoln 0 Woking 2.** Att: 2,347. City turn in another poor performance and fail to register a single shot on target. They have now taken just 3 points and scored 1 goal in the last 6 games as the play-off challenge disappears over the horizon. This turns out to be Charlee Adams' last appearance, as he is recalled a few days later. City are 12th, now 14 points behind the play-offs.

March 2015

1 Tom Davies returns to Fleetwood after his loan expires.

3 Birmingham City recall on-loan midfielder Charlee Adams before the end of his agreed loan term. They apologise to Lincoln, but feel his development needs will now be better served by playing in Birmingham's reserves.

⇒ City's visit to Torquay, which has been postponed twice, is rearranged for Tuesday 14 April.

6 City are given just 10 weeks to clear the debt owed to the Co-op Bank. They now have until the middle of May to repay the overdraft of (up to) £300,000 and the £80,000 mortgage on PlayZone.

7 **Dover Athletic 1 Lincoln 2 (Sam-Yorke, Power).** Att: 1,016. City battle back from a goal down to upset the form book on their first ever visit to Dover. Two errors by Dover keeper Andrew Rafferty hand the Imps a half time advantage after falling behind to an early goal. City are 11th, 14 points behind the play-offs.

11 City cancel the contract of Tyrell Waite to enable him to sign for Swedish club Skellefteå.

13 Ticket sales for the Madness gig at Sincil Bank are selling well, with over 4,000 sold of the 9,500 available.

14 **Lincoln 0 Welling United 2.** Att: 1,935. Normal service is resumed as City go down to a poor Welling side which started the day fourth-bottom of the league. To compound matters, Delano Sam-Yorke is sent off on the final whistle. City's poor record against Welling continues: P4 L4 F1 A7 Pts0 since relegation. Marcus Marshall makes his final appearance. Although 12th, City are now closer to the bottom four (14 points) than the play-offs (15 points).

15 City's players are brought in for training on Sunday morning after their third home defeat in a row. Chris Moyses voices his concerns that there is a lack of commitment from certain players. He adds that he will pick players he can trust for Tuesday's game at Alfreton.

17 **Alfreton Town 0 Lincoln 0.** Att: 744. City draw another blank in the game rearranged from New Year's Day. Arnaud Mendy makes his final appearance for City, who have now failed to score in 7 of the last 9 games. They slip to 13th, in no man's land.

⇒ Delano Sam-Yorke receives a four-match suspension for his red card against Welling on Saturday after an appeal against the sending-off is unsuccessful. The length of the ban is due to it being Sam-Yorke's second straight red card of the season after his red against Dartford on 22 November.

19 City launch the *Dambusters* fundraising initiative, announced on 26 February, using the Crowdfunder platform.

20 Nat Brown agrees a one-year contract extension.

⇒ City announce that they have also given one-year contract extensions to young professionals Elliot Hodge, Kegan Everington and Alex Simmons.

21 **Wrexham 1 Lincoln 1 (Tomlinson).** Att: 2,650. City earn a point with a battling performance against FA Trophy finalists Wrexham. City are up a place to 12th. In no danger of reaching the play-offs or being relegated, the target is to win as many games as possible and finish in the top half for the first time since relegation.

26 City sign 21-year-old centre back Jordan Keane on loan from Alfreton Town to the end of the season.

⇒ City sign 20-year-old defender Kieran Wallace from Sheffield United on loan to the end of the season.

⇒ Todd Jordan joins Buxton on loan until the end of the season.

28 **Lincoln 1 (Power pen) Forest Green Rovers 2.** Att: 1,938. City's poor run extends to 1 win in 8 games as they go down to their big-spending visitors. Paul Farman saves a Jon Parkin penalty in the first half but City still go in at half time two-down. On-loan centre back Jordan Keane makes his City debut - in midfield; loanee Kieran Wallace also makes his debut. John Marsden makes his final appearance before returning to Southport. City have now lost their last 4 home games (having won the previous 7) and have slipped back to 13th.

30 Grant Brown suggests that Kieran Wallace and Jordan Keane have been brought in with one eye on next season as manager Chris Moyses continues to shape his new squad.

April 2015

3 **Braintree Town 1 Lincoln 3 (Burrow 2, Tomlinson).** Att: 650. Although in the middle of a poor run, City win their seventh successive game against Braintree. They are back up to 11th with 5 games to play.

6 **Lincoln 1 (Bencherif) FC Halifax Town 1.** Att: 2,263. Jordan Cranston is sent off 3 minutes into stoppage time after play-off chasing Halifax snatch a 90th-minute equaliser. City stay 11th, in the top half by a single point.

⇒ Broadcaster BT Sports announces it is to extend its television deal for Conference Premier football for a further 3 years. In addition to the 25 regular season games plus the five play-off matches it already shows, there is to be a weekly highlights programme. The competition will also be known as the National League from 6 June 2015.

[7] Captain Alan Power is suspended for two matches after reaching his 10th booking of the season against FC Halifax. On-loan defender Jordan Cranston will miss one game following his red card.

[9] Bob Dorrian says he is thrilled that the gamble to appoint Chris Moyses has paid off, and confirms that Moyses will remain City's manager for next season.

[10] Chris Moyses reveals that he is looking to sign players from the immediate catchment area to reduce the cost of accommodation.

⇒ City announce that the price of season tickets is to be frozen for the fourth successive year.

[11] **AFC Telford United 1 Lincoln 0.** Att: 1,243. City's poor form continues with an 80th-minute defeat at relegated Telford. They slip a place to 12th, still in the top half on goal difference with 3 games to play.

⇒ City announce that their home game with promotion-chasing Eastleigh next Saturday will be shown live on BT Sport with a 12.15pm kick-off.

[13] John Marsden is recalled from his loan by Southport.

⇒ The trial of former City players Moses Swaibu and Delroy Facey gets under way at Birmingham Crown Court. Both players are charged with conspiracy to commit bribery in connection with alleged match fixing.

[14] **Torquay United 1 Lincoln 0.** Att: 1,249. City fail to score for the 9th time in 15 games as they are beaten by an 80th-minute winner at Plainmoor. This is the game rearranged from the late postponement on 24 February. City slip back into the bottom half (13th) on goal difference.

⇒ A series of text messages sent by Delroy Facey to former City striker Scott Spencer is read out in court in Birmingham. The exchange is alleged to have offered Spencer money to fix the score of a specific match involving Spencer's team Hyde FC. Spencer declined the offer. A Skype message sent by Moses Swaibu to Facey allegedly cited Whitehawk, Bromley and Lincoln as good opportunities for match fixing.

[18] **Lincoln 1 (Tomlinson) Eastleigh 2.** Att: 2,132. City lose for the third time this season to Eastleigh, this one shown live on television with a 12.15pm kick-off. City fans are angered by the presentation, which is biased totally towards Eastleigh; no one from Lincoln City is interviewed before or after the game. Jake Caprice, Kieran Wallace and Jordan Cranston make their final appearances. City slip to 15th with a game to play, but their inferior goal difference means that a top-half finish is now beyond them.

⇒ Paul Farman is voted *Player of the Season* by the fans, with Ben Tomlinson in second and Alan Power third. Farman also takes the *Away Player of the Season* award. Kegan Everington is awarded *Young Player of the Season* by the management.

⇒ Ben Tomlinson says that contract talks have taken place but he wants to keep his options open.

[20] On-loan Jordan Cranston is recalled by Notts County due to injuries at Meadow Lane.

[23] Chris Moyses labels his team's form as 'scandalous' ahead of the final game of the season at Dartford. In response to criticism from fans, Moyses asks to be judged once he has his own team. He reiterates that he will walk away if things do not improve next season.

[24] Youngsters Aidan Grant, Kegan Everington, Alex Simmons and Elliot Hodge all sign one-year contract extensions to the end of the 2015-16 season.

⇒ Jon Nolan also agrees a one-year contract extension; the move comes as a surprise to fans, who expected Nolan to be released after an indifferent season.

[25] **Dartford 0 Lincoln 0.** Att: 1,274. City's season fizzles out with a goalless draw at relegated Dartford in a game that kicks off at 5.15pm. Hamza Bencherif, Tony Diagne, Jordan Burrow, Tom Miller, Delano Sam-Yorke, Ben Tomlinson and Jordan Keane play their final games for City. Aidan Grant and Elliott Hodge make their debuts. They end the season with just 3 wins and 10 defeats from their last 17 games.

⇒ The draw at Dartford sees City finish the season in 15th place, one place lower than last season, and 13 points clear of the drop zone.

[27] Chris Moyses warns his players that he intends to complete his summer recruitment by the end of May and will not wait for those who stall on contract offers.

[29] Former City players Moses Swaibu and Delroy Facey are found guilty of conspiracy to commit bribery. Facey is jailed for two-and-a-half years and is described by the judge at Birmingham Crown Court as 'the cancer at the heart of football'. Swaibu is jailed for 16 months.

[30] Bob Dorrian is confident that the club can do a deal with the Co-op Bank after around £160,000 is raised through share and bond issues. He also confirms that the *Dambusters* scheme is destined to fail after a poor response to the appeal has left it £90,000 short of the initial target.

May 2015

[5] Legendary City goalkeeper Jimmy Jones dies at the age of 87. Jones was the last surviving member of the 1951-52 Third Division North championship-winning team, and made 80 appearances for the club between 1951 and 1954.

⇒ Former City defender Sean Newton is not offered a contract by Notts County after they are relegated to League Two. Newton is likely to be a free agent when his contract with Lincoln expires.

6 City announce the retained list for 2015-16. Under contract are Paul Farman, Alan Power, Nat Brown, Kegan Everington, Aidan Grant, Elliot Hodge, Conner Robinson and Alex Simmons.

Two players under contract for next season have been made available for immediate transfer - Tony Diagne and Jordan Burrow.

Hamza Bencherif, Tom Miller and Jon Nolan have been offered new contracts.

Youth team player Andrew Wright has been offered a first-year professional contract.

Released are Jake Caprice, Arnaud Mendy, Todd Jordan, Sean Newton, Delano Sam-Yorke and surprisingly top scorer Ben Tomlinson.

⇒ Reaction from fans to the release of Ben Tomlinson is not positive, especially as fellow striker Delano Sam -Yorke has been released as well. However, Chris Moyses responds by saying that Tomlinson was not prepared to commit to the club.

⇒ City transfer target Lee Beevers is released by Mansfield Town.

7 Stephen Tointon is appointed to the board of directors.

8 Chris Moyses announces that he is to step down from the board to avoid a potential conflict of interest.

11 Today marks the 30th anniversary of the Valley Parade fire.

12 Chris Moyses officially ceases to be a director of the club.

13 The *Dambusters* campaign closes, having failed to reach any of its targets. Just £53,960 has been pledged, meaning the scheme will not go ahead. Under the terms of the Crowdfunder mechanism, no money will be collected.

14 City sign 31-year-old ex-Imp Lee Beevers from Mansfield Town on a two-year contract. Originally signed by Keith Alexander in February 2005, Beevers spent four and a half seasons at Sincil Bank before leaving for Colchester United in 2009.

⇒ City also sign 30-year-old striker Matt Rhead from Mansfield on a two-year deal. Rhead is the player whose last-gasp equaliser for Mansfield at Sincil Bank ultimately cost City a glamour FA Cup tie against Liverpool in 2012-13.

⇒ On a busy day at Sincil Bank, City sign 21-year-old midfielder Greg Tempest from Notts County on a one-year deal.

17 City receive a boost as neighbours Grimsby Town lose the Conference play-off final on penalties to Bristol Rovers. Rovers become the first club to return to the Football League at the first attempt for 10 years, whereas Grimsby will be heading to Sincil Bank again next season.

20 City sign 29-year-old striker Liam Hearn from Mansfield Town on a one-year deal. He is the third player in a week to move to Sincil Bank from Mansfield. The move does not go down well in Grimsby, where Hearn is still regarded as a hero by Mariners fans.

21 Alan Power signs a new two-year deal.

⇒ John Schofield leaves City to become assistant manager at League Two York City. Schofield has been assisting City in a voluntary coaching capacity since the New Year.

⇒ City announce that Premier League side Leicester City are to visit Sincil Bank for a pre-season friendly on Tuesday 21 July. They have agreed to bring a full-strength squad for the game.

27 Acting managing director Kevin Cooke announces that over 7,000 tickets have been sold for Friday's Madness gig at Sincil Bank. City are set to make in excess of £25,000 from the evening, further reducing the outstanding debt to the Co-op Bank. At the same time, Cooke criticises the Co-op for what the club sees as an aggressive attitude.

28 City sign 22-year-old defender Chris Bush from Welling United on a one-year deal. Bush previously spent a month on loan at Sincil Bank in January 2013.

⇒ City also sign 26-year-old attacking midfielder Jack Muldoon from Rochdale on a one-year deal.

29 Chris Moyses confirms that Tom Miller and Hamza Bencherif have yet to sign new contracts with the club; they have been given until 5 June to accept their offers.

⇒ Pop group Madness play at Sincil Bank as the first date in their Grandslam Madness tour. Supported by Scouting For Girls and Chainska Brassika, the gig is a great success.

SEASON 2014-15

CONFERENCE

No.	Date		Opposition	Res	Att	Scorers	Townsend, N	Caprice, J	Newton, S	Power, A	Diagne, T	Brown, N	Nolan, J	Bencherif, H	Burrow, J	Marshall, M	Tomlinson, B
1	AUG	9	KIDDERMINSTER HARRIERS	0-0	2598		Y	Y	Y	Y#	Y	Y	Y	Y	Y	Y	Y
2		12	Altrincham	2-1	996	Burrow, Robinson	Y	Y	Y	Y>	Y	Y	Y	Y	Y	Y#	Y*
3		16	Barnet	2-1	1529	Burrow, Bencherif	Y	Y	Y	Y#	Y	Y	Y	Y	Y	S#	Y
4		23	BRAINTREE TOWN	3-2	2231	Newton, Bencherif, Tomlinson	Y	Y	Y	Y	Y	Y	Y	Y	Y#	S#	Y
5		25	FC Halifax	2-3	2369	Bencherif, Tomlinson (pen)	Y	Y	Y	Y#	Y	Y	Y*	Y	Y>	S#	Y
6		30	TORQUAY UNITED	1-3	2373	Tomlinson (pen)	Y	Y>	Y	Y	Y	Y	Y	Y#	Y	Y*	Y
7	SEP	6	Woking	1-3	2160	Burrow	Y	Y>	Y	Y*	Y	Y		Y	Y	S#	Y
8		9	GRIMSBY TOWN	3-2	5209	Burrow, Newton (pen), Bencherif	Y	Y	Y	Y	Y	Y	Y#	Y	Y		Y
9		13	BRISTOL ROVERS	2-3	2933	Newton (pen), Burrow	Y	Y	Y	Y	Y	Y	Y	Y	Y		Y
10		16	Welling United	0-2	504		Y	Y	Y	Y	Y		Y#	Y*	Y	Y>	S>	Y
11		20	Aldershot Town	0-1	1582		Y	S#	Y	Y	Y#			Y>	Y	Y*	Y
12		27	MACCLESFIELD TOWN	2-0	2265	Miller, Tomlinson	Y		Y		S*		Y	Y		S#	Y
13		30	GATESHEAD	1-1	2394	Anderson	Y		S#	Y		Y		Y		Y	Y
14	OCT	4	Nuneaton Town	1-2	920	Miller	Y		Y	S*	S#	Y	Y*			Y	Y
15		7	Southport	3-3	746	Sam-Yorke, Tomlinson, OG	Y		Y		Y	Y	Y			Y	Y
16		11	AFC TELFORD UNITED	2-0	2529	Newton (pen), Tomlinson	Y		Y			Y	Y		Y		Y
17		18	WREXHAM	1-1	2360	Power	Y		Y	S#		Y	Y		Y	S*	Y
18	NOV	1	Forest Green Rovers	3-3	1379	Sam-Yorke, Ledsham, Burrow			Y			Y	Y#	Y	S#	Y>	S*
19		4	ALTRINCHAM	1-2	1953	Robinson		S>	Y	Y		Y		Y	Y		S#
20		11	Gateshead	3-3	1211	Power 2 (2 pens), Sam-Yorke		Y	Y	Y		Y	S*	Y	S>	Y>	S#
21		22	DARTFORD	1-0	2483	Miller		Y	Y	Y		Y		Y	S#	Y#	Y
22		29	SOUTHPORT	1-0	2034	Miller		Y	Y	Y			Y	Y	Y	Y#	Y
23	DEC	9	NUNEATON TOWN	3-1	1421	Burrow 2, Tomlinson		Y	Y				Y	Y	Y*	Y>	Y
24		20	Kidderminster Harriers	1-2	1784	Sam-Yorke		Y	Y	Y			Y#	Y	Y		S*
25		26	ALFRETON TOWN	3-2	2685	Bencherif, Tomlinson, Marshall		Y	Y	S*		Y		Y	S>	Y	S#
26		28	Grimsby Town	3-1	7136	Adams, Power, Marshall		Y	Y	Y		Y	S#	Y	S*	Y	Y*
27	JAN	4	BARNET	4-1	2759	Tomlinson, Power, Nolan, Robinson		Y	Y	Y		Y	Y	Y	S#	Y*	Y
28		10	Eastleigh	0-4	1492			Y	Y	Y		Y	Y	Y	S*	Y#	Y
29		17	ALDERSHOT TOWN	3-0	3022	Adams, Tomlinson, Mendy		Y	Y	Y		Y#		Y	S*		Y
30		24	Macclesfield Town	0-3	1974			Y	Y	Y		Y		Y	S#	Y	Y
31		27	Chester	0-4	1569			Y	Y	Y		Y		Y		Y*	Y
32		31	DOVER ATHLETIC	1-0	2509	Tomlinson		Y	Y			Y	Y	Y		Y	Y
33	FEB	7	Bristol Rovers	0-2	6528			Y	Y#			Y	Y	Y	S*	Y>	Y
34		14	CHESTER	0-1	4568							Y	Y#	Y	Y	Y	Y*
35		28	WOKING	0-2	2347							Y	Y#	Y	Y	Y	S#
36	MAR	7	Dover Athletic	2-1	1016	Sam-Yorke, Power			Y			Y	Y*	Y		S#	Y
37		14	WELLING UNITED	0-2	1935			Y>	Y			Y		Y	S>	Y#	Y
38		17	Alfreton Town	0-0	744			Y	Y			Y		Y	Y	Y	
39		21	Wrexham	1-1	2650	Tomlinson		Y		Y		Y	Y	Y	Y		
40		28	FOREST GREEN ROVERS	1-2	1938	Power (pen)		S#		Y		Y	Y	Y	Y		
41	APR	3	Braintree Town	3-1	650	Burrow 2, Tomlinson		Y		Y		S>		S#	Y		Y*
42		6	FC HALIFAX	1-1	2263	Bencherif		Y		Y				S#	Y		Y*
43		11	AFC Telford United	0-1	1243			Y				Y		Y#	Y*		Y
44		14	Torquay United	0-1	1249			Y						S#	Y	Y	
45		18	EASTLEIGH	1-2	2132	Tomlinson		Y		Y				S*	Y		Y
46		25	Dartford	0-0	1274							Y	Y	Y	Y	Y>	S#
			Appearances				17	34	32	33	15	36	28	41	28	24	39
			Substitute appearances				0	3	0	4	3	0	6	0	11	8	7
			Goals				0	0	4	7	0	0	1	6	10	2	14

62 league goals

FA CUP

				Res	Att	Scorers			Caprice, J	Newton, S	Power, A	Diagne, T	Brown, N	Nolan, J	Bencherif, H	Burrow, J	Marshall, M	Tomlinson, B
4Q	OCT	25	Alfreton Town	1-1	886	Newton (pen)			Y	Y		Y	Y		Y	Y	Y
4QR		28	ALFRETON TOWN	5-1	1529	Newton 3 (1 pen), Sam-Yorke 2			Y	Y		Y	Y	Y*	Y#		Y>
1	NOV	8	Eastleigh	1-2	873	Sam-Yorke			Y	Y		Y		Y	Y#	Y	

FA TROPHY

| 1 | DEC | 13 | ALFRETON TOWN | 0-2 | 1243 | | | | Y | Y* | Y | | | | Y | Y | Y# | Y> | Y |

LINCOLNSHIRE CUP

| SF | JUL | 23 | Scunthorpe United | 1-0 | 729 | Newton | | | S# | Y | | Y | Y | Y | Y | | | Y |
| F | OCT | 14 | Grimsby Town | 1-2 | 652 | Marshall | Y | Y | S# | Y | Y | | Y | | | Y | S# |

Key:
Y = full appearance
Y# = full appearance, first player substituted - by substitute S#
Y* = full appearance, second player substituted - by substitute S*
Y> = full appearance, third player substituted - by substitute S>

Red Card
Yellow Card

70

	Mendy, A	Robinson, C	Ledsham, K	Kabba, S	Jordan, T	Sam-Yorke, D	Anderson, T	Miller, T	Audel, T	Farman, P	Adams, C	Simmons, A	Waite, T	Everington, K	Davies, T	Cranston, J	Marsden, J	Keane, J	Wallace, K	Grant, A	Hodge, E
	S #																				
	S #	S *	S >																		
	Y																				
	Y																				
	Y		S *	S >																	
	Y	S >	S #		S *																
	Y		S *	S >		Y #															
	Y					S #															
	Y					S #															
	Y		S #			S *															
	Y		S >			S *	Y	Y													
	Y		Y *			Y #	Y	Y													
	Y		Y			Y #	Y	Y													
	Y		Y			Y	Y #	Y													
	Y		Y			Y		Y													
	Y		Y			Y	Y	Y													
	Y					Y *	Y	Y	Y #												
	Y	S >	Y *			Y	Y	Y	Y	Y											
	Y #	S *	Y			Y *		Y	Y >	Y											
	Y *	Y #				Y		Y		Y											
						Y		Y		Y	Y										
								Y		Y	Y	S #									
	S #	S *						Y		Y	Y #		S >								
	S #					Y		Y		Y			S *								
	Y	Y *				Y >				Y	Y		Y #								
	Y #					Y				Y											
		S *				Y #				Y	Y										
		S #				Y *				Y	Y										
	Y	Y *				Y >		S #		Y	Y		S >								
	Y	S #				Y *				Y	Y #										
	Y	Y #		Y		S *				Y				S #							
	Y					Y				Y	Y										
	Y					Y *				Y	Y		S >			S #					
	Y					Y		Y		Y	Y		S *			Y	S #				
			Y #			Y		Y		Y					Y	Y	S *				
			Y *			Y		Y		Y		S #		S #	Y	Y	S *				
	Y #							Y		Y		S *			Y	Y	Y *				
		S #						Y		Y					Y	Y	Y #				
		Y *						Y		Y					Y	Y	S *	Y	Y #		
								Y		Y		S *			Y #	Y	Y	Y	Y >		
						S *		Y		Y					Y #	Y	Y	Y	Y		
						S #		Y		Y		S *			Y		Y	Y			
						Y		Y		Y		S *		Y #	Y		Y	Y *			
		S #				Y		Y		Y				Y *	Y		Y	Y #			
		Y *				S >		Y			Y #				Y		Y			Y	S *
26	**9**	**7**	**0**	**1**	**24**	**6**	**26**	**3**	**28**	**14**	**1**	**2**	**5**	**0**	**11**	**2**	**7**	**6**	**1**	**0**
4	**10**	**6**	**2**	**1**	**9**	**0**	**1**	**0**	**0**	**0**	**6**	**4**	**2**	**1**	**0**	**4**	**0**	**0**	**0**	**1**
1	**3**	**1**	**0**	**0**	**5**	**1**	**4**	**0**	**0**	**2**	**0**	**0**	**0**	**0**	**0**	**0**	**0**	**0**	**0**	**0**

	Mendy, A	Robinson, C	Ledsham, K	Kabba, S	Jordan, T	Sam-Yorke, D	Anderson, T	Miller, T	Audel, T	Farman, P											
	Y							Y	Y	Y											
	Y	S *	S >			S #		Y	Y	Y											
	Y	Y *		S *		S #		Y	Y	Y											

		Robinson, C						Miller, T	Audel, T	Farman, P	Adams, C	Simmons, A									
		S #						Y	S *	Y	Y	S >									

	Mendy, A		Ledsham, K	Kabba, S	Jordan, T	Sam-Yorke, D		Miller, T	Audel, T	Farman, P											
			S *	Y *	Y			Y #		Y											
	Y		Y			Y		Y	Y												

Appearances & Goals 2014-15

	League			FA Cup			FA Trophy			Totals			Totals		Lincolnshire Cup		
	Apps	Subs	Goals	Apps	Subs	Goals	Apps	Subs	Goals	Apps	Subs	Goals	Apps	Goals	Apps	Subs	Goals
Ben TOMLINSON	39	7	14	2	0	0	1	0	0	42	7	14	49	14	1	1	0
Hamza BENCHERIF	41	0	6	2	0	0	1	0	0	44	0	6	44	6	1	0	0
Jordan BURROW	28	11	10	3	0	0	1	0	0	32	11	10	43	10	1	0	0
Alan POWER	33	4	7	3	0	0	1	0	0	37	4	7	41	7	1	0	0
Nat BROWN	36	0	0	3	0	0	0	0	0	39	0	0	39	0	1	0	0
Jake CAPRICE	34	3	0	0	0	0	1	0	0	35	3	0	38	0	1	1	0
Jon NOLAN	28	6	1	2	0	0	1	0	0	31	6	1	37	1	2	0	0
Sean NEWTON	32	0	4	3	0	4	1	0	0	36	0	8	36	8	1	1	1
Delano SAM-YORKE	24	9	5	0	2	3	0	0	0	24	11	8	35	8	1	0	0
Marcus MARSHALL (L)	24	8	2	2	0	0	1	0	0	27	8	2	35	2	1	0	1
Arnaud MENDY	26	4	1	3	0	0	0	0	0	29	4	1	33	1	1	0	0
Paul FARMAN	28	0	0	3	0	0	1	0	0	32	0	0	32	0	1	0	0
Tom MILLER	26	1	4	3	0	0	1	0	0	30	1	4	31	4	1	0	0
Conner ROBINSON	9	10	3	1	1	0	0	1	0	10	12	3	22	3	0	0	0
Tony DIAGNE	15	3	0	0	0	0	0	0	0	15	3	0	18	0	2	0	0
Nick TOWNSEND (L)	17	0	0	0	0	0	0	0	0	17	0	0	17	0	1	0	0
Charlee ADAMS (L)	14	0	2	0	0	0	1	0	0	15	0	2	15	2	0	0	0
Karl LEDSHAM	7	6	1	0	1	0	0	0	0	7	7	1	14	1	1	1	0
Jordan CRANSTON (L)	11	0	0	0	0	0	0	0	0	11	0	0	11	0	0	0	0
Alex SIMMONS	1	6	0	0	0	0	0	1	0	1	7	0	8	0	0	0	0
Jordan KEANE (L)	7	0	0	0	0	0	0	0	0	7	0	0	7	0	0	0	0
Kegan EVERINGTON	5	2	0	0	0	0	0	0	0	5	2	0	7	0	0	0	0
Thierry AUDEL (L)	3	0	0	3	0	0	0	1	0	6	1	0	7	0	0	0	0
Tom ANDERSON (L)	6	0	1	0	0	0	0	0	0	6	0	1	6	1	1	0	0
Kieran WALLACE (L)	6	0	0	0	0	0	0	0	0	6	0	0	6	0	0	0	0
John MARSDEN (L)	2	4	0	0	0	0	0	0	0	2	4	0	6	0	0	0	0
Tyrell WAITE	2	4	0	0	0	0	0	0	0	2	4	0	6	0	0	0	0
Sahr KABBA	0	2	0	0	1	0	0	0	0	0	3	0	3	0	1	0	0
Todd JORDAN	1	1	0	0	0	0	0	0	0	1	1	0	2	0	2	0	0
Aidan GRANT	1	0	0	0	0	0	0	0	0	1	0	0	1	0	0	0	0
Tom DAVIES (L)	0	1	0	0	0	0	0	0	0	0	1	0	1	0	0	0	0
Elliot HODGE	0	1	0	0	0	0	0	0	0	0	1	0	1	0	0	0	0

Own goals: 1 | 0 | 0 | 1 | 1 | 0

Players Used	League goals	FA Cup goals	FA Trophy goals	Total goals
32	62	7	0	69

Squad Numbers 2014-15

No.	Player	No.	Player
1	Paul Farman	17	Jake Caprice
2	Tom Miller	18	Kegan Everington
3	Sean Newton	19	Alex Simmons
4	Todd Jordan	20	Charlee Adams; Jordan Keane
5	Hamza Bencherif	21	Kieran Wallace
6	Tony Diagne	22	Marcus Marshall
7	Sahr Kabba; Jordan Cranston	23	Nat Brown
8	Alan Power	24	Thierry Audel
9	Jordan Burrow	25	Tom Anderson; Tyrell Waite
10	Karl Ledsham; John Marsden	26	Nick Townsend
11	Ben Tomlinson	27	
12	Arnaud Mendy	28	Tom Davies
13		29	Elliot Hodge
14	Jon Nolan	30	Aidan Grant
15	Delano Sam-Yorke	31	David Preece
16	Conner Robinson		

Conference Final League Table 2014-15

		P	Home					Away					Totals		Pts
			W	D	L	F	A	W	D	L	F	A	F	A	
1	Barnet	46	16	2	5	54	21	12	6	5	40	25	94	46	92
P	Bristol Rovers	46	17	4	2	47	14	8	12	3	26	20	73	34	91
3	Grimsby Town	46	12	4	7	36	20	13	7	3	38	20	74	40	86
4	Eastleigh	46	12	6	5	45	28	12	4	7	42	33	87	61	82
5	Forest Green Rovers	46	12	7	4	42	27	10	9	4	38	27	80	54	79
6	Macclesfield Town	46	14	7	2	34	14	7	8	8	26	32	60	46	78
7	Woking	46	11	7	5	39	24	10	6	7	38	28	77	52	76
8	Dover Athletic	46	13	4	6	38	18	6	7	10	31	40	69	58	68
9	FC Halifax Town	46	11	7	5	38	27	6	8	9	22	27	60	54	66
10	Gateshead	46	10	6	7	38	34	7	9	7	28	28	66	62	66
11	Wrexham	46	9	8	6	27	22	8	7	8	29	30	56	52	66
12	Chester	46	11	3	9	35	36	8	3	12	29	40	64	76	63
13	Torquay United	46	10	7	6	35	26	6	6	11	29	34	64	60	61
14	Braintree Town	46	10	4	9	28	25	8	1	14	28	32	56	57	59
15	Lincoln City	46	11	4	8	35	28	5	6	12	27	43	62	71	58
16	Kidderminster Harriers	46	9	6	8	31	30	6	6	11	20	30	51	60	57
17	Altrincham	46	9	5	9	29	34	7	3	13	25	39	54	73	56
18	Aldershot Town	46	8	5	10	27	28	6	6	11	24	33	51	61	53
19	Southport	46	6	6	11	21	33	7	6	10	26	39	47	72	51
20	Welling United	46	7	8	8	29	27	4	4	15	23	46	52	73	45
21	Alfreton Town	46	6	8	9	33	40	6	1	16	16	50	49	90	45
22	Dartford	46	4	9	10	26	34	4	6	13	18	40	44	74	39
23	AFC Telford United	46	3	5	15	27	44	7	4	12	31	40	58	84	36
24	Nuneaton Town	46	7	6	10	25	33	3	3	17	13	43	38	76	36

Progress Chart 2014-15

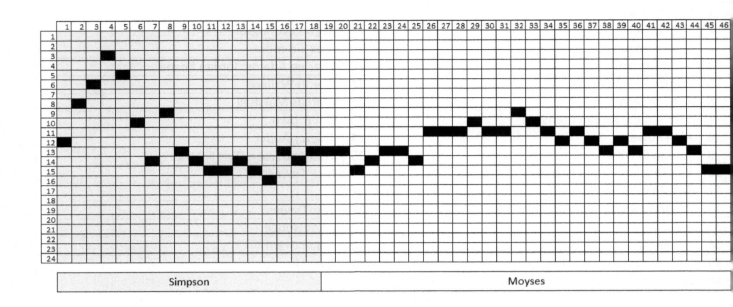

	Simpson	Moyses

Friendlies 2014-15

Jul	4	Lincoln United	3-1	650	Power, Nolan, Miller
	8	Basford United	3-4	121	Burrow, Tomlinson, Simmons
	12	DONCASTER ROVERS	2-0	1144	Burrow, Power
	19	CHESTERFIELD	2-1	952	Burrow, Power
	26	Scarborough Athletic	1-0	357	Diagne
	29	MANSFIELD TOWN	1-3	924	Bencherif
Aug	2	Stalybridge Celtic	0-1	202	
Dec	16	Lincoln United	2-1	350	Diagne, Sam-Yorke

Does not include the behind closed doors friendlies against Chesterfield (23/9/2014) and Burnley (17/2/2015).

Original Fixture List 2014-15

Aug	9	KIDDERMINSTER HARR		18	WREXHAM		31	DOVER ATHLETIC
	12	Altrincham	Nov	1	Forest Green Rovers	Feb	7	Bristol Rovers
	16	Barnet		4	ALTRINCHAM		14	CHESTER
	23	BRAINTREE TOWN		11	Gateshead		21	Macclesfield Town
	25	FC Halifax Town		15	Eastleigh		28	WOKING
	30	TORQUAY UNITED		22	DARTFORD	Mar	7	Dover Athletic
Sep	6	Woking		29	SOUTHPORT		14	WELLING UNITED
	9	GRIMSBY TOWN	Dec	6	Chester		21	Wrexham
	13	BRISTOL ROVERS		9	NUNEATON TOWN		28	FOREST GREEN ROVERS
	16	Welling United		20	Kidderminster Harriers	Apr	4	Braintree Town
	20	Aldershot Town		26	ALFRETON TOWN		6	FC HALIFAX TOWN
	27	MACCLESFIELD TOWN		28	Grimsby Town		11	AFC Telford United
	30	GATESHEAD	Jan	1	Alfreton Town		18	EASTLEIGH
Oct	4	Nuneaton Town		4	BARNET		25	Dartford
	7	Southport		17	ALDERSHOT TOWN			
	11	AFC TELFORD UNITED		24	Torquay United	Mar	29	FA Trophy Final

74

Year 5
2015-16

June 2015

1 City sign 23-year-old defender Bradley Wood from Alfreton Town on a two-year deal. The former Grimsby full-back joins for an undisclosed fee.

2 City sign 24-year-old centre-half Luke Waterfall from Wrexham on a two-year deal.

3 Tom Miller confirms that he has received offers from Football League clubs.

4 Chris Moyses reveals he is looking to sign two more players this summer. He is also leaving money in the budget to look at some trialists in pre-season.

5 City sign 32-year-old midfielder Craig Stanley from Eastleigh on a one-year deal.

7 Lincoln City supporter Andrew Helgesen launches the *Moyses Mission* campaign using the Crowdfunder platform. Supporters are invited to pledge money in exchange for a range of benefits such as VIP tickets and t-shirts. All money pledged will go straight to manager Chris Moyses' playing budget.

11 Tom Miller ends speculation by joining League Two side Carlisle United.

15 Lincoln City Supporters' Trust is hit with a further £50,000 legal bill following the Michael Foley legal action last November. Working party member Rob Bradley believes the Trust's insurers will cover the bill.

23 City announce that MANS Locations Services are to continue as back of away shirt sponsors for the 2015-16 season.

24 City sign 33-year-old midfielder Matt Sparrow from Scunthorpe United on a one-year deal.

⇒ City cancel the contract of striker Jordan Burrow to enable him to sign for FC Halifax Town.

⇒ City announce that Sleafordian Coaches are to be back of home shirt sponsors for 2015-16 season.

25 City announce that Software Europe are to be front of away shirt sponsors for 2015-16 season.

July 2015

1 Hamza Bencherif officially declines City's contract offer and signs for FC Halifax Town.

2 The players return for the start of pre-season training. Chris Moyses is also running an eye over 5 unidentified trialists as he seeks to complete his squad.

⇒ City's scheduled pre-season opener at Stamford on Saturday 11 July is cancelled due to concerns that the pitch is not up to standard at the Zeeco Stadium; low water pressure at the new ground has caused problems with the watering of the new grass.

3 City replace the cancelled match at Stamford with a game at Grantham Town on Friday evening, 10 July.

⇒ The fixture list presents City with a home game on the opening day against relegated Cheltenham Town. In a particularly curious quirk, City are to visit Cheltenham on the final day. This season's festive double-header will be against FC Halifax Town.

6 Lincoln City rubbish rumours of a £200,000 winding-up order against the club after an erroneous item appears on a non-league Facebook page.

8 City head away to Cottesmore Barracks in Rutland for three days of army training, with boss Chris Moyses hoping the experience will help bond his new squad together.

9 Defender Tony Diagne joins former club Macclesfield Town on loan until the New Year.

10 City's army training appears to have been successful, as they comfortably overcome Grantham 3-0 in the pre-season opener at South Kesteven Sports Stadium. The goals are scored by Alex Simmons, Jon Nolan and Alan Power in front of 444 fans. Trialists include former Scunthorpe defender Callum Howe, and ex-Middlesbrough defender Kieran Weledji.

⇒ City announce that Software Europe are to sponsor the St Andrews Stand for the 2015-16 season.

13 City's pre-season friendly against Leicester on 21 July is given added spice as the Foxes appoint former Chelsea and Valencia manager Claudio Ranieri to the Walkers hot seat. Bookmakers immediately install him as their favourite to be the first Premier League manager sacked in the new season.

⇒ The Moyses Mission campaign receives a boost as a mystery backer pledges an extra £10 for every pledge over £10.

15 City sign 21-year-old defender Callum Howe from Scunthorpe United on a one-year deal after a trial period. The signing has been made possible by the Crowdfunder campaign.

17 City make it two pre-season wins from two with a 2-0 victory over Lincoln United at Ashby Avenue. Goals from Luke Waterfall and trialist Shaun Harrad send the majority of the 824 fans home happy. Trialists Kieran Weledji and Nicholas Bignall also appear in the game.

21 City go down to Premier League side Leicester City 3-1 in a friendly at Sincil Bank. City take an early lead through an Alan Power penalty, but Leicester fight back with goals by Riyad Mahrez, Andrej Kramaric and Jamie Vardy in front of 3,693. Trialists Nicholas Bignall and Shaun Harrad appear as second half substitutes. Little does anyone realise that Leicester will go on to shock the football world by winning the Premier League next May.

22 Former England international Gary Charles tells Lincoln County Court that he is owed up to £50,000 in unpaid wages following a spell as assistant manager and first team coach under David Holdsworth between November 2011 and May 2012. City deny the claim, stating that Charles and fellow coach Curtis Woodhouse were working as volunteers.

23 Bob Dorrian tells Lincoln County Court that Gary Charles was never appointed assistant manager by the club. Both Dorrian and David Holdsworth confirm that Charles volunteered to help the club out. However, former City players Tyrone Thompson and Josh Gowling state that they believed Charles was a member of the coaching staff. Charles claims that Holdsworth constantly assured him he would sort out a contract for him.

24 The Gary Charles case closes with verdict pending.

25 City draw 0-0 at Boston United in the quarter-final of the Lincolnshire Cup, winning 4-1 on penalties in front of 877. Trialists Nicholas Bignall and Shaun Harrad feature as substitutes.

27 Chris Moyses decides against offering a contract to either Shaun Harrad or Nicholas Bignall, saying he was not sure they were 100% right for the team. Moyses will continue his search for another striker.

29 City play another game against an U21 side, this one from Norwich City. However, this game is better-attended, with 1,501 turning out to see a Jack Muldoon goal give City a 1-0 win.

31 The *Moyses Mission* Crowdfunder appeal closes, having raised £16, 440 for the club's playing budget. The final total eventually comes to £19,300.

August 2015

1 City come from 2-down to draw 2-2 at Scunthorpe United in the Lincolnshire Cup semi-final with goals from Alan Power and Matt Rhead, but are beaten 6-5 on penalties in front of 1,015.

5 City's pre-season schedule closes with a 6-1 win at Brigg Town. Elliot Hodge scores twice, with an own goal, Chris Bush, Conner Robinson and Liam Hearn contributing one each in front of 111.

8 **Lincoln 1 (Hearn) Cheltenham Town 1.** Att: 2,767. Liam Hearn scores a second half equaliser to earn a point against promotion favourites Cheltenham in the opening game of the season. Eight players make their debuts for City (Bradley Wood, Luke Waterfall, Jack Muldoon, Matt Sparrow, Craig Stanley, Callum Howe, Matt Rhead and Liam Hearn), while Lee Beevers makes his second debut. On a day for debuts, no fewer than ten players make their debuts for Cheltenham following their relegation from League Two last season. City are 13th in the first league table of the season, 2 points behind early leaders Eastleigh.

11 **Braintree Town 1 Lincoln 3 (Rhead 2 - 1 pen, Stanley).** Att: 657. Alan Power misses a first half penalty, so Matt Rhead takes over when City are awarded another in the second half. All four goals come after half time after Braintree are reduced to 10 men. First goals for the club by Matt Rhead and Craig Stanley give City their 8th successive win over Braintree. City are up to 6th, 2 points behind leaders Eastleigh.

15 **Eastleigh 1 Lincoln 1 (Muldoon).** Att: 1,354. Jack Muldoon scores his first goal for the club to earn a draw with the early season league leaders. City slip to 12th, 2 points behind 5th-placed Chester and 4 points behind new leaders Forest Green.

18 **Lincoln 5 (Hearn 3, Rhead 2) Macclesfield Town 3.** Att: 2,320. Liam Hearn fires a hat-trick as City fight back from an early 2-goal deficit to overpower their visitors. Greg Tempest makes his debut. City rise to 7th, 1 point behind 5th-placed Gateshead and 4 points behind leaders Forest Green.

20 Bob Dorrian believes City have the best chance of promotion this season since relegation. The board will support the manager financially in order to make the play-offs despite the current financial challenges.

22 **Forest Green Rovers 3 Lincoln 1 (Simmons).** Att: 1,385. Alex Simmons' first goal of the season is to no avail as City go down to the league leaders on a hot August day. Paul Farman saves a second half penalty from Aaron O'Connor as Tuesday's hat-trick hero Liam Hearn misses the game with a virus. City are down to 9th, 2 points behind 5th-placed Tranmere and now 7 points behind leaders Forest Green.

24 Chris Moyses reveals he may need to make changes to his defence if the goals conceded column continues to grow. Liam Hearn is fit and well again after missing the defeat at Forest Green through illness.

25 A City XI beats Gainsborough Trinity 6-1 at the Northolme in a friendly designed to give City's fringe players some game time. The goals are scored by Alex Simmons (3), Conner Robinson, youth team player Lewis Millington, and Andrew Wright.

26 Grimsby Town announce they have sold all 1,795 tickets for Saturday's game at Sincil Bank.

29 **Lincoln 1 (Rhead - pen) Grimsby Town 1.** Att: 5,849. A big police presence in the city ensures a relatively peaceful derby day. Liam Hearn fails a fitness test for the game against his former club, allegedly due to a hamstring injury. Former City captain Josh Gowling is sent-off in the first half for an alleged assault on Matt Rhead. Rhead scores the resulting penalty but City fail to hold on against 10 men. City slip to 11th, 4 points behind 5th-placed Gateshead and 9 points behind leaders Forest Green.

31 **Gateshead 2 Lincoln 0.** Att: 1,248. Chris Moyses rues another poor defensive performance as City slip to defeat in a poor game. Nat Brown and Jon Nolan make what proves to be their final appearances. City are now 12th, 6 points behind 5th-placed Cheltenham and 12 points behind leaders Forest Green.

September 2015

1 City sign 25-year-old winger Terry Hawkridge on loan from Scunthorpe United until 4 January.

5 **Lincoln 1 (Rhead) Wrexham 1.** Att: 2,628. Terry Hawkridge makes his City debut and gains an assist for City's equaliser against high-flying Wrexham. Liam Hearn is substituted after just 40 minutes. City slip into the bottom half (13th), 6 points behind 5th-placed Gateshead and a massive 14 points behind leaders Forest Green, who have won all 8 games. City are now closer to the relegation zone (5 points) than the play-offs.

7 City's away game at Boreham Wood is put back a day from Tuesday 24 November to Wednesday 25 November due to the Meadow Park ground being used by Arsenal U19s for a UEFA Youth League game.

9 Acting managing director Kevin Cooke believes the club is very close to agreeing a deal with the Co-op Bank.

10 Chris Moyses says his team has fallen two points behind the objectives set at the start of the season after a difficult opening set of fixtures. A win over Boreham Wood on Saturday will correct the deficit.

12 **Lincoln 3 (Rhead 2 - 1 pen, Simmons) Boreham Wood 1.** Att: 2,272. City trail at half time to struggling Boreham Wood despite dominating possession. Two very late goals give them the points in the first ever match between the two sides. City are back into the top half (10th), 4 points behind 5th-placed Woking and still 14 points behind leaders Forest Green, who have won their ninth straight game.

15 **Barrow 1 Lincoln 0.** Att: 1,233. A very poor performance on a very cold night sees Barrow leapfrog City into 13th place, with City slipping to 14th, their lowest position of the season. Paul Farman captains the Imps for the first time in the absence of Alan Power. They are now 6 points behind 5th-placed Wrexham, and 14 points behind leaders Forest Green, who have lost for the first time this season (2-1 at Woking).

17 City reveal that Jon Nolan put in a transfer request after the game against Wrexham on 5 September, unhappy at being rested for the game. No clubs have responded despite his name being circulated in the usual way. Nolan is willing to go out on loan but manager Moyses is keen to keep him at the club.

⇒ Liam Hearn admits to being frustrated by his continuing injury problems but asks fans to be patient.

19 **Kidderminster Harriers 0 Lincoln 2 (Power, Muldoon).** Att: 1,582. City enjoy a comfortable afternoon against bottom side Kidderminster, who are without a win all season. City are back up to 12th, 4 points behind 5th-placed Woking and 11 points behind leaders Forest Green, who have lost again (4-1 at Macclesfield).

22 **Lincoln 1 (Power) Altrincham 1.** Att: 1,893. City misfire again against struggling Altrincham, who have lost all 5 away games so far, scoring only 2 goals, and have the worst goal difference in the league. Lincoln are angered by the performance of Altrincham's Jake Moult, who somehow avoids a red card for a series of bad fouls; he is substituted after just 38 minutes to prevent him being sent off. City remain 12th, 4 points behind 5th-placed Braintree and 11 points behind leaders Forest Green, who have drawn against second-placed Cheltenham.

26 **Lincoln 2 (Hearn, Rhead) Torquay United 0.** Att: 2,467. Two goals in the first half are more than enough to see off cash-strapped strugglers Torquay. City are now up to 11th, just 3 points behind 5th-placed Wrexham and 8 points behind leaders Forest Green, who have lost again (1-0 at home to Gateshead).

29 Chris Moyses says he is unable to pursue his plans to loan out his younger players due to a raft of injuries in his squad.

October 2015

1 Jon Nolan joins Wrexham on a three-month loan with a view to a permanent transfer.

⇒ Matt Rhead says he is targeting 20 goals this season to fire the Imps into the play-offs.

2 **Guiseley 0 Lincoln 1 (Rhead).** Att: 1,279. A 14th-minute winner from Matt Rhead gives City the points in front of the BT Sport cameras. It is Rhead's 10th goal of the season. George Maris, later to join the Imps on loan from Barnsley, impresses for the home side in the first ever meeting between the clubs.

3 City sit 8th after the Saturday fixtures, just one point behind 5th-placed Dover and 6 points behind leaders Forest Green.

6 City win 3-1 at Lincoln United in an unofficial friendly to give some fringe players a run out. Alex Simmons, Callum Howe and Liam Hearn are the scorers. Approximately 250 people take advantage of free admission but donate £310 to the British Heart Foundation. Former Manchester City winger Adam Drury appears as a trialist. There is a full set of National League fixtures this evening, but for some unknown reason, City are not included. The omission gives them a game in hand for a spell.

10 **Chester 2 Lincoln 3 (Rhead, Everington, Power).** Att: 2,224. Kegan Everington scores his first goal for Lincoln. City's third successive away win sees them move back up to 8th, one point behind 5th-placed Tranmere and 9 points behind leaders Forest Green.

12 City are handed a tough draw in the fourth qualifying round of the FA Cup, away to Conference rivals Tranmere Rovers.

13 **Welling United 2 Lincoln 1 (Hearn).** Att: 702. Bradley Wood is sent off with 10 minutes to go, shortly before the relegation-threatened home side score the winner. It is yet another poor result against Welling, who have now beaten

Lincoln five times in a row. City slip back to 10th, 3 points behind 5th-placed Bromley and 9 points behind leaders Forest Green.

⇒ Striker Andrew Wright joins Lincoln United on a one-month loan.

14 Bradley Wood receives a one-match ban for his red card at Welling.

16 Defender Nat Brown joins National League strugglers FC Halifax Town on a month's loan to give him game time ahead of the busy Christmas schedule. Manager Moyses insists that Brown still has a role to play at Sincil Bank, but most fans believe they will not see him again.

⇒ BT Sport announces that City's game at Grimsby Town on 28 December is to be shown live on television.

17 **Lincoln 2 (Hawkridge, Hearn) Braintree Town 0.** Att: 2,565. Terry Hawkridge scores his first goal for City as they record their ninth straight win over high-flying Braintree. City are back up to 7th, one point behind 5th-placed Tranmere and now only 6 points behind leaders Forest Green, who have lost again (2-0 at home to Tranmere).

20 Lincoln City Supporters' Trust announces that 9 nominations have been received for membership of the Trust Board ahead of the Special General Meeting on 12 November. However, Trust rules mean that all 9 nominees will be elected unopposed. The 9 are Rob Bradley, Phillip Bird, Chris Elkington, Jean Foster, Ian Hodgson, James Lammin, Stephen Tointon, John Wilson, and Michael Foley. The last name causes much surprise among supporters.

24 **FA Cup 4Q: Tranmere Rovers 0 Lincoln 0.** Att: 3,729. An excellent rearguard action earns City a replay against their National League rivals.

26 City are drawn away to National League South side Whitehawk in the first round of the FA Cup if they can overcome Tranmere in tomorrow night's fourth qualifying round replay.

⇒ A further fund-raising campaign is launched by supporters using the Crowdfunder platform. *Moyses Mission The Next Goal* offers a similar range of benefits to the original campaign in exchange for pledges.

27 **FA Cup 4Q Replay: Lincoln 2 (Hearn, Robinson) Tranmere Rovers 0.** Att: 2,380. Two goals in the last 10 minutes see off ten-man Tranmere after goalkeeper Scott Davies is sent off for handball early in the first half. Matt Rhead misses a first half penalty but City do enough to earn an away tie at National League South side Whitehawk next month. The win also nets the club £12,500 in prize money.

28 City's scheduled game at Aldershot Town on Tuesday 10 November is put back by a day to Wednesday 11 November due to Aldershot's FA Cup tie against Bradford City being moved to Sunday 8 November.

29 City's FA Cup first round tie at Whitehawk will also be played on Sunday 8 November due to its inclusion within the BBC's interactive Final Score programme. The move earns City £12,500 in broadcasting fees.

⇒ Bob Dorrian reveals that plans for City's new 10,000-seat stadium may be lodged as early as next year after initial soil tests at the proposed site on Beevor Street prove positive.

30 Alex Simmons rejoins Boston United on a one-month loan.

⇒ City sign 19-year-old striker Kyle Wootton from Scunthorpe United on a one-month loan.

31 **Lincoln 0 Bromley 1.** Att: 2,550. City suffer their first home defeat of the season as the dangerous Moses Emmanuel strikes with 10 minutes to go for promotion rivals Bromley. Kyle Wootton makes his debut as a substitute. City are back down to 11th, 3 points behind 5th-placed Braintree and now 10 points behind leaders Forest Green.

November 2015

2 City are waiting to hear from Scunthorpe United whether they will allow on-loan striker Kyle Wootton to play in the FA Cup.

⇒ Lincoln City Supporters' Trust working party member Rob Bradley confirms that the cost of the Michael Foley court case (£95,000) was covered by insurers. Mr Bradley hopes the Trust can move forward once a new Trust board is elected at a special general meeting on 12 November.

3 Former City striker Delano Sam-Yorke is banned from driving for six months after being found guilty of speeding on Broadgate on 27 December 2014.

5 Delano Sam-Yorke appears in court again to answer a second speeding charge, this one dating from 10 December 2014 at the same location on Broadgate. He receives a fine and three penalty points.

6 Gary Charles loses his *quantum meruit* claim for £50,000 in unpaid wages against Lincoln City. The judgment in the case, which was heard over three days in July, also awards costs to the club.

8 **FA Cup 1: Whitehawk 5 Lincoln 3 (Rhead 3 - 1 pen).** Att: 1,342. Matt Rhead scores the first FA Cup hat-trick by a City player away from home for 114 years, but City go down to an embarrassing defeat to their National League South opponents. Alan Power is sent off in stoppage time after picking up a yellow card plus a straight red. 'Live' highlights of the game are shown during BBC TV's FA Cup special.

9 Alan Power receives a one-match ban for his red card at Whitehawk.

11 **Aldershot Town 1 Lincoln 2 (Wootton, Muldoon).** Att: 1,367. On-loan striker Kyle Wootton scores his first and only goal for the club. Aidan Grant makes his second and final appearance for City after Paul Farman injures a knee in training. Craig Stanley returns to action after missing two months with a hamstring injury. City are back up to 8th, one point behind 5th-placed Grimsby and 8 points behind new leaders Cheltenham. They have a game in hand over most of the sides above them.

12 Ritchie Bates is appointed City's new commercial manager.

⇒ The 9 new Lincoln City Supporters' Trust board members - Rob Bradley, Phillip Bird, Chris Elkington, Jean Foster, Ian Hodgson, James Lammin, Stephen Tointon, John Wilson, and Michael Foley - are officially confirmed at the Trust Special General Meeting this evening.

13 Elliot Hodge and Andrew Wright join Stamford on loan for one month.

⇒ Chris Moyses admits he did not always see eye-to-eye with former City striker Ben Tomlinson, but says he deserves a good reception when he returns tomorrow with Tranmere, where he is currently on loan from Barnet.

14 **Lincoln 1 (Waterfall) Tranmere Rovers 0.** Att: 3,176. Luke Waterfall scores his first goal for the club to give them their second win over Tranmere in a month. City move up a place to 7th, one point behind fifth-placed Braintree and still 8 points behind leaders Cheltenham.

16 Matt Sparrow receives a one-match ban following his fifth yellow card of the season against Tranmere.

19 Chris Moyses reveals he has five players out on loan to save on wages ahead of the transfer window opening in January. The money saved will go straight to his war chest.

⇒ Rob Bradley is appointed chairman of the Lincoln City Supporters' Trust.

21 **Torquay United 1 Lincoln 3 (Waterfall 2, Hearn).** Att: 1,752. Two more goals from defender Luke Waterfall give City their 6th away win of the season against strugglers Torquay. At long last, City have broken into the top five, and are now just 6 points behind leaders Cheltenham after they drew 1-1 with second-placed Forest Green.

25 **Boreham Wood 1 Lincoln 1 (Rhead).** Att: 681. City miss the opportunity to go third in the table as they turn in a disappointing performance against their relegation-threatened opponents in the first ever meeting between the clubs. Kyle Wootton makes the final appearance of his loan spell from Scunthorpe. With their game in hand now used up, City stay 5th, now 5 points behind leaders Cheltenham and 2 points ahead of 6th-placed Wrexham.

26 City are in shock as striker Liam Hearn announces he wants to move to National League rivals Barrow on loan. Hearn feels he is not being given enough game time as City try to manage his poor injury record. Fans feel Hearn is being lured away by the promise of more money: he has played for new Barrow manager Paul Cox before, and it is known that Cox is trying to rebuild his squad in the short-term. City manager Chris Moyses feels he has no choice but to let it happen, but the Lincoln fans are furious with Hearn. Some feel he is deliberately avoiding the game against his former club Grimsby, scheduled for 28 December. Even Chris Moyses suspects a case of 'Grimsbyitis'. Hearn's departure on the day the loan window closes leaves Moyses with no chance of finding a replacement.

⇒ City sign 25-year-old striker Nathan Blissett from Bristol Rovers on an emergency loan until 4 January. The loan is with a view to a permanent move. Chris Moyses points out that Blissett has been signed to replace Kyle Wootton, not Liam Hearn.

27 City's game at Grimsby on Monday 28 December is made all-ticket for visiting supporters.

⇒ Liam Hearn claims he is disappointed by Chris Moyses' reaction to his request to leave on loan. Countering Moyses' accusation that the move was engineered by his agent, the striker claims he does not have one. Hearn now fears that his future with Lincoln may be up in the air.

28 **Lincoln 1 (Muldoon) Welling United 1.** Att: 2,528. City's poor run against their lowly visitors continues with another disappointing result at Sincil Bank. Nathan Blissett makes his debut after joining on loan but makes little impression as a second half substitute. The midpoint of the league season is reached with City in 4th place, 7 points behind leaders Cheltenham. Unfortunately it proves to be the high point of the season, as they begin a steady descent down the table.

30 City are drawn away to either Northern Premier League Buxton or National League North Bradford Park Avenue in the first round of the FA Trophy. Saturday's third qualifying round tie between the sides was abandoned at half time due to a waterlogged pitch.

December 2015

4 City announce they have reached an agreement with the Co-op Bank regarding repayment of the outstanding debt. The deal comprises an annual payment of £25,000 per year until the debt is cleared. Chairman Bob Dorrian calls the deal 'financially damaging' but accepts that the Co-op has done all it can to assist.

⇒ City also announce that they have reached agreement with an unnamed investor to put a seven-figure sum into the club over the next five years. Acting managing director Kevin Cooke reveals that the first instalment may be available before Christmas. The investment does not involve a takeover of the club.

5 **Woking 3 Lincoln 1 (Rhead).** Att: 1,432. City's 5-game unbeaten run comes to a convincing halt with another defeat to another bogey team. Lee Beevers is sent off in stoppage time. City slip back out of the play-off places to 7th, level on points with 5th-placed Wrexham and 10 points behind leaders Cheltenham.

7 Lee Beevers receives a three-match ban for his red card at Woking on Saturday.

8 City will visit Bradford Park Avenue in the first round of the FA Trophy on Saturday 12 December after Park Avenue win 2-1 at Buxton in their third qualifying round tie.

10 Bob Dorrian confirms that some of the new investment will be used to strengthen the team with a view to reaching the play-offs, and will not be used to pay off existing debts. He also explains the deal with the Co-op Bank in more detail: the mortgage on PlayZone (£70,000) will be paid off using a loan from Dorrian; the club will then pay £25,000 per year for the next 10 years, followed by £10,000 per year for 5 years to repay the overdraft (£300,000). It emerges that Dorrian has personally guaranteed the deal against his own property.

⇒ The new investor is revealed as retired South African hedge fund manager and global equity investor Clive Nates. Nates will become a director immediately after investing an initial £300,000 in the club through his new venture Sportvest Capital LLP. His total investment will equate to around a 25% share in Lincoln City Holdings.

11 City sign 29-year-old striker Craig Reid from Brentwood Town on a non-contract basis with a view to earning a permanent deal. He has been on trial at Sincil Bank for the last couple of weeks, having originally been a transfer target during the close season.

⇒ Elliot Hodge's loan at Stamford is extended by a further two months.

⇒ City's match at Tranmere Rovers, scheduled for Saturday 26 March, is brought forward by a day to Good Friday.

⇒ Chris Moyses says a run in the FA Trophy is vital going into the second half of the season.

⇒ Clive Nates assures fans that he has no interest in taking over the club. He believes it should be run by local people and is very supportive of the role of the Supporters' Trust in it.

12 City's scheduled FA Trophy first round tie at Bradford Park Avenue is postponed due to a waterlogged pitch. The match is rescheduled for Wednesday 16 December.

14 City are drawn at home to Northern Premier League Nantwich Town in the second round of the FA Trophy if they can beat Bradford Park Avenue on Wednesday.

⇒ The second Crowdfunder appeal of the year - *Moyses Mission The Next Goal* - raises £2,680 towards the signing of a new player in the January transfer window.

16 City's rearranged FA Trophy first round tie against Bradford Park Avenue is postponed for a second time due to a waterlogged pitch. The tie will now take place on Monday 21 December.

17 Chris Moyses reveals that he has been inundated with calls from agents since the news broke of Clive Nates' investment in the club.

⇒ Lincoln City Supporters' Trust announces that Michael Foley has resigned from the Trust Board following suspension for alleged breaches of confidentiality.

19 **Lincoln 2 (Rhead 2) Barrow 2.** Att: 2,540. City throw away a 2-goal first half lead against a side with only two away wins all season. Liam Hearn is not allowed to play against his parent club, possibly for more than one reason. Matt Rhead scores both goals, the second a superb overhead kick from the edge of the box. Craig Reid makes his debut as the solitary point lifts City up a place to 7th, now 2 points behind 5th-placed Dover and 12 points behind leaders Cheltenham.

21 **FA Trophy 1: Bradford Park Avenue 2 Lincoln 1 (Muldoon).** Att: 360. City's plan to give game time to some fringe players backfires as they crash out of the Trophy to a side in the bottom half of the National League North. Reaction from fans and manager alike is not positive as City's terrible record in cup competitions continues. Chris Moyses calls the performance 'embarrassing' and apologises to fans.

22 Former Lincoln City director Keith Roe is co-opted onto the board of the Lincoln City Supporters' Trust.

24 Chris Moyses vows to strengthen his faltering side during the January transfer window, feeling that the existing players have had more than enough time to stake a claim for a place in the team.

26 **Lincoln 0 FC Halifax Town 1.** Att: 3,558. An unexpected defeat to struggling Halifax, the latest in a run of poor results at home to teams near the foot of the table. Nathan Blissett and Craig Reid fail to impress again, and make their final City appearances. City stay 7th, but are now 4 points behind 5th-placed Grimsby and 15 points behind leaders Cheltenham.

28 **Grimsby Town 2 Lincoln 0.** Att: 7,650. An early red card for defender Luke Waterfall sets the tone as the BT cameras see City go down easily to their Lincolnshire promotion rivals. Future Imps hero Nathan Arnold scores the second goal. A disastrous month has seen City pick up just 1 point from 4 games despite some relatively kind fixtures. They have now slipped to 9th, 5 points behind 5th-placed Dover Athletic and 18 points behind leaders Cheltenham. A bid for the championship, which had been so real just a month ago, is now undoubtedly over.

29 Luke Waterfall receives a one-match ban for his red card at Grimsby.

30 City announce that the home game against Forest Green Rovers, originally scheduled for Tuesday 23 February, has been brought forward to Saturday 16 January due to the fact that both teams are out of the FA Trophy.

31 Liam Hearn is recalled from Barrow, and accepts that he made a mistake in going there. A combination of bad weather, the FA Trophy and that league game against Lincoln means that Hearn has played just 80 minutes for Barrow when he could have been involved in six games had he stayed at Lincoln. He apologises to manager Moyses and to the Lincoln fans, but the fact remains that City have picked up just 2 points from their 5 league games since Hearn left, slipping from fifth to ninth. Despite Hearn alluding to personal issues that influenced his decision to leave, City supporters feel Hearn has disrupted their season and are not in a forgiving mood; they note that the Grimsby game has now been played.

January 2016

2 Wrexham decide not to extend the loan of Jon Nolan. The midfielder is now left with having to return to Lincoln, where many people feel Nolan has burned too many bridges.

⇒ City sign 19-year-old defender Patrick Brough from Carlisle United on a one-month youth loan.

⇒ **FC Halifax Town 2 Lincoln 2 (Stanley, Hearn).** Att: 1,932. Patrick Brough makes his debut, but Lincoln fail to beat 22nd-placed Halifax for the second time in a week. Substitute Liam Hearn scores in his first game since his recall, but many fans are still not happy. City are 8th, 5 points behind 5th-placed Macclesfield.

4 City cancel the contract of midfielder Jon Nolan by mutual consent. Chris Moyses feels it is in the interests of both parties that Nolan does not return to Sincil Bank.

⇒ Striker Nathan Blissett returns to Bristol Rovers at the conclusion of his loan. No move will be made to sign him permanently after he fails to make any impact.

⇒ On a busy day in the Sincil Bank departure lounge, striker Craig Reid leaves at the end of his short-term deal.

5 Legendary City striker Percy Freeman dies at the age of 70. A member of the famous Fourth Division championship-winning side of 1975-76, Percy was voted in second place in the League Legends poll. He scored 76 goals in 181 appearances, in two separate spells with the club between 1970 and 1977.

⇒ Tony Diagne formally extends his loan at Macclesfield Town until the end of the season.

⇒ Former City defender Dean West is appointed to the Academy coaching staff on a full-time basis. He has been assisting with coaching for the last 3 seasons.

6 Terry Hawkridge signs a permanent 18-month deal after his release by Scunthorpe United.

8 City sign 19-year-old striker Robbie McDaid from Leeds United on loan to the end of the season.

⇒ Alex Simmons joins Grantham Town on a month's loan.

9 **Lincoln 2 (Waterfall, Hearn) Dover Athletic 3.** Att: 2,402. Liam Hearn scores what proves to be his final goal for Lincoln as the winless run extends to 8 league games. Promotion rivals Dover twice come from behind to take the points, but are helped by a Paul Farman error and a dubious penalty. Robbie McDaid makes his first appearance after his loan move from Leeds. The game is preceded by a minute's applause for Percy Freeman. City are down to 9th, 6 points behind 5th-placed Eastleigh.

11 David Parman ceases to be a director of the club.

13 Chris Moyses reveals that he is looking to make signings in all three areas of the pitch, and has made offers for two current National League players. One is believed to be Chester striker Ross Hannah.

14 Chris Moyses misses out on one of his transfer targets, young West Bromwich Albion midfielder Samir Nabi, who is believed to be joining League Two promotion-chasers Oxford United.

15 Defender Nat Brown joins Conference North side Harrogate Town on a month's loan.

16 **Lincoln 0 Forest Green Rovers 1.** Att: 1,975. City go down to a late goal after Forest Green defender Aaron Racine is sent off. Since breaking into the top 5 in November, City have gone 9 league games without a win and slipped off the pace at the top of the table: they stay 9th, as no other fixtures have been played today, but most of the teams above them have at least one game in hand. This match has been brought forward from the scheduled Tuesday 23 February slot to fill a vacant date due to both sides being out of the FA Trophy (this is second round day).

19 City announce that they have turned down a five-figure offer from Barrow for striker Matt Rhead, which was received on Saturday morning. Chris Moyses responds by saying the offer might have bought Rhead's left leg.

21 Bob Dorrian says that Lincoln City is no longer a selling club after receiving recent investment.

⇒ Jack Muldoon agrees a one-year contract extension.

⇒ City confirm they have three players on trial this week: 22-year-old midfielder Josh Rees from Nottingham Forest, 20-year-old midfielder Billy Murphy from Bristol City, and youngster Joe Cuff who does not have a club.

⇒ Chris Moyses says he has the full backing of the board despite the current poor run.

23 **Wrexham 3 Lincoln 1 (Rhead - pen).** Att: 3,853. The bad run extends to ten league games since the last win, as City are well-beaten by a side that had lost its last 5 games. Patrick Brough plays his last match before returning to Carlisle. Liam Hearn also makes his final appearance. City are now 11th, 7 points behind 5th-placed Dover Athletic after taking just 4 points from a possible 30.

28 Scunthorpe United confirm that Lincoln have enquired about former Imp Andrew Boyce.

⇒ City sign 33-year-old defender Jamie McCombe from Stevenage on an 18-month deal. McCombe previously played for City between March 2004 and May 2006, and was part of the team that reached the League Two play-offs in 2004, 2005 and 2006. Manager Chris Moyses calls the acquisition of McCombe, 'a sign of intent'.

⇒ Chris Moyses confirms that three more players are on trial at the club this week: 25-year-old former Manchester City left-back Chris Chantler, 22-year-old winger James Caton from Shrewsbury Town, and 19-year-old midfielder George Maris from Barnsley. Maris played against the Imps for Guiseley in October.

⇒ BT Sport announces that City's game at Tranmere Rovers on Good Friday is to be shown live on television.

29 City sign 22-year-old winger James Caton on loan from Shrewsbury Town until the end of the season.

30 **Lincoln 1 (Bush) Guiseley 0.** Att: 2,265. Jamie McCombe and on-loan winger James Caton make their City debuts, as Chris Bush's first goal since his return to the club is enough to end a run of 10 games without a win. Craig Stanley breaks a foot and misses the rest of the season. Jack Muldoon captains the side following the loss of his father in the week. The play-offs are still a possibility, with City in 11th place, 5 points behind 5th-placed Tranmere.

February 2016

1 City confirm that Patrick Brough has returned to Carlisle at the end of his loan period.

⇒ City sign 19-year-old midfielder George Maris on a youth loan from Barnsley until the end of the season. Maris is the only signing on transfer deadline day.

4 Clive Nates is formally appointed to the board of directors.

6 **Lincoln 3 (Rhead, Caton, Muldoon) Eastleigh 0.** Att: 2,085. Three first half goals give City a comfortable win over play-off rivals. James Caton scores his first goal for the club, while George Maris makes his City debut as a second half substitute for Caton. City are now 9th, 2 points behind 5th-placed Eastleigh.

10 Chris Moyses intends to keep Jack Muldoon up front after his man of the match performance against Eastleigh. He also believes they can still make the play-offs, with only two matches remaining against teams in the top 5.

⇒ City reveal they are giving a trial to 23-year-old Gibraltar international Anthony Bardon. The midfielder is currently on the books at Lincoln Red Imps.

13 **Altrincham 3 Lincoln 3 (Rhead 2 - 1 pen, Muldoon).** Att: 1,293. Matt Rhead scores two goals to break Ben Tomlinson's Conference scoring record, although a missed penalty costs him a second hat-trick of the season. Future Imps Jonny Margetts and Josh Ginnelly score the first two goals, and an error by Paul Farman allows the relegation-bound hosts to snatch a point. An opportunity to close the gap on the top 5 is missed, as City slip to 10th, 3 points behind 5th-placed Dover.

15 Defender Nat Brown extends his loan at Harrogate Town by a further month; he will stay at Harrogate until 13 March.

16 City sign 19-year-old defender Courtney Wildin from Sheffield Wednesday on a one-month loan.

20 **Lincoln 3 (Caton 2, McDaid) Southport 1.** Att: 2,581. A James Caton-inspired City keep their play-off hopes firmly alive with their third win in four games. Substitute Robbie McDaid scores his first goal for the Imps. Conner Robinson appears in the first team for the last time, whilst Courtney Wildin makes his debut as a late substitute. City are up to 8th, 2 points behind 5th-placed Gateshead.

23 No game this evening due to the scheduled fixture at home to Forest Green Rovers having been brought forward to Saturday 16 January.

24 Elliot Hodge joins Gainsborough Trinity on a month's loan.

25 Saturday's scheduled game against Dover Athletic is rearranged for Tuesday 15 March due to Dover's involvement in the quarter-final of the FA Trophy.

27 No game today due to Dover's involvement in the FA Trophy. They are surprisingly beaten 2-1 at Nantwich Town of the Northern Premier League Premier Division.

March 2016

2 City slip to 10th while other clubs play their games in hand this evening.

3 City announce that Liam Hearn has rejected a loan move, preferring to stay and fight for his place. Chris Moyses reveals that two clubs were interested in taking Hearn - one from the National League, and one from the tier below.

4 Jack Muldoon reveals he has been offered a bonus by manager Chris Moyses if he can reach double figures for the season; he is currently on 7.

5 **Lincoln 2 (McCombe, Oastler own goal) Aldershot Town 0.** Att: 2,398. Jamie McCombe scores his first goal since his return to the club, while Matt Rhead misses a first half penalty. City are 8th, 5 points behind 5th-placed Tranmere, but several of the sides above them have 2 or 3 games in hand. To emphasise how badly the season has slipped since the midway point when City were 7 points behind leaders Cheltenham, the gap is now 25 points.

7 Chris Moyses confirms that Matt Rhead will take the next penalty despite having missed twice in recent games.

8 City slip back to 10th after promotion rivals Dover, Gateshead and Eastleigh all win games in hand.

10 Liam Hearn does a U-turn and joins Conference North side Harrogate Town on loan until the end of the season. City fans are adamant that he must not return.

⇒ City are giving a trial to 18-year-old Huddersfield Town defender Adam Porritt.

⇒ The AGM takes place at Sincil Bank, followed by a fans forum. The event is a far more enjoyable affair than in previous years due to the improvement in club finances, but there is still a loss of £191,595.

⇒ It is revealed at the AGM that City had agreed a deal to take a young player on loan from Everton in March 2002; unfortunately manager Walter Smith was sacked, and the loan was cancelled by new manager David Moyes. The player was a 16-year-old striker called Wayne Rooney.

12 **Macclesfield Town 1 Lincoln 1 (McCombe).** Att: 1,676. A goal from City centre-back Jamie McCombe, playing against his brother John, just about keeps City's play-off hopes alive. They stay in 10th place, 5 points behind 5th-placed Braintree, but those games in hand are beginning to look insurmountable.

15 **Dover Athletic 4 Lincoln 1 (Muldoon).** Att: 743. A heavy defeat effectively ends City's chase for a play-off position. Jamie McCombe picks up an injury as Dover's impressive form takes them up to 4th. This game was originally postponed from Saturday 27 February due to Dover's involvement in the fourth round of the FA Trophy. City are 10th, 6 points behind 5th-placed Braintree, but the games are running out. Realistically, City need 8 wins from the remaining 8 games to stand any chance of a play-off spot.

⇒ City extend the loan of Courtney Wildin from Sheffield Wednesday to the end of the season despite having used him only twice as a substitute.

16 Defender Nat Brown and striker Conner Robinson join Boston United on loan until the end of the season.

17 The Lincoln City Supporters' Trust decides to change its name to the Red Imps Community Trust at the Special General Meeting held at Sincil Bank. It also unanimously adopts a new set of Rules, which formed part of the judgement from the Michael Foley court case. The Rules will be submitted to the Financial Conduct Authority for approval.

19 **Lincoln 1 (Muldoon) Kidderminster 2.** Att: 2,178. City go down to a dreadful home defeat to bottom side Kidderminster, who are odds-on for relegation. Courtney Wildin makes his first start but it also turns out to be his final appearance for the club. The play-off dream is now well and truly over, with City in 10th place, 9 points behind 5th-placed Braintree. Questions are raised as to whether the side will actually finish in the bottom half. Fans are not impressed, and pressure grows on manager Moyses.

20 City's players are brought in for extra training sessions following their disappointing defeat yesterday. In Chris Moyses' words, "they have ruined my weekend, now I am going to ruin theirs."

21 Chris Moyses is determined not to let the season end with a whimper.

22 Clive Nates confirms he is still committed to Lincoln City despite witnessing Saturday's defeat to bottom side Kidderminster.

24 Adam Porritt joins City from Huddersfield Town on loan to the end of the season after a spell on trial.

25 **Tranmere Rovers 3 Lincoln 2 (Maris, McDaid).** Att: 5,366. City put up a brave performance in front of the BT cameras but go down to the promotion-chasing hosts. Bradley Wood is sent off for a deliberate handball, which he claims hit his chest; the TV cameras prove conclusively otherwise. George Maris scores his first goal for the club. City stay 10th, now 10 points behind 5th-placed Tranmere. A drop into the bottom half still looks unlikely, with 13th-placed Woking 7 points behind.

27 Bradley Wood is given a two-game suspension for his red card at Tranmere.

28 **Lincoln 1 (Waterfall) Gateshead 1.** Att: 2,142. The draw does neither side any favours, as City slip to 11th, 11 points behind 5th-placed Dover. They are now just 4 points ahead of 13th-placed Barrow, who are on a good run and have 2 games in hand. The bottom half beckons once more.

29 Robbie McDaid makes an appearance as a late substitute for Northern Ireland U21 in their 3-1 defeat to Scotland U21 at St Mirren Park. It is his 5th and final cap to date.

30 Chris Moyses reveals he has been involved in planning meetings this week with Bob Dorrian and Clive Nates.

April 2016

2 **Bromley 2 Lincoln 0.** Att: 1,200. Another mediocre performance sees Bromley leapfrog the Imps, who are now 12th, just a single point above Barrow and the bottom half. They are 12 points behind 5th-placed Tranmere with only 4 games remaining. Securing a place in the top half is now the Imps' main challenge.

⇒ Chris Moyses makes a cryptic comment after the game: "The results will come, maybe not with me, but they will come."

5 Manager Chris Moyses announces that he is to stand down at the end of the season. Moyses says he cannot sustain working 80 hours a week running his own business as well as managing Lincoln City. Fans are surprised, with some feeling he has taken the club as far as he can. Almost everyone acknowledges that he has been good for the club with his enthusiasm and the improvements he has made to the infrastructure.

⇒ Speculation begins immediately into who will replace Chris Moyses. Early suggestions include current managers Nicky Law (Alfreton), Billy Heath (North Ferriby), Dennis Greene (Boston United) and Gary Mills (Wrexham); out of work managers Ronnie Moore, Russ Wilcox and Rob Scott; former City stars Mick Harford and Steve Thompson; and current assistant manager Grant Brown. The debate also centres on whether City should go for an older experienced hand, or an up-and-coming younger manager with a point to prove.

6 Bob Dorrian says he is looking for an ambitious young manager, rather than a stereotypical old-school failure. He cites Braintree's Danny Cowley and Eastleigh's Chris Todd as the type he requires. The intention is to have a new manager in place by the end of the season. He also adds that he wanted Chris Moyses to carry on in the job, and is disappointed to see him go.

7 Chris Moyses says he would like to stay at Lincoln in some capacity. He does not have the time to continue coaching, but does not want to go back on the board as a director.

8 Former City captain Fred Middleton dies at the age of 85. Midfielder Middleton made 315 appearances (scoring 16 goals) for the club between 1954 and 1963, and was voted at number 60 in the Lincoln City League Legends poll.

⇒ Further speculation surrounding City's next manager is rife on social media and now includes Danny Cowley (Braintree), Paul Cox (Barrow), Marcus Bignot (Solihull) and Mark Bower (Guiseley). All four fit the profile of younger, already successful managers.

⇒ City have slipped into the bottom half of the table due to midweek results and go into the game against relegation-threatened Chester in 13th place; Chester are 17th, just 4 points clear of the drop zone and have just sacked manager Steve Burr.

9 | **Lincoln 2 (McDaid, Maris) Chester 1.** Att: 2,001. City hang on to record their first win in seven matches and lift themselves back into 11th place, but level on points with 13th-placed Barrow.

11 | Clive Nates reveals he is fully involved in the search for a new manager and will be flying over to take an active part in interviews. City intend to establish a short list of six by the end of this week. One candidate is of particular interest, having been on Nates' radar for some time. Nates is convinced that having the right man in charge will prove a big asset in attracting more investment to the club.

14 | David Preece announces that he has applied for the manager's job at Sincil Bank.

16 | **Southport 2 Lincoln 2 (McDaid, Wood).** Att: 961. Bradley Wood's first goal for City two minutes from time keeps them in the top half (11th), 1 point ahead of 13th-placed Bromley with 2 games to play. Chris Bush makes what proves to be his final appearance for City.

18 | Chris Moyses confirms that contract talks with players are on hold until City appoint a new manager.

⇒ North Ferriby manager Billy Heath is rumoured to be on City's short list. Former City player Frank Sinclair is also believed to have applied.

19 | Former Luton and Stevenage assistant manager Kevin Watson is the latest to be linked with Lincoln.

21 | City say they are expecting to announce the identity of their new manager following the May Bank Holiday. Chris Moyses confirms he is to be involved in the selection process.

⇒ Former Kidderminster and Chester manager Steve Burr and ex-Southport boss Dino Maamria are also linked with the City job.

23 | **Lincoln 2 (Rhead, Muldoon) Woking 3.** Att: 2,518. Matt Rhead becomes the first City player to score 20 league goals in a Conference season, while Jack Muldoon reaches his target of 10. Matt Sparrow makes his final appearance. City miss the opportunity to ensure a top-half finish for the first time, allowing Woking the opportunity to catch them on the final day. They are now 12th, but need at least a point at champions Cheltenham next Saturday to ensure a top half finish for the first time since relegation.

⇒ Bradley Wood is voted *Player of the Season* and *Away Player of the Season* by the fans. Elliot Hodge is handed the *Young Player of the Season* award by the management team.

24 | The Non-League Paper prints a story on its front page linking City with Liverpool legend Robbie Fowler, who is known to be looking for his first management role. It proves to be a rumour started by a photograph of Fowler with Clive Nates, taken at the Tranmere match last month.

27 | Former Macclesfield boss Steve King is believed to be on City's shortlist. King was manager of Whitehawk when they knocked City out of the FA Cup this season.

30 | **Cheltenham Town 3 Lincoln 1 (Waterfall).** Att: 5,055. City fail to spoil Cheltenham's promotion party with another disappointing performance. Greg Tempest, James Caton, Robbie McDaid and George Maris all make their final appearances for City.

⇒ City end the season by slipping into the bottom half to finish 13th; the form table over the last 10 games of the season shows City in 24th place. Over the second half of the season, only relegated sides Altrincham and Welling have picked up fewer points. City have now finished in the bottom half every year since relegation. They end the season 19 points behind the play-offs and a massive 40 points behind champions Cheltenham; the gap at the midpoint of the season had been just 7 points, with City in 4th.

May 2016

5 | Goalkeeping coach and former player David Preece leaves Lincoln after not making the shortlist for the vacant manager's job. Preece made 9 appearances for City.

⇒ North Ferriby United manager Billy Heath says he has had no contact with Lincoln about the position. Former Newcastle defender Steve Watson is believed to have applied, but it is not known whether he has been interviewed.

8 | Braintree Town's promotion dream is ended as Grimsby overturn a first leg play-off deficit to reach Wembley. Braintree's 2-0 home defeat means that manager Danny Cowley is now technically available.

⇒ Boston United's dreams of joining Lincoln in the National League are dashed as they lose 3-0 at North Ferriby United in the National League North play-off semi-final second leg; the Pilgrims lose 3-2 on aggregate. This means that Ferriby manager Billy Heath will not be available just yet, should he be offered the Lincoln job.

10 | City are linked more strongly with Danny Cowley as they move closer to naming Chris Moyses' successor. An official approach has been made, but despite confirming that talks have taken place, Cowley says it would be very hard to leave Braintree.

⇒ Braintree chairman Lee Harding believes Danny Cowley can do better than Lincoln, and adds that he is not certain Lincoln is a bigger or better club than Braintree. It is also revealed that Harding is a Lincoln City shareholder.

11 Lincoln target Danny Cowley says there are other clubs interested in him; they are believed to be League Two Notts County and National League rivals Tranmere Rovers.

12 Rumours begin to circulate that City have made their appointment, and that Danny Cowley is the man.

⇒ Danny Cowley resigns as manager of Braintree Town.

13 Danny Cowley is announced as City's new manager, to be assisted by his brother Nicky Cowley; the pair are to give up their PE teaching jobs at FitzWimarc School in Rayleigh, Essex, and go full-time with Lincoln from the 1st June. They have signed two-year contracts in the first instance. The new management team is unveiled at a specially-arranged fans forum at the Travis Perkins Suite; the appointment is extremely well-received by fans. Chairman Bob Dorrian confirms that Grant Brown's contract is due to expire shortly, the inference being that he is set to leave.

14 Danny Cowley attends the North Ferriby United v AFC Fylde National League North play-off final, ostensibly to check out one of next season's opponents. North Ferriby win 2-1.

15 City suffer a financial setback as neighbours Grimsby Town finally win promotion back to the Football League with a 3-1 play-off final win over Forest Green Rovers.

16 The players are at the club to meet the new management team; one-to-one discussions take place to enable them to assess each player's attitude.

17 Braintree Town players Matt Fry, Sam Habergham and Alex Woodyard are linked with a move to Lincoln.

18 Danny Cowley is named Fieldturf Manager of the Year at the National Game Awards, held at Chelsea's Stamford Bridge. Braintree midfielder and possible Lincoln transfer target Alex Woodyard is named Young Player of the Season.

19 The Football League announces proposals to create a new League Three from the start of the 2019-20 season; City chairman Bob Dorrian believes the changes could be positive for Lincoln, but many other club chairmen in the Football League and National League are more cautious.

⇒ Lincolnshire Co Operative Limited ceases to be a director of the club.

20 National League chairman Brian Barwick states he is 'very concerned' by the proposed reorganisation of football announced the day before.

⇒ Director Clive Nates believes City have appointed the best manager in the non-league game.

23 Lincoln announce the retained list: Matt Sparrow, Tony Diagne, Aidan Grant, Liam Hearn and Nat Brown are released; offers are made to Callum Howe, Elliot Hodge, Alex Simmons, Kegan Everington and Andrew Wright; Conner Robinson and Greg Tempest are not offered contracts but are invited back for pre-season training. Chris Bush and Craig Stanley have triggered contract extensions through appearances.

It is confirmed that Liam Hearn has already joined Ilkeston of the Northern Premier League Premier Division. Hearn leaves having scored 11 goals in 23 appearances in all competitions.

⇒ Greg Tempest immediately indicates on Twitter that he intends not to return for pre-season training. Tempest made 24 appearances in all competitions, scoring no goals.

25 Danny Cowley reveals he wants to build a squad of young, energetic players, and that he is looking to make at least 5 signings. He will operate with the same budget as Chris Moyses had last year; Cowley calls it competitive.

27 Danny Cowley promises that his Lincoln side will get better as the season progresses. His record confirms this: in 9 years as a manager, Cowley has won 6 manager of the month awards in April.

28 Conner Robinson announces on Twitter that he will not return for pre-season training. Robinson was one of only three players to have appeared for City in each of the first 5 seasons in the Conference, and scored 9 goals in 80 appearances.

29 City confirm they have accepted a transfer request from striker Matt Rhead, with Barrow and Wrexham in the hunt. Danny Cowley has already spoken to a number of potential recruits, with the intention of completing his summer business by the end of June.

30 Danny and Nicky Cowley start a week's holiday.

31 The discounted season ticket offer ends with sales up 70% on the same period in 2015.

SEASON 2015-16

NATIONAL LEAGUE

No.	Date		Opposition	Res	Att	Scorers	Farman, P	Wood, B	Waterfall, L	Muldoon, J	Beevers, L	Sparrow, M	Stanley, C	Howe, C	Rhead, M	Power, A	Simmons, A	Hodge, E
1	AUG	8	CHELTENHAM TOWN	1-1	2767	Hearn	Y	Y	Y	Y>	Y	Y*	Y	Y	Y		Y#	S>
2		11	Braintree Town	3-1	657	Rhead 2 (1 pen), Stanley	Y		Y	Y*	Y	S*	Y>	Y	Y	Y		
3		15	Eastleigh	1-1	1354	Muldoon	Y		Y	Y#	Y	Y	Y	Y	Y	S#		
4		18	MACCLESFIELD TOWN	5-3	2320	Hearn 3, Rhead 2	Y		Y	Y>	Y	Y	Y	Y	Y	S*		
5		22	Forest Green Rovers	1-3	1385	Simmons	Y	S#	Y	Y>	Y	Y	Y	Y	S*	S>		
6		29	GRIMSBY TOWN	1-1	5849	Rhead (pen)	Y	Y	Y	Y#	Y	S#	Y	Y	Y>	S*	S*	
7		31	Gateshead	0-2	1248		Y	Y>	Y	Y*	Y		Y#	Y	Y	S*		
8	SEP	5	WREXHAM	1-1	2628	Rhead	Y	Y	Y	Y	Y	Y	Y	Y		S#		
9		12	BOREHAM WOOD	3-1	2272	Rhead 2 (1 pen), Simmons	Y	Y	Y	Y#	Y	Y	Y*	Y	Y		
10		15	Barrow	0-1	1233		Y	Y	Y	S#	Y	Y	S*	Y	Y		
11		19	Kidderminster Harriers	2-0	1581	Power, Muldoon	Y	Y	Y	Y#	Y	Y	Y	Y	Y*	S#	
12		22	ALTRINCHAM	1-1	1893	Power	Y	Y	Y	Y	Y	Y#	Y	Y	Y	S#	
13		26	TORQUAY UNITED	2-0	2467	Hearn, Rhead	Y	Y	Y	Y	Y>	Y	Y*	S#	S*	
14	OCT	2	Guiseley	1-0	1279	Rhead	Y	Y	Y	Y	Y#	Y	Y	Y*	S*	
15		10	Chester	3-2	2224	Rhead, Everington, Power	Y	Y	Y	Y>	Y	Y#	Y	Y*	Y	S>	
16		13	Welling United	1-2	702	Hearn	Y	Y	Y	Y	Y	Y	Y	Y	S#	
17		17	BRAINTREE TOWN	2-0	2565	Hawkridge, Hearn	Y		Y	Y	Y	Y	Y	Y	
18		31	BROMLEY	0-1	2550		Y	Y	Y	Y*	Y	Y	Y	
19	NOV	11	Aldershot	2-1	1367	Wootton, Muldoon		Y	Y	Y>	Y	Y	Y*	Y	
20		14	TRANMERE ROVERS	1-0	3176	Waterfall	Y	Y	Y	Y>	Y	Y	Y#	Y	S#	
21		21	Torquay United	3-1	1752	Waterfall 2, Hearn	Y	Y	Y	Y	Y	Y>	Y	Y	
22		25	Boreham Wood	1-1	681	Rhead	Y	Y	Y	Y	Y	S*	Y*	Y	
23		28	WELLING UNITED	1-1	2528	Muldoon	Y	Y	Y	Y	Y	Y	Y*	Y	
24	DEC	5	Woking	1-3	1432	Rhead	Y	Y	Y	Y	Y	S*	Y	Y*	
25		19	BARROW	2-2	2540	Rhead 2	Y	Y	Y	Y	Y*	Y	Y	
26		26	FC HALIFAX	0-1	3558		Y	Y	Y	Y	Y#	Y	Y	S#	
27		28	Grimsby Town	0-2	7650		Y	Y	Y	Y*	Y>	Y	Y	
28	JAN	2	FC Halifax	2-2	1932	Stanley, Hearn	Y	Y	Y	Y	Y	Y	
29		9	DOVER ATHLETIC	2-3	2402	Waterfall, Hearn	Y	Y	Y	Y*	Y	Y	Y	
30		16	FOREST GREEN ROVERS	0-1	1975		Y	Y	Y	Y	Y*	Y	Y#	
31		23	Wrexham	1-3	3853	Rhead (pen)	Y	Y*	Y	Y	Y	Y	S*	Y	Y	
32		30	GUISELEY	1-0	2265	Bush	Y	Y	Y	S*	Y#	Y	Y*	
33	FEB	6	EASTLEIGH	3-0	2085	Rhead, Caton, Muldoon	Y	Y	Y*	Y	Y	Y	
34		13	Altrincham	3-3	1293	Rhead 2 (1 pen), Muldoon	Y	Y	Y*	Y	Y	Y	
35		20	SOUTHPORT	3-1	2581	Caton 2, McDaid	Y	Y	Y#	Y	Y>	Y*	
36	MAR	5	ALDERSHOT TOWN	2-0	2398	McCombe, OG	Y	Y	Y*	Y	Y>	Y	
37		12	Macclesfield Town	1-1	1676	McCombe	Y	Y	Y*	Y	S>	Y	Y	
38		15	Dover Athletic	1-4	743	Muldoon	Y	Y	Y	Y	Y	Y	
39		19	KIDDERMINSTER HARRIERS	1-2	2178	Muldoon	Y	Y	Y	Y	S#	Y*	Y	Y	
40		25	Tranmere Rovers	2-3	5366	Maris, McDaid	Y	Y	Y	Y	Y#	Y	S*	
41		28	GATESHEAD	1-1	2142	Waterfall	Y	Y	Y	Y*	Y	Y	Y#
42	APR	2	Bromley	0-2	1200		Y	Y	Y*	Y	Y*	Y
43		9	CHESTER	2-1	2001	McDaid, Maris	Y	Y	Y	Y	Y	S*	S>	Y*
44		16	Southport	2-2	961	McDaid, Wood	Y	Y	S#	Y*	Y	Y	S*	S>	Y
45		23	WOKING	2-3	2518	Rhead, Muldoon	Y	Y#	Y	Y>	Y	Y	Y	S#	Y
46		30	Cheltenham Town	1-3	5055	Waterfall	Y	Y	Y	Y	Y	Y
			Appearances				45	39	35	45	43	22	26	27	41	32	5	5
			Substitute appearances				0	1	1	1	1	4	2	0	2	6	12	3
			Goals				0	1	6	9	0	0	2	0	20	3	2	0

69 league goals

FA CUP

			Opposition	Res	Att	Scorers	Farman, P	Wood, B	Waterfall, L	Muldoon, J	Beevers, L	Sparrow, M	Stanley, C	Howe, C	Rhead, M	Power, A	Simmons, A	Hodge, E
4Q	OCT	24	Tranmere Rovers	0-0	3729		Y	Y	Y	Y	Y	S*	Y	Y	Y
4QR		27	TRANMERE ROVERS	2-0	2380	Hearn, Robinson	Y	Y	Y	Y#	Y	S*	Y	Y	Y
1	NOV	8	Whitehawk	3-5	1342	Rhead 3 (1 pen)	Y	Y#	Y	Y>	Y	Y	Y	Y	Y	S>

FA TROPHY

			Opposition	Res	Att	Scorers	Farman, P	Wood, B	Waterfall, L	Muldoon, J	Beevers, L	Sparrow, M	Stanley, C	Howe, C	Rhead, M	Power, A	Simmons, A	Hodge, E
1	DEC	21	Bradford Park Avenue	1-2	360	Muldoon	Y	Y	Y	S#				Y	S*	Y	Y>

LINCOLNSHIRE CUP

			Opposition	Res	Att	Scorers	Farman, P	Wood, B	Waterfall, L	Muldoon, J	Beevers, L	Sparrow, M	Stanley, C	Howe, C	Rhead, M	Power, A	Simmons, A	Hodge, E
QF	JUL	25	Boston United	0-0*	877		Y	Y	S#	Y#	Y	Y	S#	Y	S#
SF	AUG	1	Scunthorpe United	2-2#	1015	Power, Rhead	Y	Y	Y	Y#	Y	Y#	Y	Y	Y	Y	Y#

* City won 4-1 on penalties
\# City lost 5-6 on penalties

Key:
Y = full appearance
Y# = full appearance, first player substituted - by substitute S#
Y* = full appearance, second player substituted - by substitute S*
Y> = full appearance, third player substituted - by substitute S>

■ Red Card
▨ Yellow Card

88

	Nolan, J	Hearn, L	Bush, C	Everington, K	Robinson, C	Tempest, G	Brown, N	Hawkridge, T	Wootton, K	Grant, A	Blissett, N	Reid, C	Brough, P	McDaid, R	McCombe, J	Caton, J	Maris, G	Wildin, C	Harrad, S	Bignall, N
	S *		S #																	
	Y	Y #	Y	S >	S #															
	Y	Y *	Y		S *															
	Y *	Y #	Y		S #	S >														
	Y		Y #		Y															
	Y				Y *		Y													
	Y		S >	S #	Y		Y													
		Y #	Y					Y												
			Y	S *	S #			Y												
			Y	Y *	Y #			Y												
		S *	Y		S #			Y >												
		S *	Y					Y *												
		Y #	Y	S >				Y												
		S #	Y					Y												
		S *	Y		S #			Y												
		Y #	Y					Y												
		Y	Y	S #		Y #		Y												
		Y #	Y		S *			Y	S #											
		S #		S *	Y			S >	Y #	Y										
		Y *			Y			S >	S *											
		Y *		S >	Y #			S #	S *											
		Y #			S >			Y >	S #											
					Y #			S #			S *									
					S >	S #		Y #		Y >										
			Y	S *	S #			Y			Y #									
					Y			Y			S *	Y *								
			S *	S >	S #	Y		Y #												
	S *				S #	Y *		Y #					Y							
	Y				S *			Y #					Y	S #						
			S *	S #				Y					Y							
	Y #							Y					Y	S #						
			Y			Y		Y						S #	Y	Y				
			Y			Y		Y						S *	Y	Y #	S #			
			Y		S >	Y		Y #						S *	Y	Y	S #			
			Y			Y		Y						S #	Y	Y			S *	
			Y			Y #		Y						S *	Y	Y	S >		S #	
			Y			Y >		Y						S *	Y	Y #	S #			
			Y			Y *		Y						S *	Y >	Y #	S #	S >		
			Y			Y #		Y						Y			S *	Y		
			Y			Y *		Y						S #		Y				
			Y	S *				Y								S #	Y			
			Y					Y						S *		S #	Y #			
			Y					Y						Y >		Y #	S #			
			Y #					Y						S >			Y			
								Y						S >		S *	Y *			
						Y		Y #						S *	Y	S #	Y *			
	6	13	29	1	4	17	2	34	1	1	1	2	4	3	8	8	6	1	0	0
	1	7	2	12	13	3	0	4	4	0	2	0	0	13	0	4	7	3	0	0
	0	10	1	1	0	0	0	1	1	0	0	0	0	4	2	3	2	0	0	0

	Nolan, J	Hearn, L	Bush, C	Everington, K	Robinson, C	Tempest, G	Brown, N	Hawkridge, T	Wootton, K	Grant, A	Blissett, N	Reid, C	Brough, P	McDaid, R	McCombe, J	Caton, J	Maris, G	Wildin, C	Harrad, S	Bignall, N
		S #	Y #			Y *		Y												
		Y	Y *		S #	S >		Y >												
		S #	Y			S *		Y *												

	Nolan, J	Hearn, L	Bush, C	Everington, K	Robinson, C	Tempest, G	Brown, N	Hawkridge, T	Wootton, K	Grant, A	Blissett, N	Reid, C	Brough, P	McDaid, R	McCombe, J	Caton, J	Maris, G	Wildin, C	Harrad, S	Bignall, N
				Y #	Y	Y		Y		S >			Y *							

	Nolan, J	Hearn, L	Bush, C	Everington, K	Robinson, C	Tempest, G	Brown, N	Hawkridge, T	Wootton, K	Grant, A	Blissett, N	Reid, C	Brough, P	McDaid, R	McCombe, J	Caton, J	Maris, G	Wildin, C	Harrad, S	Bignall, N
	Y #	Y #	Y #		Y #	Y													S #	S #
	S #	S #	S #			S #														

Appearances & Goals 2015-16

	League			FA Cup			FA Trophy			Totals			Totals		Lincolnshire Cup		
	Apps	Subs	Goals	Apps	Subs	Goals	Apps	Subs	Goals	Apps	Subs	Goals	Apps	Goals	Apps	Subs	Goals
Jack MULDOON	45	1	9	3	0	0	0	1	1	48	2	10	50	10	2	0	0
Paul FARMAN	45	0	0	3	0	0	1	0	0	49	0	0	49	0	2	0	0
Lee BEEVERS	43	1	0	3	0	0	0	0	0	46	1	0	47	0	2	0	0
Matt RHEAD	41	2	20	3	0	3	0	1	0	44	3	23	47	23	2	0	1
Bradley WOOD	39	1	1	3	0	0	1	0	0	43	1	1	44	1	2	0	0
Terry HAWKRIDGE	34	4	1	3	0	0	0	1	0	37	5	1	42	1	0	0	0
Alan POWER	32	6	3	3	0	0	1	0	0	36	6	3	42	3	1	1	1
Luke WATERFALL	35	1	6	3	0	0	1	0	0	39	1	6	40	6	1	1	0
Chris BUSH	29	2	1	3	0	0	1	0	0	33	2	1	35	1	1	1	0
Callum HOWE	27	0	0	3	0	0	1	0	0	31	0	0	31	0	1	0	0
Matt SPARROW	22	4	0	1	2	0	0	0	0	23	6	0	29	0	2	0	0
Craig STANLEY	26	2	2	0	0	0	0	0	0	26	2	2	28	2	1	1	0
Greg TEMPEST	17	3	0	1	2	0	1	0	0	19	5	0	24	0	1	0	0
Liam HEARN	13	7	10	1	2	1	0	0	0	14	9	11	23	11	1	1	0
Conner ROBINSON	4	13	0	0	1	1	1	0	0	5	14	1	19	1	0	1	0
Alex SIMMONS	5	12	2	0	0	0	1	0	0	6	12	2	18	2	1	0	0
Robbie McDAID (L)	3	13	4	0	0	0	0	0	0	3	13	4	16	4	0	0	0
Kegan EVERINGTON	1	12	1	0	0	0	1	0	0	2	12	1	14	1	0	0	0
George MARIS (L)	6	7	2	0	0	0	0	0	0	6	7	2	13	2	0	0	0
James CATON (L)	8	4	3	0	0	0	0	0	0	8	4	3	12	3	0	0	0
Elliot HODGE	5	3	0	0	1	0	0	0	0	5	4	0	9	0	0	0	0
Jamie McCOMBE	8	0	2	0	0	0	0	0	0	8	0	2	8	2	0	0	0
Jon NOLAN	6	1	0	0	0	0	0	0	0	6	1	0	7	0	1	1	0
Kyle WOOTTON (L)	1	4	1	0	0	0	0	0	0	1	4	1	5	1	0	0	0
Patrick BROUGH (L)	4	0	0	0	0	0	0	0	0	4	0	0	4	0	0	0	0
Courtney WILDIN (L)	1	3	0	0	0	0	0	0	0	1	3	0	4	0	0	0	0
Nathan BLISSETT (L)	1	2	0	0	0	0	1	0	0	2	2	0	4	0	0	0	0
Nat BROWN	2	0	0	0	0	0	0	0	0	2	0	0	2	0	1	0	0
Craig REID	2	0	0	0	0	0	0	0	0	2	0	0	2	0	0	0	0
Aidan GRANT	1	0	0	0	0	0	0	0	0	1	0	0	1	0	0	0	0

| Own goals | | 1 | | | 0 | | | 0 | | | 1 | | | | | | 0 |

Players Used	League goals	FA Cup goals	FA Trophy goals	Total goals
30	69	5	1	75

Plus appearances in Lincolnshire Cup: Nick Bignall (1), Shaun Harrad (1).

Squad Numbers 2015-16

1	Paul Farman	16	Alex Simmons
2	Bradley Wood	17	Elliot Hodge
3	Greg Tempest	18	Lee Beevers
4	Craig Stanley	19	Robbie McDaid
5	Luke Waterfall	20	Andrew Wright
6	Chris Bush	21	Matt Sparrow
7	Jack Muldoon	22	Tony Diagne
8	Alan Power	23	Nat Brown
9	Matt Rhead	24	Kyle Wootton; Craig Reid; Courtney Wildin
10	Liam Hearn	25	Patrick Brough; Adam Porritt
11	Jon Nolan	26	Callum Howe
12	Terry Hawkridge	27	Jamie McCombe
13	Aidan Grant	28	James Caton
14	Conner Robinson	29	Nathan Blissett; George Maris
15	Kegan Everington		

National League Final League Table 2015-16

			Home					Away					Totals		
		P	W	D	L	F	A	W	D	L	F	A	F	A	Pts
1	Cheltenham Town	46	17	5	1	49	13	13	6	4	38	17	87	30	101
2	Forest Green Rovers	46	15	3	5	37	17	11	8	4	32	25	69	42	89
3	Braintree Town	46	13	6	4	24	12	10	6	7	32	26	56	38	81
P	Grimsby Town	46	13	6	4	44	17	9	8	6	38	28	82	45	80
5	Dover Athletic	46	13	5	5	43	22	10	6	7	32	31	75	53	80
6	Tranmere Rovers	46	12	2	9	31	23	10	10	3	30	21	61	44	78
7	Eastleigh	46	13	5	5	32	23	8	7	8	32	30	64	53	75
8	Wrexham	46	13	4	6	48	27	7	5	11	23	29	71	56	69
9	Gateshead	46	9	4	10	33	39	10	6	7	26	31	59	70	67
10	Macclesfield Town	46	10	5	8	28	21	9	4	10	32	27	60	48	66
11	Barrow	46	11	8	4	38	26	6	6	11	26	45	64	71	65
12	Woking	46	9	7	7	36	29	8	3	12	35	39	71	68	61
13	**Lincoln City**	**46**	**10**	**7**	**6**	**37**	**25**	**6**	**6**	**11**	**32**	**43**	**69**	**68**	**61**
14	Bromley	46	11	4	8	38	26	6	5	12	29	46	67	72	60
15	Aldershot Town	46	7	4	12	23	31	9	4	10	31	41	54	72	56
16	Southport	46	6	7	10	34	44	8	6	9	18	21	52	65	55
17	Chester	46	9	8	6	43	29	5	4	14	24	42	67	71	54
18	Torquay United	46	7	5	11	26	33	6	7	10	28	43	54	76	51
19	Boreham Wood	46	5	7	11	18	24	7	7	9	26	25	44	49	50
20	Guiseley	46	8	7	8	33	38	3	9	11	14	32	47	70	49
21	FC Halifax Town	46	6	10	7	35	43	6	2	15	20	39	55	82	48
22	Altrincham	46	8	9	6	34	30	2	5	16	14	43	48	73	44
23	Kidderminster Harriers	46	5	7	11	21	29	4	6	13	28	42	49	71	40
24	Welling United	46	5	6	12	21	33	3	5	15	14	40	35	73	35

Progress Chart 2015-16

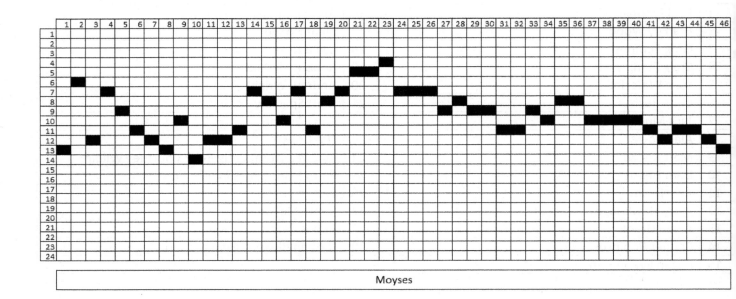

Moyses

Friendlies 2015-16

Jul	10	Grantham Town	3-0	444	Simmons, Nolan, Power
	17	Lincoln United	2-0	824	Waterfall, Harrad
	21	LEICESTER CITY	1-3	3693	Power (pen)
	29	NORWICH CITY U21	1-0	1501	Muldoon
Aug	5	Brigg Town	6-1	111	Hodge 2, Bush, Robinson, Hearn, OG
	25	Gainsborough Trinity	6-1	200	Simmons 3, Robinson, Millington, Wright
Oct	6	Lincoln United	3-1	250	Simmons, Howe, Hearn

Original Fixture List 2015-16

Aug	8	CHELTENHAM TOWN		17	BRAINTREE TOWN		13	Altrincham
	11	Braintree Town		31	BROMLEY		20	SOUTHPORT
	15	Eastleigh	Nov	10	Aldershot Town		23	FOREST GREEN ROVERS
	18	MACCLESFIELD TOWN		14	TRANMERE ROVERS		27	Dover Athletic
	22	Forest Green Rovers		21	Torquay United	Mar	5	ALDERSHOT TOWN
	29	GRIMSBY TOWN		24	Boreham Wood		12	Macclesfield Town
	31	Gateshead		28	WELLING UNITED		19	KIDDERMINSTER HARR
Sep	5	WREXHAM	Dec	5	Woking		26	Tranmere Rovers
	12	BOREHAM WOOD		19	BARROW		28	GATESHEAD
	15	Barrow		26	FC HALIFAX TOWN	Apr	2	Bromley
	19	Kidderminster Harriers		28	Grimsby Town		9	CHESTER
	22	ALTRINCHAM	Jan	2	FC Halifax Town		16	Southport
	26	TORQUAY UNITED		9	DOVER ATHLETIC		23	WOKING
Oct	2	Guiseley		23	Wrexham		30	Cheltenham Town
	10	Chester		30	GUISELEY			
	13	Welling United	Feb	6	EASTLEIGH	May	22	FA Trophy Final

Year 6

2016-17

1 Danny & Nicky Cowley officially leave their teaching jobs and are now full-time with Lincoln City.

2 Cheltenham midfielder Kyle Storer is banned for 8 matches and fined £750 for biting Bradley Wood during the National League match on 30 April.

⇒ Boston United striker Dayle Southwell reveals that Lincoln are one of the clubs chasing his signature, with other (unnamed) National League clubs also in the running.

3 Bradley Wood reveals he was left with a scar after the bite by Cheltenham's Kyle Storer.

⇒ Jack Muldoon signs the new one-year deal triggered by last season's appearances. The deal was agreed back in January.

4 Kyle Storer makes a full apology to Bradley Wood and his own club, manager and supporters.

⇒ The Red Imps Community Trust confirms that the Financial Conduct Authority has approved and registered the Trust's new rules.

7 Danny Cowley announces he is close to making three new signings: these are believed to be the three Braintree players, Sam Habergham, Matt Fry and Alex Woodyard. Cowley reiterates his desire to target players under 24 with a point to prove.

8 City deny they have received an offer of £25,000 from Barrow for striker Matt Rhead. City are still optimistic they can retain Rhead, who has a year left on his contract.

10 Managing director Kevin Cooke announces that season ticket sales are up 20% on 2015. He also confirms that every player offered terms for 2016-17 has accepted.

11 City reveal Danny Cowley's first signing: England C captain and Sportsbeat Young Player of the Season Alex Woodyard from Braintree Town signs a one-year deal with an option for a further year. Reaction from fans is very positive, and manager Cowley calls it 'a fantastic signing for the club'.

⇒ City target Sam Habergham is named in the National League All Star Team for 2015-16, but for some strange reason, Alex Woodyard - voted Player of the Season - misses out.

12 Braintree Town confirm that Sam Habergham has officially left the club, raising speculation that he is about to join former colleague Woodyard at Sincil Bank.

13 Callum Howe signs a new one-year deal.

⇒ James Caton is seen in a club video, undergoing fitness tests at Sincil Bank with the other players; speculation is rife that he is about to join the Cowley revolution.

14 Danny Cowley says Sam Habergham has received an offer from a League Two club and is on holiday considering his options. Rumour has it that Matt Fry has received an offer from York.

⇒ Cowley also confirms that they have received no bids at all for Matt Rhead and that the striker is still very much in their plans; as with the other players, he is undergoing a personal fitness plan ahead of the new season. He also states that James Caton is not due to sign despite suggestions from Radio Lincolnshire Sport that a deal is under discussion.

15 Defender Chris Bush is placed on the transfer list despite having triggered a contract extension through appearances, the first sign that the retained list may not relate too closely to the squad come August.

Cowley says that allowing him to leave will free up funds to bring in the four or five players he needs.

16 One of City's rumoured targets, former Braintree defender Matt Fry, signs for York City.

17 Danny and Nicky Cowley appear on *Friday Football* on Radio Lincolnshire. Among other topics, they state that two signings are in the pipeline for the next few days; they are hoping to sign at least one striker, possibly two; and they are looking to sign four, five or six players. Cowley also reports that striker Matt Rhead played out last season with a grade 3 tear in his groin, and has had a successful operation to repair it; and they have still received no offers for Rhead.

⇒ City launch the new kit for 2016-17: traditional red and white stripes with black shorts for home, green with white shorts for away.

20 Boston United say that City transfer target Dayle Southwell is to announce his destination in the next 48 hours.

21 City sign 20-year-old attacking midfielder Taylor Miles from Braintree Town on a one-year deal. A further signing is due to be announced tomorrow, believed to be a striker, with a further signing before the end of the week.

⇒ Danny Cowley admits he has lost out in his attempts to sign Dayle Southwell. He understands that Southwell is heading to a Football League club.

22 City miss out on another striker; a medical is planned for the player and the signing due to be announced formally, but he decides to sign for another club at the eleventh hour. The player is believed to be Pat Hoban, latterly on loan at Grimsby, who has signed for League Two Mansfield Town.

23 Transfer target Sam Habergham signs for City on a two-year deal. The 24-year old defender and current England C international joins from the Cowleys' former club Braintree Town. All three summer signings so far have come from Braintree.

⇒ Danny Cowley appoints two new members to his backroom staff: Mike Hine joins as head of medical provision and sports science, while physiotherapist Ross Poyton will assist on a consultancy basis.

24 Last season's assistant manager Grant Brown announces his departure from the club after 11 years on the coaching staff. The Imps' record appearance holder intends to stay in football in some capacity.

27 Pre-season training begins.

⇒ Fundraising initiative *Cowleys Campaign* is launched on the Crowdfunder platform, the intention being to raise funds for the playing budget. Every pound donated by fans will be matched by the mystery backer, who turns out to be supporter Ian Reeve. As previously, a range of benefits is offered in relation to the size of each donation.

⇒ Chris Bush signs for National League South side Chelmsford City.

28 City sign 25-year-old striker Adam Marriott from Stevenage on a one-year deal. Due to previous injury problems, the deal is linked to performance.

⇒ Danny Cowley says he would like to sign James Caton following his release by Shrewsbury. The 22-year-old striker is spending the week training with the Imps while Cowley tries to 'move things around' financially.

⇒ City appoint 42-year-old Jimmy Walker as their new goalkeeping coach. As well as short spells at West Ham and Tottenham, Walker made 533 first team appearances for Walsall.

29 Nottingham Forest cancel the pre-season friendly against the Imps, scheduled for 19 July. New manager Philippe Montanier has restructured his side's pre-season fixture list.

30 Ian Reeve and David Parman are appointed to the board of directors.

July 2016

1 City announce they are giving a trial to Peterborough United winger Jordan Nicholson. The 22-year-old is a similar type of player to James Caton, who is also training with the club. Danny Cowley states he is still looking to add two more signings - a left-sided player and a striker.

4 City announce they are to form an Under-21 side to play in the Lincolnshire FA U21 Development League next season. Danny Cowley aims to bridge the gap between youth team/academy football and the first team, which he feels is too wide. Up to two overage players and a goalkeeper can be fielded, providing a route back to fitness for players recovering from injury. The side will be managed by current Academy managers Damian Froggatt and Dean West.

⇒ Squad numbers are announced for 2016-17. Matt Rhead retains the No.9 shirt, increasing speculation that he is likely to remain at Sincil Bank.

6 The National League releases the fixture list for 2016-17: City start their new era away at Woking, as per the opening day three years ago. The Christmas/New Year double-header will be against minnows Guiseley, disappointing some fans who were hoping for York.

7 City announce that plans for their new stadium at Swanpool will be delayed following a decision by developers Taylor Wimpey to abandon plans to build 3,000 homes on the site. Chairman Bob Dorrian confirms that planning permission will not be applied for this year, as the club is relying on infrastructure from the housing development to make the required access to the site possible.

8 City confirm they are looking at former Hull City and Gainsborough Trinity striker Jonathon Margetts, who has been training with the club on a two-week trial. Former Chester defender Ryan Higgins is also training with the Imps. Both players are expected to appear in the two pre-season friendlies over the weekend.

⇒ City beat Grantham Town 5-1 at The Meres in the quarter-final of the Lincolnshire Cup in front of 524. Two first half goals from Terry Hawkridge, and three in the second half from Jonny Margetts (2) and James Caton earn City a semi-final against either Gainsborough or Lincoln United; therefore, the friendly already scheduled against either side will be used as the semi-final tie. City field trialists Jonny Margetts, Jordan Nicholson, James Caton, and Ryan Higgins. Paul Farman, Bradley Wood, Callum Howe and Jonny Margetts play the whole game, with the other 7 changed at half time.

⇒ Danny Cowley reveals that three proposed friendlies have been vetoed by the police on safety grounds.

9 City make it two pre-season wins from two games as they beat Worksop Town 2-0 with goals from youth team player Jack Weatherell and Peterborough United youth teamer Morgan Penfold in front of 317. City name trialists Ryan Higgins and Jordan Nicholson in the starting line-up, with the four players who played the full 90 minutes last night at Grantham - Paul Farman, Bradley Wood, Jonny Margetts and Callum Howe - not in the squad.

12 City announce the appointment of Chris Hubbard as their new company secretary. Hubbard joins from solicitors Bridge McFarland, and succeeds Jane Powell who left the post in May.

⇒ Jonny Margetts hits a first half hat-trick as City coast to a 3-0 friendly win over neighbours Boston United at York Street in front of 701. Trialists Ryan Higgins, James Caton and Jonny Margetts all start, while former Forest Green striker Aaron O'Connor plays the second half.

14 Jonny Margetts signs for City on a one-year deal. The 22-year-old striker has scored 5 goals in little over a game and a half during his trial spell. Fellow trialists Jordan Nicholson and Aaron O'Connor have left the club after failing to win deals.

⇒ BT Sport announce that the Torquay v Lincoln game on 3 September will be shown live on television with a 5.30pm kick-off.

16 City continue their promising pre-season with a 4-1 win over Championship side Reading at Sincil Bank in front of 1,239. Trialist James Caton and Jack Muldoon put City 2-0 up within the first 2 minutes against a young Reading side, with half time substitute Luke Waterfall adding a third 4 minutes after coming on. Bradley Wood adds a fourth with 6 minutes to go.

19 City draw 3-3 at Gainsborough Trinity in their latest pre-season friendly. Two goals by Jonny Margetts in the first 7 minutes are overturned as City trail 3-2 at half time. Trialist James Caton gets another run-out. Matt Rhead equalises in the second half in front of 555.

20 Manager Danny Cowley is not happy with his side's performance at Gainsborough, feeling only Matt Rhead and Jonny Margetts came out of the game with any credit.

23 Chairman of the Red Imps Community Trust Rob Bradley steps down after his position on the board of Lincoln City as Trust Supporter Director is not ratified by the club. He is replaced by Steve Tointon.

⇒ City exit the Lincolnshire Cup at the semi-final stage with a surprise 2-0 defeat at Lincoln United. The match features trialist James Caton, who plays the full 90 minutes, plus a substitutes' bench including 4 players from the youth team. Attendance: 815

25 City confirm that teenage midfielder Ellis Chapman has been sold to Premier League champions Leicester City for an undisclosed fee. The City U16 player will join Leicester's academy.

26 Young professionals Andrew Wright and Jenk Acar join Spalding United on three-month loan deals.

⇒ City come back from 2-0 down at half time to draw their penultimate pre-season friendly against an inexperienced team from League One Peterborough United. Goals from Jamie McCombe and Jack Muldoon ensure a share of the spoils, while Matt Rhead misses a second half penalty. Jordan Nicholson, who had a brief trial at Sincil Bank earlier this month, scores the second goal for the visitors. Peterborough winger Harry Anderson also catches the eye in front of 1,128.

⇒ Danny Cowley confirms that he has ended his interest in trialist James Caton after a deal could not be agreed.

29 City announce the signing of 29-year-old wide man Nathan Arnold from Grimsby Town on a two-year deal. The signing is made possible by the Crowdfunder scheme, which has raised £13,000 by this point.

30 Craig Stanley is placed on the transfer list. The 33-year-old midfielder triggered a further year through appearances but is being moved on to make way for incoming signings.

⇒ City complete their pre-season schedule with a 3-0 win over League Two Crewe Alexandra, with all three goals coming in the first 30 minutes. Adam Marriott marks his first game with a goal after 2 minutes and then adds a second, with the other goal from Jack Muldoon. Sam Habergham plays the first half, as does Nathan Arnold. Attendance: 1,058.

August 2016

2 Erstwhile City transfer target James Caton surprisingly joins Southport.

3 Matt Rhead withdraws his transfer request and signs a one-year contract extension which takes him to the end of 2017-18 season. Part of the new terms involves him training at his home in Stoke on a Monday instead of commuting to Lincoln. Manager Danny Cowley says it is 'like a new signing' for the club.

⇒ City complete the signing of 23-year-old centre half Sean Raggett from Dover Athletic on a two-year deal. The left-sided England C defender had been targeted by Liverpool, Everton and Crystal Palace towards the end of last season and is viewed as another great signing for the club. The transfer fee will be set by tribunal.

6 **Woking 1 Lincoln 3 (Rhead 2 - 1 pen, Marriott).** Att: 1,592. An excellent 407 travelling fans see City get the Cowley era under way with a fine win at bogey team Woking, their first away win since November. Adam Marriott puts City ahead on his debut, assist by Matt Rhead; Rhead scores the other two but also misses a penalty. City are 3rd in the first league table of the season. Adam Marriott, Sam Habergham, Alex Woodyard, Nathan Arnold, Jonny Margetts and Taylor Miles all make their debuts. Miles has an eventful game, appearing as a 78th-minute substitute, picking up a yellow card on 83 minutes, and breaking his ankle on 88 minutes; he will miss at least 6 weeks.

8 Danny Cowley reveals he has been watching an English player currently plying his trade in India. The search for a central midfielder has intensified following the injury to Taylor Miles.

9 **Lincoln 6 North Ferriby United 1 (Rhead 2 - 1 pen, Arnold, Waterfall, Margetts, Wood).** Att: 3,622. Danny Cowley's first home game sees the Imps 4-0 up after 24 minutes and is the first time for 10 years that City have scored 6 in a game. Sean Raggett makes his City debut while Jonny Margetts scores on his first start. An excellent attendance sees City move to the top of the table after 2 games. Matt Rhead tops the National League scoring chart with 4.

11 Kegan Everington joins Buxton on a four-week loan.

12 Taylor Miles visits a specialist in London to assess his broken ankle.

13 **Lincoln 1 (Habergham) Sutton United 3.** Att: 3,195. Nothing goes right for league leaders Lincoln as they lose Matt Rhead to a hamstring injury, go a goal down and have Bradley Wood sent off within the first 30 minutes. Very poor refereeing contributes as City equalise, only to lose to two goals in the last 7 minutes as they chase the win. City slip to 4th, 3 points behind new leaders Tranmere who are the only team left with 100% record after just 3 games.

16 City sign 19-year-old winger Harry Anderson from Peterborough United on a youth loan until the New Year. Anderson played against the Imps in a friendly at the end of last month.

⇒ **Dagenham & Redbridge 1 Lincoln 0.** Att: 1,399. City go down to their second successive defeat. Matt Rhead misses the game with his hamstring injury. City have the chances to equalise but miss them all. Harry Anderson makes his City debut as a second half substitute and impresses with his speed. City slip to 14th, 6 points behind leaders Tranmere.

| 17 | City's bid to sign former Leicester, Oldham and Shrewsbury winger James Wesolowski stalls over personal terms. The 28-year-old player has missed the majority of the last 18 months due to two serious cruciate ligament injuries.

| 20 | **Lincoln 4 (Margetts 4) Southport 0.** Att: 2,440. Jonny Margetts scores all 4, including a 'perfect' first half hat-trick (header, right foot, left foot) plus a penalty in the second half. Terry Hawkridge misses another penalty at 3-0. Margetts is the first City player to score 4 in a game since Jamie Forrester at Mansfield on 26/8/2006, and the first to score 4 at Sincil Bank since Tony Lormor against Carlisle on 11/5/1991. City move back up to 8th place, 6 points behind leaders Tranmere who still have a 100% record, and 1 point behind 5th-placed Solihull Moors.

⇒ The *Cowleys Campaign* Crowdfunder passes £25,000 in pledges.

⇒ Danny Cowley confirms there will be some ins and outs in the early part of next week as he continues to shape his squad.

| 22 | The *Cowleys Campaign* fundraiser closes with a total of £27, 522 raised; with director Ian Reeve matching the first £25,000, the total raised is £52,522.

| 23 | Craig Stanley joins National League rivals Southport on a one-month loan.

| 24 | Managing director Kevin Cooke states that an extra £90,000 will go towards the playing budget and towards running costs if attendances remain above 3,000 (current average 3,058). Cooke confirms that the club is at its most financially stable since relegation.

| 25 | Callum Howe joins Conference rivals Southport on a one-month loan, following fellow Imp Craig Stanley to Haig Avenue.

| 27 | **Macclesfield Town 1 Lincoln 2 (Anderson, Marriott).** Att: 1,650. City come back from a half time deficit to win with goals from Harry Anderson and substitute Adam Marriott. City move up to 4th, 4 points behind leaders Tranmere who lose their 100% record by drawing at struggling Southport. It is the first time since relegation that City have come back to win a league match away from home after being behind at half time; they have lost on the previous 19 occasions.

| 29 | **Lincoln 3 (Raggett, Arnold, Marriott) Gateshead 0.** Att: 3,687. The largest attendance of the season so far sees City defeat promotion rivals Gateshead with some ease. They are up to 3rd, 4 points behind leaders Tranmere.

| 31 | Top scorer Jonny Margetts joins Scunthorpe United for an undisclosed fee just 49 days after signing for the Imps. Margetts leaves having scored 5 goals in 7 appearances. Including pre-season games, he scored 12 goals in 11 games.

September 2016

| 1 | Lincoln approach Colchester United with a view to taking 20-year-old striker Macauley Bonne on loan. They are also linked with Braintree striker Simeon Akinola following last night's departure of Jonny Margetts to Scunthorpe.

| 2 | Macauley Bonne signs on a youth loan until 26 October, the day he turns 21; the loan may be converted to a full loan at that point.

| 3 | **Torquay United 1 Lincoln 2 (Rhead 2 - 1 pen).** Att: 2,061. A 93rd-minute winner by Matt Rhead on a dreadful Saturday evening moves 3rd-placed City to within one point of new leaders Forest Green, who win 2-1 at Chester. Previous leaders Tranmere are beaten 3-1 at Aldershot. Macauley Bonne makes his debut as a second half substitute in front of the BT Sport cameras. City win four successive matches for the first time since relegation.

| 7 | Elliot Hodge joins Stafford Rangers on a one-month loan.

| 8 | Taylor Miles visits a specialist with a view to returning to training by the end of this week. The news is good - the break is not as bad as originally feared.

| 10 | **Tranmere Rovers 0 Lincoln 1 (Bonne).** Att: 5,274. A second half goal from on-loan Macauley Bonne sends City to the top of the table after previous leaders Forest Green lose 4-3 at Dover in the televised lunchtime game. City have now won 5 games in a row for the first time since January/February 2011.

| 12 | City sign 30-year-old midfielder Tom Champion from Barnet on a three-month loan. The move is with a view to a permanent transfer.

| 13 | Alex Simmons joins FC Halifax Town on a three-month loan.

⇒ **Lincoln 0 Solihull Moors 0.** Att: 4,049. City misfire and fail to score against a poor Solihull team in front of the largest crowd of the season to date. Tom Champion makes a disappointing debut. Despite the draw, City stay a point clear at the top of the table on a very hot night.

| 14 | Danny Cowley denies he has made an offer for Alfreton Town midfielder Dan Bradley.

| 15 | City confirm that they have spoken to Dover Athletic about striker Ricky Miller; reaction from Dover manager Chris Kinnear is not positive.

| 17 | **Lincoln 1 (Arnold) Barrow 2.** Att: 3,578. City slip to third as a late goal against the run of play sends them to defeat. They are two points behind new leaders Dagenham & Redbridge.

| 21 | Rumoured transfer target Dan Bradley signs for AFC Fylde of the National League North for a five-figure fee. He is given a three-year contract, suggesting his choice of club may have been a financial decision.

| 24 | **Dover Athletic 2 Lincoln 0.** Att: 1,209. A poor performance sees City slip to 5th, 5 points behind leaders Dagenham & Redbridge. Sean Raggett is taken off injured against his former club after just 7 minutes.

| 26 | Craig Stanley leaves City by mutual consent after his one-month loan at Southport comes to an end.

⇒ Callum Howe extends his loan at Southport by a further four weeks.

⇒ BT Sport announces that City's game at Forest Green Rovers on Saturday 19 September will be shown live.

27 City announce that Software Europe have extended their sponsorship deal by a further two years.

28 It emerges that former Derby County striker Theo Robinson is on trial with the Imps after he scores for them in a 3-1 behind-closed-doors friendly defeat at Peterborough today.

29 Rumours circulate that Adam Marriott broke an elbow during the friendly at Peterborough; this is not confirmed by the club.

October 2016

1 **Lincoln 3 (Arnold, Waterfall, Muldoon) Braintree Town 0.** Att: 3,554. City return to winning ways with their 10th successive victory over the Essex side. City are back up to 4th in the table, 3 points behind leaders Dagenham & Redbridge.

⇒ Danny Cowley confirms that Adam Marriott did injure an elbow during the friendly at Peterborough. Initial X-rays have been inconclusive, so they are to be done again on Monday.

⇒ New Braintree Town manager Hakan Hayrettin announces that Lincoln have made a bid for striker Simeon Akinola, and that the offer will be considered by the Braintree board.

⇒ Former City manager David Herd dies at the age of 82. The former Arsenal and Manchester United legend managed the club between early 1971 and late 1972 and is remembered for reviving City's fortunes after 10 years of struggle.

3 City are drawn at home to National League rivals Guiseley in the FA Cup fourth qualifying round. It is seen as a great draw, as struggling Guiseley have just 3 points from their 13 league games so far.

4 **Wrexham 1 Lincoln 2 (Waterfall, Anderson).** Att: 3,847. A 2-0 half time lead proves enough to move City back up to 2nd in the table, 2 points behind new leaders Forest Green Rovers. Former City defender Hamza Bencherif scores a late 25-yard consolation for Wrexham. FA Cup opponents Guiseley win for the first time this season with a 6-1 thumping of York City.

7 Elliot Hodge extends his loan at Stafford Rangers to 17 January.

⇒ Danny Cowley denies he is interested in Boston United midfielder Liam Agnew.

8 City sign 27-year-old Jamaican international striker Theo Robinson on non-contract terms. Robinson has been unattached since leaving Port Vale in the summer.

⇒ **Bromley 1 Lincoln 1 (Anderson).** Att: 1,511. A defensive error by substitute Tom Champion costs City a win, while Theo Robinson makes his debut as a late substitute. City slip to 3rd in the table, 4 points behind leaders Forest Green Rovers.

11 Adam Marriott has a scan on his elbow after a second x-ray proves inconclusive.

12 Taylor Miles is set to return to full training in the next few weeks.

13 Macauley Bonne returns to Colchester United after his loan period is ended early.

⇒ City believe that Adam Marriott did not break his elbow as originally feared; a dislocation and ligament damage is the preferred diagnosis.

14 Danny Cowley reveals he is close to making a new signing, whom he describes as 'an attacking player who will help with our combination play'. The player is rumoured to be Nuneaton Town's England C midfielder Elliott Whitehouse.

15 **FA Cup 4Q: Lincoln 0 Guiseley 0.** Att: 2,629. Despite dominating the majority of the match, City are held by struggling National League side Guiseley in the FA Cup qualifier. The attendance is boosted by entry discounted to £10.

17 City will face a home tie against National League North strugglers Altrincham in the first round of the FA Cup if they can overcome Guiseley in tomorrow night's replay.

18 **FA Cup 4Q Replay: Guiseley 1 Lincoln 2 (Robinson 2).** Att: 765. Two goals from Theo Robinson on his first start are enough to put City through to host Altrincham in the first round of the FA Cup. The win earns City £12,500 in prize money.

19 Barnet recall midfielder Tom Champion from his three-month loan after a month; they have slipped into the bottom two of League Two and apparently are set to make changes. City supporters welcome the decision, feeling Champion did not fit Lincoln's style of play.

⇒ Three City players - Sam Habergham, Sean Raggett and Alex Woodyard - are called up by England C for the International Challenge Trophy game against Estonia U23 in Tallinn on 15 November. Transfer target Elliott Whitehouse of Nuneaton Town is also included in the 16-man squad.

20 City sign 22-year-old attacking midfielder Elliott Whitehouse from Nuneaton Town for an undisclosed fee. Whitehouse signs a contract to the end of the 2017-18 season after City beat off competition from National League rivals Eastleigh.

22 **Lincoln 0 Eastleigh 0.** Att: 3,180. Elliott Whitehouse makes his debut as a second half substitute as City fail to make their dominance pay against promotion rivals Eastleigh. They stay 3rd in the league, 6 points behind leaders Forest Green.

24 Danny Cowley suggests striker Adam Marriott and midfielder Taylor Miles may be back in contention for selection for the FA Cup tie against Altrincham.

⇒ Cowley also distances himself from the vacant manager's position at Grimsby Town after Paul Hurst's departure for Shrewsbury Town.

25 **Lincoln 2 (Arnold, Rhead) Boreham Wood 0.** Att: 3,014. A very good team performance inflicts the first away defeat of the season on visitors Boreham Wood; it is also the first time they have conceded more than 1 goal in a game. Lee Beevers dislocates his right knee in the first half and is out for the rest of the season. City stay 3rd in the league, 6 points behind leaders Forest Green.

⇒ Danny Cowley again reiterates his commitment to Lincoln in light of increased speculation about the vacant Grimsby job.

27 Danny Cowley confirms that Lee Beevers suffered a ruptured patella tendon against Boreham Wood and had an operation yesterday morning. No time scale has been set for his return.

28 BT Sport announces that the Lincoln City v Dover Athletic match, scheduled for Saturday 21 January, will be televised live. The game will be moved to Friday 20 January with a 7.45pm kick-off.

29 **Chester 2 Lincoln 5 (Robinson, Rhead, Raggett, Muldoon, Anderson).** Att: 2,586. An excellent display from the Imps against a side unbeaten in 9 league games takes them back up to 2nd in the table, 4 points behind leaders Forest Green. Matt Rhead scores one and has a hand in the other four against a side boasting 8 clean sheets from their last 9 games.

31 Theo Robinson is credited with Lincoln's first goal at Chester. Originally credited to Matt Rhead, television replays show the ball came back off the post and in off Robinson.

November 2016

3 Danny Cowley issues another statement dismissing speculation linking him with the vacant manager's job at Grimsby Town.

4 Danny Cowley is named Vanarama National League Manager of the Month for October.

⇒ Scunthorpe United manager Graham Alexander says Jonny Margetts is still in his plans amidst rumours of a return to Lincoln on loan. Margetts has made just one solitary appearance for the Iron since his move from Sincil Bank at the end of August.

5 **FA Cup 1: Lincoln 2 (Raggett, Power) Altrincham 1.** Att: 3,529. A host of missed chances almost costs dominant City a place in the second round as they concede a late goal. Alan Power scores his first goal of the season. Admission prices are again set at £10, but the £18,000 prize money will offset that.

⇒ City's success in reaching the second round of the FA Cup means that the scheduled National League game away to Solihull Moors on 3 December will need to be rearranged.

7 City are drawn at home to League One strugglers Oldham Athletic in the second round of the FA Cup.

8 City's game at Solihull Moors, originally scheduled for Saturday 3 December, is rearranged for Tuesday 20 December.

11 BT Sport announces that the Lincoln v Oldham FA Cup second round tie will be shown live; the game will take place on Monday 5 December. Both clubs will receive £72,000 for the broadcast.

⇒ Taylor Miles joins Boston United on a one-month loan to give him game time following his recovery from a broken ankle.

12 **Lincoln 3 (Arnold 2, Rhead) Aldershot Town 3.** Att: 3,461. An equaliser from Matt Rhead in the sixth minute of stoppage time earns the Imps a point to extend their unbeaten run to 10 games. All 7 of Nathan Arnold's goals have come at Sincil Bank. City stay 2nd in the league, 9 points behind leaders Forest Green.

⇒ Sean Raggett is forced to withdraw from the England C squad for Tuesday's game in Estonia due to a facial injury suffered towards the end of today's game against Aldershot.

13 Sam Habergham is also forced to withdraw from the England C squad following an x-ray to an ankle injury incurred against Aldershot.

15 Elliott Whitehouse and Alex Woodyard start for England C in their 2-1 win in Estonia, with Woodyard captaining the side for the third time. Whitehouse heads England in front after 7 minutes as England reach the final of the International Challenge Trophy, where they will meet Slovakia.

17 First-year professional Andrew Wright joins Grantham Town on loan until the New Year.

⇒ Director Clive Nates confirms that the television money from City's FA Cup second round tie against Oldham will go straight into Danny Cowley's playing budget.

19 **Forest Green Rovers 2 Lincoln 3 (Woodyard, Waterfall, Raggett).** Att: 2,164. City come back from 2-down with 21 minutes to go to win a crucial game that kicks off at 12.15pm for the benefit of the BT Sport cameras. A goal from Alex Woodyard means that every regular outfield player has scored this season. City remain in 2nd place, now 6 points behind leaders Forest Green with a game in hand.

21 Sean Raggett receives a one-match ban following his fifth yellow card of the season at Forest Green. He will miss Tuesday evening's game at York.

⇒ Lincoln recall centre half Callum Howe from his loan at Southport with one game of his loan spell remaining.

22 **York City 1 Lincoln 4 (Whitehouse, Arnold, Waterfall, Wood).** Att: 2,889. Callum Howe makes his first appearance of the season in place of the suspended Sean Raggett, whilst Elliott Whitehouse makes his first start. Harry Anderson misses the game through injury, but City hardly miss him as they take their goal tally to 50 for the season. The unbeaten run is now 12 games, 9 in the league. City stay in 2nd place, 4 points behind leaders Forest Green who drew 2-2 at home to third-placed Tranmere.

24 The Football Association announces that the draw for the third round of the FA Cup on Monday 5 December will take place at BT Tower in London, and not at Sincil Bank. The decision breaks the recent tradition of hosting the draw from the venue of the last televised match, which this year is the Lincoln v Oldham second round tie.

26 **Lincoln 2 (Robinson, Rhead) Maidstone United 0.** Att: 3,917. Second half goals by Theo Robinson and Matt Rhead give a dominant City the points. Rhead now has 10 for the season. City stay in 2nd place, just 1 point behind leaders Forest Green with a game in hand.

28 City are drawn away to Evo Stik League Division One (South) leaders Shaw Lane AFC in the first round of the FA Trophy.

29 **Lincoln 1 Wrexham 0.** Att: 3,344. City win their game in hand on leaders Forest Green to go top of the National League despite the 31st-minute sending-off of Sean Raggett. Matt Rhead misses a penalty but a sterling rearguard action in the second half ensures the unbeaten run is extended to 14 games. Paul Farman makes his 200th appearance for Lincoln as the season reaches the halfway stage.

30 City announce they are considering an appeal over Sean Raggett's red card against Wrexham.

⇒ City's FA Trophy tie at Shaw Lane AFC is moved to Sunday 11th December with a 1pm kick-off. The game will be all-ticket for Lincoln fans.

December 2016

1 Sean Raggett receives a three-game ban for his red card against Wrexham.

2 Elliot Hodge joins AFC Telford United on a one-month loan.

3 City have no game today by virtue of their FA Cup second round tie against Oldham being moved to Monday night for television purposes. Tranmere Rovers score a 93rd-minute winner against lowly York City to go above the Imps in the league table; York slip to the very bottom just 7 months after relegation from the Football League.

⇒ Bob Dorrian confirms that negotiations have been opened with Danny Cowley, Nicky Cowley and Alex Woodyard regarding contract extensions.

4 Barrow's 2-1 win at League One side Bristol Rovers in the second round of the FA Cup means that City's National League game at Holker Street, scheduled for Saturday 7th January, will have to be rearranged.

5 Just minutes before their second round tie is due to start, City or Oldham Athletic are drawn away to Championship side Ipswich Town in the third round of the FA Cup.

⇒ **FA Cup 2: Lincoln 3 (Robinson 2, Hawkridge) Oldham Athletic 2.** Att: 7,012. City lead 3-0 before two late goals from the League 1 side provide a nervy ending in front of the largest crowd at Sincil Bank since relegation. Jamie McCombe deputises for the suspended Sean Raggett as City reach the third round of the cup for the first time since 2009-10 season. City's unbeaten run is extended to 15 games in front of the BT Sport cameras. Admission prices are again restricted to £10 as City earn £27,000 in prize money.

7 City's FA Trophy first round tie away to Shaw Lane AFC, scheduled for Sunday 11th December, is postponed due to an FA investigation into Shaw Lane's third qualifying round tie against Nantwich Town.

9 Ipswich Town announce that they are reducing admission prices from £35 to £10 for the third round FA Cup tie against Lincoln on 7 January.

⇒ Shaw Lane AFC are removed from the FA Trophy for fielding an ineligible player (Alex Byrne) during their third qualifying round win over Nantwich Town. City will now play Northern Premier League side Nantwich away in the first round on Tuesday 13 December.

10 A blank Saturday for Lincoln due to the re-scheduling to Sunday and subsequent postponement of the FA Trophy tie at Shaw Lane.

12 Shaw Lane AFC lodge an appeal with the FA against their expulsion from the FA Trophy. The appeal will be heard on Tuesday afternoon, resulting in the postponement of City's scheduled first round tie at Nantwich that evening.

⇒ City are drawn away to National League rivals Gateshead in the second round of the FA Trophy, should they beat either Nantwich or Shaw Lane in the first round.

13 Shaw Lane lose their appeal against expulsion from the FA Trophy. City are to play Nantwich Town away on Tuesday 20 December in the first round. This means the National League game away to Solihull Moors, scheduled for the same evening, will need to be rearranged for the second time.

14 Alex Simmons extends his loan at FC Halifax Town until 21 January.

15 BT Sport announces that the Barrow v Lincoln game, which has been rescheduled for Tuesday 24 January, will be shown live on television. This will be the second Lincoln game in 5 days to be transmitted live, after the home game against Dover on Friday 20 January.

⇒ City's National League game away to Solihull Moors, postponed again due to City's FA Trophy tie at Nantwich next Tuesday, has been rearranged for Tuesday 31 January.

16 Lincoln and Nantwich agree to settle next Tuesday's FA Trophy first round tie on the night, with extra time and penalties taking place if necessary.

17 **Lincoln 2 (Arnold, Marriott) Tranmere Rovers 1.** Att: 6,335. Substitute Adam Marriott scores with his first touch one minute after coming on as City leapfrog visitors Tranmere to the top of the league. City ensure top spot at Christmas in front of the largest league attendance since relegation. The unbeaten run is now 16 games.

20 **FA Trophy 1: Nantwich Town 1 Lincoln 2 (Whitehouse, Hawkridge).** Att: 482. An own goal by goalkeeper Paul Farman in the final minute of stoppage time mars a very comfortable evening for City. The unbeaten run is extended to 17 games and earns £5,000 in prize money.

21 City and Gateshead agree to settle their FA Trophy second round tie on the day, with extra time and penalties taking place if necessary.

⇒ City announce that their initial allocation of 2,000 tickets for the FA Cup third round tie at Ipswich have sold out. A further allocation has been received, taking the total to 3,873.

22 Winger Harry Anderson is recalled from his loan by parent club Peterborough United.

23 City announce that they have sold all 3,873 tickets for the FA Cup tie at Ipswich and have requested more; a further supply is dependent on the police giving permission to open the lower tier of the Cobbold Stand at Portman Road.

26 **Guiseley 2 Lincoln 1 (Waterfall).** Att: 2,446. City suffer an unexpected defeat to bottom side Guiseley, the winner coming in the final minute of normal time. City lose top spot to Tranmere as they lose for the first time in 18 games. Elliott Whitehouse receives a second yellow card conceding the free kick that leads to the winner. The game is played in very windy conditions, and is decided by another Paul Farman error.

28 City announce that their total allocation of tickets (4,194) for the FA Cup tie at Ipswich has been sold. A decision regarding a further supply is still awaited from the police.

⇒ Elliott Whitehouse receives a one-match ban for his red card at Guiseley on Boxing Day.

⇒ It is revealed that City are running an eye over 21-year-old Hull City striker Johan ter Horst, who is training with the Imps with a view to a loan move.

29 City are to receive a further supply of 639 tickets from Ipswich Town for the FA Cup tie at Portman Road to take their final allocation to 4,833.

30 The final batch of 639 tickets for the Ipswich game sells out in 20 minutes.

⇒ City are giving a trial to former Standard Liège striker Erwin Senakuku. The 22-year-old Belgian has family in Lincoln.

31 City transfer target Simeon Akinola joins Barnet from Braintree Town for £40,000.

January 2017

1 **Lincoln 3 (Power pen, Raggett, Arnold) Guiseley 1.** Att: 5,148. City struggle again against lowly Guiseley, needing two goals in the final 3 minutes of normal time to take the points. The third successive home attendance of over 5,000 sees Nathan Arnold score his tenth goal of the season. City take over top spot from Tranmere, who lose 4-2 at Macclesfield.

3 Nathan Arnold is reportedly a target for Chesterfield, Doncaster Rovers and former club Grimsby Town.

⇒ City turn down an approach from Notts County for manager Danny Cowley.

⇒ The National League announces that all final day fixtures on Saturday 29 April will kick off at 12.15pm. The news is not well-received by fans, as many clubs have long distances to travel.

5 City sign 21-year-old full back Sean Long from Championship side Reading on loan to the end of the season. The Republic of Ireland U21 defender joins City with a view to making the loan permanent.

⇒ Chairman Bob Dorrian confirms that the overdraft has been paid off and the club is now in the black. Speaking to BBC Radio Lincolnshire, he also confirms that the club is close to agreeing new contracts with Danny and Nicky Cowley.

⇒ Ipswich Town confirm that the 4,833 supporters Lincoln are taking to Portman Road on Saturday will be the largest away following since the ground was converted to all-seated in 1992.

6 Goalkeeper Richard Walton joins Spalding United on a one-month loan.

7 **FA Cup 3: Ipswich Town 2 Lincoln 2 (Robinson 2).** Att: 16,027. City come within 4 minutes of an FA Cup victory over a team from three tiers above for the first time in their history. They lead twice in front of their largest away support for 41 years, given officially as 4,838. Theo Robinson scores two goals in an FA Cup tie for the third time this season to take his total to 6; only Isaac Moore (8 in 1890-91) has scored more FA Cup goals for City in a single season. Sean Long makes his City debut as a late substitute.

⇒ Jenk Acar joins Matlock Town on a one-month loan.

⇒ City announce that the FA Cup third round replay against Ipswich Town on 17 January will be all-ticket.

9 Bob Dorrian announces that Danny & Nicky Cowley are close to agreeing new contracts, provided some improvements to training facilities are made.

⇒ City are drawn at home to Championship leaders Brighton & Hove Albion in the fourth round of the FA Cup if they can beat Ipswich in next week's third round replay.

10 BT Sport announces that Lincoln's National League game against Forest Green Rovers on 25 March will be shown live with a 12.15pm kick-off. City will receive £6,000 in broadcasting fees.

⇒ The BBC announces that City's FA Cup third round replay against Ipswich Town on Tuesday 17 January will be shown live, with an 8.05pm kick-off. The game is worth another £72,000 in broadcasting fees. The announcement means that three successive Lincoln City matches will be shown on live television.

11 All tickets for the FA Cup replay with Ipswich Town sell out within 6 hours, suggesting the largest attendance at Sincil Bank since the FA Cup third round tie against Sunderland on 2 January 1999 (10,408). However, fans are critical of the ticket arrangements, which allow for up to 10 tickets per head; many regular supporters are unable to get one.

12 Danny and Nicky Cowley extend their contracts to the end of May 2021. The news is met with great delight from fans.

⇒ Legendary City manager Graham Taylor OBE dies of a heart attack at the age of 72. Taylor managed the team to the 1975-76 Fourth Division championship, setting several records that still stand today. He remains the only Lincoln manager to go on to manage the England team. As a player, he made 170 appearances for the Imps, scoring 2 goals.

⇒ Lincolnshire Police issues a warning against the sale of tickets for the Ipswich game on the black market after a number appear online at vastly inflated prices.

13 City sign 21-year-old winger Joe Ward on a one-month loan from Championship side Brighton & Hove Albion. He is not eligible to play against Ipswich in the FA Cup third round replay next week because he was not registered for the original tie; he will not be permitted to play against his parent club in the fourth round, should City beat Ipswich.

⇒ Kegan Everington joins Lincoln United on a one-month loan.

14 **FA Trophy 2: Gateshead 1 Lincoln 3 (Habergham, Whitehouse, Hawkridge).** Att: 578. Three second half goals overturn former City striker Jordan Burrow's third-minute opener in another dominant performance. Joe Ward makes his City debut in a side showing 6 changes from the side that drew at Ipswich. The win earns City £6,000 in prize money.

⇒ City's win over Gateshead means that the scheduled National League game at North Ferriby United on 4 February will have to be rearranged.

16 City are drawn away to National League South strugglers Welling United in the third round of the FA Trophy.

17 City trialist Johan ter Horst joins York City on loan to the end of the season after Lincoln decide not to sign him.

⇒ Lengthy articles on City manager Danny Cowley appear in The Daily Telegraph and The Times as the media frenzy continues to build ahead of tonight's FA Cup replay against Ipswich.

⇒ **FA Cup 3 Replay: Lincoln 1 (Arnold) Ipswich Town 0.** Att: 9,069. The BBC cameras see Lincoln knock a side from three tiers higher out of the FA Cup for the first time in their history. A 91st-minute goal from Nathan Arnold sees City through to the fourth round of the FA Cup for the first time since 1975-76, on a night when the fans said an emotional farewell to Graham Taylor. The win earns £67,500 in prize money in addition to the television fees. The admission price is again restricted to £10.

⇒ City's win over Ipswich means that the National League game at Braintree, scheduled for 28 January, will have to be rearranged.

18 City make available an extra 1,000 priority ticket vouchers for the fourth round FA Cup tie against Brighton. Requiring the purchase of a match ticket for the game against Dover on Friday, they sell out in less than an hour.

20 **Lincoln 2 (Hawkridge, Sterling own goal) Dover Athletic 0.** Att: 6,491. The BT Sport cameras see City extend their lead at the top of the National League to 5 points (with up to 2 games in hand on rivals) despite making several changes to the side that beat Ipswich. The game is watched by City's largest league crowd at Sincil Bank since relegation to date, and is also the fifth successive home game to be watched by over 5,000.

21 Alex Simmons joins Boston United on a three-month loan after being recalled early from his loan spell at FC Halifax.

⇒ Elliot Hodge extends his loan at AFC Telford United to the end of the season.

23 City's National League game at North Ferriby United, originally scheduled for 4 February, is rearranged for Tuesday 21 February. The game is also all-ticket.

24 City's National League game at Braintree Town, originally scheduled for 28 January, is rearranged for Tuesday 7 March.

⇒ **Barrow 3 Lincoln 0.** Att: 1,152. In City's third televised game in a row, the BT Sport cameras see Barrow win their first league game since November in a very poor game. City stay 4 points clear at the top.

26 City announce that investors linked to director Clive Nates have injected a further £150,000 into the club. A new director is also set to join the board, which will raise a further £75,000.

⇒ City confirm that all tickets for Saturday's FA Cup tie against Brighton have sold out.

⇒ Managing director Kevin Cooke announces that the entire debt due to the Co-op Bank has been paid off 14 years ahead of schedule; the club is now in the black.

28 City appear on the *You Know The Drill* feature on Sky TV's *Soccer AM*, and are also featured on *Gillette Soccer Saturday* ahead of the game against Brighton. The BBC programme *Football Focus* also comes live from Sincil Bank.

⇒ **FA Cup 4: Lincoln 3 (Power pen, Tomori own goal, Robinson) Brighton & Hove Albion 1.** Att: 9,469. City come from a goal down at half time to reach the FA Cup fifth round for the first time since 1902 and for only the fourth time in their history. Alan Power breaks Ben Tomlinson's post-relegation scoring record with his 35th goal for the club as City become only the 8th non-league club to reach the fifth round since WWII. The match is featured on BBC's Match of the Day and is also shown as BT Sport's Saturday evening programme. The admission price for this game is restricted to £15, but the win earns City £90,000 in prize money.

⇒ City's win over Brighton means that the National League match at Sutton United, scheduled for 18 February, will need to be rearranged.

29 Sutton United also reach the fifth round of the FA Cup with a 1-0 win over Leeds United.

⇒ It is revealed that the BBC wanted to show the Lincoln v Brighton tie live on television, but were refused permission by the FA who insisted they show the uninspiring Manchester United v Wigan tie instead.

30 City sign 19-year-old winger Josh Ginnelly from Burnley on loan to the end of the season.

⇒ City are drawn away to Premier League Burnley in the fifth round of the FA Cup.

⇒ City agree a permanent deal with Theo Robinson.

31 **Solihull Moors 0 Lincoln 1 (Muldoon).** Att: 1,650. 1,164 City fans see Jack Muldoon grab the winner 6 minutes into the second half. He replaces Theo Robinson in the side, who is absent from the squad 'for personal reasons'. The points total of 61 equals the total for the whole of last season. City extend their lead at the top of the table to 4 points once more, with a game in hand over second-placed Forest Green.

⇒ Late drama after the game as the management team and managing director Kevin Cooke spend an hour on the pitch apparently negotiating with Theo Robinson, who appeared at the game at half time.

⇒ Theo Robinson signs for League One side Southend United just before the 11pm transfer deadline.

February 2017

1 Tickets go on sale for City's National League game at North Ferriby on 21 February. They have been given 1,500 tickets from a capacity of 2,700.

⇒ City announce a new match ticket package in place of the Bob's Baker's Dozen and Six-Pack offerings. The *Final StrEight* tickets will guarantee a seat at each of the remaining 8 home games in the National League.

⇒ BT Sport announces it is to show City's FA Cup fifth round tie at Burnley live on television. The game will kick off at 12.30pm on Saturday 18 February. The broadcast fee for the game of £247,500 is set to take the club's earnings from this season's FA Cup run to around £900,000.

2 City sign 24-year-old left-sided midfielder Billy Knott on loan from Gillingham to the end of the season. His loan will start from 11 February to enable him to appear in the play-offs if necessary.

3 All 1,500 tickets for the game at North Ferriby have sold out. City have asked for a further allocation.

⇒ City sign 23-year-old striker Dayle Southwell from Wycombe Wanderers on a one-month loan. The former Boston star was a Danny Cowley target during the summer.

⇒ City are allocated just 3,210 tickets for the FA Cup fifth round tie at Burnley. City are to ask for more.

4 **FA Trophy 3: Welling United 1 Lincoln 3 (Ward 2, Southwell).** Att: 743. Dayle Southwell scores 8 minutes into his debut. Josh Ginnelly also makes his debut as City make 7 changes to the side that played at Solihull on Tuesday. Terry Hawkridge appears at left-back in place of the injured Sam Habergham. Joe Ward scores his first goals for the club in the second half to earn City another £7,000 in prize money.

⇒ Managing director Kevin Cooke announces that City are to show the Burnley game on a big screen at Sincil Bank.

⇒ City's win over Welling means that the National League game against Dagenham & Redbridge, scheduled for 25 February, will have to be rearranged.

6 City are drawn away to either Sutton United or Boreham Wood in the quarter-final of the FA Trophy.

7 City will head to Boreham Wood in the FA Trophy quarter-final after Wood beat Sutton 5-0 in their third round replay tonight.

⇒ City's away game at Sutton United, originally scheduled for 18 February, is rearranged for Tuesday 28 March.

8 City receive a Special Achievement Award from National League sponsors Vanarama for their FA Cup exploits.

9 Taylor Miles joins former club Concord Rangers on loan to the end of the season.

10 City extend the loan of Joe Ward from Brighton until 14 April, when the maximum 93 days will be up.

11 **Lincoln City 3 (Rhead 2, Thomas own goal) Woking 2.** Att: 5,553. Two goals from Matt Rhead, his first for 14 games, are decisive against a spirited Woking team. Billy Knott has an influential debut, but Dayle Southwell misses a penalty in the first half. City's ninth successive home win in all competitions keeps them top of the table, 3 points clear of Dagenham & Redbridge with a game in hand.

12 Danny Cowley is shown on television at the Burnley v Chelsea Premier League match, huddled under a blanket with his family. The picture is published in several national newspapers the following day.

15 All 3,210 tickets for the FA Cup fifth round tie at Burnley have sold out. City are to receive no more despite several appeals to Burnley.

16 Matt Rhead reveals that Danny Cowley went to his home in Stoke to meet him during the summer when Rhead put in a transfer request.

⇒ City announce that Vanarama will be the shirt sponsor for the Burnley game as a one-off.

17 City receive a further 200 tickets from North Ferriby for next week's game, taking the allocation to 1,700.

18 **FA Cup 5: Burnley 0 Lincoln 1 (Raggett).** Att: 19,185. An 89th-minute winner by Sean Raggett sees City become the first non-league team to reach the quarter-finals of the FA Cup since Queens Park Rangers in 1914. City create club history by reaching the quarter-finals for the first time in a game that kicks off at 12.30pm for the BT Sport cameras. The well-deserved win earns £180,000 in prize money in front of 3,213 City supporters. It is the first time they have ever knocked a side from four tiers higher out of the FA Cup, and the first time they have ever beaten a side from the top flight away from home. Burnley become the first top-flight team since the war to be knocked out of the FA Cup by a non-league team twice, after losing at home to Wimbledon in 1975.

⇒ Danny and Nicky Cowley appear in the BBC Match of the Day studio as the football world pays tribute to his record-breaking team. The media focus on City and their manager continues to reach new heights.

⇒ City's win over Burnley means that the National League game at home to Chester, scheduled for 11 March, will need to be rearranged.

19 City are drawn away to National League rivals Sutton United or Premier League giants Arsenal in the quarter-finals of the FA Cup.

20 City will travel to Arsenal in the quarter-final of the FA Cup after The Gunners beat Sutton United 2-0 at Gander Green Lane. Sutton's elimination also means that City are the only non-league side for 103 years to reach the quarter-finals of the FA Cup.

⇒ Goal hero Sean Raggett is included in the *European Team of the Week* published in the Italian newspaper *Gazzetta dello Sport*.

21 **North Ferriby United 0 Lincoln 1.** Att: 2,389. A first half header from captain Luke Waterfall is enough to seal the points and keep City clear at the top of the National League. They also have a goal disallowed and hit the woodwork three times against the league's bottom side. City set a new club record of 15 away wins in a season, surpassing the record of 14 set in 1975-76. The attendance, boosted by around 2,000 from Lincoln, is a record for North Ferriby. City's lead is still 3 points over second-placed Dagenham & Redbridge, but with 2 games in hand now.

22 City are to receive 8,942 tickets for the FA Cup quarter-final against Arsenal. The game will take place on Saturday 11 March with a 5.30pm kick-off. It will be shown live on BT Sport, earning the Imps a further television fee of £247,500.

23 City win the *LG Performance of the Week* award from the League Managers Association for their victory at Burnley. The winners are decided by a panel consisting of Sir Alex Ferguson, Howard Wilkinson, Barry Fry, Joe Royle and Dave Bassett. City are the first side from outside the Football League to win the award.

⇒ City confirm that the Stacey West Stand will be reserved for home supporters for the rest of the season.

24 Goalkeeper Richard Walton joins National League South side Bishop's Stortford on a one-month loan.

25 **FA Trophy QF: Boreham Wood 0 Lincoln 2 (Ward, Paine own goal).** Att: 901. Two second half goals ease a second-string City team to a comfortable win over their National League rivals. Dayle Southwell makes his final appearance before returning to Wycombe. The win earns a further £8,000 in prize money as City reach the semi-finals of the FA Trophy for the first time. It is City's fifth successive away win, and the seventh win in a row.

⇒ City's win over Boreham Wood means that the National League game at Maidstone United, scheduled for 18 March, will have to be rearranged: the date is needed for the second leg of the FA Trophy semi-final. The date of the first leg is moved to Tuesday 14 March, as the scheduled date of 11 March is already taken by the FA Cup quarter-final at Arsenal. Fixture congestion continues to build, meaning that City are likely to be playing Saturday-Tuesday-Thursday at least once before the end of the season. They are facing a minimum of 18 games in 60 days.

27 City are drawn against the National League's bottom club York City in the semi-finals of the FA Trophy. The first leg will take place at Bootham Crescent on Tuesday 14 March, with the second leg at Sincil Bank scheduled for Saturday 18 March.

⇒ City's National League game at home to Chester, originally scheduled for 11 March, is rearranged for Tuesday 11 April.

28 BT Sport announces that City's National League game at home to Dagenham & Redbridge, scheduled for Tuesday 4 April, will be shown live. As a consequence, the game will be brought forward 24 hours to Monday 3 April. It is the tenth Lincoln game to be shown live on television this season.

⇒ **Lincoln 1 (Power) York City 1.** Att: 6,892. City fail to overcome a dogged performance from the league's bottom team despite dominating the vast majority of possession in the second half. Results elsewhere all go City's way, as Dagenham & Redbridge, Dover and Barrow all lose. City extend their lead at the top of the National League to 4 points over Dagenham with 2 games in hand. The winning home run comes to an end at 9, and the latest overall winning run at 7. The attendance is the largest at a league game to date since relegation.

March 2017

1 Gateshead make the National League game on 17 April all-ticket for City fans, with an allocation of 3,500.

⇒ City's National League game at Maidstone United, originally scheduled for 18 March, is rearranged for Tuesday 25 April. It means that City will end the season with two away games.

⇒ Tickets for the FA Cup quarter-final against Arsenal go on sale. Restrictions placed by Arsenal mean that City can only sell them to supporters already on the club database, i.e. holders of season tickets, *Six-Packs, Bob's Baker's Dozens* and *Final StrEights*.

⇒ City re-sign striker Jonny Margetts from Scunthorpe United, initially on loan to the end of the season. The 23-year-old left Sincil Bank at the end of August 2016 after just 49 days at the club, but has received few opportunities at Glanford Park. He is eligible for both the FA Trophy and FA Cup.

3 Kegan Everington joins King's Lynn Town on loan to the end of the season.

⇒ Boreham Wood announce that the National League game against Lincoln on 21 March is to be all-ticket.

⇒ City announce that the FA Trophy semi-final first leg away to York City is to be all-ticket for Lincoln supporters.

4 **Aldershot Town 0 Lincoln 0.** Att: 3,595. City's fifth clean sheet in their last six away games sees them secure a point in a difficult game against play-off contenders Aldershot. Luke Waterfall hits the post, and Sean Raggett has a header cleared off the line two minutes into stoppage time, but City are forced to settle for a point. Jonny Margetts makes his second debut for the club. City stay top of the table, 3 points clear of Forest Green Rovers with a game in hand.

6 City sign 22-year-old striker Lee Angol from Peterborough United on loan to the end of the season. He is eligible for the FA Trophy.

⇒ Danny Cowley reveals that Sean Long is effectively a Lincoln City player; the inference is that City are taking up the option to sign the full back from Reading in the close season.

⇒ City announce that all 8,942 tickets for the FA Cup quarter-final at Arsenal have been sold.

⇒ The FA Cup tie at Arsenal will also be shown on a big screen at Sincil Bank.

7 City confirm that both legs of the FA Trophy semi-final against York City will be all-ticket. Their allocation for the first leg at Bootham Crescent is 1,900.

⇒ **Braintree Town 0 Lincoln 4 (Angol 3 - 1 pen, Arnold).** Att: 1,182. Lee Angol becomes the first Lincoln player since Billy Cobb in 1966 to score a hat-trick on his debut, and only the second ever. City extend their lead at the top of the National League to 6 points over second-placed Forest Green Rovers and third-placed Tranmere, who lose 2-1 at Barrow. City's 17th away win of the season takes them to 70 points for the first time in ten years. It is City's 11th successive win over Braintree. They have now kept 6 clean sheets in the last 7 away games.

8 Unsubstantiated rumours suggest that City have paid a loan fee in excess of £100,000 for Lee Angol.

⇒ City captain Luke Waterfall is named Vanarama National League Player of the Month for February.

⇒ Boreham Wood announce that the home game against Lincoln on 21 March will not be all-ticket after all.

9 The FA Cup pays a visit to Bishop Grosseteste University and the University of Lincoln for the day.

⇒ City confirm that Vanarama will again be the front of shirt sponsor for the game at Arsenal.

10 The Imps train at West Ham's Chadwell Heath facility ahead of their FA Cup quarter-final against Arsenal.

⇒ City sign 21-year-old left-back Riccardo Calder on loan from Aston Villa until the end of the season. He is eligible for the FA Cup and FA Trophy.

⇒ City also sign 22-year-old goalkeeper Ross Etheridge on loan from Doncaster Rovers until the end of the season. He is also eligible for the FA Cup and FA Trophy.

11 **FA Cup QF: Arsenal 5 Lincoln 0.** Att: 59,454. City hold the Premier League giants for 45 minutes but are well-beaten in the second half as Chilean international Alexis Sanchez inspires his side to a comfortable win. Manager Arsène Wenger fields his strongest side to end City's record-breaking FA Cup run in front of the second highest attendance ever to watch a Lincoln City match. The gate includes 8,942 fans from Lincoln, believed to be the biggest away support in the club's history other than for play-off finals.

⇒ Danny Cowley reveals that Aston Villa are footing the bill for Riccardo Calder's loan move.

13 Alex Woodyard signs a one-year contract extension.

14 **FA Trophy SF, 1st leg: York City 2 Lincoln 1 (Angol - pen).** Att: 3,294. City make 9 changes including a debut for on-loan goalkeeper Ross Etheridge, and throw away a half-time lead against a poor York side. A very disappointing attendance includes 1,358 from Lincoln.

⇒ In the National League, Forest Green move to within 3 points of City with a 2-1 win at Sutton, but City have 2 games in hand and a much better goal difference. Tranmere are held 0-0 at lowly Torquay.

15 Danny Cowley says he expects more players to renew their contracts now that Alex Woodyard has re-signed for next season.

16 Cowley also reveals that every player who has contributed to the club's success this season will be offered the opportunity to stay for next season. There are three different pathways available, depending upon which division the club is in next season: National League, League Two, or top seven in League Two.

18 **FA Trophy SF, 2nd leg: Lincoln 1 (Raggett) York City 1.** Att: 8,409. A ludicrous penalty decision in extra time costs City a place at Wembley: video playback clearly shows the ball hitting Luke Waterfall in the chest. Riccardo Calder makes his debut. City must now concentrate on the league.

⇒ In the National League, Forest Green draw level on points with City with a win over Wrexham, although City have three games in hand. Dagenham & Redbridge are beaten at Barrow and are slipping out of contention.

20 City have injury problems in defence ahead of the match at Boreham Wood on Tuesday: Bradley Wood and Sam Habergham are both struggling, while Sean Long is still not available.

21 **Boreham Wood 2 Lincoln 0.** Att: 1,002. City go down to two second half goals and lose top spot in the league as Forest Green go 3 points clear. City still have 3 games in hand. Tranmere win at North Ferriby to close to within 2 points of City, having played 2 games more. Dagenham & Redbridge lose at Aldershot and are almost out of contention.

22 BT Sport announces the final tranche of live matches: City's final home match against Macclesfield Town on 22 April is pencilled in at this stage in order to avoid dead rubbers.

23 Winger Joe Ward returns to parent club Brighton & Hove Albion after picking up a metatarsal injury.

⇒ City re-sign 20-year-old winger Harry Anderson on loan from Peterborough United until the end of the season. Anderson made 22 appearances during his first loan spell before being recalled in December.

24 Bradley Wood receives a 12-month drink-driving ban at Lincoln Magistrates Court after being stopped on a routine check on 12 February. Wood had been out the previous evening and was not aware the alcohol would still be in his system. He issues a public warning to others.

25 **Lincoln 3 (Angol, Habergham, Kelly own goal) Forest Green Rovers 1.** Att: 6,798. City overturn a half-time deficit to win a pivotal game in front of the BT Sport cameras. Harry Anderson makes his second debut in the lunchtime kick-off. City leapfrog Forest Green to go back to the top of the table, level on points but with three games in hand; Forest Green have only seven games remaining.

⇒ In the afternoon kick-offs, Tranmere stay third with a narrow home win over struggling Braintree; they are two points behind City, having played a game more. Dagenham & Redbridge beat York with a late goal to just about stay in touch; they are fourth, five points behind City having played three games more. Like Forest Green, they only have seven games left, one of which is at Sincil Bank a week on Monday.

27 City announce that the remaining five home games will be all-ticket with allocated seating, with the exception of the Stacey West Stand.

28 **Sutton United 1 Lincoln 1 (Whitehouse).** Att: 2,246. City concede an equaliser in the 93rd minute on the plastic pitch at Sutton. City stay top of the table, but Tranmere win 1-0 against Dover to move level on points with the Imps, who still have one game in hand.

April 2017

1 Tranmere go three points clear of Lincoln with a 1-0 win at Wrexham in the lunchtime kick-off.

⇒ **Lincoln 1 (Knott) Bromley 0.** Att: 6,843. Billy Knott scores the winner just two minutes after coming on as a 64th-minute substitute. Alan Power misses a first half penalty, but City are not troubled by a poor Bromley side. Britain's last surviving Dambuster, 95-year-old Squadron Leader George 'Johnny' Johnson DFM, is the guest of honour at the game. The attendance is the eleventh successive gate over 5,000. City return to the top of the table, level on points with Tranmere with a game in hand. Forest Green lose 1-0 at home to second-from-bottom North Ferriby and are almost out of the title race. Monday night's visitors Dagenham & Redbridge beat Eastleigh 4-0 to stay in touch, but are 6 points behind the Imps, who have two games in hand.

2 An article in the Non-League Football Paper (NLP) reports that non-league Billericay Town have made an approach for the Cowleys. Ambitious Billericay are owned by steel magnate Glenn Tamplin, who tried to buy Dagenham & Redbridge earlier in the season.

3 BT announces that City's away game at Gateshead on Monday 17 April will be broadcast live with a 3pm kick off.

⇒ **Lincoln 2 (Whitehouse, Rhead) Dagenham & Redbridge 0.** Att: 7,173. Matt Rhead heads City's 100th league and cup goal of the season in front of the largest league attendance since relegation. It is the first time the century has been achieved since 1987-88, when City lifted the Conference championship. The lead at the top of the table is extended to 3 points in a game brought forward by 24 hours for the benefit of the BT Sport cameras. City temporarily have no games in hand on Tranmere, who play tomorrow night, but the win ensures City will stay top regardless.

4 Tranmere beat Sutton United 3-2 with a 90th-minute winner to draw level on points with the Imps at the top of the league; City still have one game in hand and have a far better goal difference.

6 City announce that their penultimate away game at Maidstone United on Tuesday 25 April will be all-ticket for Lincoln fans, with an allocation of 613.

8 **Eastleigh 0 Lincoln 1 (Raggett).** Att: 2,738. Sean Raggett's 75th-minute header ensures that City have at least a play-off place. Their third successive clean sheet keeps them ahead of Tranmere on goal difference, although Tranmere reduce that deficit to three with a 9-0 win over Solihull Moors. City's current total of 85 points is a new club record under the three points for a win system.

10 Sean Raggett sees a dental specialist after suffering a dislodged front tooth during the game at Eastleigh.

11 **Lincoln 1 (Anderson) Chester 0.** Att: 7,401. A first half goal by substitute Harry Anderson is enough to give the Imps the points in front of the largest home league crowd since relegation. Alan Power is sent off two minutes after coming on as a 73rd-minute substitute, but City hold on for the win after Chester are also reduced to ten men in the closing minutes. City's fourth clean sheet in a row helps them to go three points clear at the top of the table after second-placed Tranmere lose 1-0 at home to third-placed Forest Green. City still have a game in hand on Tranmere, who have only four games remaining.

12 Alan Power receives a three-match ban for his red card against Chester.

14 **Lincoln 2 (Anderson, Habergham) Torquay United 1.** Att: 9,011. Two goals in the last four minutes of normal time give City a crucial win over their relegation-threatened visitors. The largest league crowd since relegation sees City go five points clear of second-placed Tranmere, who can only draw 2-2 at home to Aldershot. City still have a game in hand on Tranmere, who only have three games remaining. City will be champions on Monday with a win at Gateshead if Tranmere fail to beat Guiseley.

⇒ City announce that the match at Gateshead on Easter Monday will now be pay on the gate. 1,745 tickets have been sold so far of the 3,200 allocation.

15 Relegated Southport announce an allocation of 1,962 tickets for Lincoln fans for the final league game of the season at Haig Avenue on 29 April.

17 **Gateshead 1 Lincoln 2 (Rhead - pen, Arnold).** Att: 3,770. Almost 2,500 City fans see Matt Rhead and Nathan Arnold score in the final four minutes to earn all three points. The win is City's 13th away from home in the league, equalling the club record set in 1908-09, and the total of 50 goals away from home equals the club record set in 1975-76. Matt Rhead scores his 37th goal for City to overtake Alan Power (36) as City's leading scorer since relegation. The attendance of 3,770 is the largest at the Gateshead International Stadium for a regular league match, and City's following of 2,486 is the largest away support at the ground ever. Tranmere win 2-1 at Guiseley, but City remain 5 points clear with a game in hand; Tranmere have just two games remaining, and City will take the title if they beat Macclesfield Town on Saturday.

⇒ BT announces that City's final home match of the season against Macclesfield Town on Saturday will be shown live with a 12.15pm kick-off.

18 City announce that all tickets for the home match against Macclesfield Town on Saturday have been sold.

19 City confirm that the National League trophy will be presented after the Macclesfield Town game on Saturday if the Imps win to secure the championship.

⇒ City confirm that no offers have been received for defender Sean Raggett despite speculation linking him with League One side Millwall.

⇒ Contract discussions with players are put on hold until the end of the season.

20 Clive Nates confirms that City intend to build a bespoke training facility once a suitable location is found.

21 Notts County Ladies - formerly known as Lincoln Ladies until 2014 - is closed down by its parent club due to financial problems.

22 **Lincoln 2 (Hawkridge 2) Macclesfield Town 1.** Att: 10,031. Two goals from Terry Hawkridge see City crowned champions of the National League in front of the BT Sport cameras. City are forced to come from a goal down for the third game in a row and secure promotion in front of the largest crowd at Sincil Bank since re-configuration to all-seated. It is City's seventh straight win, the first time any National League side has done that this season. The championship trophy is presented to City after the final whistle amid scenes of great celebration.

⇒ Manager Danny Cowley says Lincoln must use promotion as a springboard for further success.

⇒ Director Clive Nates says City are determined to capitalise on promotion and will back Danny Cowley as much as they can.

⇒ Captain Luke Waterfall says lifting the National League championship is the proudest moment of his career, and believes City can challenge next year in League Two.

24 Danny Cowley confirms that Sam Habergham and Paul Farman will not play again this season. Habergham faces an operation and Farman a scan on muscle injuries.

⇒ Richard Ian Clarke is appointed to the board of directors.

⇒ Jeremy Simon Wright is appointed to the board of directors.

25 City announce that they have requested a further 1,000 tickets from Southport after the original allocation of 1,962 sells out.

⇒ Bob Dorrian confirms that the new stadium will hold between 12,000 and 15,000 when constructed, rather than the 10,000 planned originally. In the interim, they are to proceed with building a new training ground forthwith, which will be ready for use from October/November. He also announces that City will have a top-half of League Two budget next season.

⇒ **Maidstone United 0 Lincoln 0.** Att: 3,014. An extremely dominant performance on Maidstone's 3G pitch sees City extend their lead at the top to 6 points with one game remaining. City make 9 changes from the side that beat Macclesfield, with loanees Ross Etheridge and Riccardo Calder making their league debuts. City need a win at Southport in Saturday's final match to pass 100 points for the season.

⇒ Danny Cowley reveals that he has a competitive budget for next season and has the tools to make City a force in League Two. He appeals to fans to buy season tickets to boost the budget further.

26 Sam Habergham has a hernia operation; it emerges that he has been playing on with it for at least two months.

27 Paul Farman has a scan on his long-standing groin injury. Fortunately no operation is needed.

28 City train at Everton's Finch Farm training base ahead of tomorrow's final game at Southport.

⇒ No contact has been received from West Bromwich Albion despite speculation linking Sean Raggett with a move to The Hawthorns.

29 **Southport 1 Lincoln 1 (Angol).** Att: 3,462. City's 61st and final game of the season ends with a disappointing draw against the league's bottom side. Lee Angol scores City's 51st away goal of the season to set a new club record. A fortunate 87th-minute equaliser by the hosts does not reflect City's almost total dominance in front of Southport's largest league attendance since they left the Football League in 1978; 2,458 of them come from Lincoln. City end the season on 99 points, unbeaten in their last 11 games, with 8 wins and 3 draws.

Lincoln City end their stay in the Conference at the place it began, six long years ago.

⇒ City announce a marginal increase in season ticket prices for their first season back in League Two.

May 2017

2 Loan striker Lee Angol is transfer-listed by Peterborough United with a year of his contract remaining.

⇒ City enjoy an open top bus parade around the city to celebrate their promotion, watched by 30,000.

3 Danny Cowley meets with the players to discuss contracts; the retained list is eagerly awaited by fans.

4 Callum Howe is called up by England C for the friendly games against Punjab FA in Solihull on 28 May and Jersey FA in St Helier on 30 May. He is the only City player called up on this occasion.

⇒ The players depart for a well-earned holiday in Benidorm.

5 Danny Cowley conducts a personal tour around Lincoln primary schools with the National League trophy.

8 Nathan Arnold starts a ten-day UEFA B Licence course.

9 City are rumoured to be interested in out-of-contract Macclesfield Town midfielder Kingsley James.

⇒ Loan winger Joe Ward is released by Brighton & Hove Albion after their promotion to the Premier League.

10 Danny Cowley is in the final stages of the retained list; it should be announced by the end of the week.

⇒ Online bookmaker SkyBet makes City third favourites for the League Two title next season at 10/1, just behind Swindon and Mansfield at 9/1. Neighbours Grimsby are 33/1.

11 Lee Beevers is undergoing recuperative work at Leicester City's training base as he steps up his recovery from his ruptured patella tendon. He hopes to be able to start running within six weeks and return to pre-season training with the other players. No decision on his future with the club will be made until then.

⇒ Early season ticket sales indicate the final total may reach 3,500 ahead of the new season.

⇒ Paul Farman signs a new two-year deal.

12 Football League clubs vote to retain the much-maligned Checkatrade Trophy for next season.

13 Terry Hawkridge is rumoured to be interesting League Two rivals Notts County.

14 Forest Green Rovers join City in League Two with a 3-1 win over Tranmere Rovers in the play-off final.

15 Four City players are named in the National League Team of the Year, selected by the 24 managers: Paul Farman, Sam Habergham, Sean Raggett and Alex Woodyard.

16 Norwich City are believed to be interested in the Cowleys for their vacant manager's position.

17 Captain Luke Waterfall signs a new two-year deal. Apparently he has rejected higher financial offers from Coventry, Carlisle and Notts County to stay with the Imps.

⇒ City make a clean sweep at the National Game Awards held at Stamford Bridge. Danny Cowley is named *FieldTurf Manager of the Year* (for the second year in a row); Alex Woodyard the *Mark Harrod Player of the Year* (after winning the *Young Player* award last year); Sean Raggett the *SportsBeat Young Player of the Year*; Paul Farman the *Reusch Goalkeeper of the Year*; and - of course - the club takes the *Acerbis Cup Run of the Year* and the *Red Insure Team of the Year*.

18 The retained list is released. Under contract are Paul Farman, Alex Woodyard, Nathan Arnold, Sam Habergham, Sean Long, Sean Raggett, Matt Rhead, Luke Waterfall and Elliott Whitehouse. New contracts have been offered to Terry Hawkridge, Adam Marriott, Callum Howe, Jack Muldoon, Alan Power and Richard Walton. Released are Jenk Acar, Kegan Everington, Elliot Hodge, Taylor Miles, Alex Simmons and Andrew Wright. Jamie McCombe has been offered a coaching role, while Lee Beevers will receive a testimonial during pre-season. Bradley Wood is also out of contract, but his name is not mentioned at all.

⇒ Former loanee Lee Angol signs for League Two rivals Mansfield Town.

⇒ Terry Hawkridge rejects his contract offer and signs a two-year deal with League Two rivals Notts County.

⇒ The mystery surrounding Bradley Wood deepens as Danny Cowley reveals he has been instructed by the Football Association not to discuss the matter.

19 Bob Dorrian believes City will sell at least 4,000 season tickets for next season.

⇒ Alex Woodyard is voted supporters' *Player of the Season*, receiving his award at a celebration dinner held at the Lincolnshire Showground; Woodyard also takes the *Away Player of the Season* award. Sean Raggett is named *Young Player of the Season* by the management. General Manager John Vickers and Ticket Office Manager Dawn Cussens receive long service awards at the end of a very testing season for them, while the Lifetime Achievement Award goes to George and Doreen Ashton.

22 Danny and Nicky Cowley attend the League Managers' Association (LMA) Awards in London for the first time as members, which means that...

...LINCOLN CITY ARE BACK IN THE FOOTBALL LEAGUE AFTER SIX YEARS IN PURGATORY

SEASON 2016-17

NATIONAL LEAGUE

No.	Date		Opposition	Res	Att	Scorers	Farman, P	Wood, B	Beevers, L	Woodyard, A	McCombe, J	Waterfall, L	Muldoon, J	Habergham, S	Arnold, N	Rhead, M	Marriott, A	Margetts, J	Miles, T	Hodge, E
1	AUG	6	Woking	3-1	1592	Rhead 2 (1 pen), Marriott	Y	Y	Y	Y	Y	Y	Y*	Y	Y*	Y	Y#	S#	S*>	S>
2		9	NORTH FERRIBY UNITED	6-1	3622	Rhead 2 (1 p), Arnold, Waterfall, Margetts, Wood	Y	Y	Y	Y	S>	Y	Y*	Y	Y#	Y>		Y		S*
3		13	SUTTON UNITED	1-3	3195	Habergham	Y	Y	Y>	Y	S>	Y	Y	Y	Y*	Y#	S#	Y		
4		16	Dagenham & Redbridge	0-1	1399		Y		Y	Y		Y	Y	Y	Y		Y*	Y		
5		20	SOUTHPORT	4-0	2440	Margetts 4 (1 pen)	Y		Y	Y	S>	Y	S#	Y#		Y*	Y			
6		27	Macclesfield Town	2-1	1650	Anderson, Marriott	Y		Y	Y	Y	Y		Y	Y#	Y*	S*	Y		
7		29	GATESHEAD	3-0	3687	Raggett, Arnold, Marriott	Y	Y	Y	Y		Y		Y	Y*	Y#	Y>	S#		
8	SEP	3	Torquay United	2-1	2061	Rhead 2 (1 pen)	Y	Y	Y	Y		Y		Y	Y>	Y				
9		10	Tranmere Rovers	1-0	5274	Bonne	Y	Y>	Y	Y		Y		Y	Y#	Y	S*			
10		13	SOLIHULL MOORS	0-0	4049		Y	Y		Y		Y		Y	Y	Y	Y#			
11		17	BARROW	1-2	3578	Arnold	Y	Y		Y		Y	S*	Y	Y	Y	S>			
12		24	Dover Athletic	0-2	1209		Y	Y	S#	Y		Y	Y>	Y	Y	Y*	S*			
13	OCT	1	BRAINTREE TOWN	3-0	3554	Arnold, Waterfall, Muldoon	Y	Y	Y	Y		Y	S#	Y	Y	Y#				
14		4	Wrexham	2-1	3847	Waterfall, Anderson	Y	Y*	Y	Y		Y	S#	Y	Y	Y>				
15		8	Bromley	1-1	1511	Anderson	Y	Y>	Y	Y		Y	Y	Y#	Y*					
16		22	EASTLEIGH	0-0	3180		Y	Y	Y	Y		Y	S*	Y	Y	Y#				
17		25	BOREHAM WOOD	2-0	3014	Arnold, Rhead	Y	Y	Y#	Y		Y	S>	Y	Y	Y*				
18		29	Chester	5-2	2586	Robinson, Rhead, Raggett, Muldoon, Anderson	Y	Y		Y		Y	S#	Y	Y	Y>				
19	NOV	12	ALDERSHOT TOWN	3-3	3461	Arnold 2, Rhead	Y	Y		Y		Y	S#	Y	Y*	Y				
20		19	Forest Green Rovers	3-2	2164	Woodyard, Waterfall, Raggett	Y	Y		Y		Y		Y	Y	Y	S*			
21		22	York City	4-1	2889	Whitehouse, Arnold, Waterfall, Wood	Y	Y		Y		Y	S#	Y	Y#	Y*	S>			
22		26	MAIDSTONE UNITED	2-0	3917	Robinson, Rhead	Y	Y		Y		Y	S#	Y	Y#	Y*	S>			
23		29	WREXHAM	1-0	3344	Whitehouse	Y	Y		Y		Y	S>	Y	Y	Y*				
24	DEC	17	TRANMERE ROVERS	2-1	6335	Arnold, Marriott	Y	Y		Y	S>	Y		Y	Y	Y>	S*			
25		26	Guiseley	1-2	2446	Waterfall	Y	Y*		Y		Y	S#	Y	Y	Y				
26	JAN	1	GUISELEY	3-1	5148	Power (pen), Raggett, Arnold	Y	Y		Y		Y	S*	Y	Y>	S#				
27		20	DOVER ATHLETIC	2-0	6491	Hawkridge, OG	Y	S>		Y		Y		Y	Y	Y#	Y*			
28		24	Barrow	0-3	1152		Y	Y		Y		Y		Y	Y>	S>				
29		31	Solihull Moors	1-0	1650	Muldoon	Y	Y		Y		Y	Y#	Y	Y>	Y*	S#			
30	FEB	11	WOKING	3-2	5553	Rhead 2, OG	Y	Y		Y		Y		Y	Y	Y				
31		21	North Ferriby United	1-0	2389	Waterfall	Y			Y		Y	S>	Y	Y	S#				
32		28	YORK CITY	1-1	6892	Power	Y	S#		Y		Y		Y	Y	Y				
33	MAR	4	Aldershot Town	0-0	3595		Y	Y		Y		Y	S>	Y	Y		Y>			
34		7	Braintree Town	4-0	1182	Angol 3 (1 pen), Arnold	Y	Y		Y		Y#		Y	S*	S>	Y>			
35		21	Boreham Wood	0-2	1002		Y			Y		Y		Y	Y	S#	S>			
36		25	FOREST GREEN ROVERS	3-1	6798	Angol, Habergham, OG	Y			Y		Y	Y	Y	Y					
37		28	Sutton United	1-1	2246	Whitehouse	Y			Y		Y	Y	Y	Y	S>				
38	APR	1	BROMLEY	1-0	6843	Knott	Y			Y		Y	Y	Y	Y>					
39		3	DAGENHAM & REDBRIDGE	2-0	7173	Whitehouse, Rhead	Y	Y		Y		Y	Y	Y	Y#	S>				
40		8	Eastleigh	1-0	2738	Raggett	Y	Y		Y		Y	Y	Y	Y>	Y				
41		11	CHESTER	1-0	7401	Anderson	Y	Y		Y		Y	Y	Y	Y					
42		14	TORQUAY UNITED	2-1	9011	Anderson, Habergham	Y			Y		Y	Y>	Y	Y	S>				
43		17	Gateshead	2-1	3770	Rhead (pen), Arnold	Y			Y		Y		Y	Y	Y	S#			
44		22	MACCLESFIELD TOWN	2-1	10031	Hawkridge 2	Y	Y		Y		Y		Y	Y*	Y>				
45		25	Maidstone United	0-0	3014										Y	Y		Y#		
46		29	Southport	1-1	3462	Angol					S*	Y		Y	S>	Y				
				Appearances			44	32	14	44	3	44	10	43	43	40	8	7	0	0
				Substitute appearances			0	2	1	1	4	0	15	0	2	3	17	3	1	2
				Goals				2		1		7	3	3	12	14	4	5		

83 league goals

FA CUP

				Res	Att	Scorers	Farman, P	Wood, B	Beevers, L	Woodyard, A	McCombe, J	Waterfall, L	Muldoon, J	Habergham, S	Arnold, N	Rhead, M	Marriott, A	Margetts, J	Miles, T	Hodge, E
4Q	OCT	15	GUISELEY	0-0	2629		Y	Y*	Y	Y			Y	Y#	Y		Y			
4QR		18	Guiseley	2-1	765	Robinson 2	Y	Y	Y	Y			Y	S#	Y		Y#			
1	NOV	5	ALTRINCHAM	2-1	3529	Raggett, Power	Y	Y		Y		Y	S#	Y	Y*	Y	Y*			
2	DEC	5	OLDHAM ATHLETIC	3-2	7012	Robinson 2, Hawkridge	Y	Y		Y	Y	Y	S*	Y	Y*	Y	Y			
3	JAN	7	Ipswich Town	2-2	16027	Robinson 2	Y	Y		Y		Y	S#	Y	Y	Y*				
3R		17	IPSWICH TOWN	1-0	9069	Arnold	Y	Y		Y	S>	Y	S*	Y	Y*	Y	Y	S#		
4		28	BRIGHTON & HOVE ALBION	3-1	9469	Power (pen), OG, Robinson	Y	Y		Y	S>	Y	S#	Y	Y*	Y	Y*			
5	FEB	18	Burnley	1-0	19185	Raggett	Y	Y		Y	S>	Y	Y#	Y	Y>					
QF	MAR	11	Arsenal	0-5	59454		Y	Y		Y		Y	Y#	Y	Y	Y*	S>	S#		

FA TROPHY

				Res	Att	Scorers	Farman, P	Wood, B	Beevers, L	Woodyard, A	McCombe, J	Waterfall, L	Muldoon, J	Habergham, S	Arnold, N	Rhead, M	Marriott, A	Margetts, J	Miles, T	Hodge, E
1	DEC	20	Nantwich Town	2-1	482	Whitehouse, Hawkridge	Y	Y		S#	Y			Y>	S*	Y*	Y			
2	JAN	14	Gateshead	3-1	578	Habergham, Whitehouse, Hawkridge	Y	S#		S*			Y	Y	S>	Y>				
3	FEB	4	Welling United	3-1	743	Ward 2, Southwell	Y	S#		Y>		Y				S*				
QF		25	Boreham Wood	2-0	901	Ward, OG	Y	Y		Y		Y	Y>	Y						
SF1	MAR	14	York City	1-2	3294	Angol (pen)		Y			Y>	S>		Y	S#	Y#				
SF2		18	YORK CITY	1-1*	8409	Raggett	Y	Y>		Y		Y		Y	Y	Y				

* After extra time

LINCOLNSHIRE CUP

				Res	Att	Scorers	Farman, P	Wood, B	Beevers, L	Woodyard, A	McCombe, J	Waterfall, L	Muldoon, J	Habergham, S	Arnold, N	Rhead, M	Marriott, A	Margetts, J	Miles, T	Hodge, E
QF	Jul	8	Grantham Town	5-1	524	Hawkridge 2, Margetts 2 (1 pen), Caton	Y	Y	Y#	Y	Y#	Y#		Y#				Y	Y#	S#
SF		23	Lincoln United	0-2	815		Y	Y	Y#	Y	Y#	S#	Y	Y				Y	Y#	

Key:
Y = full appearance
Y# = full appearance, first player substituted - by substitute S#
Y* = full appearance, second player substituted - by substitute S*
Y> = full appearance, third player substituted - by substitute S>

■ Red Card
▨ Yellow Card

Attendance/register grid. Column headers (left to right):

Raggett, S · Simmons, A · Hawkridge, T · Power, A · Anderson, H · Bonne, M · Champion, T · Robinson, T · Whitehouse, E · Howe, C · Long, S · Ward, J · Ginnelly, J · Southwell, D · Knott, W · Angol, L · Etheridge, R · Calder, R · Wright, A · Stanley, C · Caton, J · Higgins, R · Andersen, L · Thompson, R · Fixter, J · Moyses, A · Nicholson, J

Main grid

Rag	Sim	Haw	Pow	And	Bon	Cha	Rob	Whi	How	Lon	War	Gin	Sou	Kno	Ang	Eth	Cal	Wri	Sta	Cat	Hig	Ande	Tho	Fix	Moy	Nic
Y	S	#																								
Y		S	*																							
Y		S	#	Y	#	S	*																			
Y	>	Y	S	*	Y																						
		Y	S	#	Y																						
		S	*	S	>	Y																					
Y		S	#	S	>	Y	#	S	*																		
Y		Y	S	>	S	#	Y	*																			
Y		Y	*		S	*	S	#	Y																		
Y			S	#	Y	*	Y	>	Y	#																	
Y	#			S	>	Y		Y																			
Y		Y	*		S	*	Y																				
Y		S	*	Y		Y	#	S	>																		
Y				Y	*	S	*	S	#	S	>																
Y				Y	*		Y		S	#																	
Y		S	#	Y		Y	>	S	*																		
Y		S	>	Y	*	Y	#	S	*																		
Y		S	*	Y	>	Y	#		S	>																	
Y		S	#	Y	>	Y	#		Y	*	S	>															
		Y	S	*			Y	>		Y	>	Y															
Y		Y	Y				Y	>		S	*																
Y		Y	#	S	*		Y	>		Y	S	#															
		Y	#		S	#	Y	*		Y																	
Y		Y	#				Y	*		Y																	
Y		Y	Y	*			Y	#				S	>														
Y		Y	>	S	*		S	#	Y			Y															
Y		Y	*	Y	#		Y					S	#		S	*											
Y		Y	*	Y			Y					Y			S	*											
Y		Y	#	S	>			S	*		Y		S	#	Y	*	Y	>									
Y			S	*				Y	>		Y		Y	Y	#	Y	*										
Y	*		Y					S	*	Y	#	S	>	Y		Y	>										
Y		Y	*	Y	#							S	*		S	#											
Y		Y					Y	S	#			Y	*		Y												
Y		S	*				Y					Y	*	Y	#	Y	>										
Y		Y	#	Y	S	#		S	*		Y				Y	*											
Y		Y	#	Y	*	S	#		S	*		Y				Y	>										
Y		Y	*	Y	#			S	>		Y		S	#	S	*	Y										
Y		Y	*					S	*		Y				S	#	Y	>									
Y		Y	#	S	>	S	*		Y	*				S	#	Y											
Y			S	>	S	#		Y	>				S	*	Y	*	Y	#									
Y			S	*				S	#		Y				Y	*	Y	#									
Y				Y	*			Y	>		Y		S	*	S	>	Y	#									
Y		Y						Y	#		S	>	S	*	S	#	Y										
Y	S	*	Y		Y			S	#	Y			Y	*	Y		Y	Y								
Y		Y	#					S	#	Y			Y	>	Y											

Totals

Rag	Sim	Haw	Pow	And	Bon	Cha	Rob	Whi	How	Lon	War	Gin	Sou	Kno	Ang	Eth	Cal	Wri	Sta	Cat	Hig	Ande	Tho	Fix	Moy	Nic
41	0	24	14	14	5	3	12	14	4	12	0	7	2	8	11	2	1	0	0	0	0	0	0	0	0	0
0	2	8	16	12	3	2	2	14	4	2	2	6	0	6	0	0	0	0	0	0	0	0	0	0	0	0
5		3	2	6	1		2	4						1	5											

Second grid

Rag	Sim	Haw	Pow	And	Bon	Cha	Rob	Whi	How	Lon	War	Gin	Sou	Kno	Ang	Eth
Y		Y	S	*	Y			S	#							
Y		Y	S	*	Y			Y	*							
Y		S	*	Y		Y		Y	#							
		Y	#	Y	S	#		Y	*							
Y		Y	Y					Y	#		S	*					
Y		Y	>	Y				Y	#							
Y		Y	Y	>				Y	#		S	*					
Y		Y	*	Y							S	*		S	#	
Y		Y	>	Y							S	*				

Third grid

Rag	Sim	Haw	Pow	And	Bon	Cha	Rob	Whi	How	Lon	War	Gin	Sou	Kno	Ang	Eth	Cal
		Y	Y				S	>	Y	#	Y						
Y		Y	*	Y	#			Y		Y	Y	Y					
S	>	Y	Y					Y		Y	Y	Y	Y	#	Y	*	
		Y	*	S	#			Y		Y	Y	Y	S	*	S	>	Y	#
			S	*				Y	Y			Y			Y	*	Y	Y
Y		Y	Y	*				S	>			S	#		S	*	Y		Y	#

Fourth grid

Rag	Sim	Haw	Pow	And	Bon	Cha	Rob	Whi	How	Lon	War	Gin	Sou	Kno	Ang	Eth	Cal	Wri	Sta	Cat	Hig	Ande	Tho	Fix	Moy	Nic
		Y	#	Y	#					Y								S	#	S	#	S	#	S	#	S	#			S	#
	S	#		Y	#					Y	#								Y				S	#	S	#	S	#		

Appearances & Goals 2016-17

	League			FA Cup			FA Trophy			Totals			Totals		Lincolnshire Cup		
	Apps	Subs	Goals	Apps	Subs	Goals	Apps	Subs	Goals	Apps	Subs	Goals	Apps	Goals	Apps	Subs	Goals
Paul FARMAN	44	0	0	9	0	0	5	0	0	58	0	0	58	0	2	0	0
Alex WOODYARD	44	1	1	9	0	0	1	2	0	54	3	1	57	1	2	0	0
Sam HABERGHAM	43	0	3	9	0	0	4	0	1	56	0	4	56	4	0	0	0
Matt RHEAD	40	3	14	9	0	0	2	2	0	51	5	14	56	14	1	0	0
Luke WATERFALL	44	0	7	9	0	0	1	1	0	54	1	7	55	7	1	0	0
Nathan ARNOLD	43	2	12	7	0	1	1	1	0	51	3	13	54	13	0	0	0
Sean RAGGETT	41	0	5	8	0	2	2	1	1	51	1	8	52	8	0	0	0
Bradley WOOD	32	2	2	9	0	0	4	2	0	45	4	2	49	2	2	0	0
Terry HAWKRIDGE	24	8	3	8	1	1	5	0	2	37	9	6	46	6	1	0	2
Alan POWER	14	16	2	7	2	2	4	2	0	25	20	4	45	4	2	0	0
Jack MULDOON	10	15	3	3	6	0	4	0	0	17	21	3	38	3	2	0	0
Elliott WHITEHOUSE	14	14	4	0	0	0	5	1	2	19	15	6	34	6	0	0	0
Adam MARRIOTT	8	17	4	0	2	0	3	1	0	11	20	4	31	4	0	0	0
Harry ANDERSON (L)	14	12	6	3	1	0	0	0	0	17	13	6	30	6	0	0	0
Theo ROBINSON	12	2	2	6	1	7	0	1	0	18	4	9	22	9	0	0	0
Sean LONG (L)	12	2	0	0	2	0	3	0	0	15	4	0	19	0	0	0	0
Lee BEEVERS	14	1	0	2	0	0	0	0	0	16	1	0	17	0	2	0	0
Josh GINNELLY (L)	7	6	0	0	0	0	2	2	0	9	8	0	17	0	0	0	0
Billy KNOTT (L)	8	6	1	0	0	0	2	1	0	10	7	1	17	1	0	0	0
Jamie McCOMBE	3	4	0	1	3	0	4	0	0	8	7	0	15	0	1	1	0
Callum HOWE	4	4	0	0	0	0	5	0	0	9	4	0	13	0	2	0	0
Lee ANGOL (L)	11	0	5	0	0	0	2	0	1	13	0	6	13	6	0	0	0
Jonny MARGETTS	7	3	5	0	1	0	0	0	0	7	4	5	11	5	1	0	2
Macauley BONNE (L)	5	3	1	0	0	0	0	0	0	5	3	1	8	1	0	0	0
Joe WARD (L)	0	2	0	0	2	0	4	0	3	4	4	3	8	3	0	0	0
Tom CHAMPION (L)	3	2	0	0	0	0	0	0	0	3	2	0	5	0	0	0	0
Dayle SOUTHWELL (L)	2	0	0	0	1	0	1	1	1	3	2	1	5	1	0	0	0
Ross ETHERIDGE (L)	2	0	0	0	0	0	1	0	0	3	0	0	3	0	0	0	0
Elliot HODGE	0	2	0	0	0	0	0	0	0	0	2	0	2	0	0	0	0
Alex SIMMONS	0	2	0	0	0	0	0	0	0	0	2	0	2	0	0	1	0
Riccardo CALDER (L)	1	0	0	0	0	0	1	0	0	2	0	0	2	0	0	0	0
Taylor MILES	0	1	0	0	0	0	0	0	0	0	1	0	1	0	2	0	0

Own goals

	League	FA Cup	FA Trophy	Totals	Lincolnshire Cup
Own goals	3	1	1	5	0

Players Used	League goals	FA Cup goals	FA Trophy goals	Total goals
32	83	14	12	109

Plus appearances in Lincolnshire Cup: James Caton 1 (1), Andrew Wright (1), Craig Stanley (1), Ryan Higgins (1), Luke Andersen (1), Ryley Thompson (1), Jack Fixter (1), Archie Moyses (1), Jordan Nicholson (1).

Squad Numbers 2016-17

1	Paul Farman	21	Richard Walton
2	Bradley Wood	22	Jack Fixter
3	Sam Habergham	23	Jimmy Walker
4	Craig Stanley; Elliott Whitehouse	24	
5	Luke Waterfall	25	Sean Raggett
6	Callum Howe	26	Tom Champion; Harry Anderson (second spell)
7	Jack Muldoon	27	Jamie McCombe
8	Alan Power	28	Nathan Arnold
9	Matt Rhead	29	Macauley Bonne
10	Adam Marriott	30	Alex Woodyard
11	Terry Hawkridge	31	Theo Robinson; Dayle Southwell; Lee Angol
12	Harry Anderson (first spell); Sean Long	32	Luke Andersen
13	Jonny Margetts	33	
14	Taylor Miles	34	Billy Knott
15	Kegan Everington	35	Archie Moyses
16	Alex Simmons	36	Josh Ginnelly
17	Elliot Hodge	37	Riccardo Calder
18	Lee Beevers	38	Joe Ward
19	Jenk Acar	39	Ross Etheridge
20	Andrew Wright		

National League Final League Table 2016-17

			Home					Away					Totals		
		P	W	D	L	F	A	W	D	L	F	A	F	A	Pts
1	**Lincoln City**	46	17	4	2	48	17	13	5	5	35	23	83	40	99
2	Tranmere Rovers	46	16	3	4	43	19	13	5	5	36	20	79	39	95
P	Forest Green Rovers	46	12	9	2	46	25	13	2	8	42	31	88	56	86
4	Dagenham & Redbridge	46	12	5	6	37	28	14	1	8	42	25	79	53	84
5	Aldershot Town	46	15	5	3	38	13	8	8	7	28	24	66	37	82
6	Dover Athletic	46	13	5	5	48	28	11	2	10	37	35	85	63	79
7	Barrow	46	12	8	3	40	20	8	7	8	32	33	72	53	75
8	Gateshead	46	9	9	5	38	23	10	4	9	34	28	72	51	70
9	Macclesfield Town	46	9	3	11	30	29	11	5	7	34	28	64	57	68
10	Bromley	46	11	3	9	33	37	7	5	11	26	29	59	66	62
11	Boreham Wood	46	8	7	8	23	21	7	6	10	26	27	49	48	58
12	Sutton United	46	13	6	4	41	25	2	7	14	20	38	61	63	58
13	Wrexham	46	10	5	8	23	24	5	8	10	24	37	47	61	58
14	Maidstone United	46	8	5	10	29	39	8	5	10	30	36	59	75	58
15	Eastleigh	46	8	7	8	28	26	6	8	9	28	37	56	63	57
16	Solihull Moors	46	8	3	12	35	38	7	7	9	27	37	62	75	55
17	Torquay United	46	9	5	9	34	28	5	6	12	20	33	54	61	53
18	Woking	46	9	7	7	32	30	5	4	14	34	50	66	80	53
19	Chester	46	8	3	12	37	35	6	7	10	26	36	63	71	52
20	Guiseley	46	9	6	8	32	31	4	6	13	18	36	50	67	51
21	York City	46	7	8	8	33	31	4	9	10	22	39	55	70	50
22	Braintree Town	46	6	4	13	23	36	7	5	11	28	40	51	76	48
23	Southport	46	7	5	11	32	41	3	4	16	20	56	52	97	39
24	North Ferriby United	46	6	2	15	17	40	6	1	16	15	42	32	82	39

113

Progress Chart 2016-17

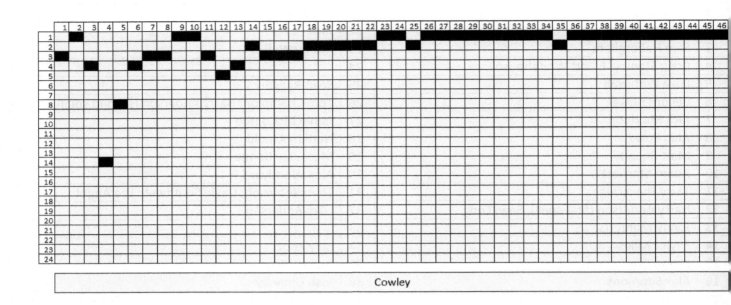

Cowley

Friendlies 2016-17

Jul	9	Worksop Town	2-0	317	Wetherell, Penfold
	12	Boston United	3-0	701	Margetts 3
	16	READING	4-1	1239	Caton, Muldoon, Waterfall, Wood
	19	Gainsborough Trinity	3-3	555	Margetts 2, Rhead
	26	PETERBOROUGH UNITED	2-2	1128	McCombe, Muldoon
	30	CREWE ALEXANDRA	3-0	1058	Marriott, Muldoon

Does not include the behind closed doors friendly against Peterborough United (28/9/2016).

Original Fixture List 2016-17

Aug	6	Woking		25	BOREHAM WOOD		18	Sutton United
	9	NORTH FERRIBY UTD		29	Chester		25	DAGENHAM & REDBGE
	13	SUTTON UNITED	Nov	12	ALDERSHOT TOWN		28	YORK CITY
	16	Dagenham & Redbridge		19	Forest Green Rovers	Mar	4	Aldershot Town
	20	SOUTHPORT		22	York City		11	CHESTER
	27	Macclesfield Town		26	MAIDSTONE UNITED		18	Maidstone United
	29	GATESHEAD		29	WREXHAM		21	Boreham Wood
Sep	3	Torquay United	Dec	3	Solihull Moors		25	FOREST GREEN ROVER
	10	Tranmere Rovers		17	TRANMERE ROVERS	Apr	1	BROMLEY
	13	SOLIHULL MOORS		26	Guiseley		8	Eastleigh
	17	BARROW	Jan	1	GUISELEY		14	TORQUAY UNITED
	24	Dover Athletic		7	Barrow		17	Gateshead
Oct	1	BRAINTREE TOWN		21	DOVER ATHLETIC		22	MACCLESFIELD TOWN
	4	Wrexham		28	Braintree Town		29	Southport
	8	Bromley	Feb	4	North Ferriby United			
	22	EASTLEIGH		11	WOKING	May	21	FA Trophy Final

Achievements

2016-17

◊ £2,500,000: The estimated earnings from the FA Cup run
◊ £639,000: Money received in live television fees from the FA Cup run
◊ £395,000: City's prize money for reaching the FA Cup quarter-final
◊ 158,834: The aggregate attendance at Sincil Bank in all matches
◊ 118,717: The aggregate attendance at Sincil Bank in the National League
◊ 59,454: The second-highest attendance ever to watch a Lincoln City match
◊ £32,000: Money received in live television fees for the 8 National League games shown
◊ £26,000: City's prize money for reaching the FA Trophy semi-final
◊ 10,031: The highest attendance at Sincil Bank since conversion to all-seated in 1999
◊ 8,942: City's away following at Arsenal, believed to be the largest in the club's history
◊ 7,442: The average home attendance since the Oldham FA Cup tie (15 matches)
◊ 5,477: The average attendance at Sincil Bank in all competitions
◊ 5,161: The average league attendance at Sincil Bank
◊ 4,838: The largest away following at Portman Road since conversion to all-seated in 1992
◊ 3,770: Gateshead's record attendance for a regular league match
◊ 3,462: Southport's record league attendance since demotion from the League in 1978
◊ 3,213: City's away following at Burnley
◊ 2,486: The largest ever away following at the Gateshead International Stadium
◊ 2,458: City's away following at Southport
◊ 2,389: North Ferriby United's record attendance, including over 2,000 from Lincoln
◊ 1,358: City's away following at York for the FA Trophy semi-final first leg
◊ 1,164: City's away following at Solihull Moors
◊ 1,068: City's away following at York for the league match in November
◊ 261: Alan Power's new club record for appearances outside the Football League
◊ 231: Paul Farman's new club record for starts outside the Football League
◊ 112: The percentage increase in attendances compared to 2015-16
◊ 103: The first non-league side for 103 years to reach the FA Cup quarter-final
◊ 99: New club record for points in a season
◊ 61: New club record for the most games played in a season
◊ 58: Paul Farman's new club record for appearances in a season by a goalkeeper
◊ 51: New club record for goals scored away from home in a season
◊ 40: New club record for wins in a season
◊ 37: Matt Rhead's new club record for goals scored outside the Football League
◊ 34: Matt Rhead's new club record for goals scored in the National League/Conference
◊ 19: New club record for the most away wins in a season
◊ 15: New club record for the most cup ties played in a season
◊ 15: The number of successive home attendances over 5,000, the best run since 1976-77
◊ 13: Equals the club record for the most away wins in the league in a season
◊ 12: New club record for matches shown live on television in a season
◊ 11: The eleventh promotion in City's history
◊ 10: The tenth divisional championship in City's history
◊ 9: New club record for the most FA Cup ties played in a season
◊ 7: The only National League side to win seven games in a row this season
◊ 6: Equals the club record for the most FA Trophy ties played in a season
◊ 3: Lee Angol the first City player to score a hat-trick away from home on his debut
◊ 2: City's second Conference/National League championship
◊ 1: First appearance in the FA Cup quarter-final
◊ 1: First appearance in the FA Trophy semi-final
◊ 1: Danny and Nicky Cowley's first season in full-time football

The Players

This section contains a detailed record for each of the 147 players to have made a first team appearance during City's six years out of the Football League. By definition, that relates to the Conference, the FA Cup and the FA Trophy. It does not include players named as unused substitutes, trialists, or those who appeared only in friendlies or Lincolnshire Cup matches; many of those will be found in the shorter section which follows.

Every effort has been made to ensure accuracy. There are many problems inherent in tracing the careers of non-league players, and I have chosen to use the month and year a player signed for a club in preference to the contract date. Where that is uncertain, the contract date is given. The first and final games stated are their first and final games for City **in non-league football**, not necessarily their first and final games for the club. For the sake of completeness, appearance statistics for Football League matches prior to relegation are also given.

Under the 'signed' and 'released' sections, the initials of the manager concerned are given in brackets: (PJ) - Peter Jackson; (CS) - Chris Sutton; (ST) - Steve Tilson; (GB) - Grant Brown; (DH) - David Holdsworth; (GS) - Gary Simpson; (CM) - Chris Moyses; (DC) - Danny Cowley.

ADAMS, Charlee

Born	16/2/1995, Redbridge
Signed	31/1/2014 (age 18) from Birmingham City on loan to the end of the season *(GS)*
First appearance	FC Halifax Town (H), Conference Premier, 1/2/2014
Final appearance	Woking (H), Conference, 28/2/2015
Released/sold	N/A

*Career: 2003 West Ham United (Y), May 2011 Birmingham City (Y), May 2013 Birmingham City (**Jan 2014 LINCOLN CITY - loan, Nov 2014 LINCOLN CITY - loan**, Aug 2016 Kilmarnock - loan).*

Young defensive midfielder who originally signed for City on a youth loan from Birmingham City on deadline day in January 2014. Quickly endeared himself to the City faithful with some committed and classy displays, earning several man of the match awards during his initial 14-game stay. He was snapped up on a further loan on 14 November 2014 until 1 January 2015, further extended on 22 December until the end of February. The loan was extended again on 21 January 2015 until the end of the season, but he was recalled on 3 March when new Birmingham manager Gary Rowett decided his development would be better served by playing in his U21 team. Charlee gained something of a name for scoring spectacular goals from distance during his two spells at Sincil Bank, with similar efforts against Grimsby and Aldershot earning him many hits on YouTube and a television interview. Broke into Birmingham's first team towards the end of the 2015-16 season, making a couple of appearances in the Championship, but was released a year later.

Lincoln City Playing Record - Conference Only

	League			FA Cup			FA Trophy			TOTALS			Lincolnshire Cup		
	App	Sub	Gls	App	Sub	Gls	App	Sub	Gls	App	Sub	Gls	App	Sub	Gls
2013-14	14	0	0	0	0	0	0	0	0	14	0	0	0	0	0
2014-15	14	0	2	0	0	0	1	0	0	15	0	2	0	0	0
TOTALS	28	0	2	0	0	0	1	0	0	29	0	2	0	0	0

ALMOND, Louis

Born	5/1/1992, Blackburn
Signed	31/1/2012 (age20) from Blackpool on loan to the end of the season *(DH)*
First appearance	Braintree Town (H), Conference Premier, 14/2/2012
Final appearance	Alfreton Town (H), Conference Premier, 10/3/2012
Released/sold	N/A

*Career: Aug 2009 Blackpool (Mar 2010 Cheltenham Town -loan, Dec 2010 Barrow - loan, Aug 2011 Barrow - loan, **Jan 2012 LINCOLN CITY - loan**, Sep 2012 Barrow - loan, Feb 2013 Hyde - loan, Aug 2013 Hyde - loan), Aug 2014 Hyde, Jan 2015 Southport, Sep 2016 Tranmere Rovers (Feb 2017 Southport - loan).*

Young striker who made just a couple of isolated appearances for Blackpool during his five years as a professional at Bloomfield Road, spending long spells on loan to clubs in the Conference Premier and below. Came on as a 67th-minute substitute against Braintree for his City debut and scored a stoppage-time equaliser. He failed to score again, and made only four more appearances for City before being recalled by Blackpool on 30 March 2012.

Lincoln City Playing Record - Conference Only

	League			FA Cup			FA Trophy			TOTALS			Lincolnshire Cup		
	App	Sub	Gls	App	Sub	Gls	App	Sub	Gls	App	Sub	Gls	App	Sub	Gls
2011-12	3	2	1	0	0	0	0	0	0	3	2	1	0	0	0
TOTALS	3	2	1	0	0	0	0	0	0	3	2	1	0	0	0

ANDERSON, Harry

Born	9/1/1997, Slough
Signed	16/8/2016 (age 19) from Peterborough United on loan to the New Year (DC)
First appearance	Dagenham & Redbridge (A), National League, 16/8/2016
Final appearance	Gateshead (A), National League, 17/4/2017
Released/sold	N/A

Career: 2013 Crawley Town (Y), Jul 2014 Peterborough United (Y), Mar 2015 Peterborough United (Jan 2016 Braintree Town - loan, Feb 2016 St Albans City - loan, **Aug 2016 LINCOLN CITY - loan, Mar 2017 LINCOLN CITY - loan**).

Strong right-sided midfielder/winger who originally signed on a youth loan until the New Year and proved to be one of the best loan signings in City's history. Was previously known to Danny Cowley, having spent a month during the 2015-16 season on loan at Braintree. Made a good impression with the fans with his pace and direct running, and it was disappointing when parent club Peterborough recalled him from his loan on 22 December 2016. Suffered a cartilage injury in his closing days at City which required an operation on his return to London Road. Re-signed for City in March for the final eleven games when Joe Ward was forced to return to Brighton, making his second City debut in the 3-1 home victory over promotion rivals Forest Green Rovers on 25 March. Scored vital goals from the substitute's bench in successive games against Chester and Torquay in April, and overall played an important role in City's promotion.

Lincoln City Playing Record - Conference Only

	League			FA Cup			FA Trophy			TOTALS			Lincolnshire Cup		
	App	Sub	Gls	App	Sub	Gls	App	Sub	Gls	App	Sub	Gls	App	Sub	Gls
2016-17	14	12	6	3	1	0	0	0	0	17	13	6	0	0	0
TOTALS	14	12	6	3	1	0	0	0	0	17	13	6	0	0	0

ANDERSON, Tom

Born	2/9/1993, Burnley
Signed	19/9/2014 (age 21) from Burnley on a one-month loan (GS)
First appearance	Aldershot Town (A), Conference, 20/9/2014
Final appearance	Wrexham (H), Conference, 18/10/2014
Released/sold	N/A

Career: 2000 Burnley (Y), May 2012 Burnley (Aug 2012 Barrow - loan, Feb 2013 Hyde - loan, Nov 2013 FC Halifax Town - loan, **Sep 2014 LINCOLN CITY - loan**, Oct 2014 Carlisle United - loan, Feb 2016 Chesterfield - loan, Aug 2016 Chesterfield - loan).

Impressive 6'4" central defender who joined City on loan from Premier League Burnley. Scored his first senior goal when he put City into the lead against Gateshead in the 1-1 draw on 30 September 2014. Returned to Burnley after a month when agreement on a loan extension could not be reached. Has since carved out a career in the lower divisions of the Football League.

Lincoln City Playing Record - Conference Only

	League			FA Cup			FA Trophy			TOTALS			Lincolnshire Cup		
	App	Sub	Gls	App	Sub	Gls	App	Sub	Gls	App	Sub	Gls	App	Sub	Gls
2014-15	6	0	1	0	0	0	0	0	0	6	0	1	0	0	0
TOTALS	6	0	1	0	0	0	0	0	0	6	0	1	0	0	0

ANGOL, Lee

Born	4/8/1994, Sutton
Signed	6/3/2017 (age 22) from Peterborough United on loan to the end of the season (DC)
First appearance	Braintree Town (A), National League, 7/3/2017
Final appearance	Southport (A), National League, 29/4/2017
Released/sold	N/A

Career: *Tottenham Hotspur (Y), Jul 2012 Wycombe Wanderers (Jan 2013 Hendon - loan, Aug 2013 Hendon - loan, Oct 2013 Maidenhead United - loan, Jan 2014 Boreham Wood - loan), Jul 2014 Luton Town (Jul 2014 Boreham Wood - loan), Jul 2015 Peterborough United (**Mar 2017 LINCOLN CITY - loan**), May 2017 Mansfield Town.*

Tall attacking midfielder/striker who joined the Imps on loan for the run-in of the 2016-17 championship season. Despite a good pedigree from the Spurs Academy, much of his early career had been spent out on loan from his various clubs. Made his name in the 2014-15 season while on loan at Conference South side Boreham Wood, scoring 30 goals in all competitions as they won promotion to the Conference. His 25 league goals earned him the Conference South Golden Boot, and he was named Young Player of the Year at the National Game Awards ahead of a number of players from the league above. Rejected a new contract offer from Luton at the end of that season and joined Peterborough. Did well in his first year in League One, but unfortunately broke an ankle in a pre-season game at Boston United in July 2016 and found it hard to regain his previous form on his return. Got his Imps career off to a terrific start by becoming only the second player in the club's history to score a hat-trick on his debut (and the first to do it away from home) in the 4-0 win at Braintree on 7 March 2017. Featured regularly as City closed in on the National League championship, leading the line ahead of strike partner Matt Rhead.

Lincoln City Playing Record - Conference Only

	League			FA Cup			FA Trophy			TOTALS			Lincolnshire Cup		
	App	Sub	Gls	App	Sub	Gls	App	Sub	Gls	App	Sub	Gls	App	Sub	Gls
2016-17	11	0	5	0	0	0	2	0	1	13	0	6	0	0	0
TOTALS	11	0	5	0	0	0	2	0	1	13	0	6	0	0	0

ANYON, Joe

Born	29/12/1986, Lytham St Annes
Signed	20/5/2010 (age 23) from Port Vale on a two-year deal (CS)
First appearance	Southport (A), Conference Premier, 13/8/2011
Final appearance	Ebbsfleet United (A), Conference Premier, 28/4/2012
Released/sold	5/5/2012 and joined Shrewsbury Town (DH)

Career: *Blackburn Rovers (Y), 2003 Port Vale (Y), 2004 Port Vale (Mar 2005 Stafford Rangers - loan, Aug 2005 Stafford Rangers - loan, Nov 2005 Harrogate Town - loan, Feb 2006 Harrogate Town - loan),* **May 2010 LINCOLN CITY** *(Mar 2011 Morecambe - loan), Jul 2012 Shrewsbury Town (Jan 2013 Macclesfield Town - loan), Jan 2015 Crewe Alexandra - non-contract, Jan 2015 Scunthorpe United, May 2017 Chesterfield.*

Highly-rated goalkeeper who found himself a remnant of City's relegation from the Football League. Having been signed by Chris Sutton on a two-year deal in May 2010, Joe originally made his debut for City in a League Two match at Rotherham on 7 August 2010. Lost his place in the closing months of the relegation season and joined Morecambe on loan, but started the new Conference season as first choice keeper despite being made available for immediate transfer by Steve Tilson in the summer. Popular with the fans, he often tried to rally supporters at a time when relationships between the club and its fan base were strained. Was voted *Player of the Season* and *Away Player of the Season* by fans in 2011-12 before leaving for Shrewsbury. Underwent three coronary operations in 2014 after being diagnosed with Wolff-Parkinson-White syndrome during a medical for a transfer from Shrewsbury to Cardiff City. The transfer fell through, but Anyon is still playing professional football today. Was capped by England at U16-level in his youth.

Lincoln City Playing Record - Conference Only

	League			FA Cup			FA Trophy			TOTALS			Lincolnshire Cup		
	App	Sub	Gls	App	Sub	Gls	App	Sub	Gls	**App**	**Sub**	**Gls**	App	Sub	Gls
2011-12	38	0	0	1	0	0	3	0	0	**42**	**0**	**0**	1	0	0
TOTALS	*38*	*0*	*0*	*1*	*0*	*0*	*3*	*0*	*0*	*42*	*0*	*0*	*1*	*0*	*0*

Lincoln City Playing Record - Football League

	League			FA Cup			League Cup			FL Trophy			TOTALS		
	App	Sub	Gls	App	Sub	Gls	App	Sub	Gls	App	Sub	Gls	**App**	**Sub**	**Gls**
2010-11	21	0	0	3	0	0	1	0	0	1	0	0	**26**	**0**	**0**
TOTALS	*21*	*0*	*0*	*3*	*0*	*0*	*1*	*0*	*0*	*1*	*0*	*0*	*26*	*0*	*0*

ARNAUD, Jean

Born	7/4/1987, Brou-sur-Chanteraine, France
Signed	27/9/2011 (age 24) from FC Libourne (France) on a four-month deal *(ST)*
First appearance	Tamworth (A), Conference Premier, 8/10/2011
Final appearance	As above - made only one appearance
Released/sold	7/12/2011 and joined KVK Tienen (Belgium) *(DH)*

Career: 2006 Racing Club Lens (France), AFC Compiègne (France), 2009 UD Melilla (Spain), Jul 2010 FC Libourne (France), Sep 2011 LINCOLN CITY, Jul 2012 KVK Tienen (Belgium), Jan 2013 RUW Ciney (Belgium).

French defender signed on a short-term contract to mid-January 2012 after a successful three-week trial. Has the dubious distinction of being the last player signed for City by Steve Tilson. Made his one and only appearance as a 63rd-minute substitute away at Tamworth just two days before Tilson was sacked. Immediately fell out of favour with caretaker manager Grant Brown and was released early from his contract by new manager David Holdsworth after less than three months with the club. Previously played with City team-mates Jean-François Christophe and Francis Laurent at French club AFC Compiègne, and the trio went on to appear for Belgian side KVK Tienen after leaving Sincil Bank. Also known by his full name - Jean Franck Arnaud - and by Arnaud Jean in Europe.

Lincoln City Playing Record - Conference Only

	League			FA Cup			FA Trophy			TOTALS			Lincolnshire Cup		
	App	Sub	Gls	App	Sub	Gls	App	Sub	Gls	**App**	**Sub**	**Gls**	App	Sub	Gls
2011-12	0	1	0	0	0	0	0	0	0	**0**	**1**	**0**	0	0	0
TOTALS	*0*	*1*	*0*	*0*	*0*	*0*	*0*	*0*	*0*	*0*	*1*	*0*	*0*	*0*	*0*

ARNOLD, Nathan

Born	26/7/1987, Mansfield
Signed	29/7/2016 (age 29) from Grimsby Town on a two-year deal *(DC)*
First appearance	Woking (A), National League, 6/8/2016
Final appearance	Southport (A), National League, 29/4/2017
Released/sold	

Career: 1999 Mansfield Town (Y), Jul 2005 Mansfield Town, Aug 2009 Hyde United, Jun 2010 Alfreton Town, Jul 2013 Cambridge United (Jul 2014 Grimsby Town - loan), May 2015 Grimsby Town, Jul 2016 LINCOLN CITY.

Skilful left-sided midfielder / striker who came to City having appeared in the National League play-off final in each of his last three seasons - once with Cambridge and twice with Grimsby, winning two of them. Also won the FA Trophy with Cambridge and reached the final with Grimsby in that same three-year period. Despite scoring in the play-off final and winning promotion to League Two, Arnold rejected a contract offer from Grimsby in the 2016 close season in search of a new challenge, and was signed by City using the money raised by the *Cowleys Campaign* Crowdfunder scheme. Immediately became an integral part of City's outstanding 2016-17 season, notably scoring the last-minute winner against Ipswich Town in the televised FA Cup third round replay and a brilliant late winner at Gateshead in April. Always intelligently-spoken and accessible to fans, he was often seen as a public representative for the players throughout the season. Frequently considered to be a manager in the making, Arnold was involved in the coaching and analysis side during the latter stages of the 2016-17 season and commenced studying for the UEFA B Licence in May 2017. Qualified as a hairdresser while playing for Alfreton in 2011, later starting his own mobile hairdressing business and working at the *Hairwayze* salon in Grimsby in his spare time. Won one England C cap in September 2008 in a 6-2 defeat to Bosnia and Herzegovina B.

Lincoln City Playing Record - Conference Only

	League			FA Cup			FA Trophy			TOTALS			Lincolnshire Cup		
	App	Sub	Gls	App	Sub	Gls	App	Sub	Gls	App	Sub	Gls	App	Sub	Gls
2016-17	43	2	12	7	0	1	1	1	0	51	3	13	0	0	0
TOTALS	43	2	12	7	0	1	1	1	0	51	3	13	0	0	0

ARTHUR, Koby

Born	31/1/1996, Kumasi, Ghana
Signed	21/3/2014 (age 18) from Birmingham City on loan to the end of the season (GS)
First appearance	Gateshead (A), Conference Premier, 22/3 2014
Final appearance	Barnet (H), Conference Premier, 26/4/2014
Released/sold	N/A

Career: *Woodford United (Y), 2012 Birmingham City (Y), Apr 2013 Birmingham City (**Mar 2014 LINCOLN CITY - loan**, Jul 2014 Cheltenham Town - loan, Aug 2016 Cheltenham Town - loan).*

Diminutive but strong attacking midfielder who became the third player to join City on loan from Birmingham City after Charlee Adams and Nick Townsend. Very highly regarded by Birmingham, having been named their Academy Player of the Season for 2012-13 shortly before signing his first professional deal. Appeared sporadically for the Blues' first team and enjoyed a couple of loan spells at Cheltenham before being released in March 2017.

Lincoln City Playing Record - Conference Only

	League			FA Cup			FA Trophy			TOTALS			Lincolnshire Cup		
	App	Sub	Gls	App	Sub	Gls	App	Sub	Gls	App	Sub	Gls	App	Sub	Gls
2013-14	2	4	0	0	0	0	0	0	0	2	4	0	0	0	0
TOTALS	2	4	0	0	0	0	0	0	0	2	4	0	0	0	0

AUDEL, Thierry

Born	15/1/1987, Nice, France
Signed	31/1/2014 (age 27) from Crewe Alexandra on a one-month loan initially (GS)
First appearance	FC Halifax Town (H), Conference Premier, 1/2/2014
Final appearance	Alfreton Town (H), FA Trophy 1, 13/12/2014
Released/sold	N/A

Career: *1992 Saint Laurent Du Var (Y), 1997 Cavigal de Nice (Y), 2001 OGC Nice (Y), 2003 FC Istres (Y), 2004 Auxerre (Y), Jun 2006 Auxerre, Jul 2007 Triestina (Italy) (Jul 2007 MNK Izola - loan, Jul 2008 San Marino - loan), Aug 2010 AC Pisa (Italy), Jan 2013 Macclesfield Town, Jun 2013 Crewe Alexandra (**Jan 2014 LINCOLN CITY - loan, Oct 2014 LINCOLN CITY - loan**), Feb 2015 Macclesfield Town, Aug 2015 Notts County, May 2017 released.*

French centre-half who had two spells on loan at Sincil Bank from parent club Crewe Alexandra. Enjoyed an intermittent career in France and Italy before trying his luck in England at the end of 2012. Originally signed on transfer deadline day in January 2014 for one month, the loan was extended to the end of the season on 4 March. Dangerous from set pieces, Audel provided a decent scoring record for a defender. Rejoined the Imps on 17 October 2014 for a three-month loan period, but injured a knee in Chris Moyses' first game as caretaker manager and never featured in a league match again. When he returned to Crewe, his contract was cancelled by mutual consent on 19 January 2015.

Lincoln City Playing Record - Conference Only

	League			FA Cup			FA Trophy			TOTALS			Lincolnshire Cup		
	App	Sub	Gls	App	Sub	Gls	App	Sub	Gls	App	Sub	Gls	App	Sub	Gls
2013-14	14	0	3	0	0	0	0	0	0	14	0	3	0	0	0
2014-15	3	0	0	3	0	0	0	1	0	6	1	0	0	0	0
TOTALS	17	0	3	3	0	0	0	1	0	20	1	3	0	0	0

AUSTIN, Mitch

Born	3/4/1991, Rochdale
Signed	2/1/2014 (age 22) from Cambridge United on a one-month loan (GS)
First appearance	Luton Town (H), Conference Premier, 4/1/2014
Final appearance	Hyde (A), Conference Premier, 8/2/2014
Released/sold	N/A

Career: Manly United (Y - Australia), 2009 Rotherham United (Y), Oct 2010 Stalybridge Celtic (Aug 2011 Worksop Town - loan), May 2013 Cambridge United (**Jan 2014 LINCOLN CITY - loan**, Mar 2014 Brackley Town - loan, Aug 2014 Brackley Town - loan, Sep 2014 Southport - loan), May 2015 Central Coast Mariners (Australia), Jun 2016 Melbourne Victory (Australia).

British-born Australian winger who signed on loan from Cambridge United with Delano Sam-Yorke in January 2014 (Austin for one month, Sam-Yorke for three). Having impressed in his first few games, the loan was extended on 3 February for a further month, but he was recalled by Cambridge on 14 February ahead of their FA Trophy semi-final against Grimsby Town. The son of Australian rugby player Greg Austin, Mitch was released by Cambridge in May 2015 and returned to Australia to play for Central Coast Mariners in the A-League.

Lincoln City Playing Record - Conference Only

	League			FA Cup			FA Trophy			TOTALS			Lincolnshire Cup		
	App	Sub	Gls	App	Sub	Gls	App	Sub	Gls	App	Sub	Gls	App	Sub	Gls
2013-14	4	2	0	0	0	0	0	0	0	4	2	0	0	0	0
TOTALS	4	2	0	0	0	0	0	0	0	4	2	0	0	0	0

BARRACLOUGH, Bradley

Born	26/5/1989, Nuneaton
Signed	1/8/2011 (age 22) on a one-year deal (ST)
First appearance	Southport (A), Conference Premier, 13/8/2011
Final appearance	Ebbsfleet United (A), Conference Premier, 5/1/2013
Released/sold	14/2/2013 and joined Gainsborough Trinity (DH)

Career: Bellarmine University Knights (USA), **Aug 2011 LINCOLN CITY** (Dec 2011 Buxton - loan, Aug 2012 Gainsborough Trinity - loan), Feb 2013 Gainsborough Trinity, Jun 2014 Bradford Park Avenue, Jul 2015 Buxton, May 2016 Spalding United.

Despite signing for City following a sports scholarship in the USA, Bradley Barraclough had lived in Lincoln since the age of four and was a Lincoln City supporter in his formative years. Won a trial and subsequent one-year contract by uploading clips of his 52 goals for Bellarmine University (Louisville, Kentucky) to YouTube and sending a link to City manager Steve Tilson. Started the 2011-12 season in the first team but was sent on loan to Buxton on 9 December until the end of the season; during his time there, he won the club's player of the season award. City took up the option in his contract for a further year on 2 May 2012, but he was soon out on loan again, this time to Gainsborough Trinity from 20 August to 2 January 2013. City released him on 14 February 2013 and he signed a permanent deal with Gainsborough in the face of competition from Boston United. City came in for severe criticism from fans when it emerged they had rejected a £6,000 offer for Barraclough on deadline day - 31 January - only to release him for free two weeks later. His last few weeks with City were marred by a disagreement with Gainsborough surrounding the financial aspects of his loan period. One of the few Lincoln City players to hold a degree, in psychology.

Lincoln City Playing Record - Conference Only

	League			FA Cup			FA Trophy			TOTALS			Lincolnshire Cup		
	App	Sub	Gls	App	Sub	Gls	App	Sub	Gls	App	Sub	Gls	App	Sub	Gls
2011-12	4	8	0	0	0	0	0	0	0	4	8	0	1	0	1
2012-13	0	1	0	0	0	0	0	0	0	0	1	0	1	0	0
TOTALS	4	9	0	0	0	0	0	0	0	4	9	0	2	0	1

BASSELE, Aristide

Born	15/7/1994, London
Signed	16/11/2012 (age 18) from AFC Bournemouth on loan until 2/1/2013 (DH)
First appearance	Hereford United (H), Conference Premier, 17/11/2012
Final appearance	Woking (H), Conference Premier, 4/12/2012
Released/sold	N/A

*Career: Bromley (Y), Jun 2011 Hayes & Yeading (Jan 2012 Burnham - loan), Jul 2012 AFC Bournemouth (**Nov 2012 LINCOLN CITY - loan**, Sep 2013 Dorchester Town - loan, Nov 2013 Welling United - loan, Mar 2014 Havant & Waterlooville - loan, Sep 2014 Welling United - loan, Mar 2015 Welling United - loan).*

Promising young striker who failed to win a regular place during his six-week loan and returned to Bournemouth in the New Year. Made several more loan moves before being released by Bournemouth in May 2015 without having made a first team appearance, his career appearing to fizzle out at that point.

Lincoln City Playing Record - Conference Only

	League			FA Cup			FA Trophy			TOTALS			Lincolnshire Cup		
	App	Sub	Gls	App	Sub	Gls	App	Sub	Gls	App	Sub	Gls	App	Sub	Gls
2012-13	1	1	0	0	0	0	1	0	0	2	1	0	0	0	0
TOTALS	1	1	0	0	0	0	1	0	0	2	1	0	0	0	0

BEARDSLEY, Jason

Born	12/7/1989, Uttoxeter
Signed	9/12/2011 (age 22) on a non-contract basis (DH)
First appearance	Grimsby Town (H), Conference Premier, 26/12/2011
Final appearance	As above - made only one appearance
Released/sold	6/1/2012 and joined Uttoxeter Town (DH)

*Career: Uttoxeter Juniors (Y), 1996 Derby County (Y), Jul 2007 Derby County (Jul 2008 Notts County - loan), Jan 2010 FC Tampa Bay (USA), Jul 2010 Macclesfield Town (Oct 2010 Eastwood Town - loan), Aug 2011 Mickleover Sports, Oct 2011 Stafford Rangers - non-contract, **Dec 2011 LINCOLN CITY - non-contract**, Aug 2012 Uttoxeter Town, Mar 2013 Eastwood Town, Mar 2013 Worcester City.*

Right-sided defender Jason Beardsley is perhaps the epitome of 'be careful what you wish for'. Beardsley left Championship club Derby County in September 2009 after allegedly telling manager Nigel Clough he was unhappy at not being in the first team. Despite a trial at Nottingham Forest shortly afterwards, Beardsley proceeded to float around the non-league scene in the Midlands for a couple of seasons without finding regular first team football at any level. Became known for unsuccessful trials with big clubs, numbering Port Vale, Oldham, Aberdeen, and a spell in the Netherlands amongst his less-successful ventures. Originally trialled for City in the summer of 2011, playing in the 2-0 pre-season friendly win at Barton Town Old Boys on 19 July, but was not offered a deal. Returned to City on non-contract terms on 9 December 2011 and made only one appearance as a substitute before his registration was cancelled on 6 January 2012. After several more unsuccessful trial periods at a variety of minor clubs, Beardsley finally admitted defeat and left football in the summer of 2013.

Lincoln City Playing Record - Conference Only

	League			FA Cup			FA Trophy			TOTALS			Lincolnshire Cup		
	App	Sub	Gls	App	Sub	Gls	App	Sub	Gls	App	Sub	Gls	App	Sub	Gls
2011-12	0	1	0	0	0	0	0	0	0	0	1	0	0	0	0
TOTALS	0	1	0	0	0	0	0	0	0	0	1	0	0	0	0

BEEVERS, Lee

Born	4/12/1983, Doncaster
Signed	14/5/2015 (age 31) from Mansfield Town on a two-year contract (CM)
First appearance	Cheltenham Town (H), National League, 8/8/2015
Final appearance	Boreham Wood (H), National League, 25/10/2016
Released/sold	

Career: *Jul 2000 Ipswich Town (Y), Mar 2001 Ipswich Town (Mar 2003 Boston United - loan), Jun 2003 Boston United,* **Feb 2005 LINCOLN CITY**, *Jun 2009 Colchester United, Jul 2011 Walsall, Jun 2012 Mansfield Town,* **May 2015 LINCOLN CITY**.

Originally signed from Boston United by Keith Alexander on 22 February 2005, Lee made his first City debut away to Leyton Orient in League Two later that day. The dependable left-sided defender became part of the most frugal City defence for many years, helping the side to reach the League Two play-offs in 2005, 2006 and 2007. The final game of his first spell with the Imps came at home to Aldershot Town in League Two on 2 May 2009. Signed for Colchester United on 29 June 2009, and has now played over 500 first-class matches. Played in almost every game in his first season back at Sincil Bank. Kept his place in the City side under Danny Cowley at right back, and was one of the stand-out performers until a ruptured patella tendon against Boreham Wood in October 2016 ended his season. Enjoyed a spell as a television pundit for BT Sport during City's FA Cup run in 2016-17, appearing alongside former England internationals Ian Wright and Michael Owen. Was awarded a testimonial in May in lieu of a contract offer, to take place in pre-season. Also won 7 caps for Wales U21, making his debut in a 4-0 home defeat to Germany on 8 February 2005. Captained the side for the first time in their 2-0 European U21 Championship qualifier defeat in Austria on 28 March 2005.

Lincoln City Playing Record - Conference Only

	League			FA Cup			FA Trophy			TOTALS			Lincolnshire Cup		
	App	Sub	Gls	App	Sub	Gls	App	Sub	Gls	App	Sub	Gls	App	Sub	Gls
2015-16	43	1	0	3	0	0	0	0	0	46	1	0	2	0	0
2016-17	14	1	0	2	0	0	0	0	0	16	1	0	2	0	0
TOTALS	57	2	0	5	0	0	0	0	0	62	2	0	4	0	0

Lincoln City Playing Record - Football League

	League			FA Cup			League Cup			FL Trophy			TOTALS		
	App	Sub	Gls	App	Sub	Gls	App	Sub	Gls	App	Sub	Gls	App	Sub	Gls
2004-05	4	6	0	0	0	0	0	0	0	0	0	0	4	6	0
2005-06	30	5	1	2	0	0	2	0	1	1	0	0	35	5	2
2006-07	44	2	5	1	0	0	1	0	1	1	0	0	47	2	6
2007-08	37	0	1	0	0	0	0	0	0	1	0	0	38	0	1
2008-09	43	1	2	2	0	0	1	0	0	1	0	0	47	1	2
TOTALS	158	14	9	5	0	0	4	0	2	4	0	0	171	14	11

BENCHERIF, Hamza

Born	2/2/1988, Paris, France
Signed	1/8/2014 (age 26) from JS Kabylie (Algeria) on a one-year deal (GS)
First appearance	Kidderminster Harriers (H), Conference, 9/8/2014
Final appearance	Dartford (A), Conference, 25/4/2015
Released/sold	1/7/2015 and joined FC Halifax Town (CM)

Career: EA Guingamp (Y), Jul 2006 Nottingham Forest (**Oct 2007 LINCOLN CITY - loan**), Jul 2009 Macclesfield Town, Jun 2011 Notts County, Sep 2013 Plymouth Argyle, Jan 2014 JS Kabylie (Algeria), **Aug 2014 LINCOLN CITY**, Jul 2015 FC Halifax Town, May 2016 Wrexham (Jan 2017 York City - loan), May 2017 released.

Solidly-built French-Algerian midfielder/defender who originally joined the Imps on loan for three months from Nottingham Forest in October 2007, making 12 League Two appearances plus one in the Football League Trophy, scoring one goal (against Chesterfield on 6 November). Made his professional debut during the loan, in the League Two game at Bury on 2 October. Unfortunately his loan period coincided with a downturn in form, with City winning just 2 of his 13 games, conceding 28 goals in the process. Joined the Imps on a permanent basis in August 2014, having played under Gary Simpson at Macclesfield between 2010 and 2011. Stayed only one season before rejecting terms to join fellow Conference side FC Halifax Town on a one-year deal. Had a mixed season with Halifax, winning the FA Trophy but suffering relegation to National League North, at which point he left for Wrexham. Won 7 caps for the Algeria U20 side in 2005/06, scoring one goal.

Lincoln City Playing Record - Conference Only

	League			FA Cup			FA Trophy			TOTALS			Lincolnshire Cup		
	App	Sub	Gls	App	Sub	Gls	App	Sub	Gls	App	Sub	Gls	App	Sub	Gls
2014-15	41	0	6	2	0	0	1	0	0	44	0	6	1	0	0
TOTALS	41	0	6	2	0	0	1	0	0	44	0	6	1	0	0

Lincoln City Playing Record - Football League

	League			FA Cup			League Cup			FL Trophy			TOTALS		
	App	Sub	Gls	App	Sub	Gls	App	Sub	Gls	App	Sub	Gls	App	Sub	Gls
2007-08	11	1	1	0	0	0	0	0	0	1	0	0	12	1	1
TOTALS	11	1	1	0	0	0	0	0	0	1	0	0	12	1	1

BLISSETT, Nathan

Born	29/6/1990, West Bromwich
Signed	26/11/2015 (age 25) from Bristol Rovers on a one-month loan (CM)
First appearance	Welling United (H), National League, 28/11/2015
Final appearance	FC Halifax Town (H), National League, 26/12/2015
Released/sold	N/A

Career: Kidsgrove Athletic (Y), Nov 2011 Romulus, Aug 2012 Kidderminster Harriers (Mar 2013 Cambridge United - loan, Dec 2013 Hednesford Town - loan, Nov 2014 Bristol Rovers - loan) Jan 2015 Bristol Rovers (Aug 2015 Tranmere Rovers - loan, **Nov 2015 LINCOLN CITY - loan**), Jan 2016 Torquay United, Jan 2017 Plymouth Argyle.

Tall striker who had impressed against the Imps for Bristol Rovers on 7 February 2015, scoring their second goal in a 2-0 win. Signed for Lincoln on an emergency loan until 4 January 2016 with a view to a permanent move, but did not do enough to win a contract. Was released by Bristol Rovers on his return and signed for Torquay United on 14 January 2016 until the end of the season. Scored 8 goals in 17 games to help keep Torquay in the National League, earning a one-year contract extension. Has since progressed to the Football League with Plymouth. The nephew of former Watford and England striker Luther Blissett.

	League			FA Cup			FA Trophy			TOTALS			Lincolnshire Cup		
	App	Sub	Gls	App	Sub	Gls	App	Sub	Gls	App	Sub	Gls	App	Sub	Gls
2015-16	1	2	0	0	0	0	1	0	0	2	2	0	0	0	0
TOTALS	1	2	0	0	0	0	1	0	0	2	2	0	0	0	0

BONNE, Macauley

Born	26/10/1995, Ipswich
Signed	2/9/2016 (age 20) from Colchester United on a two-month youth loan *(DC)*
First appearance	Torquay United (A), National League, 3/9/2016
Final appearance	Bromley (A), National League, 8/10/2016
Released/sold	N/A

*Career: 2003 Ipswich Town (Y), 2009 Norwich City (Y), 2009 Colchester United (Y), Oct 2013 Colchester United **(Sep 2016 LINCOLN CITY - loan**, Jan 2017 Woking - loan).*

Young striker signed from Colchester United on a youth loan until 26 October 2016, his 21st birthday. Became a regular squad member at Colchester from an early age, scoring his debut goal against Peterborough on his 18th birthday, and grabbing four in a 6-2 win at Wealdstone in the FA Cup First Round on 7 November 2015. Signed a new two-year contract with Colchester in June 2016 and joined the Imps to get some game time. Lincoln saw Bonne as a short-term solution following the sale of Jonny Margetts to Scunthorpe, rather than a longer-term target. Scored what proved to be a crucial winner at Tranmere but suffered concussion against Barrow and lost form thereafter. Qualifying for Zimbabwe through his parents, Bonne made a scoring debut for their U23 side in Morocco in November 2014, and has since been called up several times by the senior squad without having yet made his debut.

Lincoln City Playing Record - Conference Only

	League			FA Cup			FA Trophy			TOTALS			Lincolnshire Cup		
	App	Sub	Gls	App	Sub	Gls	App	Sub	Gls	App	Sub	Gls	App	Sub	Gls
2016-17	5	3	1	0	0	0	0	0	0	5	3	1	0	0	0
TOTALS	5	3	1	0	0	0	0	0	0	5	3	1	0	0	0

BORE, Peter

Born	4/11/1987, Grimsby
Signed	31/1/2012 (age 24) from Harrogate Town to the end of the season *(DH)*
First appearance	Braintree Town (H), Conference Premier, 14/2/2012
Final appearance	Walsall (A), FA Cup 1 Replay, 13/11/2012
Released/sold	7/1/2013 and joined Gateshead *(DH)*

*Career: 1999 Grimsby Town (Y), Aug 2006 Grimsby Town (Sep 2008 York City - loan), Aug 2011 Harrogate Town, **Jan 2012 LINCOLN CITY**, Jan 2013 Gateshead, Jun 2013 Boston United, Oct 2013 Spalding United - dual registration, Jan 2014 King's Lynn Town, Jul 2014 Spalding United, Oct 2014 retired.*

Utility man who had amassed over 170 appearances for neighbours Grimsby Town between 2006 and 2011. Although playing much of his career as a defender, Bore had started as a striker and had two hat-tricks to his name at Blundell Park. Left Grimsby in the summer of 2011 ostensibly to find a club in the Football League, but failed numerous trials and ended up at Conference North side Harrogate. One of four players signed on deadline day in January 2012 for less than half the cost of Gavin McCallum's wage, Bore signed a deal until the end of the 2011-12 season. Having signed a new one-year deal on 21 May 2012, he failed to hold down a regular place in the side and had his contract cancelled by mutual consent on 7 January 2013.

Lincoln City Playing Record - Conference Only

	League			FA Cup			FA Trophy			TOTALS			Lincolnshire Cup		
	App	Sub	Gls	App	Sub	Gls	App	Sub	Gls	App	Sub	Gls	App	Sub	Gls
2011-12	11	0	2	0	0	0	0	0	0	11	0	2	0	0	0
2012-13	5	2	0	1	1	0	1	0	0	7	3	0	0	0	0
TOTALS	16	2	2	1	1	0	1	0	0	18	3	2	0	0	0

BOYCE, Andrew

Born	5/11/1989, Doncaster
Signed	25/5/2012 (age 22) from Gainsborough Trinity on a one-year deal (DH))
First appearance	Kidderminster Harriers (H), Conference Premier, 11/8/2012
Final appearance	Plymouth Argyle (A), FA Cup 1 Replay, 20/11/2013
Released/sold	6/1/2014 and joined Scunthorpe United (GS)

Career: 2006 Doncaster Rovers (Y), May 2008 Doncaster Rovers (Sep 2008 Worksop Town L), Aug 2009 King's Lynn, Dec 2009 Gainsborough Trinity, **May 2012 LINCOLN CITY** *(Nov 2013 Scunthorpe United - loan), Jan 2014 Scunthorpe United (Mar 2014 Grimsby Town - loan, Aug 2014 Grimsby Town - loan, Aug 2015 Hartlepool United - loan, Mar 2016 Notts County - loan), Jun 2016 Grimsby Town*

One of a select number of players to have appeared for all three professional Lincolnshire clubs, centre half Boyce can also add Gainsborough Trinity to his collection. Signed for City on an initial one-year deal, with the fee eventually decided by a tribunal in August 2012 (believed to be £12,500 plus a sell-on clause). Tall and strong, he quickly became a fans' favourite with some very solid defensive displays and an eye for goal from set-pieces. Boyce signed a new two-year deal on 14 June 2013, but soon came to the attention of Scunthorpe United, whose chairman Peter Swann had been Boyce's chairman at Gainsborough. On 15 November 2013 Scunthorpe triggered a release clause in his contract, with Boyce moving to Glanford Park initially on loan from 22 November. The transfer was made permanent at the start of January 2014 for an undisclosed fee, estimated variously to be between £30,000 and £50,000. City fans were not amused when he was almost immediately loaned to Conference rivals Grimsby on 10 March, meaning he had managed to appear for all three senior Lincolnshire clubs in the space of four months.

Lincoln City Playing Record - Conference Only

	League			FA Cup			FA Trophy			TOTALS			Lincolnshire Cup		
	App	Sub	Gls	App	Sub	Gls	App	Sub	Gls	App	Sub	Gls	App	Sub	Gls
2012-13	41	0	4	6	0	0	0	0	0	47	0	4	0	0	0
2013-14	19	0	1	4	0	1	0	0	0	23	0	2	0	1	0
TOTALS	60	0	5	10	0	1	0	0	0	70	0	6	0	1	0

BOYD, Adam

Born	25/5/1982, Hartlepool
Signed	16/11/2012 (age 30) from Celtic Nation until the New Year (DH)
First appearance	Tamworth (A), FA Trophy 1, 24/11/2012
Final appearance	As above - made only one appearance
Released/sold	2/1/2013 and joined Spennymoor Town (DH)

Career: 1998 Hartlepool United (Y), 1999 Hartlepool United (Nov 2003 Boston United - loan), Jul 2006 Luton Town, Jul 2007 Leyton Orient, May 2009 Hartlepool United, Jul 2012 Celtic Nation, **Nov 2012 LINCOLN CITY,** *Jan 2013 Spennymoor Town - non-contract, Jul 2013 Bishop Auckland, May 2014 retired.*

Colourful centre forward who arrived at Lincoln towards the end of a career that had attracted as much attention for his off-field antics as on it. Had a good scoring record at hometown club Hartlepool before a long-term knee injury halted his progress. Surprisingly fetched a £500,000 transfer fee when he signed for Luton in July 2006, but failed to make the grade in the Championship and began a descent through the leagues. Came to Lincoln on trial at the start of November 2012 on the recommendation of City striker Colin Larkin, who had played with Boyd at Hartlepool. Signed a short-term deal on 16 November until 2 January, but his much-publicised fitness problems never allowed him to regain his earlier form and he was released when his contract expired.

Lincoln City Playing Record - Conference Only

	League			FA Cup			FA Trophy			TOTALS			Lincolnshire Cup		
	App	Sub	Gls	App	Sub	Gls	App	Sub	Gls	App	Sub	Gls	App	Sub	Gls
2012-13	0	0	0	0	0	0	0	1	0	0	1	0	0	0	0
TOTALS	0	0	0	0	0	0	0	1	0	0	1	0	0	0	0

BRIGHT, Kris

Born	5/9/1986, Manukau, New Zealand
Signed	8/3/2014 (age 27) from IFK Mariehamn (Finland) to the end of the season (GS)
First appearance	Welling United (H), Conference Premier, 11/3/2014
Final appearance	Barnet (H), Conference Premier, 26/4/2014
Released/sold	8/5/2014 and joined Bharat FC (India) (GS)

Career: 2002 Manurewa (New Zealand), Feb 2004 North Shore United (New Zealand), Apr 2004 Waitakere City (New Zealand), 2005 Canterbury United (New Zealand), 2005 New Zealand Knights (New Zealand), Jul 2006 Fortuna Sittard (Netherlands), Jan 2007 Kristiansund BK (Norway), Jan 2009 Panserraikos (Greece), Aug 2009 Shrewsbury Town, Feb 2011 Honved (Hungary), Oct 2011 Balzan Youths (Malta), Jan 2012 Bryne FK (Norway), Aug 2012 FC Haka (Finland), Mar 2013 IFK Mariehamn (Finland), Mar 2014 LINCOLN CITY, Nov 2014 Bharat FC (India), Jul 2015 Bidvest Wits (South Africa), Aug 2016 Linfield, May 2017 released.

Globe-trotting New Zealander who had played in New Zealand, Greece, Netherlands, Norway, Hungary, Malta and Finland before arriving at Lincoln in March 2014. Desperate to earn a career in English football, Bright had several unsuccessful trials with British clubs at various times including Gillingham, Kilmarnock, Norwich and Coventry; he had actually scored his first goal in England against Lincoln, the only goal of the game for Shrewsbury on 17 April 2010. Signed a contract at Sincil Bank until the end of the season to replace the departed Delano Sam-Yorke and scored within 5 minutes of his debut against Welling. Was then suspended for three games following a red card against Braintree and never really got going after that. Also scored in his final game for the Imps in the infamous end of season game against Barnet, but it was not enough to secure a longer-term deal and he was released at the end of his contract. Returned for pre-season training in July 2014 but finances did not allow the club to offer him a deal. Despite an excellent career scoring record of a goal every two games, he has found it impossible to settle anywhere. Played international football for New Zealand at numerous levels including 5 full caps between 2008 and 2013, and was selected as a reserve for the 2010 World Cup Finals in South Africa. His father Dave Bright also played for New Zealand, notably in the 1982 World Cup.

Lincoln City Playing Record - Conference Only

	League			FA Cup			FA Trophy			TOTALS			Lincolnshire Cup		
	App	Sub	Gls	App	Sub	Gls	App	Sub	Gls	App	Sub	Gls	App	Sub	Gls
2013-14	7	0	2	0	0	0	0	0	0	7	0	2	0	0	0
TOTALS	7	0	2	0	0	0	0	0	0	7	0	2	0	0	0

BROUGH, Patrick

Born	20/2/1996, Carlisle
Signed	2/1/2016 (age 19) from Carlisle United on a one-month youth loan (CM)
First appearance	FC Halifax Town (A), National League, 2/1/2016
Final appearance	Wrexham (A), National League, 23/1/2016
Released/sold	N/A

Young defender who signed on a one-month youth loan from Carlisle at the start of 2016. Did reasonably well in his initial matches, but did not offer anything the club did not already have on the books and returned to Carlisle at the start of February.

Lincoln City Playing Record - Conference Only

	League			FA Cup			FA Trophy			TOTALS			Lincolnshire Cup		
	App	Sub	Gls	App	Sub	Gls	App	Sub	Gls	App	Sub	Gls	App	Sub	Gls
2015-16	4	0	0	0	0	0	0	0	0	4	0	0	0	0	0
TOTALS	4	0	0	0	0	0	0	0	0	4	0	0	0	0	0

BROWN, Nat

Born	15/6/1981, Sheffield
Signed	1/3/2013 (age 31) from Macclesfield Town on loan to the end of the season *(GS)*
First appearance	Woking (A), Conference Premier, 2/3/2013
Final appearance	Gateshead (A), National League, 31/8/2015
Released/sold	23/5/2016 and joined Boston United *(DC)*

Career: 1998 Huddersfield Town (Y), Jul 2000 Huddersfield Town, **Jul 2005 LINCOLN CITY**, Jun 2008 Wrexham (Nov 2008 Macclesfield Town - loan), Jan 2009 Macclesfield Town (**Feb 2013 LINCOLN CITY - loan**), **Jun 2013 LINCOLN CITY** (Oct 2015 FC Halifax Town - loan, Jan 2016 Harrogate Town - loan, Mar 2016 Boston United - loan), Jun 2016 Boston United (Feb 2017 Hednesford Town - loan), May 2017 released.

Tall central defender who became a great servant to the club in two separate spells. Originally signed by Keith Alexander on 4 July 2005, making his City debut at home to Northampton on 6 August. Became an integral part of the side that reached the League Two play-offs in 2006 and 2007, appearing both in defence and in midfield. Had his contract cancelled by mutual consent and left for Wrexham on 27 June 2008 for a spell before rejoining Alexander at Macclesfield Town. Re-signed for Lincoln on 1 March 2013, initially on loan to the end of the season before agreeing a permanent one-year contract on 3 June. Triggered another year from 1 July 2014 through appearances, and signed a further contract extension on 20 March 2015 to take him to the end of 2015-16 season. Fell out of favour at the start of the 2015-16 season after a disappointing performance against Grimsby and played his last game for City at Gateshead two days later (as did Jon Nolan). Joined Harrogate Town on loan on 15 January 2016, extended for a further month on 15 February. Signed for Boston United on loan from 16 March until the end of the season, having been told he would not be offered a new contract. Nat impressed in their run to the Conference North play-offs, and signed a permanent one-year deal with Boston in June 2016. One of only two players to have played more than 100 games for City in two separate spells, the other being Phil Hubbard.

Lincoln City Playing Record - Conference Only

	League			FA Cup			FA Trophy			TOTALS			Lincolnshire Cup		
	App	Sub	Gls	App	Sub	Gls	App	Sub	Gls	App	Sub	Gls	App	Sub	Gls
2012-13	10	0	0	0	0	0	0	0	0	10	0	0	0	0	0
2013-14	44	0	2	4	0	0	3	0	0	51	0	2	1	0	0
2014-15	36	0	0	3	0	0	0	0	0	39	0	0	1	0	0
2015-16	2	0	0	0	0	0	0	0	0	2	0	0	1	0	0
TOTALS	92	0	2	7	0	0	3	0	0	102	0	2	3	0	0

Lincoln City Playing Record - Football League

	League			FA Cup			League Cup			FL Trophy			TOTALS		
	App	Sub	Gls	App	Sub	Gls	App	Sub	Gls	App	Sub	Gls	App	Sub	Gls
2005-06	39	2	7	2	0	0	2	0	0	1	0	1	44	2	8
2006-07	27	3	1	1	0	0	0	0	0	1	0	0	29	3	1
2007-08	23	4	0	0	0	0	1	0	0	0	0	0	24	4	0
TOTALS	89	9	8	3	0	0	3	0	0	2	0	1	97	9	9

BURROW, Jordan

Born	12/9/1992, Sheffield
Signed	21/5/2014 (age 21) from Stevenage on a two-year deal (GS)
First appearance	Kidderminster Harriers (H), Conference, 9/8/2014
Final appearance	Dartford (A), Conference, 25/4/2015
Released/sold	24/6/2015 and joined FC Halifax Town (CM)

Career: 2000 Chesterfield (Y), 2011 Chesterfield (Sep 2011 Boston United - loan), Jan 2012 Morecambe, May 2013 Stevenage, **May 2014 LINCOLN CITY**, Jun 2015 FC Halifax Town, Nov 2016 Gateshead.

Promising young striker signed on a two-year deal in May 2014. Made a very good start to his City career, scoring regularly, but fell out of favour soon after the appointment of Chris Moyses and dropped to the substitutes' bench. Despite being under contract for a further year, he was made available for immediate transfer in the retained list at the end of the season. Many supporters were surprised by this, as Burrow had been impressive leading the line at times and had also been capped three times by England C during the season: v Turkey B (A) on 14 October 2014; v Estonia U23 (H) on 18 November 2014; and v Cyprus U21 (A) on 17 February 2015. He signed for FC Halifax Town and continued to score goals in a poor side as Halifax were relegated from the National League, although he was part of the side that won the FA Trophy that same season. Made one appearance for Lincoln as a trialist against Gainsborough in a behind-closed-doors friendly in January 2012 shortly before he joined Morecambe.

Lincoln City Playing Record - Conference Only

	League			FA Cup			FA Trophy			TOTALS			Lincolnshire Cup		
	App	Sub	Gls	App	Sub	Gls	App	Sub	Gls	App	Sub	Gls	App	Sub	Gls
2014-15	28	11	10	3	0	0	1	0	0	32	11	10	1	0	0
TOTALS	28	11	10	3	0	0	1	0	0	32	11	10	1	0	0

BUSH, Chris

Born	12/6/1992, Leytonstone
Signed	7/1/2013 (age 20) from Gateshead on a one-month loan (DH)
First appearance	Southport (A), Conference Premier, 8/1/2013
Final appearance	Southport (A), National League, 16/4/2016
Released/sold	27/6/2016 and joined Chelmsford City (DC)

Career: 2008 Brentford (Y) (Feb 2010 Salisbury City - loan, Aug 2010 Woking - loan, Sep 2010 AFC Wimbledon - loan, Mar 2011 Thurrock - loan), Jun 2011 AFC Wimbledon, Jun 2012 Gateshead (**Jan 2013 LINCOLN CITY - loan,** Mar 2013 Hereford United - loan), Jun 2013 Hereford United, Jun 2014 Welling United, **May 2015 LINCOLN CITY**, Jun 2016 Chelmsford City.

Powerful defender/midfielder who originally signed on loan for a month at the start of 2013, making his debut as a substitute for Paul Robson in a 4-2 defeat at Southport. Had an eventful three games, scoring on his full debut against Newport (unfortunately City were already 4-1 down by half time) and finishing with an own goal against Forest Green. City lost all 3 games of his loan period, conceding 10 goals in the process, and Bush returned to Gateshead at the end of the month. He came back to haunt City on 24 September 2013, scoring the only goal of the game for Hereford in a dismal defeat at Edgar Street. Signed by Chris Moyses on a permanent basis from Welling United on 28 May 2015 on a one-year deal, he made his second City debut in a win at Braintree on 11 August. Although many fans felt he could be a better player than he showed, performances were disappointing despite his obvious commitment and he spent much of the season in and out of the side. Always big and strong, some felt he was too heavy; certainly his touch on the ball was often questionable. Despite triggering a contract extension through appearances, he was placed on the transfer list by new manager Danny Cowley on 15 June 2016, sparking rumours of fitness problems again. He signed for Conference South side Chelmsford City a couple of weeks later.

	League			FA Cup			FA Trophy			TOTALS			Lincolnshire Cup		
	App	Sub	Gls	App	Sub	Gls	App	Sub	Gls	App	Sub	Gls	App	Sub	Gls
2012-13	2	1	1	0	0	0	0	0	0	2	1	1	0	0	0
2015-16	29	2	1	3	0	0	1	0	0	33	2	1	1	1	0
TOTALS	31	3	2	3	0	0	1	0	0	35	3	2	1	1	0

CALDER, Riccardo

Born	26/1/1996, Birmingham
Signed	10/3/2017 (age 21) from Aston Villa on loan to the end of the season *(DC)*
First appearance	York City (H), FA Trophy semi-final second leg, 18/3/2017
Final appearance	Maidstone United (A), National League, 25/4/2017
Released/sold	N/A

*Career: 2005 Aston Villa (Y), Jul 2014 Aston Villa (Aug 2015 Dundee - loan, Mar 2016 Doncaster Rovers - loan, Jul 2016 Doncaster Rovers - loan, **Mar 2017 LINCOLN CITY - loan**).*

Left-back who came to Sincil Bank on loan as cover for Sam Habergham in the closing weeks of the 2016-17 season. Parent club Aston Villa paid his wages for the whole of his loan period, but he received very few opportunities. Capped by England U17 in 2012, playing in the Nordic Under 17 Football Championships all the way to the final, as England lost 2-0 to Sweden.

	League			FA Cup			FA Trophy			TOTALS			Lincolnshire Cup		
	App	Sub	Gls	App	Sub	Gls	App	Sub	Gls	App	Sub	Gls	App	Sub	Gls
2016-17	1	0	0	0	0	0	1	0	0	2	0	0	0	0	0
TOTALS	1	0	0	0	0	0	1	0	0	2	0	0	0	0	0

CAPRICE, Jake

Born	27/9/1993, Lambeth
Signed	1/8/2014 (age 20) from Blackpool on a one-year deal *(GS)*
First appearance	Kidderminster Harriers (H), Conference, 9/8/2014
Final appearance	Eastleigh (H), Conference, 18/4/2015
Released/sold	6/5/2015 and joined Woking *(CM)*

*Career: 2004 Crystal Palace (Y), Mar 2011 Crystal Palace, Jul 2012 Blackpool (Nov 2012 Dagenham & Redbridge - loan, Aug 2013 St Mirren - loan, Mar 2014 Tamworth - loan), **Aug 2014 LINCOLN CITY**, Jun 2015 Woking.*

Promising young right-back who joined the club after being released by Blackpool in the summer of 2014. Initially lost his place in the side to Tom Miller, but ended the season as first choice full back. Was surprisingly released at the end of the season and joined Woking. Despite his penchant for attacking down the right wing, Caprice has yet to score his first career goal in over 150 appearances.

	League			FA Cup			FA Trophy			TOTALS			Lincolnshire Cup		
	App	Sub	Gls	App	Sub	Gls	App	Sub	Gls	App	Sub	Gls	App	Sub	Gls
2014-15	34	3	0	0	0	0	1	0	0	35	3	0	1	1	0
TOTALS	34	3	0	0	0	0	1	0	0	35	3	0	1	1	0

CATON, James

Born	4/1/1994, Widnes
Signed	29/1/2016 (age 22) from Shrewsbury Town on loan until the end of the season *(CM)*
First appearance	Guiseley (H), National League, 30/1/2016
Final appearance	Cheltenham Town (A), National League, 30/4/2016
Released/sold	N/A

Career: 2003 Bolton Wanderers (Y), 2010 Bolton Wanderers, Aug 2012 Blackpool (Oct 2013 Accrington Stanley - loan, Mar 2014 Chester - loan), Jun 2014 Shrewsbury Town (Jan 2015 Southport - loan, Aug 2015 Mansfield Town - loan, Nov 2015 Wrexham - loan, **Jan 2016 LINCOLN CITY - loan**), Aug 2016 Southport, Feb 2017 Dover Athletic, May 2017 released.

Skilful left-winger who helped to revive City's play-off hopes towards the end of the 2015-16 season. Was released by Shrewsbury at the end of his loan period and started the 2016-17 pre-season training with the Imps, playing in several pre-season friendlies. Agreement on a permanent contract could not be reached, and he surprisingly signed for National League rivals Southport.

Lincoln City Playing Record - Conference Only

	League			FA Cup			FA Trophy			TOTALS			Lincolnshire Cup		
	App	Sub	Gls	App	Sub	Gls	App	Sub	Gls	App	Sub	Gls	App	Sub	Gls
2015-16	8	4	3	0	0	0	0	0	0	8	4	3	0	0	0
2016-17	0	0	0	0	0	0	0	0	0	0	0	0	1	1	1
TOTALS	8	4	3	0	0	0	0	0	0	8	4	3	1	1	1

CHAMPION, Tom

Born	15/5/1986, Barnet
Signed	12/9/2016 (age 30) from Barnet on a three-month loan *(DC)*
First appearance	Solihull Moors (H), National League, 13/9/2016
Final appearance	Bromley (A), National League, 8/10/2016
Released/sold	N/A

Career: Watford (Y), Jul 2004 Barnet (Feb 2005 Wealdstone - loan), Jul 2005 Bishop's Stortford, Jan 2010 Braintree Town, May 2010 Dartford, May 2013 Cambridge United, May 2015 Barnet (**Sep 2016 LINCOLN CITY - loan**), May 2017 released.

Signed on loan from League Two Barnet with a view to a permanent move, Tom Champion was brought in to fill a gap in central midfield. Vastly experienced in non-league football, he was part of the Cambridge United side that won promotion to League Two in 2014. Unfortunately failed to impress at Sincil Bank, with City winning just one of his five games, and returned to Barnet after one month of his intended three.

Lincoln City Playing Record - Conference Only

	League			FA Cup			FA Trophy			TOTALS			Lincolnshire Cup		
	App	Sub	Gls	App	Sub	Gls	App	Sub	Gls	App	Sub	Gls	App	Sub	Gls
2016-17	3	2	0	0	0	0	0	0	0	3	2	0	0	0	0
TOTALS	3	2	0	0	0	0	0	0	0	3	2	0	0	0	0

CHRISTOPHE, Jean-François

Born	27/6/1987, Creil, France
Signed	22/8/2011 (age 24) from AFC Compiègne (France) on a one-year deal *(ST)*
First appearance	Darlington (A), Conference Premier, 29/8/2011
Final appearance	Fleetwood Town (A), Conference Premier, 13/4/2012
Released/sold	5/5/2012 and eventually joined KVK Tienen (Belgium) *(DH)*

Career: *Racing Club Lens (Y), 2007 Portsmouth (Aug 2007 AFC Bournemouth - loan, Mar 2008 Yeovil Town - loan, Sep 2008 Southend United - loan) Dec 2008 Southend United, Sep 2010 Oldham Athletic - non-contract, Nov 2010 AFC Compiègne (France),* **Aug 2011 LINCOLN CITY,** *Jan 2013 KVK Tienen (Belgium), Mar 2013 CS Avion (France), Jun 2013 Francs-Borains (Belgium) which changed its name to RFC Seraing in 2014, Jun 2015 Arras FA (France), Jul 2016 US Vimy (France).*

Rangy midfielder who tried unsuccessfully to establish himself in English football. Signed on a one-year deal on 10 August 2011 with the deal coming into effect on 22 August. Was persuaded to join Lincoln by Francis Laurent, a former colleague from Southend United where Steve Tilson had also been their manager. Was one of the better players in a disappointing City side, but left the club when City had to reduce the wage bill at the end of the 2011-12 season. Having lost the solidarity payment (£225,000) from the Football League, Christophe was made an offer but did not wish to accept reduced terms and returned to the continent. Later played for Belgian Third Division side KVK Tienen with former City colleagues Laurent and Jean Arnaud before bouncing around lower-division and non-league football in Belgium and France.

Lincoln City Playing Record - Conference Only

	League			FA Cup			FA Trophy			TOTALS			Lincolnshire Cup		
	App	Sub	Gls	App	Sub	Gls	App	Sub	Gls	App	Sub	Gls	App	Sub	Gls
2011-12	22	5	2	2	0	0	3	0	0	27	5	2	0	0	0
TOTALS	22	5	2	2	0	0	3	0	0	27	5	2	0	0	0

COBB, Frazer

Born	5/9/1993, Newark
Signed	1/7/2012 (age 18) from the Academy on a one-year deal *(DH)*
First appearance	Hayes & Yeading United (H), Conference Premier, 21/4/2012
Final appearance	As above - made only one appearance
Released/sold	9/5/2013 and joined Sleaford Town *(GS)*

Career: *Lincoln City (Y),* **Jul 2012 LINCOLN CITY,** *Jul 2013 Sleaford Town.*

Young defender who came through the youth ranks to earn a one-year deal in summer 2012, by which time he had already made his only first team appearance - as a 62nd-minute substitute for Danny Lloyd in the Conference defeat to Hayes & Yeading on 21 April 2012. Became an estate agent in Lincoln when he left football.

Lincoln City Playing Record - Conference Only

	League			FA Cup			FA Trophy			TOTALS			Lincolnshire Cup		
	App	Sub	Gls	App	Sub	Gls	App	Sub	Gls	App	Sub	Gls	App	Sub	Gls
2011-12	0	1	0	0	0	0	0	0	0	0	1	0	0	0	0
2012-13	0	0	0	0	0	0	0	0	0	0	0	0	1	0	0
TOTALS	0	1	0	0	0	0	0	0	0	0	1	0	1	0	0

CRANSTON, Jordan

Born	11/11/1993, Wednesfield
Signed	13/2/2015 (age 21) from Notts County on loan to the end of the season (CM)
First appearance	Chester (H), Conference, 14/2/2015
Final appearance	Eastleigh (H), Conference, 18/4/2015
Released/sold	N/A

Career: Wolverhampton Wanderers (Y), Mar 2012 Wolverhampton Wanderers (Mar 2014 Nuneaton Town - loan, Aug 2014 Hednesford Town, Aug 2014 Nuneaton Town, Sep 2014 Notts County (**Feb 2015 LINCOLN CITY - loan**), Aug 2015 Gateshead, Jan 2016 Cheltenham Town.

Young left-back who was highly-rated by Wolves before he was surprisingly released in 2014. Had also won 2 caps for Wales U19 in 2011 while on the books at Molineux. Came to Lincoln on loan as part of the deal that took Sean Newton to Notts County. Although the loan was intended to run to the end of the season, he was recalled by County on 20 April 2015. Won the National League championship with Cheltenham in April 2016.

Lincoln City Playing Record - Conference Only

	League			FA Cup			FA Trophy			TOTALS			Lincolnshire Cup		
	App	Sub	Gls	App	Sub	Gls	App	Sub	Gls	App	Sub	Gls	App	Sub	Gls
2014-15	11	0	0	0	0	0	0	0	0	11	0	0	0	0	0
TOTALS	11	0	0	0	0	0	0	0	0	11	0	0	0	0	0

CUNNINGHAM, Karl

Born	4/11/1993, Lincoln
Signed	1/7/2012 (age 18) from the Academy on a one-year deal (DH)
First appearance	Alfreton Town (A), Conference Premier, 11/10/2011
Final appearance	Mansfield Town (H), Conference Premier, 18/10/2011
Released/sold	31/12/2013 and joined Gällivare Malmbergets FF (Sweden) (GS)

Career: **Lincoln City(Y)** (Jan 2012 Worksop Town - loan), **Jul 2012 LINCOLN CITY** (Aug 2012 Goole - loan, Feb 2013 Lincoln United - loan, Oct 2013 Lincoln United - loan, Nov 2013 Eastwood Town - loan), Jan 2014 Gällivare Malmbergets FF (Sweden), Jan 2015 Ånge IF (Sweden), Jan 2016 Piteå IF (Sweden), Mar 2017 Akropolis IF (Sweden).

Tall midfielder who rose through the youth ranks at Sincil Bank, being awarded a one-year professional deal in the summer of 2012. Having failed to break into the first team in 2012-13, he signed a short-term deal on 22 May 2013 until the end of December, but ironically made both his first-team appearances while still a youth team player. Had several spells out on loan to give him match time: one-month at Worksop Town from 27 January 2012, five months at Goole from 1 August 2012, three months at Lincoln United from 15 February 2013, a further month at Lincoln United from 11 October 2013, and a month at Eastwood Town from 15 November 2013, at which point he was released at the end of his contract. Joined Swedish fifth-tier side Gällivare, and had one season in the top division with Piteå. Son of City legend Tony Cunningham.

Lincoln City Playing Record - Conference Only

	League			FA Cup			FA Trophy			TOTALS			Lincolnshire Cup		
	App	Sub	Gls	App	Sub	Gls	App	Sub	Gls	App	Sub	Gls	App	Sub	Gls
2011-12	2	0	0	0	0	0	0	0	0	2	0	0	0	0	0
2012-13	0	0	0	0	0	0	0	0	0	0	0	0	0	1	0
TOTALS	2	0	0	0	0	0	0	0	0	2	0	0	0	1	0

DALEY, Luke

Born	10/11/1989, Northampton
Signed	10/8/2012 (age 22) from Plymouth Argyle on a non-contract basis *(DH)*
First appearance	Kidderminster Harriers (H), Conference Premier, 11/8/2012
Final appearance	Gateshead (A), Conference Premier, 27/8/2012
Released/sold	29/8/2012 and joined Braintree Town *(DH)*

Career: 2003 Norwich City (Y), Apr 2008 Norwich City (Jan 2011 Stevenage - loan), Jul 2011 Plymouth Argyle, **Aug 2012 LINCOLN CITY - non-contract,** *Oct 2012 Braintree Town, Jul 2014 Dartford, Jul 2015 Chelmsford City.*

Winger who had been something of a child prodigy at Norwich as a teenager, holding the distinction of being the first player ever moved to Norwich specifically to attend their academy. Joined Lincoln on a non-contract basis in August 2012 after an unsuccessful trial at Grimsby and played for no wages. Appeared in the opening five games of the season but was released on 29 August with Mark McCammon.

Lincoln City Playing Record - Conference Only

	League			FA Cup			FA Trophy			TOTALS			Lincolnshire Cup		
	App	Sub	Gls	App	Sub	Gls	App	Sub	Gls	App	Sub	Gls	App	Sub	Gls
2012-13	4	1	0	0	0	0	0	0	0	4	1	0	0	0	0
TOTALS	4	1	0	0	0	0	0	0	0	4	1	0	0	0	0

DALI, Gomez

Born	10/1/1989, Paris, France
Signed	12/3/2013 (age 24) from Droylsden on a non-contract basis *(GS)*
First appearance	Wrexham (H), Conference Premier, 12/3/2013
Final appearance	Luton Town (A), Conference Premier, 9/4/2013
Released/sold	9/5/2013 and joined UJA Maccabi Paris Métropole (France) *(GS)*

Career: 2006 Nantes (France), Aug 2010 Woking, Sep 2010 Kingstonian, Jul 2011 Aylesbury United, Jul 2012 Stockport Sports, Jan 2013 Droylsden, **Mar 2013 LINCOLN CITY - non-contract,** *Nov 2013 UJA Maccabi Paris Métropole (France).*

French striker who made several attempts at breaking into the Football League, having unsuccessful trials with a number of clubs including Tranmere and Macclesfield. Had also done the rounds of non-league football before signing for Lincoln on a non-contract basis towards the end of the 2012-13 season. Was sent off for violent conduct after 4 minutes at Braintree on 26 March - his first and only start for the Imps - although City went on to win 3-0. Received a three-match ban and made just one more appearance before being released in the close season. Returned to France after leaving Lincoln.

Lincoln City Playing Record - Conference Only

	League			FA Cup			FA Trophy			TOTALS			Lincolnshire Cup		
	App	Sub	Gls	App	Sub	Gls	App	Sub	Gls	App	Sub	Gls	App	Sub	Gls
2012-13	1	3	0	0	0	0	0	0	0	1	3	0	0	0	0
TOTALS	1	3	0	0	0	0	0	0	0	1	3	0	0	0	0

DAVIES, Tom

Born	18/4/1992, Warrington
Signed	2/2/2015 (age 22) from Fleetwood Town on a one-month loan *(CM)*
First appearance	Bristol Rovers (a), Conference, 7/2/2015
Final appearance	As above - made only one appearance
Released/sold	N/A

Career: 2001 Manchester United (Y), 2005 Blackburn Rovers (Y), 2009 Warrington Town, Jul 2010 Runcorn Town, Oct 2011 Team Northumbria, Jul 2013 FC United of Manchester, Mar 2014 Fleetwood Town (Mar 2014 FC United of Manchester - loan, Oct 2014 Alfreton Town - loan, **Feb 2015 LINCOLN CITY - loan**, Mar 2015 Southport - loan), May 2015 Accrington Stanley, Jul 2016 Portsmouth.

Young centre-back who signed from Fleetwood on a month's loan. Made his only appearance as a half-time substitute for the demotivated Sean Newton at Bristol Rovers, which turned out to be the last game for both players. Was given no other opportunities before returning to Fleetwood at the end of his loan period, leaving many supporters wondering why he was signed in the first place. Perhaps an opportunity missed, as he was playing regularly in the Football League just a few months later.

Lincoln City Playing Record - Conference Only

	League			FA Cup			FA Trophy			TOTALS			Lincolnshire Cup		
	App	Sub	Gls	App	Sub	Gls	App	Sub	Gls	App	Sub	Gls	App	Sub	Gls
2014-15	0	1	0	0	0	0	0	0	0	0	1	0	0	0	0
TOTALS	0	1	0	0	0	0	0	0	0	0	1	0	0	0	0

DIAGNE, Tony

Born	7/9/1990, Aubergenville, France
Signed	2/3/2013 (age 22) from Macclesfield Town on loan to the end of the season (GS)
First appearance	Woking (A), Conference Premier, 2/3/2013
Final appearance	Dartford (A), Conference, 25/4/2015
Released/sold	23/5/2016 and joined Hemel Hempstead Town (DC)

Career: 2007 Nottingham Forest (Y), Aug 2010 FCM Aubervilliers (France), Jan 2011 Macclesfield Town (**Mar 2013 LINCOLN CITY - loan**), Jun 2013 Morecambe, **Jun 2014 LINCOLN CITY** (Jul 2015 Macclesfield Town - loan), Aug 2016 Hemel Hempstead Town.

French centre-half who had two spells at City. Originally signed on loan from Macclesfield where Gary Simpson had been his manager. Simpson re-signed him on a permanent basis from Morecambe on a two-year deal on 30 June 2014, the contract being signed on 8 July. Although many fans considered him to be one of the better defenders at the club, he immediately lost his place under new manager Chris Moyses and hardly appeared again. Was made available for transfer in summer 2015 despite being under contract for 2015-16, and joined Macclesfield on loan on 9 July until the New Year; the loan was extended to the end of the season on 5 January 2016. He was finally released by Lincoln on 23 May 2016. Both his goals for Lincoln came in the same match, at Braintree Town on 26 March 2013.

Lincoln City Playing Record - Conference Only

	League			FA Cup			FA Trophy			TOTALS			Lincolnshire Cup		
	App	Sub	Gls	App	Sub	Gls	App	Sub	Gls	App	Sub	Gls	App	Sub	Gls
2012-13	7	0	2	0	0	0	0	0	0	7	0	2	0	0	0
2014-15	15	3	0	0	0	0	0	0	0	15	3	0	2	0	0
2015-16	0	0	0	0	0	0	0	0	0	0	0	0	0	0	0
TOTALS	22	3	2	0	0	0	0	0	0	22	3	2	2	0	0

DIXON, Bohan

Born	17/10/1989, Liverpool
Signed	15/7/2013 (age 23) from Accrington Stanley on a one-year deal (GS)
First appearance	Woking (A), Conference Premier, 10/8/2013
Final appearance	Tamworth (A), Conference Premier, 29/3/2014
Released/sold	8/5/2014 and joined Northwich Victoria (GS)

Career: *2007 Kingsley United, Jul 2008 Connah's Quay Nomads, Jul 2009 Buckley Town, local league football in 2010-11, Aug 11 Hednesford Town, Oct 2011 Burscough, May 2012 Accrington Stanley, **Jul 2013 LINCOLN CITY**, Aug 2014 Northwich Victoria, Jan 2015 Salford City, Jul 2015 Stalybridge Celtic, Mar 2016 AFC Fylde.*

Tall midfielder/striker who impressed with two goals in the pre-season friendly at Lincoln United on 13 July 2013 and signed a one-year deal two days later. Despite sporadic appearances from the substitute's bench and the occasional goal, he failed to nail down a first team place. He was released at the end of the season when City were not in a financial position to offer deals to any of their out-of-contract players. Has appeared for a number of northern clubs since, unable to quite make the grade in senior non-league football.

Lincoln City Playing Record - Conference Only

	League			FA Cup			FA Trophy			TOTALS			Lincolnshire Cup		
	App	Sub	Gls	App	Sub	Gls	App	Sub	Gls	App	Sub	Gls	App	Sub	Gls
2013-14	8	21	3	1	2	1	2	0	0	11	23	4	2	0	0
TOTALS	8	21	3	1	2	1	2	0	0	11	23	4	2	0	0

DRAPER, Nick

Born	10/12/1993, Grimsby
Signed	1/6/2011 (age 17) from the Academy on a one-year deal *(ST)*
First appearance	Alfreton Town (A), FA Cup 4Q, 29/10/2011
Final appearance	Alfreton Town (H), FA Cup 4Q Replay, 1/11/2011
Released/sold	9/5/2013 and joined Inverness Caledonian Thistle *(GS)*

Career: *2010 Lincoln City (Y), **Jul 2011 LINCOLN CITY** (Jul 2012 Sheffield FC - loan), Jun 2013 Inverness Caledonian Thistle, Oct 2014 Boston United, Nov 2014 Grimsby Town, Jul 2015 Alfreton Town (Jan 2016 Scarborough Athletic - loan), Jul 2016 Worcester City (Feb 2017 Mickleover Sports - loan).*

Youth team goalkeeper who played just a game and a half for City in the FA Cup following Joe Anyon's red card in the first match at Alfreton. Almost didn't make the replay due to illness, sparking a goalkeeping crisis - City would not have been allowed to sign a replacement under the rules of the competition, an interesting precursor to what happened against Alfreton in the FA Cup three years later. Joined Sheffield FC on 27 July 2012 on a season-long loan and was released at the end of the season. Surprisingly joined Scottish Premier League side Inverness but did not make an appearance for them. Ironically joined Alfreton Town in 2015, by which time he had not added a single first team appearance for any of his clubs since leaving Lincoln in 2013.

Lincoln City Playing Record - Conference Only

	League			FA Cup			FA Trophy			TOTALS			Lincolnshire Cup		
	App	Sub	Gls	App	Sub	Gls	App	Sub	Gls	App	Sub	Gls	App	Sub	Gls
2011-12	0	0	0	1	1	0	0	0	0	1	1	0	0	0	0
2012-13	0	0	0	0	0	0	0	0	0	0	0	0	0	0	0
TOTALS	0	0	0	1	1	0	0	0	0	1	1	0	0	0	0

DUFFY, Rob

Born	2/12/1982, Swansea
Signed	21/5/2012 (age 29) from Grimsby Town on a one-year deal *(DH)*
First appearance	Kidderminster Harriers (H), Conference Premier, 11/8/2012
Final appearance	Newport County (A), Conference Premier, 18/8/2012
Released/sold	9/4/2013 and joined King's Lynn Town *(GS)*

*Career: 1998 Charlton Athletic (Y), Jul 2000 Rushden & Diamonds (Jan 2005 Stamford - loan), Aug 2005 Cambridge United, Sep 2005 Kettering Town, Jan 2006 Gainsborough Trinity, Mar 2006 Stevenage Borough, Aug 2006 Oxford United (Jan 2008 Wrexham - loan), Jul 2008 Newport County, Jan 2009 Mansfield Town, Jan 2011 Grimsby Town, **May 2012 LINCOLN CITY**, Aug 2013 King's Lynn Town, Mar 2014 Ilkeston, Jul 2015 Nuneaton Town, Jun 2016 Basford United.*

Experienced striker who signed on a one-year deal on the same day as Ashley Westwood and Gary Mills, having formerly appeared for Mansfield under manager David Holdsworth. Started the first three games but suffered a bad ankle ligament injury in the third match at former club Newport. Once recovered, he picked up a knee injury in training and never appeared for City again. With no further opportunities forthcoming, he was released from his contract on 9 April 2013. Graduated in physiotherapy from Salford University in July 2016 and found a job as a physiotherapist; unfortunately he was forced to give the job up when he ruptured an achilles tendon fifteen minutes into his debut for Basford in August. Was appointed player-coach by Basford in May 2017.

Lincoln City Playing Record - Conference Only

	League			FA Cup			FA Trophy			TOTALS			Lincolnshire Cup		
	App	Sub	Gls	App	Sub	Gls	App	Sub	Gls	App	Sub	Gls	App	Sub	Gls
2012-13	3	0	0	0	0	0	0	0	0	3	0	0	0	0	0
TOTALS	3	0	0	0	0	0	0	0	0	3	0	0	0	0	0

ETHERIDGE, Ross

Born	14/9/1994, Derby
Signed	10/3/2017 (age 22) From Doncaster Rovers on loan to the end of the season (DC)
First appearance	York City (A), FA Trophy semi-final first leg, 14/3/2017
Final appearance	Southport (A), National League, 29/4/2017
Released/sold	N/A

*Career: Glapwell (Y), 2005 Derby County (Y), Jul 2013 Derby County (Jul 2013 Rugby Town - loan, Aug 2013 Daventry Town - loan, Aug 2013 Gresley - loan, Dec 2013 Ilkeston - loan, Nov 2014 Leek Town - loan, Jan 2015 Crewe Alexandra - loan, Mar 2015 Stalybridge Celtic - loan), Jun 2015 Accrington Stanley, May 2016 Doncaster Rovers (Dec 2016 Alfreton Town - loan, **Mar 2017 LINCOLN CITY - loan**).*

Goalkeeper who was signed in March 2017 to provide cover for Paul Farman, who had played every minute of every game to that point. Made his debut in the FA Trophy semi-final at York, conceding two second-half goals, and returned to the bench thereafter. Was recalled for the final two games of the season when Farman began treatment for a long-standing groin injury.

Lincoln City Playing Record - Conference Only

	League			FA Cup			FA Trophy			TOTALS			Lincolnshire Cup		
	App	Sub	Gls	App	Sub	Gls	App	Sub	Gls	App	Sub	Gls	App	Sub	Gls
2016-17	2	0	0	0	0	0	1	0	0	3	0	0	0	0	0
TOTALS	2	0	0	0	0	0	1	0	0	3	0	0	0	0	0

EVERINGTON, Kegan

Born	17/12/1995, Lincoln
Signed	1/7/2014 (age 18) from the Academy on a one-year deal (GS)
First appearance	Grimsby Town (A), Conference Premier, 1/1/2014
Final appearance	Gateshead (H), National League, 28/3/2016
Released/sold	18/5/2017 (DC)

*Career: 2009 Lincoln City (Y) (Feb 2014 Spalding United - loan), **Jun 2014 LINCOLN CITY** (Aug 2014 Lincoln United - loan, Aug 2016 Buxton - loan, Jan 2017 Lincoln United - loan, Mar 2017 King's Lynn Town - loan), May 2017 released.*

Local midfielder who came through the youth ranks. Made his first team debut whilst still a scholar, followed by a period on loan at Spalding United from 27 February 2014, the first of numerous loan spells away from the club. Signed his first professional contract with youth teammate Alex Simmons on 27 June 2014 (effective from 1 July), and joined Lincoln United on a three-month loan from 28 August to gain more experience. Despite being investigated by the FA in November 2014 following an unpleasant tweet about the town of Grimsby during the TV programme *Skint*, Everington was named *Young Player of the Season* in 2014-15. Signed a contract extension on 24 April 2015 to the end of the 2015-16 season along with Aidan Grant, Elliot Hodge and Alex Simmons, but failed to push on during the season. Having been on the edge of the first team for three seasons without breaking through, some fans were surprised when he was retained by new manager Danny Cowley for the 2016-17 season. Spent five months on loan at Buxton and was immediately loaned to Lincoln United on his return. Joined King's Lynn Town in March before being released at the end of the season.

Lincoln City Playing Record - Conference Only

	League			FA Cup			FA Trophy			TOTALS			Lincolnshire Cup		
	App	Sub	Gls	App	Sub	Gls	App	Sub	Gls	App	Sub	Gls	App	Sub	Gls
2013-14	0	1	0	0	0	0	0	0	0	0	1	0	0	1	0
2014-15	5	2	0	0	0	0	0	0	0	5	2	0	0	0	0
2015-16	1	12	1	0	0	0	1	0	0	2	12	1	0	0	0
2016-17	0	0	0	0	0	0	0	0	0	0	0	0	0	0	0
TOTALS	6	15	1	0	0	0	1	0	0	7	15	1	0	1	0

FAIRHURST, Waide

Born	7/5/1989, Sheffield
Signed	17/5/2013 (age 24) from Macclesfield Town on a one-year deal *(GS)*
First appearance	Forest Green Rovers (H), Conference Premier, 17/8/2013
Final appearance	Grimsby Town (A), Conference Premier, 1/1/2014
Released/sold	6/3/2014 and joined Whitehawk *(GS)*

*Career: Jul 2008 Doncaster Rovers (Jan 2009 Solihull Moors - loan, Oct 2009 Shrewsbury Town - loan, Oct 2010 Southend United - loan, Feb 2011 Hereford United - loan), Jul 2011 Macclesfield Town, **May 2013 LINCOLN CITY** (Jan 2014 Macclesfield Town - loan), Mar 2014 Whitehawk, Jul 2014 Macclesfield Town, Jul 2015 Torquay United, Feb 2016 FC Halifax Town - non-contract, Jun 2016 Boston United (Jan 2017 Frickley Athletic - loan), May 2017 released.*

Much-travelled striker who signed a one-year deal at the start of Gary Simpson's first full season. Scored twice on his debut but those turned out to be his only goals for the club. Never appeared to be fully fit, and was the subject of a strange comment from manager Simpson when he claimed he didn't know where to play him. Rejoined Macclesfield on a one-month loan on 29 January 2014 but played only one match for them. City cancelled his contract by mutual consent on 6 March and he signed for Conference South side Whitehawk.

Lincoln City Playing Record - Conference Only

	League			FA Cup			FA Trophy			TOTALS			Lincolnshire Cup		
	App	Sub	Gls	App	Sub	Gls	App	Sub	Gls	App	Sub	Gls	App	Sub	Gls
2013-14	5	7	2	0	1	0	0	1	0	5	9	2	2	0	2
TOTALS	5	7	2	0	1	0	0	1	0	5	9	2	2	0	2

FARMAN, Paul

Born	2/11/1989, North Shields
Signed	3/11/2011 (age 22) from Gateshead on a two-month loan *(DH)*
First appearance	Barrow (H), Conference Premier, 5/11/2011
Final appearance	Macclesfield Town (H), National League, 22/4/2017
Released/sold	

Career: Whitley Bay BC (Y), 2006 Monkseaton Football Academy (Y), 2007 Newcastle United (Y), Jul 2008 Blyth Spartans (Aug 2008 Washington - loan), Jun 2009 Gateshead (**Nov 2011 LINCOLN CITY - loan**), **May 2012 LINCOLN CITY** (Sep 2014 Boston United - loan).

Originally signed on loan from Gateshead following Joe Anyon's red card in the FA Cup at Alfreton, ebullient goalkeeper Paul Farman has gone on to become a Sincil Bank favourite. Farman was new manager David Holdsworth's first signing, familiar to Holdsworth from an unsuccessful week's trial at Mansfield in January 2009, and made 8 appearances for City before returning to Gateshead after picking up a groin injury. Released by Gateshead at the end of the season and signed permanently for the Imps on 23 May 2012 on a one-year deal. Continued to impress at Lincoln and signed a new two-year deal on 14 May 2013. Joined Boston United on 12 September 2014 on a three-month loan deal after losing his place to Birmingham loanee Nick Townsend, but was recalled on 22 October when Birmingham refused to allow City to play Townsend in the FA Cup. Farman has kept his place in the side ever since. Despite being known as one of the best goalkeepers in non-league football, Farman has never appeared for the England C team despite several call-ups: he was in line to make his international debut in April 2010 in a match against India U23, but the game was unfortunately cancelled; he earned a recall for the match against Albania U21 on 16 October 2012, but that game was cancelled shortly before kick-off due to flooding. Popular with the fans, he signed a new two-year deal on 26 February 2015 and was voted *Player of the Season* and *Away Player of the Season* by the fans in April. His 22 clean sheets in the championship season earned him a further two-year deal to summer 2019, and he was named *Reusch Goalkeeper of the Year* at the National Game Awards at Stamford Bridge on 17 May 2017. Farman is one of only two players (with Alan Power) to appear in each of City's six seasons in the Conference. His 231 starts in non-league football is a club record, although Power holds the overall appearance record (261). His 58 appearances in 2016-17 is a club record for a goalkeeper in a single season.

Lincoln City Playing Record - Conference Only

	League			FA Cup			FA Trophy			TOTALS			Lincolnshire Cup		
	App	Sub	Gls	App	Sub	Gls	App	Sub	Gls	App	Sub	Gls	App	Sub	Gls
2011-12	8	0	0	0	0	0	0	0	0	8	0	0	0	0	0
2012-13	39	1	0	6	0	0	1	0	0	46	1	0	0	0	0
2013-14	31	0	0	4	0	0	3	0	0	38	0	0	1	0	0
2014-15	28	0	0	3	0	0	1	0	0	32	0	0	1	0	0
2015-16	45	0	0	3	0	0	1	0	0	49	0	0	2	0	0
2016-17	44	0	0	9	0	0	5	0	0	58	0	0	2	0	0
TOTALS	195	1	0	25	0	0	11	0	0	231	1	0	6	0	0

FOFANA, Mamadou

Born	7/1/1988, Sarcelles, France
Signed	29/8/2012 (age 24) from Syrianska FC (Sweden) on a four-month deal *(DH)*
First appearance	AFC Telford United (A), Conference Premier, 8/9/2012
Final appearance	Woking (H), Conference Premier, 25/1/2014
Released/sold	8/5/2014 and joined Oxford City *(GS)*

Career: 2007 CS Sedan-Ardennes (France), 2008 Olympique Noisy-le-Sec (France), 2010 La Vitréenne (France), Jul 2011 Syrianska FC (Sweden), **Aug 2012 LINCOLN CITY**, Nov 2014 Oxford City, Jul 2015 Barrow (Nov 2015 Oxford City - loan), May 2016 released.

French midfielder, commonly known as 'Mo'. Spent a few years making very few appearances in French lower-division football before trying his luck with Swedish Premier Division side Syrianska; however, he was released by them in December 2011 after a just couple of appearances and had been a free agent before joining the Imps on a pre-season trial in July 2012. Originally signed until 2 January 2013, Fofana impressed sufficiently to earn a contract extension to the end of the season, signed on 21 December 2012. Signed a further one-year deal on 10 May 2013, but lost his place in the side at the end of January and was released in May 2014 when Gary Simpson claimed not to be able to afford to offer deals to players out of contract.

Lincoln City Playing Record - Conference Only

	League			FA Cup			FA Trophy			TOTALS			Lincolnshire Cup		
	App	Sub	Gls	App	Sub	Gls	App	Sub	Gls	App	Sub	Gls	App	Sub	Gls
2012-13	25	2	1	5	0	0	1	0	0	31	2	1	0	0	0
2013-14	19	3	0	1	1	0	2	1	1	22	5	1	2	0	0
TOTALS	44	5	1	6	1	0	3	1	1	53	7	2	2	0	0

FOSTER, Luke

Born	8/9/1985, Mexborough
Signed	1/8/2013 (age 27) from Preston North End on a one-year deal *(GS)*
First appearance	Woking (A), Conference Premier, 10/8/2013
Final appearance	Barnet (H), Conference Premier, 26/4/2014
Released/sold	8/5/2014 and joined Southport *(GS)*

Career: Jun 2002 Sheffield Wednesday (Y), Jun 2004 Sheffield Wednesday (Sep 2004 Scarborough - loan, Feb 2005 Alfreton Town - loan), **Jun 2005 LINCOLN CITY** *(Oct 2006 York City - loan), Jan 2007 Stalybridge Celtic, Feb 2007 Oxford United, Jan 2010 Mansfield Town, May 2010 Stevenage, Jun 2011 Rotherham United, Aug 2012 Matlock Town - non-contract, Dec 2012 Preston North End,* **Aug 2013 LINCOLN CITY**, *Jun 2014 Southport, Feb 2016 Harrogate Town, May 2016 Ilkeston, Nov 2016 Coalville Town.*

Much-travelled centre half who had originally joined City back in 2005 on a one-year contract from Sheffield Wednesday. Made 17 sporadic first-team appearances during 2005-06, making his original City debut in the League Two game at Notts County on 13 August 2005, and was surprisingly offered a further one-year deal in the summer of 2006. Failed to make another appearance after that and had his contract cancelled 12 January 2007 so he could join non-league Stalybridge. Won one England C cap in September 2008 v Bosnia and Herzegovina while on the books at Oxford. Suffered a serious cruciate ligament injury at Rotherham in December 2011 and struggled to regain full fitness; therefore it came as something of a surprise when he signed a one-year deal with City 1 August 2013. Was released at the end of his contract because City were not in a financial position to offer deals to the out-of-contract players. Joined Oldham Athletic as Commercial Manager in March 2017 after a few seasons playing out his career in the lower non-leagues.

Lincoln City Playing Record - Conference Only

	League			FA Cup			FA Trophy			TOTALS			Lincolnshire Cup		
	App	Sub	Gls	App	Sub	Gls	App	Sub	Gls	App	Sub	Gls	App	Sub	Gls
2013-14	25	6	1	2	1	0	3	0	1	30	7	2	2	0	0
TOTALS	25	6	1	2	1	0	3	0	1	30	7	2	2	0	0

Lincoln City Playing Record - Football League

	League			FA Cup			League Cup			FL Trophy			TOTALS		
	App	Sub	Gls	App	Sub	Gls	App	Sub	Gls	App	Sub	Gls	App	Sub	Gls
2005-06	14	2	1	0	0	0	0	0	0	1	0	0	15	2	1
2006-07	0	0	0	0	0	0	0	0	0	0	0	0	0	0	0
TOTALS	14	2	1	0	0	0	0	0	0	1	0	0	15	2	1

FUSEINI, Ali

Born	7/12/1988, Accra, Ghana
Signed	31/1/2011 (age 22) from Lewes on an 18-month deal *(ST)*
First appearance	Southport (A), Conference Premier, 13/8/2011
Final appearance	Mansfield Town (H), Conference Premier, 18/10/2011
Released/sold	25/11/2011 and joined Eastleigh *(DH)*

Midfielder who had a very interesting start to his City career. Shortly after signing in January 2011, it was revealed that he was facing trial at Blackfriars Crown Court on charges of abduction and aiding and abetting a rape; following criticism from fans, City announced they had known about the case before signing Fuseini but had been assured he was innocent. Fortunately he was cleared of all charges on 12 February 2011. It also emerged that he had been fined £1,000 by the FA in October 2008 for breaking the rules regarding agents - he had signed to two agents at the same time, and also denied the existence of the first. Legal problems aside, Fuseini had been a very promising midfielder in his early years and had been on trial at Leeds, Crystal Palace and Leyton Orient after leaving Millwall in the summer of 2010. Made his City debut in the 2-1 win at Bradford on 1 February 2011 as City headed for relegation. Despite showing flashes of ability, he was one of several players made available for transfer in May; there were no offers for him. Started the Conference season in the side, but lost his place immediately after Steve Tilson was sacked and never appeared for the Imps again. He was made available for loan by new manager David Holdsworth on 11 November 2011, but again there were no takers; he was released by mutual consent on 25 November, one of a good number to have their contracts paid up around that time. Joined Eastleigh but played only one game before being jailed for ten weeks on 8 December 2011 on two counts of driving while disqualified, incurred following a conviction for aggravated vehicle taking at the end of 2010. Ironically started a car rental business called *Go The Extra Mile* in 2014.

Lincoln City Playing Record - Conference Only

	League			FA Cup			FA Trophy			TOTALS			Lincolnshire Cup		
	App	Sub	Gls	App	Sub	Gls	App	Sub	Gls	App	Sub	Gls	App	Sub	Gls
2011-12	15	2	1	0	0	0	0	0	0	15	2	1	2	0	0
TOTALS	15	2	1	0	0	0	0	0	0	15	2	1	2	0	0

Lincoln City Playing Record - Football League

	League			FA Cup			League Cup			FL Trophy			TOTALS		
	App	Sub	Gls	App	Sub	Gls	App	Sub	Gls	App	Sub	Gls	App	Sub	Gls
2010-11	15	3	0	0	0	0	0	0	0	0	0	0	15	3	0
TOTALS	15	3	0	0	0	0	0	0	0	0	0	0	15	3	0

GARNER, Scott

Born	20/9/1989, Coventry
Signed	5/11/2012 (age 23) from Cambridge United on a two-month loan *(DH)*
First appearance	Barrow (A), Conference Premier, 10/11/2012
Final appearance	Wrexham (H), Conference Premier, 12/3/2013
Released/sold	N/A

Career: 2000 Leicester City (Y), May 2008 Leicester City (Oct 2008 Ilkeston Town - loan), Jan 2009 Mansfield Town, Jul 2010 Grimsby Town (Feb 2011 Alfreton Town - loan), Jun 2012 Cambridge United (**Oct 2012 LINCOLN CITY - loan**, Jul 2013 Boston United - loan), Jun 2014 Boston United, Jun 2016 FC Halifax Town.

Tall centre half who had played under David Holdsworth twice before, at Ilkeston Town and Mansfield. His initial two-month loan was extended to the end of the season on 3 January 2013, but Garner lost his place after a defeat to Wrexham and did not appear again. Scored the winner for FC Halifax against Chorley in the 2017 National League North play-off final. Won two England C caps during his Mansfield and Grimsby days.

Lincoln City Playing Record - Conference Only

	League			FA Cup			FA Trophy			TOTALS			Lincolnshire Cup		
	App	Sub	Gls	App	Sub	Gls	App	Sub	Gls	App	Sub	Gls	App	Sub	Gls
2012-13	12	2	0	0	0	0	1	0	0	13	2	0	0	0	0
TOTALS	12	2	0	0	0	0	1	0	0	13	2	0	0	0	0

GILBERT, Peter

Born	31/7/1983, Newcastle
Signed	4/10/2012 (age 29) from Southend United on a non-contract basis (DH)
First appearance	Luton Town (H), Conference Premier, 6/10/2012
Final appearance	Macclesfield Town (A) Conference Premier, 6/3/2013
Released/sold	9/5/2013 and eventually joined Goole (GS)

Career: 1999 Birmingham City (Y), Jul 2002 Birmingham City (Jul 2003 Plymouth Argyle - loan), Aug 2003 Plymouth Argyle, Jul 2005 Leicester City (Nov 2005 Sheffield Wednesday - loan), Jan 2006 Sheffield Wednesday (Jan 2007 Doncaster Rovers - loan), Aug 2009 Oldham Athletic, Nov 2009 Northampton Town, Jul 2010 Southend United, **Oct 2012 LINCOLN CITY** (Mar 2013 Dagenham & Redbridge - loan), Jan 2014 Goole, Jul 2014 Sacramento Republic (USA) on trial.

Well-travelled defender who had spent much of his career at Championship level, winning 10 caps for Wales U21 when on the books at Plymouth. His early promise was hampered by a series of injuries throughout his career, and he managed only 265 career appearances in 11 seasons. Had a habit of following manager Paul Sturrock around the Football League, starting at Plymouth in 2003. Notably scored two goals in four days for Plymouth in October 2003 but then went almost 8 years before his next goal, which ironically came for Southend against Plymouth in September 2011; incredibly, he scored in the next match too. Had come to the attention of David Holdsworth during an unsuccessful trial at Mansfield in September 2009. Initially joined City on 4 October 2012 on a non-contract basis. Signed a short-term permanent contract on 31 October until the New Year, which was extended to the end of the season on 21 December. Lost his place under new manager Gary Simpson, and on 28 March 2013 joined Dagenham & Redbridge on loan to the end of the season. Holding the UEFA B Licence, Gilbert joined West Bromwich Albion's Academy as a coach following a short spell in the USA.

Lincoln City Playing Record - Conference Only

	League			FA Cup			FA Trophy			TOTALS			Lincolnshire Cup		
	App	Sub	Gls	App	Sub	Gls	App	Sub	Gls	App	Sub	Gls	App	Sub	Gls
2012-13	14	0	0	5	0	0	1	0	0	20	0	0	0	0	0
TOTALS	**14**	**0**	**0**	**5**	**0**	**0**	**1**	**0**	**0**	**20**	**0**	**0**	**0**	**0**	**0**

GINNELLY, Josh

Born	24/3/1997, Coventry
Signed	30/1/2017 (age 19) from Burnley on loan to the end of the season (DC)
First appearance	Welling United (A), FA Trophy 3, 4/2/2017
Final appearance	Southport (A), National League, 29/4/2017
Released/sold	N/A

Career: 2008 Aston Villa (Y), Jan 2014 Shrewsbury Town (Y), Aug 2015 Burnley (Jan 2016 Altrincham - loan, Jul 2016 Walsall - loan, **Jan 2017 LINCOLN CITY - loan**).

Exciting young winger signed on loan from Burnley to boost City's run-in towards the National League championship. Highly-rated as an academy player, Ginnelly had rejected a professional contract offer from Shrewsbury at the age of 18 to sign for Burnley in the face of competition from Celtic, Newcastle, Stoke, Norwich and Sunderland. His pace unsettled National League defences, although his lack of experience sometimes meant that the right final ball was not always forthcoming. His scintillating performance as a second half substitute against Macclesfield in April helped City to overturn an early deficit to win the National League title. Scored for Altrincham against the Imps in February 2016.

Lincoln City Playing Record - Conference Only

	League			FA Cup			FA Trophy			TOTALS			Lincolnshire Cup		
	App	Sub	Gls	App	Sub	Gls	App	Sub	Gls	App	Sub	Gls	App	Sub	Gls
2016-17	7	6	0	0	0	0	2	2	0	9	8	0	0	0	0
TOTALS	**7**	**6**	**0**	**0**	**0**	**0**	**2**	**2**	**0**	**9**	**8**	**0**	**0**	**0**	**0**

GOWLING, Josh

Born	29/11/1983, Coventry
Signed	14/7/2011 (age 27) from Gillingham on a two-year deal *(ST)*
First appearance	Southport (A), Conference Premier, 13/8/2011
Final appearance	Ebbsfleet United (A), Conference Premier, 28/4/2012
Released/sold	31/8/2012 and joined Kidderminster Harriers *(DH)*

*Career: 1998 West Bromwich Albion (Y), Jun 2003 Herfølge BK (Denmark), Mar 2005 Ølstykke FC (Denmark), Jun 2005 AFC Bournemouth, Jun 2008 Carlisle United (Nov 2008 Hereford United - loan, Jul 2009 Gillingham - loan), Aug 2009 Gillingham (**Oct 2010 LINCOLN CITY - loan**), **Jul 2011 LINCOLN CITY**, Jan 2012 Kidderminster Harriers (Mar 2015 Grimsby Town - loan), May 2015 Grimsby Town, May 2017 released.*

Commanding centre-back who originally joined City from Gillingham on a month's loan on 28 October 2010, having lost his place in the Gillingham side following a 7-4 defeat at Accrington. Made his original City debut in the League Two match against Northampton on 2 November 2010. Returned to Gillingham after a month and scored at Sincil Bank in April as City lost 4-0. Signed on a two-year deal in the summer of 2011 after an unsuccessful trial at Crewe, and was appointed captain by Steve Tilson. Unfortunately seemed at loggerheads at times with certain sections of the club's support, becoming embroiled in a war of words on social media. Things deteriorated further in January when he was one of three City players spotted in a Lincoln nightclub in breach of club discipline. At the end of a fractious twelve months with the club, he finally departed on deadline day in August 2012, with City cancelling the second year of his contract to enable him to join Kidderminster. Was sent off at Sincil Bank playing for Grimsby on 29 August 2015 after Matt Rhead admittedly 'dropped to the floor'. Won promotion back to the Football League with Grimsby at the end of that season, winning the play-off final at Wembley against Forest Green. Has been named in the Conference team of the year on two separate occasions, in 2012-13 and 2015-16.

Lincoln City Playing Record - Conference Only

	League			FA Cup			FA Trophy			TOTALS			Lincolnshire Cup		
	App	Sub	Gls	App	Sub	Gls	App	Sub	Gls	**App**	**Sub**	**Gls**	App	Sub	Gls
2011-12	36	1	0	0	0	0	1	1	0	**37**	**2**	**0**	1	0	0
2012-13	0	0	0	0	0	0	0	0	0	**0**	**0**	**0**	1	0	0
TOTALS	**36**	**1**	**0**	**0**	**0**	**0**	**1**	**1**	**0**	**37**	**2**	**0**	**2**	**0**	**0**

Lincoln City Playing Record - Football League

	League			FA Cup			League Cup			FL Trophy			TOTALS		
	App	Sub	Gls	App	Sub	Gls	App	Sub	Gls	App	Sub	Gls	**App**	**Sub**	**Gls**
2010-11	4	0	0	2	0	0	0	0	0	0	0	0	**6**	**0**	**0**
TOTALS	**4**	**0**	**0**	**2**	**0**	**0**	**0**	**0**	**0**	**0**	**0**	**0**	**6**	**0**	**0**

GRANT, Aidan

Born	27/3/1995, South Shields
Signed	16/1/2015 (age 19) from Peterborough United initially on non-contract terms *(CM)*
First appearance	Dartford (A), Conference, 25/4/2015
Final appearance	Aldershot Town (A), National League, 11/11/2015
Released/sold	23/5/2016 and joined Corby Town *(DC)*

*Career: Whiteleas Boys Club, 2008 Newcastle United (Y), Jun 2011 Newcastle United, Mar 2013 Aston Villa (Feb 2014 Arlesey Town - loan), Jul 2014 South Shields, Sep 2014 Peterborough United - non-contract, **Jan 2015 LINCOLN CITY**, May 2016 Corby Town.*

Giant goalkeeper who was already 6'6" tall when Newcastle signed him at the age of 16. Signed by City initially on non-contract terms but on 6 February 2015 he was awarded a short-term deal to the end of the 2014-15 season. Signed a one-year extension on 24 April with Alex Simmons, Elliot Hodge, and Kegan Everington. First team opportunities were few and far between due to the form of Paul Farman, and he was eventually released in May 2016 with just two appearances to his name.

Lincoln City Playing Record - Conference Only

	League			FA Cup			FA Trophy			TOTALS			Lincolnshire Cup		
	App	Sub	Gls	App	Sub	Gls	App	Sub	Gls	App	Sub	Gls	App	Sub	Gls
2014-15	1	0	0	0	0	0	0	0	0	1	0	0	0	0	0
2015-16	1	0	0	0	0	0	0	0	0	1	0	0	0	0	0
TOTALS	2	0	0	0	0	0	0	0	0	2	0	0	0	0	0

GRAY, Dan

Born	23/11/1989, Mansfield
Signed	24/7/2012 (age 22) from Chesterfield on a one-year deal (DH)
First appearance	Kidderminster Harriers (H), Conference Premier, 11/8/2012
Final appearance	Salisbury City (A), Conference Premier, 12/4/2014
Released/sold	8/5/2014 and joined Alfreton Town (GS)

Career: Chesterfield (Y) (Mar 2008 Alfreton Town - loan), Jul 2008 Chesterfield (Jan 2011 Macclesfield Town - loan, Nov 2011 Macclesfield Town - loan), **Jul 2012 LINCOLN CITY**, Jul 2014 Alfreton Town (Jan 2015 Bradford Park Avenue - loan).

Versatile defender/midfielder who signed a one-year deal in July 2012 after a trial period in which he played in every pre-season game. Appeared in the majority of matches in the Imps' second season in the Conference and earned a further one-year deal on 15 May 2013. Appearances became more sporadic in his second season and he became one of a number of players not offered contracts in summer 2014 due to financial constraints. Joined Alfreton, but made very few appearances and drifted out of senior football soon afterwards.

Lincoln City Playing Record - Conference Only

	League			FA Cup			FA Trophy			TOTALS			Lincolnshire Cup		
	App	Sub	Gls	App	Sub	Gls	App	Sub	Gls	App	Sub	Gls	App	Sub	Gls
2012-13	31	4	1	5	0	0	0	0	0	36	4	1	0	0	0
2013-14	9	8	0	0	0	0	0	1	0	9	9	0	2	0	0
TOTALS	40	12	1	5	0	0	0	1	0	45	13	1	2	0	0

HABERGHAM, Sam

Born	20/2/1992, Rotherham
Signed	23/6/2016 (age 24) from Braintree Town on a two-year deal (DC)
First appearance	Woking (A), National League, 6/8/2016
Final appearance	Macclesfield Town (H), National League, 22/4/2017
Released/sold	

Career: 2000 Norwich City (Y), 2009 Norwich City, Jul 2011 Tamworth, Jul 2012 Braintree Town, **Jun 2016 LINCOLN CITY**.

Outstanding left-back who had enjoyed a very promising start to his career at the Norwich City Youth Academy, being part of the team that reached the quarter-finals of the FA Youth Cup in 2008-09. Was also selected for the England U17 squad for the 2009 U17 European Championships, appearing in the game against Turkey after England had been eliminated. Made one appearance for Lincoln's reserve side in 2010-11 shortly before being released by Norwich but City did not come in for him at that time. Rebuilt his career in the non-league game at Tamworth and particularly Braintree, where he was managed by Danny and Nicky Cowley. Won two caps for the England C team in 2016, against Ukraine and Slovakia, and reached the National League play-offs with Braintree. At the time he followed the Cowleys to Lincoln, Sam had neither scored a goal nor been sent off in his 226-game career. Quickly became an integral part of City's fantastic 2016-17 season, providing a potent attacking outlet in addition to his excellence in defence. His ability to deliver threatening set-pieces created many opportunities and assists, and City missed him badly on the few occasions he was unavailable. Scored a brilliant late winner against Torquay in April after City had been a goal down with four minutes remaining. Missed the final two games of the championship season after having an operation to repair a hernia. Was one of four City players called up for the England C game against Estonia on 15 November 2016 (with Alex Woodyard, Elliott Whitehouse and Sean Raggett), but was forced to withdraw through injury.

Lincoln City Playing Record - Conference Only

	League			FA Cup			FA Trophy			TOTALS			Lincolnshire Cup		
	App	Sub	Gls	App	Sub	Gls	App	Sub	Gls	App	Sub	Gls	App	Sub	Gls
2016-17	43	0	3	9	0	0	4	0	1	56	0	4	0	0	0
TOTALS	43	0	3	9	0	0	4	0	1	56	0	4	0	0	0

HAWKRIDGE, Terry

Born	23/2/1990, Nottingham
Signed	1/9/2015 (age 25) from Scunthorpe United initially on a four-month loan (CM)
First appearance	Wrexham (H), National League, 5/9/2015
Final appearance	Southport (A), National League, 29/4/2017
Released/sold	18/5/2017 and joined Notts County (DC)

*Career: Barnsley (Y), Tranmere Rovers (Y), Jul 2007 Carlton Town, Jun 2009 Hucknall Town, Sep 2010 Carlton Town, Aug 2012 Gainsborough Trinity, Jun 2013 Scunthorpe United (Mar 2015 Mansfield Town - loan, **Sep 2015 LINCOLN CITY - loan**), **Jan 2016 LINCOLN CITY**, May 2017 Notts County.*

Along with Lincoln colleague Luke Waterfall, skilful winger Terry Hawkridge was one of two Gainsborough Trinity players who had followed chairman Peter Swann to Scunthorpe in 2013. Initially played regularly at Glanford Park and earned a two-year contract extension in May 2014, but soon fell out of favour and spent the rest of the season on loan at Mansfield. Came to City on loan early in the 2015-16 season and impressed immediately, signing a permanent 18-month contract on 6 January 2016. Was one of five impressive wingers fielded by City in the 2016-17 season, interchanging roles with Harry Anderson, Nathan Arnold, Joe Ward and Josh Ginnelly. While not possessing the pace of the other four, Terry's excellent close control was a major asset in the FA Cup games against quality opposition and scored some important goals throughout the season. In particular, Terry will always be remembered at Sincil Bank as the man whose two goals against Macclesfield took City back to the Football League. Was also used as an emergency left back in the absence of Sam Habergham. Was offered a one-year deal for the 2017-18 season but chose to join hometown club Notts County on a two-year contract.

Lincoln City Playing Record - Conference Only

	League			FA Cup			FA Trophy			TOTALS			Lincolnshire Cup		
	App	Sub	Gls	App	Sub	Gls	App	Sub	Gls	App	Sub	Gls	App	Sub	Gls
2015-16	34	4	1	3	0	0	0	1	0	37	5	1	0	0	0
2016-17	24	8	3	8	1	1	5	0	2	37	9	6	1	0	2
TOTALS	58	12	4	11	1	1	5	1	2	74	14	7	1	0	2

HEARN, Liam

Born	27/8/1985, Nottingham
Signed	20/5/2015 (age 29) from Mansfield Town on a one-year deal (CM)
First appearance	Cheltenham Town (H), National League, 8/8/2015
Final appearance	Wrexham (A), National League, 23/1/2016
Released/sold	23/5/2016 and joined Ilkeston (DC)

*Career: Bulwell Rangers (Y), Hucknall Town Harriers (Y), Jul 2003 Santos FC, Jun 2006 Hucknall Town, Oct 2007 Eastwood Town, Nov 2007 Chasetown, Dec 2007 Quorn, Sep 2008 Alfreton Town, Jun 2011 Grimsby Town, Jun 2014 Mansfield Town, **May 2015 LINCOLN CITY**, May 2016 Ilkeston, Aug 2016 Alfreton Town.*

Proven goalscorer who had made his name at Alfreton Town and Grimsby Town, scoring 100 goals in four seasons and earning an England C cap in 2009. Unfortunately suffered a series of serious injuries from pre-season 2012 and never hit the same heights again. However, he made a great start to his Lincoln City career with a debut goal and then a hat-trick against Macclesfield Town in his fourth appearance. Due to his recent injury-prone record, Lincoln tried to manage his fitness and not play him in every game. Hearn appeared not to appreciate this approach, and surprisingly engineered a loan move to Barrow in November 2015 'to get more game time'. The move upset manager Chris Moyses, his Lincoln team mates and the supporters, who all felt the unity of the team had been broken. Some fans believe he did not want to play against former club Grimsby on Boxing Day, but the net result was that City's form collapsed thereafter: it may not be a coincidence that City slipped from fourth place in the league table to eventually finish in the bottom half. The move backfired spectacularly on Hearn, who managed to play just 79 minutes during the month; he could have played six games if he had stayed at Lincoln. Hearn returned and issued an apology, but was soon at it again, leading to a loan move to Harrogate in March 2016; this time, he played less than one game due to injury and was released at the end of a very disappointing season. Despite the acrimony caused by his behaviour, many City fans still rate him as one of the best players to wear the red and white stripes in recent years. Currently Head of Alfreton Town in the Community.

Lincoln City Playing Record - Conference Only

	League			FA Cup			FA Trophy			TOTALS			Lincolnshire Cup		
	App	Sub	Gls	App	Sub	Gls	App	Sub	Gls	App	Sub	Gls	App	Sub	Gls
2015-16	13	7	10	1	2	1	0	0	0	14	9	11	1	1	0
TOTALS	13	7	10	1	2	1	0	0	0	14	9	11	1	1	0

HINDS, Richard

Born	22/8/1980, Sheffield
Signed	4/11/2011 (age 31) from Sheffield Wednesday until the end of the year (DH)
First appearance	Barrow (H), Conference Premier, 5/11/2011
Final appearance	Grimsby Town (H), Conference Premier, 1/1/2012
Released/sold	4/1/2012 and joined Yeovil Town (DH)

Career: *Tranmere Rovers (Y), May 1998 Tranmere Rovers, Jul 2003 Hull City (Mar 2005 Scunthorpe United - loan), May 2005 Scunthorpe United, Jul 2007 Sheffield Wednesday, **Nov 2011 LINCOLN CITY**, Feb 2012 Yeovil Town, Jul 2013 Bury, Aug 2014 Llandudno.*

Experienced centre back who arrived on trial on 3 November 2011, having been released by Sheffield Wednesday in the summer. Signed a short-term deal the following day with a view to earning a permanent contract. However, he rejected a further contract offer on 4 January 2012 as cash-strapped City could not match his wage demands, and he left the club forthwith. Obtained a first class honours degree in Law from the Open University in 2011.

Lincoln City Playing Record - Conference Only

	League			FA Cup			FA Trophy			TOTALS			Lincolnshire Cup		
	App	Sub	Gls	App	Sub	Gls	App	Sub	Gls	App	Sub	Gls	App	Sub	Gls
2011-12	9	0	1	0	0	0	1	0	0	10	0	1	0	0	0
TOTALS	9	0	1	0	0	0	1	0	0	10	0	1	0	0	0

HOBSON, Craig

Born	25/2/1988, Bolton
Signed	8/2/2013 (age 24) from Stockport County on loan to the end of the season (DH)
First appearance	Dartford (H), Conference Premier, 9/2/2013
Final appearance	Tamworth (H), Conference Premier, 13/4/2013
Released/sold	N/A

Career: *Kendal Town, Sep 2009 Stalybridge Celtic, Jun 2012 Stockport County (**Feb 2013 LINCOLN CITY - loan**), Jun 2013 Guiseley, Mar 2014 Chester, Jun 2016 Altrincham.*

Striker who had scored 26 goals for Kendal in 2008-09, earning him a move up the non-league pyramid to Stalybridge. Joined Conference Premier side Stockport in 2012, but failed to make an impact at Edgeley Park as County were unexpectedly relegated at the end of the season, although he did score against the Imps in the 3-3 draw at Sincil Bank on 27 October 2012. His loan spell at Sincil Bank was no more successful, and he joined Guiseley in the Conference North that summer after being released by Stockport. Has since bounced between Conference Premier and the North section with various clubs.

Lincoln City Playing Record - Conference Only

	League			FA Cup			FA Trophy			TOTALS			Lincolnshire Cup		
	App	Sub	Gls	App	Sub	Gls	App	Sub	Gls	App	Sub	Gls	App	Sub	Gls
2012-13	5	7	1	0	0	0	0	0	0	5	7	1	0	0	0
TOTALS	5	7	1	0	0	0	0	0	0	5	7	1	0	0	0

HODGE, Elliot

Born	23/12/1995, Nottingham
Signed	2/2/2015 (age 19) from Notts County initially to the end of the season (CM)
First appearance	Dartford (A), Conference, 25/4/2015
Final appearance	North Ferriby United (H), National League, 9/8/2016
Released/sold	18/5/2017 (DC)

Career: *Nottingham Forest (Y), 2012 Notts County (Y), **Feb 2015 LINCOLN CITY** (Feb 2015 Spalding United - loan, Nov 2015 Stamford - loan, Feb 2016 Gainsborough Trinity - loan, Sep 2016 Stafford Rangers - loan, Dec 2016 AFC Telford United - loan), May 2017 released.*

Compact wide midfielder who came through the Nottingham Forest youth system before joining Notts County in a similar capacity. Signed for City until the end of the 2014-15 season after a successful trial, and was one of four young players to sign one-year contract extensions on 24 April 2015 (the others being Aidan Grant, Kegan Everington and Alex Simmons). Spent much of his first two seasons out on loan: Spalding United for a month with Alex Simmons from 10 February 2015; Stamford for three months from 13 November 2015; and Gainsborough Trinity from 20 February 2016 for a month. Started to appear in the first team towards the end of 2015-16 and was named *Young Player of the Season* by outgoing manager Chris Moyses. Was retained by new manager Danny Cowley in the summer of 2016 but was sent on lengthy loan spells to Stafford Rangers from 7 September and to AFC Telford United from 2 December before being released at the end of the season. Also a useful cricketer, playing for Notts and Derbyshire as a schoolboy. Son of Nottingham Forest, Leeds & England player Steve Hodge.

Lincoln City Playing Record - Conference Only

	League			FA Cup			FA Trophy			TOTALS			Lincolnshire Cup		
	App	Sub	Gls	App	Sub	Gls	App	Sub	Gls	App	Sub	Gls	App	Sub	Gls
2014-15	0	1	0	0	0	0	0	0	0	0	1	0	0	0	0
2015-16	5	3	0	0	1	0	0	0	0	5	4	0	0	0	0
2016-17	0	2	0	0	0	0	0	0	0	0	2	0	0	1	0
TOTALS	5	6	0	0	1	0	0	0	0	5	7	0	0	1	0

HONE, Danny

Born	15/9/1989, Croydon
Signed	11/12/2007 (age 18) from the Academy on a two-and-a-half-year deal (PJ)
First appearance	Southport (A), Conference Premier, 13/8/2011
Final appearance	Fleetwood Town (H), Conference Premier, 14/10/2011
Released/sold	5/5/2012 and joined Gainsborough Trinity (DH)

Career: 2006 Lincoln City (Y), 2007 LINCOLN CITY (Jul 2010 Darlington - loan, Nov 2011 Barrow - loan), Jul 2012 Gainsborough Trinity, May 2013 North Ferriby United, Jun 2016 FC Halifax Town.

Promising young centre back who came through the youth set up at Sincil Bank. Made his City debut in the League Two defeat at home to Chester on 2 November 2007 whilst still a member of the youth team. Signed his first professional contract - a two-and-a-half year deal - the following month on 11 December, his eighteenth birthday. His contract was extended on 28 November 2008 for a further year, taking him to the summer of 2011. Fell out of favour under Chris Sutton and was made available for loan on 7 May 2010, joining Darlington on 15 July until the New Year. Returned to the side under Steve Tilson and was one of only three players offered a contract for 2011-12, signing a one-year deal on 30 June 2011. Soon lost his place in the side again and joined Barrow on an emergency loan from 8 November to 8 January 2012. The loan was extended to the end of the season on 4 January 2012, and he was finally released in the summer as David Holdsworth slashed his squad. Made exactly 100 appearances for the club. Has since built a good career in senior non-league football. Won the FA Trophy with North Ferriby in 2015 and scored the goal that won them promotion to the National League in May 2016. Son of former City player Mark Hone.

Lincoln City Playing Record - Conference Only

	League			FA Cup			FA Trophy			TOTALS			Lincolnshire Cup		
	App	Sub	Gls	App	Sub	Gls	App	Sub	Gls	App	Sub	Gls	App	Sub	Gls
2011-12	9	0	1	0	0	0	0	0	0	9	0	1	2	0	0
TOTALS	9	0	1	0	0	0	0	0	0	9	0	1	2	0	0

Lincoln City Playing Record - Football League

	League			FA Cup			League Cup			FL Trophy			TOTALS		
	App	Sub	Gls	App	Sub	Gls	App	Sub	Gls	App	Sub	Gls	App	Sub	Gls
2007-08	20	3	1	2	0	0	0	0	0	0	0	0	22	3	1
2008-09	17	2	1	2	0	0	0	0	0	1	0	0	20	2	1
2009-10	16	1	1	0	0	0	0	0	0	1	0	0	17	1	1
2010-11	25	1	0	0	0	0	0	0	0	0	0	0	25	1	0
TOTALS	78	7	3	4	0	0	0	0	0	2	0	0	84	7	3

HOWE, Callum

Born	9/4/1994, Doncaster
Signed	15/7/2015 (age 21) from Scunthorpe United on a one-year deal (CM)
First appearance	Cheltenham Town (H), National League, 8/8/2015
Final appearance	Southport (H), National League, 29/4/2017
Released/sold	

Career: 2008 Scunthorpe United (Y), Jul 2012 Scunthorpe United (Dec 2012 Bradford Park Avenue - loan, Feb 2013 Frickley Athletic - loan, Nov 2013 Gainsborough Trinity - loan, Oct 2014 Gateshead - loan, Jan 2015 Alfreton Town - loan), Jul 2015 LINCOLN CITY (Aug 2016 Southport - loan).

Having been released by Scunthorpe in May 2015, centre back Howe signed a twelve-month deal in July after a successful pre-season trial. City were only able to sign Howe after fans raised almost £20,000 from a Crowdfunder scheme over the summer months. Signed a new one-year deal on 13 June 2016 but soon fell out of favour and did not appear in any of City's opening five National League games. Joined Southport on a month's loan from 25 August, which was extended for two further months after he was appointed captain. Returned to Sincil Bank at the end of his loan period to play a part in the FA Trophy run and serve as backup to the regular central defensive partnership of Luke Waterfall and Sean Raggett. Was called up by England C in May 2017 for the friendly matches against Punjab FA on 28 May and Jersey FA on 30 May, making him the last City player to represent the England non-league side. Offered a new contract in May 2017 for the first season back in the Football League.

	League			FA Cup			FA Trophy			TOTALS			Lincolnshire Cup		
	App	Sub	Gls	App	Sub	Gls	App	Sub	Gls	App	Sub	Gls	App	Sub	Gls
2015-16	27	0	0	3	0	0	1	0	0	31	0	0	1	0	0
2016-17	4	4	0	0	0	0	5	0	0	9	4	0	2	0	0
TOTALS	31	4	0	3	0	0	6	0	0	40	4	0	3	0	0

HUTCHISON, Graham

Born	17/1/1993, Bellshill
Signed	30/7/2012 (age 19) from Birmingham City on a five-month youth loan (DH)
First appearance	Macclesfield Town (H), Conference Premier, 25/8/2012
Final appearance	Tamworth (H), Conference Premier, 22/9/2012
Released/sold	N/A

*Career: Nottingham Forest (Y), **Jul 2009 Lincoln City (Y)**, Apr 2010 Birmingham City (**Jul 2012 LINCOLN CITY - loan**, Dec 2012 Worcester City - loan), Sep 2013 Worcester City, Feb 2015 FC Halifax Town (Sep 2015 AFC Telford United - loan), May 2016 Worcester City.*

Young Scottish centre back who kick-started his career in City's youth side, preferring to join Lincoln as a scholar ahead of Nottingham Forest. Soon earned a call-up to Scotland's U17 squad and attracted attention from Premier League clubs including Fulham, who took him on a four-week trial at the start of 2010. Birmingham took him on a two-week trial in March 2010 and signed him for £35,000 on 1 April, taking over his scholarship from Lincoln. Had not made an appearance in City's first team at that stage, but won 6 caps for Scotland U17 in 2009, scoring one goal in a 4-0 win over Finland on 29 July. Came back to Lincoln in July 2012 after Birmingham gave him permission to join pre-season training, and signed on a youth loan to 2 January 2013. Had a run of 7 straight games starting in the team but picked up an injury and returned to Birmingham on 13 November 2012.

Lincoln City Playing Record - Conference Only

	League			FA Cup			FA Trophy			TOTALS			Lincolnshire Cup		
	App	Sub	Gls	App	Sub	Gls	App	Sub	Gls	App	Sub	Gls	App	Sub	Gls
2012-13	7	0	0	0	0	0	0	0	0	7	0	0	0	0	0
TOTALS	7	0	0	0	0	0	0	0	0	7	0	0	0	0	0

JACKSON, Marlon

Born	6/12/1990, Bristol
Signed	25/10/2013 (age 22) from Bury on a two-month loan (GS)
First appearance	Worcester City (A), FA Cup 4Q, 26/10/2013
Final appearance	Braintree Town (A), FA Trophy 2, 14/12/2013
Released/sold	N/A

*Career: Bristol City (Y), Apr 2009 Bristol City (Aug 2009 Hereford United - loan, Nov 2009 Aldershot Town - loan, Sep 2010 Aldershot Town - loan, Sep 2011 Northampton Town - loan, Nov 2011 Cheltenham Town - loan, Jan 2012 AFC Telford United - loan, Mar 2012 AFC Telford United - loan), Jul 2012 Hereford United, Jul 2013 Bury (**OCT 2013 LINCOLN CITY - loan**), Jan 2014 FC Halifax Town, Sep 2014 Oxford City, Aug 2015 Tranmere Rovers - non-contract, Nov 2015 Oxford City, Jul 2016 Newport County.*

Quick winger signed from Bury on a two-month loan. Was released by Bury shortly after returning, and has since appeared for a number of clubs in non-league football before rejoining the Football League in 2016 with Newport. Has spent much of his career on loan to other clubs.

	League			FA Cup			FA Trophy			TOTALS			Lincolnshire Cup		
	App	Sub	Gls	App	Sub	Gls	App	Sub	Gls	App	Sub	Gls	App	Sub	Gls
2013-14	4	0	0	4	0	0	2	0	1	10	0	1	0	0	0
TOTALS	*4*	*0*	*0*	*4*	*0*	*0*	*2*	*0*	*1*	*10*	*0*	*1*	*0*	*0*	*0*

JONES, Jake

Born	6/4/1993, Solihull
Signed	21/1/2013 (age 19) from Walsall on an initial one-month loan *(DH)*
First appearance	Forest Green Rovers (H), Conference Premier, 26/1/2013
Final appearance	Hyde (A), Conference Premier, 20/4/2013
Released/sold	N/A

*Career: 2009 Walsall (Y), Jul 2011 Walsall (Nov 2011 Redditch United - loan, **Jan 2013 LINCOLN CITY - loan**), May 2013 Tamworth (Sep 2013 King's Lynn Town - loan), Jan 2014 King's Lynn Town, Jan 2015 Halesowen Town, Mar 2015 King's Lynn Town, Jun 2015 Leamington, Oct 2015 Stafford Rangers, Oct 2016 Corby Town.*

Skilful winger who joined City from Walsall on a one-month youth loan. Immediately popular with the fans for his mazy runs, his loan was extended on 26 February 2013 to the end of the season. Having been released by Walsall in May, he was offered terms by City for 2013-14 which he described as *"a no-brainer...I cannot wait to get back"*. However, given until 5pm on Friday 10 May to sign, he failed to do so, choosing to join Tamworth instead. Not the best decision of his career, as he was only at The Lamb for a few months before disappearing into junior non-league football.

Lincoln City Playing Record - Conference Only

	League			FA Cup			FA Trophy			TOTALS			Lincolnshire Cup		
	App	Sub	Gls	App	Sub	Gls	App	Sub	Gls	App	Sub	Gls	App	Sub	Gls
2012-13	7	6	0	0	0	0	0	0	0	7	6	0	0	0	0
TOTALS	*7*	*6*	*0*	*0*	*0*	*0*	*0*	*0*	*0*	*7*	*6*	*0*	*0*	*0*	*0*

JORDAN, Todd

Born	4/12/1991, Sheffield
Signed	6/3/2013 (age 21) from Shirebrook Town on non-contract terms *(GS)*
First appearance	Macclesfield Town (A), Conference Premier, 6/3/2013
Final appearance	Chester (A), Conference, 27/1/2015
Released/sold	6/5/2015 and joined Alfreton Town *(CM)*

*Career: 2000 Sheffield Wednesday (Y), 2005 Sheffield United (Y), 2007 Staveley Miners' Welfare, Oct 2011 Worsborough Bridge Athletic, Mar 2012 Parkgate, Nov 2012 Staveley Miners' Welfare, Feb 2013 Shirebrook Town, **Mar 2013 LINCOLN CITY** (Oct 2014 Stalybridge Celtic - loan, Mar 2015 Buxton - loan), Jun 2015 Alfreton Town.*

Strong left-footed utility man who originally joined on a non-contract basis from Shirebrook Town of the Northern Counties East League. Had been at Shirebrook for just two weeks when Gary Simpson, who had coached Jordan at Parkgate, came calling. Did well enough to earn a one-year deal on 23 May 2013 which was extended for a further year from 1 July 2014. Made 50 appearances for the club despite spending several periods away on loan: at Stalybridge from 17 October 2014 for one month, extended for two further months on 20 November. Jordan was occasionally criticised by fans for his lack of mobility, and despite occasional glimpses of quality, he never really made the five-division step-up to National League standard. But Todd played for the club at a time when it was unable to pay for a full squad: he was rumoured to be earning less than £100 per week, but this has never been confirmed. Was sent off after 15 minutes at Chester on 27 January 2015 and never played for the club again. Joined Buxton on loan to the end of the season on 27 March and was released when his contract expired in the summer.

Lincoln City Playing Record - Conference Only

	League			FA Cup			FA Trophy			TOTALS			Lincolnshire Cup		
	App	Sub	Gls	App	Sub	Gls	App	Sub	Gls	App	Sub	Gls	App	Sub	Gls
2012-13	10	2	1	0	0	0	0	0	0	10	2	1	0	0	0
2013-14	29	3	0	2	0	0	2	0	0	33	3	0	1	1	0
2014-15	1	1	0	0	0	0	0	0	0	1	1	0	2	0	0
TOTALS	40	6	1	2	0	0	2	0	0	44	6	1	3	1	0

KABBA, Sahr

Born	13/4/1989, Bristol
Signed	5/6/2014 (age 25) from Havant & Waterlooville on a one-year deal *(GS)*
First appearance	FC Halifax Town (A), Conference, 25/8/2014
Final appearance	Eastleigh (A), FA Cup 1, 8/11/2014
Released/sold	15/12/2014 and joined Gloucester City *(CM)*

Career: *2003 Millwall (Y), 2006 Bristol Rovers (Y), Jul 2008 Almondsbury Town, Aug 2010 Weston-super-Mare, Jul 2012 Havant & Waterlooville, **Jun 2014 LINCOLN CITY** (Sep 2014 Whitehawk - loan), Jan 2015 Gloucester City, May 2015 Welling United, Jul 2016 Wealdstone (Dec 2016 Harrow Borough - loan, Mar 2017 Hayes & Yeading United - loan).*

Diminutive striker who signed on a one-year deal in the 2014 close season, but immediately picked up an injury and struggled to reach the standard of fitness required for full-time football. Joined Whitehawk on a six-week loan on 19 September to build some match fitness, but was unable to break into the first team on his return. City decided he couldn't make the step up to professional football and released him on 15 December. All three of his first team appearances came as a substitute. He hit the headlines in September 2015 when he became the first player to be charged by the FA for feigning injury when playing for Welling against Tranmere Rovers.

Lincoln City Playing Record - Conference Only

	League			FA Cup			FA Trophy			TOTALS			Lincolnshire Cup		
	App	Sub	Gls	App	Sub	Gls	App	Sub	Gls	App	Sub	Gls	App	Sub	Gls
2014-15	0	2	0	0	1	0	0	0	0	0	3	0	1	0	0
TOTALS	0	2	0	0	1	0	0	0	0	0	3	0	1	0	0

KEANE, Jordan

Born	19/9/1993, Nottingham
Signed	26/3/2015 (age 21) from Alfreton Town on loan until the end of the season *(CM)*
First appearance	Forest Green Rovers (H), Conference, 28/3/2015
Final appearance	Dartford (A), Conference, 25/4/2015
Released/sold	N/A

Career: *Derby County (Y), Jul 2010 Wolverhampton Wanderers (Y), May 2012 Stoke City (Oct 2013 Tamworth - loan), Jul 2014 Alfreton Town (**Mar 2015 LINCOLN CITY - loan**), Aug 2015 Nuneaton Town, Dec 2016 Worcester City.*

Tall centre back who earned his loan move to Lincoln by ringing City manager Chris Moyses and asking if he was interested! Signed on transfer deadline day with Kieran Wallace until the end of the season and for some reason played the last 7 games in midfield. Unfortunately formed part of a very poor City midfield at the end of that season and failed to earn a permanent deal. Was released by Alfreton on his return and joined Nuneaton Town, unusually on the same day as his younger brother Cieron. Despite being still in his early 20s, Keane already holds the UEFA B coaching licence and at the time of writing is studying for the A licence while coaching the Notts County Under-14s.

	League			FA Cup			FA Trophy			TOTALS			Lincolnshire Cup		
	App	Sub	Gls	App	Sub	Gls	App	Sub	Gls	App	Sub	Gls	App	Sub	Gls
2014-15	7	0	0	0	0	0	0	0	0	7	0	0	0	0	0
TOTALS	7	0	0	0	0	0	0	0	0	7	0	0	0	0	0

KNOTT, Billy

Born	28/11/1992, Canvey Island
Signed	2/2/2017 (age 24) from Gillingham on loan to the end of the season (DC)
First appearance	Woking (H), National League, 11/2/2017
Final appearance	Southport (A), National League, 29/4/2017
Released/sold	N/A

Career: 1999 Concord Rangers (Y), 2003 West Ham United (Y), 2007 Chelsea (Y), Oct 2010 Sunderland (Y) (Jan 2012 AFC Wimbledon - loan, Oct 2012 Woking - loan, Aug 2013 Wycombe Wanderers - loan, Jan 2014 Port Vale - loan), May 2014 Bradford City, Jun 2016 Gillingham (Feb 2017 LINCOLN CITY - loan).

Left-sided attacking midfielder signed from Gillingham to solve Lincoln's shortage of left-footed players. Had a good youth pedigree, having come through the academy system at West Ham and Chelsea. Was released by Chelsea at the age of 17 following an unfortunate disciplinary matter and had a trial with Newcastle in August 2010 before joining the Sunderland academy. Was called into the Sunderland first team squad by Steve Bruce in February 2011 but made just one appearance in the Premier League against Spurs in May 2013 before being released. During Bradford's FA Cup run in 2014-15 he played in wins over former clubs Chelsea and Sunderland. Has also appeared for England at U16, U17 and U20 levels. Has Concord Rangers connections, having played for the youth team when his dad Steve was manager there between 1999 and 2002. His brother Sammy also played for Concord under Danny Cowley between 2012 and 2013. Signed for the Imps on 2 February but was not registered until 11 February to enable him to appear in the play-offs if necessary. Proved to be an intelligent player with good vision and passing ability, although some believed his playing style left City more exposed defensively. Came on as a second-half substitute against Bromley in April and scored the winner within two minutes, his only goal for the club.

Lincoln City Playing Record - Conference Only

	League			FA Cup			FA Trophy			TOTALS			Lincolnshire Cup		
	App	Sub	Gls	App	Sub	Gls	App	Sub	Gls	App	Sub	Gls	App	Sub	Gls
2016-17	8	6	1	0	0	0	2	1	0	10	7	1	0	0	0
TOTALS	8	6	1	0	0	0	2	1	0	10	7	1	0	0	0

LARKIN, Colin

Born	27/4/1982, Dundalk
Signed	24/8/2012 (age 30) from Hartlepool United to the end of the season (DH)
First appearance	Macclesfield Town (H), Conference Premier, 25/8/2012
Final appearance	Mansfield Town (H), Conference Premier, 26/2/2013
Released/sold	8/3/2013 and joined Harrogate Town (GS)

Career: 1999 Wolverhampton Wanderers (Sep 2001 Kidderminster Harriers - loan), Jul 2002 Mansfield Town), Jun 2005 Chesterfield, Jun 2007 Northampton Town, Aug 2009 Hartlepool United, Aug 2012 LINCOLN CITY, Mar 2013 Harrogate Town, May 2013 Gateshead, Aug 2014 Harrogate Town, Sep 2014 West Auckland Town, Jan 2015 Sunderland RCA.

Vastly experienced striker who signed on a deal until the end of the 2012-13 season. Scored two penalties in the home match against Hyde on 15 September 2012, and hit a hat-trick in the first half at Dartford on 8 December to put City 4-0 up. Four of his eight goals for City were penalties. Left the club by mutual consent on 8 March 2013, as he wanted to be closer to his home in the north-east. Joined Harrogate Town for the rest of the season before signing for Gateshead. Currently holds several coaching positions in the Sunderland area.

Lincoln City Playing Record - Conference Only

	League			FA Cup			FA Trophy			TOTALS			Lincolnshire Cup		
	App	Sub	Gls	App	Sub	Gls	App	Sub	Gls	App	Sub	Gls	App	Sub	Gls
2012-13	13	16	8	0	4	0	1	0	0	14	20	8	0	0	0
TOTALS	13	16	8	0	4	0	1	0	0	14	20	8	0	0	0

LAURENT, Francis

Born	2/1/1986, Paris, France
Signed	5/7/2011 (age 25) from Northampton Town on a one-year deal (ST)
First appearance	Alfreton Town (A), FA Cup 4Q, 29/10/2011
Final appearance	Darlington (H), Conference Premier, 9/4/2012
Released/sold	5/5/2012 and joined KVK Tienen (Belgium) (DH)

Career: 1998 US Pont-Sainte-Maxence (France) (Y), 2001 AS Beauvais Oise (France) (Y), 2004 FC Sochaux (France), Jul 2006 SV Eintracht Trier 05 (Germany), Jun 2007 1.FSV Mainz 05 (Germany), Aug 2008 Southend United, Oct 2010 AFC Compiègne (France), Jan 2011 Northampton Town, **Jul 2011 LINCOLN CITY**, Jun 2012 Doxa Katokopias (Cyprus), Aug 2012 KVK Tienen (Belgium), Jan 2013 FC Chambly (France), Jul 2014 US Pont-Sainte-Maxence (France), May 2015 retired.

Tall French winger who signed for City having played for Southend under Steve Tilson. Had previously had a short spell at French side AFC Compiègne with Jean-Francois Christophe. Signed a one-year deal with City on 5 July 2011 but struggled to win a place due to injuries. Departed in May 2012 when City could only offer reduced terms. Joined Belgian club KVK Tienen with fellow-Imps Jean-François Christophe and Jean Arnaud before finishing his career with French amateurs Pont-Sainte-Maxence, where he also began his career. Had the novel experience of playing under Jürgen Klopp when he was manager of Mainz. Currently a players' agent with Amsterdam-based Sport Entertainment Group.

Lincoln City Playing Record - Conference Only

	League			FA Cup			FA Trophy			TOTALS			Lincolnshire Cup		
	App	Sub	Gls	App	Sub	Gls	App	Sub	Gls	App	Sub	Gls	App	Sub	Gls
2011-12	5	9	1	0	2	0	1	0	0	6	11	1	0	0	0
TOTALS	5	9	1	0	2	0	1	0	0	6	11	1	0	0	0

LEDSHAM, Karl

Born	17/11/1987, Whiston
Signed	6/5/2014 (age 26) from Southport on a one-year deal (GS)
First appearance	Altrincham (A), Conference, 12/8/2014
Final appearance	Altrincham (H), Conference, 4/11/2014
Released/sold	29/12/2014 and joined Barrow (CM)

Career: 2000 Liverpool (Y), 2002 Stockport County (Y), 2004 Burscough (Y), Aug 2006 St Helens Town (Aug 2008 College of Southern Maryland (USA)), Sep 2009 Skelmersdale United (Nov 2010 Southport - loan), Jan 2011 Southport (Nov 2013 Cambridge United - loan), **May 2014 LINCOLN CITY** (Nov 2014 AFC Telford United - loan), Jan 2015 Barrow, May 2015 Stockport County, Mar 2016 retired, Nov 2016 Widnes.

Impressive midfielder who became City's first signing of the 2014 close season. Unfortunately suffered from a recurrent groin injury and never really got going at Sincil Bank. Loaned to AFC Telford for a month from 14 November to build his fitness but never appeared for the club again. He was released on 29 December and dropped to part-time football with Barrow for a few months before moving on to Stockport. The groin injury forced him to retire in March 2016 at the age of 28, upon which he headed to America to take up a coaching position in New Jersey with Advanced Total Soccer Coaching.

Lincoln City Playing Record - Conference Only

	League			FA Cup			FA Trophy			TOTALS			Lincolnshire Cup		
	App	Sub	Gls	App	Sub	Gls	App	Sub	Gls	App	Sub	Gls	App	Sub	Gls
2014-15	7	6	1	0	1	0	0	0	0	7	7	1	1	1	0
TOTALS	7	6	1	0	1	0	0	0	0	7	7	1	1	1	0

LLOYD, Danny

Born	3/12/1991, Liverpool
Signed	6/1/2012 (age 20) from Colwyn Bay to the end of the season (DH)
First appearance	York City (H), Conference Premier, 7/1/2012
Final appearance	Hayes & Yeading United (H), Conference Premier, 21/4/2012
Released/sold	14/6/2012 and joined Colwyn Bay (DH)

Career: Southport (Y), Jul 2009 Southport (Nov 2009 Chorley - loan, Aug 2010 Skelmersdale United - loan), Jul 2011 Colwyn Bay, **Jan 2012 LINCOLN CITY**, Jul 2012 Colwyn Bay, Jan 2013 Tamworth, Jun 2013 AFC Fylde, May 2016 Stockport County, May 2017 Peterborough United.

Energetic winger who signed for City on a deal to the end of the 2011-12 season a few weeks after impressing for Colwyn Bay in the FA Trophy first round tie on 10 December 2011. Became popular with fans for his committed displays, and played a part in keeping the side in the Conference Premier despite being used mainly as a substitute. Scored twice against Darlington on his first full start, but that was in April when the season was almost over. Was fully expected to rejoin the club for 2012-13, but discussions over a new contract stalled amidst claims that his wage demands were excessive in City's current financial position. In return, Lloyd claimed the offer did not value him enough and would not be enough to enable him to turn professional and move to Lincoln. Went on to score a lot of goals in non-league football, notably with AFC Fylde alongside fellow ex-Imp Danny Rowe, before making it to the Football League with Peterborough. Also known by his full name - Danny Lloyd-McGoldrick.

Lincoln City Playing Record - Conference Only

	League			FA Cup			FA Trophy			TOTALS			Lincolnshire Cup		
	App	Sub	Gls	App	Sub	Gls	App	Sub	Gls	App	Sub	Gls	App	Sub	Gls
2011-12	3	9	3	0	0	0	0	0	0	3	9	3	0	0	0
TOTALS	3	9	3	0	0	0	0	0	0	3	9	3	0	0	0

LONG, Sean

Born	2/5/1995, Dublin
Signed	5/1/2017 (age 21) from Reading on loan to the end of the season (DC)
First appearance	Ipswich Town (A), FA Cup 3, 7/1/2017
Final appearance	Southport (A), National League, 29/4/2017
Released/sold	

Career: Cherry Orchard (Ireland) (Y), Aug 2012 Reading (Y), May 2014 Reading (Oct 2015 Luton Town - loan, Mar 2016 Braintree Town - loan, Jul 2016 Cambridge United - loan, **(Jan 2017 LINCOLN CITY - loan)**, **May 2017 LINCOLN CITY.**

Having enjoyed a loan spell at Braintree under the Cowleys during the 2015-16 season, Republic of Ireland U21 international defender Sean Long joined City on loan during the January 2017 transfer window with a view to a permanent move. Initially signed to cover both full-back positions in place of long-term injury victim Lee Beevers, Long actually alternated with full back Bradley Wood to cope with the number of games the side was playing. Proved a more than capable deputy, helping City to close out the National League title, and signed on a permanent basis at the end of the season.

	League			FA Cup			FA Trophy			TOTALS			Lincolnshire Cup		
	App	Sub	Gls	App	Sub	Gls	App	Sub	Gls	App	Sub	Gls	App	Sub	Gls
2016-17	12	2	0	0	2	0	3	0	0	15	4	0	0	0	0
TOTALS	12	2	0	0	2	0	3	0	0	15	4	0	0	0	0

LOUIS, Jefferson

Born	22/2/1979, Harrow
Signed	31/1/2012 (age 32) from Brackley Town to the end of the season (DH)
First appearance	Braintree Town (H), Conference Premier, 14/2/2012
Final appearance	Ebbsfleet United (A), Conference Premier, 28/4/2012
Released/sold	5/5/2012 and joined Newport County (DH)

Career: 1996 Risborough Rangers, 1998 Thame United, Dec 2000 Aylesbury United, Jul 2001 Thame United, Feb 2002 Oxford United (Jul 2003 Woking - loan, Aug 2004 Gravesend & Northfleet - loan), Sep 2004 Forest Green Rovers, Dec 2004 Woking, May 2005 Bristol Rovers, Oct 2005 Hemel Hempstead Town, Oct 2005 Lewes, Nov 2005 Worthing, Dec 2005 Stevenage Borough, Jul 2006 Eastleigh, Sep 2006 Yeading, Jan 2007 Havant & Waterlooville, Jul 2007 Weymouth, Jan 2008 Maidenhead United, Jan 2008 Mansfield Town, Jun 2008 Wrexham, May 2009 Crawley Town (Nov 2009 Rushden & Diamonds - loan), Jun 2010 Gainsborough Trinity (Oct 2010 Darlington - loan), Jan 2011 Weymouth, Jan 2011 Hayes & Yeading, Mar 2011 Maidenhead United, Jul 2011 Brackley Town, **Jan 2012 LINCOLN CITY**, Jun 2012 Newport County (Nov 2012 Whitehawk - loan), Jan 2013 Brackley Town, Jul 2013 Hendon, Feb 2014 Margate, Jun 2014 Lowestoft Town, Dec 2014 Wealdstone, Jun 2016 Staines Town, Oct 2016 Oxford City.

Signed on 31 January 2012 until the end of the 2011-12 season, powerful striker Jefferson Louis was one of many players signed by new manager David Holdsworth in a bid to reduce the wage bill and keep struggling City in the Conference Premier. Scored within a minute on his debut against Braintree and again in his next game at Kidderminster. Played through the pain barrier after cracking a rib in training in the middle of March. City failed to hold on to him in the summer of 2012 due to offering reduced terms, and he left for Conference rivals Newport. Another City player to have served time in prison, Louis was jailed for 12 months in 2001 for dangerous driving while disqualified, and was released after serving half. The cousin of fellow City striker Richard Pacquette, the two played for Dominica together in a World Cup qualifier against Barbados in March 2008. Officially the most-travelled footballer of all time within the English game, his CV reads like a directory of non-league clubs. City were his 27th different club (his 30th in all, including returns to three previous clubs), and he signed for his 35th different club - Oxford City - in October 2016 (his 39th club in all). On the plus side, Louis has scored close to 200 goals in his career.

Lincoln City Playing Record - Conference Only

	League			FA Cup			FA Trophy			TOTALS			Lincolnshire Cup		
	App	Sub	Gls	App	Sub	Gls	App	Sub	Gls	App	Sub	Gls	App	Sub	Gls
2011-12	14	0	6	0	0	0	0	0	0	14	0	6	0	0	0
TOTALS	14	0	6	0	0	0	0	0	0	14	0	6	0	0	0

McCALLUM, Gavin

Born	24/4/1987, Mississauga, Canada
Signed	21/6/2010 (age 23) from Hereford United on a two-year deal (CS)
First appearance	Southport (A) Conference Premier, 13/8/2011
Final appearance	Alfreton Town (H), FA Cup 4Q Replay, 1/11/2011
Released/sold	30/1/2012 and later joined Woking (DH)

Career: Sep 2004 Yeovil Town (Y), Jan 2006 Yeovil Town (Aug 2006 Tamworth - loan, Mar 2007 Dorchester Town - loan, Nov 2006 Crawley Town - loan), Aug 2007 Weymouth, Feb 2008 Havant & Waterlooville, Jul 2008 Sutton United, Aug 2009 Hereford United, **Jun 2010 LINCOLN CITY** (Nov 2011 Barnet - loan), Aug 2012 Woking, Dec 2013 Sutton United (Dec 2013 Tonbridge Angels - loan), Jun 2014 Eastbourne Borough.

Canadian international striker who was signed on a notorious two-year deal by former manager Chris Sutton in summer 2010 after scoring twice against the Imps in February. The transfer fee from Hereford was set by a tribunal at around £5,000 on 26 July 2010, but the terms of the contract itself have proved controversial. Had a troubled time at Sincil Bank with fitness issues, and often appeared at loggerheads with both the club and its supporters. Made his original City debut in the League Two defeat at Rotherham on 7 August 2010. Was made available for transfer following City's relegation from the Football League in 2011, but started the season in the side when there were no offers for him. Eventually joined Barnet on loan on 22 November 2011 until the New Year, but returned to Lincoln without receiving an offer of a permanent contract. Fell foul of club discipline in January 2012 when he was seen outside a Lincoln nightclub (*Home*) with Tony Sinclair and Josh Gowling; along with Sinclair, McCallum never played for Lincoln again. His case was not helped by his refusal to go on loan to a non-league club, stating that he wanted to join a club in the Football League. Left by mutual consent on 30 January 2012 and ironically has bounced around non-league football in the south-east ever since. David Holdsworth claimed he had signed four players for less than half of what they had been paying McCallum (rumoured to be £1,200 per week). Won 4 caps for Canada U20, and 1 full cap on 29 May 2010, when he scored a 92nd-minute equaliser against Venezuela in a 1-1 draw.

Lincoln City Playing Record - Conference Only

	League			FA Cup			FA Trophy			TOTALS			Lincolnshire Cup		
	App	Sub	Gls	App	Sub	Gls	App	Sub	Gls	App	Sub	Gls	App	Sub	Gls
2011-12	17	1	3	1	0	0	0	0	0	18	1	3	1	1	0
TOTALS	17	1	3	1	0	0	0	0	0	18	1	3	1	1	0

Lincoln City Playing Record - Football League

	League			FA Cup			League Cup			FL Trophy			TOTALS		
	App	Sub	Gls	App	Sub	Gls	App	Sub	Gls	App	Sub	Gls	App	Sub	Gls
2010-11	24	12	3	0	0	0	1	0	0	0	0	0	25	12	3
TOTALS	24	12	3	0	0	0	1	0	0	0	0	0	25	12	3

McCAMMON, Mark

Born	7/8/1978, Barnet
Signed	24/2/2012 (age 33) from Sheffield FC on loan to the end of the season (DH)
First appearance	Mansfield Town (A), Conference Premier, 3/3/2012
Final appearance	Macclesfield Town (H), Conference Premier, 25/8/2012
Released/sold	29/8/2012 and retired (DH)

*Career: Aug 1997 Cambridge United, Mar 1999 Charlton Athletic (Jan 2000 Swindon Town - loan), Jul 2000 Brentford, Mar 2003 Millwall (Dec 2004 Brighton & Hove Albion - loan), Feb 2005 Brighton & Hove Albion (Feb 2006 Bristol City - loan), Aug 2006 Doncaster Rovers, Jul 2008 Gillingham (Feb 2010 Bradford City - loan), Oct 2011 Braintree Town, Feb 2012 Sheffield FC (**Mar 2012 LINCOLN CITY - loan**), **Aug 2012 LINCOLN CITY - non-contract**, Sep 2012 retired.*

Giant striker who signed on loan from Sheffield FC on 24 February 2012 and scored on his debut as a substitute at Mansfield on 3 March. Returned to Sheffield at the end of his loan period but returned for a trial at the start of the 2012-13 season on non-contract terms. Played a couple of games, but was released on 29 August and decided to retire from playing. Was awarded £68,000 in a much-publicised racial discrimination case against Gillingham FC in 2012. Had a good career in the game, appearing in the 2004 FA Cup Final while at Millwall. Also appeared in two play-off finals for Brentford and Doncaster. Won 5 full caps (scoring 4 goals) for Barbados between 2006-2008 including a hat-trick against Anguilla. Obtained a degree in Professional Sports Writing and Broadcasting after retiring and became a personal trainer with Fitness Unlimited in Sheffield.

Lincoln City Playing Record - Conference Only

	League			FA Cup			FA Trophy			TOTALS			Lincolnshire Cup		
	App	Sub	Gls	App	Sub	Gls	App	Sub	Gls	App	Sub	Gls	App	Sub	Gls
2011-12	2	4	2	0	0	0	0	0	0	2	4	2	0	0	0
2012-13	1	1	0	0	0	0	0	0	0	1	1	0	0	0	0
TOTALS	3	5	2	0	0	0	0	0	0	3	5	2	0	0	0

McCOMBE, Jamie

Born	1/1/1983, Pontefract
Signed	28/1/2016 (age 33) from Stevenage on an 18-month deal (CM)
First appearance	Guiseley (H), National League, 30/1/2016
Final appearance	York City (A), FA Trophy semi-final first leg, 14/3/2017
Released/sold	

Career: 1996 Frickley Athletic (Y), 1999 Scunthorpe United (Y), Nov 2001 Scunthorpe United (Oct 2003 Halifax Town - loan), **Mar 2004 LINCOLN CITY,** May 2006 Bristol City, Jul 2010 Huddersfield Town (Nov 2011 Preston North End - loan), Aug 2012 Doncaster Rovers, Aug 2015 Stevenage, **Jan 2016 LINCOLN CITY.**

Centre back who was originally signed for Lincoln by Keith Alexander after an unpleasant dispute with Scunthorpe, who tried to block the move. The transfer was completed only once a tribunal had ordered McCombe to sign a confidentiality agreement with the Football League preventing him from discussing the terms of the transfer. Eventually signed on 1 March 2004 and made his debut in a 4-1 win over Mansfield on 13 March. Made the play-offs in each of his three seasons with City, the last game of his first spell being the play-off semi-final defeat at Grimsby on 16 May before moving on to Bristol City later that month. After a good career in the Championship and League One, McCombe re-signed for City on 18-month contract on 28 January 2016. Made his second City debut in same game as loanee James Caton, as manager Chris Moyses tried unsuccessfully to revive City's flagging promotion challenge. Picked up an injury in the 4-1 defeat at Dover on 15 March and missed the rest of the season. Could not hold down a regular place under Danny Cowley and was officially appointed player-coach on 21 October 2016 after a period assisting with training duties. Was offered a permanent position as a coach at the end of the season in lieu of a playing contract but was expected to remain registered as a player.

Lincoln City Playing Record - Conference Only

	League			FA Cup			FA Trophy			TOTALS			Lincolnshire Cup		
	App	Sub	Gls	App	Sub	Gls	App	Sub	Gls	App	Sub	Gls	App	Sub	Gls
2015-16	8	0	2	0	0	0	0	0	0	8	0	2	0	0	0
2016-17	3	4	0	1	3	0	4	0	0	8	7	0	1	1	0
TOTALS	11	4	2	1	3	0	4	0	0	16	7	2	1	1	0

Lincoln City Playing Record - Football League

	League			FA Cup			League Cup			FL Trophy			TOTALS		
	App	Sub	Gls	App	Sub	Gls	App	Sub	Gls	App	Sub	Gls	App	Sub	Gls
2003-04	9	1	0	0	0	0	0	0	0	0	0	0	9	1	0
2004-05	40	4	3	1	0	0	2	0	1	1	0	0	44	4	4
2005-06	40	0	4	1	0	0	1	0	0	0	0	0	42	0	4
TOTALS	89	5	7	2	0	0	3	0	1	1	0	0	95	5	8

McDAID, Robbie

Born	23/10/1996, Omagh
Signed	8/1/2016 (age 19) from Leeds United on loan to the end of the season (CM)
First appearance	Dover Athletic (H), National League, 9/1/2016
Final appearance	Cheltenham Town (A), National League, 30/4/2016
Released/sold	N/A

Career: Jul 2013 Glenavon, Jul 2014 Leeds United (**Jan 2016 LINCOLN CITY - loan**), Sep 2016 Barnsley, Nov 2016 York City (Jan 2017 Chorley - loan).

Very promising young striker who was signed on a youth loan until the end of the 2015-16 season. Became popular with fans for his positive attitude and direct style of play, although he was used mainly as an impact substitute. Was linked with a permanent move to Sincil Bank when he was released by Leeds in May 2016, but the transfer never materialised. Despite playing only a handful of games for Glenavon, McDaid had attracted a lot of attention from big clubs, having trials at Southampton, Reading and Huddersfield before Leeds signed him at the age of 17 in 2014. Hit the headlines for the wrong reasons in July 2014 when he was sent off playing for Northern Ireland U19 against Mexico in a match that had to be abandoned. Capped by Northern Ireland at U17, U19 and U21 levels.

Lincoln City Playing Record - Conference Only

	League			FA Cup			FA Trophy			TOTALS			Lincolnshire Cup		
	App	Sub	Gls	App	Sub	Gls	App	Sub	Gls	App	Sub	Gls	App	Sub	Gls
2015-16	3	13	4	0	0	0	0	0	0	3	13	4	0	0	0
TOTALS	3	13	4	0	0	0	0	0	0	3	13	4	0	0	0

MARGETTS, Jonny

Born	28/9/1993, Edenthorpe
Signed	14/7/2016 (age 22) from Tranmere Rovers on a one-year deal (DC)
First appearance	Woking (A), National League, 6/8/2016
Final appearance	Boreham Wood (A), National League, 21/3/2017
Released/sold	31/8/2016 and joined Scunthorpe United (DC)

Career: 2004 Hull City (Y), Jul 2012 Hull City (Feb 2014 Gainsborough Trinity - loan, Aug 2014 Harrogate Town - loan, Dec 2014 Gainsborough Trinity - loan, Mar 2015 Cambridge United - loan), Jul 2015 Tranmere Rovers, Jul 2016 LINCOLN CITY, Aug 2016 Scunthorpe United (Mar 2017 LINCOLN CITY - loan).

Young centre forward who never broke into the first team at Hull despite scoring plenty of goals for their development team; not even three hat-tricks in a row early in 2015 could persuade Hull to keep him at the end of that season. Signed for Tranmere but had a difficult season with injuries; was loaned out to Conference rivals Southport and Altrincham before being released after a year. Signed for the Imps after a successful pre-season trial that saw him score 5 goals in less than 2 games. Made a great start to his City career, ending pre-season with 7 goals in 4 games, and started the league season in similar fashion. Became the first player in 25 years to score four goals in a match at Sincil Bank when he scored all four against Southport on 20 August 2016. After just 49 days at Lincoln, he joined Scunthorpe United on transfer deadline day for a fee rumoured to be in the region of £50,000 to £100,000. Received few opportunities at Glanford Park, and on 1 March 2017 he returned to City on loan to the end of the season with a view to a permanent transfer thereafter. Appeared only sporadically in his second spell and failed to add to his excellent early season goal tally.

Lincoln City Playing Record - Conference Only

	League			FA Cup			FA Trophy			TOTALS			Lincolnshire Cup		
	App	Sub	Gls	App	Sub	Gls	App	Sub	Gls	App	Sub	Gls	App	Sub	Gls
2016-17	7	3	5	0	1	0	0	0	0	7	4	5	1	0	2
TOTALS	7	3	5	0	1	0	0	0	0	7	4	5	1	0	2

MARIS, George

Born	6/3/1996, Sheffield
Signed	1/2/2016 (age 19) from Barnsley on loan to the end of the season (CM)
First appearance	Eastleigh (H), National League, 6/2/2016
Final appearance	Cheltenham Town (A), National League, 30/4/2016
Released/sold	N/A

Career: 2010 Barnsley (Y), May 2014 Barnsley (Jan 2015 Nuneaton Town - loan, Sep 2015 Guiseley - loan, Feb 2016 LINCOLN CITY - loan), Jun 2016 Cambridge United.

Young midfielder signed on loan until the end of the 2015-16 season. Scored a lot of goals for Barnsley's academy side, several of which feature on YouTube. Had impressed when playing against Lincoln for Guiseley in the televised game on 2 October 2015. Did well during his loan spell at Sincil Bank, scoring a couple of well-taken goals including a televised header at Tranmere that alerted other clubs to his ability. Released by Barnsley at the end of his loan and signed for League Two Cambridge.

Lincoln City Playing Record - Conference Only

	League			FA Cup			FA Trophy			TOTALS			Lincolnshire Cup		
	App	Sub	Gls	App	Sub	Gls	App	Sub	Gls	App	Sub	Gls	App	Sub	Gls
2015-16	6	7	2	0	0	0	0	0	0	6	7	2	0	0	0
TOTALS	6	7	2	0	0	0	0	0	0	6	7	2	0	0	0

MARRIOTT, Adam

Born	14/4/1991, Brandon, Suffolk
Signed	28/6/2016 (age 25) from Stevenage on a one-year deal (DC)
First appearance	Woking (A), National League, 6/8/2016
Final appearance	Maidstone United (A), National League, 25/4/2017
Released/sold	

Career: Norwich City (Y), 2006 Cambridge United (Y), Jul 2009 Cambridge United (Mar 2012 Cambridge City - loan, Aug 2012 Bishop's Stortford - loan, Nov 2012 Cambridge City - loan), Jan 2013 Cambridge City, Jul 2014 Stevenage, **Jun 2016 LINCOLN CITY.**

Prolific striker who scored 90 goals in three seasons for Cambridge United's youth team. Broke into their first team but was used mainly as a substitute before spending several periods on loan elsewhere. Scored 62 goals in two seasons for Cambridge City, breaking the club's scoring record in 2013-14 with 41 in 38 league games including four hat-tricks. Earned a move to League Two Stevenage in the summer of 2014 but his time there was badly affected by injury. Joined Lincoln on a performance-based deal accordingly. Made a great start to his City career, scoring on his debut at Woking, but injured an arm in a friendly against Peterborough in September and failed to win back a regular place in the side. Despite his obvious technical ability, Marriott gained a reputation more as an impact substitute rather than as a starter, and delivered some important cameos against Tranmere, Ipswich and Torquay in particular. Despite an intermittent season, Marriott was offered a new contract in the summer of 2017.

Lincoln City Playing Record - Conference Only

	League			FA Cup			FA Trophy			TOTALS			Lincolnshire Cup		
	App	Sub	Gls	App	Sub	Gls	App	Sub	Gls	App	Sub	Gls	App	Sub	Gls
2016-17	8	17	4	0	2	0	3	1	0	11	20	4	0	0	0
TOTALS	8	17	4	0	2	0	3	1	0	11	20	4	0	0	0

MARSDEN, John

Born	9/12/1992, Liverpool
Signed	12/2/2015 (age 22) from Southport on loan to the end of the season (CM)
First appearance	Chester (H), Conference, 14/2/2015
Final appearance	Forest Green Rovers (H), Conference, 28/3/2015
Released/sold	N/A

Career: 2000 Wrexham (Y), 2004 Wigan Athletic (Y), Feb 2009 Glasgow Celtic (Aug 2010 Hamilton Academical - loan), Feb 2011 Rochdale - non-contract, Aug 2011 Aberystwyth Town, Jul 2012 Stockport Sports, Feb 2013 Stoke City, Jul 2013 Shrewsbury Town, Aug 2014 Southport (**Feb 2015 LINCOLN CITY - loan**), Aug 2015 Macclesfield Town, Sep 2015 Colwyn Bay, Jan 2016 Stockport County (Mar 2017 AFC Telford United - loan), May 2017 released.

Teen prodigy whose prolific goalscoring record for Wigan's academy and Liverpool Schoolboys had earned a three-year professional contract with Celtic at the age of 16. His time at Celtic was affected by injury and he moved back to England when he was released in January 2011. Did the rounds of numerous clubs close to his Liverpool home, eventually joining Lincoln on loan until the end of the 2014-15 season. Failed to make any impact at all at Sincil Bank and was recalled by Southport on 13 April 2015.

	League			FA Cup			FA Trophy			TOTALS			Lincolnshire Cup		
	App	Sub	Gls	App	Sub	Gls	App	Sub	Gls	App	Sub	Gls	App	Sub	Gls
2014-15	2	4	0	0	0	0	0	0	0	2	4	0	0	0	0
TOTALS	2	4	0	0	0	0	0	0	0	2	4	0	0	0	0

MARSHALL, Marcus

Born	7/10/1989, Hammersmith
Signed	1/8/2014 (age 24) from Morecambe on loan for the season *(GS)*
First appearance	Kidderminster Harriers (H), Conference, 9/8/2014
Final appearance	Welling United (H), Conference, 14/3/2015
Released/sold	N/A

*Career: Blackburn Rovers (Y), Aug 2008 Blackburn Rovers (Jan 2010 Rotherham United - loan), Jul 2010 Rotherham United (Jan 2012 Macclesfield Town - loan), Jul 2012 Bury (Nov 2012 Grimsby Town - loan, Jan 2013 Grimsby Town - loan), Jun 2013 Morecambe (**Aug 2014 LINCOLN CITY - loan**), Jun 2015 Grimsby Town, Aug 2016 Boston United (Mar 2017 Coalville Town - loan), May 2017 released.*

Winger who signed on a season-long loan from League Two side Morecambe, having previously played for Gary Simpson at Macclesfield. Played the majority of the season due to his ability to operate down either flank, and notably scored in the 3-1 win at Grimsby. Another ex-City player who won promotion back to the League with Grimsby in 2015-16, but was immediately released by The Mariners in the close season. Has since begun to slip down the non-league ladder.

	League			FA Cup			FA Trophy			TOTALS			Lincolnshire Cup		
	App	Sub	Gls	App	Sub	Gls	App	Sub	Gls	App	Sub	Gls	App	Sub	Gls
2014-15	24	8	2	2	0	0	1	0	0	27	8	2	1	0	1
TOTALS	24	8	2	2	0	0	1	0	0	27	8	2	1	0	1

MEDLEY, Luke

Born	21/6/1989, Greenwich
Signed	17/11/2011 (age 22) from Kidderminster Harriers on loan to the New Year *(DH)*
First appearance	Wrexham (H), Conference Premier, 19/11/2011
Final appearance	Grimsby Town (H), Conference Premier, 1/1/2012
Released/sold	N/A

*Career: 2005 Welwyn Garden City, Jun 2005 Protec Academy, Barnet (Y), Nov 2006 Tottenham Hotspur (Y), Jul 2007 Bradford City (Jan 2008 Cambridge City - loan), Jun 2008 Barnet (Mar 2009 Havant & Waterlooville - loan, Jul 2009 Woking - loan, Feb 2010 Havant & Waterlooville - loan), Aug 2010 Mansfield Town (Feb 2011 Aldershot Town - loan), Jun 2011 Kidderminster Harriers (**Nov 2011 LINCOLN CITY - loan**, Jan 2012 Woking - loan), Feb 2012 Bromley, Jul 2013 Hayes & Yeading United, Oct 2013 Goole, Nov 2013 Crawley Down Gatwick, Mar 2014 Margate, Jul 2014 Chatham Town, Oct 2014 Walton Casuals, Jan 2016 Chatham Town, Jan 2017 Cray Wanderers.*

Journeyman striker who had previously played under David Holdsworth at Mansfield. Signed on loan to 1 January 2012, but failed to impress after 6 short appearances from the substitute's bench and returned to Kidderminster. Has since returned to his roots, playing for a number of minor clubs around south-east London.

	League			FA Cup			FA Trophy			TOTALS			Lincolnshire Cup		
	App	Sub	Gls	App	Sub	Gls	App	Sub	Gls	**App**	**Sub**	**Gls**	App	Sub	Gls
2011-12	0	6	0	0	0	0	0	0	0	**0**	**6**	**0**	0	0	0
TOTALS	*0*	*6*	*0*	*0*	*0*	*0*	*0*	*0*	*0*	*0*	*6*	*0*	*0*	*0*	*0*

MENDY, Arnaud

Born	10/2/1990, Évreux, France
Signed	10/2/2014 (age 24) to the end of the season *(GS)*
First appearance	Braintree Town (A), Conference Premier, 18/3/2014
Final appearance	Alfreton Town (A), Conference, 17/3/2015
Released/sold	6/5/2015 and joined Whitehawk *(CM)*

*Career: ALM Évreux (Y) (France), 2007 FC Rouen (France), Jun 2008 Derby County (Oct 2009 Grimsby Town - loan, Sep 2010 Tranmere Rovers - loan), Jul 2011 Macclesfield Town (Oct 2012 Luton Town - loan), Jan 2013 Luton Town, **Feb 2014 LINCOLN CITY**, Jul 2015 Whitehawk, Jul 2016 Hemel Hempstead Town.*

Another player previously known to Gary Simpson from his time as Macclesfield manager, rangy midfielder Arnaud Mendy made the headlines in 2011 when he returned to Macclesfield with an unidentified tropical disease after trips to Africa on international duty with Guinea-Bissau. His last club before linking up with Simpson again at Lincoln was Luton Town, with whom he had an unsettled spell. Luton eventually cancelled his contract on 27 December 2013, after which he spent several months out of the game due to family issues. After a short trial, Mendy signed for City on 10 February 2014 on a deal to the end of the 2013-14 season. Took time to find his feet in the National League but fought back well, winning his first cap for Guinea-Bissau since 2011 when he played in the African Nations qualifier against Botswana on 19 July 2014; the appearance made him the 11th player to receive a full international cap whilst on City's books. Signed a further one-year deal on 8 July 2014 but was released in the summer of 2015. That decision came back to bite City, as he was an integral part of the Whitehawk team that knocked City out of the FA Cup in November 2015.

Lincoln City Playing Record - Conference Only

	League			FA Cup			FA Trophy			TOTALS			Lincolnshire Cup		
	App	Sub	Gls	App	Sub	Gls	App	Sub	Gls	**App**	**Sub**	**Gls**	App	Sub	Gls
2013-14	7	0	0	0	0	0	0	0	0	**7**	**0**	**0**	0	0	0
2014-15	26	4	1	3	0	0	0	0	0	**29**	**4**	**1**	1	0	0
TOTALS	*33*	*4*	*1*	*3*	*0*	*0*	*0*	*0*	*0*	*36*	*4*	*1*	*1*	*0*	*0*

MILES, Taylor

Born	11 July 1995, Watford
Signed	21/6/2016 (age 20) from Braintree Town on a one-year deal *(DC)*
First appearance	Woking (a), National League, 6/8/2016
Final appearance	As above - made only one appearance
Released/sold	18/5/2017 and joined Hemel Hempstead Town *(DC)*

*Career: 2012 West Ham United (Y) (Feb 2014 Concord Rangers - loan), Sep 2014 Concord Rangers, Jul 2015 Braintree Town, **Jun 2016 LINCOLN CITY** (Nov 2016 Boston United - loan, Feb 2017 Concord Rangers - loan), May 2017 Hemel Hempstead Town.*

Young right-sided midfielder who had shown great promise in his early years at West Ham, gaining a reputation for tough-tackling and scoring goals from distance. Played regularly in the academy and U21 sides, but was surprisingly released in May 2014. Slipped into the non-league scene in Essex with Danny Cowley's Concord Rangers, where he had enjoyed a loan spell during his time at West Ham. Followed Cowley to Braintree and then to Lincoln, signing on an initial one-year deal. Had a very eventful debut at Woking, coming on as a 78th-minute substitute, collecting a yellow card in the 83rd minute, and breaking an ankle after 88 minutes. Joined Boston United on a one-month loan on 11

November 2016 as part of his recovery from the injury and returned to former club Concord in February to give him more game time. Released at the end of the season without adding to his solitary appearance.

Lincoln City Playing Record - Conference Only

	League			FA Cup			FA Trophy			TOTALS			Lincolnshire Cup		
	App	Sub	Gls	App	Sub	Gls	App	Sub	Gls	App	Sub	Gls	App	Sub	Gls
2016-17	0	1	0	0	0	0	0	0	0	0	1	0	2	0	0
TOTALS	*0*	*1*	*0*	*0*	*0*	*0*	*0*	*0*	*0*	*0*	*1*	*0*	*2*	*0*	*0*

MILLER, Tom

Born	29/6/1990, Ely
Signed	21/3/2012 (age 21) from Newport County to the end of the season *(DH)*
First appearance	Newport County (H), Conference Premier, 24/3/2012
Final appearance	Dartford (A), Conference, 25/4/2015
Released/sold	11/6/2015 and joined Carlisle United *(CM)*

Career: *1999 Ipswich Town (Y), 2005 Norwich City (Y), Apr 2008 Glasgow Rangers (Dec 2009 Brechin City - loan), Feb 2010 Dundalk, Jan 2011 Newport County,* **Mar 2012 LINCOLN CITY,** *Jun 2015 Carlisle United.*

Popular centre back who earned a two-year deal at Glasgow Rangers at the age of 18. Suffered from a string of serious injuries at Ibrox and joined Dundalk initially for a trial period that turned into a permanent contract. Rebuilt his career in Ireland and made his way back into English football with Newport. Was involved in a serious injury to Bolton's South Korean international Chung-Yong Lee in a pre-season friendly in July 2011, and things deteriorated for him at Newport from then on, resulting in his contract being cancelled on 4 January 2012. Originally signed for Lincoln on 21 March to the end of the season, and ironically made his City debut in a 2-0 win over former club Newport. Quickly became popular with the fans for his obvious defensive ability and developed a knack of scoring goals. Signed a permanent one-year deal on 25 July 2012 and a new two-year contract on 6 June 2013. Attracted a lot of interest from other clubs, but his loyalty to Lincoln in the face of better offers from elsewhere was rewarded by the supporters' *Player of the Season* award in 2013-14. Was offered terms in the summer of 2015 but eventually decided to join Carlisle in League Two.

Lincoln City Playing Record - Conference Only

	League			FA Cup			FA Trophy			TOTALS			Lincolnshire Cup		
	App	Sub	Gls	App	Sub	Gls	App	Sub	Gls	App	Sub	Gls	App	Sub	Gls
2011-12	8	0	1	0	0	0	0	0	0	8	0	1	0	0	0
2012-13	38	0	1	6	0	0	1	0	0	45	0	1	1	0	0
2013-14	37	1	5	4	0	0	3	0	0	44	1	5	0	0	0
2014-15	26	1	4	3	0	0	1	0	0	30	1	4	1	0	0
TOTALS	*109*	*2*	*11*	*13*	*0*	*0*	*5*	*0*	*0*	*127*	*2*	*11*	*2*	*0*	*0*

MILLS, Gary

Born	20/5/1981, Isle of Sheppey
Signed	21/5/2012 (age 31) from Nuneaton Town on a one-year deal *(DH)*
First appearance	Kidderminster Harriers (H), Conference Premier, 11/8/2012
Final appearance	Gateshead (H), Conference Premier, 29/12/2012
Released/sold	1/3/2013 and joined Brackley Town *(GS)*

Career: *Coventry City (Y), Northampton Spencer, Jul 1997 Rushden & Diamonds (Y), Jun 1999 Rushden & Diamonds, Apr 2006 Crawley Town - non-contract, Aug 2006 Crawley Town, Jan 2007 Rushden & Diamonds, May 2007 Tamworth, Oct 2007 Kettering Town, May 2008 Stevenage Borough, May 2009 Mansfield Town (Oct 2010 Forest Green Rovers - loan), Jan 2011 Rushden & Diamonds, May 2011 Bath City, Sep 2011 Nuneaton Town,* **May 2012 LINCOLN CITY,** *Mar 2013 Brackley Town, May 2013 Boston United (Aug 2013 King's Lynn Town - loan), Jan 2014 King's Lynn Town, May 2014 retired. May 2016 King's Lynn Town, Oct 2016 Corby Town manager, April 2017 sacked.*

Abrasive midfielder who came to Lincoln with a good track record in non-league football, having won promotion at Rushden & Diamonds in 2001 and 2003, Kettering in 2008, Nuneaton in 2012, and the FA Trophy with Stevenage in 2009. However, he failed to settle at any club for long after originally leaving Rushden & Diamonds in 2006, appearing for thirteen different clubs in a seven-year period. Famously had a public spat with namesake manager Gary Mills at Tamworth that resulted in his dismissal. Signed for City on a one-year deal on 21 May 2012 and was appointed captain by David Holdsworth, who had managed Mills at Mansfield. Lost his place in the side after picking up a serious knee ligament injury against Gateshead at the end of December and never appeared for the club again, his contract cancelled by mutual consent two days after Gary Simpson became manager. Retired from playing when he became assistant manager at Wrexham in May 2014 but re-registered as a player upon rejoining King's Lynn as player-coach in May 2016. Became player-assistant manager at Kings Lynn before joining Corby Town as player-manager in October 2016. Was dismissed by Corby in April 2017 as they headed for relegation from the Northern Premier League Premier Division.

Lincoln City Playing Record - Conference Only

	League			FA Cup			FA Trophy			TOTALS			Lincolnshire Cup		
	App	Sub	Gls	App	Sub	Gls	App	Sub	Gls	App	Sub	Gls	App	Sub	Gls
2012-13	17	1	0	6	0	0	0	0	0	23	1	0	0	0	0
TOTALS	17	1	0	6	0	0	0	0	0	23	1	0	0	0	0

MORGAN, David

Born	4/7/1994, Belfast
Signed	13/9/2012 (age 18) from Nottingham Forest on a one-month youth loan (DH)
First appearance	Hyde (H), Conference Premier, 15/9/2012
Final appearance	Gateshead (H), Conference Premier, 29/12/2012
Released/sold	N/A

*Career: Ards (Y), 2008 Nottingham Forest (Y), 2012 Nottingham Forest (**Sep 2012 LINCOLN CITY - loan**, Jan 2013 Dundee - loan, Oct 2013 Tamworth - loan), Aug 2014 Ilkeston, Jul 2015 Nuneaton Town, Mar 2017 AFC Fylde.*

Combative young midfielder who spent a period on loan from Nottingham Forest shortly after signing his first professional deal with them. Originally signed on a 28-day youth loan, the loan was extended until 1 January on 19 October 2012. Was sent off in the FA Cup fourth qualifying round tie against FC Halifax Town, having come on as a substitute, and received a three-match ban. Appeared only sporadically after that and returned to Forest at the end of the year. A Northern Ireland international at U17 level (5 caps), U19 (4 caps), and U21 (4 caps). Wrote an interesting column on football for the Nuneaton News as part of his Professional Sports Writing and Broadcasting degree course at Staffordshire University.

Lincoln City Playing Record - Conference Only

	League			FA Cup			FA Trophy			TOTALS			Lincolnshire Cup		
	App	Sub	Gls	App	Sub	Gls	App	Sub	Gls	App	Sub	Gls	App	Sub	Gls
2012-13	6	2	0	0	1	0	1	0	0	7	3	0	0	0	0
TOTALS	6	2	0	0	1	0	1	0	0	7	3	0	0	0	0

MULDOON, Jack

Born	19/5/1989, Scunthorpe
Signed	28/5/2015 (age 26) from Rochdale on a one-year deal (CM)
First appearance	Cheltenham Town (H), National League, 8/8/2015
Final appearance	Southport (A), National League, 29/4/2017
Released/sold	

Career: 1997 Scunthorpe United (Y), Dec 2006 Doncaster Rovers, Mar 2007 Brigg Town, Dec 2008 Sheffield FC, Jul 2009 Glapwell, Jan 2010 Alfreton Town, Jun 2010 Stocksbridge Park Steels, Jun 2012 North Ferriby United (Dec 2012 Sheffield FC - loan), Jul 2013 Worksop Town, May 2014 Rochdale (Jan 2015 FC Halifax Town - loan), **May 2015 LINCOLN CITY.**

If rewards were given for sheer effort and determination to succeed, Jack Muldoon would be a wealthy man. The attacking midfielder/striker reached the professional game the hard way, having been diagnosed with Type 1 diabetes at the age of 13, and being released by Scunthorpe at 17. Played his way back up through non-league football while earning a living as a plasterer. Earned a deal at Rochdale after scoring 25 goals for Stocksbridge in 2011-12, 24 for North Ferriby and Sheffield FC in 2012-13, and 21 for Worksop the following season. Unfortunately suffered a bad groin injury in pre-season and never managed to force his way into the Rochdale first team on a regular basis. Snapped up by Chris Moyses on a one-year deal and proceeded to become a real fans' favourite with his powerful running and 100% commitment. Was the only player in 2015-16 to appear in every league and cup game and became only the seventh player since relegation to score 10 goals in a season (Ben Tomlinson, Jamie Taylor, Vadaine Oliver, Jordan Burrow, Matt Rhead, and Liam Hearn being the others at that point). Deservedly earned a further one-year deal in summer 2016 under Danny Cowley, signed on 3 June 2016, but appeared less frequently in the championship season. Was still offered a new contract for 2017-18 nonetheless.

Lincoln City Playing Record - Conference Only

	League			FA Cup			FA Trophy			TOTALS			Lincolnshire Cup		
	App	Sub	Gls	App	Sub	Gls	App	Sub	Gls	App	Sub	Gls	App	Sub	Gls
2015-16	45	1	9	3	0	0	0	1	1	48	2	10	2	0	0
2016-17	10	15	3	3	6	0	4	0	0	17	21	3	2	0	0
TOTALS	55	16	12	6	6	0	4	1	1	65	23	13	4	0	0

NELSON, Mitchell

Born	31/8/1989, London
Signed	31/8/2011 (age 22) from AFC Bournemouth on a one-month loan (ST)
First appearance	Braintree Town (A), Conference Premier, 3/9/2011
Final appearance	Wrexham (A), Conference Premier, 19/11/2011
Released/sold	N/A

Career: Jun 2007 Colchester United (Y), Jul 2009 Tooting & Mitcham United, Jun 2010 AFC Bournemouth (Oct 2010 Eastbourne Borough - loan, **Aug 2011 LINCOLN CITY - loan, Oct 2011 LINCOLN CITY - loan**), Dec 2011 Eastleigh, May 2013 Sutton United, Jan 2014 Margate, Jun 2015 Dulwich Hamlet, May 2016 Welling United.

Young defender who initially signed for City on a one-month loan on his 22nd birthday. Returned for a further month from 11 October 2011 to 8 November, extended further until 5 December. Fell out with new manager David Holdsworth over limited opportunities to play one hour before the game at Newport County on 3 December and was sent back to Bournemouth 30 minutes before kick-off. His contract was cancelled by Bournemouth two weeks later. Has since turned out for a host of non-league clubs in the south, missing the whole of the 2014-15 season with a cruciate ligament injury.

Lincoln City Playing Record - Conference Only

	League			FA Cup			FA Trophy			TOTALS			Lincolnshire Cup		
	App	Sub	Gls	App	Sub	Gls	App	Sub	Gls	App	Sub	Gls	App	Sub	Gls
2011-12	9	1	0	2	0	0	0	0	0	11	1	0	0	0	0
TOTALS	9	1	0	2	0	0	0	0	0	11	1	0	0	0	0

NEWTON, Sean

Born	23/9/1988, Liverpool
Signed	13/5/2013 (age 24) from Stockport County on a two-year deal (GS)
First appearance	Woking (A), Conference Premier, 10/8/2013
Final appearance	Bristol Rovers (A), Conference, 7/2/2015
Released/sold	6/5/2015 and joined Wrexham (CM)

Career: 2005 Chester City (Y), May 2007 Chester City (Aug 2007 Southport - loan, Feb 2008 Droylsden - loan), Aug 2008 Droylsden, Jun 2009 Barrow, Aug 2009 AFC Telford United (Mar 2012 Stockport County - loan), May 2012 Stockport County, **May 2013 LINCOLN CITY** (Feb 2015 Notts County - loan), May 2015 Wrexham (Oct 2016 York City - loan), Jan 2017 York City.

One of the better players to appear for City since relegation, left back Sean Newton signed on a two-year contract from relegated Stockport. Soon gained plaudits for his attacking displays, although some fans felt he was not so good at the day job of defending. Dangerous from free kicks, Newton had an unusually good scoring record, due in part to being the team's penalty taker for a spell. Became the first and only defender in the club's history to date to score a hat-trick, in the 5-1 win over Alfreton Town in the FA Cup on 28 October 2014. The hat-trick was also notable for being scored against an outfield player: Alfreton midfielder Anthony Howell was pressed into service as an emergency goalkeeper when the Reds were left without a recognised keeper for the game. Unfortunately his time at the club came to a disappointing end, becoming unsettled and asking for a move. After a poor performance at Bristol Rovers, he was substituted at half-time and never appeared for the club again. He was loaned to League One side Notts County on 13 February 2015 to the end of the season for a fee with a view to a permanent transfer, with young defender Jordan Cranston coming the other way on loan. However, Newton did not make the step up to League One standard and the move was cancelled. City were left with little option but to release him at the end of the season, as he clearly did not want to stay. Rumour was that he wanted to be closer to his base in Liverpool, and he eventually signed for Conference rivals Wrexham. Was involved in FA Cup controversy in December 2008 when he scored both goals for Droylsden in a famous 2-1 second round win over Chesterfield when he should have been suspended. Had a lengthy involvement with England C, appearing in the matches against Malta U21 on 17 February 2009 (scored one goal), Belgium U21 on 19 May 2009 (lost 0-1), East of Scotland on 22 May 2010 (won 1-0), Republic of Ireland U23 on 26 May 2010 (won 2-1), and Gibraltar on 15 November 2011 (lost 1-3) in addition to being named in contingency squads for games against Wales U23 and Turkey.

Lincoln City Playing Record - Conference Only

	League			FA Cup			FA Trophy			TOTALS			Lincolnshire Cup		
	App	Sub	Gls	App	Sub	Gls	App	Sub	Gls	App	Sub	Gls	App	Sub	Gls
2013-14	45	0	2	4	0	0	3	0	0	52	0	2	1	0	0
2014-15	32	0	4	3	0	4	1	0	0	36	0	8	1	1	1
TOTALS	77	0	6	7	0	4	4	0	0	88	0	10	2	1	1

NICOLAU, Nicky

Born	12/10/1983, St Pancras
Signed	12/7/2011 (age 27) from Boreham Wood on a one-year deal (ST)
First appearance	AFC Telford United (A), Conference Premier, 23/8/2011
Final appearance	Hyde (A), Conference Premier, 20/4/2013
Released/sold	9/5/2013 and joined Chelmsford City (GS)

Career: 1994 Arsenal (Y), 2002 Arsenal (Mar 2004 Southend United - loan), May 2004 Southend United, Jul 2005 Swindon Town (Jan 2006 Hereford United - loan), Jul 2006 Barnet, Aug 2009 Maidenhead United, Sep 2009 Woking, Aug 2010 Dover Athletic, Dec 2010 Boreham Wood, **Jul 2011 LINCOLN CITY**, May 2013 Chelmsford City, Aug 2014 Welling United, Sep 2014 Chelmsford City, Jan 2015 Bishop's Stortford, May 2015 retired.

London-born Cypriot midfielder who first came to the attention of Imps fans as part of the Southend team that beat City in the League Two play-off final in 2005. Rejoined his former manager Steve Tilson at Lincoln and signed a one-year contract in July 2011. Proved to be a solid performer when called upon and earned a one-year extension on 11 May 2012. Was capped by Cyprus at U17, U19 and U21 levels, and won the FA Youth Cup with Arsenal in 2001.

Lincoln City Playing Record - Conference Only

	League			FA Cup			FA Trophy			TOTALS			Lincolnshire Cup		
	App	Sub	Gls	App	Sub	Gls	App	Sub	Gls	App	Sub	Gls	App	Sub	Gls
2011-12	14	5	0	2	0	0	0	1	0	16	6	0	1	1	0
2012-13	18	8	4	1	1	0	0	1	0	19	10	4	1	0	1
TOTALS	32	13	4	3	1	0	0	2	0	35	16	4	2	1	1

NOLAN, Jon

Born	22/4/1992, Huyton
Signed	20/5/2013 (age 21) from Stockport County on a one-year deal *(GS)*
First appearance	Woking (A), Conference Premier, 10/8/2013
Final appearance	Gateshead (A), National League, 31/8/2015
Released/sold	4/1/2016 and joined Grimsby Town *(CM)*

Career: *1999 Everton (Y), Jul 2011 Stockport County, **May 2013 LINCOLN CITY** (Oct 2015 Wrexham - loan), Jan 2016 Grimsby Town, May 2016 Chesterfield.*

Enigmatic midfielder initially signed from relegated Stockport on a one-year contract, which was extended on 7 February 2014 to the end of the 2014-15 season. Despite being one of the more naturally talented players to appear for City in recent years, Nolan divided opinion among supporters and managers alike, and spent periods in and out of the side. Known for his undoubted skill on the ball, the problems appeared to lie in his work-rate, which was often open to question within the requirements of the Conference. Unexpectedly agreed a further year's contract extension on 24 April 2015 when the majority of fans expected to see him leave the club. Put in a transfer request in September 2015 and joined Wrexham on loan for three months from 1 October with a view to a permanent transfer; unfortunately his performances for them were not up to par and he returned to Lincoln at the end of his loan. His acrimonious departure to Wrexham left Lincoln with no option but to cancel his contract by mutual consent, which they did on 4 January 2016. Joined Grimsby on 21 January and regained his form in time to play a pivotal role in their promotion via the National League play-off final in May. Was offered a permanent deal by Grimsby, but declined and signed for League One Chesterfield. Won one England C cap whilst on Lincoln's books, appearing alongside Imps colleague Jordan Burrow in the 4-2 win over Estonia U23 on 18 November 2014.

Lincoln City Playing Record - Conference Only

	League			FA Cup			FA Trophy			TOTALS			Lincolnshire Cup		
	App	Sub	Gls	App	Sub	Gls	App	Sub	Gls	App	Sub	Gls	App	Sub	Gls
2013-14	28	4	5	3	0	0	2	0	0	33	4	5	1	0	0
2014-15	28	6	1	2	0	0	1	0	0	31	6	1	2	0	0
2015-16	6	1	0	0	0	0	0	0	0	6	1	0	1	1	0
TOTALS	62	11	6	5	0	0	3	0	0	70	11	6	4	1	0

NUTTER, John

Born	13/6/1982, Taplow
Signed	8/7/2011 (age 29) from Gillingham on a two-year deal *(ST)*
First appearance	Southport (A), Conference Premier, 13/8/2011
Final appearance	Walsall (A), FA Cup 1 Replay, 13/11/2012
Released/sold	4/1/2013 and joined Woking *(DH)*

Career: *1998 Blackburn Rovers (Y), Feb 2001 Wycombe Wanderers, May 2001 Aldershot Town (Feb 2002 St Albans City - loan, Nov 2002 Gravesend & Northfleet - loan, Jan 2003 Grays Athletic - loan), Jun 2004 Grays Athletic, Jun 2006 Stevenage Borough (Nov 2007 Gillingham - loan), Jan 2008 Gillingham, **Jul 2011 LINCOLN CITY** (Nov 2012 Woking - loan), Jan 2013 Woking, May 2015 retired.*

Experienced defender signed on a two-year contract following City's relegation from the League. Appeared in every game in City's first season back in the Conference, the only player to do so. Was appointed captain for the 2012-13 season, but his family had problems relocating to Lincoln and he asked for a move back south in November 2012. He joined Woking on a two-month loan on 16 November before City released him from his contract on 4 January 2013 to enable the transfer to be made permanent. Retired at 32 to become a full-time PE teacher.

Lincoln City Playing Record - Conference Only

	League			FA Cup			FA Trophy			TOTALS			Lincolnshire Cup		
	App	Sub	Gls	App	Sub	Gls	App	Sub	Gls	App	Sub	Gls	App	Sub	Gls
2011-12	46	0	2	2	0	0	3	0	0	51	0	2	1	0	0
2012-13	12	0	1	1	2	0	0	0	0	13	2	1	0	0	0
TOTALS	58	0	3	3	2	0	3	0	0	64	2	3	1	0	0

O'KEEFE, Josh

Born	22/12/1988, Whalley
Signed	17/5/2010 (age 21) from Walsall on a two-year deal (CS)
First appearance	Southport (A), Conference Premier, 13/8/2011
Final appearance	Wrexham (A), Conference Premier, 19/11/2011
Released/sold	26/12/2011 and joined Southport (DH)

*Career: 2001 Blackburn Rovers (Y), 2007 Blackburn Rovers, Jul 2009 Walsall, **May 2010 LINCOLN CITY**, Mar 2012 Southport, Sep 2012 Hereford United, Jan 2014 Kidderminster Harriers (Sep 2014 AFC Telford United - loan, Nov 2014 Chester - loan), May 2015 Altrincham, Jun 2016 Chorley.*

Tall box-to-box midfielder who was one of the players left over from the relegation season, making his City debut in the League Two game at Rotherham United on 7 August 2010. Known by Chris Sutton from his playing days at Blackburn, O'Keefe signed on a two-year deal in the summer of 2010 which hung over into the Conference years. One of four players still on Football League contracts, he quickly became surplus to requirements as David Holdsworth tried to restructure the playing budget, and left by mutual consent on 26 December 2011 with his contract paid up. Has since spent his career in the non-league game in his native north-west, latterly linking up with former Blackburn colleague Matt Jansen at Chorley. Won one cap for Republic of Ireland U21 against Austria in 2008. The son of former Blackburn goalkeeper Vince O'Keefe.

Lincoln City Playing Record - Conference Only

	League			FA Cup			FA Trophy			TOTALS			Lincolnshire Cup		
	App	Sub	Gls	App	Sub	Gls	App	Sub	Gls	App	Sub	Gls	App	Sub	Gls
2011-12	4	6	1	2	0	0	0	0	0	6	6	1	1	1	0
TOTALS	4	6	1	2	0	0	0	0	0	6	6	1	1	1	0

Lincoln City Playing Record - Football League

	League			FA Cup			League Cup			FL Trophy			TOTALS		
	App	Sub	Gls	App	Sub	Gls	App	Sub	Gls	App	Sub	Gls	App	Sub	Gls
2010-11	33	4	4	1	0	0	1	0	0	1	0	0	36	4	4
TOTALS	33	4	4	1	0	0	1	0	0	1	0	0	36	4	4

OLIVER, Vadaine

Born	21/10/1991, Sheffield
Signed	3/8/2012 (age 20) from Sheffield Wednesday on a one-year deal (DH)
First appearance	Kidderminster Harriers (H), Conference Premier, 11/8/2012
Final appearance	Hyde (A), Conference Premier, 20/4/2013
Released/sold	10/6/2013 and joined Crewe Alexandra (GS)

Career: *Sheffield Wednesday (Y), 2010 Sheffield Wednesday, **Aug 2012 LINCOLN CITY**, Jun 2013 Crewe Alexandra (Oct 2014 Mansfield Town - loan), May 2015 York City (Aug 2016 Notts County - loan).*

Powerful striker who made a significant impact in his only season with the club. Joined from Sheffield Wednesday, where his opportunities had been restricted by injury. Was used mainly as a substitute until he scored two goals from the bench in the cup win at Walsall, after which he secured a regular starting place in the side. Scored a second-half hat-trick in his last game for the club at Hyde, which City won 5-1 to secure their Conference status on the final day of the season. Was only the third City player to reach double figures in a season in the Conference era after Jamie Taylor and Alan Power, who reached the milestone earlier that same season. Offered terms by City for 2013-14 but signed for Crewe on 10 June for an appearance-related fee reported to be in the region of £45,000. Ended up back in non-league football when relegated from the Football League with York in 2016, and suffered a second successive relegation to National League North in 2017.

Lincoln City Playing Record - Conference Only

	League			FA Cup			FA Trophy			TOTALS			Lincolnshire Cup		
	App	Sub	Gls	App	Sub	Gls	App	Sub	Gls	App	Sub	Gls	App	Sub	Gls
2012-13	22	15	11	0	5	2	0	1	0	22	21	13	0	1	0
TOTALS	**22**	**15**	**11**	**0**	**5**	**2**	**0**	**1**	**0**	**22**	**21**	**13**	**0**	**1**	**0**

PACQUETTE, Richard

Born	28/1/1983, Kilburn
Signed	4/1/2012 (age 28) from Maidenhead United to the end of the season *(DH)*
First appearance	York City (H), Conference Premier, 7/1/2012
Final appearance	Ebbsfleet United (A), Conference Premier, 28/4/2012
Released/sold	5/5/2012 and joined Bromley *(DH)*

Career: *1996 Queens Park Rangers (Y), Feb 2000 Queens Park Rangers (Oct 2002 Stevenage Borough - loan, Dec 2003 Dagenham & Redbridge - loan, Feb 2004 Mansfield Town - loan), Sep 2004 Milton Keynes Dons, Nov 2004 Fisher Athletic, Nov 2004 Brentford - non-contract, Dec 2004 Farnborough Town, Jan 2005 Stevenage Borough - non-contract, Feb 2005 St Albans City, Mar 2005 Hemel Hempstead Town, Mar 2005 Hampton & Richmond Borough, Jul 2005 Worthing (Feb 2006 Thurrock - loan), Mar 2006 Havant & Waterlooville (Mar 2008 Maidenhead United - loan), Jun 2008 Maidenhead United (Feb 2009 Histon - loan), May 2009 York City, Jun 2010 Eastbourne Borough, Aug 2011 Hayes & Yeading United, Dec 2011 Maidenhead United, **Jan 2012 LINCOLN CITY**, Aug 2012 Bromley, Dec 2012 Eastleigh, Jan 2012 Sutton United, Mar 2013 Maidenhead United, Jun 2014 Eastbourne Borough, Jul 2015 Hampton & Richmond Borough (Nov 2015 Lewes - loan), Jan 2016 Walton & Hersham, Mar 2016 Hampton & Richmond Borough, Jul 2016 Metropolitan Police, Oct 2016 Grays Athletic, Dec 2016 Egham Town.*

Like his cousin Jefferson Louis, striker Richard Pacquette had already done the football rounds by the time he signed for City in 2012. City were his 20th different club in 8 years, and he appeared for an incredible 8 clubs in 2004-05 alone. Had a good early pedigree, appearing for QPR in the old Second Division play-off final defeat to Cardiff in 2003. Won two full caps for Dominica in 2008 in World Cup qualifiers against Barbados, playing with cousin Louis in the first leg and scoring Dominica's goal. Famously gave Havant & Waterlooville the lead at Anfield in the 4th round of the FA Cup on 26 January 2008 before losing 5-2. Signed for Lincoln on a deal until the end of the 2011-12 season, Richard was one of several players who left City in the close season due to the reduced terms on offer. By the end of the 2016-17 season, he had scored over 150 goals in almost 500 career matches.

Lincoln City Playing Record - Conference Only

	League			FA Cup			FA Trophy			TOTALS			Lincolnshire Cup		
	App	Sub	Gls	App	Sub	Gls	App	Sub	Gls	App	Sub	Gls	App	Sub	Gls
2011-12	9	4	3	0	0	0	0	0	0	9	4	3	0	0	0
TOTALS	**9**	**4**	**3**	**0**	**0**	**0**	**0**	**0**	**0**	**9**	**4**	**3**	**0**	**0**	**0**

PEARSON, Matty

Born	3/8/1993, Keighley
Signed	5/1/2012 (age 18) from Blackburn Rovers on a three-month loan *(DH)*
First appearance	Carshalton Athletic (H), FA Trophy 2, 14/1/2012
Final appearance	Carshalton Athletic (A) FA Trophy 2 Replay, 18/1/2012
Released/sold	N/A

*Career: 2003 Blackburn Rovers (Y), Jul 2010 Blackburn Rovers (**Jan 2012 LINCOLN CITY - loan**), Aug 2012 Rochdale (Mar 2013 FC Halifax Town - loan), Jun 2013 FC Halifax Town, May 2015 Accrington Stanley.*

Promising young centre back who had won one cap for the England U18 side in 2010. Was signed on a three-month youth loan / trial from Blackburn with a view to a permanent move, but Matty never had the opportunity to show what he was capable of in a poor Imps side. Had the misfortune of making his two appearances for City in the dismal FA Trophy matches against Carshalton. Was recalled by Blackburn on 31 January 2012, probably because he was not getting any game time. Has since gone on to build a good career in the game, winning two England C caps in 2013-14 (scoring 1 goal) before advancing to the Football League.

Lincoln City Playing Record - Conference Only

	League			FA Cup			FA Trophy			TOTALS			Lincolnshire Cup		
	App	Sub	Gls	App	Sub	Gls	App	Sub	Gls	App	Sub	Gls	App	Sub	Gls
2011-12	0	0	0	0	0	0	2	0	0	2	0	0	0	0	0
TOTALS	0	0	0	0	0	0	2	0	0	2	0	0	0	0	0

PERRY, Kyle

Born	5/3/1986, Birmingham
Signed	8/7/2011 (age 25) from Tamworth on a two-year deal *(ST)*
First appearance	Southport (A) Conference Premier, 13/8/2011
Final appearance	Grimsby Town (H), Conference Premier, 26/12/2011
Released/sold	5/5/2012 and joined Nuneaton Town *(DH)*

*Career: 1997 Walsall (Y) (Sep 2004 AFC Telford United - loan), Jul 2005 AFC Telford United (Oct 2005 Sutton Coldfield Town - loan), Jul 2006 Hednesford Town, Sep 2006 Willenhall Town, Jul 2007 Chasetown, Jan 2008 Port Vale (Mar 2009 Northwich Victoria - loan), Jun 2009 Mansfield Town, Jul 2010 Tamworth, **Jul 2011 LINCOLN CITY** (Jan 2012 AFC Telford United - loan), Jul 2012 Nuneaton Town (Oct 2012 Hereford United - loan, Feb 2013 Tamworth - loan), May 2013 Altrincham, May 2015 Hednesford Town, May 2015 Hednesford Town, Mar 2016 Worcester City, Aug 2016 Stafford Rangers.*

Much-travelled striker with frequent moves around the Midlands non-league scene. Signed for Port Vale a few weeks after knocking Vale out of the FA Cup with Chasetown but famously failed to score in his 33 appearances at Vale Park. Signed for City on a two-year deal on 8 July 2011 and scored on his debut at Southport on the opening day. Unfortunately he never seemed fully fit, and after being told by David Holdsworth that he could leave, he joined AFC Telford on loan for the rest of the season on 6 January. Perry had scored twice for City against Telford as a late substitute back in August, and ironically scored for Telford at Sincil Bank in a 1-1 draw on 25 February, drawing criticism from City fans for allowing him to play. Released in the summer of 2012 and joined Nuneaton. Also known for playing rhythm guitar and singing lead vocals for erstwhile Midlands rock band *Stubblemelt*. Now a freelance graphic and web designer under the name *Make Me Original*.

Lincoln City Playing Record - Conference Only

	League			FA Cup			FA Trophy			TOTALS			Lincolnshire Cup		
	App	Sub	Gls	App	Sub	Gls	App	Sub	Gls	App	Sub	Gls	App	Sub	Gls
2011-12	14	10	3	0	2	0	0	0	0	14	12	3	1	0	1
TOTALS	14	10	3	0	2	0	0	0	0	14	12	3	1	0	1

PLATT, Conal

Born	14/10/1986, Preston
Signed	4/11/2011 (age 25) from Cambridge United on a two-month loan *(DH)*
First appearance	Barrow (H), Conference Premier, 5/11/2011
Final appearance	Southport (A), Conference Premier, 8/1/2013
Released/sold	7/3/2013 and joined Gainsborough Trinity *(GS)*

*Career: 1998 Liverpool (Y), May 2006 AFC Bournemouth (Nov 2006 Morecambe - loan, Feb 2007 Weymouth - loan), Jul 2007 Weymouth (Feb 2008 Rushden & Diamonds - loan), May 2008 Forest Green Rovers, Jun 2010 Cambridge United (Sep 2011 AFC Telford United - loan, **Nov 2011 LINCOLN CITY - loan), Jan 2012 LINCOLN CITY**, Mar 2013 Gainsborough Trinity, Jul 2013 Stalybridge Celtic.*

Skilful winger who originally signed on loan from Cambridge. Released by Cambridge at the end of the loan and signed an 18-month deal with Lincoln on 6 January 2012. Unfortunately suffered a broken leg in a behind closed doors friendly against Doncaster on 21 February and had psychological problems regaining his fitness. Recovery took a year, and he made only one more substitute appearance before being released on 7 March 2013. Returned to Sincil Bank in November 2013 as part of the Stalybridge team beaten 5-1 in the FA Trophy, before leaving senior football at the end of that season.

Lincoln City Playing Record - Conference Only

	League			FA Cup			FA Trophy			TOTALS			Lincolnshire Cup		
	App	Sub	Gls	App	Sub	Gls	App	Sub	Gls	App	Sub	Gls	App	Sub	Gls
2011-12	14	0	2	0	0	0	3	0	1	17	0	3	0	0	0
2012-13	0	1	0	0	0	0	0	0	0	0	1	0	0	0	0
TOTALS	**14**	**1**	**2**	**0**	**0**	**0**	**3**	**0**	**1**	**17**	**1**	**3**	**0**	**0**	**0**

POWER, Alan

Born	23/1/1988, Dublin
Signed	6/7/2011 (age 23) from Rushden & Diamonds on a one-year deal *(ST)*
First appearance	Southport (A), Conference Premier, 13/8/2011
Final appearance	Southport (A), National League, 29/4/2017
Released/sold	

*Career: Belvedere (Y), 2005 Nottingham Forest (Y), 2006 Nottingham Forest (Nov 2007 Grays Athletic - loan), Jun 2008 Hartlepool United, Jun 2010 Rushden & Diamonds, **Jul 2011 LINCOLN CITY**.*

One of the true stalwarts of City's Conference era, midfielder Alan Power has written his name into the club's record books as the only player to have been with the club since the summer of 2011. Signing for City on a one-year contract on the same day as Rushden & Diamonds team mate Sam Smith, he has seldom been out of the side since. As well as scoring close to 40 goals for City, Alan holds the club record for the most appearances outside the Football League. His penalty against Brighton in the FA Cup fourth round on 28 January 2017 made him City's leading aggregate scorer since relegation for a short time (with 36), before being overtaken by Matt Rhead (37). Has had several spells as penalty taker, which partly accounts for his good scoring record. Signed a one-year contract extension on 2 May 2012, two years on 24 May 2013, and a further two years on 21 May 2015. Won the supporters' *Player of the Season* award in 2012-13 but has drawn criticism at times for trying to be over-elaborate. Spent three seasons as team captain until losing the role to Luke Waterfall in August 2016. Was initially sidelined under Danny Cowley but eventually won his place back after a string of fine performances during the FA Cup run of 2016-17. He is one of only two players to have appeared in each of City's six Conference seasons (the other being Paul Farman), and is the only player to appear in City's first game in the Conference and their last, both at Southport. Offered a new contract at the end of the championship season, thereby providing him with the opportunity to be the only player to survive the non-league experience in its entirety and appear in the Football League thereafter. Capped by the Republic of Ireland at U17, U18, U19 and U21 levels.

	League			FA Cup			FA Trophy			TOTALS			Lincolnshire Cup		
	App	Sub	Gls	App	Sub	Gls	App	Sub	Gls	App	Sub	Gls	App	Sub	Gls
2011-12	42	0	4	2	0	0	2	1	0	46	1	4	1	1	0
2012-13	34	3	8	5	0	3	1	0	1	40	3	12	0	0	0
2013-14	36	2	3	4	0	0	1	0	3	41	2	6	0	0	0
2014-15	33	4	7	3	0	0	1	0	0	37	4	7	0	0	0
2015-16	32	6	3	3	0	0	1	0	0	36	6	3	1	1	1
2016-17	14	16	2	7	2	2	4	2	0	25	20	4	2	0	0
TOTALS	191	31	27	24	2	5	10	3	4	225	36	36	4	2	1

PREECE, David

Born	26/8/1976, Sunderland
Signed	4/12/2012 (age 36), from Barnsley initially on non-contract terms *(DH)*
First appearance	Dartford (A), Conference Premier, 8/12/2012
Final appearance	Welling United (A), Conference Premier, 2/11/2013
Released/sold	N/A

Career: Nov 1991 Sunderland (Y), Jul 1994 Sunderland, Aug 1997 Darlington, Jul 1999 Aberdeen, Jul 2005 Silkeborg IF (Denmark), Aug 2008 Odense BK (Denmark), Jul 2009 Barnsley, **Dec 2012 LINCOLN CITY** *(Apr 2013 Keflavik IF (Iceland) - loan), May 2014 retired.*

One of a very rare breed of erudite footballers, David Preece originally signed for City as a player on non-contract terms on 4 December 2012, signing a permanent contract as player/coach for the rest of the season on 21 December. Joined Icelandic Premier Division team Keflavik to regain fitness during summer 2013, and re-signed for City on a one-year deal on 8 August 2013. Officially became the club's goalkeeping coach at the same time, and received very few first team opportunities due to the form of protégé Paul Farman. Took a step backwards in 2014, intending to retire as a player and focus on coaching and a burgeoning career in the media, and became an integral part of the three-man management team under Chris Moyses. Always popular with the fans, Preece left the club on 5 May 2016 after applying for the vacant manager's job and not receiving an interview. Currently writes a weekly column for the Sunderland Echo, having completed a Professional Sportswriting and Broadcasting course at Staffordshire University in 2012. Has also guested regularly on BBC Radio 5Live and Talksport.

Lincoln City Playing Record - Conference Only

	League			FA Cup			FA Trophy			TOTALS			Lincolnshire Cup		
	App	Sub	Gls	App	Sub	Gls	App	Sub	Gls	App	Sub	Gls	App	Sub	Gls
2012-13	7	1	0	0	0	0	0	0	0	7	1	0	0	0	0
2013-14	1	0	0	0	0	0	0	0	0	1	0	0	1	0	0
TOTALS	8	1	0	0	0	0	0	0	0	8	1	0	1	0	0

RAGGETT, Sean

Born	25/1/1994, Gillingham
Signed	3/8/2016 (age 22) from Dover Athletic on a two-year deal *(DC)*
First appearance	North Ferriby United (H), National League, 9/8/2016
Final appearance	Maidstone United (A), National League, 25/4/2017
Released/sold	

Career: Gillingham (Y), 2010 Dover Athletic (Y), Jan 2012 Dover Athletic (Sep 2012 Herne Bay - loan, Nov 2012 Whitstable Town - loan), **Aug 2016 LINCOLN CITY.**

Giant centre back who joined on a two-year deal on the eve of the 2016-17 season. Something of a coup for Lincoln, Raggett had been on the radar of numerous top clubs including Liverpool and Everton just a few months earlier, and reportedly had been on his way to sign for Barrow when he literally diverted to speak to Lincoln. Unable to agree a figure with former club Dover, a tribunal eventually set his transfer fee at a rumoured £50,000 plus add-ons. Made his

City debut in a 6-1 win over North Ferriby, which was the first time City had scored six for a decade, and alongside Luke Waterfall formed one of the best central defensive partnerships in recent years. Also had a good scoring record and headed the iconic 89th-minute goal at Burnley which took City to the quarter-finals of the FA Cup for the first time in their history. Became the focus of transfer speculation as City closed in on the National League title, attracting interest from Premier League clubs once more. Raggett had been called up by England C on four occasions prior to joining the Imps, appearing once against the Republic of Ireland U21 on 1 June 2015, and was one of four City players called up for the game against Estonia on 15 November 2016, the others being Alex Woodyard, Elliott Whitehouse and Sam Habergham. Was named *SportsBeat Young Player of the Year* at the National Game Awards on 17 May 2017, taking the award that was won by Alex Woodyard twelve months before. Capped a fine season by being named City's *Young Player of the Season* by the management.

Lincoln City Playing Record - Conference Only

	League			FA Cup			FA Trophy			TOTALS			Lincolnshire Cup		
	App	Sub	Gls	App	Sub	Gls	App	Sub	Gls	App	Sub	Gls	App	Sub	Gls
2016-17	41	0	5	8	0	2	2	1	1	51	1	8	0	0	0
TOTALS	41	0	5	8	0	2	2	1	1	51	1	8	0	0	0

REID, Craig

Born	17/12/1985, Coventry
Signed	11/12/2015 (age 29) from Brentwood Town on a non-contract basis *(CM)*
First appearance	Barrow (H), National League, 19/12/2015
Final appearance	FC Halifax Town (H), National League, 26/12/2015
Released/sold	4/1/2016 and joined Gainsborough Trinity *(CM)*

*Career: 2000 Coventry City (Y), Jul 2002 Ipswich Town (Y), Apr 2004 Coventry City (Mar 2006 Tamworth - loan), Jan 2007 Cheltenham Town, Aug 2008 Grays Athletic (Sep 2008 Newport County - loan), Dec 2008 Newport County, Jan 2011 Stevenage, Jul 2012 Aldershot Town, Aug 2013 Southend United, Feb 2014 Stevenage, May 2014 Kidderminster Harriers, Oct 2015 Brentwood Town, **Dec 2015 LINCOLN CITY**, Jan 2016 Gainsborough Trinity, Jun 2016 Gloucester City, Jan 2017 Newport County, May 2017 released.*

Experienced striker who had been a transfer target during the 2015 close season. Eventually joined City on a non-contract basis with a view to earning a permanent deal, but was released after just a few weeks after being substituted in both of his appearances. Enjoyed the majority of his success in a two-year spell at Newport County, and was Stevenage's record signing when he joined them in 2011. Surprisingly re-signed for League Two side Newport in January 2017 after three years in non-league football.

Lincoln City Playing Record - Conference Only

	League			FA Cup			FA Trophy			TOTALS			Lincolnshire Cup		
	App	Sub	Gls	App	Sub	Gls	App	Sub	Gls	App	Sub	Gls	App	Sub	Gls
2015-16	2	0	0	0	0	0	0	0	0	2	0	0	0	0	0
TOTALS	2	0	0	0	0	0	0	0	0	2	0	0	0	0	0

RHEAD, Matt

Born	31/5/1984, Stoke-on-Trent
Signed	14/5/2015 (age 30) from Mansfield Town on a two-year deal *(CM)*
First appearance	Cheltenham Town (H), National League, 8/8/2015
Final appearance	Southport (A), National League, 29/4/2017
Released/sold	

*Career: Norton United, July 2004 Kidsgrove Athletic, Oct 2007 Eastwood Town (Sep 2008 Kidsgrove Athletic - loan), Jun 2009 Nantwich Town (Dec 2009 Congleton Town - loan), Jan 2010 Congleton Town, Jul 2010 Eastwood Town, Jun 2011 Corby Town, Jan 2012 Mansfield Town, **May 2015 LINCOLN CITY**.*

Vastly experienced in non-league football, colossus Matt Rhead was one of three players to join the club in the summer of 2015 from Mansfield (the others being Liam Hearn and former City favourite Lee Beevers). Rhead had won the Conference title with Mansfield in 2013, and had famously broken Lincoln hearts with a last-minute equaliser in the FA Cup tie at Sincil Bank on 1 December 2012, which cost City a plum third round home tie against Liverpool. Rhead proved extremely effective in the rough and tumble of the National League and was instrumental in helping City to fourth place in the table at the midway point of the 2015-16 season. His total of 23 goals in 2015-16 included 20 in the league, making him the only City player in their Conference history to reach that milestone. Became hugely popular with the fans because of his robust style of play, although his touch on the ball and ability in the air were far and away beyond what opposing fans and managers were prepared to allow him credit for. Unfortunately became unsettled by an approach from Barrow in January 2016, a saga that continued for the rest of the season before Rhead eventually put in an official transfer request at the end of May. After new manager Danny Cowley visited him at his Stoke home to discuss a way forward, Rhead finally put an end to transfer speculation on 3 July 2016 by signing a contract extension to the summer of 2018. Played a deeper role under Cowley, with quick strikers like Theo Robinson and Lee Angol playing off him, and scored fewer goals as a consequence. Scored the 100th goal of the 2016-17 season in the 2-0 win over Dagenham & Redbridge in April, and holds the club record for the most goals scored outside the Football League (37). One of only six players to make over 100 appearances for the Imps in the Conference years.

Lincoln City Playing Record - Conference Only

	League			FA Cup			FA Trophy			TOTALS			Lincolnshire Cup		
	App	Sub	Gls	App	Sub	Gls	App	Sub	Gls	App	Sub	Gls	App	Sub	Gls
2015-16	41	2	20	3	0	3	0	1	0	44	3	23	2	0	1
2016-17	40	3	14	9	0	0	2	2	0	51	5	14	1	0	0
TOTALS	81	5	34	12	0	3	2	3	0	95	8	37	3	0	1

ROBINSON, Conner

Born	11/10/1994, Lincoln
Signed	11/8/2012 (age 17) from the Academy on a two-year deal (DH)
First appearance	Hayes & Yeading (H), Conference Premier, 21/4/2012
Final appearance	Southport (H), National League, 20/2/2016
Released/sold	23/5/2016 and joined North Ferriby United (DC)

Career: 2006 Lincoln City (Y), Aug 2012 LINCOLN CITY (Mar 2013 Worksop Town - loan, Aug 2013 Gainsborough Trinity - loan, Sep 2014 Boston United - loan, Mar 2016 Boston United - loan), Jun 2016 North Ferriby United, Jan 2017 Lincoln United.

Promising young striker who came through the youth ranks at Sincil Bank but never quite realised his potential, creating a club record for appearances from the substitute's bench in the Conference era. Signed a two-year deal prior to the season opener against Kidderminster on 11 August 2012 and initially put in some impressive performances. Was handed the Young Player of the Season award by Gary Simpson in 2012-13, but his career was badly affected by a broken leg against Worcester City in the FA Cup fourth qualifying round replay on 29 October 2013. Signed a new two-year contract on 7 March 2014 but never regained the necessary momentum and made very few starts from then on. Spent numerous spells on loan to maintain his match fitness in the absence of a reserve team. Along with Alan Power and Paul Farman, was one of only three players to appear in City's first 5 seasons in the Conference. Was not offered a contract in May 2016 but was invited back for pre-season training; on 28 May, he announced on his Twitter account that he was leaving.

Lincoln City Playing Record - Conference Only

	League			FA Cup			FA Trophy			TOTALS			Lincolnshire Cup		
	App	Sub	Gls	App	Sub	Gls	App	Sub	Gls	App	Sub	Gls	App	Sub	Gls
2011-12	0	1	0	0	0	0	0	0	0	0	1	0	0	0	0
2012-13	5	12	4	1	1	0	0	0	0	6	13	4	1	0	0
2013-14	9	7	1	1	1	0	1	0	0	11	8	1	0	0	0
2014-15	9	10	3	1	1	0	0	1	0	10	12	3	0	0	0
2015-16	4	13	0	0	1	1	1	0	0	5	14	1	0	1	0
TOTALS	27	43	8	3	4	1	2	1	0	32	48	9	1	1	0

ROBINSON, Theo

Born	22/1/1989, Birmingham
Signed	7/10/2016 on a non-contract basis (DC)
First appearance	Bromley (A), National League, 8/10/2016
Final appearance	Brighton & Hove Albion (H), FA Cup 4, 28/1/2017
Released/sold	31/1/2017 and joined Southend United (DC)

Career: 2004 Stoke City (Y), 2005 Watford (Y), Jan 2007 Watford (Feb 2007 Wealdstone - loan, Aug 2007 Hereford United - loan, Jan 2009 Southend United - loan), Jul 2009 Huddersfield Town (Sep 2010 Millwall - loan), Jan 2011 Millwall (Feb 2011 Derby County - loan), May 2011 Derby County (Feb 2013 Huddersfield Town - loan), Aug 2013 Doncaster Rovers (Mar 2015 Scunthorpe United - loan), Aug 2015 Motherwell, Jan 2016 Port Vale, **Oct 2016 LINCOLN CITY**, Jan 2017 Southend United.

Quick striker with an excellent pedigree, having played in the Premier League with Watford at the start of his career. Signed for City on monthly non-contract terms after a two-week trial at Sincil Bank in October 2016. Scored two goals on his first full start for the Imps to win the FA Cup fourth qualifying round tie at Guiseley and went on to secure a regular place in the side. Impressed fans with his strong running and created space for strike partner Matt Rhead. Had an extraordinary scoring record in the FA Cup, netting seven times in 2016-17 which left him one goal behind the club record set by Isaac Moore in 1890-91. Despite helping City to the top of the National League and the FA Cup fifth round, Robinson rejected a permanent contract offer to sign a far more lucrative two-and-a-half-year deal with League One side Southend just two minutes before the transfer window closed on deadline day. Interestingly, City received a substantial transfer fee for Robinson despite not having him under contract, as Southend had to pay to waive the standard seven-day approach restriction. Ultimately played an important part in City's promotion, inspiring the side throughout the middle of the season with his FA Cup exploits. Won 7 caps for Jamaica in 2013.

Lincoln City Playing Record - Conference Only

	League			FA Cup			FA Trophy			TOTALS			Lincolnshire Cup		
	App	Sub	Gls	App	Sub	Gls	App	Sub	Gls	App	Sub	Gls	App	Sub	Gls
2016-17	12	2	2	6	1	7	0	1	0	18	4	9	0	0	0
TOTALS	12	2	2	6	1	7	0	1	0	18	4	9	0	0	0

ROBSON, Paul

Born	4/8/1983, Kingston-upon-Hull
Signed	13/1/2012 (age 28) from Newport County on non-contract terms (DH)
First appearance	Carshalton Athletic (H), FA Trophy 2, 14/1/2012
Final appearance	Newport County (H), Conference Premier, 12/1/2013
Released/sold	29/1/2013 and joined North Ferriby United (DH)

Career: May 1999 Doncaster Rovers (Y), May 2001 Charlton Athletic, Jul 2004 Bridlington Town, Apr 2005 Long Island Rough Riders (USA), Feb 2008 Crystal Palace Baltimore (USA), Jul 2011 Newport County, **Jan 2012 LINCOLN CITY**, Feb 2013 North Ferriby United, Jun 2014 Scarborough Athletic.

Right back who signed originally on non-contract terms. Signed a permanent one-year deal in May 2012, but was released on 29 January 2013 with youngsters Dan Coupland, Elliot Green and Jake Turner as manager David Holdsworth attempted to cut City's cloth. Made very few appearances in professional football in this country despite being attached to Charlton and Crystal Palace at various times. Became assistant manager at Brigg Town in October 2016 after damaging knee ligaments in the 2016-17 pre-season.

Lincoln City Playing Record - Conference Only

	League			FA Cup			FA Trophy			TOTALS			Lincolnshire Cup		
	App	Sub	Gls	App	Sub	Gls	App	Sub	Gls	App	Sub	Gls	App	Sub	Gls
2011-12	16	0	0	0	0	0	2	0	0	18	0	0	0	0	0
2012-13	10	1	0	0	1	0	0	0	0	10	2	0	0	0	0
TOTALS	26	1	0	0	1	0	2	0	0	28	2	0	0	0	0

RODNEY, Nialle

Born	28/2/1991, Nottingham
Signed	31/1/2012 (age 20) from Bradford City to the end of the season (DH)
First appearance	Braintree Town (H), Conference Premier, 14/2/2012
Final appearance	Hayes & Yeading United (H), Conference Premier, 21/4/2012
Released/sold	5/5/2012 and later joined AFC Telford United (DH)

Career: 2004 Nottingham Forest (Y), 2009 Nottingham Forest (Mar 2010 Ilkeston Town - loan, Mar 2011 Burton Albion - loan), Jul 2011 Bradford City (Oct 2011 Darlington - loan, Nov 2011 Mansfield Town - loan), **Jan 2012 LINCOLN CITY**, Feb 2013 AFC Telford United, Jul 2013 Hartlepool United, Oct 2014 Ilkeston, Dec 2014 Greyhounders FC, Sep 2015 Spalding United, Nov 2015 Coalville Town.

One of four players allegedly signed by David Holdsworth on transfer deadline day for less than half of Gavin McCallum's wage, quick young striker Nialle Rodney signed a deal to the end of the season on 31 January 2012. Failed to pin down a regular spot in the first team and was released when his contract expired. Had shown great promise at Nottingham Forest as a teenager but never really gained a foothold in the professional game once he had left the City Ground. Outside of football, he founded clothing company ENOS and high net worth concierge service Grandeur Living.

Lincoln City Playing Record - Conference Only

	League			FA Cup			FA Trophy			TOTALS			Lincolnshire Cup		
	App	Sub	Gls	App	Sub	Gls	App	Sub	Gls	App	Sub	Gls	App	Sub	Gls
2011-12	2	4	0	0	0	0	0	0	0	2	4	0	0	0	0
TOTALS	2	4	0	0	0	0	0	0	0	2	4	0	0	0	0

ROWE, Danny L

Born	29/1/1989, Blackpool
Signed	13/5/2013 (age 24) from Fleetwood Town on a one-year deal (GS)
First appearance	Macclesfield Town (H), Conference Premier, 13/8/2013
Final appearance	Barnet (H), Conference Premier, 26/4/2014
Released/sold	8/5/2014 and joined AFC Fylde (GS)

Career: 1996 Preston North End (Y), 2001 Manchester United (Y), 2005 Wren Rovers, Jul 2010 Kendal Town, Dec 2010 Fleetwood Town, (Aug 2011 Droylsden - loan, Jan 2012 Stockport County - loan, Jul 2012 Stockport County - loan, Jan 2013 Barrow - loan), **May 2013 LINCOLN CITY**, Aug 2014 AFC Fylde.

A prime contender for the Lincoln City 'one who got away' award, talented ball-playing midfielder/striker Danny Rowe signed for City on a one-year deal on the same day as his former Stockport colleague Sean Newton. Scored the only goal of the game against Macclesfield on his debut and became popular with the fans for his obvious footballing ability. Picked up an ankle injury at Luton in September and never really won his place back. Was released at the end of his contract because Gary Simpson claimed not to be in a financial position to offer deals to the out-of-contract players. This one proved a real shame, as he joined bankrolled AFC Fylde and proceeded to score 68 goals in the next two seasons. He topped that with 50 in all competitions in 2016-17 as Fylde won the National League North championship; Rowe's 47 league goals was a new record for the National League North, and he was named player of the season for the North division for his achievements. Had also scored 111 in five seasons for Wren Rovers prior to joining Kendal Town in summer 2010. Danny hit the headlines in May 2001 when Manchester United were ordered by a tribunal to pay Preston a financial package totalling up to £136,000 to sign him. He was just 12 at the time. Frequently confused with fellow player Danny M Rowe, even by current club AFC Fylde, whose website gives the playing career of his namesake in place of the correct information.

	League			FA Cup			FA Trophy			TOTALS			Lincolnshire Cup		
	App	Sub	Gls	App	Sub	Gls	App	Sub	Gls	App	Sub	Gls	App	Sub	Gls
2013-14	15	8	3	0	0	0	0	2	0	15	10	3	0	0	0
TOTALS	15	8	3	0	0	0	0	2	0	15	10	3	0	0	0

RUSSELL, Simon

Born	19/3/1985, Kingston-upon-Hull
Signed	20/7/2011 (age 26) from Cambridge United on a one-year deal *(ST)*
First appearance	Southport (A), Conference Premier, 13/8/2011
Final appearance	Mansfield Town (A), Conference Premier, 3/3/2012
Released/sold	5/5/2012 and joined Alfreton Town *(DH)*

*Career: Jul 2001 Hull City (Y), Jun 2002 Hull City, Jul 2004 Kidderminster Harriers, Aug 2008 York City (Sep 2009 Tamworth - loan, Jan 2010 Cambridge United - loan), May 2010 Cambridge United, **Jul 2011 LINCOLN CITY**, Jul 2012 Alfreton Town, Jan 2013 Gainsborough Trinity, Jun 2016 North Ferriby United.*

Midfielder/winger with vast experience of the Conference, having played in the division since being relegated from League Two with Kidderminster in 2005. Signed a one-year deal with Lincoln but was one of the players released in 2012 when City could only offer reduced terms. Also appeared in the FA Trophy Final with York in 2008-2009 (lost 2-0 to Stevenage). As at the end of 2016-17 season, Russell had played well over 400 games at Conference/Conference North level.

Lincoln City Playing Record - Conference Only

	League			FA Cup			FA Trophy			TOTALS			Lincolnshire Cup		
	App	Sub	Gls	App	Sub	Gls	App	Sub	Gls	App	Sub	Gls	App	Sub	Gls
2011-12	17	9	1	1	0	0	2	1	0	20	10	1	2	0	1
TOTALS	17	9	1	1	0	0	2	1	0	20	10	1	2	0	1

SAM-YORKE, Delano

Born	20/1/1989, London
Signed	2/1/2014 (age 24) from Cambridge United on a three-month loan *(GS)*
First appearance	Luton Town (H), Conference Premier, 4/1/2014
Final appearance	Dartford (A), Conference, 25/4/2015
Released/sold	6/5/2015 and joined Forest Green Rovers *(CM)*

*Career: 2006 Woking (Y), 2008 Woking (Nov 2009 Cray Wanderers - loan), Jul 2010 AFC Wimbledon (Sep 2010 Basingstoke Town - loan), Jun 2011 Basingstoke Town, May 2013 Cambridge United (**Jan 2014 LINCOLN CITY - loan**, **Aug 2014 LINCOLN CITY - loan**), **Jan 2015 LINCOLN CITY**, May 2015 Forest Green Rovers (Jan 2016 Boreham Wood - loan), Jul 2016 Woking (Jan 2017 Maidstone United - loan), May 2017 Maidstone United.*

Powerful striker originally signed by Gary Simpson on loan from Cambridge on 2 January 2014 for three months; signed for City at the same time as his Cambridge team-mate Mitch Austin, who came for a month. After some impressive early performances, City tried to sign him permanently but could not agree personal terms with the player, who apparently wanted to be closer to his home in London. Was recalled by Cambridge on 26 February, but was re-signed by Gary Simpson for a second loan spell on 29 August, this time until 17 January 2015. After a period of negotiation, Sam-Yorke signed permanently on 20 January on a deal to the end of the season. Formed a good partnership with Ben Tomlinson but was released in the summer of 2015. Between his two loan spells at Sincil Bank, Sam-Yorke played in Cambridge's 2-1 victory over Gateshead in the Conference play-off final on 18 May 2014. His legacy to Lincoln was not so memorable - a 6-month driving ban in November 2015 for two speeding offences on Broadgate.

	League			FA Cup			FA Trophy			TOTALS			Lincolnshire Cup		
	App	Sub	Gls	App	Sub	Gls	App	Sub	Gls	App	Sub	Gls	App	Sub	Gls
2013-14	9	0	3	0	0	0	0	0	0	9	0	3	0	0	0
2014-15	24	9	5	0	2	3	0	0	0	24	11	8	1	0	0
TOTALS	33	9	8	0	2	3	0	0	0	33	11	11	1	0	0

SHARP, Chris

Born	19/6/1986, Liverpool
Signed	11/11/2013 (age 27) from Hereford United on a one-month loan *(GS)*
First appearance	Southport (A), Conference Premier, 12/11/2013
Final appearance	Braintree Town (A), FA Trophy 2, 14/12/2013
Released/sold	N/A

Career: *Vauxhall Motors (Y), 2004 Capenhurst Villa, Sep 2005 Rhyl, Aug 2008 Bangor City, Jan 2010 The New Saints, Aug 2011 AFC Telford United, Jan 2013 Hereford United (**Nov 2013 LINCOLN CITY - loan**), Jul 2014 Stockport County, Jun 2015 Colwyn Bay, Oct 2015 Salford City, Dec 2015 Marine, Jun 2016 Bradford Park Avenue, May 2017 released.*

Journeyman striker who came to City's attention when he scored two second-half goals against the Imps for Hereford United in their 3-2 win on 16 February 2013, which is notable for being manager David Holdsworth's final game. Signed on a month's loan, extended for a second month on 11 December, but was recalled eight days later. Appeared in European competitions by virtue of early success with his three Welsh clubs, and missed the whole of the 2006-07 season with a double leg break sustained in Rhyl's UEFA Cup tie against Lithuanian side FK Suduva. Notably received a red card playing for Bangor against Carmarthen in 2009 while being carried off, having badly broken his arm committing the foul. Son of former Everton & Scotland striker Graeme Sharp.

	League			FA Cup			FA Trophy			TOTALS			Lincolnshire Cup		
	App	Sub	Gls	App	Sub	Gls	App	Sub	Gls	App	Sub	Gls	App	Sub	Gls
2013-14	3	0	1	0	0	0	2	0	1	5	0	2	0	0	0
TOTALS	3	0	1	0	0	0	2	0	1	5	0	2	0	0	0

SHERIDAN, Jake

Born	8/7/1986, Nottingham
Signed	17/11/2011 (age 25) from Eastwood Town initially on loan to the New Year *(DH)*
First appearance	Ebbsfleet United (H), Conference Premier, 26/11/2011
Final appearance	Barnet (H), Conference Premier, 26/4/2014
Released/sold	8/5/2014 and joined Alfreton Town *(GS)*

Career: *Dunkirk FC, Aug 2005 Notts County, Jul 2007 Tamworth, Aug 2011 Eastwood Town (**Nov 2011 LINCOLN CITY - loan**), **Jan 2012 LINCOLN CITY,** Jun 2014 Alfreton Town (Mar 2015 Boston United - loan), 2015 Boston United, Jul 2016 Basford United.*

Popular attacking midfielder/winger who was initially signed on loan by David Holdsworth on 17 November 2011. Impressed sufficiently to earn a permanent deal to the end of the season from 3 January 2012. Proved a consistent performer who always played with 100% commitment, which sometimes manifested itself as a goal, sometimes as a yellow card. Signed a one-year deal on 11 May 2012 and another on 16 May 2013, but spent many long hours on the substitutes' bench. One of only six players to play over 100 games during the Imps' Conference era. Had previously played under former City manager Steve Thompson at Notts County. Was appointed captain at Basford but unfortunately suffered a double compound fracture of his right leg in October 2016 which necessitated four operations. The incident hit the headlines due to Sheridan having to wait on the pitch for more than an hour for an ambulance to arrive.

Lincoln City Playing Record - Conference Only

	League			FA Cup			FA Trophy			TOTALS			Lincolnshire Cup		
	App	Sub	Gls	App	Sub	Gls	App	Sub	Gls	App	Sub	Gls	App	Sub	Gls
2011-12	12	8	0	0	0	0	0	3	1	12	11	1	0	0	0
2012-13	30	10	1	5	0	1	0	0	0	35	10	2	1	0	0
2013-14	20	9	1	1	2	0	2	1	0	23	12	1	2	0	0
TOTALS	62	27	2	6	2	1	2	4	1	70	33	4	3	0	0

SIMMONS, Alex

Born	13/3/1996, Lincoln
Signed	27/6/2014 (aged 18) from the Academy on a one-year deal *(GS)*
First appearance	Braintree Town (A), Conference Premier, 18/3/2014
Final appearance	Maidstone United (A), National League, 25/4/2017
Released/sold	18/5/2017 *(DC)*

Career: *2005 Lincoln City (Y) (Nov 2013 Lincoln United - work experience),* **Jun 2014 LINCOLN CITY** *(Aug 2014 Grantham Town - loan, Dec 2014 Boston United - loan, Feb 2015 Spalding United - loan, Oct 2015 Boston United - loan, Jan 2016 Grantham Town - loan, Sep 2016 FC Halifax Town - loan, Jan 2017 Boston United - loan), May 2017 released.*

Promising attacking midfielder/left winger who came through the youth ranks at Sincil Bank. Was part of the side that won the Midland Youth Cup in March 2014, the same month in which he made his first team debut. Was named *Young Player of the Season* in 2013-14, and signed his first professional contract shortly afterwards, on 27 June. Signed a contract extension on 20 April 2015 to the end of the 2015-16 season, and was given a further year in the summer of 2016. Despite being a professional at the club for three seasons, Simmons was given very few runs in the first team, sprinkled with regular spells on loan at various Lincolnshire non-league clubs. Released in the summer of 2017. Son of former City player Tony Simmons.

Lincoln City Playing Record - Conference Only

	League			FA Cup			FA Trophy			TOTALS			Lincolnshire Cup		
	App	Sub	Gls	App	Sub	Gls	App	Sub	Gls	App	Sub	Gls	App	Sub	Gls
2013-14	0	1	0	0	0	0	0	0	0	0	1	0	0	1	0
2014-15	1	6	0	0	0	0	0	1	0	1	7	0	0	0	0
2015-16	5	12	2	0	0	0	1	0	0	6	12	2	1	0	0
2016-17	0	2	0	0	0	0	0	0	0	0	2	0	0	1	0
TOTALS	6	21	2	0	0	0	1	1	0	7	22	2	1	2	0

SINCLAIR, Tony

Born	5/3/1985, Lewisham
Signed	8/7/2011 (age 26) from Gillingham on a one-year deal *(ST)*
First appearance	Kidderminster Harriers (H), Conference Premier, 16/8/2011
Final appearance	York City (H), Conference Premier, 7/1/2012
Released/sold	5/5/2012 and joined Carshalton Athletic *(DH)*

Career: *2001 Gillingham (Y), 2004 Beckenham Town, Jul 2006 Maidstone United, Aug 2006 Beckenham Town, Mar 2007 Fisher Athletic, Jul 2007 Welling United, May 2009 Woking, Jul 2010 Gillingham,* **Jul 2011 LINCOLN CITY,** *Aug 2012 Carshalton Athletic, Oct 2012 Dulwich Hamlet, 2013 Greenwich Borough, Feb 2014 Carshalton Athletic, Oct 2015 Carshalton Athletic.*

Athletic defender who started well but picked up an ankle injury in December 2011 which needed an operation. Compounded matters by falling out of favour after being spotted outside a Lincoln nightclub on 12 January 2012 with Gavin McCallum and Josh Gowling, and never played for City again. Was finally released in May 2012. Has since played for a number of non-league clubs in the south east.

Lincoln City Playing Record - Conference Only

	League			FA Cup			FA Trophy			TOTALS			Lincolnshire Cup		
	App	Sub	Gls	App	Sub	Gls	App	Sub	Gls	App	Sub	Gls	App	Sub	Gls
2011-12	23	1	0	2	0	0	1	0	0	26	1	0	0	0	0
TOTALS	23	1	0	2	0	0	1	0	0	26	1	0	0	0	0

SMITH, Adam

Born	20/2/1985, Huddersfield
Signed	21/6/2012 (age 27) from Mansfield Town on a one-year deal (DH)
First appearance	Kidderminster Harriers (H), Conference Premier, 11/8/2012
Final appearance	Kidderminster Harriers (A), Conference Premier, 6/4/2013
Released/sold	9/5/2013 and joined FC Halifax Town (GS)

Career: Kirkheaton, 2001 Chesterfield (Y), Mar 2004 Chesterfield (**Jan 2008 LINCOLN CITY - loan**), Aug 2008 Gainsborough Trinity (Nov 2008 York City - loan), Jan 2009 York City, May 2010 Mansfield Town (Oct 2011 Aldershot Town - loan, Nov 2011 Aldershot Town - loan), **Jun 2012 LINCOLN CITY**, Jul 2013 FC Halifax Town, Jun 2015 Wrexham (Nov 2015 Guiseley - loan), Jan 2016 Guiseley, Oct 2016 Alfreton Town.

Speedy winger who had originally made four appearances for City on loan from Chesterfield in 2007-08, making his first City debut as a substitute in the 2-0 win at Rochdale on 5 January 2008. All four of his loan appearances came as a substitute before he returned to Chesterfield after a month. Signed a one-year deal in June 2012 after being chased by David Holdsworth for much of the previous season, and apparently took a significant pay cut to sign, the reason being that he had played under Holdsworth at Mansfield. Was sent off in the match at Grimsby on New Year's Day 2013 for a foul on Bradley Wood, receiving a three-match ban after an appeal by Lincoln failed to overturn his red card. His poor scoring record and inconsistent delivery led to him being released at the end of his contract, one of many players who always appeared to play better against City than he did for them. Smith hit the headlines for the wrong reasons in January 2017 when he received a suspended two-year prison sentence at Derby Crown Court for a £22,278 credit card scam against clothing retailer TK Maxx.

Lincoln City Playing Record - Conference Only

	League			FA Cup			FA Trophy			TOTALS			Lincolnshire Cup		
	App	Sub	Gls	App	Sub	Gls	App	Sub	Gls	App	Sub	Gls	App	Sub	Gls
2012-13	19	11	1	6	0	1	1	0	0	26	11	2	0	0	0
TOTALS	19	11	1	6	0	1	1	0	0	26	11	2	0	0	0

Lincoln City Playing Record - Football League

	League			FA Cup			League Cup			FL Trophy			TOTALS		
	App	Sub	Gls	App	Sub	Gls	App	Sub	Gls	App	Sub	Gls	App	Sub	Gls
2007-08	0	4	0	0	0	0	0	0	0	0	0	0	0	4	0
TOTALS	0	4	0	0	0	0	0	0	0	0	0	0	0	4	0

SMITH, Sam

Born	20/5/1990, Derby
Signed	6/7/2011 (age 21) from Rushden & Diamonds on a one-year deal (ST)
First appearance	Southport (A), Conference Premier, 13/8/2011
Final appearance	Hayes & Yeading United (H), Conference Premier, 21/4/2012
Released/sold	1/8/2012 and joined Cambridge United (DH)

Career: Jan 2008 Rushden & Diamonds (Oct 2009 Corby Town - loan, Dec 2009 Hinckley United - loan), **Jul 2011 LINCOLN CITY**, Aug 2012 Cambridge United (Jun 2013 Hereford United - loan), Jun 2014 AFC Telford United (Sep 2014 Brackley Town - loan), Jun 2015 Brackley Town, Feb 2016 Woking, Jul 2016 Kettering Town, Feb 2017 Gold Coast City (Australia).

Tall 6'3" striker who signed from Rushden & Diamonds on a one-year deal on the same day as his Diamonds colleague Alan Power. Made a good start to his City career, having the distinction of scoring City's first goal back in non-league football after 29 minutes of his debut at Southport. Unfortunately his season was badly affected by breaking the same foot twice: first against Wrexham on 19 November, missing six weeks, and again against Southport on 24 January, which kept him out for three months. Despite missing half the season, Smith still managed to finish top scorer with 9 goals. Signed a further one-year contract on 2 May 2012 but was sold to Cambridge in August 2012 for an undisclosed fee (rumoured to be £25,000) after City reportedly turned down two initial offers for him. Emigrated to Australia towards the end of 2016 after leaving Kettering. Currently holds the UEFA B coaching licence.

Lincoln City Playing Record - Conference Only

	League			FA Cup			FA Trophy			TOTALS			Lincolnshire Cup		
	App	Sub	Gls	App	Sub	Gls	App	Sub	Gls	App	Sub	Gls	App	Sub	Gls
2011-12	18	6	7	2	0	2	2	0	0	22	6	9	2	0	1
TOTALS	18	6	7	2	0	2	2	0	0	22	6	9	2	0	1

SOUTHWELL, Dayle

Born	20/10/1993, Louth
Signed	3/2/2017 (age 23) from Wycombe Wanderers on a one-month loan (DC)
First appearance	Welling United (A), FA Trophy 3, 4/2/2017
Final appearance	Boreham Wood (A), FA Trophy 4, 25/2/2017
Released/sold	N/A

Career: 2004 Grimsby Town (Y), Apr 2012 Grimsby Town (Oct 2013 Harrogate Town - loan), May 2014 Boston United, Jun 2016 Wycombe Wanderers (Feb 2017 LINCOLN CITY - loan).

Local striker who made his name through a couple of prolific seasons at Boston United. Was originally a target for Danny Cowley in the summer of 2016 but chose to move up to the Football League with League Two Wycombe. Suffered an injury early in the 2016-17 season and hardly appeared for Wycombe before his loan move to Sincil Bank. City originally wanted to sign him to the end of the season but Wycombe manager Gareth Ainsworth preferred to restrict the move to a month. Scored just 8 minutes into his debut at Welling, but failed to score again before being recalled by his parent club. Won one England C cap against Slovakia in June 2016 prior to his move to Wycombe.

Lincoln City Playing Record - Conference Only

	League			FA Cup			FA Trophy			TOTALS			Lincolnshire Cup		
	App	Sub	Gls	App	Sub	Gls	App	Sub	Gls	App	Sub	Gls	App	Sub	Gls
2016-17	2	0	0	0	1	0	1	1	1	3	2	1	0	0	0
TOTALS	2	0	0	0	1	0	1	1	1	3	2	1	0	0	0

SPARROW, Matt

Born	3/10/1981, Wembley
Signed	24/6/2015 (age 33) from Scunthorpe United on a one-year deal (CM)
First appearance	Cheltenham Town (H), National League, 8/8/2015
Final appearance	Woking (H), National League, 23/4/2016
Released/sold	23/5/2016 and joined Sorrento (Australia) (DC)

Career: Scunthorpe United (Y), 1999 Scunthorpe United, Jun 2010 Brighton & Hove Albion, Jan 2013 Crawley Town, Jul 2013 Scunthorpe United (Feb 2015 Cheltenham Town - loan), Jun 2015 LINCOLN CITY, May 2016 Sorrento (Australia), Oct 2016 Gainsborough Trinity, Nov 2016 Sorrento (Australia), Jan 2017 Joondalup United (Australia).

Very experienced midfielder who had scored for neighbours Scunthorpe in the 2009 League One play-off final against Millwall (won 3-2). Also won the League One championship with Brighton in 2011 and spent several years playing successfully at Championship level. Unfortunately his best days were well behind him by the time he arrived at Sincil

Bank, although the quality was still visible at times. Was released by City in the close season of 2016 when he did not fit the style of play favoured by new boss Danny Cowley. One of several players on City's books to have served a prison sentence in his early years, having been jailed for 9 months for assault whilst on the books at Scunthorpe in August 2001. Won five promotions and played over 500 professional games before moving to Australia upon his release from the Imps. Currently holds the UEFA B coaching licence.

Lincoln City Playing Record - Conference Only

	League			FA Cup			FA Trophy			TOTALS			Lincolnshire Cup		
	App	Sub	Gls	App	Sub	Gls	App	Sub	Gls	App	Sub	Gls	App	Sub	Gls
2015-16	22	4	0	1	2	0	0	0	0	23	6	0	2	0	0
TOTALS	22	4	0	1	2	0	0	0	0	23	6	0	2	0	0

STANLEY, Craig

Born	2/3/1983, Nuneaton
Signed	5/6/2015 (age 32) from Eastleigh on a one-year deal (CM)
First appearance	Cheltenham Town (H), National League, 8/8/2015
Final appearance	Guiseley (H), National League, 30/1/2016
Released/sold	26/9/2016 and joined Barwell (DC)

Career: Walsall (Y), Jul 2002 Walsall (Jul 2003 Raith Rovers - loan), Feb 2004 Telford United, Jun 2004 Hereford United, Jun 2006 Morecambe (Jan 2011 Torquay United - loan), Jun 2011 Bristol Rovers, Jul 2012 Aldershot Town, Jul 2014 Eastleigh, Jun 2015 LINCOLN CITY (Aug 2016 Southport - loan), Sep 2016 Barwell.

Popular strong-tackling defensive midfielder who played a key role in City's midfield until a broken foot at the end of January 2016 ruled him out for the rest of the season. City won just four of their remaining fourteen games without him and slipped into the bottom half. Had been signed on an initial one-year deal, but triggered a second year through appearances despite the injury. However, new manager Danny Cowley decided Craig was not suitable for City's new high-pressing style of play and placed him on the transfer list at the end of July 2016. After a one-month loan at Southport in August, he left the club by mutual consent. Built a good career in football despite being diagnosed with Type 1 diabetes whilst playing for Walsall in 2002. Won 4 caps for England C including a period as captain, and won the European Challenge Trophy in 2006. Twice won promotion from the Conference through the play-offs, with Hereford in 2006 and Morecambe in 2007. Coached the Notts County U16 team after leaving Lincoln and is currently head coach at the Deon Burton Football Academy.

Lincoln City Playing Record - Conference Only

	League			FA Cup			FA Trophy			TOTALS			Lincolnshire Cup		
	App	Sub	Gls	App	Sub	Gls	App	Sub	Gls	App	Sub	Gls	App	Sub	Gls
2015-16	26	2	2	0	0	0	0	0	0	26	2	2	1	1	0
2016-17	0	0	0	0	0	0	0	0	0	0	0	0	0	1	0
TOTALS	26	2	2	0	0	0	0	0	0	26	2	2	1	2	0

TAYLOR, Jamie

Born	16/12/1982, Crawley
Signed	1/7/2011 (age 28) from Eastbourne Borough on a two-year deal (ST)
First appearance	Southport (A), Conference Premier, 13/8/2011
Final appearance	Hyde (A), Conference Premier, 20/4/2013
Released/sold	9/5/2013 and joined Sutton United (GS)

Career: Broadbridge Heath, Jul 2001 Horsham, Aug 2002 Aldershot Town (Feb 2003 Horsham - loan, Dec 2003 Carshalton Athletic - loan), Mar 2004 AFC Wimbledon, Oct 2004 Horsham, Dec 2006 Woking, Mar 2007 Dagenham & Redbridge (Feb 2008 Grays Athletic - loan), May 2008 Grays Athletic, Jul 2009 Eastbourne Borough, Jul 2011 LINCOLN CITY, May 2013 Sutton United (Dec 2013 Eastbourne Borough - loan), Sep 2014 Margate (Jan 2016 Eastbourne Borough - loan), Feb 2016 Eastbourne Borough.

Clever striker who signed on a two-year deal following City's relegation from the FL. Had an intermittent first season due to a succession of injuries and never really won a regular starting place. Fortunately came good in the second season, becoming the first City player since relegation to score 10 goals in a season when he scored against Braintree on 6 November 2012. Considering that Alan Power and Vadaine Oliver also reached double figures that season, it is hard to understand how City needed to win on the final day to keep themselves in the Conference. City intended to offer new terms for the 2013-14 season, but Taylor decided to leave Lincoln and return to his native south-east when his partner was expecting twins. Turning down an offer from Luton, he joined Sutton United to be closer to his home. Has scored over 250 goals in a 15-year career.

Lincoln City Playing Record - Conference Only

	League			FA Cup			FA Trophy			TOTALS			Lincolnshire Cup		
	App	Sub	Gls	App	Sub	Gls	App	Sub	Gls	App	Sub	Gls	App	Sub	Gls
2011-12	10	14	4	0	1	0	2	0	2	12	15	6	1	0	0
2012-13	33	7	13	6	0	3	0	0	0	39	7	16	1	0	0
TOTALS	43	21	17	6	1	3	2	0	2	51	22	22	2	0	0

TEMPEST, Greg

Born	28/12/1993, Nottingham
Signed	14/5/2015 (age 21) from Notts County on a one-year deal (CM)
First appearance	Macclesfield Town (H), National League, 18/8/2015
Final appearance	Cheltenham Town (A), National League, 30/4/2016
Released/sold	23/5/2016 and joined Nuneaton Town (DC)

Career: Mansfield Town (Y), 2010 Notts County (Y), May 2012 Notts County (Nov 2012 Ilkeston - loan, Sep 2014 Boston United - loan, Jan 2015 Boston United - loan), May 2015 LINCOLN CITY, Jun 2016 Nuneaton Town (Mar 2017 Gainsborough Trinity - loan), May 2017 released.

Tough young midfielder known as much for his wild hairstyle as for his playing ability. Earned plaudits for his better displays but was too inconsistent and inexperienced to hold down a regular place in the side. Despite supposedly being offered a new contract by outgoing manager Chris Moyses, Tempest was released by new manager Danny Cowley in May 2016, but was invited back for pre-season training along with Conner Robinson. Both players declined, and Tempest signed for Nuneaton. Had hit the local headlines in October 2014 when he went in goal in the closing minutes of Boston United's game against Hyde and kept a clean sheet. Won 6 caps for Northern Ireland U21 in 2013 whilst on the books at Notts County, qualifying through his grandfather Bill Corkhill; Corkhill played 287 FL games for Notts County and Cardiff between 1931 and 1952, and managed Scunthorpe United between 1952 and 1956.

Lincoln City Playing Record - Conference Only

	League			FA Cup			FA Trophy			TOTALS			Lincolnshire Cup		
	App	Sub	Gls	App	Sub	Gls	App	Sub	Gls	App	Sub	Gls	App	Sub	Gls
2015-16	17	3	0	1	2	0	1	0	0	19	5	0	1	0	0
TOTALS	17	3	0	1	2	0	1	0	0	19	5	0	1	0	0

THOMAS, Jordan

Born	8/8/1995, Grantham
Signed	20/10/2012 (age 17) from the Academy on a two-year deal (DH)
First appearance	Mansfield Town (H), Conference Premier, 18/10/2011
Final appearance	Carshalton Athletic (H), FA Trophy 2, 14/1/2012
Released/sold	8/5/2014 and joined Spalding United (GS)

Career: 2007 Lincoln City (Y), Oct 2012 LINCOLN CITY (Nov 2012 Sheffield FC - loan, Sep 2013 Gainsborough Trinity - loan, Nov 2013 Eastwood Town - loan, Jan 2014 Spalding United - loan), Jul 2014 Spalding United, Sep 2014 Newark Town, Jul 2015 Harrowby United, Aug 2015 Holbeach United.

Young striker who was a prolific scorer in youth football for City. Became the youngest player to make an appearance in Lincoln's first team in a competitive fixture when he made his debut against Mansfield, aged 16 years and 71 days. Signed a two-year professional contract on 20 October 2012 but never appeared for the first team again. Spent lengthy spells out on loan to various Lincolnshire non-league clubs to gain experience and game time. It was during his spell at Gainsborough in 2013-14 that he became the subject of Trinity's expulsion from the FA Cup, when beaten second qualifying round opponents Rushall Olympic claimed he wasn't registered in time for the game. Despite Lincoln sending evidence to the FA that they had submitted the relevant paperwork ahead of the deadline, the FA claimed they had not received it and bizarrely expelled Trinity from the competition. Was released in 2014 and has continued to score goals for a succession of local clubs.

Lincoln City Playing Record - Conference Only

	League			FA Cup			FA Trophy			TOTALS			Lincolnshire Cup		
	App	Sub	Gls	App	Sub	Gls	App	Sub	Gls	App	Sub	Gls	App	Sub	Gls
2011-12	0	1	0	0	0	0	0	1	0	0	2	0	0	0	0
2012-13	0	0	0	0	0	0	0	0	0	0	0	0	0	0	0
2013-14	0	0	0	0	0	0	0	0	0	0	0	0	0	0	0
TOTALS	0	1	0	0	0	0	0	1	0	0	2	0	0	0	0

THOMPSON, Curtis

Born	2/9/1993, Nottingham
Signed	21/10/2011 (age 18) from Notts County on a one-month loan (GB)
First appearance	Cambridge United (A), Conference Premier, 21/10/2011
Final appearance	As above - made only one appearance
Released/sold	N/A

Career: 2005 Leicester City (Y), 2009 Notts County (Y), Oct 2011 Notts County (**Oct 2011 LINCOLN CITY - loan,** Nov 2012 Ilkeston - loan).

Young midfielder who joined the club on loan from Notts County having just signed his first professional contract, but was caught up in a change of management at Sincil Bank. Signed by caretaker manager Grant Brown, Thompson appeared just once - as an 88th-minute substitute for Josh O'Keefe at Cambridge on the day he signed - before his loan was cut short by new manager David Holdsworth. Has since gone on to establish himself in Notts County's first team.

Lincoln City Playing Record - Conference Only

	League			FA Cup			FA Trophy			TOTALS			Lincolnshire Cup		
	App	Sub	Gls	App	Sub	Gls	App	Sub	Gls	App	Sub	Gls	App	Sub	Gls
2011-12	0	1	0	0	0	0	0	0	0	0	1	0	0	0	0
TOTALS	0	1	0	0	0	0	0	0	0	0	1	0	0	0	0

THOMPSON, Reece

Born	11/11/1993, Worksop
Signed	1/7/2010 (age 16) from Retford United Youth (CS)
First appearance	Carshalton Athletic (A), FA Trophy 2 Replay, 18/1/2012
Final appearance	As above - made only one appearance
Released/sold	5/5/2012 and joined Retford United (DH)

Career: Retford United (Y), **2010 Lincoln City (Y)**, Jul 2012 Retford United, Oct 2014 Frickley Athletic, Aug 2015 York City, Sep 2016 North Ferriby United.

Small striker who came through the Imps youth system after joining from Retford. Unfortunately, his only appearance came as an 89th-minute substitute in the dismal defeat at Carshalton in the FA Trophy and he never made the first team again. Holds the dubious distinction of having played the fewest minutes for Lincoln City during the Conference era. Rebuilt his playing career in non-league football with Retford and Frickley before attracting interest from numerous League clubs in 2014-15. Chose to join York in the summer of 2015, but suffered from an undisclosed illness from October and missed much of the season as York were relegated to the National League. Later joined North Ferriby and scored regularly as they were relegated back to National League North after one solitary season at the top level.

Lincoln City Playing Record - Conference Only

	League			FA Cup			FA Trophy			TOTALS			Lincolnshire Cup		
	App	Sub	Gls	App	Sub	Gls	App	Sub	Gls	App	Sub	Gls	App	Sub	Gls
2011-12	0	0	0	0	0	0	0	1	0	0	1	0	0	0	0
TOTALS	0	0	0	0	0	0	0	1	0	0	1	0	0	0	0

THOMPSON, Tyrone

Born	8/5/1982, Sheffield
Signed	17/11/2011 (age 29) from FC Halifax Town on a short-term deal (DH)
First appearance	Ebbsfleet United (H), Conference Premier, 26/11/2011
Final appearance	Ebbsfleet United (A), Conference Premier, 28/4/2012
Released/sold	5/5/2012 and joined Sheffield FC (DH)

Career: 1991 Sheffield United (Y), Jul 2000 Sheffield United (Oct 2002 LINCOLN CITY - loan, Mar 2003 Doncaster Rovers - loan), Jul 2003 Huddersfield Town, Jun 2004 Scarborough, Aug 2005 Halifax Town, Jun 2007 Crawley Town, May 2008 Torquay United, Jul 2010 Mansfield Town, Aug 2011 Grimsby Town, Oct 2011 FC Halifax Town, **Nov 2011 LINCOLN CITY**, Aug 2012 Sheffield FC, Jan 2013 Gainsborough Trinity, Jan 2014 Goole.

Tenacious midfielder who ironically made his professional debut for Sheffield United in a 6-1 win over Lincoln in the League Cup first round, first leg tie on 22 August 2000. Originally signed for Lincoln on a month's loan in October 2002 and made his debut v York City in the Football League Trophy first round on 22 October. Made one FL appearance and two in the Football League Trophy before returning to United. Initially joined City on a deal until 8 January 2012 as a free agent following his release by FC Halifax, which was then extended to the end of the season on 9 January. Another player who played under David Holdsworth at Mansfield. Could not agree a deal for 2012-13 and joined former City coach Curtis Woodhouse at Sheffield FC. Became a football agent after retirement, numbering City strikers Jack Muldoon and Nathan Arnold among his clients.

Lincoln City Playing Record - Conference Only

	League			FA Cup			FA Trophy			TOTALS			Lincolnshire Cup		
	App	Sub	Gls	App	Sub	Gls	App	Sub	Gls	App	Sub	Gls	App	Sub	Gls
2011-12	26	0	1	0	0	0	3	0	0	29	0	1	0	0	0
TOTALS	26	0	1	0	0	0	3	0	0	29	0	1	0	0	0

Lincoln City Playing Record - Football League

	League			FA Cup			League Cup			FL Trophy			TOTALS		
	App	Sub	Gls	App	Sub	Gls	App	Sub	Gls	App	Sub	Gls	App	Sub	Gls
2002-03	0	1	0	0	0	0	0	0	0	2	0	0	2	1	0
TOTALS	0	1	0	0	0	0	0	0	0	2	0	0	2	1	0

THOMSON, Jake

Born	12/5/1989, Portsmouth
Signed	2/1/2013 (age 23) from Newport County on a one-month loan (DH)
First appearance	Ebbsfleet United (A), Conference Premier, 5/1/2013
Final appearance	Forest Green Rovers (H), Conference Premier, 26/1/2013
Released/sold	N/A

Career: *2005 Southampton (Y), 2008 Southampton (Jan 2009 AFC Bournemouth - loan, Oct 2009 Torquay United - loan), Jul 2010 Exeter City (Feb 2011 Cheltenham Town - loan), Sep 2011 Kettering Town (Sep 2011 Forest Green Rovers - loan), Jan 2012 Forest Green Rovers, Jun 2012 Newport County (**Jan 2013 LINCOLN CITY - loan**), Aug 2013 Salisbury City, Jan 2014 AFC Portchester, Jul 2014 Bognor Regis Town, Sep 2015 Havant & Waterlooville, Jan 2017 Gosport Borough.*

Midfielder who had originally been a transfer target for David Holdsworth in the summer of 2012. Signed on a month's loan in January 2013, and did well enough for City to want to extend his spell at the club; however, the money was not available as City continued to trim their squad, and Thomson and fellow-loanee Chris Bush returned to their parent clubs in early February. Failed to fulfil his early potential in football, appearing for 13 different clubs in 7 years. Started his international career with the England U17 side (4 caps, 1 goal), but later switched to Trinidad & Tobago for whom he qualified through his parents, winning 4 caps for the U20s and 2 full caps in 2009.

Lincoln City Playing Record - Conference Only

	League			FA Cup			FA Trophy			TOTALS			Lincolnshire Cup		
	App	Sub	Gls	App	Sub	Gls	App	Sub	Gls	App	Sub	Gls	App	Sub	Gls
2012-13	3	0	0	0	0	0	0	0	0	3	0	0	0	0	0
TOTALS	3	0	0	0	0	0	0	0	0	3	0	0	0	0	0

TOMLINSON, Ben

Born	31/10/1989, Dinnington
Signed	23/7/2013 (age 23) from Alfreton Town on a two-year deal *(GS)*
First appearance	Woking (A), Conference Premier, 10/8/2013
Final appearance	Dartford (A), Conference, 25/4/2015
Released/sold	6/5/2015 and joined Barnet *(CM)*

Career: *Worksop Town (Y), Jul 2008 Worksop Town, Jun 2011 Macclesfield Town, Aug 2012 Alfreton Town,* **Jul 2013 LINCOLN CITY,** *May 2015 Barnet (Sep 2015 Grimsby Town - loan, Oct 2015 Tranmere Rovers - loan, Feb 2016 Barrow - loan), Mar 2017 Carlisle United.*

Lively striker signed from Alfreton on a two-year deal for an undisclosed sum (believed to be £6,000), and went on to become one of the most popular players of the Conference era. Had a very good scoring record in both of his seasons, becoming the first player since relegation to reach 20 in a season. Of less use was his poor disciplinary record, picking up regular yellow cards and suspensions because of his aggressive style of play. Was less effective in his second season due to being played out wide, but was surprisingly released at the end of his contract and joined newly-promoted Barnet in League Two. Failed to settle at The Hive and spent most of his first season out on loan, scoring just 4 goals in 37 appearances for four different clubs, before being released in January 2017. Had previously played for Gary Simpson at Macclesfield, and later had a spell on loan at Barrow where Simpson was the assistant manager. Held both of the club's Conference scoring records until overtaken by Matt Rhead in 2015-16 (most goals in a season) and by first Alan Power and then by Rhead again in 2016-17 (most goals in the Conference era).

Lincoln City Playing Record - Conference Only

	League			FA Cup			FA Trophy			TOTALS			Lincolnshire Cup		
	App	Sub	Gls	App	Sub	Gls	App	Sub	Gls	App	Sub	Gls	App	Sub	Gls
2013-14	39	0	18	4	0	2	1	0	0	44	0	20	1	0	0
2014-15	39	7	14	2	0	0	1	0	0	42	7	14	1	1	0
TOTALS	78	7	32	6	0	2	2	0	0	86	7	34	2	1	0

TOWNSEND, Nick

Born	1/11/1994, Solihull
Signed	13/2/2014 (age 19) from Birmingham City on a one-month youth loan *(GS)*
First appearance	Kidderminster Harriers (H), Conference Premier, 15/2/2014
Final appearance	Wrexham (H), Conference, 18/10/2014
Released/sold	N/A

Career: *2007 Birmingham City (Y) (Mar 2013 Oxford City - loan), May 2013 Birmingham City (**Feb 2014 LINCOLN CITY - loan, Aug 2014 LINCOLN CITY - loan**, Aug 2015 Barnsley - loan), Sep 2015 Barnsley.*

Outstanding young goalkeeper initially signed on a one-month youth loan following an injury to Paul Farman at Hyde. Impressed immediately and stayed until the end of the 2013-14 season. Re-signed on a season-long youth loan on 2 August 2014, with manager Gary Simpson publicly announcing he would be number one for the season. However, Birmingham would not give Lincoln permission to play him in the FA Cup following the dismissal of manager Lee Clark, and he lost his place to Paul Farman. He never played another game for Lincoln, and Birmingham recalled him on 4 January 2015.

Lincoln City Playing Record - Conference Only

	League			FA Cup			FA Trophy			TOTALS			Lincolnshire Cup		
	App	Sub	Gls	App	Sub	Gls	App	Sub	Gls	App	Sub	Gls	App	Sub	Gls
2013-14	14	0	0	0	0	0	0	0	0	14	0	0	0	0	0
2014-15	17	0	0	0	0	0	0	0	0	17	0	0	1	0	0
TOTALS	31	0	0	0	0	0	0	0	0	31	0	0	1	0	0

TURNBULL, Paul

Born	23/1/1989, Handforth
Signed	25/1/2013 (age 24) from Northampton Town on loan to the end of the season *(DH)*
First appearance	Forest Green Rovers (H), Conference Premier, 26/1/2013
Final appearance	Hyde (A), Conference Premier, 20/4/2013
Released/sold	N/A

Career: *2000 Stockport County (Y), 2005 Stockport County (Mar 2008 Altrincham - loan), Jun 2011 Northampton Town (Jan 2012 Stockport County - loan, Sep 2012 Stockport County - loan, **Jan 2013 LINCOLN CITY - loan**), Jul 2013 Macclesfield Town, Jun 2016 Barrow.*

Combative midfielder signed on loan until the end of the 2012-13 season. Contributed some solid performances as City avoided relegation from the Conference under new manager Gary Simpson. Was released by Northampton on his return and joined Macclesfield. Has the distinction of being Stockport County's youngest ever Football League player at the age of 16 years and 97 days, and being team captain at 21.

Lincoln City Playing Record - Conference Only

	League			FA Cup			FA Trophy			TOTALS			Lincolnshire Cup		
	App	Sub	Gls	App	Sub	Gls	App	Sub	Gls	App	Sub	Gls	App	Sub	Gls
2012-13	14	1	0	0	0	0	0	0	0	14	1	0	0	0	0
TOTALS	14	1	0	0	0	0	0	0	0	14	1	0	0	0	0

WAITE, Tyrell

Born	1/7/1994, Derby
Signed	27/11/2014 (age 20) from Notts County initially on a one-month loan *(CM)*
First appearance	Nuneaton Town (H), Conference, 9/12/2014
Final appearance	Chester (H), Conference, 14/2/2015
Released/sold	11/3/2015 and joined Skellefteå (Sweden) *(CM)*

*Career: Ilkeston (Y), Mar 2012 Ilkeston, Mar 2012 Notts County (Oct 2012 Nuneaton Town - loan, Dec 2013 Ilkeston - loan, Aug 2014 Nuneaton Town - loan, Oct 2014 Ilkeston - loan, **Nov 2014 LINCOLN CITY - loan), Jan 2015 LINCOLN CITY**, Mar 2015 Skellefteå (Sweden), Jan 2016 Nuneaton Town, Jul 2016 Kidderminster Harriers.*

Young striker who signed initially on loan until 4 January 2015. Ironically made his City debut in a 3-1 win over his former club Nuneaton. Despite not appearing regularly during his loan spell, City surprisingly signed him permanently on 16 January 2015 on a deal until the end of the season. Less surprisingly he made only three more very brief appearances from the substitutes' bench before the club cancelled his contract on 11 March to allow him to join Swedish second division club Skellefteå.

Lincoln City Playing Record - Conference Only

	League			FA Cup			FA Trophy			TOTALS			Lincolnshire Cup		
	App	Sub	Gls	App	Sub	Gls	App	Sub	Gls	App	Sub	Gls	App	Sub	Gls
2014-15	2	4	0	0	0	0	0	0	0	2	4	0	0	0	0
TOTALS	2	4	0	0	0	0	0	0	0	2	4	0	0	0	0

WALLACE, Kieran

Born	26/1/1995, Nottingham
Signed	26/3/2015 (age 20) from Sheffield United on loan to the end of the season *(CM)*
First appearance	Forest Green Rovers (H), Conference, 28/3/2015
Final appearance	Eastleigh (H), Conference, 18/4/2015
Released/sold	N/A

*Career: Nottingham Forest (Y), Jul 2014 Ilkeston - non-contract, Nov 2014 Sheffield United **(Mar 2015 LINCOLN CITY - loan, Aug 2016 Fleetwood Town - loan).***

Young defender signed on transfer deadline day until the end of the season. Unfortunately played in a poor City side and won just one of his six games. Returned to Sheffield United and forced his way into their first team in August 2015. Had a very promising start to his career at Nottingham Forest, being capped by England at U16 level (6 caps) and U17 (7 caps). Also appeared in both legs of Forest's FA Youth Cup semi-final defeat to eventual winners Norwich in April 2013.

Lincoln City Playing Record - Conference Only

	League			FA Cup			FA Trophy			TOTALS			Lincolnshire Cup		
	App	Sub	Gls	App	Sub	Gls	App	Sub	Gls	App	Sub	Gls	App	Sub	Gls
2014-15	6	0	0	0	0	0	0	0	0	6	0	0	0	0	0
TOTALS	6	0	0	0	0	0	0	0	0	6	0	0	0	0	0

WARD, Joe

Born	22/8/1995
Signed	13/1/2017 (age 21) from Brighton & Hove Albion on a one-month loan *(DC)*
First appearance	Gateshead (A), FA Trophy 2, 14/1/2017
Final appearance	York City (A), FA Trophy semi-final first leg, 14/3/2017
Released/sold	N/A

*Career: Chelmsford City (Y), Dec 2013 Chelmsford City, Jun 2015 Brighton & Hove Albion (**Jan 2017 LINCOLN CITY - loan**), May 2017 released.*

Lightning-fast young right-sided midfielder/winger who joined on a month's loan from Brighton's U23 side. Scored twice in as many minutes in his second start at Welling in the FA Trophy. City extended his loan to the maximum 93 days on 10 February 2017, keeping him at the club until 14 April. Unfortunately picked up a metatarsal injury in March and returned to Brighton a month early. Was released by Brighton at the end of the season amidst speculation linking him with a permanent move to Sincil Bank.

Lincoln City Playing Record - Conference Only

	League			FA Cup			FA Trophy			TOTALS			Lincolnshire Cup		
	App	Sub	Gls	App	Sub	Gls	App	Sub	Gls	App	Sub	Gls	App	Sub	Gls
2016-17	0	2	0	0	2	0	4	0	3	4	4	3	0	0	0
TOTALS	0	2	0	0	2	0	4	0	3	4	4	3	0	0	0

WATERFALL, Luke

Born	30/7/1990, Sheffield
Signed	2/6/2015 (age 24) from Wrexham on a two-year deal *(CM)*
First appearance	Cheltenham Town (H), National League, 8/8/2015
Final appearance	Southport (A), National League, 29/4/2017
Released/sold	

*Career: Jul 2006 Barnsley (Y), Jul 2008 Tranmere Rovers (Oct 2008 Altrincham - loan), Jul 2009 Ilkeston Town, Jul 2010 Gainsborough Trinity, Jul 2013 Scunthorpe United (Aug 2014 Macclesfield Town - loan, Nov 2014 Mansfield Town - loan), Jan 2015 Wrexham, **Jun 2015 LINCOLN CITY.***

Right-sided centre half signed from National League rivals Wrexham on a two-year deal. Waterfall and fellow-Imp Terry Hawkridge had followed Gainsborough chairman Peter Swann to Scunthorpe in the summer of 2013, making Lincoln the third club they had played for together. Made his debut in the opening game of the 2015-16 season against eventual champions Cheltenham and held down his place for the rest of the season. Commanding in the air, Waterfall scored some useful goals from set-pieces including two at Torquay in November 2015. Was appointed team captain early in the 2016-17 season under Danny Cowley and turned in some impressive performances in partnership with Sean Raggett, the pair also adding an outstanding 15 goals between them. Became the first City captain for 29 years to lift a championship trophy when City beat Macclesfield to win the National League in April 2017. Signed a new two-year contract on 17 May 2017 after rejecting higher financial offers from Coventry, Carlisle and Notts County.

Lincoln City Playing Record - Conference Only

	League			FA Cup			FA Trophy			TOTALS			Lincolnshire Cup		
	App	Sub	Gls	App	Sub	Gls	App	Sub	Gls	App	Sub	Gls	App	Sub	Gls
2015-16	35	1	6	3	0	0	1	0	0	39	1	6	1	1	0
2016-17	44	0	7	9	0	0	1	1	0	54	1	7	1	0	0
TOTALS	79	1	13	12	0	0	2	1	0	93	2	13	2	1	0

WATSON, Karlton

Born	30/4/1992, Peterborough
Signed	4/1/2012 (age 19) from Nottingham Forest to the end of the season *(DH)*
First appearance	York City (H), Conference Premier, 7/1/2012
Final appearance	Ebbsfleet United (A), Conference Premier, 28/4/2012
Released/sold	5/5/2012 and later joined Leicester City *(DH)*

Career: Apr 2005 Nottingham Forest (Y) (Sep 2011 Eastwood Town - loan), **Jan 2012 LINCOLN CITY**, Nov 2012 Leicester City (Feb 2013 AFC Telford United), Aug 2014 Boston United - non-contract, Sep 2014 retired.

Promising young centre back whose career was wrecked by injury. Had been Nottingham Forest's *Young Player of the Season* in 2009-10, but had then missed most of 2010-11 with an ankle injury that necessitated 5 operations and 18 months of recuperation. Was released by Forest on 16 December 2011 and Joined Lincoln on a short-term deal until the end of the season. Made his first class debut while on City's books but was given very few opportunities after that. Was surprisingly signed by Leicester when he left Sincil Bank after a short spell at the Nike Academy. Was also called up by England U19 during his time at Forest.

Lincoln City Playing Record - Conference Only

	League			FA Cup			FA Trophy			TOTALS			Lincolnshire Cup		
	App	Sub	Gls	App	Sub	Gls	App	Sub	Gls	App	Sub	Gls	App	Sub	Gls
2011-12	3	2	0	0	0	0	2	0	0	5	2	0	0	0	0
TOTALS	3	2	0	0	0	0	2	0	0	5	2	0	0	0	0

WATTS, Adam

Born	4/3/1988, Hackney
Signed	2/10/2009 (age 21) from Fulham initially on a one-month loan (CS)
First appearance	Southport (A), Conference Premier, 13/8/2011
Final appearance	Alfreton Town (H), FA Cup 4Q Replay, 1/11/2011
Released/sold	26/12/2011 and joined Gainsborough Trinity (DH)

Career: Fulham (Y), Feb 2007 Fulham (Mar 2007 MK Dons - loan, Mar 2009 Northampton Town - loan, **Oct 2009 LINCOLN CITY - loan**), **Jan 2010 LINCOLN CITY**, Jan 2012 Gainsborough Trinity, Oct 2012 Eastbourne Borough, Nov 2015 contract cancelled.

Central defender Adam Watts has the dubious distinction of being Chris Sutton's first signing when he joined originally on a month's loan from Fulham, making his City debut the following day at home to Aldershot in League Two. The loan was extended until the New Year, but was made permanent on 5 January 2010 when he signed a deal to the end of 2012. Suffered a bad leg break at Grimsby on 20 February 2010, and missed the rest of the season. Was told he could leave on 11 May 2011 following City's relegation from the Football League but could not find a club; he eventually left on 26 December by mutual consent. Played on for four more seasons at Eastbourne before a series of injuries led to the cancellation of his contract by mutual consent on 26 November 2015.

Lincoln City Playing Record - Conference Only

	League			FA Cup			FA Trophy			TOTALS			Lincolnshire Cup		
	App	Sub	Gls	App	Sub	Gls	App	Sub	Gls	App	Sub	Gls	App	Sub	Gls
2011-12	11	0	0	2	0	0	0	0	0	13	0	0	2	0	0
TOTALS	11	0	0	2	0	0	0	0	0	13	0	0	2	0	0

Lincoln City Playing Record - Football League

	League			FA Cup			League Cup			FL Trophy			TOTALS		
	App	Sub	Gls	App	Sub	Gls	App	Sub	Gls	App	Sub	Gls	App	Sub	Gls
2009-10	18	0	0	2	0	0	0	0	0	0	0	0	20	0	0
2010-11	40	0	1	2	0	0	1	0	0	1	0	0	44	0	1
TOTALS	58	0	1	4	0	0	1	0	0	1	0	0	64	0	1

WHITEHOUSE, Elliott

Born	27/10/1993, Worksop
Signed	20/10/2016 (age 22) from Nuneaton Town to the end of 2017-18 season (DC)
First appearance	Eastleigh (H), National League, 22/10/2016
Final appearance	Southport (A), National League, 29/4/2017
Released/sold	

Career: *Sheffield United (Y), 2012 Sheffield United (Sep 2013 York City - loan, Mar 2014 Alfreton Town - loan), Jul 2014 Notts County (Jan 2015 Nuneaton Town - loan), May 2015 FC Halifax Town, Sep 2015 Nuneaton Town,* **Oct 2016 LINCOLN CITY**.

Attacking midfielder signed from Nuneaton for an undisclosed fee. Reportedly turned down more lucrative offers from other clubs including National League rivals Eastleigh to sign for the Imps. Shared a central midfield role with Alan Power, but scored some useful goals despite his limited number of appearances. Enjoyed a good start in football, and was captain of Sheffield United's youth team when they lost to Manchester United in the 2010-11 FA Youth Cup final. Made his debut for the England C team in a 4-3 defeat to Slovakia on 5 June 2016. Was one of four City players called up for the England C game against Estonia on 15 November 2016, scoring England's opening goal in a 2-1 win.

Lincoln City Playing Record - Conference Only

	League			FA Cup			FA Trophy			TOTALS			Lincolnshire Cup		
	App	Sub	Gls	App	Sub	Gls	App	Sub	Gls	App	Sub	Gls	App	Sub	Gls
2016-17	14	14	4	0	0	0	5	1	2	19	15	6	0	0	0
TOTALS	14	14	4	0	0	0	5	1	2	19	15	6	0	0	0

WILDIN, Courtney

Born	30/3/1996, Crewe
Signed	16/2/2016 (age 19) from Sheffield Wednesday on a one-month loan (CM)
First appearance	Southport (H), National League, 20/2/2016
Final appearance	Kidderminster Harriers (H), National League, 19/3/2016
Released/sold	N/A

Career: *Coventry City (Y), Highfield Rangers (Y), 2011 Aston Villa (Y), Aug 2015 Sheffield Wednesday, (Jan 2016 Gainsborough Trinity - loan,* **Feb 2016 LINCOLN CITY - loan**), *May 2016 Boston United (Dec 2016 Hednesford Town - loan, Jan 2017 Corby Town - loan), May 2017 Nuneaton Town.*

Young left-back signed initially on a one-month loan, which was extended to the end of the 2015-16 season on 15 March. Hardly had a look-in at Sincil Bank, leaving fans to wonder why he was signed in the first place. Released by Wednesday on his return and joined Boston. Had the unusual experience of signing for Nuneaton on the same day as his brother Luther. Made his full international debut for Antigua and Barbuda against Puerto Rico on 4 June 2016.

Lincoln City Playing Record - Conference Only

	League			FA Cup			FA Trophy			TOTALS			Lincolnshire Cup		
	App	Sub	Gls	App	Sub	Gls	App	Sub	Gls	App	Sub	Gls	App	Sub	Gls
2015-16	1	3	0	0	0	0	0	0	0	1	3	0	0	0	0
TOTALS	1	3	0	0	0	0	0	0	0	1	3	0	0	0	0

WILLIAMS, Robbie

Born	6/7/1987, Blackpool
Signed	1/1/2012 (age 24) from AFC Telford United on loan to the end of the season *(DH)*
First appearance	Grimsby Town (A), Conference Premier, 1/1/2012
Final appearance	Fleetwood Town (A), Conference Premier, 13/4/2012
Released/sold	N/A

Career: *Wren Rovers, 2005 The New Saints (Y), 2006 The New Saints (Nov 2006 Newtown - loan, Nov 2008 Caersws - loan), Jul 2009 Altrincham, Jun 2011 AFC Telford United (Sep 2011 Altrincham - loan,* **Jan 2012 LINCOLN CITY - loan***), Aug 2012 Hyde, Jan 2013 Colwyn Bay, Mar 2013 Hyde, Jun 2013 Barrow, Jun 2015 Kendal Town, Jan 2016 Newtown, May 2016 retired.*

Defender brought in on loan in January 2012 until the end of the season with a view to a permanent transfer. Failed to earn a deal, not helped by the fact that City lost six of his first ten games before he lost his place in the side to new signing Tom Miller. Returned to Telford once the loan expired. Had more success in Welsh football, winning the league and cup double in 2006-07 with TNS and appearing in the Champions League qualifiers in 2006-07 and 2007-08. Also won 3 caps for the Welsh U23 non-league side. Now works for Manchester City's academy.

Lincoln City Playing Record - Conference Only

	League			FA Cup			FA Trophy			TOTALS			Lincolnshire Cup		
	App	Sub	Gls	App	Sub	Gls	App	Sub	Gls	App	Sub	Gls	App	Sub	Gls
2011-12	10	1	0	0	0	0	0	0	0	10	1	0	0	0	0
TOTALS	10	1	0	0	0	0	0	0	0	10	1	0	0	0	0

WOOD, Bradley

Born	2/9/1991, Leicester
Signed	1/6/2015 (age 23) from Alfreton Town on a two-year deal *(CM)*
First appearance	Cheltenham Town (H), National League, 8/8/2015
Final appearance	Macclesfield Town (H), National League, 22/4/2017
Released/sold	

Career: *2007 Grimsby Town (Y), Oct 2009 Grimsby Town, May 2013 Alfreton Town,* **Jun 2015 LINCOLN CITY.**

Very experienced young right back who already had well over 200 first team appearances to his name by the time he joined City in June 2015. One of the best players to appear for the Imps since their Football League days, Bradley Wood has proved to be a tenacious defender with a penchant for attacking down the flanks. Quickly became popular with the fans as City had an excellent first half to the 2015-16 season, and was voted both *Player of the Season* and *Away Player of the Season* in April. Was used intermittently in central midfield at the start of the 2016-17 season, and played a key role as City stormed to the National League championship. Unfortunately blotted his copy book with an unfortunate drink-driving conviction and slipped out of favour in the closing stages of the championship season. Won 1 England C cap v Latvia in September 2013.

Lincoln City Playing Record - Conference Only

	League			FA Cup			FA Trophy			TOTALS			Lincolnshire Cup		
	App	Sub	Gls	App	Sub	Gls	App	Sub	Gls	App	Sub	Gls	App	Sub	Gls
2015-16	39	1	1	3	0	0	1	0	0	43	1	1	2	0	0
2016-17	32	2	2	9	0	0	4	2	0	45	4	2	2	0	0
TOTALS	71	3	3	12	0	0	5	2	0	88	5	3	4	0	0

WOODYARD, Alex

Born	3/5/1993, Gravesend
Signed	11/6/2016 (age 23) from Braintree Town on a one-year deal (DC)
First appearance	Woking (A), National League, 6/8/2016
Final appearance	Southport (A), National League, 29/4/2017
Released/sold	

Career: *Charlton Athletic (Y), 2009 Southend United (Y), 2011 Southend United (Sep 2011 Farnborough - loan, Mar 2013 Braintree Town - loan), Aug 2013 Dartford, Jun 2014 Concord Rangers, Aug 2015 Braintree Town,* **Jun 2016 LINCOLN CITY.**

England C captain Alex Woodyard was new manager Danny Cowley's first signing, bringing the talented midfielder with him from Braintree. Signing a one-year deal with an option for a further year, the defensive midfielder had just been named *FieldTurf Young Player of the Season* for 2015-16 after playing an integral role in Braintree's run to the National League play-offs. Turned down better financial offers from other National League clubs in order to continue his relationship with Cowley, having also played for him at Concord Rangers. Played a significant role in City's fantastic 2016-17 season, signing a further one-year contract on 13 March 2017 despite a lot of attention from Football League clubs, and was deservedly voted *Player of the Season* by the supporters for his inspirational performances. Already had 3 England C caps to his name when he joined the Imps (Cyprus U21 in February 2015, Ukraine U20 in March 2016, and Slovakia U21 in June 2016). Was one of four City players called up for the England C game against Estonia on 15 November 2016, the others being Sean Raggett, Elliott Whitehouse and Sam Habergham. Capped another fine season on 17 May 2017 by being named the *Mark Harrod Player of the Year* at the National Game Awards at Stamford Bridge to add to the *Young Player* award he won twelve months ago.

Lincoln City Playing Record - Conference Only

	League			FA Cup			FA Trophy			TOTALS			Lincolnshire Cup		
	App	Sub	Gls	App	Sub	Gls	App	Sub	Gls	App	Sub	Gls	App	Sub	Gls
2016-17	44	1	1	9	0	0	1	2	0	54	3	1	2	0	0
TOTALS	44	1	1	9	0	0	1	2	0	54	3	1	2	0	0

WOOTTON, Kyle

Born	11/10/1996, Kidderminster
Signed	30/10/2015 (age 19) from Scunthorpe United on a one-month loan (CM)
First appearance	Bromley (H), National League, 31/10/2015
Final appearance	Boreham Wood (A), National League, 25/11/2015
Released/sold	N/A

Career: *2007 Scunthorpe United (Y), Jan 2015 Scunthorpe United (**Oct 2015 LINCOLN CITY - loan**, Sep 2016 North Ferriby United - loan, Jan 2017 Cheltenham Town - loan).*

Tall striker signed on a month's youth loan. Scored on his only start in the game at Aldershot but returned to Scunthorpe at the end of the loan period.

Lincoln City Playing Record - Conference Only

	League			FA Cup			FA Trophy			TOTALS			Lincolnshire Cup		
	App	Sub	Gls	App	Sub	Gls	App	Sub	Gls	App	Sub	Gls	App	Sub	Gls
2015-16	1	4	1	0	0	0	0	0	0	1	4	1	0	0	0
TOTALS	1	4	1	0	0	0	0	0	0	1	4	1	0	0	0

WRIGHT, Nick

Born	25/11/1987, Birmingham
Signed	1/7/2013 (age 25) from Mansfield Town on a one-year deal (GS)
First appearance	Woking (A), Conference Premier, 10/8/2013
Final appearance	North Ferriby United (H), FA Trophy 3, 11/1/2014
Released/sold	8/5/2014 and joined Worcester City (GS)

*Career: Birmingham City (Y), 2005 Birmingham City (Jan 2006 Tamworth - loan, Oct 2006 Bristol City - loan, Nov 2006 Northampton Town - loan, Apr 2007 Ashford Town (Kent) - loan), Aug 2007 Halesowen Town - non-contract, Oct 2007 Tamworth, Jul 2010 Kidderminster Harriers, Jun 2012 Mansfield Town, **Jul 2013 LINCOLN CITY** (Mar 2014 Kidderminster Harriers), Aug 2014 Worcester City, Mar 2015 Gloucester City, Aug 2015 Corby Town - non-contract, Aug 2015 Kettering Town, Sep 2015 Rushall Olympic, Dec 2015 Alvechurch, May 2016 released.*

Rangy striker who signed a one-year deal in July 2013, revealing he had turned down offers to play in India. Hit a hat-trick in a pre-season friendly against Harrogate two weeks after signing, but things were all downhill after that. Had a disappointing scoring record at Lincoln and became known for a profligate penalty against Southport. Struggled to win a regular place in the side and joined Kidderminster Harriers on 10 March 2014 on loan until his contract ran out at the end of the season. Played for a large number of non-league clubs in the Midlands as his career wound down, appearing for eight clubs in two seasons. Won 3 caps for England C in 2008 and 2009, scoring no goals.

Lincoln City Playing Record - Conference Only

	League			FA Cup			FA Trophy			TOTALS			Lincolnshire Cup		
	App	Sub	Gls	App	Sub	Gls	App	Sub	Gls	App	Sub	Gls	App	Sub	Gls
2013-14	8	11	2	2	2	0	1	2	0	11	15	2	1	1	0
TOTALS	8	11	2	2	2	0	1	2	0	11	15	2	1	1	0

YUSSUF, Adi

Born	20/2/1992, Zanzibar
Signed	23/5/2013 (age 21) from Burton Albion on a one-year deal (GS)
First appearance	Salisbury City (H), Conference Premier, 7/9/2013
Final appearance	Aldershot Town (H), Conference Premier, 12/10/2013
Released/sold	8/5/2014 and joined Oxford City (GS)

*Career: 2008 Leicester City (Y) (Jan 2011 Tamworth - loan), Aug 2011 Burton Albion, **May 2013 LINCOLN CITY** (Nov 2013 Gainsborough Trinity - loan, Jan 2014 Harrogate Town - loan, Feb 2014 Histon - loan), Aug 2014 Oxford City, Jun 2015 Mansfield Town (Aug 2016 Crawley Town - loan), Jan 2017 Grimsby Town.*

Signed on a one-year deal on the same day as Jon Nolan. Had struggled with fitness and injuries in his career, and City knew they were taking a gamble which unfortunately did not come off. Injured a hamstring during a pre-season County Cup match against Boston United and never really made it back. Had numerous loan spells to try to build some match fitness but he was released at the end of his contract with very few appearances to his name. Finally started to realise his potential after leaving the Imps. Joined Oxford City and scored 27 goals in 2014-15, earning a transfer to League Two Mansfield Town. He made the headlines for the wrong reasons on 11 March 2016 when he was given a five-match ban for urinating behind a stand during a match at Plymouth whilst warming up as a substitute.

Lincoln City Playing Record - Conference Only

	League			FA Cup			FA Trophy			TOTALS			Lincolnshire Cup		
	App	Sub	Gls	App	Sub	Gls	App	Sub	Gls	App	Sub	Gls	App	Sub	Gls
2013-14	1	1	0	0	0	0	0	0	0	1	1	0	1	0	0
TOTALS	1	1	0	0	0	0	0	0	0	1	1	0	1	0	0

Appearances 2011-2017

#	Name	League Apps	League Subs	League Goals	FA Cup Apps	FA Cup Subs	FA Cup Goals	FA Trophy Apps	FA Trophy Subs	FA Trophy Goals	Totals Apps	Totals Subs	Totals Goals	Totals Apps	Totals Goals
1	Alan POWER	191	31	27	24	2	5	10	3	4	225	36	36	261	36
2	Paul FARMAN	195	1	0	25	0	0	11	0	0	231	1	0	232	0
3	Tom MILLER	109	2	11	13	0	0	5	0	0	127	2	11	129	11
4	Matt RHEAD	81	5	34	12	0	3	2	3	0	95	8	37	103	37
	Jake SHERIDAN	62	27	2	6	2	1	2	4	1	70	33	4	103	4
6	Nat BROWN (NL only)	92	0	2	7	0	0	3	0	0	102	0	2	102	2
7	Luke WATERFALL	79	1	13	12	0	0	2	1	0	93	2	13	95	13
8	Bradley WOOD	71	3	3	12	0	0	5	2	0	88	5	3	93	3
	Ben TOMLINSON	78	7	32	6	0	2	2	0	0	86	7	34	93	34
10	Jack MULDOON	55	16	12	6	6	0	4	1	1	65	23	13	88	13
	Sean NEWTON	77	0	6	7	0	4	4	0	0	88	0	10	88	10
	Terry HAWKRIDGE	58	12	4	11	1	1	5	1	2	74	14	7	88	7
13	Jon NOLAN	62	11	6	5	0	0	3	0	0	70	11	6	81	6
14	Conner ROBINSON	27	43	8	3	4	1	2	1	0	32	48	9	80	9
15	Jamie TAYLOR	43	21	17	6	1	3	2	0	2	51	22	22	73	22
16	Andrew BOYCE	60	0	5	10	0	1	0	0	0	70	0	6	70	6
17	John NUTTER	58	0	3	3	2	0	3	0	0	64	2	3	66	3
18	Lee BEEVERS (NL only)	57	2	0	5	0	0	0	0	0	62	2	0	64	0
19	Mamadou FOFANA	44	5	1	6	1	0	3	1	1	53	7	2	60	2
20	Dan GRAY	40	12	1	5	0	0	0	1	0	45	13	1	58	1
21	Alex WOODYARD	44	1	1	9	0	0	1	2	0	54	3	1	57	1
22	Sam HABERGHAM	43	0	3	9	0	0	4	0	1	56	0	4	56	4
23	Nathan ARNOLD	43	2	12	7	0	1	1	1	0	51	3	13	54	13
24	Sean RAGGETT	41	0	5	8	0	2	2	1	1	51	1	8	52	8
25	Nicky NICOLAU	32	13	4	3	1	0	0	2	0	35	16	4	51	4
26	Todd JORDAN	40	6	1	2	0	0	2	0	0	44	6	1	50	1
27	Callum HOWE	31	4	0	3	0	0	6	0	0	40	4	0	44	0
	Hamza BENCHERIF (NL only)	41	0	6	2	0	0	1	0	0	44	0	6	44	6
	Delano SAM-YORKE	33	9	8	0	2	3	0	0	0	33	11	11	44	11
30	Jordan BURROW	28	11	10	3	0	0	1	0	0	32	11	10	43	10
	Vadaine OLIVER	22	15	11	0	5	2	0	1	0	22	21	13	43	13
32	Joe ANYON (NL only)	38	0	0	1	0	0	3	0	0	42	0	0	42	0
33	Arnaud MENDY	33	4	1	3	0	0	0	0	0	36	4	1	40	1
34	Josh GOWLING (NL only)	36	1	0	0	0	0	1	1	0	37	2	0	39	0
35	Chris BUSH	31	3	2	3	0	0	1	0	0	35	3	2	38	2
	Jake CAPRICE	34	3	0	0	0	0	1	0	0	35	3	0	38	0
37	Luke FOSTER (NL only)	25	6	1	2	1	0	3	0	1	30	7	2	37	2
	Adam SMITH	19	11	1	6	0	1	1	0	0	26	11	2	37	2
39	Marcus MARSHALL (L)	24	8	2	2	0	0	1	0	0	27	8	2	35	2
40	Bohan DIXON	8	21	3	1	2	1	2	0	0	11	23	4	34	4
	Colin LARKIN	13	16	8	0	4	0	1	0	0	14	20	8	34	8
	Elliott WHITEHOUSE	14	14	4	0	0	0	5	1	2	19	15	6	34	6
43	Jean-Francois CHRISTOPHE	22	5	2	2	0	0	3	0	0	27	5	2	32	2
44	Nick TOWNSEND (L)	31	0	0	0	0	0	0	0	0	31	0	0	31	0
	Adam MARRIOTT	8	17	4	0	2	0	3	1	0	11	20	4	31	4
46	Paul ROBSON	26	1	0	0	1	0	2	0	0	28	2	0	30	0
	Simon RUSSELL	17	9	1	1	0	0	2	1	0	20	10	1	30	1
	Harry ANDERSON (L)	14	12	6	3	1	0	0	0	0	17	13	6	30	6
49	Matt SPARROW	22	4	0	1	2	0	0	0	0	23	6	0	29	0
	Alex SIMMONS	6	21	2	0	0	0	1	1	0	7	22	2	29	2
	Charlee ADAMS (L)	28	0	2	0	0	0	1	0	0	29	0	2	29	2
	Tyrone THOMPSON	26	0	1	0	0	0	3	0	0	29	0	1	29	1
53	Craig STANLEY	26	2	2	0	0	0	0	0	0	26	2	2	28	2
	Sam SMITH	18	6	7	2	0	2	2	0	0	22	6	9	28	9
55	Tony SINCLAIR	23	1	0	2	0	0	1	0	0	26	1	0	27	0
56	Nick WRIGHT	8	11	2	2	2	0	1	2	0	11	15	2	26	2
	Kyle PERRY	14	10	3	0	2	0	0	0	0	14	12	3	26	3
58	Tony DIAGNE	22	3	2	0	0	0	0	0	0	22	3	2	25	2
	Danny ROWE	15	8	3	0	0	0	0	2	0	15	10	3	25	3
60	Greg TEMPEST	17	3	0	1	2	0	1	0	0	19	5	0	24	0
	Gary MILLS	17	1	0	6	0	0	0	0	0	23	1	0	24	0
62	Liam HEARN	13	7	10	1	2	1	0	0	0	14	9	11	23	11
	Jamie McCOMBE (NL only)	11	4	2	1	3	0	4	0	0	16	7	2	23	2
64	Kegan EVERINGTON	6	15	1	0	0	0	1	0	0	7	15	1	22	1
	Theo ROBINSON	12	2	2	6	1	7	0	1	0	18	4	9	22	9

	League			FA Cup			FA Trophy			Totals			Totals	
	Apps	Subs	Goals	Apps	Subs	Goals	Apps	Subs	Goals	Apps	Subs	Goals	Apps	Goals
66 Thierry AUDEL (L)	17	0	3	3	0	0	0	1	0	20	1	3	21	3
Peter BORE	16	2	2	1	1	0	1	0	0	18	3	2	21	2
68 Peter GILBERT	14	0	0	5	0	0	1	0	0	20	0	0	20	0
69 Gavin McCALLUM (NL only)	17	1	3	1	0	0	0	0	0	18	1	3	19	3
Sean LONG (L)	12	2	0	0	2	0	3	0	0	15	4	0	19	0
71 Conal PLATT	14	1	2	0	0	0	3	0	1	17	1	3	18	3
72 Ali FUSEINI (NL only)	15	2	1	0	0	0	0	0	0	15	2	1	17	1
Francis LAURENT	5	9	1	0	2	0	1	0	0	6	11	1	17	1
Josh GINNELLY (L)	7	6	0	0	0	0	2	2	0	9	8	0	17	0
Billy KNOTT (L)	8	6	1	0	0	0	2	1	0	10	7	1	17	1
76 Robbie McDAID (L)	3	13	4	0	0	0	0	0	0	3	13	4	16	4
77 Paul TURNBULL (L)	14	1	0	0	0	0	0	0	0	14	1	0	15	0
Scott GARNER (L)	12	2	0	0	0	0	1	0	0	13	2	0	15	0
79 Karl LEDSHAM	7	6	1	0	1	0	0	0	0	7	7	1	14	1
Waide FAIRHURST	5	7	2	0	1	0	0	1	0	5	9	2	14	2
Jefferson LOUIS	14	0	6	0	0	0	0	0	0	14	0	6	14	6
82 George MARIS (L)	6	7	2	0	0	0	0	0	0	6	7	2	13	2
Jake JONES (L)	7	6	0	0	0	0	0	0	0	7	6	0	13	0
Bradley BARRACLOUGH	4	9	0	0	0	0	0	0	0	4	9	0	13	0
Richard PACQUETTE	9	4	3	0	0	0	0	0	0	9	4	3	13	3
Adam WATTS (NL only)	11	0	0	2	0	0	0	0	0	13	0	0	13	0
Lee ANGOL (L)	11	0	5	0	0	0	2	0	1	13	0	6	13	6
88 James CATON (L)	8	4	3	0	0	0	0	0	0	8	4	3	12	3
Elliot HODGE	5	6	0	0	1	0	0	0	0	5	7	0	12	0
Craig HOBSON (L)	5	7	1	0	0	0	0	0	0	5	7	1	12	1
Danny LLOYD	3	9	3	0	0	0	0	0	0	3	9	3	12	3
Mitchell NELSON (L)	9	1	0	2	0	0	0	0	0	11	1	0	12	0
Josh O'KEEFE (NL only)	4	6	1	2	0	0	0	0	0	6	6	1	12	1
94 Jordan CRANSTON (L)	11	0	0	0	0	0	0	0	0	11	0	0	11	0
Robbie WILLIAMS (L)	10	1	0	0	0	0	0	0	0	10	1	0	11	0
Jonny MARGETTS	7	3	5	0	1	0	0	0	0	7	4	5	11	5
97 Marlon JACKSON (L)	4	0	0	4	0	0	2	0	1	10	0	1	10	1
David MORGAN (L)	6	2	0	0	1	0	1	0	0	7	3	0	10	0
Richard HINDS	9	0	1	0	0	0	1	0	0	10	0	1	10	1
100 David PREECE	8	1	0	0	0	0	0	0	0	8	1	0	9	0
Danny HONE (NL only)	9	0	1	0	0	0	0	0	0	9	0	1	9	1
102 Mark McCAMMON	3	5	2	0	0	0	0	0	0	3	5	2	8	2
Macauley BONNE (L)	5	3	1	0	0	0	0	0	0	5	3	1	8	1
Joe WARD (L)	0	2	0	0	2	0	4	0	3	4	4	3	8	3
105 Jordan KEANE (L)	7	0	0	0	0	0	0	0	0	7	0	0	7	0
Kris BRIGHT	7	0	2	0	0	0	0	0	0	7	0	2	7	2
Graham HUTCHISON (L)	7	0	0	0	0	0	0	0	0	7	0	0	7	0
Karlton WATSON	3	2	0	0	0	0	2	0	0	5	2	0	7	0
109 Tom ANDERSON (L)	6	0	1	0	0	0	0	0	0	6	0	1	6	1
Kieran WALLACE (L)	6	0	0	0	0	0	0	0	0	6	0	0	6	0
John MARSDEN (L)	2	4	0	0	0	0	0	0	0	2	4	0	6	0
Tyrell WAITE	2	4	0	0	0	0	0	0	0	2	4	0	6	0
Mitchell AUSTIN (L)	4	2	0	0	0	0	0	0	0	4	2	0	6	0
Koby ARTHUR (L)	2	4	0	0	0	0	0	0	0	2	4	0	6	0
Nialle RODNEY	2	4	0	0	0	0	0	0	0	2	4	0	6	0
Luke MEDLEY (L)	0	6	0	0	0	0	0	0	0	0	6	0	6	0
117 Kyle WOOTTON (L)	1	4	1	0	0	0	0	0	0	1	4	1	5	1
Chris SHARP (L)	3	0	1	0	0	0	2	0	1	5	0	2	5	2
Luke DALEY	4	1	0	0	0	0	0	0	0	4	1	0	5	0
Louis ALMOND (L)	3	2	1	0	0	0	0	0	0	3	2	1	5	1
Tom CHAMPION (L)	3	2	0	0	0	0	0	0	0	3	2	0	5	0
Dayle SOUTHWELL (L)	2	0	0	0	1	0	1	1	1	3	2	1	5	1
123 Patrick BROUGH (L)	4	0	0	0	0	0	0	0	0	4	0	0	4	0
Courtney WILDIN (L)	1	3	0	0	0	0	0	0	0	1	3	0	4	0
Nathan BLISSETT (L)	1	2	0	0	0	0	1	0	0	2	2	0	4	0
Gomez DALI	1	3	0	0	0	0	0	0	0	1	3	0	4	0
127 Sahr KABBA	0	2	0	0	1	0	0	0	0	0	3	0	3	0
Rob DUFFY	3	0	0	0	0	0	0	0	0	3	0	0	3	0
Jake THOMSON (L)	3	0	0	0	0	0	0	0	0	3	0	0	3	0
Aristide BASSELE (L)	1	1	0	0	0	0	1	0	0	2	1	0	3	0
Ross ETHERIDGE (L)	2	0	0	0	0	0	1	0	0	3	0	0	3	0

		League			FA Cup			FA Trophy			Totals			Totals	
		Apps	Subs	Goals	Apps	Subs	Goals	Apps	Subs	Goals	Apps	Subs	Goals	Apps	Goals
132	Craig REID	2	0	0	0	0	0	0	0	0	2	0	0	2	0
	Aidan GRANT	2	0	0	0	0	0	0	0	0	2	0	0	2	0
	Adi YUSSUF	1	1	0	0	0	0	0	0	0	1	1	0	2	0
	Karl CUNNINGHAM	2	0	0	0	0	0	0	0	0	2	0	0	2	0
	Jordan THOMAS	0	1	0	0	0	0	0	1	0	0	2	0	2	0
	Nick DRAPER	0	0	0	1	1	0	0	0	0	1	1	0	2	0
	Matty PEARSON (L)	0	0	0	0	0	0	2	0	0	2	0	0	2	0
	Riccardo CALDER (L)	1	0	0	0	0	0	1	0	0	2	0	0	2	0
140	Tom DAVIES (L)	0	1	0	0	0	0	0	0	0	0	1	0	1	0
	Adam BOYD	0	0	0	0	0	0	0	1	0	0	1	0	1	0
	Jean ARNAUD	0	1	0	0	0	0	0	0	0	0	1	0	1	0
	Jason BEARDSLEY	0	1	0	0	0	0	0	0	0	0	1	0	1	0
	Frazer COBB	0	1	0	0	0	0	0	0	0	0	1	0	1	0
	Reece THOMPSON	0	0	0	0	0	0	0	1	0	0	1	0	1	0
	Curtis THOMPSON (L)	0	1	0	0	0	0	0	0	0	0	1	0	1	0
	Taylor MILES	0	1	0	0	0	0	0	0	0	0	1	0	1	0

#	Player	League Apps	League Subs	League Goals	FA Cup Apps	FA Cup Subs	FA Cup Goals	FA Trophy Apps	FA Trophy Subs	FA Trophy Goals	Totals Apps	Totals Subs	Totals Goals	Totals Apps	Totals Goals
1	Matt RHEAD	81	5	34	12	0	3	2	3	0	95	8	37	103	37
2	Alan POWER	191	31	27	24	2	5	10	3	4	225	36	36	261	36
3	Ben TOMLINSON	78	7	32	6	0	2	2	0	0	86	7	34	93	34
4	Jamie TAYLOR	43	21	17	6	1	3	2	0	2	51	22	22	73	22
5	Jack MULDOON	55	16	12	6	6	0	4	1	1	65	23	13	88	13
	Luke WATERFALL	79	1	13	12	0	0	2	1	0	93	2	13	95	13
	Vadaine OLIVER	22	15	11	0	5	2	0	1	0	22	21	13	43	13
	Nathan ARNOLD	43	2	12	7	0	1	1	1	0	51	3	13	54	13
9	Liam HEARN	13	7	10	1	2	1	0	0	0	14	9	11	23	11
	Delano SAM-YORKE	33	9	8	0	2	3	0	0	0	33	11	11	44	11
	Tom MILLER	109	2	11	13	0	0	5	0	0	127	2	11	129	11
12	Jordan BURROW	28	11	10	3	0	0	1	0	0	32	11	10	43	10
	Sean NEWTON	77	0	6	7	0	4	4	0	0	88	0	10	88	10
14	Conner ROBINSON	27	43	8	3	4	1	2	1	0	32	48	9	80	9
	Sam SMITH	18	6	7	2	0	2	2	0	0	22	6	9	28	9
	Theo ROBINSON	12	2	2	6	1	7	0	1	0	18	4	9	22	9
17	Colin LARKIN	13	16	8	0	4	0	1	0	0	14	20	8	34	8
	Sean RAGGETT	41	0	5	8	0	2	2	1	1	51	1	8	52	8
19	Terry HAWKRIDGE	58	12	4	11	1	1	5	1	2	74	14	7	88	7
20	Jon NOLAN	62	11	6	5	0	0	3	0	0	70	11	6	81	6
	Hamza BENCHERIF (NL only)	41	0	6	2	0	0	1	0	0	44	0	6	44	6
	Andrew BOYCE	60	0	5	10	0	1	0	0	0	70	0	6	70	6
	Jefferson LOUIS	14	0	6	0	0	0	0	0	0	14	0	6	14	6
	Elliott WHITEHOUSE	14	14	4	0	0	0	5	1	2	19	15	6	34	6
	Harry ANDERSON (L)	14	12	6	3	1	0	0	0	0	17	13	6	30	6
	Lee ANGOL (L)	11	0	5	0	0	0	2	0	1	13	0	6	13	6
27	Jonny MARGETTS	7	3	5	0	1	0	0	0	0	7	4	5	11	5
28	Robbie McDAID (L)	3	13	4	0	0	0	0	0	0	3	13	4	16	4
	Jake SHERIDAN	62	27	2	6	2	1	2	4	1	70	33	4	103	4
	Bohan DIXON	8	21	3	1	2	1	2	0	0	11	23	4	34	4
	Nicky NICOLAU	32	13	4	3	1	0	0	2	0	35	16	4	51	4
	Sam HABERGHAM	43	0	3	9	0	0	4	0	1	56	0	4	56	4
	Adam MARRIOTT	8	17	4	0	2	0	3	1	0	11	20	4	31	4
34	Bradley WOOD	71	3	3	12	0	0	5	2	0	88	5	3	93	3
	James CATON (L)	8	4	3	0	0	0	0	0	0	8	4	3	12	3
	Thierry AUDEL (L)	17	0	3	3	0	0	0	1	0	20	1	3	21	3
	Danny ROWE	15	8	3	0	0	0	0	2	0	15	10	3	25	3
	Conal PLATT	14	1	2	0	0	0	3	0	1	17	1	3	18	3
	John NUTTER	58	0	3	3	2	0	3	0	0	64	2	3	66	3
	Kyle PERRY	14	10	3	0	2	0	0	0	0	14	12	3	26	3
	Gavin McCALLUM (NL only)	17	1	3	1	0	0	0	0	0	18	1	3	19	3
	Richard PACQUETTE	9	4	3	0	0	0	0	0	0	9	4	3	13	3
	Danny LLOYD	3	9	3	0	0	0	0	0	0	3	9	3	12	3
	Joe WARD (L)	0	2	0	0	2	0	4	0	3	4	4	3	8	3
45	Chris BUSH	31	3	2	3	0	0	1	0	0	35	3	2	38	2
	Craig STANLEY	26	2	2	0	0	0	0	0	0	26	2	2	28	2
	Alex SIMMONS	6	21	2	0	0	0	1	1	0	7	22	2	29	2
	George MARIS (L)	6	7	2	0	0	0	0	0	0	6	7	2	13	2
	Jamie McCOMBE (NL only)	11	4	2	1	3	0	4	0	0	16	7	2	23	2
	Nat BROWN (NL only)	92	0	2	7	0	0	3	0	0	102	0	2	102	2
	Marcus MARSHALL (L)	24	8	2	2	0	0	1	0	0	27	8	2	35	2
	Tony DIAGNE	22	3	2	0	0	0	0	0	0	22	3	2	25	2
	Charlee ADAMS (L)	28	0	2	0	0	0	1	0	0	29	0	2	29	2
	Luke FOSTER (NL only)	25	6	1	2	1	0	3	0	1	30	7	2	37	2
	Mamadou FOFANA	44	5	1	6	1	0	3	1	1	53	7	2	60	2
	Nick WRIGHT	8	11	2	2	2	0	1	2	0	11	15	2	26	2
	Waide FAIRHURST	5	7	2	0	1	0	0	1	0	5	9	2	14	2
	Kris BRIGHT	7	0	2	0	0	0	0	0	0	7	0	2	7	2
	Chris SHARP (L)	3	0	1	0	0	0	2	0	1	5	0	2	5	2
	Adam SMITH	19	11	1	6	0	1	1	0	0	26	11	2	37	2
	Peter BORE	16	2	2	1	1	0	1	0	0	18	3	2	21	2
	Mark McCAMMON	3	5	2	0	0	0	0	0	0	3	5	2	8	2
	Jean-Francois CHRISTOPHE	22	5	2	2	0	0	3	0	0	27	5	2	32	2

	League			FA Cup			FA Trophy			Totals			Totals	
	Apps	Subs	Goals	Apps	Subs	Goals	Apps	Subs	Goals	Apps	Subs	Goals	Apps	Goals
64 Kegan EVERINGTON	6	15	1	0	0	0	1	0	0	7	15	1	22	1
Kyle WOOTTON (L)	1	4	1	0	0	0	0	0	0	1	4	1	5	1
Arnaud MENDY	33	4	1	3	0	0	0	0	0	36	4	1	40	1
Karl LEDSHAM	7	6	1	0	1	0	0	0	0	7	7	1	14	1
Tom ANDERSON (L)	6	0	1	0	0	0	0	0	0	6	0	1	6	1
Todd JORDAN	40	6	1	2	0	0	2	0	0	44	6	1	50	1
Dan GRAY	40	12	1	5	0	0	0	1	0	45	13	1	58	1
Marlon JACKSON (L)	4	0	0	4	0	0	2	0	1	10	0	1	10	1
Craig HOBSON (L)	5	7	1	0	0	0	0	0	0	5	7	1	12	1
Tyrone THOMPSON	26	0	1	0	0	0	3	0	0	29	0	1	29	1
Simon RUSSELL	17	9	1	1	0	0	2	1	0	20	10	1	30	1
Ali FUSEINI (NL only)	15	2	1	0	0	0	0	0	0	15	2	1	17	1
Francis LAURENT	5	9	1	0	2	0	1	0	0	6	11	1	17	1
Josh O'KEEFE (NL only)	4	6	1	2	0	0	0	0	0	6	6	1	12	1
Danny HONE (NL only)	9	0	1	0	0	0	0	0	0	9	0	1	9	1
Richard HINDS	9	0	1	0	0	0	1	0	0	10	0	1	10	1
Louis ALMOND (L)	3	2	1	0	0	0	0	0	0	3	2	1	5	1
Alex WOODYARD	44	1	1	9	0	0	1	2	0	54	3	1	57	1
Billy KNOTT (L)	8	6	1	0	0	0	2	1	0	10	7	1	17	1
Macauley BONNE (L)	5	3	1	0	0	0	0	0	0	5	3	1	8	1
Dayle SOUTHWELL (L)	2	0	0	0	1	0	1	1	1	3	2	1	5	1
85 Paul FARMAN	195	1	0	25	0	0	11	0	0	231	1	0	232	0
Lee BEEVERS (NL only)	57	2	0	5	0	0	0	0	0	62	2	0	64	0
Callum HOWE	31	4	0	3	0	0	6	0	0	40	4	0	44	0
Matt SPARROW	22	4	0	1	2	0	0	0	0	23	6	0	29	0
Greg TEMPEST	17	3	0	1	2	0	1	0	0	19	5	0	24	0
Elliot HODGE	5	6	0	0	1	0	0	0	0	5	7	0	12	0
Patrick BROUGH (L)	4	0	0	0	0	0	0	0	0	4	0	0	4	0
Courtney WILDIN (L)	1	3	0	0	0	0	0	0	0	1	3	0	4	0
Nathan BLISSETT (L)	1	2	0	0	0	0	1	0	0	2	2	0	4	0
Craig REID	2	0	0	0	0	0	0	0	0	2	0	0	2	0
Aidan GRANT	2	0	0	0	0	0	0	0	0	2	0	0	2	0
Jake CAPRICE	34	3	0	0	0	0	1	0	0	35	3	0	38	0
Nick TOWNSEND (L)	31	0	0	0	0	0	0	0	0	31	0	0	31	0
Jordan CRANSTON (L)	11	0	0	0	0	0	0	0	0	11	0	0	11	0
Jordan KEANE (L)	7	0	0	0	0	0	0	0	0	7	0	0	7	0
Kieran WALLACE (L)	6	0	0	0	0	0	0	0	0	6	0	0	6	0
John MARSDEN (L)	2	4	0	0	0	0	0	0	0	2	4	0	6	0
Tyrell WAITE	2	4	0	0	0	0	0	0	0	2	4	0	6	0
Sahr KABBA	0	2	0	0	1	0	0	0	0	0	3	0	3	0
Tom DAVIES (L)	0	1	0	0	0	0	0	0	0	0	1	0	1	0
Mitchell AUSTIN (L)	4	2	0	0	0	0	0	0	0	4	2	0	6	0
Koby ARTHUR (L)	2	4	0	0	0	0	0	0	0	2	4	0	6	0
Adi YUSSUF	1	1	0	0	0	0	0	0	0	1	1	0	2	0
David PREECE	8	1	0	0	0	0	0	0	0	8	1	0	9	0
Paul TURNBULL (L)	14	1	0	0	0	0	0	0	0	14	1	0	15	0
Peter GILBERT	14	0	0	5	0	0	1	0	0	20	0	0	20	0
Scott GARNER (L)	12	2	0	0	0	0	1	0	0	13	2	0	15	0
Jake JONES (L)	7	6	0	0	0	0	0	0	0	7	6	0	13	0
Paul ROBSON	26	1	0	0	1	0	2	0	0	28	2	0	30	0
David MORGAN (L)	6	2	0	0	1	0	1	0	0	7	3	0	10	0
Graham HUTCHISON (L)	7	0	0	0	0	0	0	0	0	7	0	0	7	0
Luke DALEY	4	1	0	0	0	0	0	0	0	4	1	0	5	0
Gomez DALI	1	3	0	0	0	0	0	0	0	1	3	0	4	0
Rob DUFFY	3	0	0	0	0	0	0	0	0	3	0	0	3	0
Jake THOMSON (L)	3	0	0	0	0	0	0	0	0	3	0	0	3	0
Aristide BASSELE (L)	1	1	0	0	0	0	1	0	0	2	1	0	3	0
Bradley BARRACLOUGH	4	9	0	0	0	0	0	0	0	4	9	0	13	0
Adam BOYD	0	0	0	0	0	0	0	1	0	0	1	0	1	0
Joe ANYON (NL only)	38	0	0	1	0	0	3	0	0	42	0	0	42	0
Josh GOWLING (NL only)	36	1	0	0	0	0	1	1	0	37	2	0	39	0
Tony SINCLAIR	23	1	0	2	0	0	1	0	0	26	1	0	27	0
Adam WATTS (NL only)	11	0	0	2	0	0	0	0	0	13	0	0	13	0
Robbie WILLIAMS (L)	10	1	0	0	0	0	0	0	0	10	1	0	11	0
Mitchell NELSON (L)	9	1	0	2	0	0	0	0	0	11	1	0	12	0
Nialle RODNEY	2	4	0	0	0	0	0	0	0	2	4	0	6	0

	League			FA Cup			FA Trophy			Totals			Totals	
	Apps	Subs	Goals	Apps	Subs	Goals	Apps	Subs	Goals	Apps	Subs	Goals	Apps	Goals
Luke MEDLEY (L)	0	6	0	0	0	0	0	0	0	0	6	0	6	0
Karlton WATSON	3	2	0	0	0	0	2	0	0	5	2	0	7	0
Karl CUNNINGHAM	2	0	0	0	0	0	0	0	0	2	0	0	2	0
Jordan THOMAS	0	1	0	0	0	0	0	1	0	0	2	0	2	0
Jean ARNAUD	0	1	0	0	0	0	0	0	0	0	1	0	1	0
Jason BEARDSLEY	0	1	0	0	0	0	0	0	0	0	1	0	1	0
Frazer COBB	0	1	0	0	0	0	0	0	0	0	1	0	1	0
Nick DRAPER	0	0	0	1	1	0	0	0	0	1	1	0	2	0
Matty PEARSON (L)	0	0	0	0	0	0	2	0	0	2	0	0	2	0
Reece THOMPSON	0	0	0	0	0	0	0	1	0	0	1	0	1	0
Gary MILLS	17	1	0	6	0	0	0	0	0	23	1	0	24	0
Curtis THOMPSON (L)	0	1	0	0	0	0	0	0	0	0	1	0	1	0
Sean LONG (L)	12	2	0	0	2	0	3	0	0	15	4	0	19	0
Josh GINNELLY (L)	7	6	0	0	0	0	2	2	0	9	8	0	17	0
Tom CHAMPION (L)	3	2	0	0	0	0	0	0	0	3	2	0	5	0
Ross ETHERIDGE (L)	2	0	0	0	0	0	1	0	0	3	0	0	3	0
Riccardo CALDER (L)	1	0	0	0	0	0	1	0	0	2	0	0	2	0
Taylor MILES	0	1	0	0	0	0	0	0	0	0	1	0	1	0

Trialists & Others

The following players all spent time at Sincil Bank but never appeared in a first class match for City (Conference / FA Cup / FA Trophy) during the Conference era. Some are trialists, others signed on a non-contract basis, and others signed on permanent contracts who failed to make the grade. The list cannot be comprehensive, as some trialists were never formally named on team sheets; for example, the two Belgian defenders who appeared in several pre-season games during 2014 remained unidentified. Furthermore, a number of players only appeared in behind-closed-doors friendlies, and were not confirmed in the public domain. The list does not include members of the Academy team used in friendlies, although those who appeared in Lincolnshire Cup games are included.

Acar, Jenk: Signed as a first-year professional in summer 2016 after coming through the City Academy. Scored two goals in the U18 Midland Youth Cup win over Shrewsbury in March 2014. Enjoyed loan spells at Spalding United (11 goals in 23 games) and Matlock Town during 2016-17, but was released at the end of the season.

Andersen, Luke: Youth team midfielder who appeared in the Lincolnshire Cup quarter-final win over Grantham Town and the friendly against Worksop in July 2016.

Armstrong-Ford, Matt: Trialist goalkeeper who linked up with City in July 2013 after leaving Hastings United. Appeared for the final 15 minutes of the pre-season defeat at Grantham, but immediately gifted the winning goal and never appeared for the Imps again. Interesting character who is a qualified zoologist, and has worked extensively as a safari guide in Africa. Returned to play for Margate for a few months in January 2015. His father Gerry Armstrong was a top tennis umpire who famously disqualified John McEnroe from the 1990 Australian Open, and Matt himself has sat as a line judge in major tournaments.

Belkouche, Zakaria: French defender who arrived at Sincil Bank on trial in July 2014. Had tried his luck in British football before, having spent a few months at Stranraer towards the end of the 2011-12 season, before returning to France with Olympique Noisy-le-Sec. Made a brief substitute appearance in the friendly win over Chesterfield but was not offered a contract. Returned to Noisy-le-Sec before moving on to US Créteil-Lusitanos.

Bannister, Phil: Striker who arrived at Lincoln on trial during the 2012 close season after a year with Blyth Spartans. Scored in a pre-season game at Worksop but did not earn a contract. Returned to his native north-east to sign for Bedlington Terriers before setting off on a non-league odyssey through AFC Fylde, Prescot Cables, West Auckland, Warrington Town, and current club Burscough. Like Bradley Barraclough, Bannister had played college soccer in the USA, for Loyola University in Maryland.

Biggins, Harrison: Trialist midfielder who played against Lincoln United in July 2014 after leaving Barnsley. Did not impress, and quickly moved on to Stocksbridge Park Steels, where he still plays. The son of former City striker Wayne.

Bignall, Nicholas: Much-travelled striker who arrived at Sincil Bank on trial in the summer of 2015. Despite having spent six seasons at Reading, Bignall had made very few appearances for a dozen different clubs, many of whom he had joined on loan from the Royals. Appeared in the friendlies against Lincoln United and Leicester City, and in the Lincolnshire Cup match against Boston United. Manager Chris Moyses said there was only one contract available between Bignall and fellow trialist Shaun Harrad; as it happened, he signed neither. Joined Gainsborough Trinity for a season before moving back south to play for Hungerford Town, his 14th different club.

Butler, Jamie: Trialist goalkeeper who arrived from Tooting & Mitcham with Stefan Cox in the summer of 2011. Appeared in one half of the friendly at Gainsborough but had a poor game. Went on to appear for Metropolitan Police and Concord Rangers. Currently in his second spell with Hemel Hempstead in National League South after a very brief stay at Braintree Town at the start of 2016-17. Hit the headlines in February 2016 when he scored a last-minute equaliser from his own area for Hemel against Sutton United. Made his England C debut against Slovakia U21 in June 2016.

Chambers, Luke: Young goalkeeper who came through the academies at Derby County, Arsenal and Southend United. Spent periods on loan at Bishops Stortford, Concord Rangers and Grays Athletic before leaving Roots Hall at the end of 2013-14 season. Enjoyed an extended trial at Sincil Bank in summer 2014, appearing in the friendlies against Lincoln United, Doncaster Rovers, Chesterfield and Scarborough Athletic. Joined Dunstable Town before moving on to Wealdstone. Won 2 caps for Wales at U16 and U17 levels.

Clucas, Sam: A real contender for the Lincoln City 'one who got away' award, midfielder Sam was originally signed for City by Peter Jackson in 2009. Unfortunately made his debut in Jackson's final game as City manager, and immediately fell out of favour under Chris Sutton. Was released at the end of the season and went to the Glenn Hoddle Academy in Spain in an attempt to salvage his career. Returned to Sincil Bank on trial in the summer of 2011 and played in the friendly against Barton Town OB. Was not offered a contract, and eventually signed for League Two Hereford United.

Following spells at Mansfield and Chesterfield, Sam joined Premier League Hull City in July 2015 for £1.3 million, where he features regularly.

Coupland, Dan: Another member of the Midland Youth Cup-winning team of 2011-12, full-back Dan was signed as a first-year professional in summer 2012. Spent the early part of 2012-13 season on loan at Goole with teammate Karl Cunningham, but never came into contention for a first team place and was released as a cost-cutting measure on 29 January 2013. Joined home town club Harrogate Railway Athletic until the end of the season, upon which he moved to America to attend Bellevue University, Nebraska.

Cox, Stefan: Left winger who tried his luck with City during the 2011 pre-season after three years with Lewes, Beaconsfield, Dulwich Hamlet, Sutton United and Tooting & Mitcham. Was recommended to Steve Tilson along with Tooting teammate Jamie Butler and featured in the friendlies against Brigg Town, Gainsborough Trinity and Nottingham Forest. Did well enough to earn a short term deal to allow him to play in the Lincolnshire Cup Final - which he did not do - but was snapped up by Conference rivals Fleetwood Town on a one-year deal. Has since played for a number of non-league clubs including Chester, Hyde, Metropolitan Police, Crawley Down Gatwick, Carshalton Athletic, Merstham and Walton Casuals.

Drury, Adam: 22-year-old former Grimsby and Manchester City winger who joined City on trial in October 2015, appearing in the friendly with Lincoln United. Stayed for three weeks but was unable to earn a contract. Prior to joining up with the Imps, he had relatively brief spells at St Mirren, Burton Albion and Bristol Rovers, but could not settle anywhere. Spent two months at Gainsborough Trinity after leaving Sincil Bank before moving on to Grimsby Borough.

Eckhardt, Sam: Promising right back who came through the Sheffield United and Sheffield Wednesday academy systems. Had a lengthy trial in summer 2011, appearing in several friendlies. Signed a short-term deal in order to appear in the Lincolnshire Cup Final defeat to Grimsby but departed soon afterwards. Spent a few seasons as a striker for Sheffield FC, Hallam, Parkgate and Shirebrook Town before becoming better known as male model Sam Reece. Besides becoming the face of a number of consumer brands such as *Next*, *Gap*, *Police* and *Paul Smith*, Sam appears frequently in various celebrity magazines and featured notoriously on the television show *First Dates* in 2015.

Fernades, Vincent: Centre half who was given a brief pre-season trial under Steve Tilson in 2011. Played in the defeat at Gainsborough, but was not offered a deal.

Fixter, Jack: Youth team centre half who appeared in the pre-season game at Worksop and the Lincolnshire Cup semi-final defeat to Lincoln United in July 2016.

Fox, Joe: Midfielder who played as a trialist against Barton Town OB in the summer of 2011 after leaving the Hull City Academy. Later appeared for Hyde, Worksop Town, Ossett Albion, Frickley Athletic, FC United of Manchester and Scarborough Athletic.

Gouveia, Geoffrey: American midfielder who signed a one-year deal in summer 2012 after a period playing in Madeira for 1° Maio Funchal, Santana and Pontassolense. Never made an appearance for City's first team and was released early from his contract in March 2013. Later appeared for Matlock Town and Glapwell, as well as seeking work as a male model.

Green, Elliot: Young centre back who was signed as a first year professional in 2012 following success with the Midland Youth Cup-winning side of 2011-12. Despite loan spells at Eastwood Town and Sheffield FC, he failed to break into the first team and was released as a cost-cutting measure on 29 January 2013. Has also played for Stamford, Lincoln United and Grantham Town; Swedish sides Ånge IF, Gällivare Malmbergets FF and Sollefteå; Canadian side Whitecaps FC2; and most recently Guiseley in the National League.

Green, Nick: Full-back who spent ten years in the Lincoln City youth/academy system. Appeared as a substitute in the Lincolnshire Cup Final win over Gainsborough in October 2013 but received no more first team opportunities. Was a member of the team which won the Midland Youth Cup in March 2014 but was not offered a professional contract that summer.

Guerin-Lokonga, Aristote: Tall striker who came through the ranks at the Wolverhampton Wanderers Academy. Played for City as a trialist against Barton Town OB in July 2011 but did not impress. Also had unsuccessful trials with Sunderland, Plymouth and Bristol Rovers in 2011. Settled in the north-east and has since appeared for a number of Northern League sides including Jarrow Roofing, Consett, Sunderland RCA, Newcastle Benfield and South Shields.

Hatfield, Will: Skilful midfielder who joined Lincoln on trial with Leeds United teammate Sanchez Payne in December 2011. Was released by Leeds on his return in January 2012, and signed for League Two side Accrington after a very brief spell at FC Halifax. Scored both goals for Guiseley in their shock 2-1 win over the promotion-chasing Imps in December 2016.

Harrad, Shaun: Striker with lots of Football League experience who spent time on trial at the same time as Nicholas Bignall during the 2015 pre-season. Appeared in the friendlies against Lincoln United and Leicester City and made a reasonable impression. City manager Chris Moyses said there was only one contract available for either Bignall or Harrad, and that they were competing for it; as it happened, he signed neither. Eventually signed for Worcester City, where he failed to score in 17 appearances, before moving on to short spells with Torquay and Wrexham.

Higgins, Ryan: Attacking right-back who had an extended trial with City during the summer of 2016 as Danny Cowley built his first squad. Had a good pedigree from the Birmingham City Academy, and plenty of National League experience with Tamworth, AFC Telford and latterly Chester, scoring against the Imps in January 2015 in the 4-0 defeat at the Deva Stadium. Played in the friendlies against Grantham, Worksop and Boston, but was not offered a deal and eventually signed for Southport.

Hollingsworth, Michael: Young midfielder who had a trial at Sincil Bank in the summer of 2014 after ten years at Nottingham Forest. Appeared in the friendlies against Lincoln United and Basford United, but failed to earn a contract and signed for home town club Boston United. Joined Grantham Town in May 2015, where he still plays.

Hutchinson, Andrew: Promising striker who came through the youth set-up. Scored on his first Football League start for the Imps at Bradford City in April 2009 at the age of 17, and signed a one-year professional deal during the close season of 2011. Unfortunately picked up an injury in a pre-season friendly at Ilkeston and never appeared for the first team again. Had short spells with Lincoln United, Eastwood Town and Coalville before returning to Ashby Avenue in summer 2014. Made 22 first team appearances in City's Football League days, scoring one goal.

Kelly, Danny: Former Norwich City and Barnet striker who appeared as a trialist in the pre-season game against Barton Town OB in 2011. Eventually signed for Cambridge City before heading to play in Australia for two years. Returned for two more seasons at Cambridge City before signing for current club St Ives Town.

King, Gary: Striker who came through the youth ranks at Lincoln, eventually making 12 appearances for the first team before being released in the summer of 2009. Played for a large number of Lincolnshire non-league clubs before returning to Sincil Bank on trial in July 2013. Appeared in the game against Lincoln United but was not offered a deal by new manager Gary Simpson. Recommenced his journey around the local non-league scene, appearing for Lincoln United, Stamford, and in the 2017 FA Vase Final for Cleethorpes Town.

Leggett, Ryan: Youth team right back who appeared in the Lincolnshire Cup Final defeat to Grimsby in July 2012. Spent time on loan at Boston Town and Grantham later that season, but was not offered a professional contract by City in the summer of 2013. Signed permanently for Boston Town before moving on to Holbeach United and Pinchbeck in quick succession.

Lindberg, Doug: Australian goalkeeper who appeared in several pre-season games in 2011 as well as the Lincolnshire Cup Final. City signed him on non-contract terms for that game and kept him on the books in order to have a better look at him. Had a loan spell at Sleaford from 9 September before being released on 22 November, whereupon he returned to Sleaford for the rest of the season. Joined Boston Town in September 2012 for a short period before returning to Australia.

McCashin, Sean: Northern Irish defender who spent a short period on trial at Sincil Bank in July 2013. Attended the Glenn Hoddle Academy in Spain after leaving Nottingham Forest, returning to his home country in January 2012 to play for Lisburn and Glenavon. Was not offered a contract by Lincoln, and had a short spell with Antrim side Chimney Corner before joining Dungannon Swifts in January 2014. Won two caps for Northern Ireland U21 in 2010-11.

Meadows, Danny: Former Alfreton Town midfielder who appeared in the pre-season games against Lincoln United and Basford United in summer 2014. Was not offered a deal and joined Boston United for a few months before moving on to Grantham Town where he still plays.

Moore, Dallas: Young Californian defender who appeared as a trialist in the pre-season game at Gainsborough in 2011. Came through the youth ranks at Grimsby Town before being released in 2010, after which he spent a season in non-league with Halesowen Town and St Neots. Was not offered a contract by Lincoln, and signed for Histon a few weeks later before returning to America in January 2012.

Moyses, Archie: Young midfielder who appeared as a substitute in the Lincolnshire Cup semi-final defeat to Lincoln United and the friendly against Crewe in July 2016 as a second-year scholar. Son of former City boss Chris.

Nicholson, Jordan: Young winger from Peterborough United who spent a brief spell training with Lincoln in the summer of 2016 with a view to a long-term loan. Appeared in the first two pre-season games at Grantham and Worksop before returning to Peterborough. Actually scored for them against City in a 2-2 draw at the end of July. Another Peterborough winger caught the eye in that game - Harry Anderson, who signed for the Imps in August.

O'Connor, Aaron: Very experienced non-league striker who joined up with the Imps for pre-season training in 2016 after being released by Stevenage. Made one appearance at Boston as a second half substitute but departed soon afterwards. Eventually signed for Kettering Town, ironically to replace former Imp Sam Smith who was heading to Australia.

Payne, Sanchez: Young midfielder who had a trial for the Imps with his Leeds United teammate Will Hatfield in December 2011 and January 2012 as new City manager David Holdsworth tried to reorganise his squad. Appeared in a behind-closed-doors friendly at Gainsborough but failed to earn a permanent move. Later appeared for a host of northern non-league clubs including Buxton, Stockport, Frickley, Ossett Town and Bradford Park Avenue.

Penfold, Morgan: Highly-rated 17-year-old Peterborough United youth team striker who had a very brief trial with City in July 2016, appearing and scoring in the second half of the 2-0 win at Worksop. Made his debut for Peterborough as a late substitute in their 6-1 home defeat to Norwich U23 in the Checkatrade Cup the following month. Joined St Ives Town on loan in October 2016 and signed a two-and-a-half-year professional deal with Peterborough in January 2017.

Porritt, Adam: 18-year-old defender who joined City on loan from Huddersfield in March 2016 after a brief trial. Made no appearances for the first team. Was not offered a professional contract by Huddersfield in the summer of 2016, and had a short spell at Liversedge before moving on to Goole AFC in February 2017. He currently plays for Harrogate Town.

Rawdon, Will: Youth teamer who appeared in the Lincolnshire Cup Final defeat to Grimsby in July 2012. Spent time on loan at Sleaford Town and Grantham Town in 2013 but was not offered a professional deal.

Richardson, Tom: Young midfielder who had been the captain of York City's youth team before being released in the summer of 2011. Signed for Lincoln from Sheffield FC on 10 January 2012 on a contract to the end of the season, and was immediately loaned to Blyth Spartans for a month from 13 January. Made only one brief appearance as a substitute at Blyth before returning to Sincil Bank. Had a loan spell at North Ferriby in March 2012, but failed to make any impact at Lincoln and was released when his contract expired.

Roberts, Jack: Former Lincoln City Academy midfielder who trialled for the Imps in the summer of 2015 after spending four years in the US. Appeared in the pre-season game against Grantham, but failed to win a contract and signed for AFC Telford United. Later appeared for Rushall Olympic and Stratford Town.

Rooney, Matthew: Northern Irish striker who came up through the Manchester United Academy. Joined City on trial with Glenavon teammate Sean McCashin in July 2013 after spells with Cliftonville and Derry City. Failed to secure a deal and returned to Northern Ireland to play for Portadown. Later moved on to Drogheda United, Warrenpoint and back to Portadown before joining Cowdenbeath in January 2017 after an unsuccessful trial with St Mirren.

Smith, Adam C: 19-year-old goalkeeper signed from Leicester on loan from 5 January 2012 as cover to the end of the season after spending two weeks training with the Imps. Never made an appearance for the first team and returned to Leicester at the end of his loan. Had several more loan spells with a number of clubs before being sacked by Leicester for his part in a sex tape scandal. Signed for Northampton in June 2015, where he is currently number one choice.

Thompson, Ryley: Youth team full back who appeared as a substitute in the friendly at Worksop and the Lincolnshire Cup semi-final defeat to Lincoln United in July 2016.

Turner, Jake: Former Scunthorpe, Brigg and Winterton goalkeeper who signed for City in July 2012 after a short trial period. Played in the Lincolnshire Cup Final defeat to Grimsby, but found first team opportunities non-existent behind Paul Farman and David Preece. Spent a month on loan at Grantham before being released early from his contract on 29 January 2013 as a cost-cutting measure. Signed for Worksop Town, and has since appeared for Grantham and Lincoln United.

Walton, Richard: Highly-rated young goalkeeper who signed his first professional deal with the Imps in the summer of 2016. Appeared in the pre-season games against Worksop, Boston, Reading and Gainsborough and was a mainstay of the new U21 Development team. Joined Spalding United on loan in January 2017 and Bishop's Stortford in February, where he conceded a nightmare 26 goals in his 9 appearances as Stortford headed for relegation. Was offered a new contract at the end of the season.

Ward, Callum: Defender who made one appearance in City's Lincolnshire Cup final win over Gainsborough in October 2013. Was a member of the U18 side which won the Midland Youth Cup in March 2014. Surprisingly declined a professional contract from City in the summer of 2014 and left professional football to train as a teacher at Bishop Grosseteste University. Joined Lincoln United later in 2014.

Weledji, Kieran: Young centre half who trialled with City after spending 5 years with the Middlesbrough Academy. Appeared in the pre-season friendlies at Grantham and Lincoln United in July 2015 but failed to win a contract. Signed for Whitby Town in August 2015, where he still plays.

Williams, Tom: Non-league striker from the north-west who was given a brief trial in July 2013. Clubs have included Kendal Town, Chorley and Bamber Bridge.

Wilson, James: Young striker who originally joined the Imps in May 2008 following spells as a trainee at Leicester and Nottingham Forest. Signed a one-year professional deal with the Imps during the summer of 2011, and appeared in a number of pre-season friendlies including as substitute in the Lincolnshire Cup Final defeat to Grimsby. Never appeared for the first team in a competitive fixture and had a loan spell at Worksop Town from 29 November 2011 and two spells with Holbeach from 27 January 2012. Was not offered a deal in summer 2012 as City's financial position worsened, and left football.

Wright, Andrew: Attacking midfielder who came through the academy system. Earned his first professional deal in summer 2015, signing up for a further year in 2016. Spent the majority of his senior Imps career out on loan: one month at Lincoln United from October 2015, one month at Stamford from November 2015, three months at Spalding United from July 2016, and two months at Grantham Town from November 2016. Was released in May 2017 without making a first team appearance for City.

The Managers

TILSON, Steve

Born	27/7/1966, Wickford
Appointed	15/10/2010 on a two-and-a-half-year contract
Appointed by	Bob Dorrian
Previous club	Southend United
Departed	10/10/2011 (sacked)
Next club	Basildon Ladies

Playing Career	Basildon United, Bowers United, 1986 Witham Town, Feb 1989 Southend United (Sep 1993 Brentford - loan), Jul 1997 Canvey Island, Oct 2002 Southend United, Mar 2004 retired.

Managerial Career	Nov 2003 Southend United, **Oct 2010 LINCOLN CITY**, Jun 2012 Basildon Ladies head coach, Jul 2012 Canvey Island manager (concurrent with duties at Basildon Ladies), Jul 2015 Basildon Ladies manager.

First City game	Southport (A), Conference Premier, 13/8/2011 (post-relegation)
Final City game	Tamworth (A), Conference Premier, 8/10/2011

It is entirely possible that Steve Tilson would never have darkened the Sincil Bank door, had City not lost to his Southend United side in the League Two play-off final in 2005. The defeat catapulted Tilson to the attention of City's directors and supporters, creating an impression that was further enhanced a year later when he took his side straight up to the Championship. A holder of the UEFA A Licence, many were surprised when he parted company with cash-strapped Southend in acrimonious circumstances in July 2010, with legal wrangling continuing into the autumn. Looking for a new manager following Chris Sutton's unexpected departure, City moved quickly to secure their man, his appointment being confirmed on 15 October. The appointment was met with delight by supporters, who felt the club had appointed the right man to take them straight back to League One. Unfortunately, Steve Tilson will be remembered as the man who took Lincoln straight back to non-league football, and to six years in purgatory.

Taking over Sutton's expensively assembled squad with the side in 21st place in the League Two table, initial results were encouraging and City climbed slowly to a mid-table position. A 2-1 win over former club Southend on 12 March left City just 10 points off the play-offs with games in hand on many of the teams above them; a late run to promotion looked just possible. No one considered it worth looking at the foot of the table; they were 11 points clear of danger with 11 games to play, with no cause for alarm whatsoever.

How quickly that optimism disappeared into thin air. Tilson may claim to have been unlucky with injuries, having lost influential captain Delroy Facey for the season with a dislocated shoulder during the 1-1 draw with Macclesfield on 16 March, but a series of inexplicable team selections led to an astonishing run that saw City plummet down the table. His insistence on playing teenage loan goalkeeper Elliot Parish ahead of the experienced Joe Anyon resulted in some heavy home defeats - 6-0 to Rotherham, and 4-0 to Gillingham - and City's relegation from the Football League was confirmed following a 3-0 capitulation at home to Aldershot on the final day. City had picked up just 2 points from their last 11 games, and shell-shocked fans awaited the inevitable dismissal of the manager who had been its architect.

Incredibly, Tilson received the backing of the board of directors and set about building a squad capable of taking the club back to the Football League at the first attempt. The expectation was certainly there, as City had regained their League place at the first time of asking on all four previous occasions. Despite the need for a much-reduced playing budget, Tilson did have the added bonus of the £225,000 parachute payment from the Football League to invest in his players.

Sadly, the record books show that City's descent towards oblivion continued unabated, with some poor signings producing some dreadful performances. Having sunk to 19th place, just 1 point clear of the Conference Premier relegation zone, Tilson and assistant manager Paul Brush were finally sacked on 10 October 2011 after another dismal defeat, this one by 4-0 at Tamworth. With the parachute payment gone and the budget stretched, whichever manager came in to replace him was facing a Herculean task to reverse City's breathtaking downward momentum.

Many supporters feel Tilson never bonded with the city or its supporters, a problem exacerbated by his weekly commute from Essex. At the time of his dismissal, chairman Bob Dorrian called him 'a disaster for Lincoln City', and his record during his solitary year in charge does little to refute the assertion. Always eager to blame the budget and the attitude of his players, his reign will be remembered for all the wrong reasons.

After Lincoln, the likelihood of finding a suitable position in management was obviously not high, and in March 2012 he chose to launch a football academy back in Essex with his former Southend colleague Danny Greaves. His first coaching role followed in June as head coach with Basildon Ladies, and he returned to men's management with former club Canvey Island the following month. His tenure at Canvey came to a disappointing end after just one season, since when he has continued his role with Basildon Ladies. The Ladies have risen through the ranks of women's football since he became involved with the club, from the Eastern Region Premier League to the FA Women's Premier Southern Division. He was appointed manager in the summer of 2015, where he remains today.

Lincoln City Record - Conference Only

	P	W	D	L	F	A	Pts	PPG	Win%
League	14	3	3	8	11	20	12	0.86	21.4
FA Cup	0	0	0	0	0	0	N/A	N/A	0
FA Trophy	0	0	0	0	0	0	N/A	N/A	0
Totals	*14*	*3*	*3*	*8*	*11*	*20*	*N/A*	*N/A*	*21.4*

Lincoln City Record - Football League

	P	W	D	L	F	A	Pts	PPG	Win%
League	34	10	6	18	38	66	36	1.05	29.4
FA Cup	3	1	1	1	6	6	N/A	N/A	33.3
League Cup	0	0	0	0	0	0	N/A	N/A	0
League Trophy	0	0	0	0	0	0	N/A	N/A	0
Totals	*37*	*11*	*7*	*19*	*44*	*72*	*N/A*	*N/A*	*29.7*

BROWN, Grant

Born	19/11/1969, Sunderland
Appointed	10/10/2011 and 18/2/2013 on a caretaker basis
Appointed by	Bob Dorrian
Previous club	Grantham Town
Departed	24/6/2016 (contract not renewed)
Next club	N/A

Playing Career	1984 Leicester City (Y), Jul 1988 Leicester City (**Aug 1989 LINCOLN CITY - loan**), **Jan 1990 LINCOLN CITY**, Jul 2002 Telford United, Jun 2003 Alfreton Town, Jul 2005 Worksop Town, Aug 2005 Grantham Town, May 2006 retired.

Managerial Career	**Aug 2005 LINCOLN CITY youth team coach, Oct 2007 caretaker manager, Jul 2009 assistant head of youth, Jun 2010 head of youth, Oct 2010 caretaker manager, Feb 2013 caretaker manager, Feb 2013 assistant manager.**

First City game	Alfreton Town (A), Conference Premier, 11/10/2011 (post-relegation)
Last City game	Mansfield Town (H), Conference Premier, 26/2/2013

If anyone can lay legitimate claim to legendary status at Lincoln City, it is Grant Brown. Originally joining as a player on an extended loan from Leicester City in August 1989, uncompromising central defender Brown was signed on a permanent basis in January 1990 for a then club record £63,000. It proved to be a sound investment, as Brown was named club captain in 1992 and went on to break the club's appearance record, making a total of 407 in the Football League (469 in all competitions, scoring 18 goals). After being awarded a testimonial season in 1999-2000, he fell victim to the club's parlous financial position and was released in the summer of 2002 as the Imps hurtled towards administration. After a short period away during which he wound down his playing career in non-league football, Brown returned to Lincoln as youth team coach in August 2005. Over the next 11 years, he would serve variously as youth team coach, assistant head of youth, head of youth, assistant manager and caretaker manager for three separate spells, but never managed to secure the hot seat on a permanent basis despite numerous applications.

Brown's first spell as caretaker manager had come in October 2007 following the dismissal of management duo John Schofield and John Deehan, and he managed the Imps to a draw and a defeat before Peter Jackson was appointed. Brown returned to a minor management role when Jackson was diagnosed with throat cancer in February 2008, assisting caretaker manager Iffy Onuora until Jackson was well enough to return.

Brown's second spell as caretaker manager - and his first with City as a non-league club - came in October 2011 following the dismissal of Steve Tilson. Brown got off to a great start with a 3-1 win at Alfreton and was interviewed for the job the following week along with Martin Foyle, former City manager Steve Thompson, and former Sheffield United defender David Holdsworth, who was appointed to the role two days later. Brown returned to his position as head of youth, as Holdsworth chose to proceed without an assistant manager.

His third and final spell in the manager's chair came when Holdsworth was sacked 16 months later, when he was assisted by director Chris Moyses. City failed to score in Brown's two games in charge, and the job went to former City assistant manager Gary Simpson. Brown took a step up at that point, officially taking the role of assistant manager to Simpson alongside Moyses as coach. However, when Simpson was placed on garden leave in November 2014, it was Moyses who received the caretaker role with Brown assisting. It appeared his chances of getting the role on a permanent basis had gone, and he was forced to settle for a part in Moyses' new three-man coaching team alongside goalkeeping specialist David Preece. Ironically, he found himself in a more public role as Moyses encouraged Brown and Preece to take on some of the pre- and post-match media responsibilities in his place.

With the departure of Moyses at the end of the 2015-16 season and the appointment of Danny Cowley, it became increasingly unlikely that Brown would form part of the management structure as Cowley set about building an extensive support network of sports science and fitness staff. His departure was confirmed at the end of June 2016 when his contract with the club officially expired, ending a total of 24 years as player, coach and manager.

Wishing to stay in football in some capacity, Brown was named as the new manager of the FootballCV Academy near Stamford on 12 July, where he remains today.

Lincoln City Record - Conference Only

	P	W	D	L	F	A	Pts	PPG	Win%
League	6	1	2	3	5	8	5	0.83	16.7
FA Cup	0	0	0	0	0	0	N/A	N/A	0
FA Trophy	0	0	0	0	0	0	N/A	N/A	0
Totals	*6*	*1*	*2*	*3*	*5*	*8*	*N/A*	*N/A*	*16.7*

Lincoln City Record - Football League

	P	W	D	L	F	A	Pts	PPG	Win%
League	2	0	1	1	1	2	1	0.50	0
FA Cup	0	0	0	0	0	0	N/A	N/A	0
League Cup	0	0	0	0	0	0	N/A	N/A	0
League Trophy	0	0	0	0	0	0	N/A	N/A	0
Totals	*2*	*0*	*1*	*1*	*1*	*2*	*N/A*	*N/A*	*0*

HOLDSWORTH, David

Born	8/11/1968, Walthamstow
Appointed	24/10/2011 initially to the end of the season
Appointed by	Bob Dorrian
Previous club	Mansfield Town
Departed	17/2/2013 (mutual consent)
Next club	Goole AFC

Playing Career	Free United, Jul 1986 Watford, Oct 1996 Sheffield United, Mar 1999 Birmingham City (Jan 2002 Walsall - loan), Aug 2002 Bolton Wanderers, Nov 2002 Scarborough, Jul 2003 Gretna, May 2005 retired.

Managerial Career	Jul 2004 Gretna coach, May 2006 Gretna director of youth development, May 2008 Ilkeston Town manager, Dec 2008 Mansfield Town manager, **Oct 2011 LINCOLN CITY manager**, Oct 2013 Goole AFC manager, Jan 2014 resigned.

First City game	Alfreton Town (A) FA Cup 4Q, 29/10/2011
Last City game	Hereford United (A), Conference Premier, 16/2/2013

Originally taken to Watford from local football in the east end of London by former Imps legend Graham Taylor, David Holdsworth had a relatively distinguished career in football, playing for many years in the top flight and winning one cap for the England U21 side, a 1-0 defeat in Greece on 7 February 1989. Having made over 500 appearances at centre half for a number of clubs, Holdsworth stepped into a coaching role for the first time whilst playing north of the border for ambitious Gretna. His first significant post came at Mansfield in December 2008, with the Stags sitting 18th in the Conference Premier; they recovered well to finish 12th, but failed to push on the following season when they finished on the same points total as the year before (62). He left by mutual consent in November 2010 with the side in 10th place, the board at Field Mill unable to see firm evidence of progress after two years. After a brief spell out of football, he beat Grant Brown, Martin Foyle and Steve Thompson to the Sincil Bank hot seat on 24 October 2011 and set about correcting the immense problems caused by Steve Tilson's disastrous reign.

Holdsworth's task was simple: keep the club in the Conference Premier. It was far from simple, of course, as the legacy of a huge Football League wage bill combined with further lack of success on the pitch had left the club on a financial knife-edge. At his first press conference, Holdsworth confirmed he would have no money to spend unless he made substantial savings first. He also announced that he would be working without an assistant manager due to financial constraints (with the budget for the management team rumoured to be £50,000), and 'would have to call in a few favours from friends'. Those favours proved to be Curtis Woodhouse and Gary Charles working for the club on a casual basis, the result of which would come back to haunt the club at a later date.

Nicknamed 'the tinkerer' by the fans at Mansfield, the dressing room door at Sincil Bank soon became a revolving one as a stream of players came and went. The whole period can be summed up by Holdsworth's activity on transfer deadline day (31 January 2012), when he claimed to have brought in four players - Jefferson Louis, Peter Bore, Louis Almond and Nialle Rodney - for less than half what they were paying recently-departed striker Gavin McCallum. Whatever the case, a series of well-known non-league journeymen came in for very short periods before moving on; Holdsworth justified his methodology by saying he did not want to pay players throughout the summer. The result was a very unsettled team with many new faces and inconsistent performances, but somehow they struggled to safety, securing Conference Premier status with a 2-2 draw at champions-elect Fleetwood on 13 April. The inevitable outcome was that City had just nine players remaining under contract when the retained list was announced in May.

Holdsworth agreed a one-year contract on 18 May and immediately set off on a new signing spree. In came Rob Duffy, Gary Mills, Ashley Westwood, Paul Farman, Andrew Boyce, Adam Smith, Dan Gray, Geoffrey Gouveia, Graham Hutchison, Jake Turner, Vadaine Oliver and Luke Daley before the season even got under way. With so many new faces,

City supporters were unsure how the season would progress. The answer was not well, and by the second week of October they were back in the bottom four. Calls for Holdsworth's head were becoming louder when the team suddenly embarked on a six-game unbeaten run that took them into the top half. Holdsworth was even named Manager of the Month for November. The improvement was reinforced by a minor run in the FA Cup during which they won a first round replay at League One side Walsall before exiting the competition to former club Mansfield in a second round replay. With Liverpool awaiting the winners, it was a pivotal point in the season and in terms of Holdsworth's tenure; it will never be known whether that tie against Liverpool would have changed anything, but the defeat kick-started another poor run which saw City nosedive back down the league table. After just one win in ten, Holdsworth parted company with the club by mutual consent on 17 February 2013 after a dismal showing at Hereford.

At the time of his appointment, Mansfield Town supporters warned that Holdsworth would make a lot of signings on short-term deals, and that is exactly what he proceeded to do. It must be remembered that his remit was to avoid relegation and try to reduce the amount of money leaving the club on the playing side. Although his hands were undoubtedly tied by the poor squad inherited from Steve Tilson, Holdsworth's period in charge was characterised by some very poor signings who added nothing to an already weak mix. On the positive side, he made several good signings for the club including Paul Farman and Andrew Boyce, although cynics might say it was inevitable he would find one or two worth keeping from amongst the multitude. Memorable for the minor FA Cup run and reasonable league position over the first half of the 2012-13 season, Holdsworth was City's manager at a very difficult time in its history. He may be credited ultimately with halting the club's slide down the non-league pyramid for a time, although the hard black and white reality is that City were in 19th place in the league table when he joined the club, and 18th when he left it.

To a certain extent, Holdsworth was on a hiding to nothing at Lincoln. Whilst it is always incumbent upon the manager to create wealth and success for the club by signing the right players, some semblance of investment is needed to set that going, and Holdsworth had none. His remit was to avoid relegation, and he did that. His departure the following season became increasingly inevitable despite the cup run, and the experience at Lincoln added very little to his CV. He struggled to find another job after leaving Sincil Bank, and qualified as a fitness instructor in September 2013. He then endured a very undistinguished few months as manager of Goole AFC before that ended in acrimony in January 2014, since when he has not worked in football.

Lincoln City Record - Conference Only

	P	W	D	L	F	A	Pts	PPG	Win%
League	59	18	14	27	87	99	68	1.15	30.5
FA Cup	8	2	4	2	12	11	N/A	N/A	25.0
FA Trophy	4	1	1	2	5	7	N/A	N/A	25.0
Totals	*71*	*21*	*19*	*31*	*104*	*117*	*N/A*	*N/A*	*29.5*

SIMPSON, Gary

Born	11/4/1961, Sheffield
Appointed	27/2/2013 initially to the end of the season
Appointed by	Bob Dorrian
Previous club	Parkgate
Departed	3/11/2014 (sacked)
Next club	Barrow

Playing Career	1977 Stoke City (Y), Jun 1980 Boston United, Jul 1985 Stafford Rangers, Jul 1986 Weymouth, Dec 1986 Stafford Rangers, Jul 1988 Boston United, Oct 1989 Altrincham, 1991 Gainsborough Trinity, Dec 1993 Arnold Town, Sep 1994 Hyde United. Oct 1994 retired.

Managerial Career	1991 Gainsborough Trinity player/manager, 1996 Ilkeston Town assistant manager, Oct 2000 Northwich Victoria assistant manager, **Jul 2002 LINCOLN CITY assistant manager, Nov 2003 LINCOLN CITY caretaker manager,** May 2006 Peterborough United assistant manager, Jul 2007 Bury reserve team coach, Feb 2008 Macclesfield Town assistant manager, Mar 2010 Macclesfield Town caretaker manager, Apr 2010 Macclesfield Town manager, 2012 Parkgate coach on a casual basis, **Feb 2013 LINCOLN CITY manager,** Feb 2016 Barrow assistant manager.

First City game	Woking (A), Conference Premier, 2/3/2013
Last City game	Forest Green Rovers (A), Conference, 1/11/2014

A genuine non-league specialist, midfielder Gary Simpson spent the vast majority of his playing career outside the Football League despite having one of the better playing records of his day. In addition to picking up 9 England C caps, Simpson was well-known to Lincolnshire football fans as the captain of Boston United when they lost 2-1 to Wealdstone in the 1985 FA Trophy final. After a lengthy playing career, Simpson went into management for the first time at the age of 30 as player/manager at Gainsborough. But the most significant event was playing in the Boston United team alongside a powerful winger named Keith Alexander. It was the start of a managerial relationship that would take them to six different clubs together.

His first involvement with Lincoln City came in the close season of 2002 when new manager Alexander appointed Simpson as his assistant on a part-time basis due to the club's poor financial position. Against all odds, the duo led City to three successive Division Three/League Two play-offs between 2003 and 2005, losing in the final twice. Simpson stepped into the manager's chair in November 2003 when Alexander suffered a brain aneurysm, and managed to keep the momentum going with five wins, four draws and two defeats from his eleven games before Alexander was well enough to return. Things turned sour unexpectedly when, on 2 January 2006, Simpson and Alexander were placed on garden leave; after an internal investigation, Alexander returned while Simpson was dismissed from his post 'for footballing reasons'. No formal explanation has ever been given for the decision.

Simpson went on to work with Alexander at three more clubs before taking over as Macclesfield Town manager upon Keith's death on 3 March 2010. Simpson did well to keep Macclesfield afloat in the Football League on a tiny budget, suffering a raft of injuries before losing his job in March 2012 as the side headed for relegation. He had been helping with coaching duties at non-league Parkgate when the opportunity came to return to Sincil Bank in February 2013 following the departure of David Holdsworth. Taking the job initially to the end of the season, Simpson had just 13 games to keep City in the Conference Premier. His return of 20 points from those 13 games kept them up by 6 points, safety only being secured with a 5-1 win at Hyde on the final day of the season. Simpson asked for a permanent contract and was rewarded with a three-year deal.

Simpson set about creating his own squad in the close season of 2013, with just two players remaining under contract. Some impressive signings were made including defender Sean Newton, midfielders Danny Rowe and Jon Nolan, and strikers Waide Fairhurst and Ben Tomlinson. City made a very good start to the season and were sitting in 7th place after the first two months. However, a run of just one win in fourteen games saw the Imps slip to just above the relegation zone by the turn of the year. A series of mainly forgettable loan signings were made in an effort to revive the team's fortunes, and calls for Simpson's dismissal became loud and clear after a dismal 4-0 home defeat to Conference North village side North Ferriby in the FA Trophy. The loan signings of Charlee Adams and Nick Townsend from Birmingham helped City to struggle to mid-table, but a draw on the final day against Barnet saw the Imps fail to finish in the top half for the third successive season.

With the nucleus of the squad retained on two-year deals, signings during the 2014 close season were fewer in number with defender Hamza Bencherif and striker Jordan Burrow the most notable; goalkeeper Nick Townsend returned from Birmingham on loan. The Imps got off to an excellent start to the season, a 3-2 win over neighbours Grimsby leaving them just outside the play-offs. Unfortunately, a series of desperately poor performances saw the side slip into the bottom half by the end of October. Losing a three-goal lead at Forest Green with 20 minutes remaining proved the final straw, and Simpson was placed on garden leave with a view to leaving the club.

Although working with a restricted budget, Simpson was not helped by some poor media interviews which convinced some supporters that he did not know how to correct the obvious problems that first appeared during 2013-14. His regular references to the budget eventually wore thin, and his tactical ability was frequently called into question with supporters feeling there was no plan B. There is no doubt that Gary Simpson moved Lincoln City further away from the wrong end of the Conference table during his tenure, and in that sense was good for the club. There was no danger that City would be relegated with Simpson in charge, but there was no chance they would be promoted either, and that was always the main problem. It really was time for plan B.

Lincoln City Record - Conference Only

	P	W	D	L	F	A	Pts	PPG	Win%
League	77	29	21	27	108	106	108	1.40	37.6
FA Cup	6	2	3	1	10	8	N/A	N/A	33.3
FA Trophy	3	2	0	1	8	6	N/A	N/A	66.6
Totals	*86*	*33*	*24*	*29*	*126*	*120*	*N/A*	*N/A*	*38.3*

Lincoln City Record - Football League

	P	W	D	L	F	A	Pts	PPG	Win%
League	11	5	4	2	14	10	19	1.72	45.4
FA Cup	2	1	0	1	3	4	N/A	N/A	50.0
League Cup	0	0	0	0	0	0	N/A	N/A	0
League Trophy	2	1	0	1	4	4	N/A	N/A	50.0
Totals	*15*	*7*	*4*	*4*	*21*	*18*	*N/A*	*N/A*	*46.7*

MOYSES, Chris

Born	1/11/1965, Lincoln
Appointed	3/11/2014 initially as caretaker manager
Appointed by	Bob Dorrian
Previous club	Lincoln Moorlands Railway
Departed	30/4/2016 (resigned)
Next club	N/A

Playing Career	**1980 Lincoln City (Y)**, Jul 1984 Halifax Town, Jul 1985 Boston United, Oct 1985 Shepshed Charterhouse, Oct 1985 Grantham.

Managerial Career	2008 Lincoln United assistant manager, Feb 2010 Lincoln Moorlands Railway manager, **May 2011 Lincoln City Academy coach, Nov 2014 LINCOLN CITY caretaker manager, Dec 2014 LINCOLN CITY manager, Apr 2016 resigned.**

First City game	Altrincham (H), Conference, 4/11/2014
Last City game	Cheltenham Town (A), National League, 30/4/2016

Lincoln born and bred, Chris Moyses has served Lincoln City as supporter, apprentice, player, academy coach, director, first-team coach, caretaker manager and manager. Having made a handful of appearances in a relatively short playing career, defender Moyses hung up his boots in 1986 and found work outside football as a roofer. Spells with the Royal Mail and as an HGV driver followed before he found a job as a pipe layer. From that beginning grew his own utilities contracting company East Midlands Contracting Limited, which he founded in 1998. Having made a success in the world of business, he decided to put some money back into Lincolnshire football by investing in first Lincoln United and then Lincoln Moorlands Railway, also taking a coaching role at each club.

His first involvement with Lincoln City came shortly after relegation when his commitment helped to secure the future of the Academy following the loss of central funding from the Football League. The arrangement included coaching, forcing him to resign as manager of Moorlands where he had enjoyed several successful seasons. As his connection with the club grew closer, he was appointed to the board in October 2012. As director, he also held an unofficial role as director of football, acting as a point of liaison between the board and the coaching staff. At a time when City could not afford an assistant manager, Moyses also took on a minor coaching role with the first team.

Following the suspension on garden leave of Gary Simpson on 3 November 2014, Moyses was appointed caretaker manager with Grant Brown assisting. Having lost his first game at home to relegation-bound Altrincham, Moyses confirmed that he had been given four matches to earn the job on a permanent basis, suggesting he was now ahead of Brown in the pecking order. After two wins and a draw from the next three games, he was formally appointed on 8 December 2014 on a twelve-month rolling contract. Grant Brown and David Preece completed his coaching team.

There were to be no quick fixes. Despite a brief foray into the top ten at the end of January, City fell away to finish 15th as a succession of disappointing loan signings came and went. As the 2014-15 season drew to a very slow close, Moyses answered criticism from fans by asking to be judged once he had his own team. Hinting at a lack of commitment from certain unnamed players, he made a good number of changes to his squad in the close season of 2015. Out went popular striker Ben Tomlinson and defenders Sean Newton and Hamza Bencherif, whilst striker Jordan Burrow was made available for transfer. In came some experienced National League players in Liam Hearn, Matt Rhead, Bradley Wood, and former City favourite Lee Beevers. Optimism was high that 2015-16 could be a good season.

It so nearly was. At the exact midpoint of the season, a 1-1 draw at home to Welling left City in 4th place in the National League, just 7 points behind leaders Cheltenham, and hopes were high that a play-off place as a minimum could be achieved. However, just two days prior to the game against Welling, striker Liam Hearn announced he wanted to join National League rivals Barrow on loan because he felt he was not being given enough game time. The move certainly backfired on Hearn, who played just 80 minutes for Barrow when he could have played in six games for Lincoln. Many fans feel Hearn's behaviour disturbed the squad unity that Moyses had worked so hard to create, and the striker was never forgiven. A dramatic collapse ensued, which saw City pick up just 21 more points over the second half of the season; only relegated clubs Welling and Altrincham earned fewer. Another bottom-half finish was the eventual result, and with just four games remaining, Moyses announced that he was to stand down at the end of the season.

Criticism of Chris Moyses and in particular how he became Lincoln City manager has filled many pages on social media. Accusations that he had a hand in the departures of David Holdsworth and Gary Simpson are unfounded, and have been denied many times by Moyses and the club. Moyses has stressed how he deliberately had no part in determining their futures because of his involvement on the coaching side, although he would have been entitled to do so by virtue of his position as director. Cynics often repeat how Moyses bought his position as manager, but there is no foundation to that either. It is almost always forgotten that he did the job for free at a time when City could not afford a full-time manager, and at the same time as he was running his own company. It was the problems caused by effectively running two businesses simultaneously that led to his resignation in April 2016. Despite their poor form over the second half of the 2015-16 season, Bob Dorrian has confirmed that the club would have persisted with Chris into 2016-17 had he not taken the decision to step down.

Although ultimately ending in disappointment - and a fifth successive bottom half finish - there can be no doubt that Chris Moyses improved Lincoln City both on and off the pitch during his 18 months at the helm. Improvements to training facilities were made - allegedly at his personal expense - including the opening of the Sobraon Barracks site which enabled the players to train on grass instead of the artificial surface at Sincil Bank. The atmosphere changed noticeably around the club, leading to investment from Clive Nates and his consortium. And he signed some very good players: Matt Rhead, Bradley Wood, Lee Beevers, Jack Muldoon, Luke Waterfall, Terry Hawkridge and Callum Howe were all to play significant roles under Danny Cowley.

Lincoln City Record - Conference Only

	P	W	D	L	F	A	Pts	PPG	Win%
League	74	26	18	30	102	108	96	1.30	35.1
FA Cup	4	1	1	2	6	7	N/A	N/A	25.0
FA Trophy	2	0	0	2	1	4	N/A	N/A	0
Totals	*80*	*27*	*19*	*34*	*109*	*119*	*N/A*	*N/A*	*33.7*

Born	22/10/1978, Havering
Appointed	13/5/2016 on a two-year deal
Appointed by	Bob Dorrian
Previous club	Braintree Town
Departed	N/A
Next club	N/A

Playing Career	Hornchurch, Wimbledon, Dagenham & Redbridge, Purfleet, Barking, 1997 Harlow Town, Tilbury, 2003 Hornchurch, Jul 2004 Boreham Wood, Oct 2004 Romford, Jun 2005 AFC Hornchurch, Jul 2006 Brentwood Town, Jun 2007 Concord Rangers, May 2008 retired.

Managerial Career	Jun 2007 Concord Rangers joint-manager, May 2012 Concord Rangers manager, Apr 2015 Braintree Town manager, **May 2016 LINCOLN CITY manager.**

First City game	Woking (A), National League, 6/8/2016
Last City game	Southport (A), National League, 29/4/2017

When Lincoln announced the appointment of Danny Cowley on a two-year contract on 13 May 2016, the reaction from supporters should have been muted. They were getting a PE teacher with nine years of part-time non-league management behind him, yet the excitement and optimism generated that day was unprecedented. City had bucked the trend of appointing tired journeymen, and instead had gone for a younger manager they had targeted deliberately. Cowley was the man Clive Nates had said was on his radar, and the directors made an immediate bee-line for him. The fact that Danny signed his contract sitting at a table at Cambridge Services at 11.30pm confirms that there was really only one candidate. And City were not getting just the one Cowley, they were getting two: any discussion of Danny Cowley must include brother Nicky, who had signed up as assistant manager. They resigned their teaching positions at FitzWimarc School in Rayleigh, and started the immense task of turning Lincoln City into a viable football club again.

Who was Danny Cowley? He came from Essex, and a similar appointment had not worked out too well for Lincoln a few seasons earlier. But this man was different. Always active in coaching from his early teens, Cowley had spent his entire playing career in the non-league scene in the south-east after failing to make the grade at Wimbledon. Nearing the end of his career with a persistent hamstring injury, he joined Concord Rangers as joint-manager (with Danny Scopes) in the summer of 2007 and proceeded to take the Essex Senior League club to promotion to the Isthmian League at the first attempt. They also reached the quarter-final of the FA Vase, giving him an early scent of Wembley. The play-offs were reached the following season, unsuccessfully, but they won promotion again in 2009-10. They spent a couple of seasons consolidating in the Isthmian Premier Division before winning promotion to Conference South in 2013 in Danny's first season as sole manager. From the Essex Senior League to Conference South in six seasons was startling for such a small club, and they also added the Isthmian League Cup with a win over Dulwich.

Having turned down the manager's position at Chelmsford City, there followed two seasons of steady improvement which ended in a close call for the Conference South play-offs in 2015. But it was becoming inevitable that Cowley would need to move on if he were to test his abilities at a higher level. Perhaps the most significant event came in September 2014: his brother Nicky was forced to retire as a player with Concord and took over the assistant manager's post. When National League side Braintree Town came calling in April 2015, the pair moved as an established management team. In their only season at Braintree, they astounded the football world by taking the tiny Essex club to third place in the National League, suffering defeat to full-time Grimsby only when their part-time players tired in the second leg of the play-off semi-final. 'The non-league Ranieri' was now a marked man, and City faced competition from a number of National and Football League clubs before they persuaded him to sign on the dotted line that night at Cambridge Services.

The Cowleys immediately set about building a squad capable of delivering their renowned high-pressing game, and there were few surprises in the retained list. In came England C captain Alex Woodyard from Braintree, followed by several other experienced National League players including skilful Grimsby winger Nathan Arnold, England C left-back Sam Habergham (also from Braintree), and towering centre half Sean Raggett from Dover. The season got under way with an excellent 3-1 win away to bogey team Woking, and City were up and running. The crowds came back in big numbers as City shot to the top of the National League with a series of outstanding displays. Cowley continued to refine his squad as the number of games increased, bringing in Elliott Whitehouse from Nuneaton, exciting young winger Harry Anderson on loan from Peterborough, and vastly experienced striker Theo Robinson, who would have a big impact during his short stay at the club. Even the FA Cup held no terrors as the Imps embarked on a record-breaking run that saw them reach the quarter-final for the first time in their history. At the same time, the club also reached the semi-final of the FA Trophy despite fielding a second-string. For the first time ever, City were still in all three competitions at the beginning of March.

The media frenzy that surrounded City's FA Cup run shone a very bright spotlight onto Danny Cowley, and numerous approaches for him from Football League clubs were rejected outright. City supporters received some great news on the morning of 12 January 2017 as the Cowleys extended their contracts to the end of the 2020-21 season. The news was in stark contrast to the announcement of the passing of legendary City manager Graham Taylor later that same day; perhaps new legends were being created at Sincil Bank. Television crews seemed to be camped outside the ground as Cowley became a well-known figure in the media with regular appearances on the BBC, BT Sport and Sky Sports. No fewer than twelve Lincoln City matches were shown live on television, winning praise from the highest of quarters; when Premier League giants Arsenal ended City's astonishing FA Cup run with a 5-0 win on 11 March, even the great Arsène Wenger tipped them for the National League title.

With the FA Cup run over, and with an estimated £2.5 million in the bank, debt-free Lincoln City could now focus on a return to the Football League, and they had the money to do it. A number of quality loan signings arrived in the final three months of the season to boost player numbers for the run-in and crucially provide cover for every position. Despite extreme fatigue from the sheer number of games played (61), the players got City over the line with an astonishing seven straight wins. A 2-1 win over Macclesfield Town on 22 April in front of over 10,000 at Sincil Bank took Lincoln City back to the Football League, an astonishing achievement in Cowley's first season as a professional football manager. To cap a tremendous season, on 17 May Cowley was named *FieldTurf Manager of the Year* at the National Game Awards for the second year running. His side also collected the *Red Insure Team of the Year* and *Acerbis Cup Run of the Year* awards in addition to individual awards for Paul Farman, Alex Woodyard and Sean Raggett.

Danny Cowley very quickly proved to be very different to anything seen previously at Sincil Bank. His eloquent and always approachable personality won over even the most cynical of critics, while his approach to medical care, sports science and general fitness work was akin to a Premier League club. His playing philosophy came straight from the Jürgen Klopp school of football, while his previous experience as a school teacher was always visible in the way he handled players and supporters alike. He immediately created ties to a number of organisations around the city that he knew could be of service, including sports scientists and statisticians from the local universities and training facilities that could be utilised at low cost. He reconnected the club with its local community in a way that had not been seen since Graham Taylor's day, witnessed by the huge queues snaking around the ground for the big games that came thick and fast over the second half of the 2016-17 season. Supported wonderfully by brother Nicky, Lincoln City was transformed from a moribund former Football League club into a vibrant, exciting club of the future within a matter of months. Cowley believes the journey has just begun, and fans are already dreaming of reaching the Championship; with a new training ground, money in the bank and even a new stadium on the horizon, it would take a brave soul to bet against him doing just that.

Lincoln City Record - Conference Only

	P	W	D	L	F	A	Pts	PPG	Win%
League	46	30	9	7	83	40	99	2.15	65.2
FA Cup	9	6	2	1	14	12	N/A	N/A	66.7
FA Trophy	6	4	1	1	12	6	N/A	N/A	66.7
Totals	*61*	*40*	*12*	*9*	*109*	*58*	*N/A*	*N/A*	*65.6*

Imperama

The general information section

Appearances

The record for the most appearances during City's six-year stay in the Conference is held by Alan Power, who is the longest-serving player on the books. Power made a total of 261 league and cup appearances, scoring 36 goals. Paul Farman holds the record for the most starts, with 231 in all competitions compared to Power's 225. Power and Farman are the only players to appear in all six seasons. In 2016-17, Farman also set the club record for appearances in a season by a goalkeeper (58).

Alan Power holds the club records for the most appearances in the Conference (222) and the FA Trophy (13). Power's total in the FA Cup (26) is just one short of the club record of 27 held by George Fraser (1901-1911).

Attendances

Having plummeted following relegation, average home attendances remained relatively consistent until 2016-17:

2011-12 2,347 (2,298 including cup matches)

2012-13 2,181 (2,241 including cup matches)

2013-14 2,353 (2,276 including cup matches)

2014-15 2,562 (2,468 including cup matches)

2015-16 2,594 (2,585 including cup matches)

2016-17 5,161 (5,477 including cup matches)

The largest attendance for a league game since relegation came at the championship-winning game against Macclesfield Town on 22 April 2017 (10,031). This is also the largest attendance at any league game in the six years in the Conference, home or away, and the largest attendance since Sincil Bank was re-configured to all-seated in 1999.

The smallest for a home league game since relegation was 1,379 against Wrexham on 12 March 2013.

The smallest attendance for any home game since relegation was 1,023 for the FA Trophy first round tie against Stalybridge Celtic on 30 November 2013.

The sudden upsurge in attendances over the second half of the 2016-17 season caused the club numerous problems with ticketing. The sale of packages such as the *Bob's Baker's Dozen* and *Six-pack* meant that the club did not have an accurate idea of how many match tickets had already been sold. As a consequence, many matches during the run-in were made either all-ticket or all-ticket for certain areas of the ground.

Captain

The role of captain has sometimes been divided between two areas - club captain and team captain, with the latter being the most recognised designation. The following players have officially been appointed team captain, but numerous others have taken over the role on a temporary basis in the absence of the appointee (*shown in brackets*).

2011-12   Josh Gowling (*John Nutter*), John Nutter

2012-13   Gary Mills (*Andrew Boyce, Tom Miller*), Alan Power (*Andrew Boyce, Nat Brown*)

2013-14   Alan Power (*Nat Brown, Tom Miller*)

2014-15   Alan Power (*Nat Brown, Hamza Bencherif*)

2015-16   Alan Power (*Craig Stanley, Paul Farman, Matt Rhead, Jack Muldoon*)

2016-17   Luke Waterfall (*Bradley Wood, Alan Power, Sam Habergham*)

Clive Nates

Quite how an Everton supporter from Johannesburg came to be involved with Lincoln City was originally a mystery. Retired hedge fund manager and global equity investor Clive Nates had been watching from afar ever since Everton and Lincoln agreed a tenuous alliance in the early 2000s, and the draw had become stronger. He approached Bob Dorrian in 2015 when the City chairman was coincidentally in South Africa, and informal discussions commenced with a view to investing in Lincoln City. The move officially took place in late 2015/early 2016, and Nates became a director on 4 February 2016 just as the settlement deal was agreed with the Co-op Bank. Believed to be around £1m, the investment was to come from a small consortium under the Sportvest LLP name, and was to be spread sensibly over a five-year period.

Since that time, Clive Nates has brought much more than money to Sincil Bank. Many observers feel the club has become more professional in a number of ways, including external communication. Fully engaged with the fans through various social media, Clive was heavily involved in the search for a new manager and was instrumental in identifying and persuading Danny and Nicky Cowley to move to Sincil Bank. Despite continuing to live in his homeland, his arrival at the club undoubtedly kick-started a dramatic revival in Lincoln City's fortunes, and he continues to play a leading role in carrying the club forward.

Conference / National League

England's senior non-league competition has undergone several changes in name and sponsor during City's membership:

2011-12	Blue Square Bet Conference Premier
2012-13	Blue Square Bet Conference Premier
2013-14	Skrill Conference Premier
2014-15	Vanarama Conference
2015-16	Vanarama National League
2016-17	Vanarama National League

The Co-operative Bank

In early February 2015, City announced that they had to find around £380,000 urgently to repay all monies owed to their bankers, Co-operative Bank. The problem had arisen around a year earlier when the Co-op had asked City to find alternative banking facilities following a change in business strategy; unfortunately City had been unable to do so, which is hardly surprising, given the size of the debt. The bank had now decided to call in the full amount of the debt, which was money the club did not have. The debt consisted of an £80,000 mortgage on the PlayZone facility at Sincil Bank, plus an overdraft of up to £300,000, which was essentially fully utilised.

With the Co-op pressing for the sale of club assets, City appealed to fans for support by offering 50p shares and three-year bonds offering a 3% return, although the bonds were delayed due to problems finalising the correct security for them. The problem was exacerbated in early March when City were given just ten weeks to clear the debt. The various appeals raised around £160,000, topped up by an estimated £25,000 from the Madness gig on 29 May. Other attempts to raise funds through a *Save The Imps* Crowdfunder appeal and the ill-fated *Dambusters* scheme were not successful.

Although well short of the £380,000 needed, the improvement in finances eventually enabled the club to agree a fifteen-year settlement with the Co-op after a fraught and protracted period of negotiation. In early December 2015, Bob Dorrian announced that the club would repay the debt at the rate of £25,000 per year for the next ten years, followed by £10,000 for five years to repay the outstanding overdraft. Dorrian effectively took over the mortgage on

PlayZone by loaning the club the money to pay it off. He called the deal 'financially damaging' to the club, but at least its short-term future had been secured. What Bob did not reveal is that he had offered his own property as security.

On the same day, City announced that agreement had been reached with an unnamed investor to put a seven-figure sum into the club over the next five years; the unnamed investor turned out to be Clive Nates, and things were finally looking up.

As things turned out, the deal with the Co-op Bank was short-lived. City's dramatic run to the quarter-finals of the FA Cup in 2016-17 enabled the club to clear the debt completely, fourteen years early.

Cowley's Campaign

Following the success of the *Moyses' Mission* Crowdfunder appeal in the summer of 2015, a similar fundraising initiative was launched on 27 June 2016 to provide funds for new manager Danny Cowley's playing budget. Also using the Crowdfunder platform, a range of benefits including signed match balls and shirts were offered in exchange for donations from supporters. An added dimension this time was the matching of donations to a maximum of £25,000 by a mystery backer, who turned out to be new City director Ian Reeve. By the time the campaign closed on 22 August, donations had reached £27,522; including the £25,000 from the mystery backer, a sum of £52,522 went to the playing budget. The club later revealed that the money had already been used to sign Nathan Arnold, who proved to be a key signing in the unforgettable 2016-17 season.

The Dambusters Appeal

Following the club's announcement that the debt to the Co-op Bank was being called in, one of the ideas to raise funds very quickly was to superimpose an image of a Lancaster bomber onto the seats in the Co-op Stand. Announced on 26 February 2015, the idea came from Preston North End, who had created an image of legendary winger Sir Tom Finney for seats at their Deepdale ground. With the painting of the Lancaster coming from the talented brush of renowned aviation artist Simon Atack, fans were invited to sponsor individual seats ranging from £40 to £250. With the target set at £150,000, it would be the largest scheme of its kind if successful.

Again using the Crowdfunder platform, the scheme was officially open to donations from 19 March 2015. Despite the subject matter and the extensive publicity surrounding it, the scheme failed to capture the imagination of the Lincoln public. Supporters remained unconvinced by the idea, one problem being the proposed move to a new stadium within five years. By the time the scheme closed on 13 May, just £53,960 had been pledged and no money was collected.

Delroy Facey & Moses Swaibu

The problem of match-fixing has reared its ugly head at various times in British football, most notably following allegations against former Lincoln players John Fashanu and Bruce Grobbelaar - and Wimbledon goalkeeper Hans Segers - in the second half of the 1990s. Rumours abounded after that, but the only high-profile cases were in other sports.

That changed on 28 November 2013 when six people were arrested on suspicion of football match-fixing on behalf of an international betting syndicate. One of those named was former City captain Delroy Facey, who had played for the club in their relegation season of 2010-11. As the investigation continued, it emerged that another of the accused was Facey's erstwhile City teammate Moses Swaibu, and that one of the players they had tried to recruit was another former City striker, Scott Spencer, who had refused point-blank to be involved. Although there was never any real suspicion that games involving Lincoln City were targeted, it cast a shadow over City's presence in non-league football as supporters wondered whether the pair could be responsible for that fate. That suspicion was refuted, as the investigation concentrated on a number of non-league matches played in 2013.

At the end of a protracted and at times complex series of trials and re-trials, both players were found guilty of conspiracy to commit bribery: on 29 April 2015 at Birmingham Crown Court, Facey was jailed for two-and-a-half years for his central role in the scheme, and Swaibu for sixteen months.

England C

The England C team is specifically for players outside the Football League under the age of 23; up to three overage players may also be used at any one time. Matches are largely played against the U23 and U21 teams from eastern European countries, with sides from the former Soviet states and the former Yugoslavia providing regular opponents.

The following players have made appearances for the England C team while on the books at Lincoln:

Jordan Burrow (3): v Turkey B, 14/10/2014; v Estonia U23, 18/11/2014; v Cyprus U21, 17/2/2015.

Jon Nolan (1): v Estonia U23, 18/11/2014.

Elliott Whitehouse (1): v Estonia U23, 15/11/2016 (1 goal).

Alex Woodyard (1): v Estonia U23, 15/11/2016 (captain).

Adam Watts was called up to the contingency squad for the home game against India on 6/9/2011.

Paul Farman was called up for the game in Albania on 16/10/2012, only to have the game postponed due to flooding.

Tom Miller was placed on standby for the game against Jordan U23 on 4/3/2014, and again for the games against Slovakia U23 on 24/5/2014 and Hungary on 28/5/2014.

Sam Habergham and Sean Raggett were called up for the game against Estonia U23 on 15/11/2016 alongside Elliott Whitehouse and Alex Woodyard, but were both forced to withdraw through injury.

Callum Howe became the final City player to be called up to the squad when he was selected for the friendlies against Punjab FA on 28/5/2017 and Jersey FA on 30/5/2017.

FA Cup

The Football Association Challenge Cup is England's premier cup competition and consists of two preliminary and four qualifying rounds prior to the FA Cup proper, which commences with the first round. National League clubs enter at the fourth qualifying round stage, one round before the first round proper when clubs from the lower two divisions of the Football League enter the competition.

City's record in the competition has been poor historically. Prior to the incredible run in 2016-17 which saw the Imps reach the quarter-final, their best run since relegation came in 2012-13 when they reached the second round. A win over Conference rivals Mansfield Town would have brought City a home tie against Premier League giants Liverpool in the third round, but a last-gasp equaliser at Sincil Bank by future City legend Matt Rhead earned Mansfield a replay, which City lost 2-1.

Between seasons 2010-11 and 2014-15, 8 consecutive Lincoln City FA Cup ties went to replays, which is believed to be a record for the competition. The opponents concerned were: Hereford United (2010-11); Alfreton Town (2011-12); FC Halifax Town, Walsall and Mansfield Town (2012-13); Worcester City and Plymouth Argyle (2013-14); and Alfreton Town again in 2014-15. The run was ended by Eastleigh in the first round on 8 November 2014 when a 90th minute goal by Ben Strevens gave the home side a 2-1 win.

Since relegation, City have beaten five clubs from the Football League: Walsall in 2012-13, and Oldham Athletic, Ipswich Town, Brighton & Hove Albion and Burnley in 2016-17.

The astonishing run to the quarter-final in 2016-17 set a number of records:

The official away contingent of 4,838 at the third round tie at Championship side Ipswich Town on 7 January 2017 was the largest away following at Portman Road since the ground was converted to all-seater in 1992.

The win over Ipswich in the third round replay on 17 January 2017 was the first time in City's history that they had knocked a team from three tiers higher out of the FA Cup. They took exactly eleven days to do it again by beating Brighton.

The attendance of 9,469 for the fourth round win over Brighton & Hove Albion on 28 January 2017 was the highest at Sincil Bank since the ground was reconfigured to an all-seated stadium. That record was surpassed by the 10,031 which attended the championship-winning game against Macclesfield Town on 22 April 2017.

The win over Brighton made City only the eighth non-league team to reach the last 16 since the Second World War.

The win over Premier League Burnley in the fifth round on 18 February 2017 was the first time in City's history that they had knocked a team from four tiers higher out of the FA Cup.

The win over Burnley put City through to the quarter-finals of the FA Cup for the first time in their 133-year history. It was only the second time in City's history that they had beaten a top-flight side in the FA Cup (the other being West Bromwich Albion in 1960-61), and the first time they had done it away from home.

The win over Burnley also made City the first non-league club to reach the quarter-final of the FA Cup since Queens Park Rangers in 1914, and the first since the competition was reorganised into its present format in 1925.

The official total of 8,942 supporters at the quarter-final tie at Arsenal on 11 March 2017 is believed to be the largest away following in City's history, other than for the two play-off finals in 2003 and 2005.

The attendance at the Emirates Stadium of 59,454 is the second-highest attendance ever at any game involving Lincoln City, surpassed only by the Second Division match at Everton on 16 April 1954 (61,231).

The Game at Arsenal was City's ninth FA Cup match of the season, setting a new club record.

The FA Cup run in 2016-17 earned City an estimated £2.5 million, enabling them to pay off the Co-op debt fourteen years early.

Record since relegation: P27 W11 D10 L6 F42 A38.

Fourth qualifying round: 1

First round proper: 3

Second round proper: 1

Third round proper: 0

Fourth round proper: 0

Fifth round proper: 0

Quarter-final: 1

FA Trophy

The Football Association Challenge Trophy is the main cup competition for non-league clubs and is open to clubs from tiers 5 to 8 of the English football league system. The competition consists of one preliminary and three qualifying rounds prior to the competition proper. National League clubs enter at the first round proper stage.

As per the FA Cup, City's limited record in the competition has been poor. Although they reached the quarter-final in 1987-88, they had made little headway since relegation in 2011 with some notorious defeats, notably to Carshalton Athletic and North Ferriby United.

Like everything else, that all changed in 2016-17 as City surged to the semi-final. Ironically, the team that reached the semi-final was essentially a second-string consisting of squad players and loanees. With the demands of the National League promotion campaign increasing as the season progressed, it was the sensible approach to a competition that inevitably took third place behind the league and the incredible FA Cup run. The run was all the more remarkable because City were drawn away in every round including the semi-final first leg.

Record since relegation: P15 W7 D2 L6 F26 A23.

First round proper: 3

Second round proper: 1

Third round proper: 1

Fourth round proper (quarter-final):

Semi-final: 1

Gary Charles

City were rocked in 2014 by a claim for unpaid wages from former England international Gary Charles, who had served as coach and assistant manager under David Holdsworth between November 2011 and May 2012. Charles was claiming £50,000, based upon the legal principle of *quantum meruit* - a reasonable sum of money to be paid for services rendered or work done when the amount due is not stipulated in a legally enforceable contract. There were several obvious flaws with the claim, including the fact that Charles had never formally been appointed by the club in any capacity regardless of the existence of a contract, and that the amount of £50,000 was far more than Holdsworth himself had earned as manager. Nevertheless, the case cost City a substantial sum of money in legal costs regardless of the outcome, and a judgment in favour of Charles would have been very serious financially.

The case was heard over three days at Lincoln Magistrates Court, between 22 and 24 July 2015. City insisted that Charles and Curtis Woodhouse were assisting the club on a voluntary basis, and that no offers for a permanent contract were ever made. Charles claimed that Holdsworth had promised to arrange a contract for him after an initial trial period of four to six weeks, together with retrospective payment if the club remained in the Conference Premier. This was denied by Holdsworth on the basis that he was only on a short-term contract himself to the end of the season and was in no position to make such assurances. Former players Tyrone Thomson and Josh Gowling spoke in support of Charles, believing him to have been a coach at the club. However, Charles' case was not helped by Curtis Woodhouse not bringing a similar claim on his own part.

When the judgment was finally handed down 6 November 2015, it was in City's favour with costs. Giving his response to the outcome, chairman Bob Dorrian confirmed the case would have cost the club over £80,000 had the claim been successful.

Hat-tricks

Nine hat-tricks were scored during City's six years out of the Football League, scored by nine different players:

3/8/2012	Colin Larkin	3 v Dartford (A)	Conference Premier
20/4/2013	Vadaine Oliver	3 v Hyde (A)	Conference Premier
30/11/2013	Alan Power	3 v Stalybridge Celtic (H)	FA Trophy 1
1/2/2014	Ben Tomlinson	3 v FC Halifax Town (H)	Conference Premier
28/10/2014	Sean Newton	3 v Alfreton Town (H)	FA Cup 4Q Replay
18/8/2015	Liam Hearn	3 v Macclesfield Town (H)	National League

8/11/2015	Matt Rhead	3 v Whitehawk (A)	FA Cup 1
20/8/2016	Jonny Margetts	4 v Southport (H)	National League
7/3/2017	Lee Angol	3 v Braintree Town (A)	National League

Larkin's hat-trick came in the first half, while Oliver's came in the second half. Newton is the only defender in the club's history to score a hat-trick, and it came against an outfield player standing in for the regular goalkeeper, who was missing through injury. Margetts is the only player of the nine to score 4 in a match, with the unusual combination of header-left foot-right foot-penalty. Angol became only the second player in the club's history to hit a hat-trick on debut, and the first to do it away from home. Angol was also the 100th different player to score a competitive hat-trick for the club. Rhead is the only one to finish on the losing side, with the other eight being wins.

Leading Goalscorers

The record for the most goals scored during City's six-year stay in the Conference is held by Matt Rhead with 37 in all competitions between August 2015 and April 2017. Rhead holds the record for the most goals in the Conference itself (34) and is also the club's all-time record goalscorer in non-league football. Theo Robinson holds the record for the most goals in the FA Cup during the six-year exile (7), and Alan Power the record for the FA Trophy (4).

Leading goalscorers by season are:

2011-12	Sam Smith, 9 (7 Conference Premier, 2 FA Cup)
2012-13	Jamie Taylor, 16 (13 Conference Premier, 3 FA Cup)
2013-14	Ben Tomlinson, 20 (18 Conference Premier, 2 FA Cup)
2014-15	Ben Tomlinson, 14 (14 Conference)
2015-16	Matt Rhead, 23 (20 National League, 3 FA Cup)
2016-17	Matt Rhead, 14 (14 National League)

Some databases credit Matt Rhead with 15 league goals in 2016-17, but this is incorrect. The extra goal stems from City's 5-2 win at Chester on 29 October when Rhead was initially credited with City's 42nd-minute equaliser. Television replays clearly showed Rhead's effort hit the post and rebounded into the net off Theo Robinson, and the goal was correctly allocated to Robinson two days later.

Lincoln City Holdings

Better known as 'the holding company', Lincoln City Holdings was created in January 2012 primarily to facilitate a cash injection of £522,000 into the club from chairman Bob Dorrian, Lincolnshire Co-operative and the Lindum Group. The move was deemed necessary to secure the immediate future of the club following the financial privations of relegation, with Dorrian casting doubts over the club's ability to pay its way in February and March otherwise. The move was also made as a vehicle to facilitate further investment into the club, although its very existence has been controversial and subject to various challenges since its formation. The investment process involves the purchase of shares in Lincoln City, then converting those into shares in Lincoln City Holdings, thereby giving the shareholder more say in the running of the club. Many people feel the formation of the holding company has devalued shares in Lincoln City Football Club, but in reality those shares held very little value for most shareholders anyway.

The decision by Lincoln City Supporters' Trust to move a large number of its shares into the holding company divided opinion, considering late chairman John Reames had gifted the shares to it in order to preserve independence from the club and maintain a critical say in its running.

Lincoln City Holdings owns a controlling interest of three million shares in the club, meaning a takeover would cost a minimum of £1.5 million. The influx of capital following the advent of Clive Nates and Sportvest LLP in February 2016 further secured the importance of the holding company at the heart of Lincoln City.

Lincoln City Supporters' Trust

Better known as 'the Trust', Lincoln City Supporters' Trust was founded in 2001 in an attempt to raise funds to keep the club in existence. Its foundation lay in shares donated by former chairman John Reames, which gave the supporters a powerful voice in the running of Lincoln City as its major shareholder. Widely credited with saving the club following administration in 2002, it made City the first community-owned club in the Football League and allowed fans to place two members on the board. One million of its shares were transferred to Lincoln City Holdings upon its formation in January 2012.

The existence of the Trust has been somewhat chequered in recent years, marred at times by internal conflict, personality clashes, numerous changes to its board of directors, and legal battles that had nothing to do with football. Membership of the Trust stood at more than 1,000 in its heyday, although that reduced rapidly as things turned sour. In June 2014, the position had deteriorated to the point at which an emergency working party had to be set up to keep it going. The involvement of former City chairman Rob Bradley at that point gave credence to the project, and an open meeting that month gave the working party a mandate to continue. A successful legal challenge by businessman Michael Foley to the way in which the Trust had operated resulted in a large legal bill in November 2014, but also cleared the way to resuscitate the organisation and regain the confidence of the supporters once more. A new Trust Board was elected in November 2015, and despite further problems in establishing a settled personnel, was officially re-launched as the Red Imps Community Trust in March 2016. A further setback followed in July 2016 when Lincoln City refused to ratify the appointment of Trust chairman Rob Bradley to its board of directors; Bradley was forced to resign as chairman, to be replaced by Steve Tointon. Since that time, the Trust appears to have abandoned squabbling and acting beyond its powers as its main activities, and returned to its appointed duty of supporting Lincoln City once more.

Lincoln Lizards

A nickname given to the FA Trophy team in 2016-17. In order to protect his key players from the negative effects of playing too many games, manager Danny Cowley chose to field a team made up of fringe players and loanees in what was viewed as the least important competition in City's season. For some reason, the team became known as the Lincoln Lizards.

Lincolnshire Cup

As members of the Lincolnshire Football Association, Lincoln City are obliged to take part in the Lincolnshire Senior Cup each season, which is intended primarily as a pre-season competition. Although of very little importance to senior clubs Grimsby, Scunthorpe and Lincoln, the rules of the competition impose certain conditions on participants including the requirement to field strong sides at all times. This has often thrown the senior clubs into conflict with the Lincolnshire FA, particularly when the latter stages of the competition have taken place within the regular football season. One such conflict took place in July/August 2011 when Steve Tilson planned to field a youth team in the final against Grimsby; he was prevented from doing so.

The structure of the competition has also changed regularly over the years, with numerous changes in category. As of 2015, the Senior Cup is contested between Lincoln City, Grimsby Town, Scunthorpe United, Boston United, Gainsborough Trinity, Stamford, Lincoln United, Spalding United, and Grantham Town, although Scunthorpe paid a fee to be exempt from the 2016-17 competition. As one of the three most senior clubs, City are exempt to the semi-final stage.

City's record since relegation:

2011-12: Losing finalists

2012-13: Losing finalists

2013-14: Winners

2014-15: Losing finalists

2015-16: Semi-finalists

2016-17: Semi-finalists

Lincolnshire FA U21 Development League

The Lincolnshire FA U21 Development League was formed in 2015 to provide local clubs with low-cost competitive football for their youth teams. Although largely for players under the age of 21, up to three overage players may be fielded including a goalkeeper. The first champions in 2015-16 were Boston United.

City took the decision to join the league in July 2016 for various reasons. First of all, it provided competitive football for the development players who were not in the picture at first team level. With no reserve team, new manager Danny Cowley felt the gap between the two levels was too wide. Secondly, it gave City a vehicle for giving first team players some valuable game time to build match fitness after injury. The side is managed by Academy managers Damian Froggatt and Dean West.

Managers

Lincoln City have had five permanent managers since relegation, with Grant Brown stepping in as caretaker following the departures of Steve Tilson and David Holdsworth. Chris Moyses was effectively the caretaker following the dismissal of Gary Simpson, with Brown assisting, before his appointment on a permanent basis. Detailed information on each can be found in *The Managers* chapter.

Steve Tilson: 15 October 2010 to 10 October 2011

Grant Brown (caretaker): 10 October 2011 to 24 October 2011

David Holdsworth: 24 October 2011 to 17 February 2013

Grant Brown (caretaker): 18 February 2013 to 27 February 2013

Gary Simpson: 27 February 2013 to 3 November 2014

Chris Moyses (caretaker): 3 November 2014 to 8 December 2014

Chris Moyses: 8 December 2014 to 30 April 2016

Danny Cowley: 13 May 2016 to present

Their records are as follows:

Conference/National League games only:

		P	W	D	L	F	A	Pts	PPG	Win%
1	Danny Cowley	46	30	9	7	83	40	99	2.15	65.2
2	Gary Simpson	77	29	21	27	108	106	108	1.40	37.6
3	Chris Moyses	74	26	18	30	102	108	96	1.30	35.1
4	David Holdsworth	59	18	14	27	87	99	68	1.15	30.5
5	Steve Tilson	14	3	3	8	11	16	12	0.86	21.4
6	Grant Brown	6	1	2	3	5	8	5	0.83	16.7

All games (Conference/FA Cup/FA Trophy):

		P	W	D	L	F	A	Win%
1	Danny Cowley	61	40	12	9	109	58	65.6
2	Gary Simpson	86	33	24	29	126	120	38.3
3	Chris Moyses	80	27	19	34	109	119	33.7
4	David Holdsworth	71	21	19	31	104	117	29.5
5	Steve Tilson	14	3	3	8	11	16	21.4
6	Grant Brown	6	1	2	3	5	8	16.7

Manager of the Month

Two Lincoln managers have won the prestigious monthly award from the Conference / National League:

November 2012: David Holdsworth

October 2016: Danny Cowley

Manager of the Year

Danny Cowley was named *FieldTurf Manager of the Year* at the National Game Awards for the second year running at a ceremony held at Stamford Bridge on 17 May 2017.

Moyses' Mission

The first of the really successful Crowdfunder campaigns, *Moyses' Mission* was launched on 7 June 2015 with the objective of raising funds for manager Chris Moyses' playing budget. The brainchild of supporter Andrew Helgeson, supporters were invited to make donations in exchange for a range of benefits including VIP tickets and t-shirts. A further boost came on 12 July when a mystery backer pledged an extra £10 for every pledge over £10. When the appeal closed on 31 July, a total of £16,440 had been pledged, which increased to £19,300 once the mystery backer was included.

The money had already been used to sign defender Callum Howe on 15 July.

Moyses' Mission The Next Goal

This Crowdfunder campaign was launched on 26 October 2015 to raise further funds to support the team's excellent start to the season. Intending to fund the signing of a new player during the January transfer window, it offered similar benefits to the original campaign. Unfortunately this one proved an appeal too far, and closed on 14 December having realised just £2,680.

New Stadium

Although Sincil Bank appears to be a fine modern stadium - and by comparison to the majority of grounds in the National League, it is - it has become increasingly apparent that the majority of small clubs need to generate alternative sources of income to enable survival. Many new stadia built within the last ten years have been conceived as multi-purpose venues capable of providing income streams outside of match days. Function suites, restaurants and rentable office accommodation can create revenue over and above that generated from football activities. Within that context, City have decided that Sincil Bank is no longer fit for purpose.

Several sites around the city have been assessed but nothing concrete has been determined at the time of writing. Discussions with the city council over a site at Swanpool were proceeding well until July 2016 when builders Taylor Wimpey pulled out of a plan to build 3,000 homes on the site; without the infrastructure created by the development, plans for the new stadium could not proceed. Funding is still to be secured, but the intention is to move into a new stadium within the next five to ten years.

The question of capacity came under scrutiny following the huge surge in attendances experienced during the 2016-17 season. Originally intended to seat 10,000, the current view suggests that may be amended to 15,000 or more if City's upturn in fortunes continues into the Football League.

Parachute Payment

The parachute payment is a sum of money paid by the Football League to a club relegated to the Conference, intended to help the club settle into life outside the protective financial blanket of the League. City received £225,000 but the amount varies each year. Clubs relegated from 2016 onwards receive a further payment in their second season after relegation provided they are not promoted at the first attempt.

Player of the Month

Two Lincoln players have won the Conference / National League Player of the Month award:

October 2012: Jamie Taylor

February 2017: Luke Waterfall

Player of the Season

The Player of the Season award is voted for by the supporters and dates back to 1969-70 when the first winner was goalkeeper John Kennedy. The winners since relegation are:

2011-12	Joe Anyon
2012-13	Alan Power
2013-14	Tom Miller
2014-15	Paul Farman
2015-16	Bradley Wood
2016-17	Alex Woodyard

PlayZone

PlayZone is an indoor soft-play area for adults and children, situated adjacent to Sincil Bank Stadium. Although the owners of the business itself were independent, the building was owned by the club, and formed part of the original debt owed to the Co-op Bank. City chairman Bob Dorrian took over the mortgage on the building at the time of the deal in December 2015, before it was sold to the owners of the PlayZone business in 2017.

Reserve Team

One of the inevitable casualties of City's relegation from the Football League was the club's reserve team. In its final season of 2010-11, the reserve team finished in fifth place (out of eight) in the Central League Eastern Division with 20 points from its 14 games.

Although there was an urgent need to cut costs throughout the club, the decision has often meant a lack of regular football for those not involved with the first team on a weekly basis. Problems have also arisen with moving players back to full fitness following injury.

In an effort to overcome these problems, and also to narrow the gap between first team and academy levels, City entered the Lincolnshire FA U21 Development League for the 2016-17 season.

Save The Imps

The *Save The Imps* Crowdfunder appeal was launched on 5 February 2015, the day after City announced they had to find £380,000 to repay the debt to the Co-op Bank. Intending to raise £350,000 by 5 March, the campaign never got going and closed having received just £2,740 in pledges.

Television

Several television companies have been involved in the broadcasting of non-league football. Coverage of the Conference Premier was initially the preserve of Premier Sports, a division of Luxembourg-based Setanta Sports, who held the rights between the start of the 2010-11 season and the end of 2012-2013. The fee payable to the home club was £5,000, with £1,000 going to the away club. In May 2013 the rights were awarded to fledgling broadcaster BT Sport, who increased the fees payable to £6,000 and £2,000 respectively.

Rights for the FA Cup proper have usually been shared between competing companies, with ITV and satellite broadcaster ESPN holding sway until 2013. BT Sport took over sharing live matches with ITV from 2013 after it purchased ESPN's UK and Ireland operation. Since 2014 BT has shared live coverage with the BBC. Fees for the FA Cup are far more lucrative than the National League, with the fee set at £72,000 per club for the Oldham match in the second round in the 2016-17 season, £72,000 for the replay victory over Ipswich in the third round (half of the £144,000 fee for an original third round tie), and £247,500 for the fifth and sixth round ties at Burnley and Arsenal.

The following matches featuring Lincoln City have been shown live on television since relegation:

19/8/11	Lincoln 1 Wrexham 2	Conference Premier	Premier Sports
3/9/11	Braintree Town 1 Lincoln 0	Conference Premier	Premier Sports
14/10/11	Lincoln 1 Fleetwood Town 3	Conference Premier	Premier Sports
13/4/12	Fleetwood Town 2 Lincoln 2	Conference Premier	Premier Sports
28/9/12	Forest Green Rovers 3 Lincoln 0	Conference Premier	Premier Sports
18/4/15	Lincoln 1 Eastleigh 2	Conference	BT Sport
2/10/15	Guiseley 0 Lincoln 1	National League	BT Sport
28/12/15	Grimsby Town 2 Lincoln 0	National League	BT Sport
25/3/16	Tranmere Rovers 3 Lincoln 2	National League	BT Sport
3/9/16	Torquay United 1 Lincoln 2	National League	BT Sport
19/11/16	Forest Green Rovers 2 Lincoln 3	National League	BT Sport

5/12/16	Lincoln 3 Oldham Athletic 2	FA Cup 2	BT Sport
17/1/17	Lincoln 1 Ipswich Town 0	FA Cup 3 Replay	BBC
21/1/17	Lincoln 2 Dover Athletic 0	National League	BT Sport
24/1/17	Barrow 3 Lincoln 0	National League	BT Sport
18/2/17	Burnley 0 Lincoln 1	FA Cup 5	BT Sport
11/3/17	Arsenal 5 Lincoln 0	FA Cup QF	BT Sport
25/3/17	Lincoln 3 Forest Green Rovers 1	National League	BT Sport
3/4/17	Lincoln 2 Dagenham & Redbridge 0	National League	BT Sport
17/4/17	Gateshead 1 Lincoln 2	National League	BT Sport
22/4/17	Lincoln 2 Macclesfield Town 1	National League	BT Sport

City's FA Cup first round defeat at Whitehawk on 8 November 2015 was featured by the BBC on their Sunday afternoon FA Cup special. The programme featured 'live highlights' from a number of games.

City's away game at Southport, scheduled for Friday 30 November 2012, was selected originally for live broadcast but was postponed due to City's involvement in the second round of the FA Cup.

Three successive City games were shown on live television in 2016-17 season: the FA Cup third round replay against Ipswich Town on BBC TV followed by the National League games against Dover and Barrow on BT Sport.

2016-17 was the most profitable season, the twelve live games earning a massive £671,000 in broadcasting fees.

Training Ground

The club's modern training ground on Carlton Boulevard was mothballed in June 2011 in order to save money following City's relegation from the Football League. The club was faced with a bill for £250,000 when soil samples revealed work would need to take place to make the pitches fit for purpose, and it was money the club did not have. As a result, City were forced to take advantage of various training facilities around the city whenever possible, using the 3G pitch at Sincil Bank as base.

However, Chris Moyses realised the problems inherent in training on an artificial surface but playing matches on grass, and took steps to establish facilities at the Sabraon Barracks on Burton Road in the summer of 2015. Rumours that Moyses paid for the facility out of his own pocket have not been substantiated officially, yet it would appear in keeping with his previous actions at Lincoln Moorlands Railway. Whatever the truth, the facility was certainly a step in the right direction.

The subject of training facilities arose again during contract negotiations with Danny and Nicky Cowley in December 2016 and January 2017. Although very willing to agree new deals with the club, the Cowleys made it a condition that the club would improve both its training facilities and the medical care provided for the players. The club readily agreed, and the pair signed contracts to the end of the 2020-21 season in return. In April 2017 the club confirmed that a purpose-built training centre is to be built at a site just outside the city, with its opening set for October/November 2017.

The Dorrian Review

For the first time, Bob gives his thoughts on his time as chairman - the managers, the players, and the reasons behind those landmark financial decisions.

At five o'clock after the Aldershot game, I was shell-shocked. I couldn't believe that a team that had been in with a chance of the play-offs with twelve games to go - and that out of those twelve games probably needed another four or five points to avoid relegation - had been relegated.

My comments after the game were probably true when I said it would take us two or three years to get back to the Football League. When Lincoln went straight back up in 1988 after the previous relegation, there were only one or two professional clubs in the division. Obviously that has a great bearing on your ability to bounce back. And that whilst a lot of clubs in the National League claim to be part-time, when you ask what their players do for a full-time job, they struggle to answer. You will find that a lot of these so-called part-time clubs are paying wages that are almost the equivalent of what we pay our players for full-time football. So the reality was that it was going to be a lot tougher to get out of the Conference this time than it had been twenty-three years earlier.

I also knew that we would be in severe financial difficulty. I had considered the unthinkable - what would happen if we did go down - and the consequences were horrific. In that last season in the Football League we received a solidarity payment, which is a combination of television money and FA money, of around £670,000 just for being in the League. That was obviously gone. We received a parachute payment of £225,000 in lieu, so we were already £445,000 down on where we were the previous season before we had even started. I also knew that gates would be down, and that all other incidental income streams such as catering and sponsorship would fall as a result.

What we also had to factor in, and what was worse, was the second season when we received no parachute payment at all. Had we been in the Football League, over those first two seasons in non-league we would have received £1.35 million; what we actually received was £225,000. Therefore we were more than a million pounds short of what was needed. Over those first two seasons, we lost between £1.5 million and £1.8 million in revenue and were still running a full-time football club with a big stadium and all its infrastructure costs. The crunch came in October/November 2011 when we realised we were simply going to run out of money over the second half of the season, and there would be no money to pay wages from February. We had some serious thinking to do.

That was when we began to consider the vehicle that became Lincoln City Holdings. In addition to the urgent need for working capital, we needed a way to make ourselves attractive to investors by giving them a significant say in the running of the football club in return; that could be achieved by becoming a director of the football club and exchanging those shares for shares in the holding company. Prior to the holding company, even a purchase of one million shares in the football club would secure only 12% ownership and no say whatsoever. No one in their right mind would do that. It is also a vehicle for selling the club. As things stand today, the holding company controls 60% of the football club and is therefore an attractive proposition should anyone feel inclined to buy. It is not that simple of course - we would require massive assurances and guarantees in writing, and we would only sell the club to an individual capable of taking the club further than we are able to do.

So there were two very good reasons for forming the holding company. I was the only person likely to invest in Lincoln City at that time. I put £500,000 into the club in January 2012 simply to make sure it survived, for without that money we would almost certainly have gone into administration. It was needed to ensure we could complete the season and re-group in the summer. Had we gone into administration, we would have suffered a points deduction and undoubtedly a further relegation. However, a little-known fact is this: even if we had enjoyed a good season on the pitch and gates had held up reasonably well, we would still have been in a similar financial position. The reality is, as a full-time professional football club in non-league, you are almost certain to lose money. It is simply a question of how much, and how much can you afford to lose, because it is about cash flow. As long as you have enough money coming in to replace those losses, theoretically you are fine.

Was Chris Sutton in any way to blame for our relegation? Some people believe he only came to Lincoln to gain experience in management and had not really expected to get the job in the first place, but his presentation to the board had been very professional, and he had been impressive at both interviews. Martin O'Neill even rang me to recommend him; Roy Hodgson spoke to one of our other directors to recommend Ian Pearce too, and we would be getting a Premier League centre half into the bargain, so there were several very good reasons why we felt Chris was the right man for the job. We reached the third round of the FA Cup, but consistency in the league was harder to establish. Somehow, it never quite worked out for him or for us.

Although I would never blame Chris, some of the signings that were made under his tenure were certainly a catalyst for what happened next. He did what he thought was right at the time. He has been accused in some quarters of offering deals to players that were outside the financial remit we had given him, but I never saw any evidence of that. He signed some good players - Mustapha Carayol and Albert Jarrett to name two - but he also signed too many who were not. He plundered Fulham using his Roy Hodgson connection, but were those players ultimately any better than who we already had? It was inevitable that the contracts we had agreed with players as a Football League club would have financial consequences after relegation, which is why we tried to move them all on in the summer of 2011.

I always remember his departure as a key moment. We were playing Burton Albion - who have since risen to the Championship - on a Tuesday night. I saw Chris as usual before the game, and he seemed fine. Despite being in the bottom four, we drew 0-0 and I thought we played really well. I went in to see him after the game to congratulate him, and he told me he was resigning. There was a reason, which we have mutually agreed not to broadcast, but it came as a complete surprise. I tried to persuade Chris to stay, but he was adamant. Out of the blue, we were facing the unenviable task of having to find a new manager mid-season who was capable of carrying us clear of the foot of the table using players signed by another manager. In no way would we have chosen to do that, and I still believe we would have remained in the Football League if Chris had stayed.

So when we appointed Steve Tilson, I thought we had done really well to get him. Here was a man who had taken Southend from League Two to the Championship in successive seasons on a comparatively small budget, and we all thought that there must be a good manager in there. To see him fail at the first hurdle with us was quite shattering. Watching that final game against Aldershot was like we were all watching a car crash in slow motion, including the manager. Although he never said anything to me, I think even Steve would admit that he had lost the dressing room by that stage, and there was nothing he could have said or done prior to the game - or even during it - that would have influenced the outcome. There were things going on that he had no control over.

At the end of that disastrous season, we all sat down as a board to decide what we were going to do next. The problem was, who were we going to get if we sacked Steve? The world of football awaited his dismissal, and perhaps Steve did too, but I gave him my backing in the immediate aftermath of relegation because I felt he had been unlucky. A lot of the things I said post-relegation were possibly ill-considered, but I believed Tilson had suffered a lot of critical injuries to key players in the last twelve games of that season. The most critical of all, and what started everything off, happened at Macclesfield on a cold Tuesday evening. We were leading 1-0 with about five minutes to go when Delroy Facey, who was our captain and who had built a great understanding with Ashley Grimes, was carried off, never to play for Lincoln City again. Ben Hutchinson had been sent off for two yellow cards earlier in the half, and we had used all our substitutes, so we had to see the game out with nine men. In the third minute of injury time Macclesfield scored an equaliser, costing us two vital points. That game to me was the most critical game of the season for Lincoln City in terms of its later demise. It was a massive turning point in our fortunes and in relation to the ensuing eleven games.

Unfortunately, we never managed to find anyone to fill Delroy's role up front, and I thought Steve committed a major error when he brought Drewe Broughton back from a loan spell at AFC Wimbledon for the final four games. Broughton had been ineffective before being shipped out to Wimbledon, and was never going to be the answer. But the ill-fortune continued in other ways. Gavin Hoyte and Stephen Hunt both picked up injuries. Then Sunderland recalled Trevor Carson. We had agreed to keep him until the end of the season when they suddenly claimed to need him back; two days later he went out on loan to Brentford. It was their prerogative of course, but if Carson had stayed, we might have been looking at a different scenario today. It left us having to find a replacement before the transfer deadline, and we ended up with young Elliot Parish, who had never played a first team game for anyone. He conceded six at home to Rotherham on his debut, which should have sounded a warning; but for some reason Steve chose to persist with Elliot in preference to Joe Anyon, whom he had fallen out with. Mistakes and misfortune, we suffered from them both.

I had several long conversations with Steve immediately after relegation and he was adamant he was going to give it his all the following season. The reality was, we knew there was a good manager in there, and we felt he had the motivation to rescue his reputation as well as that of our football club. Therefore we decided to give him another chance.

Steve made some good signings in the close season, although he left it very late to sign anyone, not before July if I remember rightly. He brought Alan Power to the club, and Alan was very good that first season. In the first six or seven games of the new season, we played really good football but we could not win games. I remember absolutely paralysing Wrexham at Sincil Bank in the second home match and losing 2-1, and that was symptomatic of that opening period. We were dominating 75% of a game and losing, every week. Eventually we got to a point where we knew we could not carry on like that. We decided it would be cheaper to pay Steve off and start again, and that is what we did following a dismal defeat at Tamworth in October 2011.

When we took the decision to sack Steve, I said I regretted not having sacked him earlier, immediately after relegation. That was obviously at odds with the backing we had given him at the time, but things deteriorated massively. I also said his reign had been a disaster for Lincoln City, which by that stage was certainly true. He had continued to live in Essex and stayed in Lincoln two or three nights per week, which was never going to provide the most effective foundation for doing the job or for building any sort of relationship with either his players or with the people of Lincoln. Danny Cowley has shown the right way to achieve all of those things, but Steve simply got it wrong. I don't think he ever bonded at all with the club or the city, and I think it came as a relief to him when I finally sacked him.

David Holdsworth came in a few weeks later, and he did a specific job for us. First and foremost, his remit from me was to ease out of the club as many of the higher earners as he possibly could; to bring in some players who were a lot less expensive, but still able to do a job in the Conference; and to maybe give us a shot at a top five spot. We knew pretty quickly that was not going to happen, because the quality he was able to bring in simply did not compare to the other clubs in the Conference. So our *raison d'être* soon became to survive in that league on virtually no money: we were running on empty.

David was quite imaginative in the way he managed the club, and was capable of pulling off little coups here and there, bringing players into the club even for short periods of time. That enabled us to maintain our status in that league, although at one stage we feared he was not going to do it. He did clear the high earners off the wage roll, the most notorious being Gavin McCallum who had been signed by Chris Sutton on £1,200 per week, and replaced them with players of a certain kind. Most of the replacements were traditional football journeymen who stayed for a few months until a better offer came along, and were not concerned about their careers as footballers per se. The departures of some of those high earners did cause a lot of grievances that we were forced to address. But that had been David's remit when we appointed him, and we were still in the Conference the following August. It was now time to move the club forward, and that was David's remit for 2012-13.

There was a glimmer of improvement in some of the early league performances, but the team failed to sustain what had been a reasonably promising first half of the season. That season is memorable only for the cup run that almost brought Liverpool to Sincil Bank. I remember Jamie Taylor missing a golden opportunity to equalise at Mansfield, putting a header wide of the post, and that highlights the very small margin between success and failure at our level. But sixteen months after David joined us, the reality was that we were still in the bottom eight in the Conference and seemingly no further forward on the pitch. By the time we lost at Hereford in February, regrettably we knew we had to make another change.

Although very effective in his first season, I felt David had lost momentum by the time we sacked him. He was never going to take us anywhere, which we probably knew when we appointed him. We needed someone to sort out the mess left by the previous manager, and he did that, but that was as far as it was likely to go. He signed some good players amidst the dross, such as the clever Colin Larkin, but the majority left a lot to be desired. The rapid turnover made it impossible to achieve a settled side, and the result of that manifested itself visibly on the pitch through some increasingly poor performances in early 2013. There was little to persuade us that things were going to get any better, and the spectre of relegation was again on the horizon. Whatever David had brought to the club was no longer working, and it was time to part company.

Gary Simpson had been part of a successful duo that had taken Lincoln to the play-offs four times. Arguably, he was the talent-spotter in the Alexander-Simpson partnership but never got the credit for his role. He had been sacked as manager of Macclesfield the previous season as they headed for relegation to the Conference, but had been desperately unlucky with a raft of injuries. They had been on a run of nineteen games without a win, but drew a lot of those despite the injury problems. We felt his record at Macclesfield therefore stood up reasonably well, and he was available. He also lived in Sheffield, which would be a cheap appointment, and he wanted to come. I thought he was well worth a try, and at interview he told us he had a point to prove. He came in until the end of the season initially and did a great job, keeping us up by six clear points.

Gary felt he could get us to the play-offs in his first full season once he had brought in his own players, and without question he signed some good ones. Sean Newton, Jon Nolan, Danny Rowe and Ben Tomlinson all came in during that first close season. On the negative side he did sign Todd Jordan, who I thought had very limited ability for Conference football, and insisted on playing him every week. He also signed Nick Wright, Bohan Dixon and Adi Yussuf, none of whom had any real impact, so there was quite a contrast between the better players and the rest. For the first time since relegation, we actually finished closer to the play-offs in terms of points than to the bottom four, but Gary's assertion that the play-offs were a possibility was not borne out, and we finished well off the pace in fourteenth. That was very disappointing, but it did give us hope that we could close the gap the following season and make that play-off challenge. Nothing else would have been good enough really, in what would be his second full season, and perhaps he had made a rod for his own back with his play-off promise the previous summer.

Unfortunately, I felt some of the signings made in the 2014 close season were never going to move us forward. There were numerous trialists coming in and out of the club, most of whom were nowhere near the right standard; we even had some unnamed Belgians for a short time. Sahr Kabba came on the basis of a video from an agent, and he hardly kicked a ball for the club. Hamza Bencherif was a decent player, but the likes of Arnaud Mendy and Marcus Marshall were not likely to rip open opposing defences on a regular basis. And so it proved, and by the end of October we were essentially where we had been for most of the previous season - exactly in the middle of the table. The football was very difficult to watch, and I sensed the supporters had lost patience. After losing a three-goal lead at Forest Green with twenty minutes to go, we put Gary on garden leave while we sorted out some contractual issues with him, although the decision had been made prior to that match. That result confirmed to us that we were making the right decision.

Regrettably we never really achieved an effective working relationship with Gary. A chairman needs to have an open, honest and frank conversation with his manager at all times, and for whatever reason it never seemed to work that way. Perhaps he thought he was being criticised or undermined in some way, but that was not the case at all. His first defence in public was always the budget, it was always the fault of the board. It reached the point of walking on egg shells, and that could only end one way.

Five or six weeks before we sacked him, we realised he was never going to get us out of this league, not with his style of play and philosophy. Although the results kept us in mid-table, the performances were hard to watch, and that difficult relationship kept rearing its head. We were never going to be relegated with Gary in charge, but that should be a given at a club of this size with the budget we gave him. We were past that stage, and we now wanted to press on for promotion. I liken him to Tony Pulis, who perennially keeps clubs in the Premiership without challenging the leaders. Gary had turned us into a solid mid-table side, but we now needed a manager who could not only carry the club forward, but could initiate the journey back to the Football League in earnest.

It has been widely intimated that Chris Moyses only got the manager's job at Lincoln City because we could not afford to appoint a full-time manager from outside the club. That is not strictly true. Chris had been assisting with some of the coaching under Gary Simpson and acted as a form of liaison between the board and the management. He had been in the dressing room, in and around the players, for the previous two years and had sufficient knowledge of how things worked at player-management interaction level. He was popular with the players and was also a Lincoln man through and through. Most managers are basically mercenaries who come just to do a job, and normally they are not successful. Therefore we felt Chris had as good a chance of making a success of being Lincoln City manager as anyone else, and he cared deeply. The fact that he did the job for nothing was as much a point of honour as anything else - he felt it was a genuine honour to be the manager of this club, and that was the offer he made to us. Chris was certainly different to anything we had seen before, and we all felt it was worth trying.

His first few months in the job were really a settling-in period for him, the task being to get us to the end of that season in a reasonable position, and he achieved that after some difficult results. The Gary Charles situation which arose around the same time was potentially very damaging, and would have cost us over £100,000 had we lost because we would have been obliged to pay his costs as well as our own. It hung over our heads for almost a year, but despite the financial uncertainty of the outstanding tribunal, we backed Chris with a very good budget in the summer of 2015. He used it well to sign some very good players. Matt Rhead and Liam Hearn came in from Mansfield with old favourite Lee Beevers, plus Luke Waterfall, Jack Muldoon, Bradley Wood and Callum Howe. It must not be forgotten that most of those players were to form the backbone of Danny Cowley's side the following season. The fans rallied round with a superb Crowdfunder appeal, and things were looking good for the new season.

As the record books show, we got off to a great start and spent much of the opening half of the season in and around the top five. I actually felt we were in a false position with the side we had, but Chris appeared to be working miracles. By direct contrast, the second half of the season was a mystery to all of us. To be in the top four at the halfway stage and ultimately finish in the bottom half again defied explanation. It was hard to identify any one thing as the cause, but in my opinion the Liam Hearn affair was the catalyst. Perhaps the sense of unity between the players had been broken irreparably, and it never looked the same after that. It caused us a lot of problems at the time and contributed to an immediate loss of form thereafter.

Shortly before the end of the season, Chris told me he was standing down. It was entirely his decision, we would have persevered with Chris for the 2016-17 season, but the pressures of effectively running two businesses were proving too great. Being the manager of a professional football club is a 24/7 job, and Chris felt he would not be able to give it 100%. Within that context it was the right decision, and it gave us ample time to find the right man to take his place.

Chris worked really hard for Lincoln City, and he put a lot of money into the youth department previously. It was no great risk to have appointed him manager, and in my opinion he did better than any of the managers who preceded him since our relegation. Chris was always ready to stand down, should things have gone horribly wrong at any stage, and we would then have been in the position of having to appoint from outside the club. Contrary to popular belief, we would have found the money to do that. There were obviously gaps in his knowledge as a manager, and as a rookie he was bound to make mistakes. Because he treated the players really well as people, he expected that to be returned in terms of effort. For the most part it was, but I am not sure he knew how to address it when that was not forthcoming. We are very grateful to Chris for what he did for this club. He left a genuine legacy in terms of some good players and improved facilities. Although he may well have been a stop-gap initially, his reign as manager proved significant in terms of building the platform from which the next manager could drive the club to the next level.

We knew that we needed a young up-and-coming manager with genuine ambition, not a tired journeyman looking for his latest temporary staging post. There were two managers I had identified during the initial stages of the process, one of whom was Danny Cowley, but I never thought for one moment we could get him. He was top of my list, but even after speaking to Danny initially, I thought we had little chance of getting a deal over the line. Much has been made of the fact that Danny and Nicky gave up their teaching careers to come here, but the truth is that Danny had identified Lincoln City already as a club where he could commence his career as a full-time football manager. In no way did we have to persuade him to leave his teaching job, and contrary to what the supporters feared at the time, in no way was that an obstacle to his appointment.

Another concern we had was the challenge of working in Lincoln and leaving their families in Essex, but the Cowleys are professional sportspeople. Danny's wife Kate is an international athlete who is used to being away from home for long periods. As a group of people, the Cowleys understand implicitly what it takes to succeed in professional sport, and they accepted the negatives a long time ago. If it means coming to Lincoln for a period in order to achieve their ambitions, then that is what they will do. They had already turned down a couple of Football League clubs prior to our initial contact, but we knew none of this at the time. We interviewed four candidates - the Cowleys, Richard Hill, Billy

Heath and Steve Watson - but there was only going to be one winner from the moment we met them. Once they assured us that Lincoln was the club for them, and that the negatives in our minds were nothing of the kind, we knew we had our men.

There was obviously a greater cost involved in paying the wages of two managers, which had to be sufficient to compensate for the loss of their relatively secure teaching careers. Furthermore, we had to consider the cost of travel and housing, but by this stage we were in a fortunate position. Without the advent of Clive Nates to the board a few months earlier, we would not have been able to afford the Cowleys. Investment in a football club does not have to be in eight figures: just enough to enable you to move to the next stage of your journey is plenty, provided you have the right man to spend it. We knew we had the right man, and Clive's investment enabled us to make the right offer.

We worked very hard to conclude the appointment because we knew there would be lots of other clubs interested. After three meetings and numerous telephone calls, Roger Bates and I went down to meet them again at Cambridge Services one evening with the forms to sign. We were there for two hours talking to Danny and Nicky about a whole range of positive subjects relating to their prospective roles. At an opportune moment, I got the forms out, handed Danny a pen, and asked him whether he was going to sign. He did. It was half past eleven at night.

Danny set about building his squad with some judicious signings, and another Crowdfunder provided a further £50,000 to add to his war chest. In came England C internationals instead of the knackered journeymen we had become used to. Who could have imagined Alex Woodyard, Sam Habergham and Sean Raggett in Lincoln City's colours just a few months earlier? We won at Woking on the opening day, the fans came out in large numbers for the first home game, and the rest is history.

The cup-tie against Oldham was a seminal game in as much as it opened the club up once again to those lapsed fans who probably would not have darkened our door again without the publicity and television exposure. We had more than 7,000 at the match, which is far more than we expected, and we realised that the people of Lincoln were back on board. The Lincoln Loco was gathering speed, and the fans had a club they could be proud of to a certain degree. Winning that tie was the first of four giant-killings that led us to the quarter-finals of the FA Cup for the first time in our history and that immense game at Arsenal. To have made £2.5 million from the FA Cup run alone - plus the increased revenues from sponsorship and higher gates at league matches - has completely transformed Lincoln City from financial also-rans to a club ready and able to meet the challenge of the Football League. The club has become attractive to potential signings once more; every player in the lower divisions will want to play for Danny Cowley, and there is a fan base three times its size at the start of the season. The television exposure from the cup run has made the Lincoln City name known all over the world. As I was saying, a little investment has enabled us to employ the right man to spend it.

On that subject, one of the most important roles of a football club chairman is to secure investment, and I often hold discussions with investors with regard to Lincoln City. There are a lot of people around who call themselves investors who actually have no money to invest whatsoever, and you can waste a lot of time with those people. They see a club either in financial trouble or simply short of money, and think they can buy it for a pound. Some of them are nothing more than asset-strippers, and I see it as my responsibility to ensure those people are kept away from Lincoln City.

Some investors are very genuine, of course. I had a five hour meeting with Peter Swann and it seemed a meeting of minds. At the end of the meeting we shook hands, and I welcomed him to Lincoln City. Without betraying any confidences, the intention was for Peter to replace me as chairman for a year and then possibly buy the club, and I thought the deal was concluded. A few days later he joined Scunthorpe on a similar deal. It was disappointing at the time, as I believe Peter could have been good for Lincoln City, but I also believe these things happen for a reason.

Strangely enough, I was in South Africa when we received an email from a local investor who was interested in putting money into the club. I have a house in South Africa and I spend quite a lot of time there. I was down in Cape Town, so I gave him a ring at his home in Johannesburg. His name was Clive Nates, by some strange quirk of fate he was a Lincoln City supporter, and he seemed very genuine. We had numerous telephone calls at the initial stage, and after about a year of discussions we finally had the paperwork completed to everyone's satisfaction. He is actually part of a small consortium operating under the name Sportvest Capital LLP, so there were many legal obligations to consider. Clive became a director of both Lincoln City Football Club and Lincoln City Holdings, and by the end of February 2016 a very significant event in the history of the club had taken place.

I know it has been very difficult for a lot of our fans to accept our time out of the Football League: non-league football is not palatable for most fans, and it has been unpalatable for us as well. There have been mountains to climb, and for much of that time, success has been simply to stay in existence and to stay in the National League. The directors are charged with ensuring the future of the football club first and foremost, and that has been our guiding light. Any other course of action would have been reckless in terms of the responsibility incumbent upon us as directors.

In spite of all the financial challenges since relegation, I think we have done very well to manage the club the way we have, and keep the club afloat at the same time. It has been no mean feat, I can assure you. At every stage of my chairmanship, I have tried to make the right decisions for the future of Lincoln City, and I stand by them all. Therefore I am extremely relieved that this season we have finally arrived at the stage we have been working towards for six years. All the hard work that the board has carried out in terms of safeguarding the future of the football club has started to bear fruit. The football side of the club is probably the best it has been for thirty years or more, so the patience of the fans and the patience of the board has finally been rewarded.

I am very proud to be chairman of this great club, the club I have supported all my life. I came from Vernon Street, within earshot of the ground, and even had a short spell on the club's books in Ron Gray's time. It is my club, it has been in my blood for over sixty years. I have never regretted becoming chairman in 2010 despite everything that has happened since. It was an honour to be offered the position, and it gives me a great sense of satisfaction to see Lincoln City on the rise again. It is easy to forget that the majority of our directors are local people who are lifelong supporters too, and we are there every week cheering the team on with the rest of you. Lincoln City is back where it belongs, and long may that continue.

Bob Dorrian, Lincoln, May 2017

Vital Lincoln City:
Welcome Danny Cowley

The following article was first published on the Vital Lincoln City social media site on the day Danny Cowley was unveiled, 13 May 2016. At the time, we knew very little about our new manager, and the article drew together the limited information available and tried to place the appointment into some kind of perspective. Just twelve months on, and at the end of an extraordinary season, we thought the article was well worth reproducing here.

Welcome: Danny Cowley

As soon as Chris Moyses announced on 5 April that he was to step down at the end of the season, the search was on to find the next Lincoln City manager. The inward groan from thousands of die-hard supporters could be heard for miles around as the anticipated influx of applications from the usual dire suspects landed with an extremely dull thud on the doormat at Sincil Bank. Which desperate journeyman would Bob Dorrian choose this time? Many names were bandied about, ranging from the experienced (but strangely unsuccessful) Ronnie Moore to some Argentinian bloke who had just taken the caretaker reins at City's cup conquerors Whitehawk. Were we really that desperate? Were we really that stupid? Fortunately a man from Johannesburg called Clive Nates was involved, and he was never likely to allow anything like that to happen to his investment.

Who, then? Bob Dorrian stated unequivocally that the club wanted a young, eager manager who could offer new ideas and new methods rather than those tired old journeymen. Someone from non-league circles who knew what was required; someone who knew the clubs, the players, the tactics, all of it. Perhaps someone who was not currently a manager; Clive even stated that he had one name on his radar, and that name had applied. The sigh of relief was tangible. This time, Lincoln were going to take the search for their new manager the length and breadth of the country, rather than the length and breadth of the boardroom. This time, Lincoln meant business.

Interviews took place, and rumours abounded as the media and fans alike came up with some extraordinary names. But there was a delay in the announcement with no updates from the club, leading to the conclusion that it had to be someone involved in the play-offs. That narrowed it down a bit to the prime candidate Danny Cowley of Conference rivals Braintree, but surely he would never come? He had a full-time job as Head of PE at a school in Essex, and he would never give that up to go full-time. Next on the list was Billy Heath from nearby North Ferriby, but this suggestion elicited a curiously lukewarm response from fans despite his obvious success with the Villagers. Dennis Greene, then? That was a possibility but seemed second-best, somehow. Surely not Simon Weaver from Harrogate? The presence of a millionaire father made this rather extreme suggestion more plausible, but garnered almost no support from Imps anywhere. The wait has been almost unbearable.

Well, this evening the dust has settled to reveal none other than Danny Cowley in the Sincil Bank hot seat. This is an appointment that should generate great excitement amongst City fans who have been used to mediocre managerial appointments for far too long. Somehow, Bob and Clive have pulled off something very special: this time, we have the right one. Or should we say the right two? Nicky Cowley is our new assistant manager this evening.

So, who is Danny Cowley? A lot has been written of late about the polite, dignified young man from Essex; one newspaper referred to him as 'the non-league Ranieri', but who exactly is he? Although he has become a familiar face on our TV screens recently as his team of bakers and candlestick-makers repeatedly put the wind up their supposedly more professional full-time opponents, very little is known about the man who has seemingly come from nowhere in no time at all.

It never is that simple, of course. Although still only 37, Danny has been a manager for an incredible nine full seasons, overseeing a total of 435 competitive matches in that time (see the statistical section at the end for full details). If ever a manager has served an apprenticeship, it is Danny. Taking over the manager's position at Essex Senior League also-rans Concord Rangers in summer 2007 in conjunction with Danny Scopes, the learning stage appears to have been very short as his side romped to the championship and promotion to the Isthmian League Division One North at the first attempt. They also reached the quarter-final of the FA Vase, losing to Lowestoft Town by a single goal. To call this a promising start would be an understatement.

Consolidation might have been the objective in their first season in the Isthmian League, but a play-off place was the reality; however, hopes of a second successive promotion ended with a 5-4 penalty shoot-out defeat to Waltham Abbey in the final. The play-offs were reached the following season and promotion secured with a win over Enfield Town. Consolidation in the Isthmian Premier, then? Not a bit of it, as Concord missed a play-off spot by just two points at the first attempt. In the summer of 2012 Glen Alzapiedi joined Danny as his assistant and helped the club to yet another promotion, this time with a play-off final win at old foes Lowestoft. From Essex Senior League to Conference

South in just six seasons might have been enough, but the club added the Isthmian League Cup to their collection with a 3-2 win over Dulwich.

The simple aim for the first ever season in tier 6 was survival, but that was achieved by a margin of 21 points; indeed, another 8 points would have seen the club make the play-offs and challenge for the Conference Premier. By way of compensation, the club won the Essex Senior Cup for the first time, beating a certain Braintree Town in the final. The team fell just 5 points short of the play-offs in 2014-15 but retained the Essex Senior Cup with a storming win over Billericay. Concord also reached the first round of the FA Cup for the first time in its history, going down to a narrow 1-0 defeat at home to Mansfield after a 1-1 draw at Field Mill. Another significant event took place in September 2014 as assistant Glen Alzapiedi took the manager's position at Cheshunt; he was replaced by Danny's brother Nicky, who had been forced to retire as a player with Concord; the management team was complete.

From the Essex Senior League to seventh place in Conference South, one championship, two play-off final wins and six trophies in eight incredible seasons. So it came as no surprise that bigger clubs were interested. Going full-time was not an option, as both Cowleys shared their football duties with full-time jobs in the PE department at the FitzWimarc School in Rayleigh, so a position at the highest level within the realms of part-time football was the next-best thing: Braintree Town came calling.

Everyone knows what Danny has achieved this season. One prize idiot, writing a season preview for Vital Lincoln last summer, even tipped Braintree for relegation following the departure of Alan Devonshire to Maidenhead. What fools we were. OK, what a fool I was. The record books will show that everything went wrong for them in the second leg of the play-off semi-final, as the part-timers were outrun by a resurgent - and full-time - Grimsby. But Danny had written his name firmly into the frame for any lower division or senior non-league job going. Including ours. Rumours of Notts County and Tranmere did not bode well (not least for Gary Brabin), but at least Danny appeared to be considering going full-time. He wanted to test his methods in full-time football; he wanted away.

Could Bob and Clive possibly pull it off?

Probably not.

But they have.

Danny and Nicky Cowley - welcome to Lincoln City. We are very pleased to have you.

Is Danny Cowley the right appointment for Lincoln City?

There is no way of knowing, of course.

But what we do know is that the last 13 managers to win promotion from the Conference all conform to the same profile: a track record of promotions lower down the non-league pyramid and the majority had at least one play-off campaign in the Conference Premier. On that basis, Cowley is an absolute bullseye.

All Lincoln or any club can do is build the right profile and find a manager who fits that. In no way does it guarantee success and could end in desperate failure (again). But what you have to do is give yourself the best chance of success by appointing the right people in certain positions, and it looks as if Lincoln (almost unbelievably) have done exactly that.

With Cowley's appointment, we have given ourselves the best possible chance of moving forward because he conforms to the profile of a successful Conference manager. Unfortunately, Tilson, Holdsworth, Simpson and Moyses were not even close to conforming with that profile and were all unsuccessful. You don't have to be a genius to work that out.

For once, Lincoln City have done this exactly right. If Danny Cowley's appointment turns out to be unsuccessful, Lincoln could have done no more than they have.

So why is Danny Cowley coming to Lincoln?

The doubters may ask how anyone could give up the security of a full-time job in teaching to become a professional football manager; some may even suspect a touch of insanity; or did Bob Dorrian hire a shaman to cast a spell over the FitzWimarc Head of PE? The answer lies in a statement Danny made upon joining Braintree almost exactly a year ago this week:

"You only get one life and I want to make the most of mine."

Perhaps he feels he has done all he can at Braintree after one solitary season. Could it be repeated? With Cowley's record, it probably could, but there is as great a personal risk involved in staying at Braintree as moving into full-time football. He has stated on several occasions that he is ambitious. A mediocre season at Braintree would certainly see his personal stock fall; he would not be as much in demand from professional clubs as at the present time, and perhaps it is now or never. Timing can be everything, and he feels his time is now.

The natural progression is to a full-time club with potential. Danny has said within the last few days that he and Nicky wanted to join a club where they could really add value. Can they do that at Lincoln? Can they win football matches and put significant numbers on the gate? Their record to date says they can. The support is certainly still there, waiting. Can they blow a breath of fresh air through the club and its supporters and galvanise the city behind them? There is no reason why not. But the idea of restoring Lincoln City to its rightful place in the Football League must be irresistible for them. That is the definition of adding real value. They have a great opportunity to write themselves into the history of our great club, to join Anderson and Taylor, Murphy and Alexander. They can be the ones to lead us back to the League and into our new stadium. To add real value. To become legends.

And we love our legends at Lincoln City.

We have him for two years, at least to begin with. But now he has turned professional, he will be on the radar of every club in the lower divisions of the Football League, who will be monitoring his progress in full-time football very closely. Presumably he has an objective to take us back to the Football League, or at least make a serious challenge, within those two years. If he fails, we will not have lost very much; two years of Clive Nates' investment will have been used, but we can hardly be in a worse position than in any of the last five years; Danny's outstanding record almost guarantees that. And if other clubs come calling at the end of those two years, very few will begrudge him a move if Lincoln City are back in the Football League.

Danny Cowley: Personal profile

Age: 37 (DOB: 22 October 1978)

Wife: Great Britain athlete Kate (Brewington) Cowley, also a PE teacher at FitzWimarc.

Children: Isabella (7) and George (3)

PE teacher at FitzWimarc School, Rayleigh, since 2001, latterly department head.

Playing career: Dagenham, Purfleet, Barking, Harlow Town, Boreham Wood, Romford, AFC Hornchurch, Brentwood, Concord Rangers (retired 2007 due to hamstring injury).

Nicky Cowley: Personal profile

Age: 34

Wife: Lauren (Powell) Cowley

Children: Harry (5) and Betsy (2)

Head of Boys PE at FitzWimarc School, Rayleigh.

Playing career: Witham Town, Boreham Wood, Romford, Brentwood, AFC Hornchurch, Concord Rangers (retired 2014 due to knee injury).

Danny Cowley: Statistics Section

Section A: League games only (play-offs and cup matches not included):

By Season			Pos	P	W	D	L	PPG	
2007-08	Concord Rgs	Essex Snr League (Tier 9)	1st (P)	32	25	2	5	2.406	
2008-09	Concord Rgs	Isthmian Div 1N (Tier 8)	5th (F)	42	23	10	9	1.880	
2009-10	Concord Rgs	Isthmian Div 1N (Tier 8)	2nd (PO)	42	26	8	8	2.047	
2010-11	Concord Rgs	Isthmian Premier (Tier 7)	8th	42	21	8	13	1.690	
2011-12	Concord Rgs	Isthmian Premier (Tier 7)	14th	42	16	9	17	1.357	
2012-13	Concord Rgs	Isthmian Premier (Tier 7)	4th (PO)	42	22	10	10	1.809	
2013-14	Concord Rgs	Conference South (Tier6)	9th	42	17	10	15	1.452	
2014-15	Concord Rgs	Conference South (Tier6)	7th	40	18	11	11	1.625	RESD
2015-16	Braintree Town	Conference Prem (Tier5)	3rd (SF)	46	23	12	11	1.761	RESD

Key: P = Promoted; R = Relegated; SF = Lost in play-off semi-final; F = Lost in play-off final; PO = Won play-off final; D = Demoted.

Summary		P	W	D	L	F	A	PPG	GFPG	GAPG	CLEAN
2007-15	Concord Rgs	324	168	68	88	613	380	1.765	1.891	1.172	121
2015-16	Braintree Town	46	23	12	11	56	38	1.761	1.217	0.826	21
		370	191	80	99	669	418	1.765	1.808	1.130	142

Key: PPG = Points earned per game; GFPG = Goals scored per game; GAPG = Goals conceded per game; CLEAN = clean sheets.

Win ratio (league games only): 51.6%
Draw ratio (league games only): 21.6%
Loss ratio (league games only): 26.8%
Clean sheets (league games only): 38.4%

Section B: Cup matches and play-offs

FA Cup	P	W	D	L	Best season
Concord Rangers	27	14	5	8	1R 2014-15
Braintree Town	2	1	0	1	1R 2015-16
TOTALS	29	15	5	9	

** Cowley has never gone out of the FA Cup at the first time of asking: has won at least one round each season.*

FA Trophy / Vase	P	W	D	L	Best season
Concord Rangers	26	16	2	8	QF 2007-08 (Vase); R2 2014-15 (Trophy)
Braintree Town	2	1	0	1	R2 2015-16
TOTALS	28	17	2	9	

Play-offs	P	W	D	L	Best season
Concord Rangers	6	5	0	1	Winners 2009-10, 2012-13.
Braintree Town	2	1	0	1	Semi-final 2015-16
TOTALS	8	6	0	2	

All matches	P	W	W%	D	D%	L	L%
Concord Rangers	383	203	53.0%	75	19.6%	105	27.4%
Braintree Town	52	26	50.0%	12	23.0%	14	27.0%
TOTALS	435	229	52.6%	87	20.0%	119	27.4%

Other Football Books

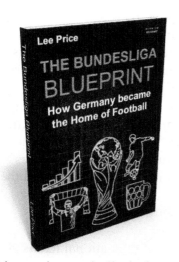

The Bundesliga Blueprint: How Germany became the Home of Football
by Lee Price

German Football is on a roll: winners of the 2014 World Cup, Bundesliga club sides leading the way in Europe, a production line of superb talent coming through the system. Yet, fifteen years ago – at Euro 2000 – it was all so different. Germany suffered one of their most humiliating tournament exits as dismal performances saw them finish bottom of their group with just one point… Immediately, the German FA set about fixing things. And rather than fudging matters, they introduced a raft of major changes designed to return German football to its sporting pinnacle in just 10 years.

In this entertaining, fascinating, and superbly-researched book, sportswriter Lee Price explores German football's 10–year plan. A plan that forced clubs to invest in youth, limit the number of foreign players in teams, build success without debt, and much more. The Bundesliga Blueprint details how German fans part-own and shape their clubs, how football is affordable, and the value of beer and a good sausage on match days. The book includes interviews from Michael Ballack, Jens Nowotny and Christoph Kramer, and the movers-and-shakers behind Germany's leading clubs including Schalke, Dortmund, and Paderborn. There is no doubt that German football is the envy of many nations. There is no doubt that, thanks to them, lessons should be learned by everyone else.

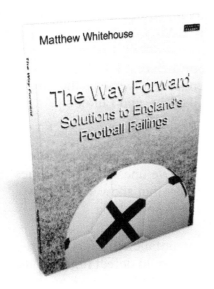

The Way Forward: Solutions to England's Football Failings
by Matthew Whitehouse

English football is in a state of crisis. It has been almost 50 years since England made the final of a major championship and the national sides, at all levels, continue to disappoint and underperform. Yet no-one appears to know how to improve the situation.

In *The Way Forward*, football coach Matthew Whitehouse examines the causes of English football's decline and offers a number of areas where change and improvement need to be implemented immediately. With a keen focus and passion for youth development and improved coaching he explains that no single fix can overcome current difficulties and that a multi-pronged strategy is needed. If we wish to improve the standards of players in England then we must address the issues in schools, the grassroots, and academies, as well as looking at the constraints of the Premier League and English FA.

Unafraid to speak his mind, Matthew Whitehouse makes a well researched and compelling case for all footballing parties to work together to improve standards and modernise their approach. Improvements need to come from the FA and their work with grassroots football to increase the quality of coaching, as well as from the academies who need to do more in terms of the environments they create for producing elite players. An improvement in scouting, talent identification, sport science, and attitudes is also long overdue.

Unless change is implemented soon, England will continue to exist in the backwaters of international football – enviously watching the likes of Spain, Germany, Holland and others, as they deliver high quality teams that are able to win tournaments.

"Whitehouse, while still relatively unknown, has written a masterpiece… Young, forward thinking and passionate about the English game, this is a book you'll be hearing a lot more about over the coming years"
These Football Times

Worst in the World: International Football at the bottom of the FIFA Rankings by Aidan Williams

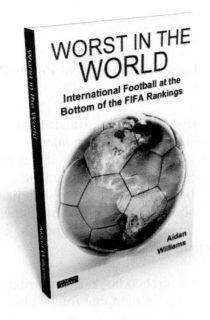

The fate of sporting underdogs has long stirred the passions of many a follower. There is something pleasing about watching apparently 'ordinary' people taking on the sporting elite. Teachers, accountants, fishermen and waiters – they play for the love of football and the pride in their nation.

For footballing countries stuck at the bottom of FIFA's world rankings – life can be hard. Sporadic fixtures against far better equipped sides can be a soul-destroying enterprise with frequent defeat, sometimes bordering on humiliation, the regular outcome for these teams and their players. But when that positive result finally arrives, it can mean so much: unbridled joy, national glory, and even… redemption.

In *Worst in the World*, Aidan Williams looks at the national teams at the wrong end, so to speak, of FIFA's rankings. In doing so, he brings attention to those nations whose footballing aspirations lie not in trophies or even qualification, but simply in the love of the game and the pride of representing their country.

Conference Season by Steve Leach

Disillusioned with the corporate ownership, mega-bucks culture, and overpaid prima donnas, of the Premiership, Steve Leach embarked on a journey to rediscover the soul of professional football. His journey, over the 2012/13 season, took him to twenty-four different Football Conference towns and fixtures, visiting venues as diverse as the Impact Arena in Alfreton, Stonebridge Road in Ebbsfleet, and Luton's Kenilworth Road.

Encountering dancing bears at Nuneaton, demented screamers at Barrow, and 'badger pasties' at rural Forest Green – Steve unearthed the stories behind the places and people – it was a journey that showed just how football and communities intertwine, and mean something.

As the season progressed Steve relished how unfancied teams of part-timers, such as Braintree Town and Dartford, could defeat higher status opponents, and watched 'big name' clubs such as Luton Town and Lincoln City struggle to make an impact. Throughout all this, his anguish grew at the prospect of his beloved Stockport County getting relegated.

Conference Season is a warm and discerning celebration of the diversity of towns and clubs which feature in the Conference, and of the supporters who turn up week-after-week to cheer their teams on.

www.BennionKearny.com/Soccer

Lightning Source UK Ltd.
Milton Keynes UK
UKOW07f1857170717

305505UK00008B/412/P